A-Z NEWPORT

CONTENTS

Key to Map Pages	2-3
Large Scale Cardiff City Centre	4-5
Map Pages	6-120
Index to Streets, Towns, Villages, Hospitals and selected Places of Interest	121-168

REFERENCE

Motorway	M4
Proposed	
A Road	A48
Proposed	
B Road	B4562
Dual Carriageway	
One-way Street Traffic flow on A Roads is also indicated by a heavy line on the driver's left.	
Restricted Access	
Pedestrianized Road	
Track / Footpath	
Residential Walkway	
Railway	Station, Level Crossing, Tunnel
Built-up Area	BRIAR CL.
Local Authority Boundary	
National Boundary	
National Park Boundary	
Posttown Boundary	
Postcode Boundary (within Posttown)	
Map Continuation	15 / Large Scale City Centre 5
Car Park (selected)	P
Church or Chapel	†
Cycleway (selected)	
Fire Station	■
Hospital	H
House Numbers (A & B Roads only)	13 8
Information Centre	i
National Grid Reference	320
Police Station	▲
Post Office	★
Toilet: without facilities for the Disabled with facilities for the Disabled	
Viewpoint	
Educational Establishment	
Hospital or Hospice	
Industrial Building	
Leisure or Recreational Facility	
Place of Interest	
Public Building	
Shopping Centre or Market	
Other Selected Buildings	

SCALE

Map Pages 6-120 1:15,840

0 ¼ ½ Mile

0 250 500 750 Metres

4 inches (10.16 cm) to 1 mile 6.31 cm to 1 kilometre

Map Pages 4-5

8 inches (2

Copyright of Geographers' A-Z Map C

Fairfield Road, Borough Green, Sevenoaks, Kent TN15 8PP
Telephone: 01732 781000 (Enquiries & Trade Sales)
01732 783422 (Retail Sales)
www.a-zmaps.co.uk

Edition 3 2003, Edition 3C 2007 (Part Revision)

BRECON BEACONS NATIONAL PARK
MERTHYR TYDFIL
(Merthyr Tudful)
Hirwaun
ABERTILLERY
(Abertyleri)
New Tredegar
Cwm
Aberdare
(Aberdar)
Bargoed
(Bargod)
Oakdale
Treherbert
Mountain Ash
(Aberpennar)
Treharris
Newbridge
(Cefn Bychan)
Treorchy
(Treoci)
RHONDDA
St.Gwynno Forest
Blackwood
(Coed Duon)
Ton-Pentre
Abercynon
Nelson
Pontllanfraith
Abercarn
Ynysbwl
Tonypandy
Glyncoch
Cwmfelinfach
Crosskeys
PONTYPRIDD
Llanbradach
Risca
Gilfach Goch
Bedwas
Machen
Rhydyfelin
Treforest
Penyrheol
CAERPHILLY
(Caerffili)
Church Village
Nantgarw
Beddau
Llantrisant
Taff's Well
Thornhill
CARDIFF GATE
Pencoed
INSET PAGE 78
Talbot Green
Pentyrch
Llanishen
Rhiwbina
Pentwyn
St. Mellons
Llanharry
Pontyclun
CARDIFF WEST
Radyr
Birchgrove
Cyncoed
Whitchurch
Rumney
Llandaff
Roath
Tremorfa
Canton
COWBRIDGE
(Y Bont-Faen)
Caerau
CARDIFF
(Caerdydd)
Grangetown
Bonvilston
(Tresimwn)
Wenvoe
Llandough
(Llandoch)
Llanblethian
(Llanfleiddan)
Dinas Powys
Penarth
Colcot
Palmerston
Cosmeston
Llantwit Major
(Llanilltud Fawr)
St. Athan
(Sain Tathan)
CARDIFF INTERNATIONAL AIRPORT
BARRY (Barri)
Sully
Rhoose
(Y Rhws)
Barry Island
(Ynys y Barri)
BRISTOL CHANNEL
(MÔR HAFREN)
River Taff
Ebbw River
Rhymney River
Sirhowy River
Ely River
A465
A470
A4059
A4233
A4054
A469
A4048
A4046
A467
B4256
B4276
B4275
B4263
B4471
A472
B4251
A4061
A4064
B4224
B4254
B4273
B4451
A4058
A4093
A4119
B4280
A473
A4222
A48
B4270
A4226
B4268
B4265
M4
14 15 16 17
24 25 26 27 28 29 30 31 32 33
40 41 42 43 44 45 46 47 48 49 50 51
64 65 66 67 68 69 70 71 72 73 74 75
78 79 80 81 82 83 84 85 86 87 88 89
90 91 92 93 94 95 96 97
98 99 100 101 102 103
104 105 106 107 108 109
110 111 112 113
114 115 116 117 118 119 120

KEY TO MAP PAGES *Allwedd i Dudalennau'r Map*

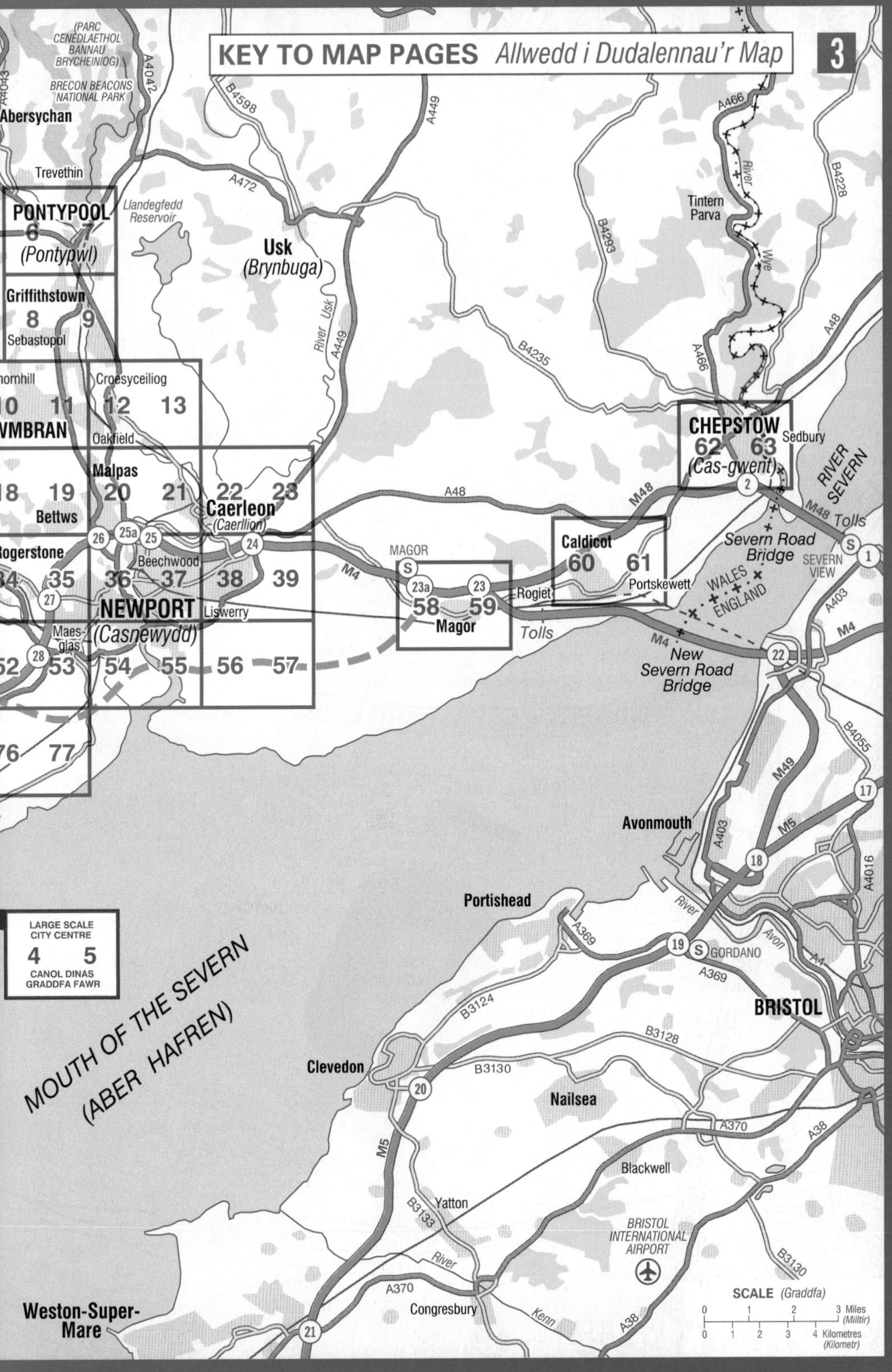

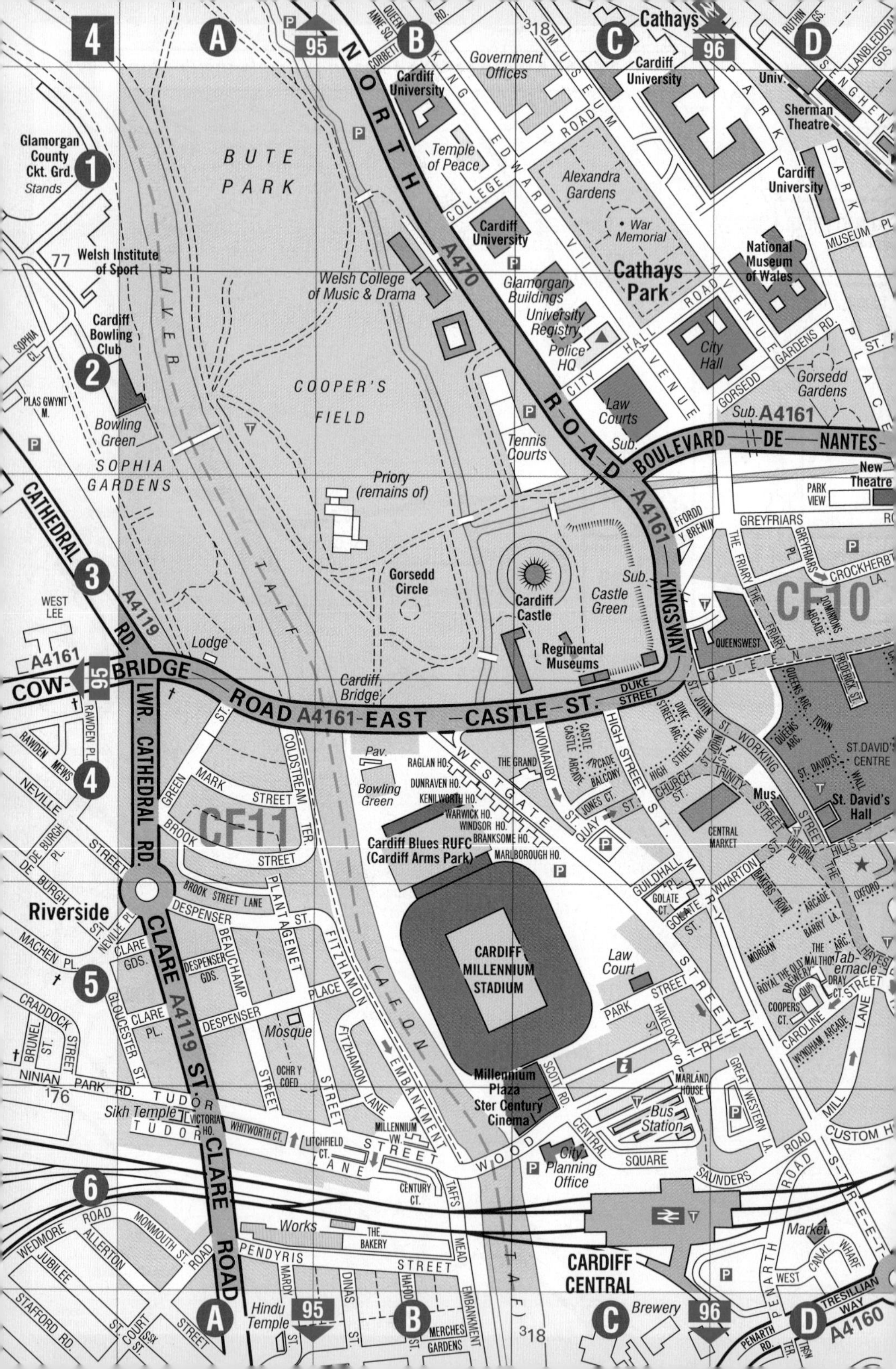

A
B
C
D
95
96
Cathays
Government Offices
Cardiff University
Univ.
Sherman Theatre
BUTE PARK
Temple of Peace
Alexandra Gardens
War Memorial
Cathays Park
National Museum of Wales
Glamorgan County Ckt. Grd.
Stands
Welsh Institute of Sport
Welsh College of Music & Drama
Glamorgan Buildings
University Registry
Police HQ
City Hall
Law Courts
Gorsedd Gardens
Cardiff Bowling Club
Bowling Green
SOPHIA GARDENS
COOPER'S FIELD
Tennis Courts
Priory (remains of)
BOULEVARD DE NANTES
A4161
A470
NORTH ROAD
New Theatre
Gorsedd Circle
Cardiff Castle
Castle Green
Regimental Museums
KINGSWAY
CF10
CF11
Lodge
Cardiff Bridge
COW-BRIDGE ROAD A4161-EAST-CASTLE-ST.
CATHEDRAL RD.
A4119
LWR. CATHEDRAL RD.
Riverside
Queenswest
St. David's Centre
St. David's Hall
Central Market
Cardiff Blues RUFC (Cardiff Arms Park)
CARDIFF MILLENNIUM STADIUM
Law Court
Millennium Plaza Ster Century Cinema
Bus Station
Central Square
City Planning Office
Mosque
Sikh Temple
CLARE ROAD
CLARE ST.
Works
The Bakery
CARDIFF CENTRAL
Brewery
Market
Hindu Temple
Tabernacle
TRESILLIAN WAY
A4160
318
1
2
3
4
5
6

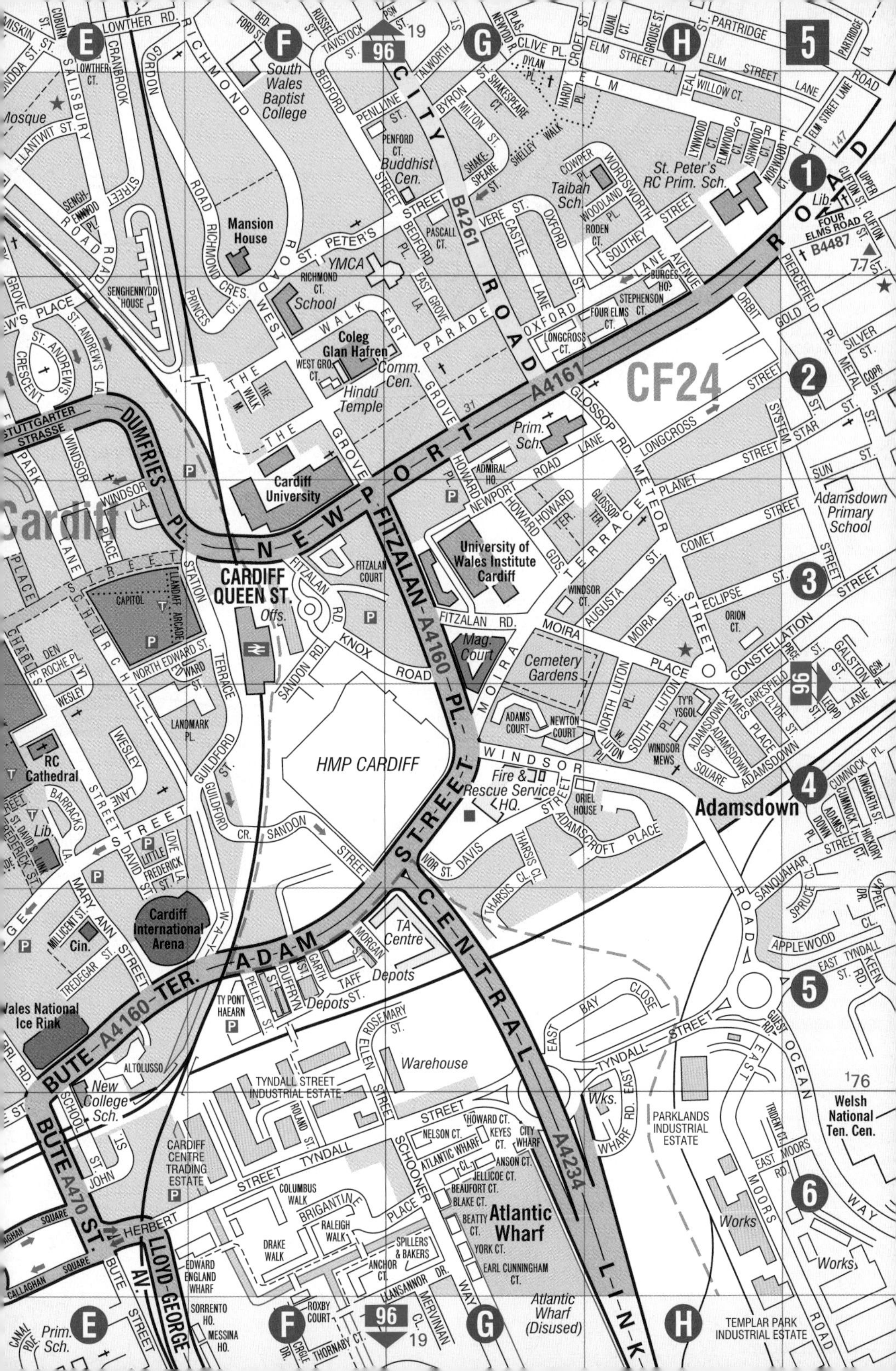
E
F
G
H
5
96
19
1
2
3
4
5
6
CF24
Cardiff
South Wales Baptist College
Mosque
Mansion House
Buddhist Cen.
YMCA
School
Coleg Glan Hafren
Comm. Cen.
Hindu Temple
St. Peter's RC Prim. Sch.
Taibah Sch.
Lib.
Prim. Sch.
Cardiff University
CARDIFF QUEEN ST.
Offs.
University of Wales Institute Cardiff
Mag. Court
Cemetery Gardens
Adamsdown Primary School
HMP CARDIFF
Fire & Rescue Service HQ.
Adamsdown
RC Cathedral
CAPITOL
Cardiff International Arena
Cin.
Wales National Ice Rink
TA Centre
Depots
Warehouse
New College Sch.
TYNDALL STREET INDUSTRIAL ESTATE
CARDIFF CENTRE TRADING ESTATE
Atlantic Wharf
Atlantic Wharf (Disused)
Wks.
PARKLANDS INDUSTRIAL ESTATE
Works
Welsh National Ten. Cen.
TEMPLAR PARK INDUSTRIAL ESTATE
Prim. Sch.
176
77
147
31
LOWTHER RD.
RICHMOND ROAD
CITY ROAD
B4261
NEWPORT ROAD
A4161
FITZALAN PL.
A4160
ADAM ST.
BUTE TER.
BUTE ST.
A470
CENTRAL LINK
A4234
LLOYD GEORGE AV.
DUMFRIES PL.
STUTTGARTER STRASSE
CHURCHILL WAY
ELM STREET
CLIVE PL.
PARTRIDGE ROAD
FOUR ELMS ROAD
B4487
GLOSSOP RD.
METEOR STREET
MOIRA PLACE
CONSTELLATION STREET
WINDSOR ROAD
TYNDALL STREET
EAST TYNDALL ST.
OCEAN WAY
EAST MOORS RD.
MOORS ROAD
SANDON STREET
KNOX ROAD
FITZALAN RD.
STATION TERRACE
GUILDFORD ST.
DAVID STREET
MARY ANN STREET
TREDEGAR ST.
SCHOONER WAY
HERBERT ST.
CALLAGHAN SQUARE

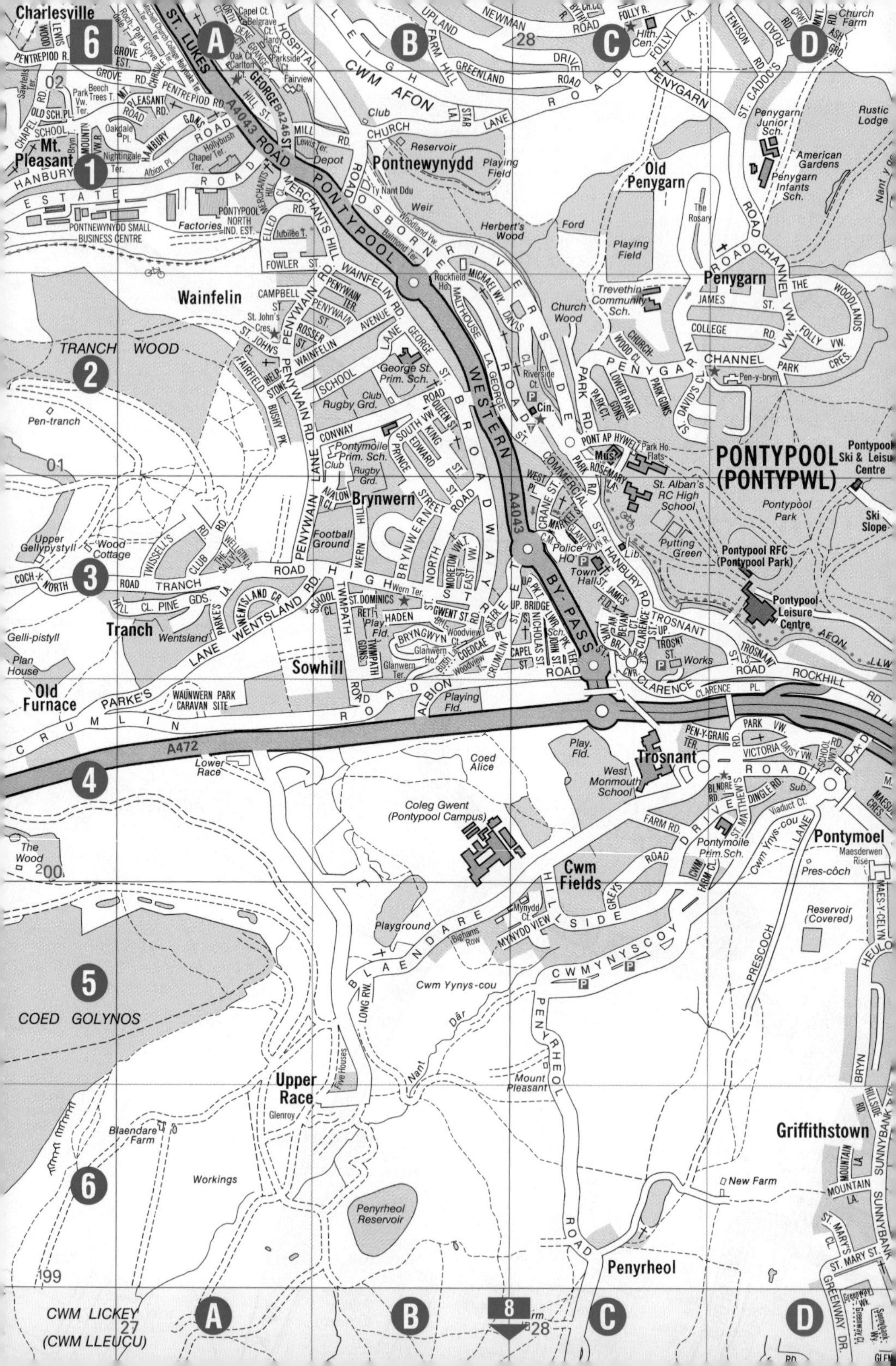

6
Charlesville
A
B
C
D
28
Mt. Pleasant
Hanbury Road
Estate
Pontnewynydd Small Business Centre
Pontypool North Ind. Est.
Factories
St. Lukes
A4043 Road
George St.
B4246
Pontypool Road
Merchants Hill
Fowler St.
Jubilee T.
Elled Rd.
Wainfelin
Wainfelin Rd.
Wainfelin Avenue
Campbell St.
Penywain Rd.
Penywain Ter.
Rosser St.
St. Johns Cl.
St. John's Cres.
Fairfield Cl.
Bushy Pk.
Help Stone
Tranch Wood
Pen-tranch
01
Upper Gellypystyll
Wood Cottage
Coch-y-North
Tranch Road
Twissell's Rd.
Club Rd.
The Sally
Wellgrig Cl.
Hill Cl.
Pine Gds.
Tranch
Wentsland
Wentsland Cr.
Wentsland Rd.
Parke's La.
Parke's Lane
Gelli-pistyll
Plan House
Old Furnace
Waunwern Park Caravan Site
Crumlin Road
A472
Sowhill
Albion Road
Playing Fld.
School Cl.
Twmpath
St. Dominics
Haden
Bryngwyn
Coedcae
Glanwern Ter.
Glanwern Ho.
Woodview
Gwent St.
Brynwern
Brynwern Street
Football Ground
Wern Hill
Avalon Cl.
Conway
Pontymoile Prim. Sch.
Rugby Grd.
Prince
Edward
King
Queen St.
South Vw.
School Lane
George St. Prim. Sch.
Club
Rugby Grd.
Broadway
Western By-Pass
A4043
North St.
Moreton Vw.
East Vw.
Up. Bridge St.
Nicholas St.
John St.
Capel St.
Crumlin Pl.
Hanbury Rd.
Commercial St.
Crane St.
Market St.
Police HQ
Town Hall
St. James' Fld.
Lib.
Cin.
Riverside Ct.
Park Rd.
Pont Ap Hywel
Park Ho. Flats
Mus.
Rosemary La.
St. Alban's RC High School
Putting Green
Trosnant
Trosnant St.
Clarence St.
Clarence Pl.
Works
Rockhill Rd.
Upland
Newman
Hospital
Leigh Road
Cwm Afon
Greenland
Farm Hill
Star La.
Church Lane
Mill Rd.
Reservoir
Depot
Pontnewynydd
Playing Field
Osborne Road
Ty Nant Ddu
Weir
Woodland Vw.
Balmond Ter.
Herbert's Wood
Riverside
Michael Wy.
Malthouse La.
Davis Cl.
Church Wood
Ford
Old Penygarn
Playing Field
Trevethin Community Sch.
The Rosary
Penygarn
Penygarn Junior Sch.
Penygarn Infants Sch.
American Gardens
Rustic Lodge
St. Cadoc's Road
Tenison Rd.
Folly La.
Folly R.
Hlth. Cen.
Church Farm
Channel Road
James St.
College Rd.
The Woodlands
Folly Vw.
Channel Vw.
Park Cres.
Penygarn
Pen-y-bryn
St. David's Cl.
Lower Park Gdns.
Park Gdns.
Park Ct.
Church Wood Cl.
PONTYPOOL (PONTYPWL)
Pontypool Park
Pontypool Ski & Leisure Centre
Ski Slope
Pontypool RFC (Pontypool Park)
Pontypool Leisure Centre
Afon Llwyd
Play. Fld.
Trosnant
West Monmouth School
Pen-y-graig Ter.
Park Vw.
Victoria Road
Daisy Vw.
School Rd.
Coed Alice
Lower Race
Coleg Gwent (Pontypool Campus)
The Wood
200
Farm Rd.
Drive
St. Matthew's
Dingle Rd.
Viaduct Ct.
Pontymoile Prim. Sch.
Cwm Ynys-cou Lane
Pontymoel
Maesderwen Rise
Pres-côch
Maes-y-Celyn
Reservoir (Covered)
Cwm Fields
Hillside
Greys Road
Mynydd Ct.
Mynydd View
Bighams Row
Blaendare Road
Playground
Cwmynyscoy
Cwm Yynys-cou
Long Rw.
Nant Dâr
Penyrheol Road
Prescoch
Coed Golynos
Upper Race
Five Houses
Glenroy
Mount Pleasant
Blaendare Farm
Workings
Penyrheol Reservoir
Penyrheol
Griffithstown
Mountain La.
New Farm
Hillside Rd.
Sunnybank Rd.
St. Mary's Cl.
St. Mary St.
Greenway Dr.
Bryn
99
Cwm Lickey (Cwm Lleucu)
27
8
28

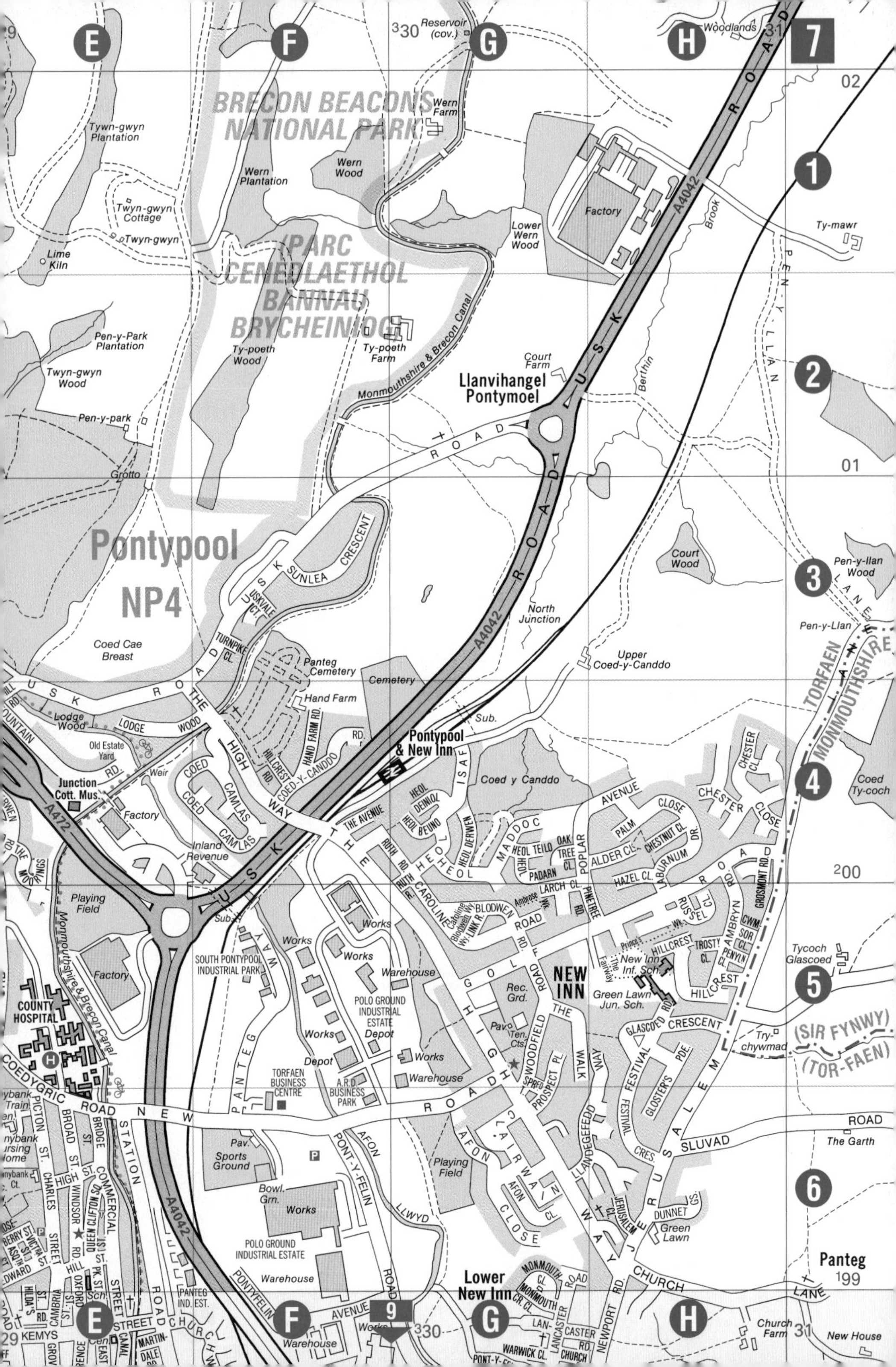
BRECON BEACONS NATIONAL PARK
(PARC CENEDLAETHOL BANNAU BRYCHEINIOG)
Pontypool
NP4
Llanvihangel Pontymoel
Pontypool & New Inn
NEW INN
Lower New Inn
Panteg
COUNTY HOSPITAL
TORFAEN
MONMOUTHSHIRE
(SIR FYNWY)
(TOR-FAEN)
A4042
A472
USK ROAD
NEW ROAD
COEDYGRIC ROAD
GOLF ROAD
HIGH WAY
THE HIGHWAY
JERUSALEM LANE
CHURCH LANE
SLUVAD ROAD
PEN-Y-LLAN LANE
Monmouthshire & Brecon Canal
Factory
Works
Warehouse
Depot
SOUTH PONTYPOOL INDUSTRIAL PARK
POLO GROUND INDUSTRIAL ESTATE
TORFAEN BUSINESS CENTRE
A.R.D. BUSINESS PARK
PANTEG IND. EST.
Wern Plantation
Wern Wood
Wern Farm
Tywn-gwyn Plantation
Twyn-gwyn Cottage
Twyn-gwyn
Lime Kiln
Pen-y-Park Plantation
Twyn-gwyn Wood
Pen-y-park
Grotto
Ty-poeth Wood
Ty-poeth Farm
Lower Wern Wood
Court Farm
Court Wood
Ty-mawr
Woodlands
Reservoir (cov.)
Pen-y-llan Wood
Pen-y-Llan
North Junction
Upper Coed-y-Canddo
Coed y Canddo
Coed Ty-coch
Tycoch Glascoed
Try-chywmad
The Garth
Church Farm
New House
Coed Cae Breast
Panteg Cemetery
Cemetery
Hand Farm
Lodge Wood
Old Estate Yard
Junction Cott. Mus.
Inland Revenue
Playing Field
Sports Ground
Bowl. Grn.
Rec. Grd.
New Inn Inf. Sch.
Green Lawn Jun. Sch.
Green Lawn
Berthin
Brook
Sub.
330
31
02
01
200
199
1
2
3
4
5
6
9
E
F
G
H

CWM LICKEY
(CWM LLEUCU)
Cwm Lickey Pond
MYNYDD TWYN - GLAS
Penyrheol
GRIFFITHSTOWN
Hill Farm
CWRDY ROAD
CWRDY LANE
Cwrdy Wood
White House
Cefn-llwyd
The Bungalow
Ysgubor-goed
Pontypool
NP4
Whitehall
Capel-llwyd
Oaklands
Quarries (dis.)
Uplands
Wain Hywel
Little Greenmeadow Farm
Mountain Farm
Bryn
COED GWAUN-Y-FFEIRIAD
PONTNEWYDD GOLF COURSE
Tunnel
Wren's Nest Farm
Glyn Bran Cottage
Yewtree
MOUNTAIN ROAD
Maes-gwyn
Weir
Blaen Bran Reservoirs
Mine Slope Cottages
Upper Cwmbran
Pencoed
Cwm Bran
Blaen
Upper Cwmbran Inf. Sch.
Five Locks
Club House
FIVE LOCKS CL.
GREENFIELD CL.
MAESGWYN
FIVE LOCKS ROAD
Locks
PENYPARC
Coed Gwern-Esgob
The Square
Works
UPPER CWMBRAN ROAD
TY PWCA
Playing Field
The Hawthorns
MAENDY
Lowlands
Football Ground
Penywaun Farm
Resr. (covered)
Woodlands Junior & Infants Schools
Bellevue
Gorse House
Gelli-gravog
The Graigs
West Pontnewydd
Pontnewydd Prim. Sch.
Garn-Wen
Park House Farm
Football Ground
Church Wood
Church Wood
Graig Fawr
Subway
Hillside Cottage
Thornhill
Brook
Works
Forge
Graig Fawr

6
10
11

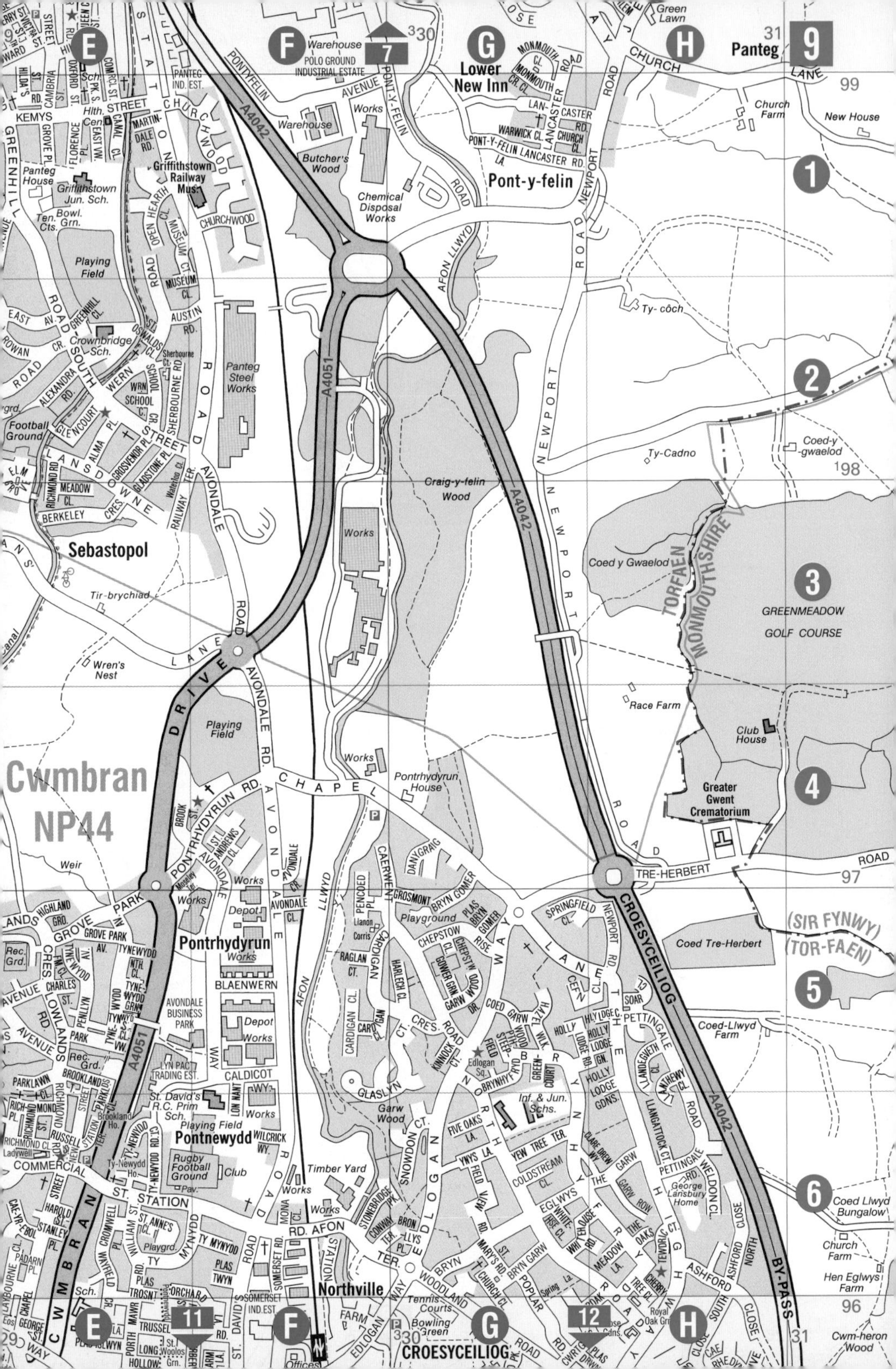

Panteg
9
Lower New Inn
Pont-y-felin
Griffithstown
Griffithstown Railway Mus.
Warehouse
POLO GROUND INDUSTRIAL ESTATE
Butcher's Wood
Chemical Disposal Works
Church Farm
New House
Ty-coch
Panteg Steel Works
Playing Field
Crownbridge Sch.
Football Ground
Sebastopol
Tir-brychiad
Wren's Nest
Craig-y-felin Wood
Coed y Gwaelod
Ty-Cadno
Coed-y-gwaelod
TORFAEN
MONMOUTHSHIRE
GREENMEADOW GOLF COURSE
Race Farm
Club House
Greater Gwent Crematorium
Pontrhydyrun House
Cwmbran
NP44
Pontrhydyrun
AVONDALE BUSINESS PARK
LYN PACT TRADING EST.
St. David's R.C. Prim Sch.
Pontnewydd
Rugby Football Ground
Timber Yard
Garw Wood
Edlogan Sq.
Inf. & Jun. Schs.
Coed Tre-Herbert
(SIR FYNWY)
(TOR-FAEN)
Coed-Llwyd Farm
George Lansbury Home
Coed Llwyd Bungalow
Church Farm
Hen Eglwys Farm
Cwm-heron Wood
Northville
CROESYCEILIOG
Tennis Courts
Bowling Green
SOMERSET IND.EST
A4042
A4051
CWMBRAN DRIVE
CROESYCEILIOG BY-PASS
NEWPORT ROAD
TRE-HERBERT ROAD
CHAPEL LANE
AVONDALE ROAD
7
11
12

Thornhill
Greenmeadow
Fairwater
Coed Eva
Henllys
Graig Fawr
Greenmeadow Community Farm
Greenmeadow Wood
Greenmeadow Primary Sch.
Fairwater High School
Fairwater Leisure Centre
Fairwater Sports & Social Club
Football Ground
Coed Eva Jun. & Inf. Schs.
Henllys C in W Sch.
Maes-y-Rhiw Resr. (covered)
Tranch Wood
Coed Waun-fyr
Coed Meyrick-moel
Coed Caeau-duon
EBBW FOREST
Park House Farm
Hillside Cottage
Pen-llan-gwyn
Llanderfel Farm
Craig-Llywarch
Upper House Farm
Pen-y-wyrlod Farm
Tunley
Old Row
New Row
Four Houses
Incline Farm
Penheol-y-badd-fach
Penheol-y-badd-fawr
Blaen-y-cwm
Coed y Tranch
Ty-trappau
Pensarn Farm
Pen-y-werlod
Pant-yr-heol
Cock-y-north
Springfield Hall
Green Court Farm
Pentrefield Cott.
Cefn Perthy
Gelli-fach
Coed Mary-David
Sunnybank
Vale Vw.
Dowlais Brook
Nant y Milwr
Fairwater Sq. Shops
Ty Gwyn
Sports Grd.
Comm. Cen.
Ty-Canol Ct.
Craig Road
Ty Canol Way
Gwyn Road
Ty Gwyn Way
Thornhill Road
Henllys Way
Henllys Lane
Pensarn Way
Penyland Road
Glan Rhyd
Rhyd Road
Bellevue Ter.
Doralltt
Greenwood Dr.
Marlborough Rd.
Fairwater Way
Brunel Road
Ton Road
Oaksford
Neerings Way
Tolpath
Farlays
Tramway
Ashleigh Ct.
Windsor Rd.
Granston Sq.
Teynes
Willins
Tydies
Stiels
Oxtens
Penylan Ct.
Meyricks
Pentre Close
Perthy Cl.
Llys Gwyrdd
Oakleigh Ct.
Sycamore Ct.
Rosemead
Penmaes
Spring Grove
Oaklands
Beechleigh Cl.
Hafren
Usk
Wye Ct.
Trannon Ct.
Stour Court
Rhymney Court
Leadon Court
Monnow Ct.
Bristol View
Huntingdon Cl.
Exeter Cl.
Warwick Cl.
Leicester Dr.
Edinburgh Dr.
Arundel Ct.
Norfolk Cl.
Wellington
Bedford Cl.
York Pl.
Maes y Rhiw Ct.
Woolpitch
Bowleaze
Ravenscourt
Archer Rd.
Moss Rd.
Berthin
Littledene
St. Peters Cl.
Subway
Bluebell Court
Rose Ct.
Daffodil
Thistle Ct.
Major Cl.
Primrose Court
Saffron Ct.
Heather Ct.
Buttercup Court
Clover Ct.
Hawkes Ridge
Celandine Ct.
Orchid Ct.
Blaen-y-cwm Vw.
Pant Gwyn Cl.
Henllys Village Rd.
Longhouse Gro.
Park Cl.
Forest Vw.
Briers Ga.
Twmbarlwm Ri.
Gelli Fawr Ct.
Pensarn
Wern Fach Ct.
Hendre Ct.
Castle Ct.
Laburnum Dr.
Oak Gro.
Birch Gro.
Campion Cl.
Juniper Cres.
Dean Ct.
Brynonnen Ct.
Tegfan Ct.
Nant-y-Milwr Cl.
Pant-yr-Heol Cl.
Glade
Forest Cl.
Rede Rd.
Jule
Long Acre
Pace Rd.
Newton
Crofton Mede
Ladybench
Rushbrook
Deerbrook

8

18

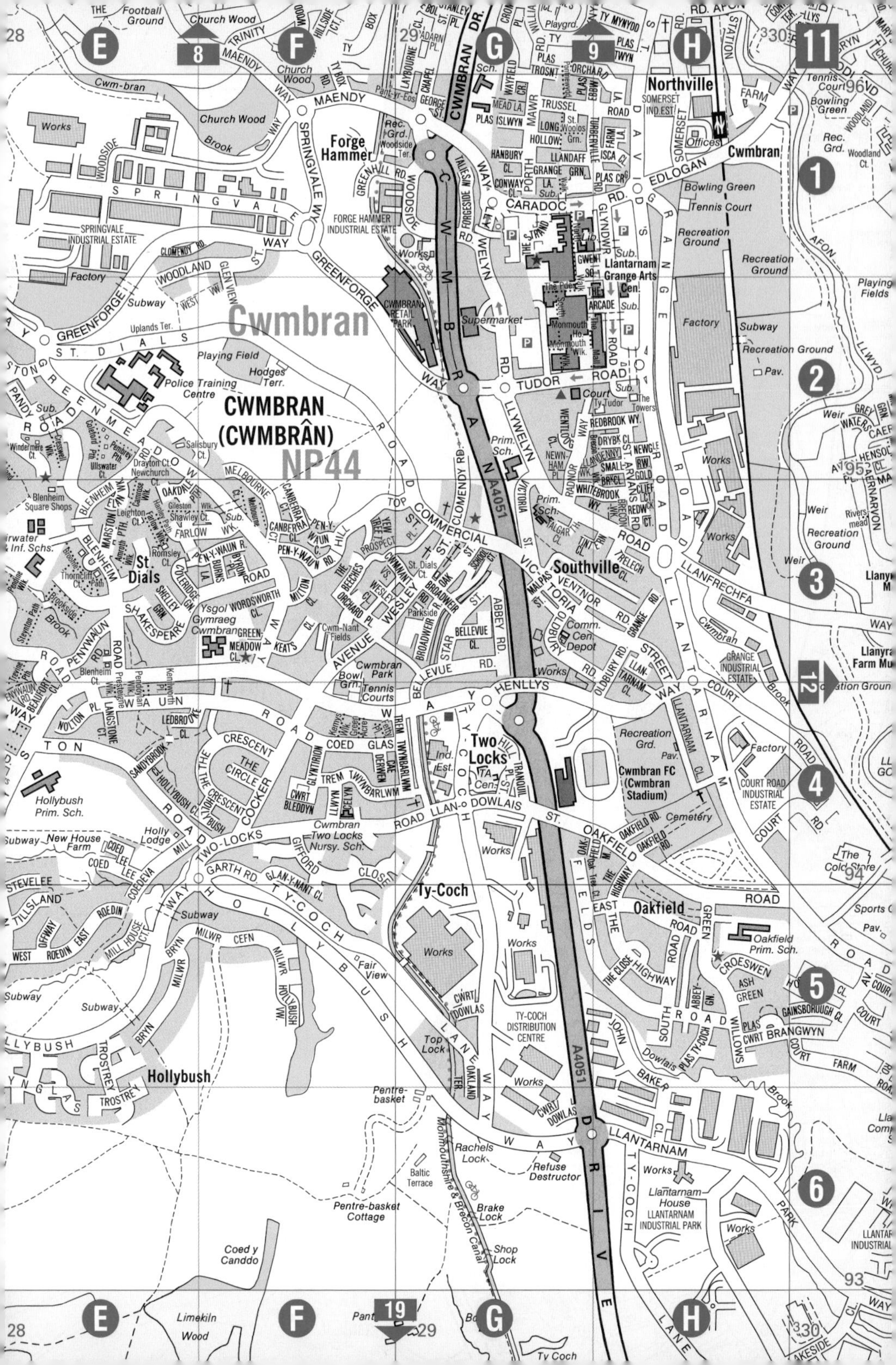

11
Cwmbran
CWMBRAN
(CWMBRÂN)
NP44
Northville
Southville
Oakfield
Two Locks
Ty-Coch
Hollybush
St. Dials
Forge Hammer
Llantarnam Grange Arts Cen.
Cwmbran FC (Cwmbran Stadium)
Springvale Industrial Estate
Forge Hammer Industrial Estate
Cwmbran Retail Park
Police Training Centre
Ty-Coch Distribution Centre
Llantarnam Industrial Park
Court Road Industrial Estate
Grange Industrial Estate
Llantarnam House
Monmouthshire & Brecon Canal
A4051
Cwmbran Drive
Llanfrechfa Way
Greenforge Way
St. Dials Road
Henllys Way
Two-Locks Road
Llantarnam Way
Oakfield Road
Edlogan Way
Commercial St.
Victoria St.
Hollybush Way
Ty-Coch Lane
8
9
12
19
E
F
G
H
1
2
3
4
5
6
28
29
330
93
94
95
96

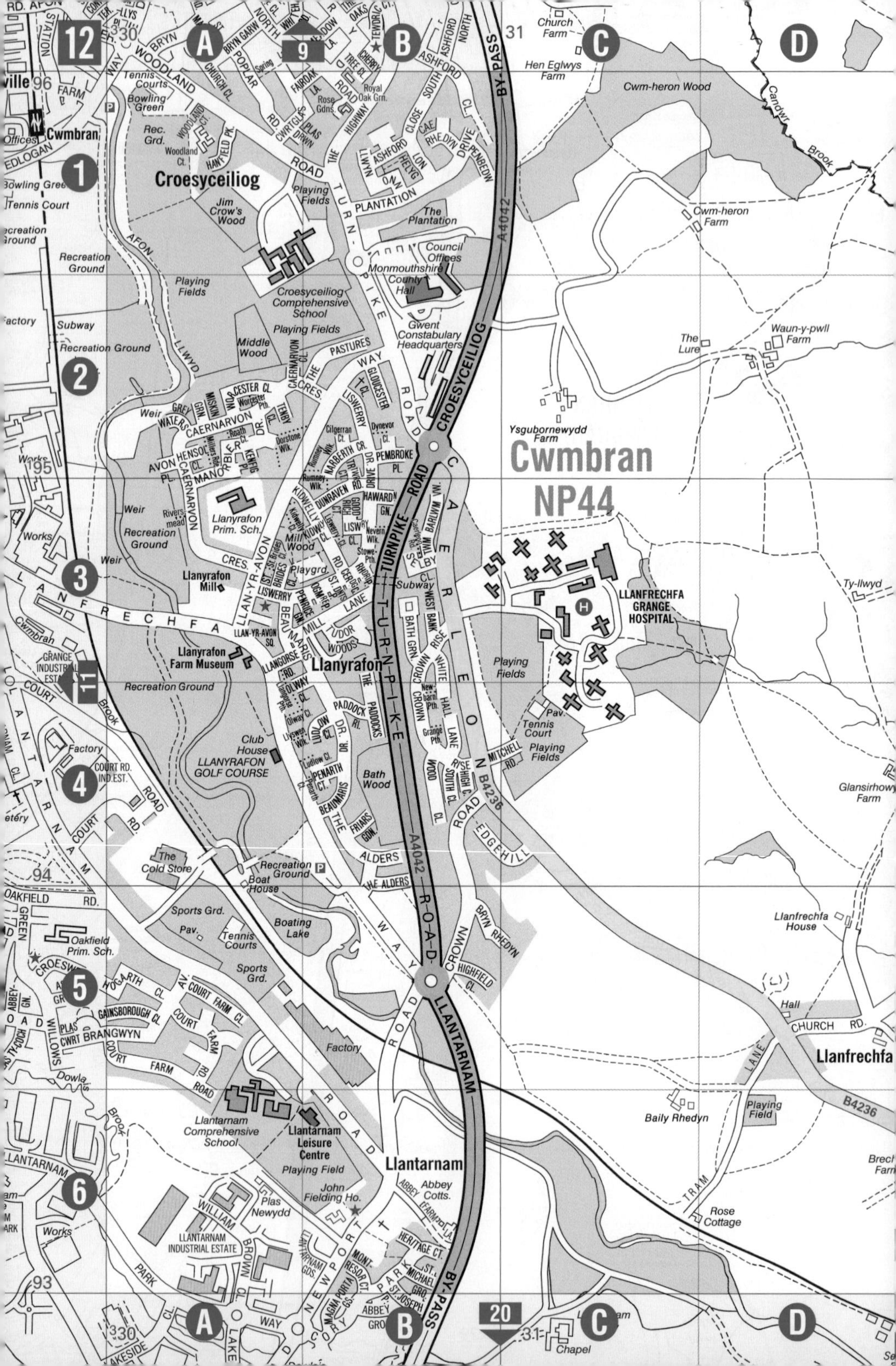

12
A
B
C
D
9
20
11
1
2
3
4
5
6
Cwmbran
NP44
Croesyceiliog
Llanyrafon
Llantarnam
Llanfrechfa
Cwmbran
Church Farm
Hen Eglwys Farm
Cwm-heron Wood
Candwr Brook
Cwm-heron Farm
The Lure
Waun-y-pwll Farm
Ysgubornewydd Farm
Ty-llwyd
Glansirhowy Farm
Llanfrechfa House
Hall
Baily Rhedyn
Rose Cottage
Chapel
Playing Field
LLANFRECHFA GRANGE HOSPITAL
Playing Fields
Tennis Court
Pav.
Monmouthshire County Hall
Council Offices
Gwent Constabulary Headquarters
The Plantation
Croesyceiliog Comprehensive School
Playing Fields
Jim Crow's Wood
Middle Wood
Rec. Grd.
Woodland Ct.
Tennis Courts
Bowling Green
Royal Oak Grn.
Rose Gdns.
Recreation Ground
Subway
Factory
Works
Weir
Rivers mead
Llanyrafon Prim. Sch.
Mill Wood
Playgrd.
Llanyrafon Mill
Llanyrafon Farm Museum
Club House
LLANYRAFON GOLF COURSE
Bath Wood
The Cold Store
Recreation Ground
Boat House
Boating Lake
Sports Grd.
Tennis Courts
Oakfield Prim. Sch.
Factory
Llantarnam Comprehensive School
Llantarnam Leisure Centre
Playing Field
John Fielding Ho.
Plas Newydd
Abbey Cotts.
LLANTARNAM INDUSTRIAL ESTATE
GRANGE INDUSTRIAL ESTATE
COURT RD. IND.EST.
Offices
Bowling Green
Tennis Court
Dowlais Brook
Brook
A4042
B4236
CROESYCEILIOG BY-PASS
TURNPIKE ROAD
LLANTARNAM BY-PASS
CAERLEON ROAD
LLANFRECHFA WAY
WOODLAND ROAD
PLANTATION
THE HIGHWAY
CHURCH RD.
EDGEHILL
BRYN RHEDYN
HIGHFIELD CL.
CROWN RISE
MITCHELL RD.
THE PASTURES
LLAN-YR-AVON
CAERNARVON CRES.
AVON LLWYD
OAKFIELD RD.
COURT FARM RD.
GAINSBOROUGH CL.
HOGARTH CL.
BRANGWYN
CWRT
WILLIAM BROWN CL.
LAKE
NEWPORT RD.
PARK
CORY PARK
MAGNA PORTA GS.
MONTRESOR CT.
HERITAGE CT.
ST. MICHAEL GRO.
ST. JOSEPH
ABBEY GRO.
ABBEY FARM
THE ALDERS
ALDERS
BEAUMARIS DR.
PENARTH CT.
LUDLOW CL.
THE PADDOCKS
PADDOCK RI.
TUDOR WOODS
MILL LANE
BATH GRN.
WEST BANK
WHITE HALL LANE
SOUTH CL.
HIGH C.
LLANGORSE RD.
OLWAY CL.
LLYSWEN WK.
LISWERRY
KIDWELLY
DUNRAVEN RD.
NARBERTH CR.
PEMBROKE PL.
HAWARDN GN.
GOODRICH
CILGERRAN CT.
DYNEVOR CL.
GLOUCESTER CT.
WORCESTER CL.
MISKIN GRN.
CAERNARVON
HENSOL CL.
MANORBIER DR.
KENFIG
TENBY
GREY WATERS
AVON PL.
TURNPIKE
ASHFORD CL.
LLWYN ASHFORD
HELYG
LON CAE
RHEDYN DRIVE
PENBEDW
SOUTH CLOSE
NORTH
POPLAR RD.
FAIROAK LA.
PLAS DRWN
CWRT GLAS
BRYN GARW
CHURCH CL.
WOODLAND CT.
HANFIELD PK.
CHERRY TREE CL.
TEWDRIC CT.
OAKS
STATION RD.
RD. AFON
EDLOGAN
FARM
COURT RD.
LLANTARNAM
ABBEY GN.
WILLOWS
PLAS
LAKESIDE CL.
LLANFRECHFA
TRAM LANE
31
330
96
95
94
93

13
E
F
G
H
32
33
34
96
The Old Rectory
Perthellic Farm
Celynen
Llanthewy Vach
TRE-HERBERT
Sor Brook
Court Perrott
Llandegveth
1
Cefn-tila
Cefn-tila-bach
PENYGLOG
Weir
Court Perrott Cottages
ROAD
White House
TRE-HERBERT
NANTSOR ROAD
Pont Waun-y-pwll
Lan-y-nant
2
Weir
Sor Brook
Gwern Dywyll
Ty-Capten Farm
ROAD
195
Candwr Brook
Pont Lan Sor
Berth-llwyd
Pen-y-wain Farm
3
Little Creigydd Farm
Roughton Farm
Lan-Sor Wood
Creigydd Farm
Roughton House
The Hollies
Cefn Llwyn
Newport
Pen-y-banc
Sarelle Cottage
4
MONMOUTHSHIRE
TORFAEN
NP18
94
(SIR FYNWY)
(TOR-FAEN)
Lindens
GATLAS
Pentopyn
CANDWR
Candwr Farm
5
Reservoir
Church Farm
Pant-yr-eos Farm
Gilwern Brake
Candwr Brook
Pen-y-banc
Shaftesbury Farm
Waterworks
ROAD
LANE
Sunny Pl.
BADGER MDW
CANDWR
6
LAMB
BRECHFA CL
GILWERN FM. CL
Gilwern Farm
Cassandra
Ponthir Primary School
PARK
93
LANE
LANE
CAERLEON
Brook Farm
Ponthir
21
OAKLANDS
E
F
G
H
32
33
34

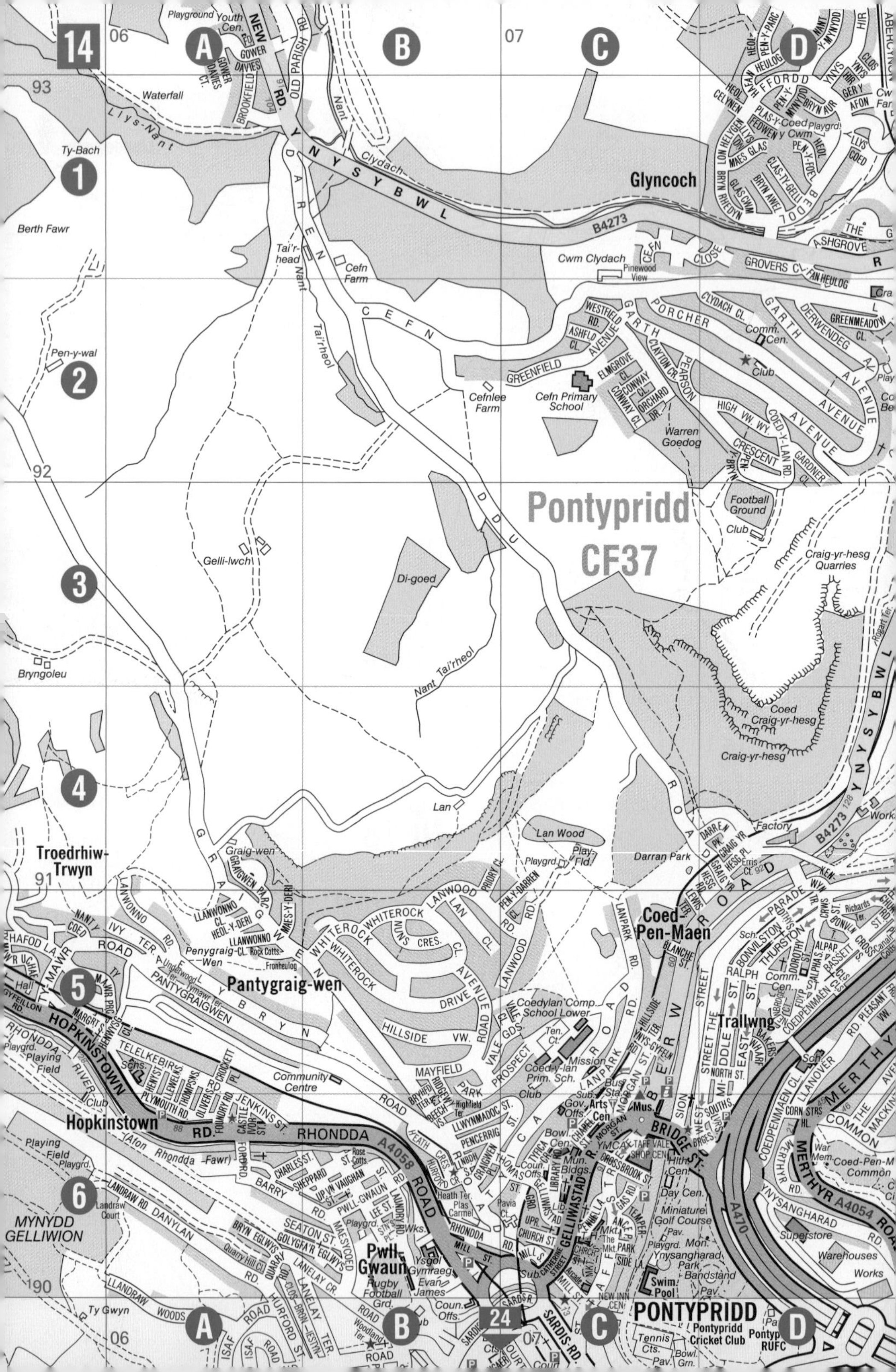
Playground
Youth Cen.
NEW RD.
OLD PARISH RD.
GOWER DAVIES CT.
BROOKFIELD
Waterfall
Llys-Nant
Ty-Bach
Berth Fawr
Nant Clydach
YNYSYBWL
DAREN
Glyncoch
B4273
Tai'r-head
Cefn Farm
Cwm Clydach
Pinewood View
CEFN CLOSE
GROVERS CL.
ASHGROVE
FAN HEULOG
CEFN
Tai'rheol
WESTFIELD RD.
ASHFLD CL.
AVENUE
GREENFIELD
GARTH
PORCHER
CLYDACH CL.
DERWENDEG
GREENMEADOW CL.
Comm. Cen.
Club
Cefnlee Farm
Cefn Primary School
ELMGROVE CL.
CONWAY CL.
ORCHARD DR.
CLAYTON CR.
PEARSON
HIGH VW. WY.
COED-Y-LAN RD.
CRESCENT
GARDNER CL.
Warren Goedog
Pen-y-wal
DDU
Pontypridd
CF37
Football Ground
Club
Craig-yr-hesg Quarries
Gelli-lwch
Di-goed
Bryngoleu
Nant Tai'rheol
Coed Craig-yr-hesg
Craig-yr-hesg
ROAD
Lan
Lan Wood
Factory
Work
Darran Park
Play Fld.
Playgrd.
GRAIG-WEN
Graig-wen
Troedrhiw-Trwyn
Pantygraig-wen
PANTYGRAIGWEN
BRYN
LLANWONNO
IVY TER.
ROAD
Penygraig-Wen
Rock Cotts.
Fronheulog
WHITEROCK
NUNS CRES.
LANWOOD
AVENUE
DRIVE
HILLSIDE VW.
MAYFIELD PARK
PRIORY CL.
PEN-Y-DARREN CL.
LANPARK RD.
Coed-Pen-Maen
BLANCHE ST.
BERW
STREET
ROAD
Coedylan Comp. School Lower
Coed-y-lan Prim. Sch.
Mission
Trallwng
BONVILSTON
THURSTON
PARADE
RALPH
Comm. Cen.
HILLSIDE
Bus Sta.
Arts Cen.
Mus.
BRIDGE ST.
TAFF VALE SHOP CEN.
Day Cen.
Miniature Golf Course
Ynysangharad Park
Bandstand
Swim. Pool
PONTYPRIDD
Pontypridd Cricket Club
RUFC
Tennis Cts.
Bowl. Grn.
A470
MERTHYR
A4054
ROAD
COEDPENMAEN CL.
LLANOVER
THE COMMON
War Mem.
Coed-Pen-Maen Common
YNYSANGHARAD RD.
Superstore
Warehouses
Works
HOPKINSTOWN
Hopkinstown
RHONDDA
A4058
ROAD
Playing Field
Playgrd.
Community Centre
Club
MYNYDD GELLIWION
Landraw Court
DANYLAN
LLANDRAW WOODS
Ty Gwyn
Pwll-Gwaun
Ysgol Gymraeg Evan James
Rugby Football Grd.
Coun. Offs.
SARDIS RD.
Heath Ter.
Plas Carmel
GELLIWASTAD
TAFF ST.
Mkt.
Mun. Bldgs.
Lib.
CHURCH ST.
MILL ST.
NEW INN CEN.
93
92
91
190
06
07

24

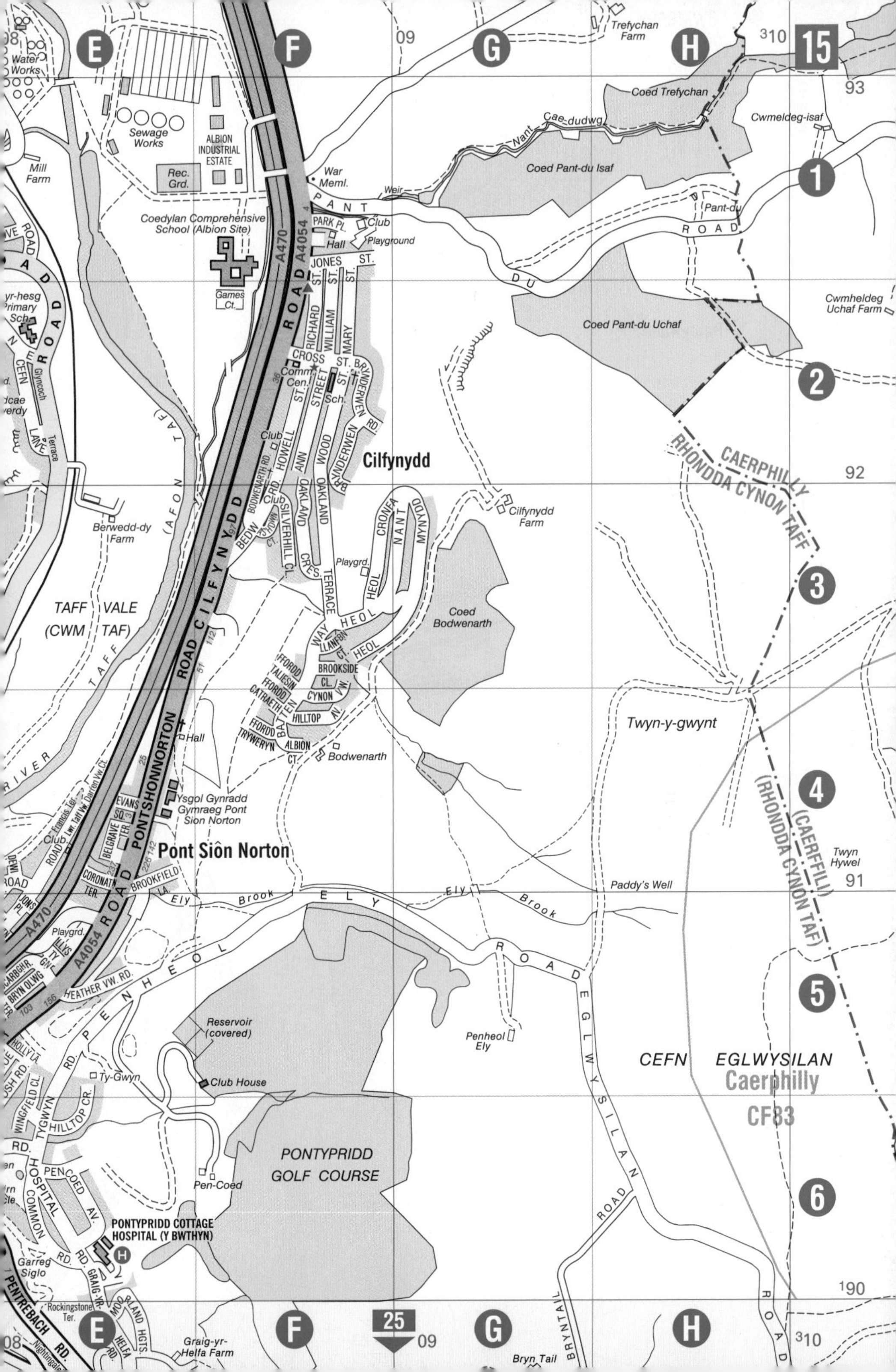
E
F
G
H
Trefychan Farm
Coed Trefychan
Cwmeldeg-isaf
Nant Cae-dudwg
Coed Pant-du Isaf
Water Works
Sewage Works
ALBION INDUSTRIAL ESTATE
Rec. Grd.
Mill Farm
War Meml.
Weir
PANT DU ROAD
Pant-du
PARK PL.
Club
Playground
Hall
Coedylan Comprehensive School (Albion Site)
A470
A4054
JONES ST.
Games Ct.
RICHARD ST.
WILLIAM ST.
MARY ST.
Coed Pant-du Uchaf
Cwmheldeg Uchaf Farm
CROSS ST.
Comm. Cen.
Sch.
BRYNDERWEN RD.
HOWELL ST.
ANN STREET
WOOD ST.
Club
Cilfynydd
CAERPHILLY
RHONDDA CYNON TAF
OAKLAND TERRACE
OAKLAND CRES.
SILVERHILL CL.
BODWENARTH RD.
BEDW
CRONFA
NANT
MYNYDD
HEOL
Cilfynydd Farm
Playgrd.
Berwedd-dy Farm
AFON TAF
ROAD CILFYNYDD
TAFF VALE (CWM TAF)
Coed Bodwenarth
LLANFBN WAY
HEOL
BROOKSIDE
FFORDD TALIESIN
FFORDD CATRAETH
BAYTEN
CYNON VW.
HILLTOP AV.
FFORDD TRYWERYN
ALBION CT.
Bodwenarth
Twyn-y-gwynt
RIVER TAFF
PONTSHONNORTON ROAD
Hall
Ysgol Gynradd Gymraeg Pont Sion Norton
EVANS SQ.
BELGRAVE TER.
Pont Siôn Norton
CORONATN TER.
BROOKFIELD LA.
Club
Playgrd.
(CAERFFILI)
(RHONDDA CYNON TAF)
Twyn Hywel
Paddy's Well
Ely Brook
ELY ROAD
PENHEOL
HEATHER VW. RD.
BRYN OLWG
Reservoir (covered)
Penheol Ely
EGLWYSILAN ROAD
CEFN EGLWYSILAN
Caerphilly
CF83
Club House
Ty-Gwyn
HILLTOP CR.
WINGFIELD CL.
TYGWYN RD.
PENCOED AV.
HOSPITAL RD.
COMMON
PONTYPRIDD GOLF COURSE
Pen-Coed
PONTYPRIDD COTTAGE HOSPITAL (Y BWTHYN)
Garreg Siglo
PENTREBACH RD.
Rockingstone Ter.
GRAIG-YR-HELFA RD.
MOORLAND HGTS.
Graig-yr-Helfa Farm
BRYNTAIL
Bryn Tail
1
2
3
4
5
6
93
92
91
190
310
08
09
25

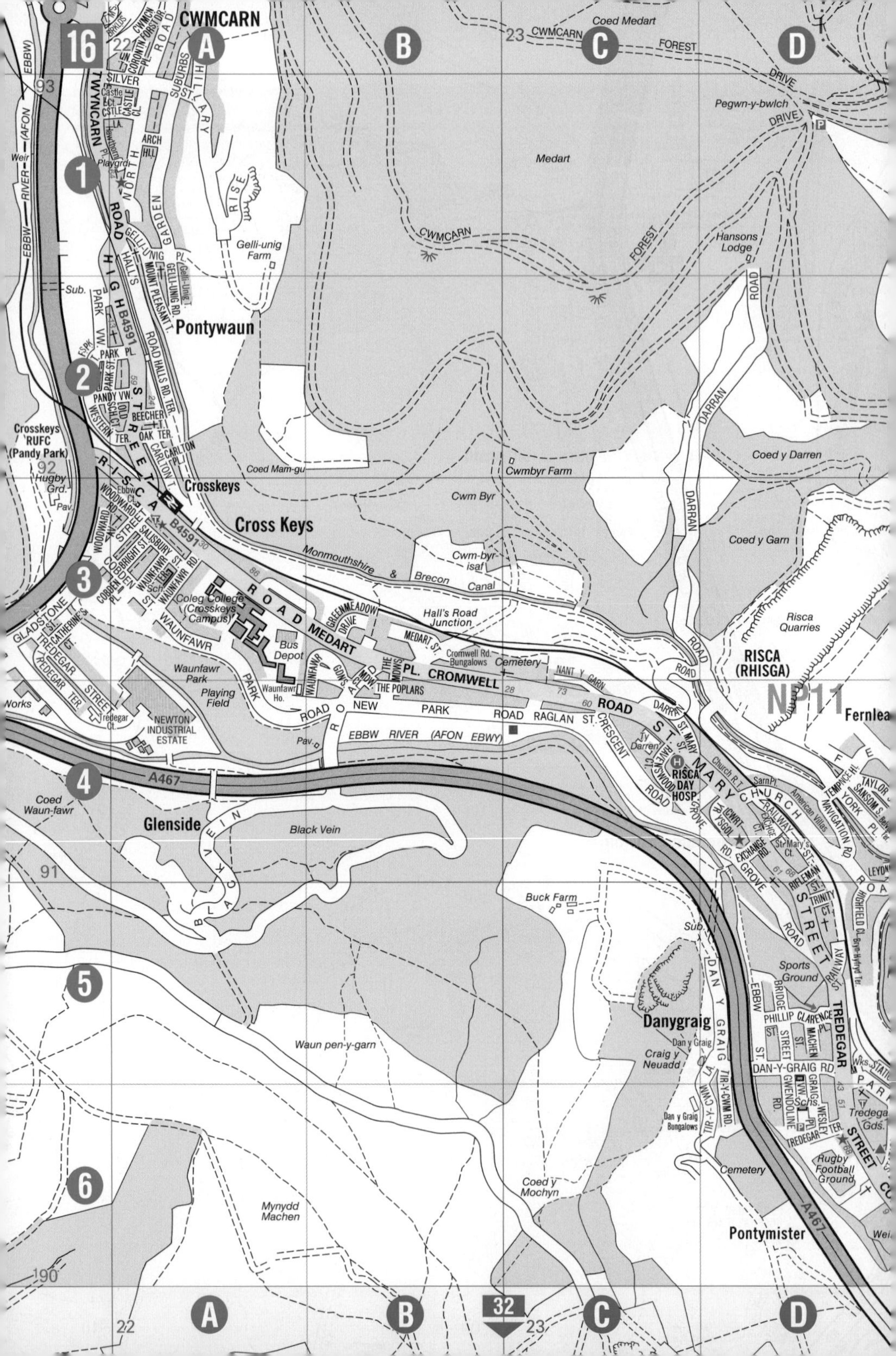
16
CWMCARN
A
B
C
D
1
2
3
4
5
6
93
92
91
190
22
23
32
Coed Medart
CWMCARN FOREST DRIVE
Pegwn-y-bwlch
Medart
Hansons Lodge
Gelli-unig Farm
Pontywaun
TWYNCARN
SILVER
SUBURBS ST.
HILLARY RISE
NORTH ARCH HLL.
GARDEN
Playgrd.
HIGH STREET
ROAD
B4591
HALLS ROAD
HALLS RD. TER.
MOUNT PLEASANT T.
GELLI-UNIG RD.
GELLI-UNIG PL.
PARK VW.
PARK PL.
PARK ST.
PANDY VW.
BEECHER T.
OAK TER.
CARLTON T.
CARLTON PL.
WESTERN TER.
Sub.
Weir
EBBW RIVER (AFON EBBW)
Crosskeys RUFC (Pandy Park)
Hugby Grd.
Pav.
RISCA STREET
Crosskeys
Cross Keys
Coed Mam-gu
Cwmbyr Farm
Cwm Byr
Cwm-byr-isaf
Coed y Darren
Coed y Garn
DARRAN ROAD
Monmouthshire & Brecon Canal
Hall's Road Junction
WOODWARD RD.
SALISBURY ST.
BRIGHT ST.
COBDEN ST.
COBDEN PL.
WAUNFAWR RD.
WAUNFAWR ST.
WAUNFAWR TER.
Coleg College (Crosskeys Campus)
ROAD MEDART
GREENMEADOW DRIVE
MEDART ST.
Bus Depot
Cromwell Rd. Bungalows
Cemetery
CROMWELL PL.
NANT Y GARN
THE POPLARS
THE MEWS
WAUNFAWR PARK
Waunfawr Park
Playing Field
Waunfawr Ho.
GLADSTONE ST.
ST. CATHERINE'S CT.
TREDEGAR CT.
TREDEGAR TER.
TREDEGAR STREET
Tredegar Ct.
Works
NEWTON INDUSTRIAL ESTATE
NEW PARK ROAD
RAGLAN ST.
ROAD
EBBW RIVER (AFON EBWY)
CRESCENT ROAD
Ty Darren
RAVENSWOOD CT.
RISCA DAY HOSP
ST. MARY ST.
ST. MARY STREET
CHURCH
Church R.T.
Sarn Pl.
American Villas
RISCA (RHISGA)
Risca Quarries
NP11
Fernlea
A467
Coed Waun-fawr
Glenside
BLACK VEIN
Black Vein
Buck Farm
Waun pen-y-garn
Danygraig
Dan y Graig
Craig y Neuadd
DAN Y GRAIG
TIR-Y-CWM LA.
TIR-Y-CWM RD.
Dan y Graig Bungalows
Cemetery
Coed y Mochyn
Mynydd Machen
Pontymister
GROVE RD.
CWRT RYSGOL
EXCHANGE RD.
RIFLEMAN ST.
TRINITY CT.
STREET
RAILWAY ST.
RAILWAY
NAVIGATION RD.
TEMPANCE HL.
TAYLOR
SANSOM S.
YORK PL.
LEYON
HIGHFIELD CL.
Sports Ground
BRIDGE ST.
EBBW ST.
PHILLIP ST.
CLARENCE PL.
MACHEN ST.
DAN-Y-GRAIG RD.
GWENDOLINE RD.
GRAIG ST.
WESLEY PL.
TREDEGAR TER.
TREDEGAR STREET
Rugby Football Ground
Tredegar Gds.

E
F
G
H
325
26
93
92
91
190
Craig y Dyffryn
Coed Mary-David
Pandy-mawr
Dyffryn-ffynnonau
Twmbarlwm
TORFAEN
CAERPHILLY
Cwmbran
NP44
(TOR-FAEN)
(CAERFFILI)
Cwrt Henllys
Coed Pren-nimran
Ysgubor-newydd
Craig y Lan
Coed y Cwrt
Coed Pant-yr-eos
(TOR-FAEN)
(CASNEWYDD)
Pant-yr-eos Reservoir
Upper Grippath
Cribarth Villa
Cwm-y-nant
Newport
Pantyreos Farm
Cribarth
Penrhiw
Pen-twyn
Little Pentwyn
Lower Pen-twyn Farm
NEWPORT
CAERPHILLY
MOUNTAIN ROAD
Upper Wenallt
Craig y Wenallt
Lower Wenallt Farm
Ty'n-y-pwll
(CASNEWYDD)
(CAERFFILI)
NP10
HOLLY ROAD
FAIRVIEW AVENUE
BIRCH GRO.
ROWAN RD.
HIGH TREES
ELM AVENUE
PINE CL.
ROSEMONT AV.
MOUNT PENRHIW RD.
PENRHIW RD.
Ty-Sign Jun. & Inf. Schs.
ASTER CL.
Ty-Sign
Manor Ct.
Play-grd.
SNOWDON CL.
GELLI CR.
GELLI CL.
LLWYN GELLI
WOOD
ALMOND
MAPLE AVENUE
PARK ROAD Hillside IND. EST.
PRIORY ST.
HILL ST.
VIEW RD
VIEW CR.
WYNDHAM T.
WYNDHAM TER.
Factory Cotts
THISTLE WAY
Risca & Pontymister
Hillside Wks.
MANOR
HAFOD
LWR.
MILL STREET
CHANNEL
CORONATION ST
Inf. Sch.
Brittania
EPPYNT CL.
PRESCELI CL.
CADER IDRIS CL.
TWM BARLWM CL.
CHEVIOT CL.
PENNINE CL.
QUANTOCK CL.
BRIERLEY CL.
CLEVELAND DR
PENTLAND CL.
BREDON CL.
MENDIP CL.
ARRAN CL.
MALVERN CL.
COTSWOLD WAY
CHILTERN CL.
MOUNTSIDE
PONTYMASON
MANOR WY.
Ty-Sign
Risca Leisure Centre
Sch.
Tennis Cts.
Ysgubor-w
Playing Field
FORSYTHIA CL.
SYCAMORE CLOSE
Play-grd.
CRES
Monmouthshire & Brecon Canal
Graig
SEVERN
MACHEN
CHARTIST CT.
MALVERN TER.
PARK PLACE
LYNE RD.
BROOKLAND RD.
Youth Cen.
Lib.
CLYDE ST.
WELLSPRING
MARYLAND RD.
LLANARTH SQ.
TRAFALGAR ST.
FRANCIS
ISAF RD
Recreation Ground
SPRINGFIELD RD.
COMMERCIAL B4591
COMMERCIAL ST. CARAVAN SITE
PONTYMISTER INDUSTRIAL ESTATE
STREET
SPRINGFIELD
TY-ISAF CR.
HERBERT
PARK
ROAD
Works
CLIFTON ST.
AVENUE
Pen y van
LANE
18
33

18
A
B
C
D
10
27
26
93
92
91
190
1
2
3
4
5
6
17
34
Coed Caeau-duon
Hall
Gelli-fach
Coed Mary-David
Pandy-mawr
Pandy-bach
Coed y Bedw
Castell Farm
Greenmeadow
Castell-y-Bŵch
Cwm Farm
Henllys Vale House
Henllys Vale
Primrose Cottage
PENTRE LANE
CRAIG-CEILIOG LANE
Ffynnon Erw-wen
COED Y TWRCH
Nant-y-Pandy
Nant Henllys
Coed Shon Uchaf
Coed Pren-nimran
Ffynnon-dwyn
(TOR-FAEN)
(CASNEWYDD)
TORFAEN
NEWPORT
Cefn Adam
Lan-is-haul
Coed Pant-yr-eos
Mill Cottage
Tynewydd
Pantyreos Farm
Pantyreos Brook
MILL WOOD
COED CRAIG CEILIOG
Church Farm
Tregwillym House
Park Farm
Craig y Wenallt
Lower Wenallt Farm
Coed Bedw
Garth
Maes-y-coed
HENLLYS LANE
COED BALD
Garth Fach
Golynos
NP10
Golynos Fach Farm
Golynos Fawr Farm
GROES ROAD
Betws Brook
MOUNTAIN ROAD
MALVERN CL.
MOUNTSIDE
PONTYMASON LANE
Risca Leisure Centre
Heol-fawr
Golynos Cottage
Ysgubor-wen
Tennis Cts.
Mescoed Bach
MESCOED MAWR
Playing Field
NEWPORT GOLF COURSE
Gwern-y-

E
F
G
H
11
35
29
330
190
1
2
3
4
5
6
20
93
92
91
Cwmbran
NP44
Newport
NP20
Bettws
Croes-y-mwyalch
Coed y Canddo
Limekiln Wood
Pantglas
Bottom Lock
Ty Coch Wood
Tredeger Lock
Monmouthshire & Brecon Towing Path
Draper's Lock
Cidermill
Wheatsheaf Cottage
Eureka Ho.
Canal
Tamplin Lock
Pentre Bach
Cwrt-Bach
Ty-gwyn
Craig-y-ceiliog Farm
Craig-y-ceiliog Cottage
Traws Mawr House
Ty'n-y-pwll
Bettws Reservior
Yewtree Cottage
Bettws Rugby Club
Wood-side
Green Court Farm
Pentwyn Cottage
Tynyffynon
Ty-ffynonn Lock
Rougemont School
Sneyd Lodge
Sneyd Park
Sneyd Ho.
Malpas Court Primary School
Malpas Court
Lodge Farm
Cottage Farm
INDUSTRIAL PARK
Works
LLANTARNAM INDUSTRIAL EST.
A4051
CWMBRAN DRIVE
PENTRE LANE
PANT GLAS ROAD
TRAWS MAWR LANE
LEACH ROAD
ITCHEN RD.
PEN-TWYN LANE
MILL HEATH
MONNOW WAY
LAMBOURNE WAY
BETTWS LANE
BETTWS HILL
MALPAS ROAD
NEWPORT RD.
Millbrook Jun. & Inf. Schs.
Comm. Cen.
St. David Lewis R.C. Prim. Sch.
Civil Service Sports Ground
Playing Field
Malpas Brook
Monnow Jun.& Inf. Schs.
Social Club
Lib.
BETTWS CENTRE
Hlth. Cen.
Nursy. Sch.
Church Cott.
Llwynaid
Weir
Hazel Wood
Games Courts
Bettws High School
Leisure Centre
Cricket Grd
Woodstock Pond
Woodstock Pool
Morgans Pool
Coed Kemeys
PARC Y BRAIN
Childs Ho.
Willowbrook

A
B
C
D
12
1
2
3
4
5
6
19
36
M4
Cwmbran
Croes-y-mwyalch
Malpas
Bryglas
NP44
NP20
TORFAEN
NEWPORT
LLANTARNAM INDUSTRIAL ESTATE
Works
LLANTARNAM PK. WAY
LAKESIDE
LAKEVIEW ROAD
NEWPORT RD.
HERITAGE CT.
MAGNA PORTA GS.
CORY PARK
ABBEY GRO.
Llantarnam Abbey
Chapel
Dowlais Bri.
Dowlais Brook
Graig Wood
Lodge Farm
Ty-Isaf
Graig Wood House
Cottage Farm
TY-COCH LANE
Croes-y-mwyalch Farm
MALTHOUSE ROAD
LLANTARNAM BY-PASS
A4042
Pen-y-Parc
CWMBRAN DRIVE
PENTRE LANE
BLACKBIRDS CL.
THE MANOR
NEWPORT ROAD
LANSDOWNE GDS.
Brooklands Farm
BRYNGLAS TUNNELS & MALPAS RELIEF ROAD
A4051
Rougemont School
Sneyd Lodge
Sneyd Park
Sneyd Ho.
MALPAS ROAD
WAVELL DRIVE
HORROCKS CL.
ROBERTSON WAY
CLAREMONT
MONTGOMERY RD.
ARLINGTON CL.
ANDERSON PL.
WOODLANDS DR.
HARDING AV.
ST. JOSEPH'S HOSPITAL
ST. ANNE'S HOSPICE
Malpas Court Prim. Sch.
Malpas Pk. Prim. Sch.
CATALPA CL.
WISTARIA
CIRCLE WHITTLE DR.
EDISON
BACON PLACE
Malpas Court
ROWAN WAY
SYLVAN CL.
JAPONICA
MAGNOLIA CL.
LARCH CT.
ASPEN WY.
PILTON VALE
CHERRY TREE CL.
FERN RISE
THE COPPINS
BIRCH GRO
BIRCHGROVE CL.
PENNY CRESCENT
BAIRD CL.
BLACKETT AV.
CHAPMAN CL.
RIDGE
DAVY CL.
MT. PLNT.
CURIE CL.
RUSSELL DR.
RUTHERFORD HILL
DARWIN DR.
KELVIN CL.
MARCONI CL.
RANKINE CL.
BOYLE CL.
NEWTON WAY
FLEMING
HARVEY CL.
LISTER GREEN
HALDANE PL.
CHADWICK CL.
FARADAY
WESTFIELD DR.
WESTFIELD WAY
WESTFIELD AV.
Playing Field
St. David Lewis R.C. Prim. Sch.
GROVE
LAUREL CL.
PINEWOOD CL.
THE SPINNEY
ALDER GRO.
CRES.
Playground
PILLMAWR ROAD
PILLMAWR CIRCLE
Lib.
YEWBERRY
Comm. Cen.
Recreation Ground
Malpas C in W Junior & Infants Schools
HOLLYBUSH AV.
CRES.
GRAIG PARK AV.
GRAIG PARK CIRCLE
GRAIG PK. LA.
GRAIG PK. HILL
GRAIG WOOD CL.
Bryglas Prim. Sch.
BRYNGLAS DR.
BRYNGLAS CT.
BRYNGLAS AV.
BRYN BEVAN
BRYNGLAS RD.
GROVE PARK DR.
Grove Park
THE FIRS
Adult Training Centre
Tennis Courts
Community Centre
Brook
BETTWS LANE
Malpas Brook
Towing Path
Cricket Grd
Leisure Centre
MON ROAD
LLANOVER CL.
Woodstock Pond
Woodstock Pool
BLAEN-Y-PANT CR.
Mount Pleasant
Pill Mawr Farm
Pillmawr House
Park Farm
Lodge Wood
RIVER USK
ST. JULIAN'S GLEBELANDS (Recreation Ground)
Junction 25a
M4 MOTORWAY
Indoor Bowls Cen.
St. Julian's Glebelands Rec. Grd.
Works
93
92
91
90
330
31

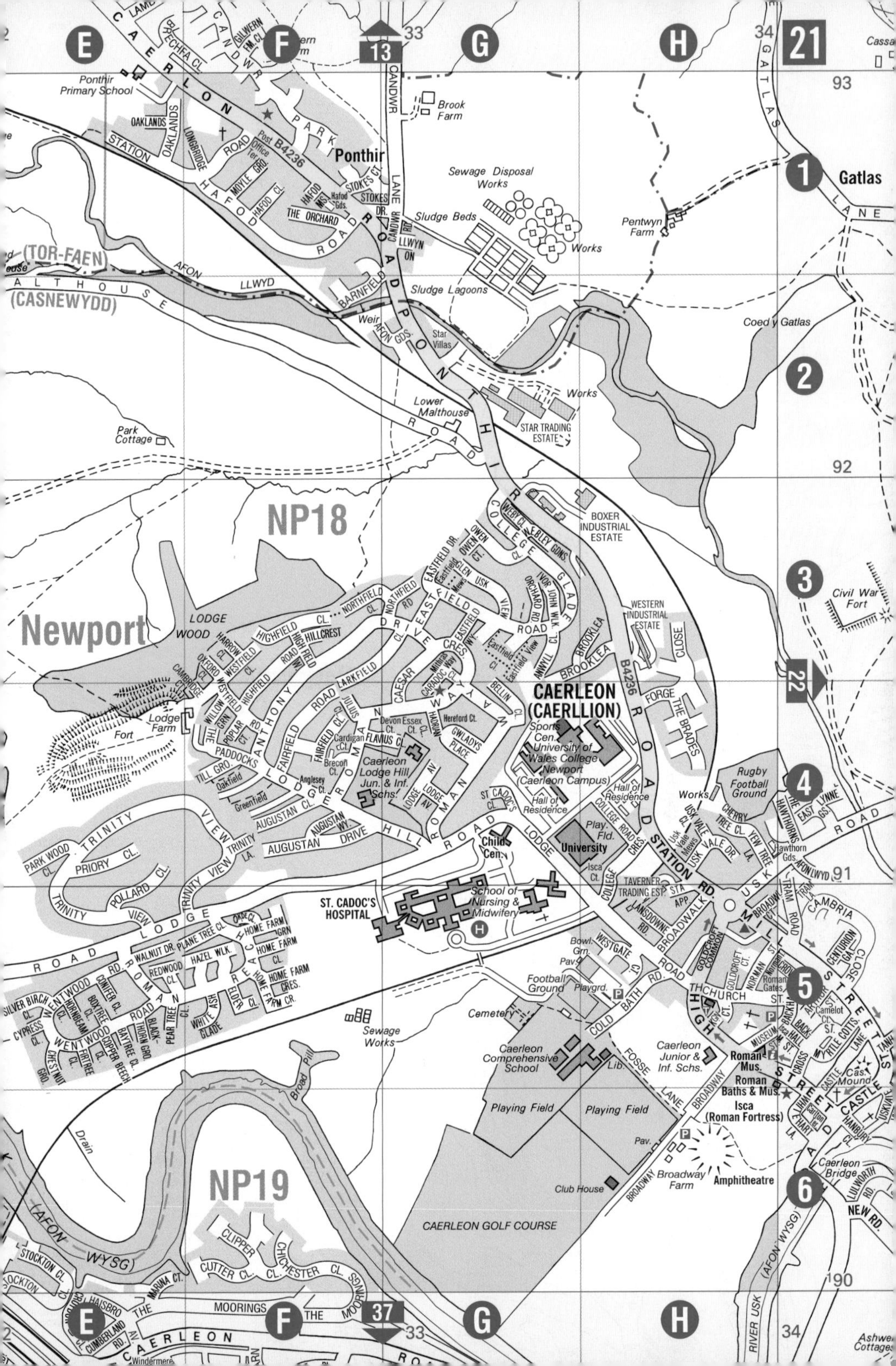

E
F
G
H
13
33
34
93
92
91
90
1
2
3
4
5
6
22
37
Ponthir
Ponthir Primary School
Brook Farm
Sewage Disposal Works
Sludge Beds
Works
Pentwyn Farm
Gatlas
GATLAS LANE
CAERLEON ROAD
B4236
PARK
STATION ROAD
HAFOD ROAD
OAKLANDS
LONGBRIDGE
MOYLE GRO.
HAFOD CL.
THE ORCHARD
STOKES CT.
STOKES DR.
LLWYN ON
CANDWR LANE
PONTHIR ROAD
Post Office
(TOR-FAEN)
(CASNEWYDD)
AFON LLWYD
MALTHOUSE ROAD
Sludge Lagoons
BARNFIELD
Weir
AFON GDS.
Star Villas
Coed y Gatlas
Works
Lower Malthouse
STAR TRADING ESTATE
Park Cottage
NP18
BOXER INDUSTRIAL ESTATE
COLLEGE GLADE
WEBLEY GDNS.
Civil War Fort
Newport
LODGE WOOD
WESTERN INDUSTRIAL ESTATE
CLOSE
BROOKLEA
FORGE
THE BRADES
CAERLEON (CAERLLION)
Sports Cen.
University of Wales College Newport (Caerleon Campus)
Hall of Residence
Lodge Farm
Fort
HIGHFIELD CL.
HILLCREST
NORTHFIELD CL.
NORTHFIELD RD
EASTFIELD DR.
EASTFIELD DRIVE
EASTFIELD WY.
ANTHONY DRIVE
LARKFIELD
CAESAR CRES.
FAIRFIELD ROAD
FAIRFIELD CL.
ROMAN WAY
Devon Ct.
Essex Ct.
Hereford Ct.
GWLADYS PLACE
FLAVIUS CL.
Cardigan Ct.
Brecon Ct.
Anglesey Ct.
Caerleon Lodge Hill Jun. & Inf. Schs.
LODGE AV.
LODGE HILL
ROMAN WAY
TILL GRO.
Oakfield
Greenfield
THE PADDOCKS
AUGUSTAN CL.
AUGUSTAN DRIVE
AUGUSTAN WY.
HILL ROAD
LODGE ROAD
TRINITY VIEW
TRINITY LA.
PARK WOOD CL.
PRIORY CL.
POLLARD CL.
TRINITY VIEW
Child. Cen.
University
Play. Fld.
Isca Ct.
COLLEGE CRES.
COLLEGE ROAD
STATION RD.
USK VALE DR.
USK VALE CL.
Usk Vale Mews
Works
Rugby Football Ground
EAST LYNNE GDS.
THE HAWTHORNS
CHERRY TREE CL.
YEW TREE LA.
Hawthorn Gds.
USK ROAD
AFON LWYD
TRAM ROAD
CAMBRIA CLOSE
CENTURION GA.
TAVERNER TRADING EST.
STA. APP.
LANSDOWNE RD.
BROADWALK
GOLDCROFT COMMON
GOLDCROFT CT.
NORMAN ST.
MILL STREET
ST. CADOC'S HOSPITAL
School of Nursing & Midwifery
LODGE ROAD
PLANE TREE CL.
WALNUT DR.
HAZEL WLK.
REDWOOD CL.
HOME FARM GRN
HOME FARM CL.
HOME FARM CRES.
ROMAN REACH
Bowl. Grn.
Pav.
WESTGATE CT.
Football Ground
Playgrd.
COLD BATH RD.
CHURCH ST.
HIGH STREET
Roman Gates
Camelot Ct.
Cemetery
Sewage Works
Caerleon Comprehensive School
Lib.
FOSSE LANE
Caerleon Junior & Inf. Schs.
Roman Mus.
Roman Baths & Mus.
Isca (Roman Fortress)
MUSEUM ST.
BACKHALL ST.
CROSS ST.
CASTLE ST.
Cas. Mound
HANBURY CL.
Playing Field
Playing Field
Pav.
Club House
Broadway Farm
Amphitheatre
Caerleon Bridge
LULWORTH RD.
NEW RD.
BROADWAY
SILVER BIRCH CL.
CYPRESS CL.
WENTWOOD RD.
WENTWOOD ROAD
CONIFER CL.
BOXTREE CL.
HORNBEAM CL.
PEAR TREE CL.
BLACKTHORN GRO.
WHITE ASH GLADE
ELDER CL.
CHESTNUT GRO.
FIR TREE CL.
COPPER BEECH CL.
BAYTREE CL.
Drain
Broad Pill
NP19
(AFON WYSG)
CAERLEON GOLF COURSE
CLIPPER CL.
CUTTER CL.
CHICHESTER CL.
MARINA CT.
STOCKTON CL.
THE MOORINGS
HAISBRO AV.
CUMBERLAND RD.
CAERLEON ROAD
RIVER USK (AFON WYSG)
Ashwell Cottages

22
34
335
A
B
C
D
93
92
91
190
1
2
3
4
5
6
Cassandra
Gatlas
Pentwyn Cottage
GATLAS LANE
Brook
Sor
The Chymes
Garth
USK ROAD
Little Farm
Cwm-y-gwcw
Home Farm
Ivybridge
Ivybridge Wood
Cheshire Home
Llanhennock
Caeryder Oak
Coed y Gatlas
Ty-coch
Nant-y-mynydd
Pencraig Farm
Lower Pencreeg
Drain
Oaklands Lodge
Sor Mill Farm
Sor Brook Bridge
Penrhos Farm
Civil War Fort
MONMOUTHSHIRE
NEWPORT
(AFON WYSG)
Great Bulmore Farm
Newport
NP18
Ysgubar Newydd Farm
21
Rugby Football Ground
Works
Ty Fferm
TWYN OAKS
THE HAWTHORNS
EAST LYNNE GS
CHERRY TREE CL.
YEW TREE LA.
USK VALE CL.
Usk Vale Mews
USK VALE DR.
STATION RD.
Hawthorn Gds.
AFON LWYD CL.
TRAM ROAD
CAMBRIA CLOSE
CENTURION GA.
BROADWALK
GOLDCROFT COMMON
B4236
MILL STREET
AFON LWYD
Little Bulmore
Caer Eithin
Little Bulmore Wood
Catsash House
RIVER USK
BULMORE ROAD
CAERLEON (CAERLLION)
Roman Gates
Camelot Ct.
Caerleon Junior & Inf. Schs.
Roman Mus.
Roman Baths & Mus.
Isca (Roman Fortress)
Amphitheatre
Cas. Mound
Uskside
Broadway Farm
BROADWAY
Caerleon Bridge
LULWORTH RD.
ISCA ROAD
NEW ROAD
CAERLEON ROAD
B4596
Chepstow Hill
Clawdd
Roman Road
Club House
Driving Range
Pen-y-lan
Welsh Golfing Union
CELTIC MANOR GOLF COURSE
CATSASH ROAD
Ashwell Cottages
38
Coldra Wood

Garn-fawr
Garn-fach
Glen Usk
Pant-gwyn
Castle Mill
RIVER USK (AFON WYSG)
(SIR FYNWY)
(CASNEWYDD)
Redland Pool
Underpass
A449
Kemeys Farm
Kemeys House
Depot
KEMEYS GRAIG
LANE
Abernant Farm
ROAD
Woodward's Farm
Great Bulmore
GOLF COURSE
Pen-toppen-ash
NEW WOOD
COED Y CAERAU
Chapel Cottage
Treclover
Crows Ridge
Mount Tudor
Pen-y-Bryn
Sleepyhollow
Woodville Bungalow
Reservoir (covered)
Cat's Ash
Draenllwyn
OLD ROMAN ROAD
Langstone Prim. Sch.
Windy Ridge
Cat's Ash Farm
CATSASH ROAD
Caeffynnon
The Gorelands
Langstone
TREGARN RD.
MAGOR RD.
B4245
CELTIC MANOR GOLF COURSE
Priory Wood
Priory Farm
A48
CHEPSTOW ROAD
THE GLEN
Langstone Park
Columbus House
PRIORY GS.
STOCKWOOD CL.
SILURE WY.
ROSECROFT DRIVE
PARK END
Delbury
PRIORY DR.
PRIORY WALK
PRIORY WY.
PRIORY GRO.
LANGSTONE BUS. VILLAGE
CRES.
STOCKWOOD WY.
Garden Centre
39
SPARTAN CL.
GRENADIER DR.
Rec. Grd.
THE PADDOCK
OLD CHEPSTOW
THE NURSERIES
Langstone
E F G H
1 2 3 4 5 6
37 38 93 92 91 90

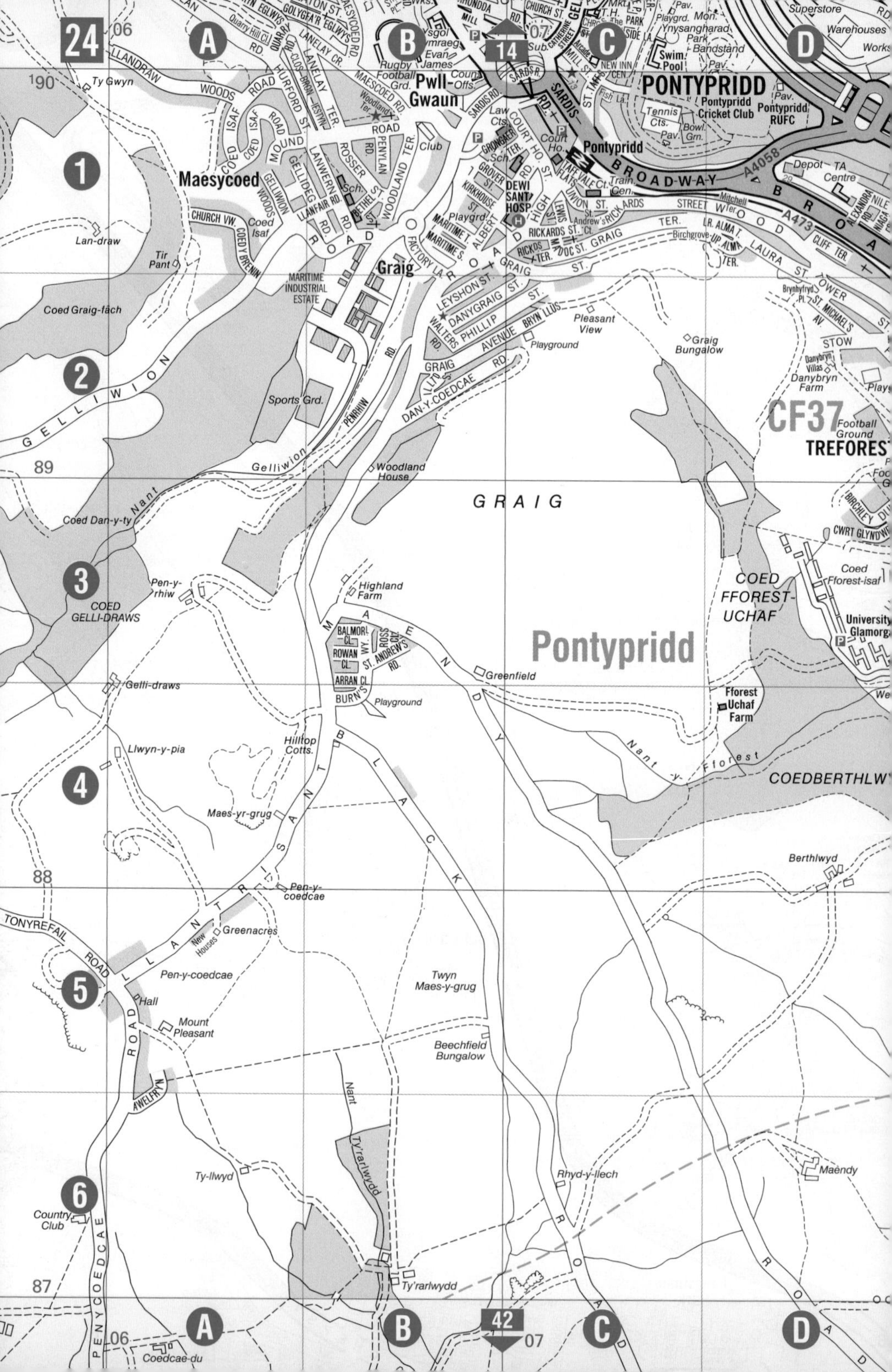

A
B
C
D
1
2
3
4
5
6
06
07
190
89
88
87
14
42
PONTYPRIDD
Pontypridd
Pontypridd Cricket Club
Pontypridd RUFC
Ynysangharad Park
Bandstand
Swim. Pool
Tennis Cts.
Bowl. Grn.
Superstore
Warehouses
Works
BROADWAY
A4058
A473
Depot
TA Centre
Pwll-Gwaun
Maesycoed
Graig
Rugby Football Grd.
Ysgol Gymraeg Evan James
Couny Offs.
Law Cts.
Court Ho.
DEWI SANT HOSP.
Train Cen.
MARITIME INDUSTRIAL ESTATE
Sports Grd.
Ty Gwyn
Lan-draw
Tir Pant
Coed Graig-fâch
Coed Isaf
GELLIWION
Gelliwion
Coed Dan-y-ty
Nant
Woodland House
GRAIG
Pleasant View
Playground
Graig Bungalow
CF37
TREFOREST
Football Ground
Danybryn Farm
Danybryn Villas
COED FFOREST-UCHAF
Coed Fforest-isaf
CWRT GLYNDWR
BIRCHLEY DR.
University of Glamorgan
Fforest Uchaf Farm
Nant-y-Fforest
COEDBERTHLWYD
Berthlwyd
Pen-y-rhiw
COED GELLI-DRAWS
Gelli-draws
Highland Farm
MAENDY
BALMORL CL.
ROWAN CL.
ARRAN CL.
BURNS
ST. ANDREW'S RD.
Greenfield
Playground
Hilltop Cotts.
LLANTRISANT
BLACK
Llwyn-y-pia
Maes-yr-grug
Pen-y-coedcae
Greenacres
New Houses
TONYREFAIL ROAD
Pen-y-coedcae
Hall
Mount Pleasant
Twyn Maes-y-grug
Beechfield Bungalow
AWELFRYN
Ty-llwyd
Nant Ty'rarlwydd
Rhyd-y-llech
Maendy
Country Club
PENYCOEDCAE
Ty'rarlwydd
Coedcae-du
ROAD

E
F
G
H
15
43
26
1
2
3
4
5
6
PONTYPRIDD COTTAGE HOSPITAL (Y BWTHYN)
Pentrebach
Graig-yr-Helfa Farm
Hillside View
Bryn Tail
Hendre-Prosse
Tir Cae-mawr
Craig-fach
Coleg Morgannwg (Centre for Art & Design Technology)
Cemetery
Glyntaff Crematorium
Offices
Coed Glyn-Taf
Ffynnon-Rhingyll
Glyn-Taf
GLYNTAFF
Treforest
Machine Bri.
Lewistown Park
Comm. Cen.
Coed Craig-lwyd
GLYNTAFF HOUSING EST.
Ysgol Gyfun Rhydfelen
Coleg Morgannwg
Heol-y-Celyn Prim. & Rhydyfelin Nursy. Schs.
Treharne Flats
RHYDYFELIN
Playing Field
Newman R.C. Comp. Sch.
Michael's R.C.Prim. Sch.
Govt. Offices
Works
Hawthorn Leisure Cen.
Comm.Cen.
Rec. Grd.
Glen Afon
Hawthorn
Factory
Hawthorn Primary & High Schools
Caeglas
Recreation Ground
Graig y Fforest Farm
Heol-y-Cawl Bungalow
Heol-y-cawl
Coed Tir-isaf
Lowlands
CF38
Coed y Fardre
TONTEG INDUSTRIAL ESTATE
TAFF BUSINESS CEN.
Kidz Playgrd.
Upper Boat
TREFOREST IND. EST.
Fardre-uchaf
A4054
A470
A473
CARDIFF ROAD
BRYNTAIL
EGLWYSILAN ROAD
GRAIG Y FFOREST
RIVER TAFF
DYNEA ROAD
LLANTWIT ROAD

310
11
A
B
C
D
1
2
3
4
5
6
190
89
88
87
Rugby Field
Ckt. Grd.
Ty'n-y-parc
Nant Corrwg
EGLWYSILAN ROAD
Garth
Tir Cae-mawr
Ffynnon Llan
Ffynnon-Rhingyll
The Old Rectory
Nant Llan
Aber-Fawr
Pumping Station
Greenfield Pl.
HILLSIDE AV.
GARTH ESTATE
HENDRE RD.
Garth Villas
WINDSOR PL.
Coed Ty'n-y-parc
Abertrid
WOODLAND TER.
CHURCH RD.
UP. FRANCIS ST.
EGLWYSILAN WY.
FRANCIS
TRIDWR RD.
DAN-Y-MYNYDD
TY'N Y PARC
Gleneagles
Coed Craig-lwyd
Pant-drain
Nant Corrwg
Senghenrdd Dyke
Mynydd Meio
CAERPHILLY
RHONDDA CYNON TAFF
Taff Valley Quad Bike & Activity Centre
RHYDYFELIN
FFORESTNEWYDD
FFYNNONBWLA
DYNEA WAY
HEOL-Y-BRYN
25
DYNEA CT.
DYNEA CL.
Playgrd.
DAN-YR-ALLT CL.
ELM ST.
DYNEA ROAD
PINEWOOD CR.
BRYNFAB R.
ARFONFAB CR.
CLOS ANEURIN
CORRWG
GLAN Y NANT
Gelli Hirion
MAES YR AWEL
MAES GANOL
MAES UCHAF
MAES Y FELIN
R.C. Ch.
Ffynnonbwla
Mynydd-mayo
GELLI HIRION INDUSTRIAL ESTATE
Depot
Superstore
Pontypridd
CF37
Ffynnon-isaf
LAUREL AV.
CRES.
Playgrd.
CARDIFF ROAD
County Vw.
Nant
THE RISE
A470
A4054
Caeglas
Pav.
Recreation Ground
Lonydd
Williams Pl.
UPPER BOAT IND. PK.
CRWYS CR.
GWILI RD.
Midway Park
HIRAETHOG RD.
HEOL-Y-BWNSI
Llwyn Onn Farm
Pen-y-groes
Upper Boat
West Winds
Tai'r Level
RIVER TAFF
Upper Boat
Works
TAFF BUSINESS CEN.
Kidz Playgrd.
TONTEG INDUSTRIAL ESTATE
TREFOREST IND. EST.
Factories
TONTEG ROAD
SEVERN RD.
Works
GWAELOD-Y-GARTH RD.
MAIN AV.
HEOL GRDESWEN
HEOL TY MAEN
44
Factories
Heol-y-bwnsy
Crossroads
Nant
Ffynnonwen
TAFFS FALL
AFON TAF

E
F
G
H
13
14
190
1
2
3
4
5
6
Cwm yr Aber
Cae'r-llwyn
Waterfall
Cwmceffy
BRYNCOED TER.
HIGH STREET
EDWARD TER.
ABER TER.
BRYN ABER
BRYNGELLI
Cwmaber Infants School
Nant
Cwmaber Junior Sch.
FFORDD LAS PL.
FFORDD LAS
CAE-BRYN
ANNES GDS.
YMCA
KING ST.
THOMAS ST.
DAN-Y-GRAIG
B4263
UNDERWOOD TER.
GRAIGWEN CRESCENT
Sunnybank
Mountain Vw.
Craigyfedw
GRAIG-Y-FEDW
Graigwen Ct.
Pav.
Library
Rec. Grd.
Pont y Felin
ABERFAWR ROAD
ABERFAWR TER.
COEDCAE RD.
COED-Y-PICA
BRONMYNNYD
ILAN ROAD
Caerphilly CF83
Coed Cae pica
Graig-wen
Cwm-Ifor
Pen yr Heol Las Farm
Cwarrau-mawr
BOWLS LANE
Waterfall
CWM FFOR
HEOL CWARREL
CLARK
89
HENFRON
BLAEN
BRYNAWEL
PEN-Y-BRYN
HEOL FAWR
HEOL FER
ANEURIN
GLAN FFRWD
CAE CARADOG
BRYN NANT
BRYN-YR-YSGOL
CALEDFRYN
HEOL TIR BACH
PEN-Y-GROES
CEFN-Y-LON
HEOL GRAIG-WEN
28
Cwm yr Aber
Hendredenny-uchaf Farm
Plymouth House
Hendredenny-ganol
Nant yr Aber
B4263
HEOL SERTH
BRYN SIRIOL
CLYD
Ty-isaf
BRYN IFOR
Cwn Ifor Primary Sch.
WAY
Penyrheol
TROED-Y-BRYN
RHIW FACH
Pav.
Bowl. Grn.
Aneurin Park
BOWLS CL.
Bowls Terrace
BRYNHYFRYD
88
Ty Isaf Bungalows
Hendredenny Park
CHESTER CT.
GOLWG Y COED
RHUDDLAN CT.
DUNRAVEN CT.
HENDREDENNY DRIVE
TENBY CT.
CAERNARVON CT.
KIDWELLY CT.
CLOS GWERNYDD
BROOKSIDE CL.
STATION TER.
Orchards Poultry Farm
BRIGHAM CT.
CAERLEON CT.
NARBERTH CT.
DENBIGH CT.
OGMORE CT.
MORLAIS CT.
HARLECH CT.
CONWAY CT.
CARMARTHEN CT.
CHEPSTOW CT.
CALDICOT CT.
RAGLAN CT.
MONMOUTH CT.
GROESWEN ROAD
PEMBROKE CT.
HOLYHEAD CT.
WHITE CROSS LA.
OLD FURNACE RD.
CENYDD CL.
CENYDD R.
St. Cenydd Comprehensive School
Hendredenny Park Primary Sch.
St. Cenydd Leisure Cen.
Hendre Jun. Sch.
Ty-newydd
Playing Fields
BY-PASS
A468
CAERPHILLY
ST. CENYDD
HEOL-Y-PIA
MAES-Y-SIGLEN
TRESIGLEN
CAE'R FFERM
LON ROBIN GOCH
87
(CAERFFILI)
(RHONDDA CYNON TAF)
Pantyrefin Cottage
Cardiff CF15
GYPSY LANE
Tai Cae bryn
Ty-llwyd
Cartref
Bryngolau
Y Groes-wen
Groes-wen Farm
GROESWEN
SWORD HILL
45
Gledyr

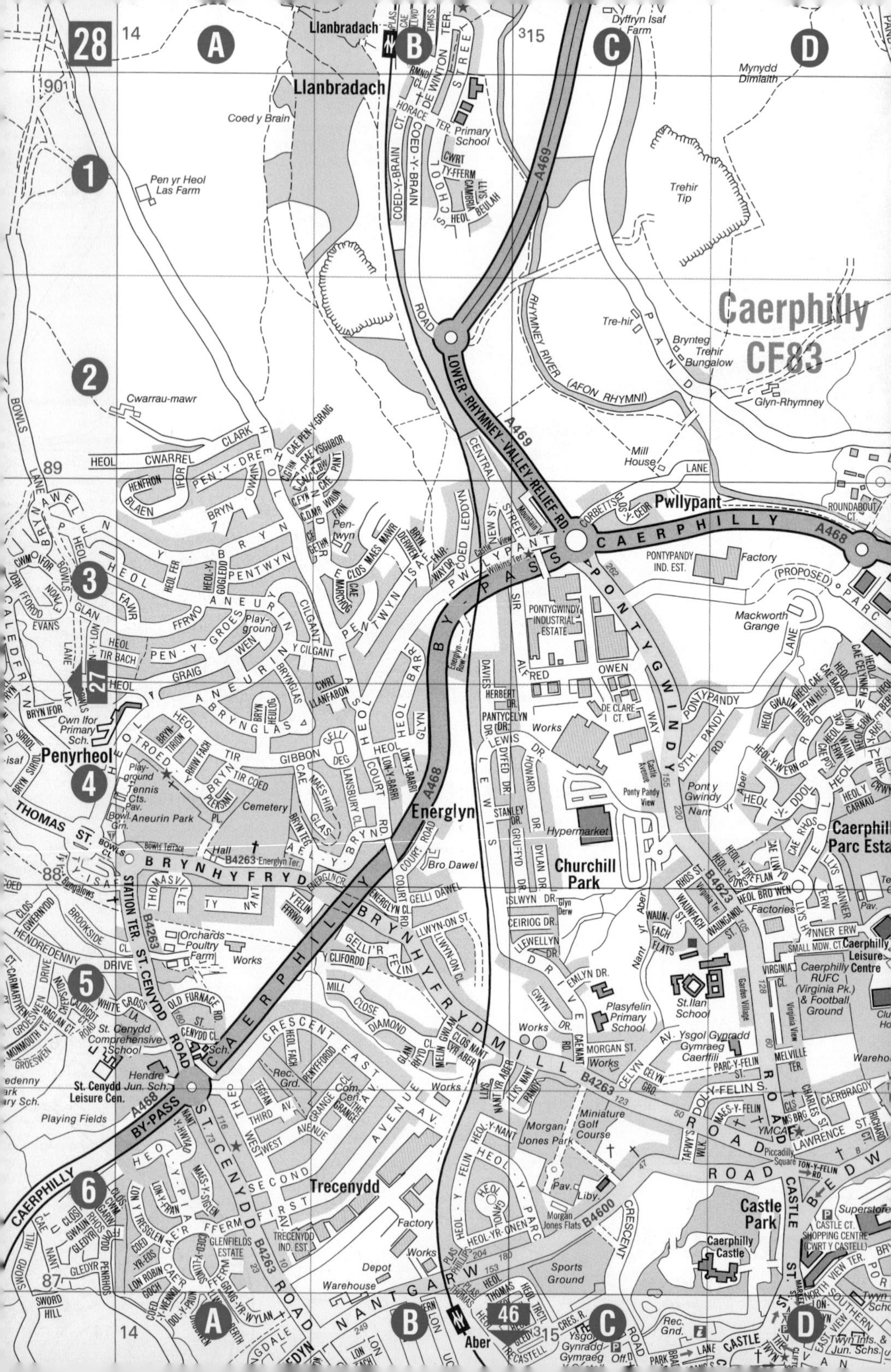
28
A
B
C
D
1
2
3
4
5
6
14
315
901
89
88
87
Llanbradach
Coed y Brain
Pen yr Heol Las Farm
Cwarrau-mawr
Dyffryn Isaf Farm
Mynydd Dimlaith
Trehir Tip
Tre-hir
Brynteg
Trehir Bungalow
Glyn-Rhymney
Caerphilly
CF83
Mill House
Pwllypant
RHYMNEY RIVER (AFON RHYMNI)
LOWER-RHYMNEY-VALLEY-RELIEF-RD.
A469
A468
CAERPHILLY
BY-PASS
CAERPHILLY BY-PASS
PONTYPANDY IND. EST.
Factory
PONTYGWINDY INDUSTRIAL ESTATE
PONTYGWINDY
Mackworth Grange
Primary School
Penyrheol
Cwn Ifor Primary Sch.
Aneurin Park
Tennis Cts.
Cemetery
Energlyn
Hypermarket
Churchill Park
Caerphilly Parc Estate
Caerphilly Leisure Centre
Caerphilly RUFC (Virginia Pk.) & Football Ground
St. Ilan School
Plasyfelin Primary School
Ysgol Gynradd Gymraeg Caerffili
Miniature Golf Course
Morgan Jones Park
Morgan Jones Flats
Castle Park
Caerphilly Castle
CASTLE CT. SHOPPING CENTRE (CWRT Y CASTELL)
Superstore
St. Cenydd Comprehensive School
Hendre Jun. Sch.
St. Cenydd Leisure Cen.
Playing Fields
Orchards Poultry Farm
Trecenydd
TRECENYDD IND. EST.
GLENFIELDS ESTATE
Sports Ground
Depot
Warehouse
Works
Aber
46
27
BRYNHYFRYD
B4263
B4623
B4600
NANTGARW ROAD
ST. CENYDD ROAD
STATION TER.
THOMAS ST.
CASTLE ST.
Piccadilly Square

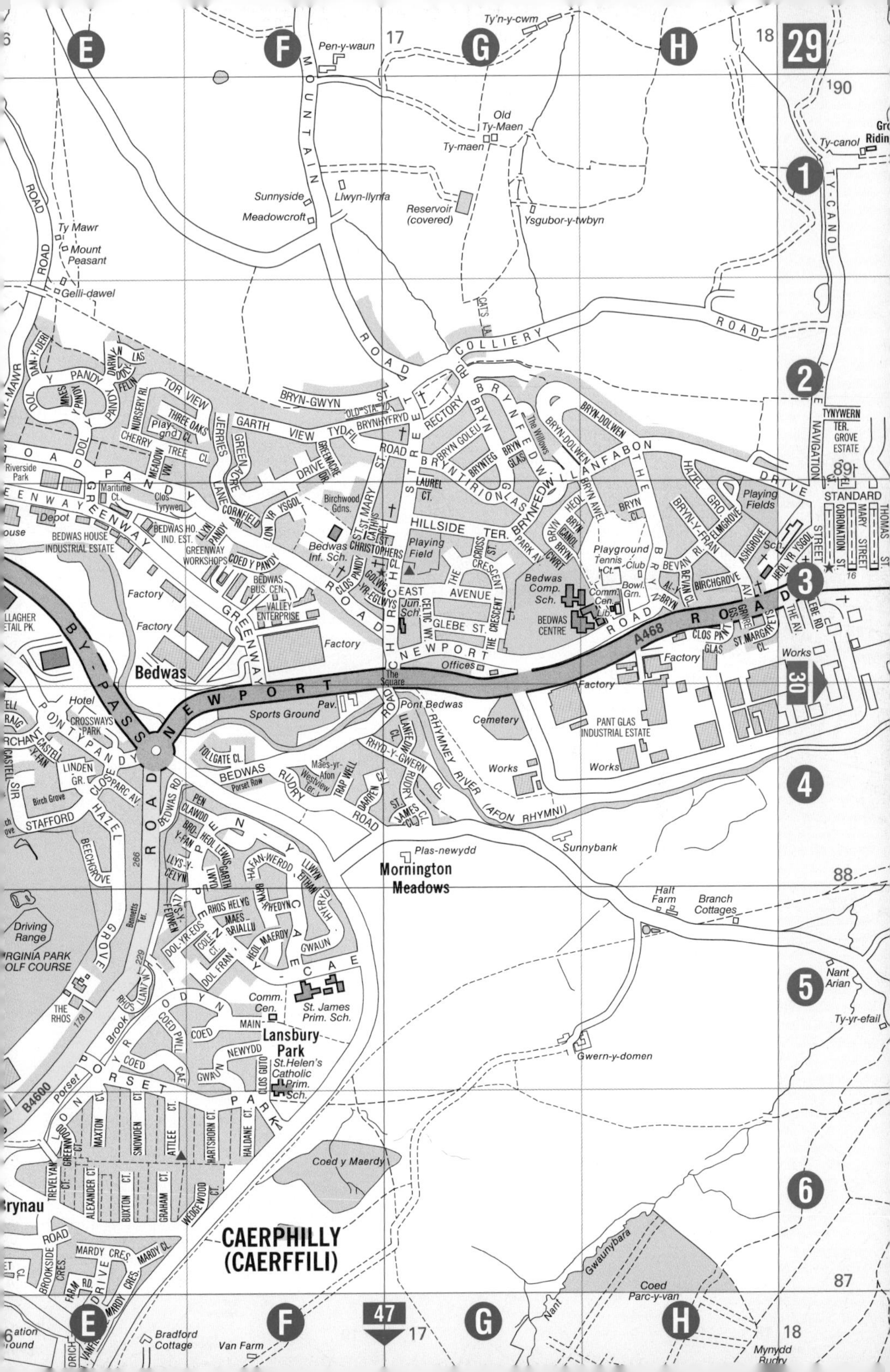
E
F
G
H
17
18
190
89
88
87
1
2
3
4
5
6
Pen-y-waun
Ty'n-y-cwm
MOUNTAIN ROAD
Old Ty-Maen
Ty-maen
Ty-canol
TY-CANOL
Sunnyside
Meadowcroft
Llwyn-llynfa
Reservoir (covered)
Ysgubor-y-twbyn
Ty Mawr
Mount Peasant
Gelli-dawel
CATS LA.
COLLIERY ROAD
BRYN-GWYN ST.
OLD STA. YD.
TOR VIEW
THREE OAKS
CHERRY TREE CL.
GARTH VIEW DRIVE
TYDFIL
BRYNHYFRYD
RECTORY RD.
BRYNFEDW
The Willows
BRYN-DOLWEN
TYNYWERN TER.
GROVE ESTATE
NAVIGATION
DOL Y PANDY
PANDY ROAD
Riverside Park
Maritime Ct.
Clos Tyrywen
GREENWAY
Depot
BEDWAS HOUSE INDUSTRIAL ESTATE
BEDWAS HO. IND. EST.
GREENWAY WORKSHOPS
COED Y PANDY
CORNFIELD RI.
LON YR YSGOL
Birchwood Gdns.
Bedwas Inf. Sch.
ST. CHRISTOPHERS CL.
CHURCH STREET
LAUREL CT.
BRYNTIRION
BRYNTEG
BRYN GOLEU
HILLSIDE TER.
PARK AV.
Playing Field
CROSS ST.
CRESCENT
THE AVENUE
EAST
Jun. Sch.
CELTIC WY.
GLEBE ST.
THE CRESCENT
Bedwas Comp. Sch.
BEDWAS CENTRE
Comm. Cen.
Lib.
Playground
Tennis Ct.
Club
Bowl. Grn.
BRYN AWEL
BRYN CL.
LLANFABON DRIVE
HAZEL GRO.
BRYN-Y-FRAN
ELMGROVE
ASHGROVE
BIRCHGROVE
BEVAN RI.
BEVAN CL.
Playing Fields
HEOL YR YSGOL
STANDARD
CORONATION ST.
MARY STREET
THOMAS ST.
THE AV.
GLEBE RD.
ST. MARGARETS CL.
CLOS PANT GLAS
A468
NEWPORT ROAD
Offices
Factory
Works
BEDWAS BUS. CEN.
VALLEY ENTERPRISE
Bedwas
The Square
Pont Bedwas
Sports Ground
Pav.
Cemetery
PANT GLAS INDUSTRIAL ESTATE
30
BY-PASS
Hotel
CROSSWAYS PARK
PONTYPANDY
LINDEN GR.
PARC AV.
Birch Grove
STAFFORD
HAZEL CLOSE
BEECHGROVE
GROVE
TOLLGATE CL.
BEDWAS RD.
Porset Row
RUDRY ROAD
Maes-yr-Afon
Westview Ter.
TRAP WELL
BARREN CL.
RHYD-Y-GWERN
LLANFEDW CL.
RUDRY CL.
ST. JAMES CL.
RHYMNEY RIVER (AFON RHYMNI)
Sunnybank
Plas-newydd
Mornington Meadows
Halt Farm
Branch Cottages
Nant Arian
Ty-yr-efail
Gwern-y-domen
Driving Range
VIRGINIA PARK GOLF COURSE
THE RHOS
RHOS LLAN
Bennetts Ter.
266
229
178
B4600
LLYS-Y-CELYN
HEOL LEWIS
HAFAN-WERDD
LLWYN EITHIN
RHOS HELYG
MAES BRIALLU
BRYN-RHEDYN
HEOL MAERDY
GWAUN
DOL-YR-EOS
DOL FRAN
CAE
Comm. Cen.
St. James Prim. Sch.
Lansbury Park
St. Helen's Catholic Prim. Sch.
CLOS GUTO
MAIN
NEWYDD
COED
GWAUN
PORSET PARK
Brook
MAXTON CT.
SNOWDEN CT.
ATTLEE CT.
HARTSHORN CT.
HALDANE CT.
TREVELYAN CT.
GREENWOOD CT.
ALEXANDER CT.
BUXTON CT.
GRAHAM CT.
WEDGEWOOD CT.
Coed y Maerdy
Brynau
BROOKSIDE CRES.
MARDY CRES.
MARDY CL.
FARM RD.
DRIVE
CAERPHILLY (CAERFFILI)
Nant Gwaunybara
Coed Parc-y-van
Bradford Cottage
Van Farm
Mynydd Rudry
47

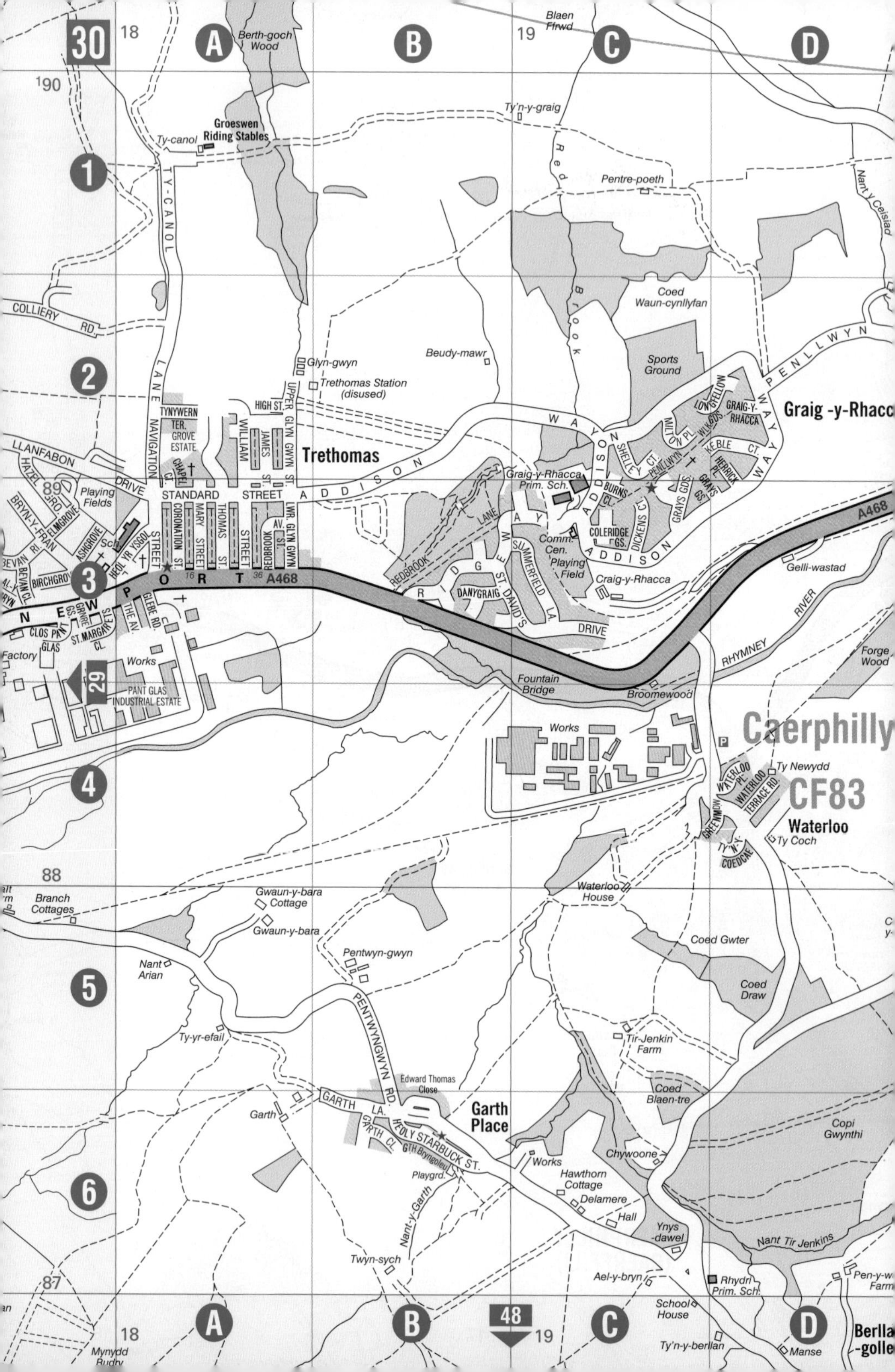
30
18
19
A
B
C
D
1
2
3
4
5
6
190
89
88
87
Berth-goch Wood
Blaen Ffrwd
Groeswen Riding Stables
Ty-canol
Ty'n-y-graig
Red Brook
Pentre-poeth
Nant y Ceisiad
Coed Waun-cynllyfan
COLLIERY RD.
TY-CANOL LANE
Glyn-gwyn
Trethomas Station (disused)
Beudy-mawr
Sports Ground
PENLLWYN WAY
Graig -y-Rhacca
Trethomas
TYNYWERN TER.
GROVE ESTATE
NAVIGATION
WILLIAM
JAMES ST.
HIGH ST.
UPPER GLYN GWYN ST.
LLANFABON DRIVE
HAZEL GRO.
Playing Fields
STANDARD STREET
ADDISON WAY
Graig-y-Rhacca Prim. Sch.
Comm. Cen.
Playing Field
Craig-y-Rhacca
COLERIDGE GS.
DICKENS CT.
BURNS CL.
SHELLEY CT.
MILTON PL.
LONGFELLOW
GRAIG-Y-RHACCA
KEBLE CT.
HERRICK PL.
GRAYS GDS.
CORONATION ST.
MARY STREET
THOMAS ST.
STREET
REDBROOK AV.
LWR. GLYN GWYN ST.
BRYN-Y-FRAN
ELMGROVE
ASHGROVE
HEOL YR YSGOL
Sch.
BEVAN RI.
BEVAN CL.
BIRCHGROVE
PORT STREET
A468
REDBROOK LANE
RIDGEWAY
DANYGRAIG
ST. DAVID'S
SUMMERFIELD LA.
DRIVE
NEW
CLOS PANT GLAS
ST. MARGARET'S CL.
THE AV.
GLEBE RD.
Factory
Works
29
PANT GLAS INDUSTRIAL ESTATE
Gelli-wastad
RHYMNEY RIVER
Forge Wood
Fountain Bridge
Broomewood
Works
Caerphilly
CF83
Ty Newydd
WATERLOO PL.
WATERLOO TERRACE RD.
GREENMOW
TY'N-Y-COEDCAE
Waterloo
Ty Coch
Waterloo House
Branch Cottages
Gwaun-y-bara Cottage
Gwaun-y-bara
Pentwyn-gwyn
Coed Gwter
Coed Draw
Nant Arian
PENTWYNGWYN RD.
Ty-yr-efail
Tir-Jenkin Farm
Coed Blaen-tre
Edward Thomas Close
Garth Place
GARTH LA.
GARTH CL.
HEOL Y STARBUCK ST.
Garth
Playgrd.
Works
Chywoone
Copi Gwynthi
Hawthorn Cottage
Delamere
Hall
Nant-y-Garth
Ynys -dawel
Nant Tir Jenkins
Twyn-sych
Ael-y-bryn
Rhydri Prim. Sch.
Pen-y-w Farm
School House
Ty'n-y-berllan
Manse
Berlla -golle
Mynydd Budy
48

E
F
G
H
21
22
Pen-rhiw
Pen-rhiw Warren
Newport
NP11
190
Ty'r-ffynnon Farm
Ty-draw
Cwm Fedw
Ty-canol Farm
Bovil-uchaf
Coed y Fedw
Machen
Chatham
Coed Pen-llwyn
Shake Holes
Rhyd y Gwern
Generals Well
Rhyd-y-Gwern Farm
Machen Mill
Greenwood
Ty Ffern
Forge Bridge
Plas Newydd
Forge Wood
Cwm-diffrwyth
Cwmnofydd Farm
Woodland Cottage
Mynydd y Bwlch
Coed Cefn-pwll-du
Copi Gwynthi
Penhow Farm
Coed Llwyn-hir
Dan-y-Graig
Cwm Leyshon
Cwm-Leyshon Quarry
Yew Tree Cottage
Draethen
Cardiff CF3
Coed Craig-Ruperrat
Playground
Nant y Draethen
The Row
COMMERCIAL ROAD
WESLEY HILL
CHATHAM
COMMERCIAL RD. A468
ROYAL OAK
THE OAKS
A468
32
49
88
89
87
1
2
3
4
5
6

22
A
B
16
23
C
Pontymister
D
190
1
Bovil-uchaf
Caerphilly
Castle Farm
NP11
Upper Ochrwyth
2
Coed Pen-llwyn
Shake Holes
Ffwrwm
CF83
CAERPHILLY
NEWPORT
Llan-danglws
CROWN WK.
LLANARTH ST.
89
OAKFIELD GDNS.
OAK CL.
ROYAL OAK LA.
THE OAKS
COMMERCIAL RD.
Stone Quarry
Pen-y-parc
The Park
Upper Park Cottage
Twyn Pant-
3
Park Cottages
Ty'n-y-berllan
Pan-teg
A468
31
The Volland
Old Station House
4
Maendy-uchaf
Lower Machen
Maendy-fach
Maendy-isaf
88
A468
Cricket Ground
Pav.
5
Machen-fach
Plas Cottages
Pont y Draethen
Plas Machen
RHYMNEY RIVER (AFON RHYMNI)
Cardiff
CF3
Wern
The Row
MELIN DWR
Playground
Tre'sguthan
6
Draethen
Iron Bridge Cottage
Coed Craig-Ruperrat
87
PARK
A
B
50
C
D
22
23
Gwern-y-Goytre

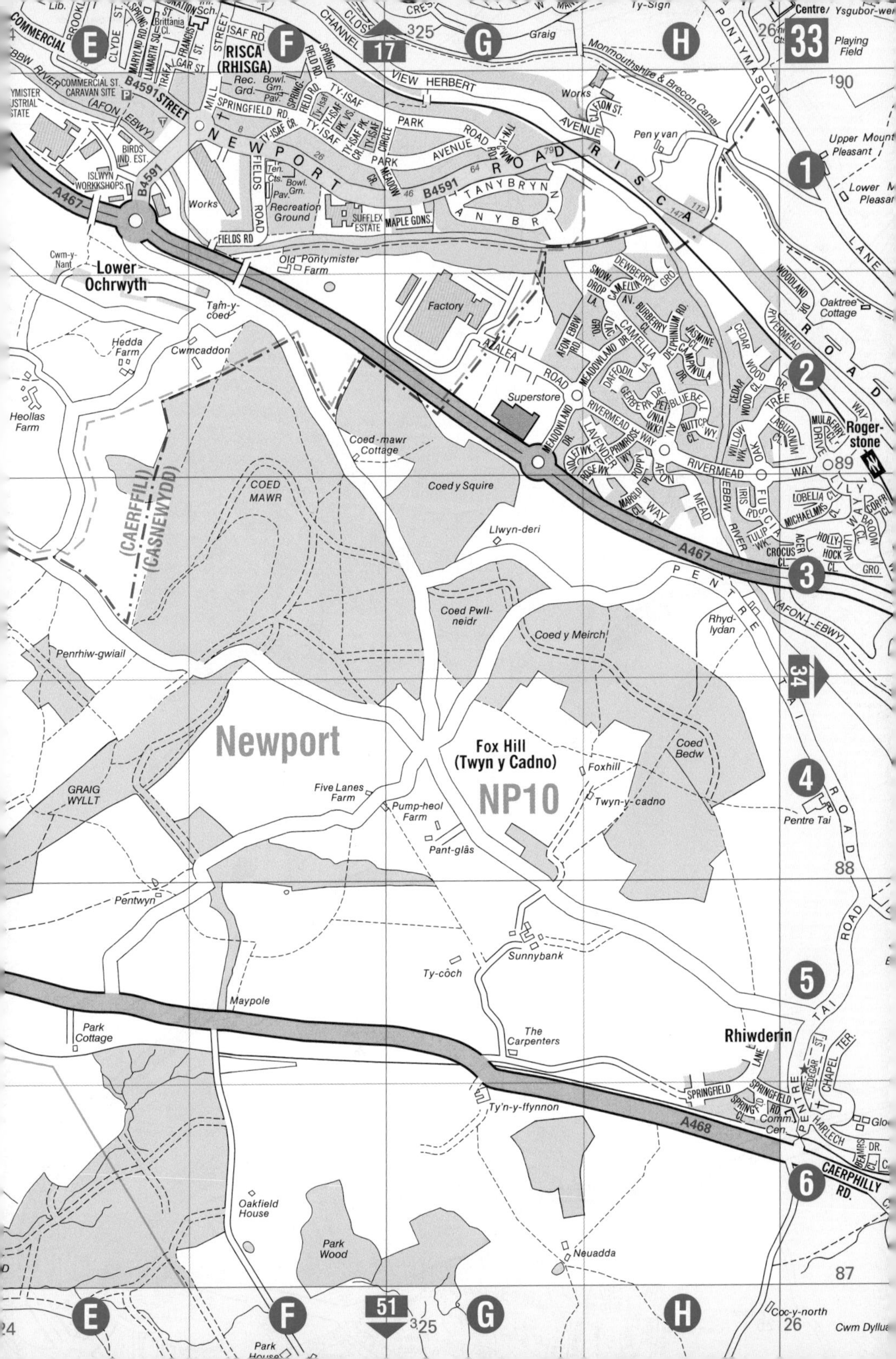

33
17
51
34
E
F
G
H
1
2
3
4
5
6
325
26
190
89
88
87
24
RISCA
(RHISGA)
COMMERCIAL
STREET
B4591
EBBW RIVER
(AFON EBWY)
COMMERCIAL ST. CARAVAN SITE
BIRDS IND. EST.
ISLWYN WORKKSHOPS
A467
A468
B4591
NEWPORT ROAD
RISCA ROAD
SPRINGFIELD RD.
MILL STREET
ISAF RD.
CLYDE ST.
Rec. Grd.
Bowl. Grn.
Pav.
TY-ISAF
VIEW HERBERT
PARK AVENUE
PARK ROAD
MEADOW CR.
CIRCLE
TANYBRYN
FIELDS ROAD
FIELDS RD
Recreation Ground
SUFFLEX ESTATE
MAPLE GDNS.
Works
Ten. Cts.
Bowl. Grn.
Pav.
Monmouthshire & Brecon Canal
CHANNEL
CLOSE
Graig
Ty-Sign
Centre/Ysgubor-wen
Playing Field
PONTYMASON
Pen y van
CLIFTON ST.
AVENUE
Upper Mount Pleasant
Lower Mount Pleasant
LANE
WOODLAND DR.
Oaktree Cottage
RIVERMEAD
ROAD
Lower Ochrwyth
Cwm-y-Nant
Old Pontymister Farm
Tam-y-coed
Hedda Farm
Cwmcaddon
Heollas Farm
Factory
AZALEA ROAD
Superstore
SNOWDROP LA.
DEWBERRY GRO.
CAMELLIA AV.
BURBERRY CL.
DELPHINIUM RD.
JASMINE CL.
CAMPANULA DR.
AFON EBBW RD
LILAC GRO.
MEADOWLAND DR.
DAFFODIL LA.
GERBERA DR.
BLUEBELL WY.
BUTTCP. CL.
RIVERMEAD WAY
LAVENDER
PRIMROSE WY.
ROSE WK.
POPPY PL.
MARGLD. CL.
VIOLET WK.
AFON MEAD
CEDAR WOOD
CEDAR WOOD CL.
TREE
LABURNUM CL.
MULBERRY DRIVE
Rogerstone
WILLOW WK.
OAK
RIVERMEAD WAY
IRIS RD.
FUSCIA
LOBELIA CL.
MICHAELMAS CL.
LILY WAY
CORFRI
BROOM CL.
LUPIN
HOLLYHOCK CL.
ACER
CROCUS CL.
TULIP WK.
GRO.
EBBW RIVER
(AFON EBWY)
Coed-mawr Cottage
Coed y Squire
COED MAWR
(CAERFFILI)
(CASNEWYDD)
Llwyn-deri
Coed Pwll-neidr
Coed y Meirch
PENTRE TAI ROAD
Rhyd-lydan
Penrhiw-gwiail
Newport
Fox Hill
(Twyn y Cadno)
NP10
Foxhill
Twyn-y-cadno
Coed Bedw
Pentre Tai
GRAIG WYLLT
Five Lanes Farm
Pump-heol Farm
Pant-glâs
Pentwyn
Sunnybank
Ty-côch
Maypole
Park Cottage
The Carpenters
Rhiwderin
LANE
SPRINGFIELD
SPRINGFIELD RD.
SPRING CL.
Comm. Cen.
TREDEGAR ST.
CHAPEL TER.
HARLECH
BEAMRS CL.
DR.
CAERPHILLY RD.
Ty'n-y-ffynnon
Oakfield House
Park Wood
Neuadda
Coc-y-north
Cwm Dyllu
Park House

34
A
B
C
D
18
27
26
190
89
88
87
100
1
2
3
4
5
6
33
52
Ysgubor-wen
Playing Field
Mescoed Bach
MESCOED MAWR
NEWPORT GOLF COURSE
MOUNTAIN ROAD
Upper Mount Pleasant
Lower Mount Pleasant
Llwyni Wood
Grove House
Forest Lodge
PARC Y BRAIN
Great Oak (Newport Golf Club)
Oaktree Cottage
Monmouthshire & Brecon Canal
Culvert Cottage
RISCA ROAD
B4591
Rogerstone
CEFN ROAD
The Uplands
Mount Pleasant Prim. Sch.
Cefn Cott.
Greendale
Fourteen Locks
Cwm
A467
Football Ground
Comm. Cen.
Cricket Ground
Works
WERN INDUSTRIAL ESTATE
WERN TRADING ESTATE
Cefn Wood
Playing Field
HIGHCROSS ROAD
CHARTIST DRIVE
Rogerstone Primary School & Cefn Wood Comm. Cen.
High Cross
Bowling Grn.
PENTRE TAI ROAD
Rhyd-lydan
Coed Bedw
Pentre Tai
Earth Works
NP10
Aluminium Works
EBBW RIVER (AFON EBWY)
TREGWILYM ROAD
Lib.
TREGWILYM INDUSTRIAL ESTATE
Rhiwderin
Gloch-wen
Garth Wood
Mineral Railway
CAERPHILLY ROAD
A468
Garth
Pentrepoeth Prim. Sch.
Baytree Cottage
Garthfields Cottages
Coc-y-north
Cwm Dylan
Pentre-poeth
Bassaleg Bri.
Bassaleg School

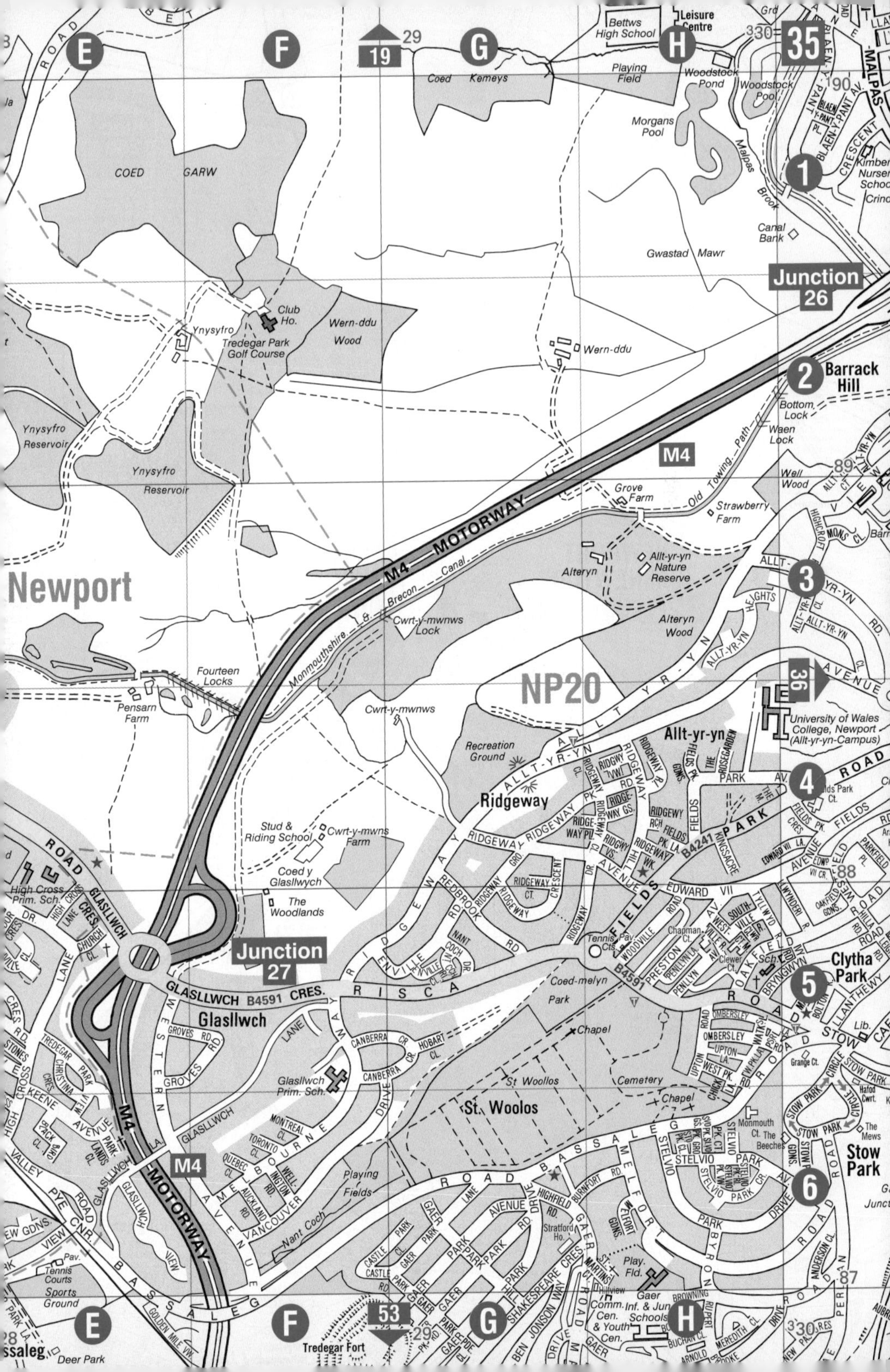

35
19
53
36
Newport
NP20
Junction 26
Junction 27
M4 MOTORWAY
Coed Kemeys
Bettws High School
Leisure Centre
Playing Field
Woodstock Pond
Woodstock Pool
Morgans Pool
Malpas Brook
Canal Bank
Gwastad Mawr
COED GARW
Club Ho.
Tredegar Park Golf Course
Ynysyfro
Wern-ddu Wood
Wern-ddu
Ynysyfro Reservoir
Barrack Hill
Bottom Lock
Waen Lock
Old Towing Path
Grove Farm
Strawberry Farm
Well Wood
Alteryn
Allt-yr-yn Nature Reserve
Alteryn Wood
Monmouthshire & Brecon Canal
Cwrt-y-mwnws Lock
Cwrt-y-mwnws
Fourteen Locks
Pensarn Farm
University of Wales College, Newport (Allt-yr-yn-Campus)
Allt-yr-yn
Recreation Ground
Ridgeway
Stud & Riding School
Cwrt-y-mwns Farm
Coed y Glasllwych
The Woodlands
High Cross Prim. Sch.
Glasllwch
Glasllwch Prim. Sch.
Coed-melyn Park
Chapel
St Woolos
St. Woolos
Cemetery
Clytha Park
Stow Park
Lib.
Grange Ct.
Hafod Cwrt.
The Mews
Monmouth Ct.
The Beeches
Chapman Ct.
Clewer Ct.
Playing Fields
Nant Coch
Stratford Ho.
Play. Fld.
Gaer Inf. & Jun. Schools
Hillview Comm. Cen. & Youth Cen.
Tennis Courts
Sports Ground
Tredegar Fort
Deer Park
Kimber Nursery School
B4591
B4241
GLASLLWCH CRES.
RISCA ROAD
BASSALEG ROAD
ALLT-YR-YN AVENUE
FIELDS PARK ROAD
FIELDS ROAD
EDWARD VII AVENUE
RIDGEWAY
WESTERN AVENUE
MELBOURNE WAY
CANBERRA DRIVE
STOW HILL
STOW PARK
STELVIO PARK
BYRON ROAD
GAER PARK
SHAKESPEARE CRES.
BEN JONSON WAY
GAER ROAD
PYE CNR.
VALLEY VIEW
BLAEN-Y-PANT AV.
MALPAS RD.
HIGHCROFT
MONS CL.
OAKFIELD RD.
BRYNGWYN RD.
PRESTON AV.
WOODVILLE RD.
UPTON RD.
OMBERSLEY RD.
GROVES RD.
HOBART CL.
MONTREAL CL.
TORONTO CL.
QUEBEC CL.
AUCKLAND RD.
WELLINGTON RD.
VANCOUVER
GOLDEN MILE VW.

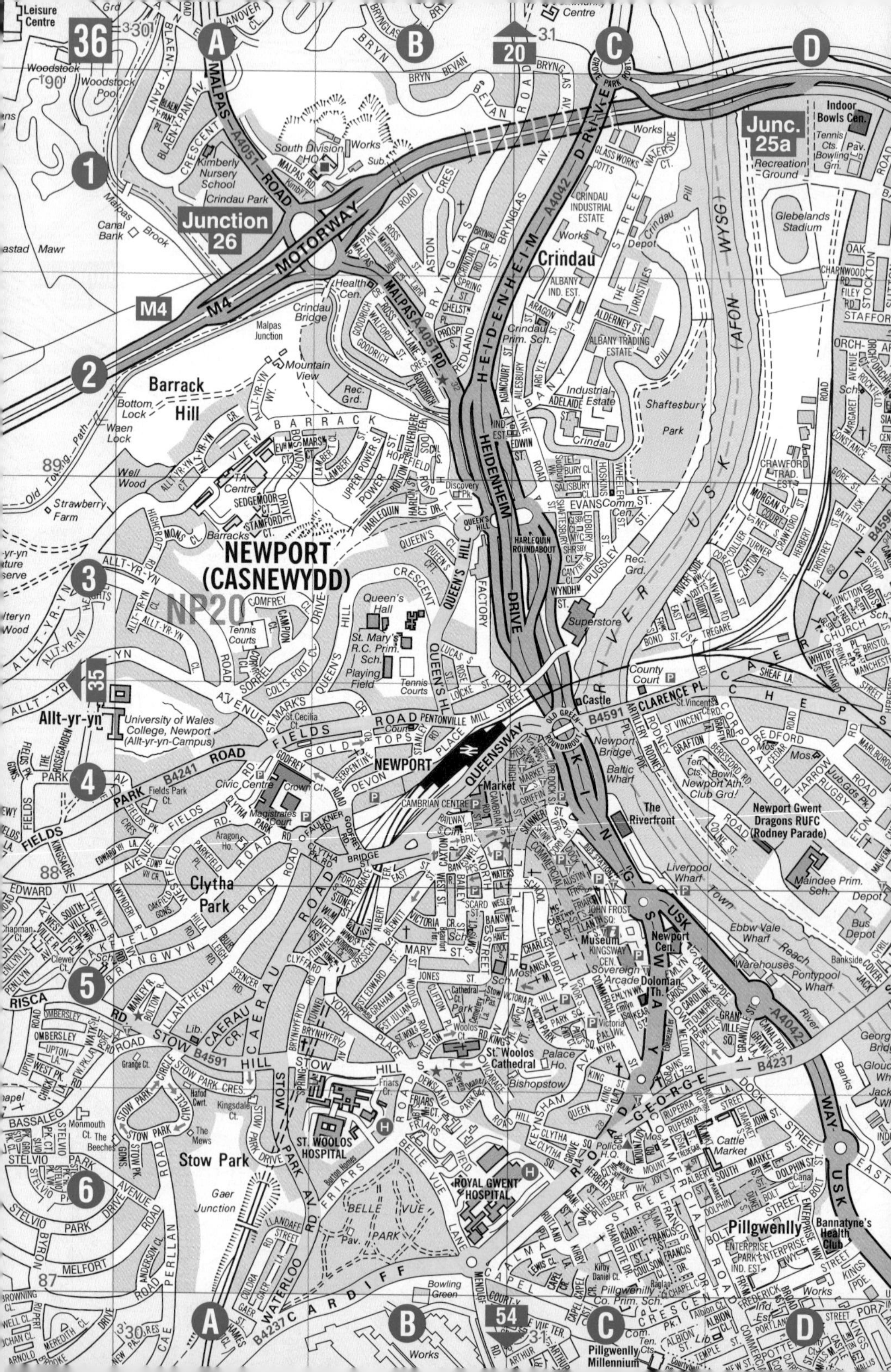
36
20
54
35
Junction 26
Junc. 25a
M4
MOTORWAY
NEWPORT (CASNEWYDD)
NP20
Crindau
Barrack Hill
Clytha Park
Stow Park
Pillgwenlly
Allt-yr-yn
ST. WOOLOS HOSPITAL
ROYAL GWENT HOSPITAL
St. Woolos Cathedral
Newport Gwent Dragons RUFC (Rodney Parade)
Glebelands Stadium
Shaftesbury Park
The Riverfront
HARLEQUIN ROUNDABOUT
OLD GREEN ROUNDABOUT
University of Wales College, Newport (Allt-yr-yn-Campus)
RIVER USK
AFON WYSG
HEIDENHEIM DRIVE
QUEENSWAY
KINGSWAY
GEORGE STREET
CARDIFF ROAD
STOW HILL
CAERAU ROAD
MALPAS ROAD
BARRACK HILL
CLARENCE PL.
CORPORATION ROAD
COMMERCIAL ROAD

E
F
G
H
21
33
34
CAERLEON GOLF COURSE
NP18
1
2
3
4
5
6
RIVER USK (AFON WYSG)
CAERLEON ROAD B4596
M4 MOTORWAY
Junc. 25
St. Julian's Sch. Play Fields
St. Julian's Jun. and Inf. Schs.
ST. JULIANS PARK
St. Julians Wood
Christchurch Cemetery
Newport
St. Julians
Summer Hill
Maindee
Beechwood
BEECHWOOD PARK
Miniature Golf Course
Woodland Park
Gaer Wood
Lawrence Hill
38
NP19
CHEPSTOW ROAD
ROAD B4237
B4591
Maindee Swim. Pool
HOSPICE
Eveswell Prim. Sch.
Somerton Prim. Sch.
Alway
Alway Jun. & Inf. Schs.
LISWERRY PARK
Pond
Somerton
Works
Recreation Ground
JOHNSEY TRADING ESTATE
Great Western Wharf
Blaina Wharf
Spytty Pill
St.Patrick's R.C. Prim. Sch.
Playing Field
Jun. & Inf. Schs.
Lisweryy Pill Bridge
Depot Liswerry
Liswerry Jun. & Inf. Schs.
Playing Fields
Old Town Dock
55
33
34
WHARF ROAD
CORPORATION ROAD
CHRISTCHURCH ROAD
LISWERRY ROAD
NASH ROAD
M4

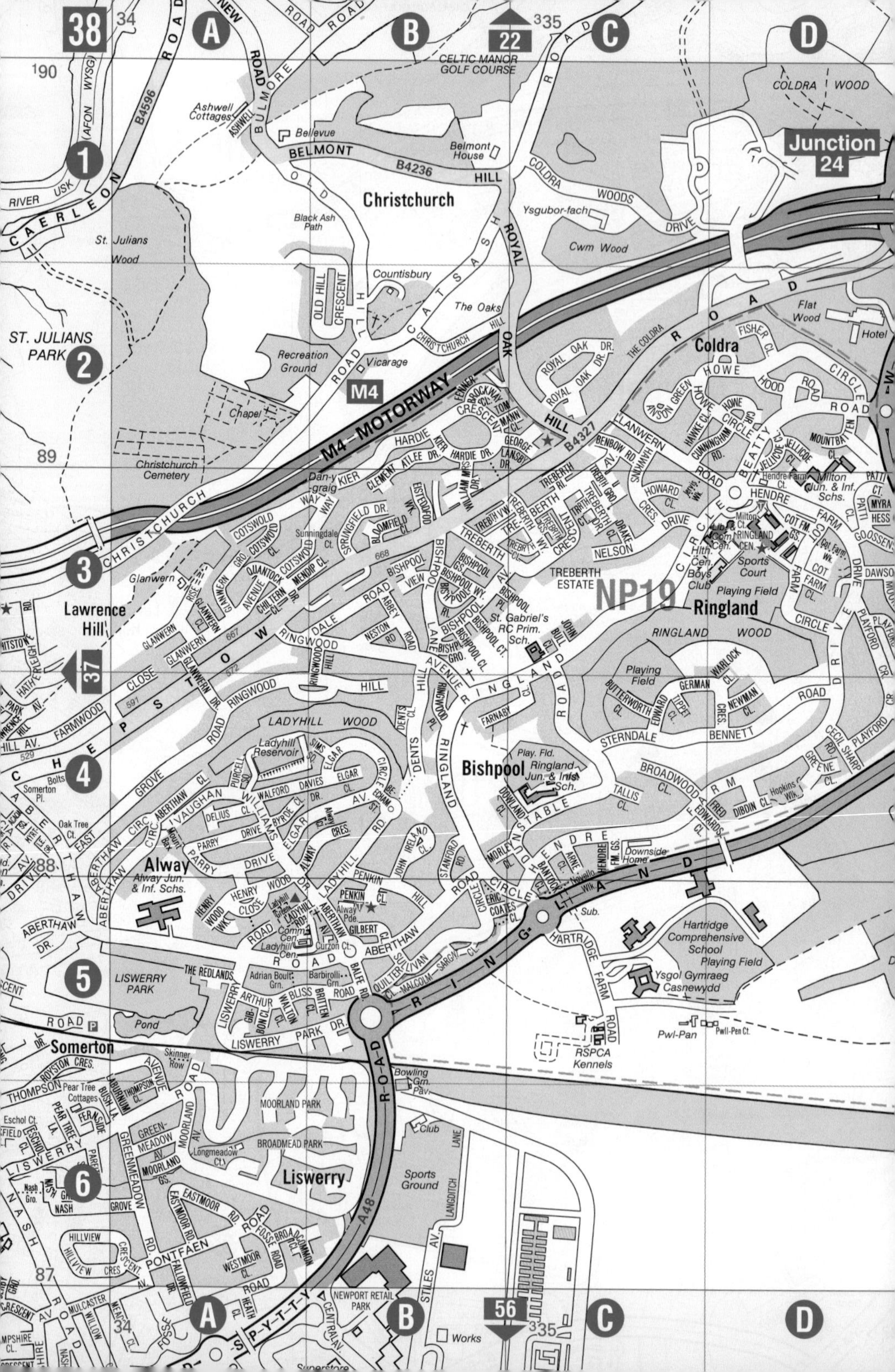

Christchurch
Celtic Manor Golf Course
Coldra Wood
Junction 24
St. Julians Park
St. Julians Wood
Cwm Wood
Recreation Ground
Christchurch Cemetery
M4 Motorway
Coldra
Lawrence Hill
Ringland
Treberth Estate
NP19
Ringland Wood
Ladyhill Wood
Bishpool
Alway
Liswerry Park
Somerton
Liswerry
Moorland Park
Broadmead Park
Sports Ground
Newport Retail Park
Hartridge Comprehensive School
Ysgol Gymraeg Casnewydd
RSPCA Kennels
Pwl-Pan
22
56
37

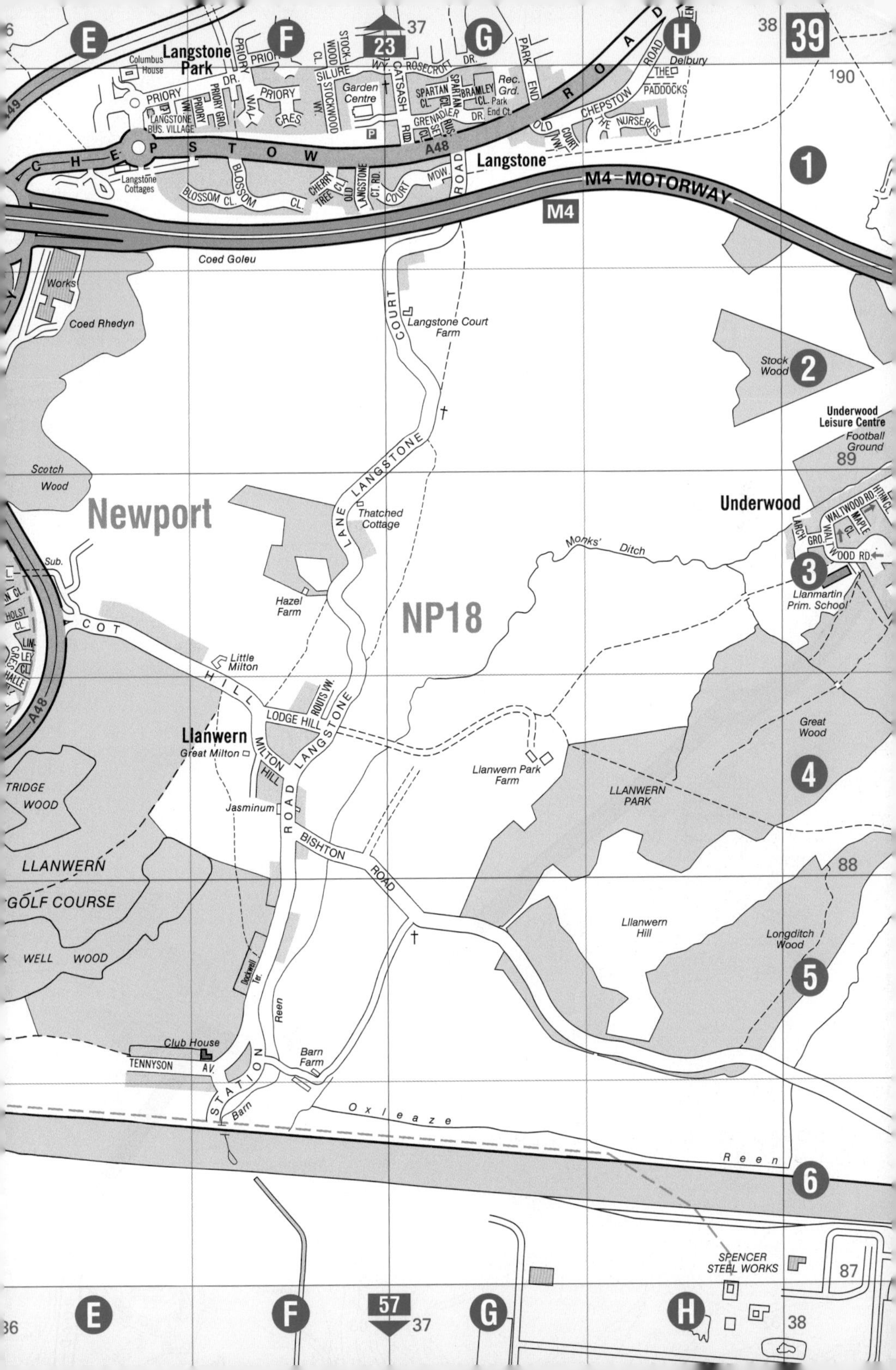

39
23
57
E
F
G
H
1
2
3
4
5
6
36
37
38
190
89
88
87
Langstone Park
Columbus House
LANGSTONE BUS. VILLAGE
PRIORY DR.
PRIORY WALK
PRIORY CRES.
PRIORY GRO.
SILURE WY.
STOCKWOOD CL.
STOCKWOOD WY.
Garden Centre
CATSASH RD.
ROSECROFT DR.
SPARTAN CL.
BRAMLEY CL.
GRENADIER DR.
Rec. Grd.
Park End Ct.
PARK END
OLD COURT VW.
CHEPSTOW ROAD
THE NURSERIES
THE PADDOCKS
Delbury
CHEPSTOW ROAD
A48
Langstone
Langstone Cottages
BLOSSOM CL.
CHERRY TREE CL.
OLD LANGSTONE CT. RD.
COURT MDW.
M4 MOTORWAY
M4
Coed Goleu
Works
Coed Rhedyn
Langstone Court Farm
Stock Wood
Underwood Leisure Centre
Football Ground
Scotch Wood
Newport
LANGSTONE COURT LANE
Thatched Cottage
Underwood
WALTWOOD RD.
MAPLE CL.
LARCH GRO.
Monks' Ditch
Sub.
Hazel Farm
NP18
Llanmartin Prim. School
COT HILL
Little Milton
ROUTS VW.
LODGE HILL
LANGSTONE ROAD
Llanwern
Great Milton
MILTON HILL
Llanwern Park Farm
Great Wood
TRIDGE WOOD
Jasminum
LLANWERN PARK
BISHTON ROAD
LLANWERN GOLF COURSE
Lllanwern Hill
Longditch Wood
WELL WOOD
Dockwell Ter.
Reen
Club House
TENNYSON AV.
STATION
Barn Farm
Barn
Oxleaze Reen
SPENCER STEEL WORKS

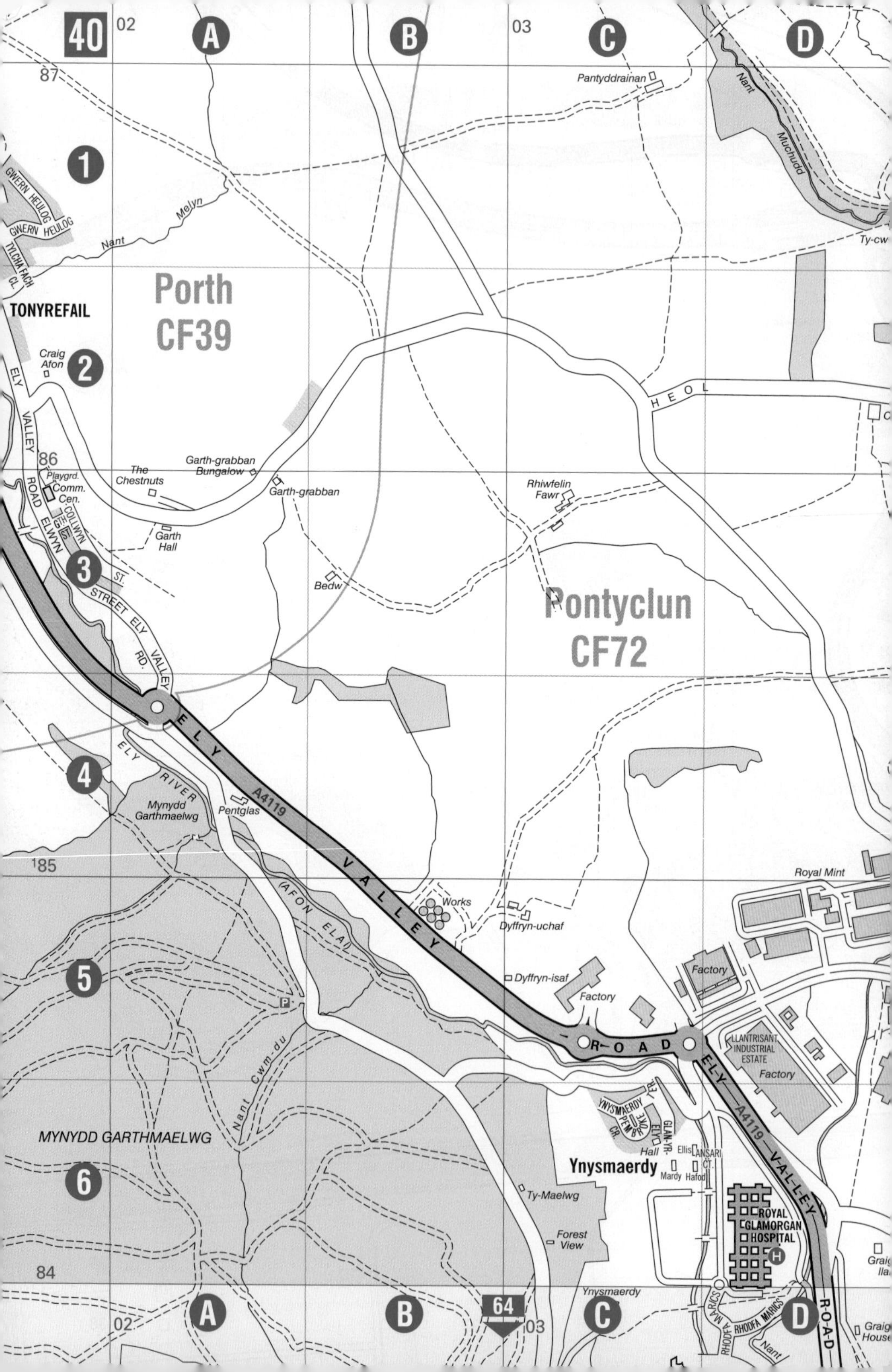
02
03
A
B
C
D
87
86
85
84
1
2
3
4
5
6
Porth
CF39
Pontyclun
CF72
TONYREFAIL
Pantyddrainan
Nant Muchudd
Ty-cw
Nant Melyn
GWERN HEULOG
TYLCHA FACH CL.
Craig Afon
ELY VALLEY ROAD
HEOL
Garth-grabban Bungalow
The Chestnuts
Garth-grabban
Garth Hall
Playgrd.
Comm. Cen.
ELWYN ST.
COLLWYN ST.
GTH ST.
STREET ELY
VALLEY RD.
Rhiwfelin Fawr
Bedw
ELY RIVER
Mynydd Garthmaelwg
Pentglas
A4119
ELY VALLEY ROAD
(AFON ELAI)
Works
Dyffryn-uchaf
Dyffryn-isaf
Factory
Royal Mint
LLANTRISANT INDUSTRIAL ESTATE
MYNYDD GARTHMAELWG
Nant Cwm-du
YNYSMAERDY TR.
PEMBROKE CR.
ELY CT.
GLAN-YR-
Hall
Ellis
ANSARI CT.
Ynysmaerdy
Mardy
Hafod
Ty-Maelwg
Forest View
ROYAL GLAMORGAN HOSPITAL
Graig
Ynysmaerdy
RHODFA MARICS
Graig House
Nant
64

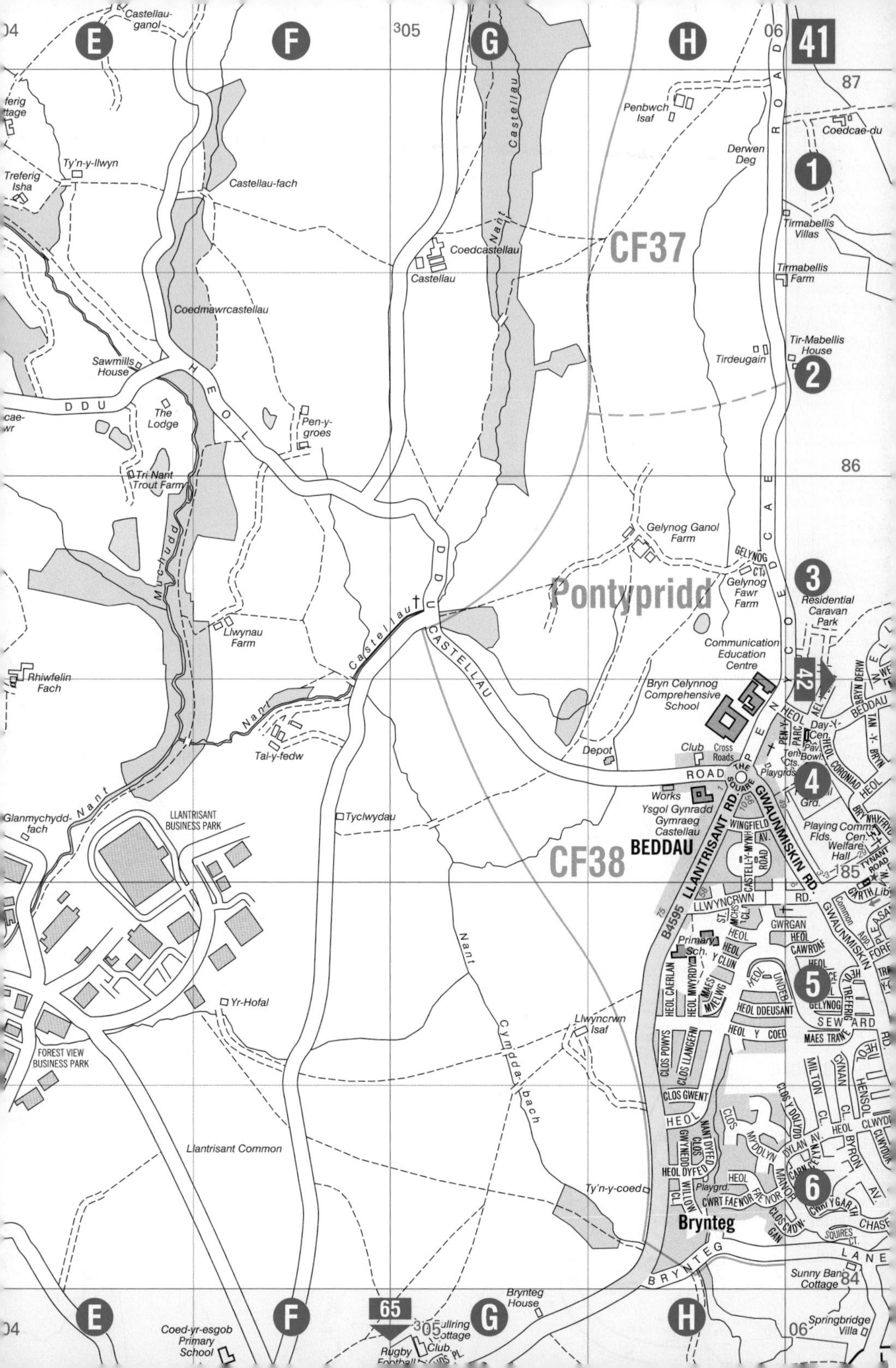

E
F
G
H
305
06
87
86
185
84
04
Castellau-ganol
Treferig Cottage
Ty'n-y-llwyn
Treferig Isha
Castellau-fach
Coedcastellau
Castellau
Coedmawrcastellau
Sawmills House
DDU
HEOL
The Lodge
Pen-y-groes
Tri Nant Trout Farm
Murhudd
Llwynau Farm
Rhiwfelin Fach
Nant
Tal-y-fedw
Castellau
CASTELLAU
Glanmychydd-fach
LLANTRISANT BUSINESS PARK
FOREST VIEW BUSINESS PARK
Tyclwydau
Yr-Hofal
Llantrisant Common
Nant Cymdda-bach
Llwyncrwn Isaf
Ty'n-y-coed
Brynteg House
Coed-yr-esgob Primary School
Rugby Club
Penbwch Isaf
Derwen Deg
Coedcae-du
Tirmabellis Villas
Tirmabellis Farm
Tir-Mabellis House
Tirdeugain
CF37
Gelynog Ganol Farm
GELYNOG CT.
Gelynog Fawr Farm
Pontypridd
Residential Caravan Park
Communication Education Centre
Bryn Celynnog Comprehensive School
ROAD
PENYCOEDCAE
Club
Cross Roads
Depot
Works
Ysgol Gynradd Gymraeg Castellau
THE SQUARE
BEDDAU
CF38
LLANTRISANT RD.
GWAUNMISKIN RD.
B4595
WINGFIELD AV.
CASTELL-Y-MYNACH ROAD
LLWYNCRWN
Primary Sch.
HEOL Y CLUN
HEOL CAERLAN
HEOL MWYRDY
MAES MAELWG
HEOL DDEUSANT
HEOL Y COED
CLOS POWYS
CLOS LLANGEFNI
CLOS GWENT
CLOS GWYNEDD
HEOL DYFED
WILLOW CL.
Playgrd.
MANOR
Brynteg
BRYNTEG LANE
GWRGAN
HEOL CAWRDAF
HEOL TREFERIG
GELYNOG
SEWARD
MAES TRANE
MILTON CL.
CYNAN CL.
HENSOL
BYRON AV.
DYLAN AV.
CLWYDIAN
SQUIRES CT.
CHASE
Day-Y-Cen.
Pav. Bowls
Playgrds
HEOL CORONIAD
Playing Flds.
Comm. Cen.
Welfare Hall
TYNANT ROAD
Lib.
Sunny Bank Cottage
Springbridge Villa
BRYN DERW
TAN-Y-BRYN
BEDDAU

42
65

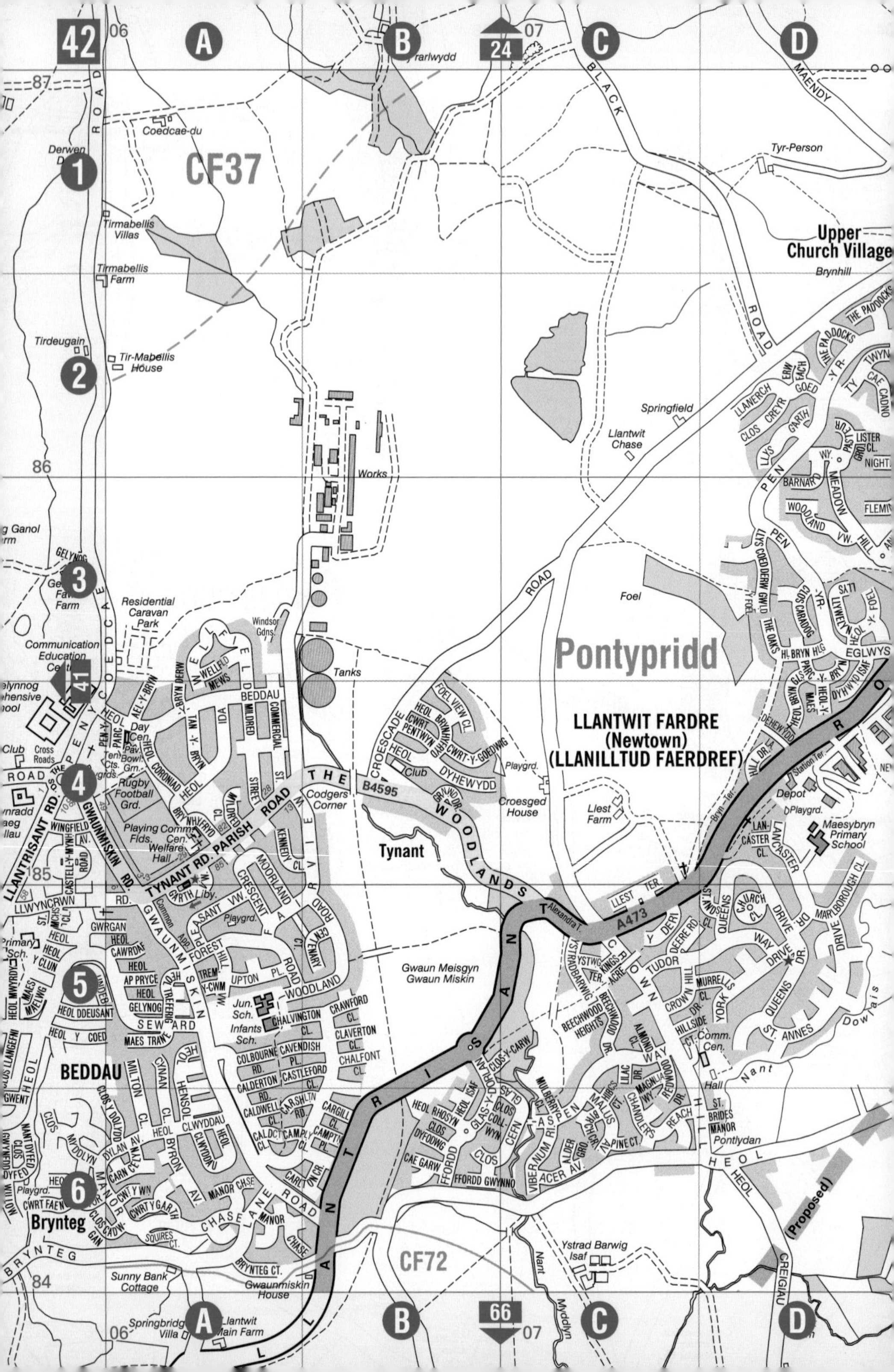
A
B
C
D
24
06
07
87
86
85
84
1
2
3
4
5
6
41
66
CF37
CF72
Coedcae-du
Derwen
Tirmabellis Villas
Tirmabellis Farm
Tirdeugain
Tir-Mabellis House
Residential Caravan Park
Communication Education Centre
Works
Tanks
Windsor Gdns.
Springfield
Llantwit Chase
Tyr-Person
Upper Church Village
Brynhill
Foel
Pontypridd
LLANTWIT FARDRE
(Newtown)
(LLANILLTUD FAERDREF)
Llest Farm
Croesged House
Playgrd.
Club
Codgers Corner
Tynant
B4595
A473
THE WOODLANDS
TYNANT RD. PARISH ROAD
Gwaun Meisgyn
Gwaun Miskin
Maesybryn Primary School
Depot
Station Ter.
Comm. Cen.
Hall
Pontlydan
(Proposed)
BEDDAU
Brynteg
Day Cen.
Rugby Football Grd.
Playing Flds.
Comm. Cen.
Welfare Hall
Liby.
Jun. Sch.
Infants Sch.
Cross Roads
Sunny Bank Cottage
Gwaunmiskin House
Springbridge Villa
Llantwit Main Farm
Ystrad Barwig Isaf
BLACK ROAD
MAENDY
ROAD
PEN-Y-COEDCAE ROAD
LLANTRISANT RD.
GWAUNMISKIN RD.
GWAUNMISKIN
LLANTRISANT
BRYNTEG
CHASE LANE ROAD
HEOL CREIGIAU
Nant Myddlyn
Dowlais

E
F
G
H
25
67
44
08
09
10
310
87
86
185
84
1
2
3
4
5
6
TONTEG INDUSTRIAL ESTATE
TREFOREST IND. ESTATE
Factories
Fardre-uchaf
GRAIG Y FFOREST
THE DELL
FFORDD-Y-GOLLEN
HEOL-Y-FEDWEN
HEOL DDERWEN
THE COPPICE
FFORDD YR-YWEN
Playgrd.
BRYN RHEDYN
THE RISE
CHURCH ROAD
MILFORD CL.
MANOR CL.
RUTHIN
NEYLAND CL.
TOWYN WY.
TOWYN CL.
ANGLESEY CL.
HOLYWELL RD.
Tir-y-graig
CLOSE
TONTEG ROAD
A473
LLANBERIS CL.
CONWAY CRES.
MENAI CL.
BRECON
CARMARTHEN DR.
MONMOUTH CL.
PEMBROKE CL.
DENBIGH CL.
BEAUMARIS DR.
RADNOR
CARDIGAN CL.
PRESTEIGNE AV.
FFORDD GERDINAN
GERDINAN CR.
HEOL DEG
Gwauncelyn Jun. and Inf. Schs.
CAE FARDRE
VICARAGE CT.
WELLFIELD CT.
DOLGELLAU AV.
Summer Dale Cl.
ST. ILLTYD
SWN-Y-NANT
CAE FFYNNON
HEOL-Y-FRO
EGLWYS DRAW
MAINDY CT.
FARDRE CT.
CASTLE CT.
ABBEY CT.
MANOR CT.
FARDRE CR.
FARDRE
Llantwit Fardre Sports Cen.
Central Park
Llantwit Fardre Sports Club
HOLLYBUSH TER.
HOLLYBUSH CL.
SALEM LA.
Hollybush Villas
The Precinct
Nant Ty-crwyn
Nant y Arian
Springfield Ct.
TY-GWYN RD.
Hall
BIRCH GRO.
CAE
Rec. Grd.
Playgrd.
Llanilltud Faerdref Prim. Sch.
Brook Ter.
Comm. Cen.
Liby.
Ysgol Gynradd Gymraeg
Offices
THE PARADE
Club
LEWIS S.
Alma Ter.
JENNER WK.
WAKELIN CL.
HEOL
MAIN ROAD
COED Y DYFFRYN
CWRT COED-Y-BRENIN
HEOL LODWIG
FACH
LLYS
STATION ROAD
DAVIDS AV.
CHURCH VILLAGE
CRWYN
Dyffryn Dowlais
ACORN GRO.
Y COED
BUTTERFLY CL.
ALLT Y WINER
LON Y CROWN
HEOL Y COED WIG
Depot
Dyffryn Bach Ter.
Offices
Bute Farm
The Old Forge
Dyffryn-bach
BROOKDALE
BROOKDALE CT.
HEOL SALEM
HEOL MYNYDD
HEOL NANT
CELYN
Playgrd.
BROOMFIELD
CEDAR CR.
THE RIDINGS
RIDINGS
BIRCHFIELD
CEDAR CL.
RIDGEWAY PL.
BRIAR
Playgrds.
Rec. Grd.
Comm. Cen.
BROOKSIDE
HIGHFIELD CL.
BROOKWAY
LOWLAND DR.
LANSDALE DR.
FAIRHILL DR.
WAY
UNDERHILL DR.
MEADOW CRES.
FAIRMOUND
FAIRMOUND PL.
OAKFIELD CRES.
MAESTEG GRO.
MAESTEG GDNS.
MAESTEG CRES.
CHERITON GRO.
CHERITON
Ysgol Ty Coch
Playgrd.
TON-TEG
TONTEG
(Proposed)
Pound
Ty-isaf Farm
Bryn Glas
Reservoir
Maes-m
SEVERN
Dowlais
Nant
Playground
CF38
NANT CELYN
PARC NANT CELYN
PARC
PARC ROAD
HEOL-Y-PARC
Dryscoed
Celyn Farm
Ty-newydd Farm
Playgrd.
Hall
HEOL-Y-FFEYNNON
FFORDD-Y-CAPEL
DOWLAIS
HEOL TIR COCH
FELIN
PENYWAUN
NANT Y HEOL ISCOED
HEOL FFRWD
WAUN HIR
PHILIP
Efail Isaf
Cwm Uchaf Farm
New House Cwm Mill
Cwm-Isaf
Nant y Felin
Garth-Isaf
Coedgae Bassett
Ty Mawr
OWN INDUSTRIAL ESTATE

A
B
C
D
26
1
2
3
4
5
6
43
68
CF37
CF38
Pontypridd
THE WILLOWFORD
Treforest Estate
TREFOREST INDUSTRIAL ESTATE
Factories
Works
Factory
Depot
RIVERSIDE IND. PARK
THE OED CEN.
Club House
Crossroads
Heol-y-bwnsy
Tai'r Level
Ffynnon-Wen
Tai Pen-twyn
Tir-Thomas James
Cae Tŷ-du
Bowlplex Cardiff
Showcase Cinema
PARC NANTGARW
Multi-Trade Centre
Playground
Day Centre
OXFORD ST.
CARDIFF RD
A4054
A470
MAIN AVENUE
Bryn Glas
Lower Incline House
The Warren
Warren
Reservoir
Maes-mawr
Coed Maes-bach
Maesbach
Willowford Cottages
Gedrys
Tai Crib-y-lan
Coed y Gedrys
Nant-y-Gedrys
Ty-newydd Farm
Lan Farm
Garth-fawr
Tyisaf
Craig y Lan
Salem Row
Salem Ter.
Ynys-gau
RHONDDA CYNON TAF
CARDIFF
(RHONDDA CYNON TAF)
(CAERDYDD)
Nant y Felin
Gwaelod-y-garth
GARTH HILL
MAIN ROAD
Post Office Row
Bristol Ter.
RIVERSIDE ST.
Pant Pl.
Garth Vw.
Cules Ter.
Club
Rec. Grd.
Ffynnon Taf Prim. Sch.
AFON TAF
RIVER TAFF
TONTEG RD.
SEVERN RD.
TAFFS MEAD RD.
GARTH ROAD
TAFFS FALL RD.
FORD RD.
TAFFS BRIDGE RD.
GWAELOD-Y-MEAD
WILLOWFORD ROAD
HEOL GROESWEN
HEOL TY MAEN
POWYS RD.
GWENT RD.
HEOL CROCHENDY
HEOL Y GAMLAS
HEOL PARDOE
HEOL BILLINGSLEY
ST. DAVIDS CL.
THE WILLOWFORD
Centre Ct.
RHYD-YR-HELYG
HEOL Y PWLL
HEOL YR ODYN
CROCHENDY
FFYNNONBWLA ROAD
Nant Ffynnon-wen
Kidz Playgrd.
Williams Pl.
87
86
185
84
310
11

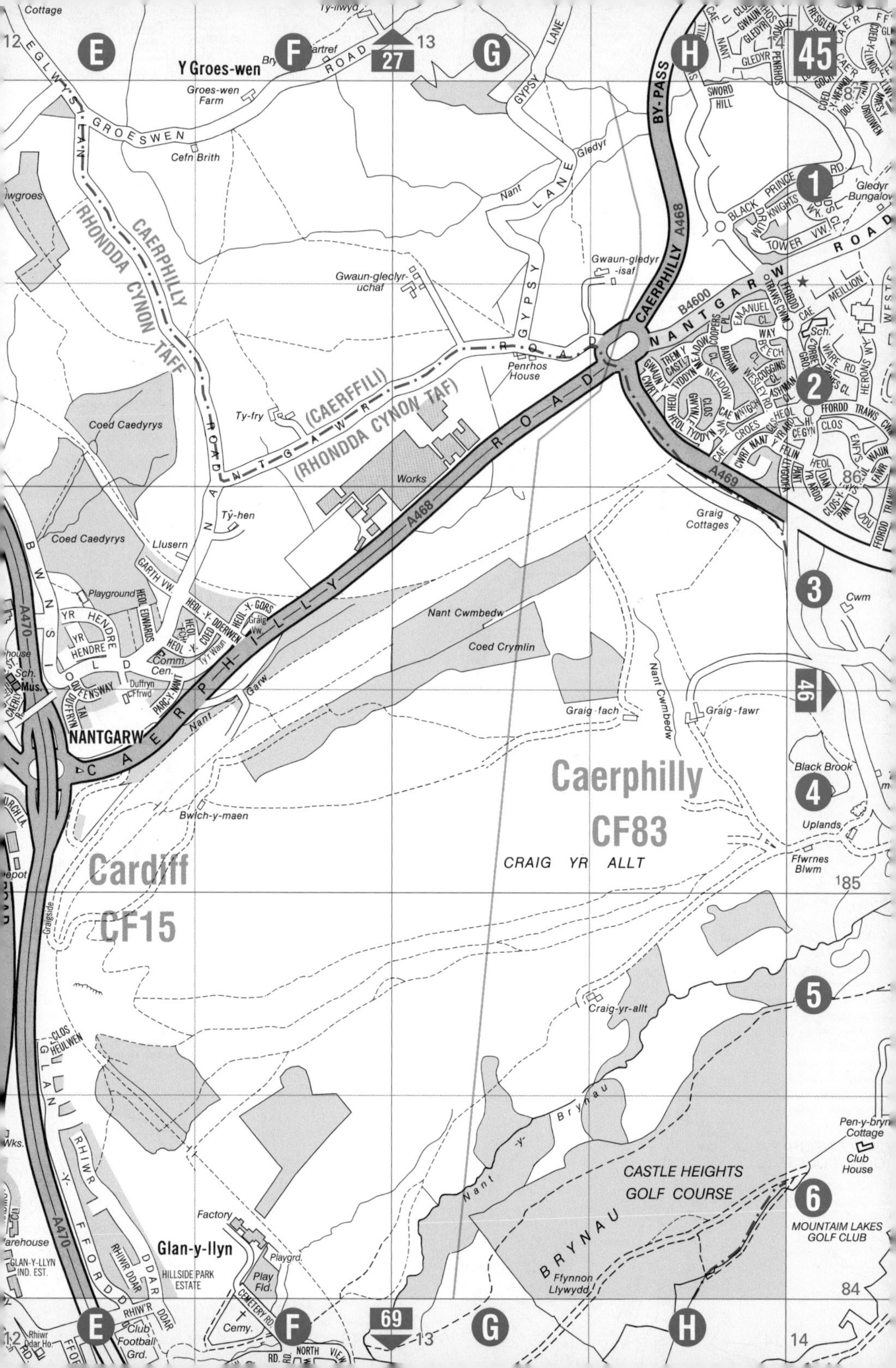
Y Groes-wen
Groes-wen Farm
Cefn Brith
GROESWEN
EGLWYS ILAN ROAD
CAERPHILLY
RHONDDA CYNON TAFF
(CAERFFILI)
(RHONDDA CYNON TAF)
NANTGARW ROAD
GYPSY LANE
Gwaun-gledyr-uchaf
Gwaun-gledyr-isaf
Penrhos House
Ty-fry
Works
Coed Caedyrys
Tŷ-hen
Llusern
Playground
NANTGARW
CAERPHILLY ROAD
A468
A469
A470
B4600
BY-PASS
SWORD HILL
BLACK PRINCE RD.
TOWER VW.
Gledyr Bungalow
Graig Cottages
Nant Cwmbedw
Coed Crymlin
Graig-fach
Graig-fawr
Cwm
Black Brook
Uplands
Ffwrnes Blwm
Caerphilly CF83
Cardiff CF15
CRAIG YR ALLT
Bwlch-y-maen
Craig-yr-allt
Nant-y-Brynau
BRYNAU
CASTLE HEIGHTS GOLF COURSE
MOUNTAIN LAKES GOLF CLUB
Pen-y-bryn Cottage
Club House
Ffynnon Llywydd
Factory
Glan-y-llyn
HILLSIDE PARK ESTATE
Playgrd.
Play Fld.
Cemy.
CEMETERY RD.
RHIW'R DDAR
RHIWR-Y-FFORDD
GLAN-Y-LLYN IND. EST.
Club Football Grd.
Rhiwr Ddar Ho.
CLOS HEULWEN
Graigside
E
F
G
H
1
2
3
4
5
6
12
13
14
27
46
69
84
85
86
87

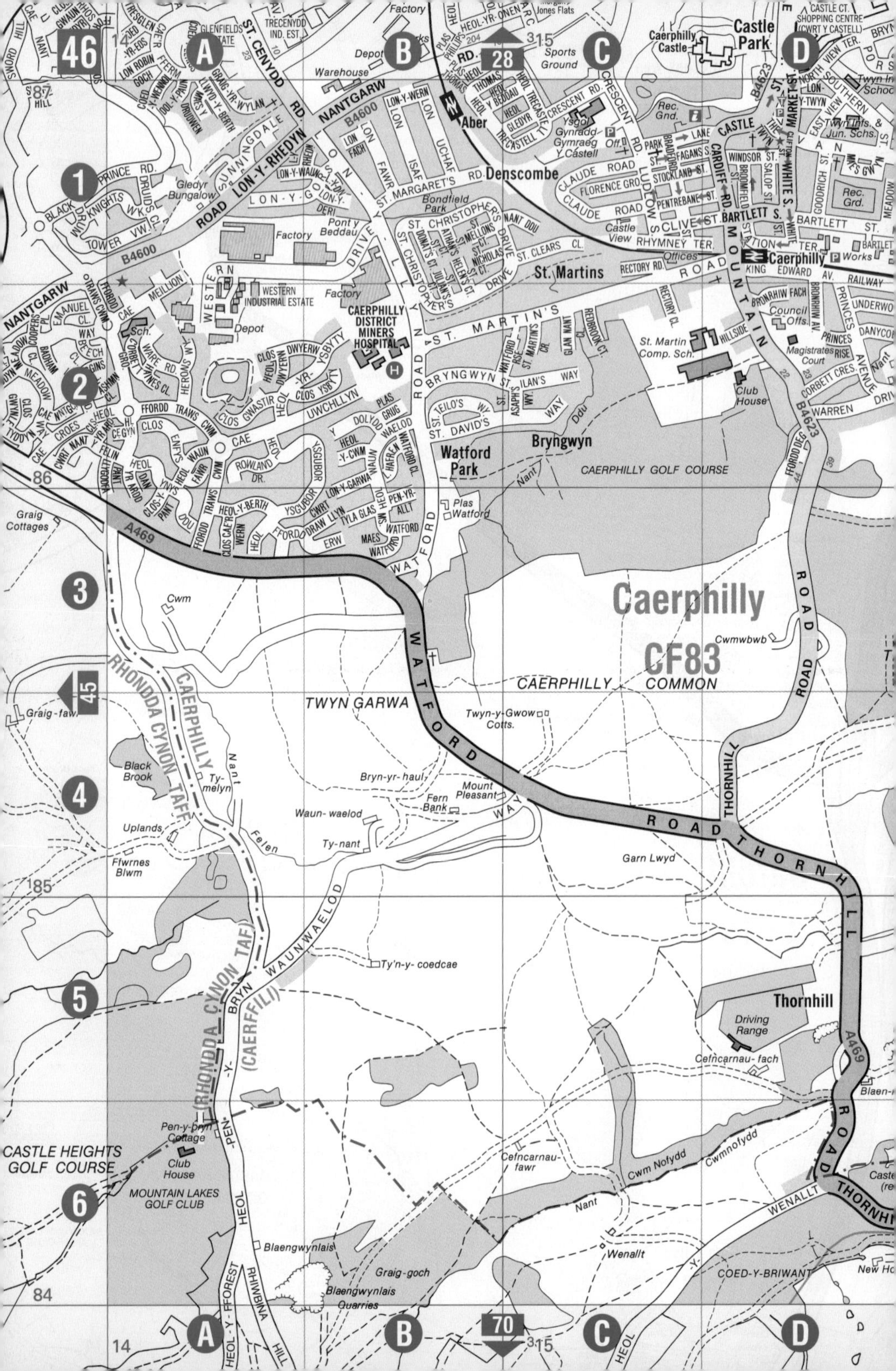

46
A
B
C
D
1
2
3
4
5
6
28
45
70
14
315
87
86
185
84
Factory
TRECENYDD IND. EST.
Depot
Warehouse
ST. CENYDD RD.
NANTGARW
B4600
LON-Y-RHEDYN ROAD
Aber
Sports Ground
Castle Park
Caerphilly Castle
CASTLE CT. SHOPPING CENTRE (CWRT Y CASTELL)
Twyn Inf. & Jun. Schs.
Rec. Gnd.
Rec. Grd.
Ysgol Gynradd Gymraeg Y Castell
Denscombe
ST. MARGARET'S RD.
Bondfield Park
Pont y Beddau
Gledyr Bungalow
PRINCE RD.
TOWER VW.
SUNNINGDALE
CRESCENT RD.
CLAUDE ROAD
FLORENCE GRO.
PENTREBANE ST.
BRADFORD ST.
STOCKLAND ST.
CLIVE ST.
BARTLETT ST.
CARDIFF RD.
MOUNTAIN ROAD
Castle View
RHYMNEY TER.
Offices
Caerphilly
KING EDWARD AV.
RAILWAY
Works
St. Martins
RECTORY RD.
ST. MARTIN'S ROAD
St. Martin Comp. Sch.
Council Offs.
Magistrates Court
PRINCES AVENUE
Club House
B4623
WARREN
CORBETT CRES.
Factory
WESTERN INDUSTRIAL ESTATE
Depot
CAERPHILLY DISTRICT MINERS HOSPITAL
ST. CHRISTOPHER'S DRIVE
BRYNGWYN ST.
ST. DAVID'S WAY
Watford Park
Bryngwyn
CAERPHILLY GOLF COURSE
Plas Watford
FFORDD TRAWS CWM
ROWLAND DR.
A469
Graig Cottages
Cwm
WATFORD ROAD
Caerphilly
CF83
CAERPHILLY COMMON
Cwmwbwb
TWYN GARWA
Twyn-y-Gwow Cotts.
RHONDDA CYNON TAFF
CAERPHILLY
Graig-fawr
Black Brook
Ty-melyn
Nant
Bryn-yr-haul
Mount Pleasant
Fern Bank
Waun-waelod
Ty-nant
Uplands
Felen
Ffwrnes Blwm
WATFORD WAY
THORNHILL ROAD
Garn Lwyd
WAUNWAELOD
BRYN
Ty'n-y-coedcae
(RHONDDA CYNON TAF)
(CAERFFILI)
Thornhill
Driving Range
Cefncarnau-fach
PEN-Y-BRYN
HEOL
Pen-y-bryn Cottage
CASTLE HEIGHTS GOLF COURSE
Club House
MOUNTAIN LAKES GOLF CLUB
Cefncarnau-fawr
Cwm Nofydd
Cwmnofydd
Nant
WENALLT
Wenallt
Blaengwynlais
Graig-goch
Blaengwynlais Quarries
HEOL-Y-FFOREST
RHIWBINA HILL
COED-Y-BRIWANT

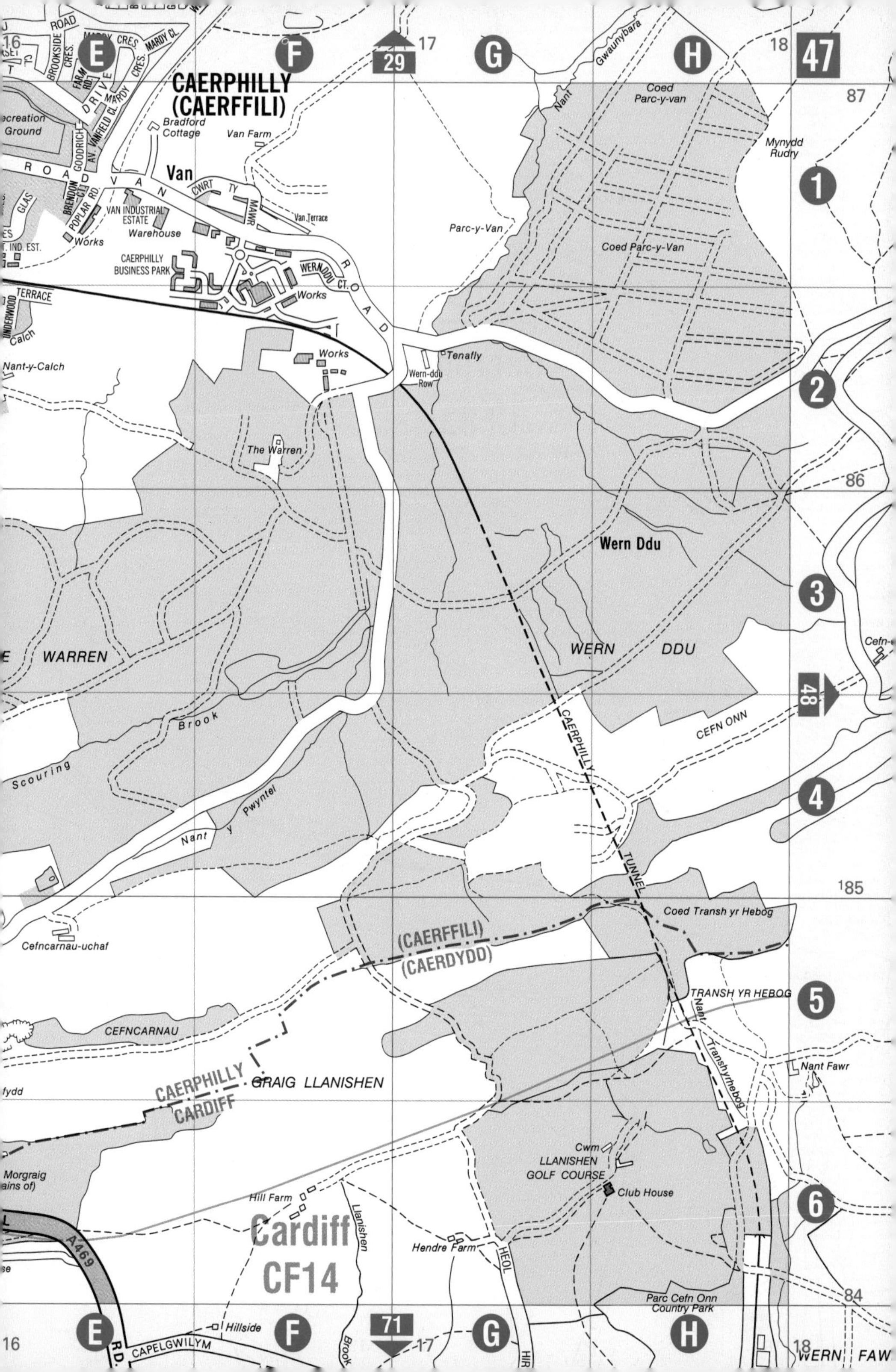
CAERPHILLY
(CAERFFILI)
Bradford Cottage
Van Farm
Van
VAN ROAD
CWRT TY MAWR
Van Terrace
VAN INDUSTRIAL ESTATE
Warehouse
Works
CAERPHILLY BUSINESS PARK
WERN DDU CT.
Works
Recreation Ground
BROOKSIDE CRES.
MARDY CRES.
MARDY CL.
MARDY CRES.
FARM RD.
DRIVE
VANFIELD CL.
GOODRICH AV.
BRENDON CL.
POPLAR RD.
GLAS
UNDERWOOD TERRACE
Calch
Nant-y-Calch
Works
Tenafly
Wern-ddu Row
The Warren
Parc-y-Van
Coed Parc-y-van
Coed Parc-y-Van
Nant Gwaunybara
Mynydd Rudry
Wern Ddu
WARREN
WERN DDU
CAERPHILLY TUNNEL
CEFN ONN
Brook
Scouring
Nant y Pwyntel
Cefncarnau-uchaf
(CAERFFILI)
(CAERDYDD)
Coed Transh yr Hebog
TRANSH YR HEBOG
Nant Transhyrhebog
Nant Fawr
CEFNCARNAU
GRAIG LLANISHEN
CAERPHILLY
CARDIFF
Morgraig
Cwm
LLANISHEN GOLF COURSE
Club House
Hill Farm
Cardiff
CF14
Llanishen Brook
Hendre Farm
HEOL HIR
A469
Parc Cefn Onn Country Park
Hillside
CAPELGWILYM RD.
WERN FAW
Cefn
E
F
G
H
16
17
18
29
71
48
1
2
3
4
5
6
87
86
185
84

48
A
B
30
C
D
1
2
3
4
5
6
72
47
18
19
87
86
185
84
Ynys-dawel
Twyn-sych
Nant Tir Jenkins
Pen-y-waun Farm
Rhydri Prim. Sch.
Ael-y-bryn
School House
Ty'n-y-berllan
Manse
Mynydd Rudry
RUDRY COMMON
Rudry
Green Yard Farm
CWRT GRIFFIN
Llwyn Gwyn
Craig y Llan
Caerphilly
CF83
Gwaun-y-grisal
Coed Cefn-onn
Nant-y-Cwm
Pant-glas-bach
Ty'n-y-graig
WERN DDU
Cefn-onn
CEFN ONN
Coed Llwyn-celyn
Pant-glas
Coed Siencyn
Pentwyn
CAERPHILLY
CARDIFF
Craig-Llysfaen
Coed y Graig
Coed Transh yr Hebog
TRANSH YR HEBOG
Tai-mawr
Brynhill Farm
Springmeadow
Mount Pleasant
Nant Fawr
Windylaw
Nant Transhyrhebog
CF14
GRAIG ROAD
RUDRY ROAD
Green Meadow Farm
Coedcefnpor
Fair Oak Farm
Nant-tydraw-fach
Pant Teg Farm
The Hollies
WERN FAWR

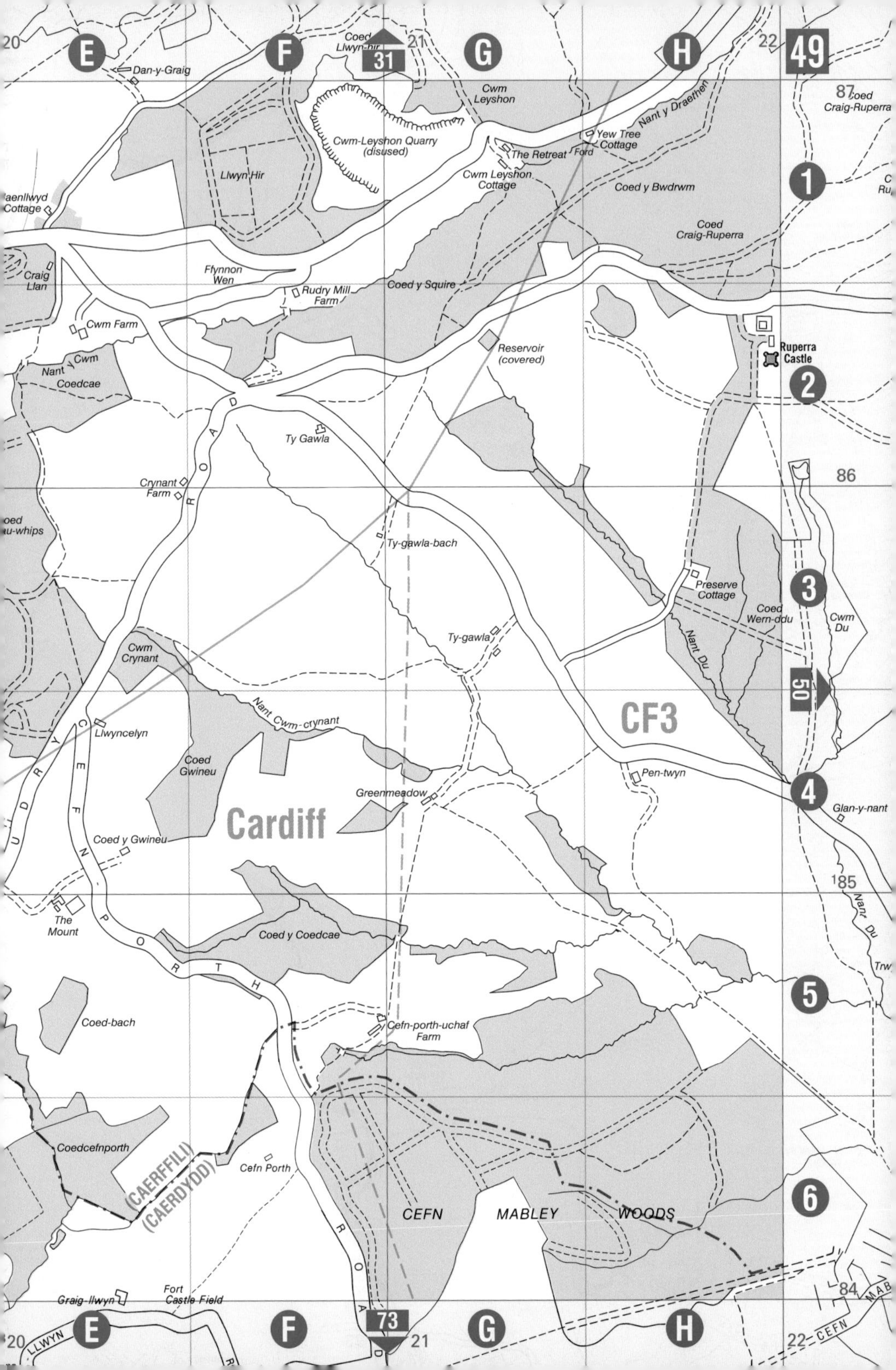

Dan-y-Graig
Coed Llwyn-hir
31
Cwm Leyshon
Cwm-Leyshon Quarry (disused)
Yew Tree Cottage
Nant y Draethen
The Retreat
Ford
Cwm Leyshon Cottage
Coed y Bwdrwm
Coed Craig-Ruperra
Llwyn Hir
Cottage
Craig Llan
Ffynnon Wen
Rudry Mill Farm
Coed y Squire
Cwm Farm
Nant y Cwm
Coedcae
Reservoir (covered)
Ruperra Castle
Ty Gawla
Crynant Farm
Ty-gawla-bach
Preserve Cottage
Coed Wern-ddu
Nant Du
Cwm Du
Ty-gawla
Cwm Crynant
Nant Cwm-crynant
CF3
50
Llwyncelyn
Coed Gwineu
Pen-twyn
Glan-y-nant
Greenmeadow
Cardiff
Coed y Gwineu
The Mount
Coed y Coedcae
Coed-bach
Cefn-porth-uchaf Farm
Coedcefnporth
(CAERFFILI)
(CAERDYDD)
Cefn Porth
CEFN MABLEY WOODS
Craig-llwyn
Fort Castle Field
73
RUDRY ROAD
CEFN PORTH ROAD
LLWYN
CEFN MAB
E F G H
1 2 3 4 5 6
20 21 22
87 86 185 84

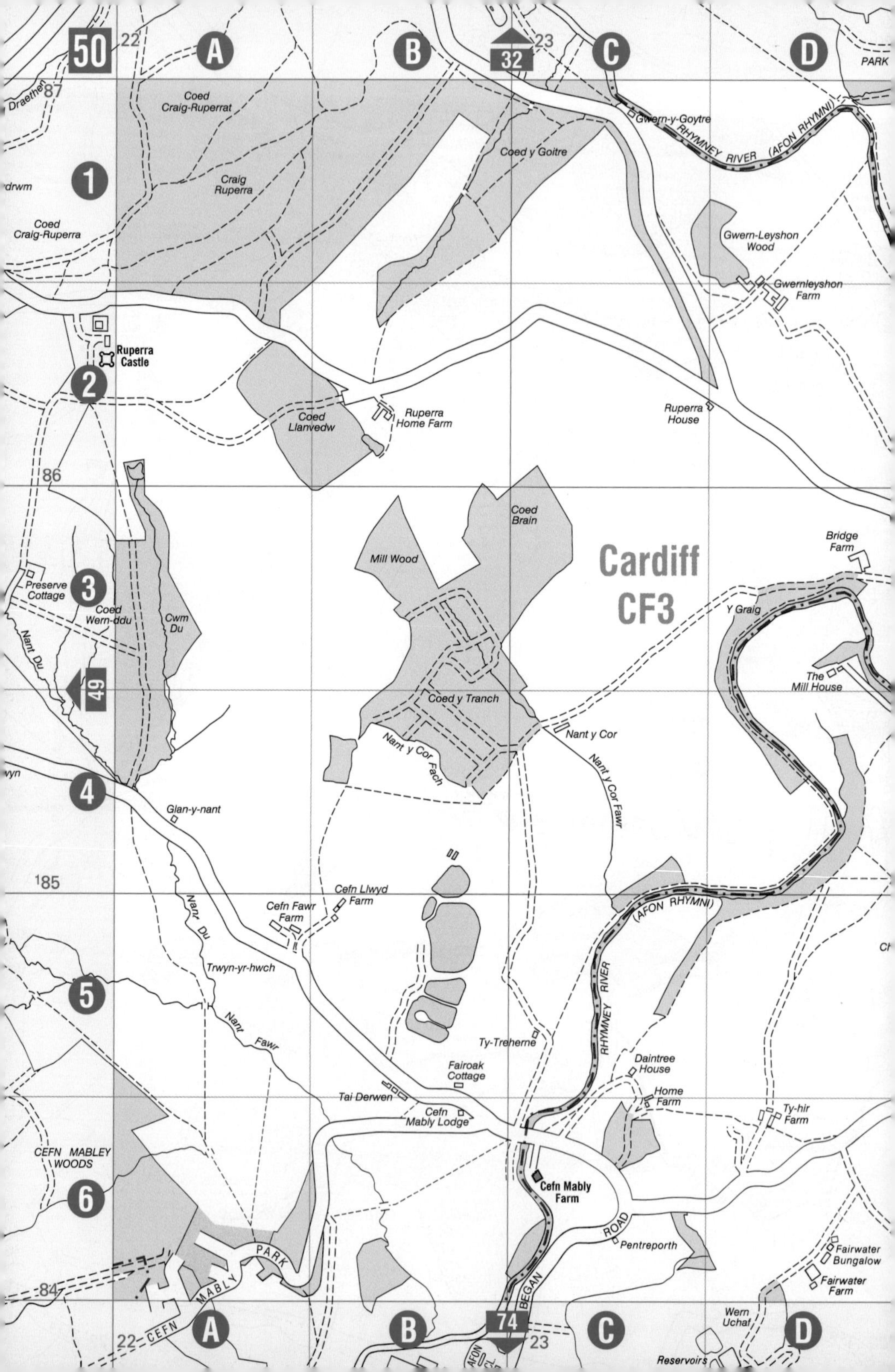
50
22
A
B
32
23
C
D
PARK
Draethen
87
Coed Craig-Ruperrat
Craig Ruperra
Coed y Goitre
Gwern-y-Goytre
RHYMNEY RIVER (AFON RHYMNI)
1
Coed Craig-Ruperra
Gwern-Leyshon Wood
Gwernleyshon Farm
Ruperra Castle
2
Coed Llanvedw
Ruperra Home Farm
Ruperra House
86
Coed Brain
Mill Wood
Cardiff CF3
Bridge Farm
Preserve Cottage
3
Coed Wern-ddu
Cwm Du
Y Graig
Nant Du
49
Coed y Tranch
The Mill House
Nant y Cor
Nant y Cor Fach
Nant y Cor Fawr
4
Glan-y-nant
85
Cefn Llwyd Farm
Cefn Fawr Farm
Nant Du
(AFON RHYMNI)
RHYMNEY RIVER
Trwyn-yr-hwch
5
Nant Fawr
Ty-Treherne
Daintree House
Fairoak Cottage
Home Farm
Tai Derwen
Cefn Mably Lodge
Ty-hir Farm
CEFN MABLY WOODS
6
Cefn Mably Farm
ROAD
Pentreporth
PARK
MABLY
CEFN
BEGAN
Fairwater Bungalow
Fairwater Farm
84
22
A
B
74
23
C
Wern Uchaf
D
Reservoirs

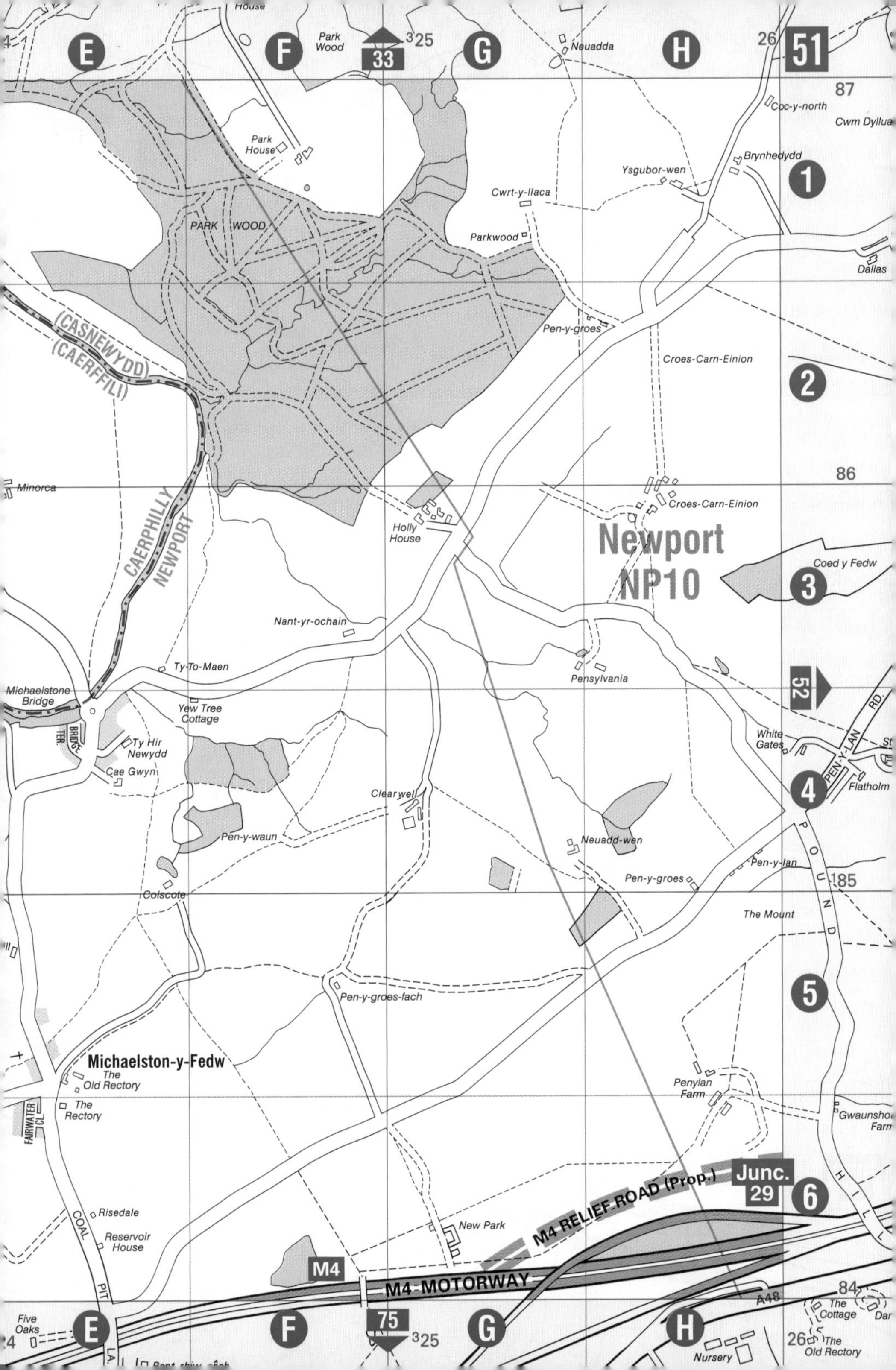
51
E
F
G
H
33
325
26
87
Park Wood
Neuadda
Coc-y-north
Cwm Dyllua
Brynhedydd
Ysgubor-wen
Park House
Cwrt-y-llaca
PARK WOOD
Parkwood
Dallas
(CASNEWYDD)
(CAERFFILI)
Pen-y-groes
Croes-Carn-Einion
1
2
86
Minorca
Croes-Carn-Einion
Holly House
Newport NP10
Coed y Fedw
3
CAERPHILLY
NEWPORT
Nant-yr-ochain
Ty-To-Maen
Pensylvania
52
Michaelstone Bridge
Yew Tree Cottage
Ty Hir Newydd
BRIDGE TER.
Cae Gwyn
White Gates
PEN-Y-LAN RD.
Flatholm
4
Clearwell
Pen-y-waun
Neuadd-wen
Pen-y-lan
Pen-y-groes
POUND HILL
185
Colscote
The Mount
5
Pen-y-groes-fach
Michaelston-y-Fedw
The Old Rectory
The Rectory
FAIRWATER CL.
Penylan Farm
Gwaunsho Farm
Junc. 29
6
M4 RELIEF ROAD (Prop.)
Risedale
New Park
Reservoir House
COAL PIT LA
M4
M4-MOTORWAY
A48
84
The Cottage
Five Oaks
75
325
26
The Old Rectory
Nursery

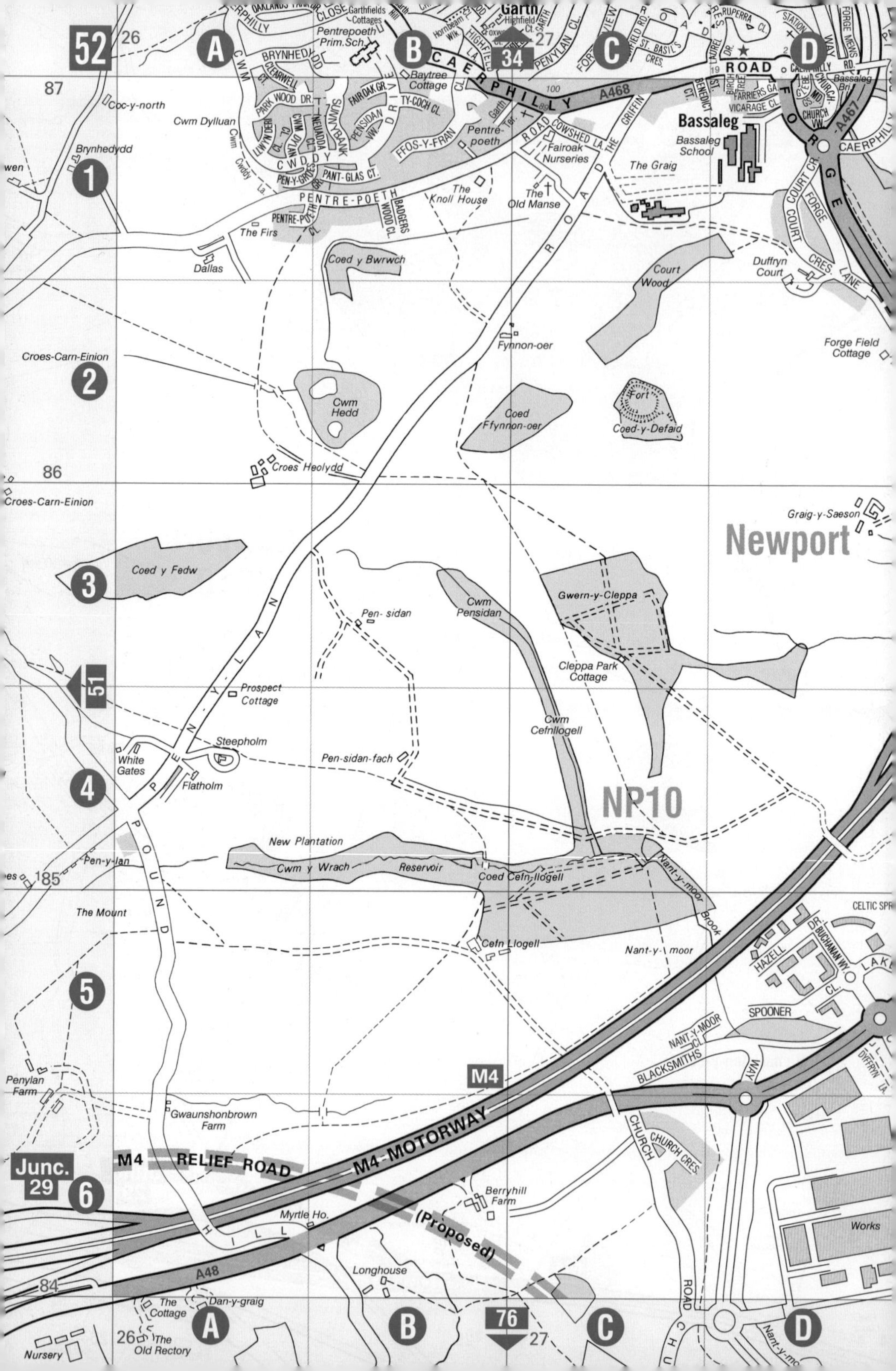
Garthfields Cottages
Pentrepoeth Prim.Sch.
Garth
Highfield
34
Baytree Cottage
CAERPHILLY ROAD
A468
Cwm Dylluan
Coc-y-north
Brynhedydd
CWDDY
PENTRE-POETH
The Firs
Dallas
The Knoll House
The Old Manse
Fairoak Nurseries
COWSHED LA.
THE GRIFFIN
Bassaleg
Bassaleg School
The Graig
Coed y Bwrwch
Court Wood
Duffryn Court
Forge Field Cottage
Fynnon-oer
Croes-Carn-Einion
Cwm Hedd
Coed Ffynnon-oer
Fort
Coed-y-Defaid
Croes Heolydd
Graig-y-Saeson
Newport
Coed y Fedw
Cwm Pensidan
Gwern-y-Cleppa
Pen- sidan
Cleppa Park Cottage
Prospect Cottage
Steepholm
White Gates
Flatholm
Pen-sidan-fach
Cwm Cefnllogell
NP10
New Plantation
Cwm y Wrach
Reservoir
Coed Cefn-llogell
Nant-y-moor Brook
Pen-y-lan
PEN-Y-LAN
POUND HILL
The Mount
Cefn Llogell
Nant-y-moor
CELTIC SPR
HAZELL DR.
BUCHANAN WY.
SPOONER CL.
NANT-Y-MOOR CL.
BLACKSMITHS WAY
Penylan Farm
Gwaunshonbrown Farm
M4
M4-MOTORWAY
M4 RELIEF ROAD (Proposed)
Junc. 29
CHURCH ROAD
CHURCH CRES.
Berryhill Farm
Myrtle Ho.
Works
A48
Longhouse
The Cottage
Dan-y-graig
The Old Rectory
Nursery
76
51
Nant-y-mo

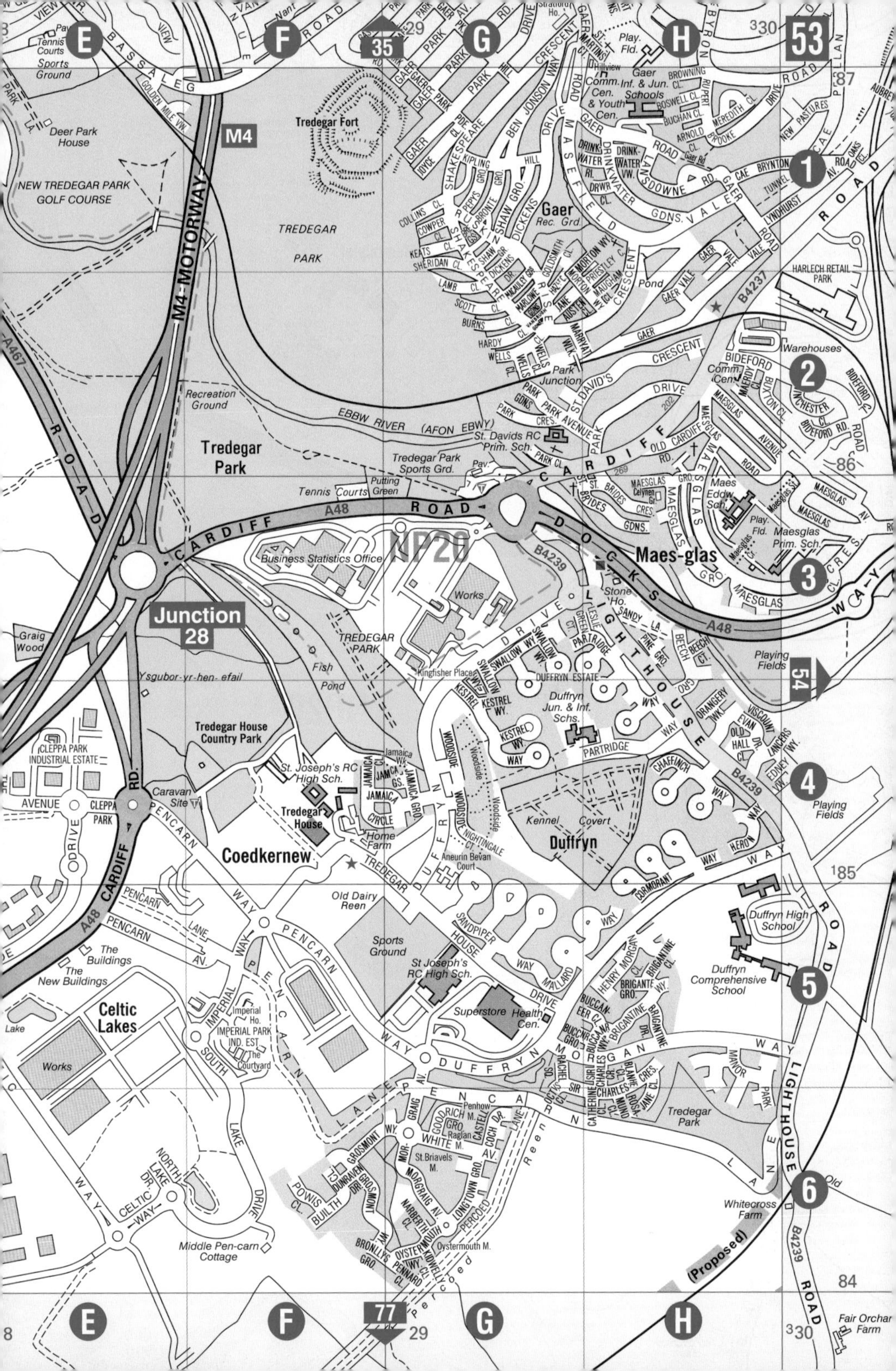
E
F
G
H
35
29
330
87
1
2
3
4
5
6
86
185
84
54
77
M4
M4-MOTORWAY
Junction 28
A48
A467
B4237
B4239
NP20
Sports Ground
Tennis Courts
Deer Park House
NEW TREDEGAR PARK GOLF COURSE
Tredegar Fort
TREDEGAR PARK
Gaer
Rec. Grd.
Gaer Inf. & Jun. Schools
Comm. Cen. & Youth Cen.
Play. Fld.
Pond
HARLECH RETAIL PARK
Warehouses
Comm. Cen.
Park Junction
EBBW RIVER (AFON EBWY)
Recreation Ground
Tredegar Park
St. Davids RC Prim. Sch.
Tredegar Park Sports Grd.
Putting Green
Tennis Courts
CARDIFF ROAD
Maes Eddw. Sch.
Maesglas Prim. Sch.
Maes-glas
Business Statistics Office
Works
Stone Ho.
Playing Fields
Graig Wood
Ysgubor-yr-hen-efail
Fish Pond
Kingfisher Place
DUFFRYN ESTATE
Duffryn Jun. & Inf. Schs.
Tredegar House Country Park
CLEPPA PARK INDUSTRIAL ESTATE
St. Joseph's RC High Sch.
Tredegar House
Caravan Site
Home Farm
Coedkernew
Kennel Covert
Duffryn
Aneurin Bevan Court
Old Dairy Reen
Sports Ground
St Joseph's RC High Sch.
Duffryn High School
Duffryn Comprehensive School
The Buildings
The New Buildings
Celtic Lakes
Lake
Works
Imperial Ho.
IMPERIAL PARK IND. EST.
The Courtyard
Superstore
Health Cen.
Tredegar Park
Whitecross Farm
(Proposed)
St.Briavels M.
Oystermouth M.
Middle Pen-carn Cottage
Fair Orchard Farm
LIGHTHOUSE ROAD
DOCKS WAY
DUFFRYN WAY
PENCARN WAY
PENCARN LANE
CELTIC WAY
LAKE DRIVE

A
B
C
D
1
2
3
4
5
6
36
53
Newport
NP20
NP10
Pillgwenlly
Mendalgief
Maes-glas
M4 RELIEF ROAD (Proposed)
(Proposed)
DOCKS WAY
USK WAY
WEST WAY
EAST WAY
A48
B4237
B4591
B4239
WATERLOO RD.
BELLE VIEW PARK
Bowling Green
Works
HARLECH RETAIL PARK
MENDALGIEF RETAIL PARK
MAESGLAS RETAIL PARK
MAESGLAS INDUSTRIAL ESTATE
New Sidings
Depots
Warehouses
PORT ROAD
Level of Mendalgief
Ebbw Junction
East Mendalgief Junction
Retail Park
Sports Ground
YMCA
Pillgwenlly Millennium Centre
Transporter Bridge
Crow Point
Tredegar Wharf
Neptune Works
Old Jetties
RIVER USK
River Wharf
Dock Offices
North Quay
North Dock
Swing Bridge
EBBW RIVER (AFON EBWY)
Tredegar Pill
Playing Fields
Duffryn High School
Duffryn Comprehensive School
MORGAN WAY
Tredegar Park
PENCARN
Whitecross Farm
LIGHTHOUSE ROAD
HEOL PONT-Y-CWCW
Old Dairy
Reen
New Dairy Farm
Fair Orchard Farm
Newport Pill
South Lock
Power Station
West Pier
East Pier
330
31
87
86
85
84

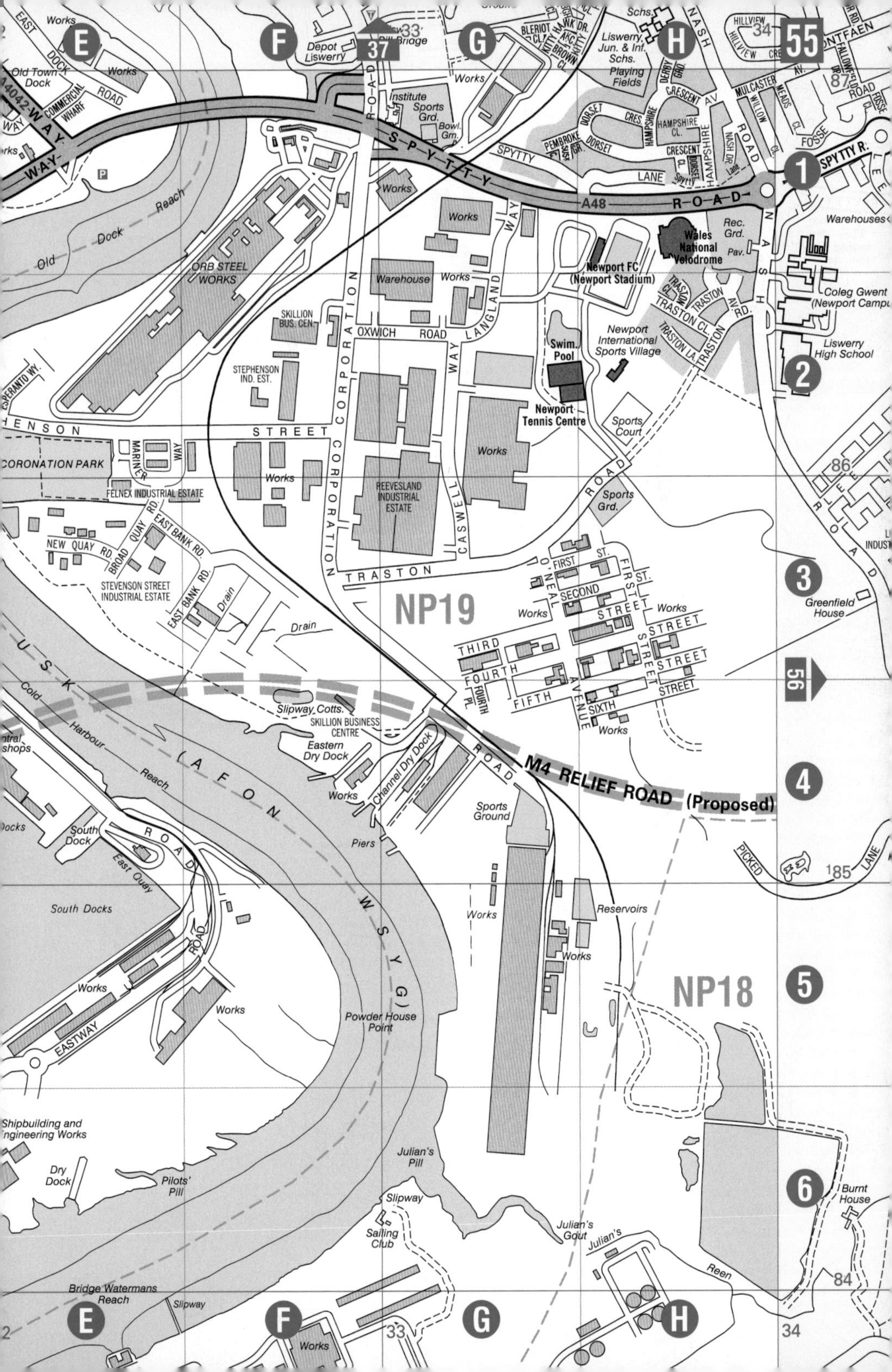

55
37
56
NP19
NP18
ORB STEEL WORKS
Wales National Velodrome
Newport FC (Newport Stadium)
Newport International Sports Village
Newport Tennis Centre
REEVESLAND INDUSTRIAL ESTATE
STEVENSON STREET INDUSTRIAL ESTATE
FELNEX INDUSTRIAL ESTATE
CORONATION PARK
SKILLION BUSINESS CENTRE
M4 RELIEF ROAD (Proposed)
SPYTTY ROAD
CORPORATION ROAD
TRASTON ROAD
NASH ROAD
STEPHENSON STREET
Coleg Gwent (Newport Campus)
Liswerry High School
South Docks
Powder House Point
Julian's Pill
Sailing Club
Reservoirs
Burnt House
Greenfield House

56
A
B
C
D
38
Liswerry
PONTFAEN
WESTMOOR CL.
FALLOWFIELD DR.
FOSSE ROAD
BROADCOMMON CL.
MULCASTER AV.
CRESCENT
HAMPSHIRE CL.
HAMPSHIRE CRESCENT
DORSET CL.
NASH DR.
WILLOW CL.
MEADS CL.
FOSSE CL.
HEATH CL.
A48 ROAD
SPYTTY ROAD
SPYTTY
LEE WAY
QUEENSWAY
NEWPORT RETAIL PARK
CENTRAL AVENUE
STILES AVENUE
SEVEN STILES AVENUE
Works
Superstore
Megabowl Newport
Cineworld Cinema
Warehouses
Rec. Grd.
Pav.
Wales National Velodrome
TRASTON AV.
TRASTON RD.
TRASTON CL.
TRASTON LA.
Coleg Gwent (Newport Campus)
Lliswerry High School
Warehouse
QUEENSWAY MEADOWS INDUSTRIAL ESTATE
LEEWAY CT.
NEWPORT INDUSTRIAL ESTATE
MEADOWS ROAD
QUEEN'S WAY
Longditch Reen
LONGDITCH RD.
CURLEW CL.
PLOVER CL.
Hoyley Stadium
NP19
ESTUARY ROAD
BROADWATER RD.
FRESHWATER RD.
Factories
LAKE ROAD
CLEARWATER ROAD
LEE WAY INDUSTRIAL ESTATE
Reen
Tatton Farm
Julians
TATTON ROAD
Newport
Greenfield House
NASH MEAD
Catnic Site
Works
STREET
55
M4 RELIEF ROAD (Proposed)
PICKED LANE
BROADSTREET
Pye Corner
Picked Lane Farm
The Elms
Yewtree Farm
Richmond
Broadway Farm
Greenacres Park
COMMON
Chapel Farm
Common
Fair Orchard
The Poplars
Common Farm
Home Farm
Common House
LANE
Ty Du Farm
Reen
Old Farm House
The Shrubbery
Burnt House
Julian's
NASH ROAD
Marieville
Morfa
STRAITS
Little Cross Farm
The Vines
WEST NASH RD.
GOLDCLIFF RD.
Henton Farm
Nash
1
2
3
4
5
6
34
335
87
86
185
84

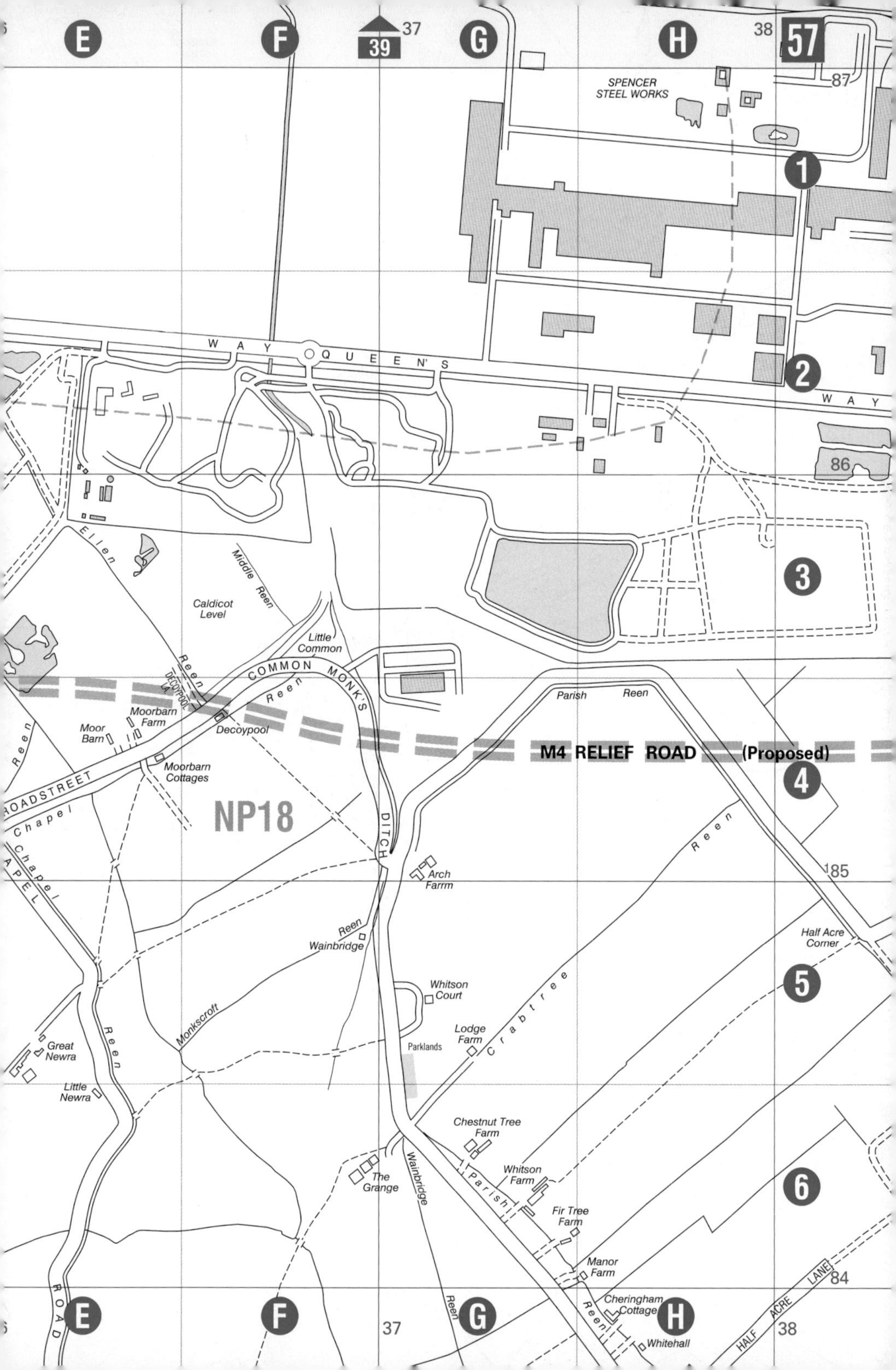
E
F
39
37
G
H
38
SPENCER
STEEL WORKS
87
1
WAY QUEEN'S
2
WAY
86
3
Ellen
Middle Reen
Caldicot
Level
Little
Common
COMMON
MONK'S
Reen
DECOYPOOL LA
Reen
Moorbarn
Farm
Moor
Barn
Decoypool
Parish
Reen
M4 RELIEF ROAD (Proposed)
4
Reen
Moorbarn
Cottages
ROADSTREET
Chapel
NP18
DITCH
Chapel
APEL
Reen
Arch
Farrm
185
Reen
Wainbridge
Half Acre
Corner
5
Whitson
Court
Crabtree
Great
Newra
Reen
Monkscroft
Lodge
Farm
Parklands
Little
Newra
Chestnut Tree
Farm
Whitson
Farm
Parish
6
The
Grange
Wainbridge
Fir Tree
Farm
Manor
Farm
84
HALF ACRE LANE
ROAD
E
F
37
Reen
G
Reen
Cheringham
Cottage
H
38
Whitehall

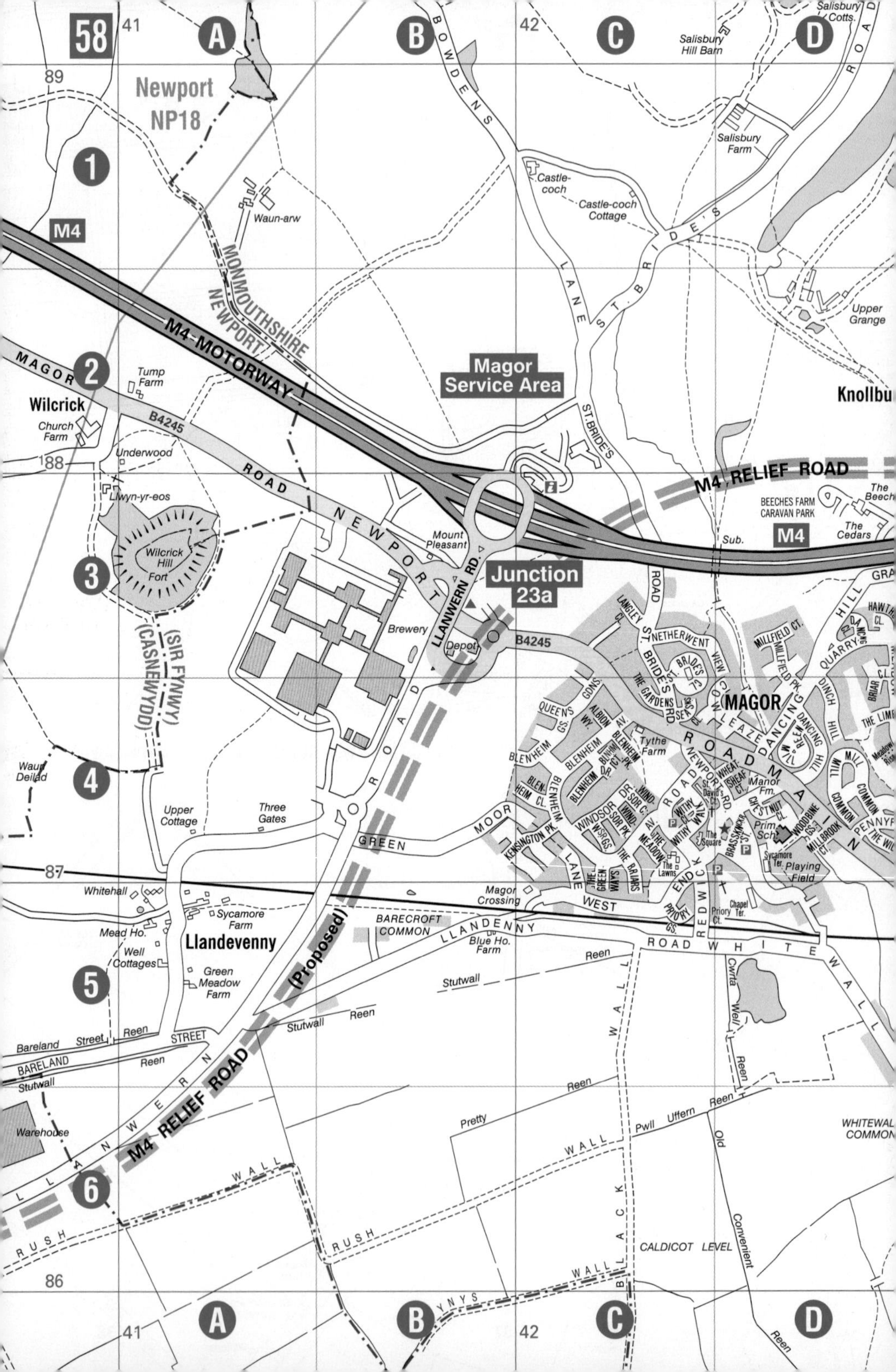

Newport NP18
M4 MOTORWAY
MONMOUTHSHIRE
NEWPORT
Magor Service Area
Junction 23a
M4 RELIEF ROAD
M4 RELIEF ROAD (Proposed)
Wilcrick
Church Farm
Tump Farm
Underwood
Llwyn-yr-eos
Wilcrick Hill Fort
Waun-arw
Waun Deilad
(SIR FYNWY)
(CASNEWYDD)
MAGOR ROAD
NEWPORT ROAD
B4245
Mount Pleasant
Brewery
Depot
LLANWERN RD.
BOWDENS LANE
Castle-coch
Castle-coch Cottage
ST. BRIDE'S
Salisbury Cotts.
Salisbury Hill Barn
Salisbury Farm
Upper Grange
Knollbu
BEECHES FARM CARAVAN PARK
The Beech
The Cedars
Sub.
MAGOR
Tythe Farm
Manor Fm.
The Square
Prim. Sch.
Sycamore Ter.
Playing Field
Priory Ct.
Chapel Ter.
The Lawns
Magor Crossing
WEST END
GREEN MOOR LANE
Upper Cottage
Three Gates
Whitehall
Sycamore Farm
Mead Ho.
Well Cottages
Llandevenny
Green Meadow Farm
BARECROFT COMMON
LLANDENNY ROAD
Blue Ho. Farm
WHITEWALL
Reen
Stutwall
Stutwall Reen
Bareland Street
BARELAND STREET
Warehouse
LLANWERN
RUSH WALL
BLACK WALL
Pretty
Pwll Uffern Reen
Cwrt-y-Well Reen
Old Convenient
CALDICOT LEVEL
WHITEWALL COMMON
YNYS WALL
41
42
89
88
87
86

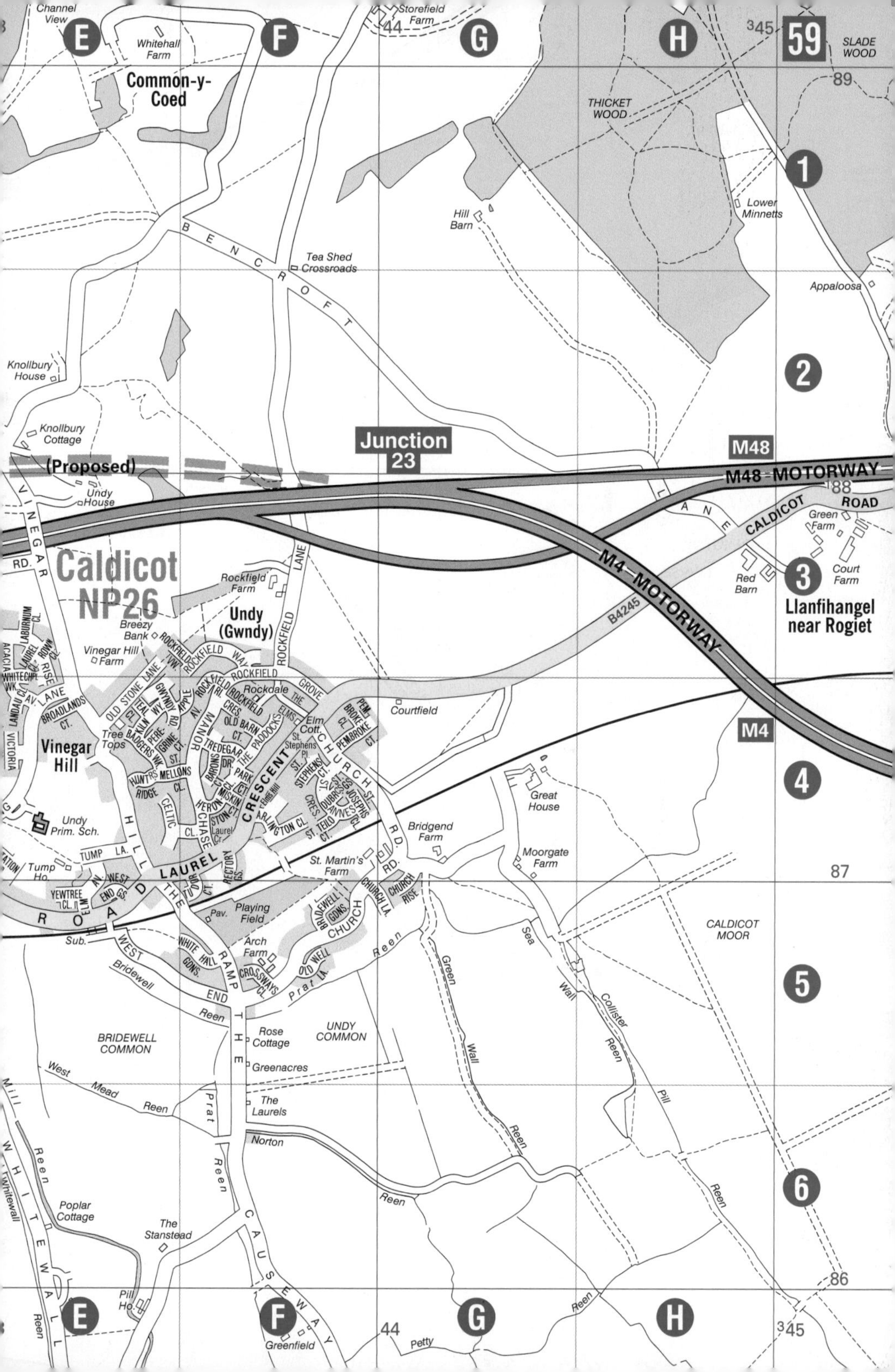

E
F
G
H
1
2
3
4
5
6
345
44
89
88
87
86
Channel View
Whitehall Farm
Common-y-Coed
Storefield Farm
SLADE WOOD
THICKET WOOD
Lower Minnetts
Hill Barn
BENCROFT
Tea Shed Crossroads
Appaloosa
Knollbury House
Knollbury Cottage
Junction 23
M48
(Proposed)
Undy House
M48 MOTORWAY
M4 MOTORWAY
LANE
CALDICOT ROAD
Green Farm
Red Barn
Court Farm
Llanfihangel near Rogiet
B4245
VINEGAR RD.
Caldicot NP26
Rockfield Farm
Undy (Gwndy)
ROCKFIELD LANE
Breezy Bank
Vinegar Hill Farm
ROCKFIELD WAY
ROCKFIELD GROVE
Rockdale
Courtfield
Elm Cott.
THE ELMS
THE PADDOCKS
St. Stephens Pl.
CHURCH RD.
PEMBROKE CT.
OLD STONE LANE
OLD BARN CT.
MANOR CHASE
BROADLANDS CT.
LANE
Vinegar Hill
Tree Tops
BADGERS WK.
HUNTERS RIDGE
MELLONS CL.
CELTIC CL.
TREDEGAR PARK
CRESCENT
ST. STEPHENS CT.
DUBRICIUS GS.
ST. ANNES CL.
ST. JOSEPHS CL.
ST. TEILO CRES.
ARLINGTON CL.
Great House
Bridgend Farm
Moorgate Farm
Undy Prim. Sch.
TUMP LA.
Tump Ho.
HILL
LAUREL ROAD
WEST END GS.
YEWTREE CL.
ELM AV.
TUDOR CT.
RECTORY GS.
St. Martin's Farm
CHURCH LA.
CHURCH RISE
Playing Field
Pav.
BRIDEWELL GDNS.
CHURCH
Sub.
WEST END
WHITE HALL GDNS.
THE RAMP
Arch Farm
CROSSWAYS CL.
OLD WELL
Prat LA.
Reen
Bridewell Reen
BRIDEWELL COMMON
Rose Cottage
UNDY COMMON
Greenacres
Green Wall Reen
Sea Wall
Collister Reen
CALDICOT MOOR
West Mead Reen
Prat
The Laurels
Norton
Pill
Mill Reen
WHITEWALL
Whitewall Reen
Poplar Cottage
The Stanstead
Pill Ho.
CAUSEWAY
Greenfield
Petty

60
A
B
C
D
1
2
3
4
5
6
47
48
190
89
88
Ten Elms
Westgate Farm
St. Stephen's Church
Great House Farm
Caer-went
VENTA SILVRVM
(Roman Town)
Rodge Farm
Nedern Brook
Upper Rodge Wood
Sea View
Llantwinatt
Brockwells Farm
Reservoir (covered)
Club House
DEWSTOW GOLF COURSE
Driving Range
Little Dewstow
Keepers Lodge
Dewstow Farm
Gate Ho.
Rustic Lodge
Dewstow House
Dewstow Lodge
Ifton Quarries
Ifton Crest
Works
Elms Farm
New House Farm
Highfield
Slough Farm
A48
Mayfield
The Grange
Caerwent Brook Cottages
East View
The Woodlands
Caerwent Quarries (stone)
Woodland Valley
Rock House
The Elms
Caldicot NP26
Brookside
Church Farm
Caldicot St. Mary's Jun. Sch.
M48 MOTORWAY
M48
Cemy.
Inf. Sch.
King George's Field
Bowl Grn.
Albion Ho.
Wesley Bldgs.
Lib.
CALDICOT
Caldicot Comprehensive School
Caldicot Community College & Leisure Centre
Hall
Durand Prim. Sch.
Court Ho.
Caldicot West End Inf. Sch.
Playground
Pav.
Cwrt Severn
Rugby Ground
Depot
IFTON INDUSTRIAL PARK
CHEESEMAN'S TRAD. EST.
IFTON QUARRY IND. EST.
ROGIET RD. B4245
NEWPORT ROAD
CALDICOT
Ifton Manor
Rogiet
Playing Field
Severn Tunnel Junction
GARTHALAN DRIVE
STATION RD.
Caldicot
Ifton Bank Reen
Summerway Reen
Sewage Works
DEWSTOW ROAD
CALDICOT ROAD
SANDY LANE
CHURCH ROAD
CHEPSTOW ROAD
WOODSTOCK WAY
CALDICOT
GOLDFINCH CLOSE
LONGCROFT ROAD
CAE MAWR ROAD
WOODLAND ROAD
PARK RD.
FERNLEIGH RD.
WESTFIELD RD.
GREEN LANE
SHAKESPEARE DR.
LONGFELLOW RD.
BYRON PL.
MASEFIELD RD.
BETJEMAN AV.
WORDSWORTH CL.
CHAUCER CL.
TENNYSON RD.
KEATS
KIPLING
SHELLY CL.
FERNEY CROSS
BIRBECK
DEWSTON CL.
DEWSTON GDNS.
FERNEY KIRR. CR.
LACH CL.
FAIRFIELD
OAKLEY CLOSE
OAKLEY ROAD
SYCAMORE AV.
HAZEL AV.
BEECH RD.
ELM RD.
FIRS ROAD
HERBERT RD.
ASH GROVE
WILLOW CL.
MAPLE CL.
NEDDERN WY.
AVON CLOSE
BROOKSIDE
CAS TROGGI
NEDDERN CL.
NEDDERN GDS.
CASTLE LEA
WENTWOOD VW.
EBBW
TRODDI
HONDDU CL.
ANGIDDY CL.
USK CL.
ELAN WAY
TAFF RD.
CLOS ALWEN
HEOL GLASLYN
HEOL TOWY
CLOS RHEIDOL
CLOS ALED
HEOL TEIFI
MARGRET T'S WY.
PRIORY CL.
BUDDEN CR.
CHURCHFIELD AV.
DANCARGA DR.
MONKS CRES.
GROVE GDS.
LLANTHONY CL.
COURT HOUSE CL.
CASTLE LEA
PROSPECT CR.
JUBILEE WY.
GREENFIELD
CAE MAWR AV.
CAE MAWR GR.
GREEN AV.
WESTFIELD AV.
WAGHAUSEL CL.
NORMAN CT.
ORCHARD CL.
YEW TREE CL.
WOODSTOCK CT.
DURAND RD.
FITZWALTER RD.
COBB CR.
ALIANORE RD.
STAFFORD R.
LINNET RD.
MALLARD AV.
CURLEW AV.
KINGFISHER CL.
NIGHTINGALE CL.
FALCON CL.
EAGLE CL.
PLOVER CR.
SWALLOW DR.
SWAN CL.
HERON RD.
KESTREL CL.
BLACKBIRD
PLUM TREE LA.
THE AVENUE
BURNS CR.
LONGFELLOW CL.
Longfellow Place
IFTON LA.
CHESTNUT
POPLAR CL.
YEW TREE RI.
DRIVE
IFTON CROSSWY.
LAND VW.
WOOD-
GRENVILLE TER.
WEST WAY
IFTON TER.
IFTON AV.
Manor Ct.
CWRT MORGAN
CENTURIONS CT.
HIGHFIELD LANE
VERNON GRO.
MARTINS RD.
BISHOP CL.
CADOC CL.
CANNON
ST. TATHAN'S PL.
Play Area
Playing Field
VICARAGE GDNS.
EAST GATE CR.
ST. STEPHEN'S CL.
CAER-WENT GS.
BURTON HOMES
POUND LA.

61
E
F
G
H
49
350
190
89
88
1
2
3
4
5
6
NP16
Traskney
Slidyhill Wood
Verlands Wood
Hawthorn
Little Peterstow Farm
Lorna Doone
Parkwall Farm
Parkwall Lodge
Parkwall Cott.
A48
M48
M48-MOTORWAY
Crick
Depot
OLD SHIRENEWTON RD.
Wks.
Bentley Green
Woodside
Sunny Bank
The Croft
Uplands
Severn Farm
Crick Ho.
Bradbury's Farm
West View
Killcrow Hill
CRICK
WALNUT GRO.
ROAD
B4245
Oak Grove
Hill Barn
Ballan Wood
CRICK RD.
Central Farm
Little Ballan
MOUNT
Crown Hill Nurseries
Coltshay Hill
LAN
OR
The Berries
Motte & Bailey
Cartref
Crown Hill Farm
Crown Hill
Rectory Farm
Leechpool
Harpson Barn
Leechpool House
LEECHPOOL ROAD
Nedern
The Bungalow
Mount Ballan
Crossways
BALLAN
Farthing Hill
Ruffets
Brook
Lower Leechpool Farm
Withy Beds
Red Gates
CALDICOT
CALDICOT CASTLE COUNTRY PARK
PORTSKEWETT HILL
Caldicot Castle
STOW BALL HILL
Archbishop Rowan Williams C. in W. Prim. Sch.
BLACK ROCK RD
HODGES CL.
CROFT
LABNM GR.
LABURNUM T.
HESTN
Lodge
MITEL BUSINESS PARK
PORTSKEWETT
TREE TOPS
CRICK RD.
Hall
Manor Farm
STATION VW.
HILL BARN
SUNNYBANK RD.
Station Bungalows
CASTLE LEA
LODGE CR.
CASTLE LODGE CL.
CASTLE WAY
PILL WAY
Arthurs Ct.
CASTLE CT.
GRAY HILL VW.
OAKLANDS PK.
ROAD
MAIN
WEDGEWOOD DR.
HILL BARN VW.
Nedern Bri.
LODGE WAY
St. Mary's Pl.
ST. MARY'S CLOSE
MANOR WY.
SUDBROOK RD.
CANTERBURY WAY
ORCHARD GDS.
THE SOUTHBROOK VIEW
Hillhouse Barn
DEEPWEIR DR.
DEEPWEIR
PASS
PILL
Castertown Pill
Ebley Gdns.
CASTLE COURT
SEVERN BRIDGE INDUSTRIAL ESTATE
Hall
Rec. Grd.
NORMAN WAY
Southbrook
DEEPWEIR GDS.
DENNY VW.
REDMEADOW CR.
MOORLANDS
Deepweir
ESTUARY VW.
RAILWAY VW.
ROW
SYMONDSCLIFF
Electricity Sub Station
AV.
ORCHID DRIVE
OLD PILL FARM IND. EST.
Severn
Tunnel
The Terrace
Marine Ter.
Sea View
SUDBROOK
Sudbrook
Severn Tunnel
The Pill
Factory
PILL FARM ESTATE
Paper Mill
Church Row
Ysgol y Ffin
The Villas
ROAD
Stone Cotts.
CAMP RD
Post Office Row
Walker Flats
Old Row
Fort
M4

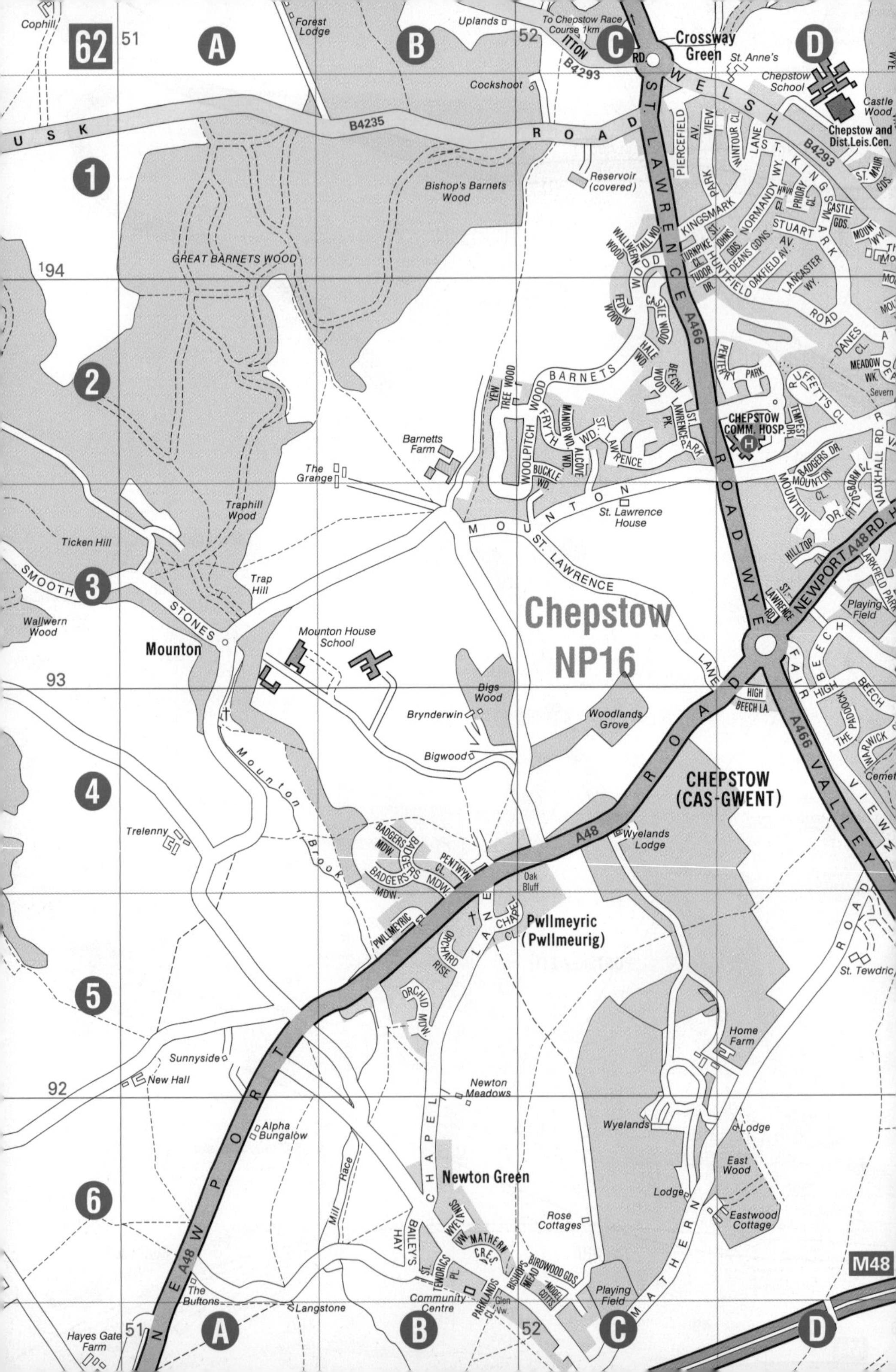

62
51
52
A
B
C
D
1
2
3
4
5
6
194
93
92
Cophill
Forest Lodge
Uplands
To Chepstow Race Course 1km
ITTON RD.
B4293
Crossway Green
St. Anne's
Chepstow School
Castle Wood
Chepstow and Dist.Leis.Cen.
Cockshoot
USK ROAD
B4235
WELSH ST.
ST. LAWRENCE
A466
Reservoir (covered)
Bishop's Barnets Wood
GREAT BARNETS WOOD
PIERCEFIELD AV.
VIEW
WINTOUR CL.
LANE
PARK
KINGS PARK
ST. MAUR GDS.
NORMANDY WY.
KINGSMARK
STUART
AV.
CASTLE GDS.
MOUNT WY.
TURNPIKE CL.
ST. JOHNS GDS.
DEANS GDS.
OAKFIELD AV.
LANCASTER WY.
TUDOR DR.
HUNTFIELD
ROAD
WALLWERN WOOD
TALL WD.
FEDW WOOD
CASTLE WOOD
HALE WD.
BEECH WOOD
DANES CL.
MEADOW WK.
Severn
PENTERRY PARK
RUFFETT'S CL.
TEMPEST DR.
BARNETS
YEW TREE WOOD
WOOLPITCH WOOD
FRYTH
MANOR WD.
ALCOVE WD.
ST. LAWRENCE PK.
LAWRENCE PARK
ST. LAWRENCE
CHEPSTOW COMM. HOSP.
BUCKLE WD.
Barnetts Farm
The Grange
Traphill Wood
Ticken Hill
SMOOTH STONES
Trap Hill
MOUNTON
St. Lawrence House
ST. LAWRENCE LANE
MOUNTON DR.
BADGERS DR.
MOUNTON CL.
FITZOSBORN CL.
VAUXHALL RD.
HILLTOP
NEWPORT A48 RD.
LARKFIELD PARK
Playing Field
Wallwern Wood
Mounton
Mounton House School
Chepstow NP16
ROAD WYE
RD.
FAIR VIEW
HIGH BEECH
BEECH HIGH
HIGH BEECH LA.
THE PADDOCK
WARWICK
Cemet
Bigs Wood
Brynderwin
Bigwood
Woodlands Grove
CHEPSTOW (CAS-GWENT)
A466 VALLEY
Mounton Brook
Trelenny
BADGERS MDW.
PENTWYN CL.
A48
Wyelands Lodge
Oak Bluff
PWLLMEYRIC CL.
CHAPEL CL.
LANE
ORCHARD RISE
Pwllmeyric (Pwllmeurig)
ROAD
St. Tewdric
ORCHID MDW.
Home Farm
Sunnyside
New Hall
Newton Meadows
Alpha Bungalow
Wyelands
Lodge
NEWPORT
CHAPEL
Mill Race
Newton Green
East Wood
Lodge
Rose Cottages
Eastwood Cottage
WYELANDS VW.
BAILEY'S HAY
MATHERN CRES.
BIRDWOOD GDS.
BISHOPS MEAD
MODEL COTTS.
ST. TEWDRICS PL.
MATHERN
M48
Playing Field
The Buftons
Langstone
Community Centre
PARKLANDS CL.
Glen Vw.
NEWPORT A48
Hayes Gate Farm

TUTSHILL
B4228
Castleford Hill
Wyecliffe House
St. John's on the Hill Sch.
Bigstone
Granville Ter.
Sedbury Lane
Castle Vw.
Severn Avenue
Mead Farm
Tump Farm
Sedbury Lane
Upper Sedbury House
The Poplars
Elmdale
Chepstow Castle
Castle Dell
The Dell Prim. Sch.
The Gables
Mus.
Badmington Villas
Factory
Kendall Sq.
Slipway
River Vw.
The Back
St. Ann St.
A48
Wyebank Road
Sedbury Business Park
Works
Wydean School
Grahamstown Rd.
Badams Court
The Elms
Buffer Wharf
Depot
Superstore
Sch. Hill Trad. Est.
Station Ind. Est.
Chepstow
Moor St.
High St.
Place de Cormeilles
Thomas Sq.
Albion
Restway Wall
Port Wall
Portwall Rd.
Green Street
Caird Street
Avenue
Sports Field
Playgrnd.
Pav.
Hardwick
Mount Pleasant
Works
Offa's Mead Prim. Sch.
Playing Field
Wyebank Way
Tallard's Pl.
Alfreds Rd.
Penda Pl.
Tylers Way
Park View
Depot
SEDBURY
The Lodge
Arlington Ct.
Sedbury Lane
Sewage Works
Football Field
Tallard's Marsh
Buttington Rd.
Mercian Wy.
Norse Wy.
Bridget Dr.
Offa's Dyke
Pennsylvania Farm
Standing Stone
Barnes Cottage
Buttington Lodge
Buttington Tump
Buttington Cottages
Buttington Ter.
Buttington Farm
Buttington Hill
Varteg Cott.
Garden Cottage
Dairy Cott.
Sedbury Park
The Coombe
Sedbury Cliffs
MONMOUTHSHIRE (SIR FYNWY)
FOREST OF DEAN
ENGLAND (LLOEGR)
WALES (CYMRU)
Works
Beaufort Quarry
Hardwick Cliffs
Strongbow Rd.
Marten Rd.
Fairfield Rd.
Pavilion Sports Ground
Pembroke Primary Sch.
Bulwark Industrial Estate
The Bulwarks Play. Fld.
Alpha Road
Camp Rd.
Alexandra Rd.
Victoria Road
Middle Way
St. George Rd.
Bulwark Road
Prim. Sch.
Pembroke Rd.
Mathern Way
Thornwell Road
Bulwark
Cromwell Rd.
Burnt Barn Rd.
The Octagon
Raglan Way
Warren Slade
Thornwell Prim. Sch.
Park Redding
Denbigh Dr.
Valentine Lane
Mariners Reach
Grasmere Wy.
Hall
Aust Cr.
Western Avenue
Somerset Road
Chartists Wy
Playgrd.
Playing Field
Club Ho.
Rugby Football Ground
The Old Fm. Shop. Cen.
Beaufort Park
Sports Ground
Pav.
Loop Road
Inner Loop Road
Beachley Road
Slimeroad Pill
Salmon Catch
Severn Bridge Park Residential Homes
Engineering Works
Gibraltar Wy.
St. Georges Wy.
Ferry Way
Beachley
Slipway
Slipway
Army Apprentices College
RIVER SEVERN
Junction 2
A466 Link Road
A48 MOTORWAY
Newhouse Farm Industrial Estate
Sewage Works
E F G H
1 2 3 4 5 6
54
355
194
93
92

A
B
C
D
40
Forest View
ROYAL GLAMORGAN HOSPITAL
MYNYDD GARTHMAELWG
Ynysmaerdy
RHODFA MARICS
Welsh Blood Service
Ely Meadow (Gwaun Eli)
Machudd
Nant
A4119
ELY VALLEY ROAD
Coed-Cae Farm
Weirs
Works
Graig-lwyd
Coedynysmaerdy
(AFON ELAI)
ELY RIVER
LLANTRISANT & PONTYCLUN GOLF COURSE
PINE COURT ROAD
FIRBANKS WY.
FAIRWAYS
Garth-uchaf
The Kennels
Garth-isaf Farm
Club Ho.
Talbot Green
Lanelay Farm
LANELAY CT.
Fire Service HQ
FOREST WLK.
FOREST HILLS DR.
WOODFIELD
PINEWOOD HILL
DUNRAVEN CRES.
LANELAY CL.
TALBOT SQUARE
ROAD
Prim. Sch.
Halls
Hall
Comm. Cen.
Play. Fld.
Garth Maelwg
Works
Factory
Lanelay Hall Playing Fields
LANELAY
LANELAY PK.
LANELAY GRO.
CLOS
SPRING FIELD
COWBRIDGE
FANHEULOG
A473
GREEN
Sewage Works
PARK
LANE
LANELAY INDUSTRIAL ESTATE
COEDCAE LANE INDUSTRIAL ESTATE
THE BEECHES INDUSTRIAL ESTATE
Mwyndy Junction
Factory
Hypermarket
A4222
COWBRIDGE ROAD
Hendre Owen
Nant Melyn
Woodland Workshop Cen.
CAMBRIAN IND. EST. (WEST SIDE)
CAMBRIAN IND. EST. (EAST SIDE)
PANT Y DDERWEN
School House
COED TRECASTELL
YNYSDDU
CLOS YNYSDDU
COEDCAE
ASH GRO.
LLWYN
COED MIERI
GARTH
UNNO
TYLAGARW
ELY VALLEY IND. ESTATE
MAELOG CL.
MERTHYR ST.
LEWIS ST.
ELY ST.
LON ELAI
SCHOOL ST.
STATION APP.
HEOL
David's Ct.
CLUN CRES.
CLUN AVENUE
WINDSOR CT.
LLANTRISANT ROAD
Works
Tylagarw Terrace
TYLE
Trecastle
Pontyclun
JUNCTION INDUSTRIAL ESTATE
Railway Ter.
Playgrd.
STATION T.
STUART ST.
HEOL YR ORSAF
CERDIN
PONTYCLUN
Club
Playgrd.
Rugby Ground
ELY RIVER (AFON ELAI)
MILLFIELD
RIVER'S EDGE
Hall
CASTAN
PALALWYF
Club
Bowl. Grn.
DERWEN AV.
FAIR VIEW CL.
LLWYNFEN RD.
RHYD Y NANT
TIR-AFON
PARK CR.
Prim. Sch.
Lib.
Heol Dafydd
Pontyclun Prim. Sch.
Ty-du
Ty-draw
War Meml.
Playgrd.
Pav.
HEOL-Y-FELIN
TALYGARN
FFORDD GLAN YRAFON
Sports Ground
CLOS BRENIN
TEGFAN
Brow-Dawel Cl.
MAES-YR-AFON
Tyna Cottage
Nant Felin-fach
DANYBRYN
78
Depot
Football Ground
HEOL GLAN ELAI
1
2
3
4
5
6
84
83
82
81
02
03

E
F
G
H
41
305
65
Brynteg
Brynteg House
Bullring Cottage
Rugby Football Ground
Club
Coed-yr-esgob Primary School
Malthouse
Tanks
LLANTRISANT
Llantrisant Castle
Ysgol Gynradd Gymraeg Llantrisant
NEWBRIDGE ROAD
B4595
DAN CAERLAN
Playgrd.
Playground
East Caerlon
Caeau'r-llan
ERW HIR
Erw Hir
Gwern-y-Moel
Gwern-y-Moel Uchaf
Rhiwbrwdwal Farm
Springbridge Villa
84
Cymdda-bach
Nant
A473
Coedcaerau-bach
83
CROSS INN ROAD
Cross Inn
Dairy
LLANTRISANT RD.
HIGH STREET
TALBOT RD.
Llantrisant Leisure Cen.
Penygawsi
Penygawsi Primary Sch.
CARDIFF ROAD
SOUTHGATE DR.
Bus Sta.
PARC MANWERTHU TONYSGYBORIAD (TALBOT GREEN RETAIL PK.)
Lib.
Sub.
Sewage Works
GLAMORGAN VALE RETAIL PARK
RHIWSAESON ROAD
Tondrugwaer
Taff Cotts.
1
2
3
4
5
6
66
Pontyclun
CF72
Sewage Works
Afon Clun
A4119
ROAD
Subway
Cefn-y-Parc Cemetery
Depot
Lynwood
182
Cefn-parc Farm
Superstore
Works
Coed-yr-hendy
Mwyndy
Mwyndy Cross
Mwyndy Ter.
Long Acre
Bute Farm Cottage
Bute Cottages
Mwyndy House
Ty-Newydd Woods
Llwyn saer
Cefnyrhendy
Playgrd.
Vehicle Testing Centre
B4264
SCHOOL ROAD
Hendy
MISKIN ROAD
Miskin
Hendy Quarry
LLANTRISANT A4119 ROAD
81
Tynewydd
Croffta
PENDOYLAN RD.
College House
06
79
War Meml.
Ceulan

Brynteg
66
A
B
C
D
42
06
07
Sunny Bank Cottage
Gwaunmiskin House
Springbridge Villa
Llantwit Main Farm
BRYNTEG
BRYNTEG CT.
SQUIRES CT.
LANE
CHASE
ROAD
LLANTRISANT
A473
Ystrad Barwig Isaf
Nant
Brook Farm
Westmoor
(Proposed)
Pontypridd
84
1
Cymdda-bach
Myddlyn
Rhiwbrwdwal Farm
Disgwylfa
Gwern-y-Moel Uchaf
Ty uchaf
Hendrescy
2
Fort
The Lodge
Coedcaerau-bach
83
Ty-Mawr Farm
Coed-y-Graig
Pontyclun
CF72
Hillcroft
RHIWSAESON
Rhiwsaeson
Tondrugwaer
ROAD
RHONDDA CYNON TAFF
CARDIFF
Sports Ground
Ty'n y Ca Farm
3
Afon
Tor-y-coed Farm
Pav.
Sewage Works
Clun
65
Llwyn-y-brain-mawr
Llwyn-y-brain-bach
HEOL CREIGIAU
Llwynmilwas Farm
Smithy
Llwynmilwas
4
(RHONDDA CYNON TAFF)
(CAERDYDD)
182
Porthandro
5
Ty-Newydd Woods
CREIGIAU GOLF COURSE
PARC-Y-
Llwyn-saer
Ford
Club House
Brofiscin Farm
TRE GARTH CT.
Creigiau Primary School
Maendy Farm
CREIGIAU
6
PARC-Y-FELIN
HEOL BROFISCIN
HEOL-YR-HAUL
GLAN CREIGIAU
BRYN CREIGIAU
Groesfaen
PEN Y GROES
PARK LA.
FFORDD
DOL-Y-FELIN
LLANTRISANT
Llwyn yr Eos
ROAD
MAIN
A4119
ROAD
PARC
81
Maes Mawr
Tynewydd
Croffta
The Smithy
PENDOYLAN RD.
80
TYNANT
A
B
C
D
College House
06
07
Cottages
Hill

67
43
81
68
CF38
Cardiff
CF15
PENTYRCH
Mavrid
Woodbury
Cwm Uchaf Farm
New House Cwm Mill
Ty Mawr
Coedgae Bassett
Coed Hendre-'sguthan
Bwlch-y-gwynt
Garth-uchaf
Craig Gwilym
Pump House
Soar
Brynhyfryd
Reservoir
Ty'n-y-ffald
Silverbrook
Warren House
Craig-Gwilym
Mountain Ash Cottage
Ty'n-y-coed
Ty'n-y-Coed
Aqueduct
TYN-Y-COED ROAD
MOUNTAIN ROAD
GARTH HILL
Y Graig
Coed y Creigiau
Quarry
Penllwyn
Pentyrch Prim. Sch.
Creigiau Farm
Craig-yr-yd
Pav.
Ten. Cts.
Sports Ground
Craig Ffynnon-dwym
Ffynnon Dwym
Station Houses
Reservoir
PANT-Y-GORED
HEOL PANT-Y-GORED
PENUEL ROAD
HEOL-Y-PARC
BRONLLWYN
Playground
Sports Ground
Pentwyn
Pentwyn Farmhouse
Pant-y-gored
Rhuddin
Craig-y-parc School
MAES-Y-SARN
TROED-Y-GARTH
HEOL PENLLWYN
HEOL GAM
HEOL-Y-BRYN
TEMPERANCE CT.
HIGH CNR.
HEOL-Y-PENTRE
FIELD TER.
BRYN SIRIOL
PENMAES
BRYN-YR-EGLWYS
PENFFORDD
HAUL
PANTEG
AEL-Y-BRYN
BRON-Y-FRO
CEFN PENUEL
LON BRODOG
PANT BACK
PEN-Y-WAUN
Erw Wen Cottages
PARC-Y-FRO
CASTLE TER.
CASTLE CL.
WOODLAND
TERRACE
THE
CLOS DARNAU
Hall
STA. RD.
HEOL
CARDIFF ROAD
CASTELL-Y-MYNACH
PARC
GREEN ACRE
Castell-y-mynach
COED-Y-
MAES-Y-
MAES CADWGAN
HAFOD
CLOS LLEWELLYN
DERWEN

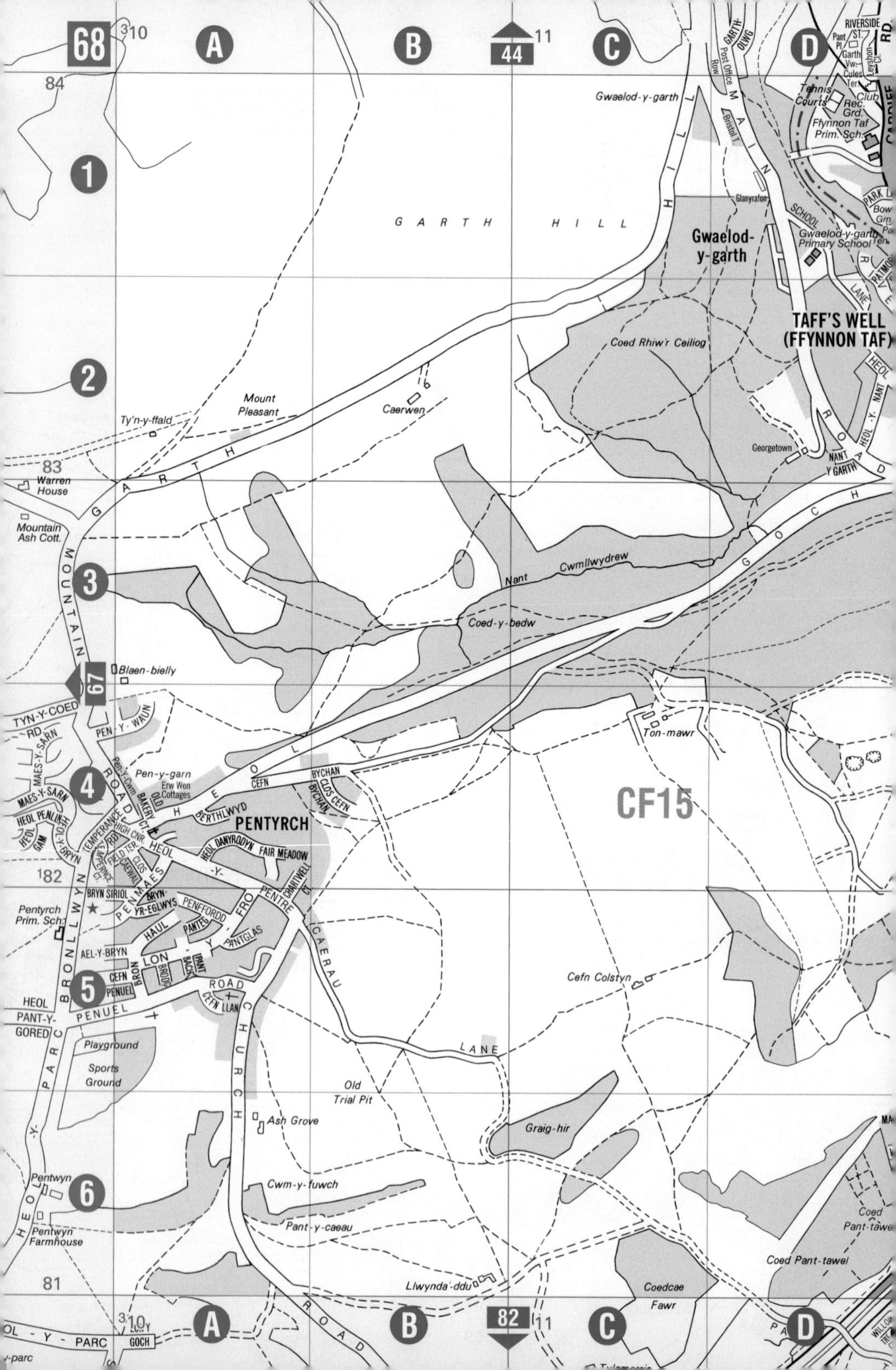
A
B
C
D
44
1
2
3
4
5
6
GARTH HILL
Gwaelod-y-garth
TAFF'S WELL (FFYNNON TAF)
PENTYRCH
CF15
Mount Pleasant
Caerwen
Ty'n-y-ffald
Warren House
Mountain Ash Cott.
Coed Rhiw'r Ceiliog
Nant Cwmllwydrew
Coed-y-bedw
Blaen-biellу
Ton-mawr
Pen-y-garn
Erw Wen Cottages
Pentyrch Prim. Sch.
Playground
Sports Ground
Old Trial Pit
Ash Grove
Cefn Colstyn
Graig-hir
Cwm-y-fuwch
Pant-y-caeau
Pentwyn
Pentwyn Farmhouse
Llwynda'-ddu
Coedcae Fawr
Coed Pant-tawel
Tennis Courts
Rec. Grd.
Ffynnon Taf Prim. Sch.
Gwaelod-y-garth Primary School
Georgetown
Glanyrafon
67
82

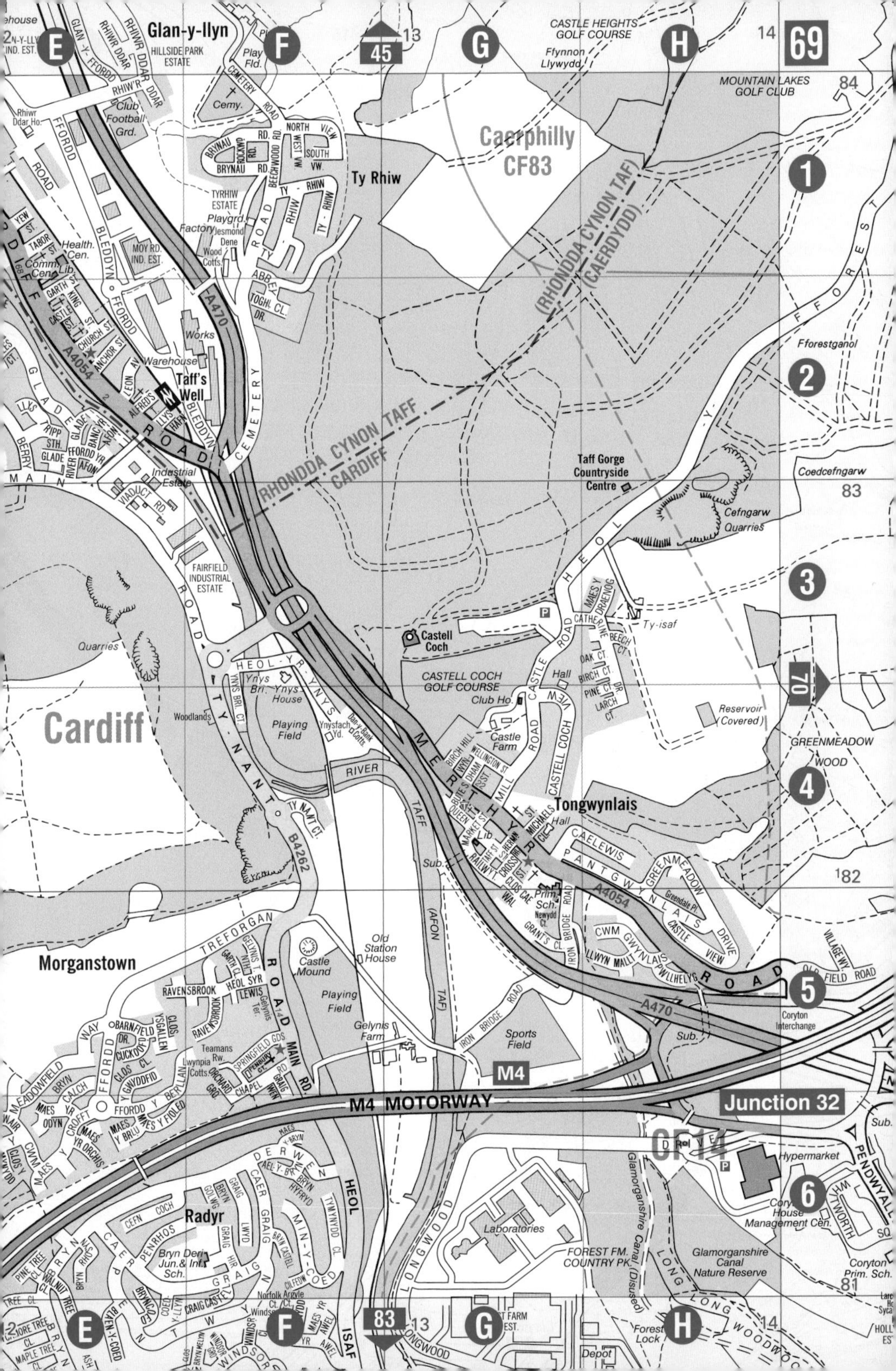

Glan-y-llyn
HILLSIDE PARK ESTATE
45
CASTLE HEIGHTS GOLF COURSE
Ffynnon Llywydd
MOUNTAIN LAKES GOLF CLUB
Caerphilly CF83
Ty Rhiw
TYRHIW ESTATE
MOY RD. IND. EST.
Taff's Well
RHONDDA CYNON TAFF
CARDIFF
(RHONDDA CYNON TAF) (CAERDYDD)
Fforestganol
Taff Gorge Countryside Centre
Coedcefngarw
Cefngarw Quarries
FAIRFIELD INDUSTRIAL ESTATE
Industrial Estate
Castell Coch
CASTELL COCH GOLF COURSE
Ty-isaf
Reservoir (Covered)
70
GREENMEADOW WOOD
Cardiff
Quarries
Tongwynlais
Morganstown
Castle Mound
Old Station House
Playing Field
Gelynis Farm
Sports Field
Coryton Interchange
M4 MOTORWAY
Junction 32
CF14
Hypermarket
Coryton House Management Cen.
Radyr
Bryn Deri Jun.& Inf. Sch.
Laboratories
FOREST FM. COUNTRY PK.
Glamorganshire Canal (Disused)
Glamorganshire Canal Nature Reserve
Coryton Prim. Sch.
Forest Lock
Depot
83
A470
A4054
B4262
M4

70
46
69
84
M4
Junction 32
Caerphilly
CF83
MOUNTAIN LAKES GOLF CLUB
Blaengwynlais
Blaengwynlais Quarries
Graig-goch
Wenallt
COED-Y-BRIWANT
New Ho
FFOREST
RHIWBINA
HEOL-Y-WENALLT
Bwlch-y-cwm
CWM NOFYDD
Cwmnofydd
Twynavgwynion
Radio Station
Briwnant
Nant-y-briwnant
Fforestganol
Coed-y-wenallt
Glan-y-nant
Craigbriwnant
Briwnant-fach
Coedcefngarw
Cefngarw Quarries
Old Quarries
RHIWBINA HILL
WENALLT
Rhiwbina
Woodhill
Graig Farm
Reservoir (Covered)
GREENMEADOW WOOD
Pant-mawr Wood
Pine Croft
Nant Cwmnofydd
Castle Mound
M4 MOTORWAY
MERTHYR RD.
OLD FIELD ROAD
VILLAGE WY.
Coryton Interchange
Pant Mawr Cemetery
Pantmawr
NORTHERN AVENUE
A470
PENDWYALLT
A4054 ROAD
Hypermarket
Coryton House Management Centre
Glamorganshire Canal Nature Reserve
Coryton Prim. Sch.
HOLLYBUSH ESTATE
Coryton
Club House
WHITCHURCH (CARDIFF) GOLF COURSE
Greenhill School
Rhiwbeina Jun. & Inf. Schs.
RHIWBINA GARDEN VILLAGE
Coryton
Whitchurch
Rhiwbina
PEN-Y-DRE

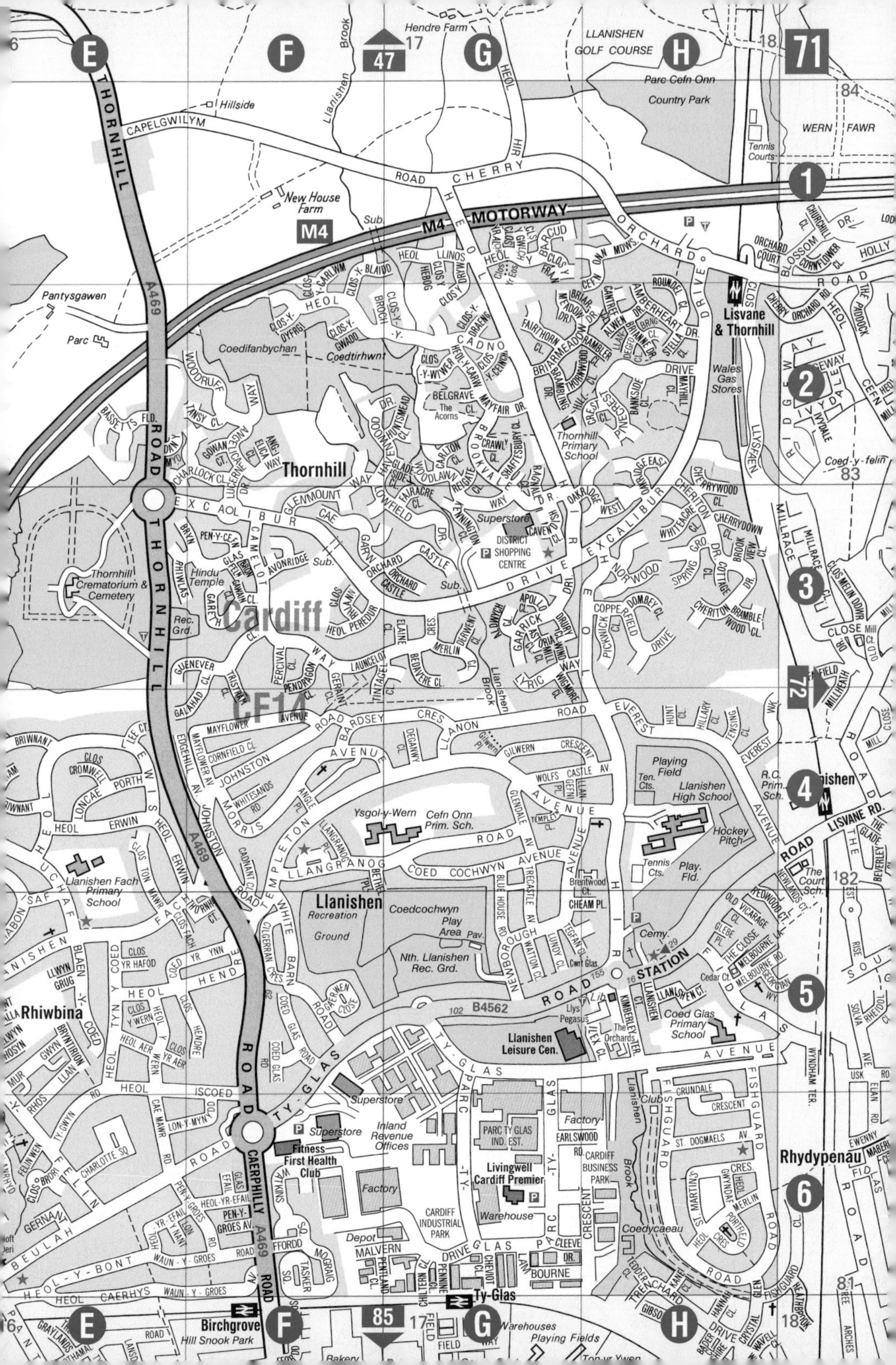
71
47
85
72
E
F
G
H
1
2
3
4
5
6
LLANISHEN GOLF COURSE
Hendre Farm
Parc Cefn Onn Country Park
WERN FAWR
Tennis Courts
Hillside
New House Farm
Pantysgawen
Parc
M4
M4 MOTORWAY
CAPELGWILYM
ROAD CHERRY
ORCHARD DRIVE
THORNHILL ROAD
A469
Coedifanbychan
Coedtirhwnt
Thornhill
Lisvane & Thornhill
Wales Gas Stores
Thornhill Primary School
Thornhill Crematorium & Cemetery
Hindu Temple
Rec. Grd.
Cardiff
CF14
EXCALIBUR DRIVE
Superstore
DISTRICT SHOPPING CENTRE
Llanishen Brook
Coed-y-felin
Playing Field
Ten. Cts.
Llanishen High School
Hockey Pitch
Tennis Cts.
Play. Fld.
R.C. Prim. Sch.
Llanishen
LISVANE RD.
The Court Sch.
Ysgol-y-Wern
Cefn Onn Prim. Sch.
Llanishen Fach Primary School
Llanishen
Recreation Ground
Coedcochwyn Play Area
Nth. Llanishen Rec. Grd.
Cemy.
STATION ROAD
B4562
Llanishen Leisure Cen.
Lib.
Llys Pegasus
The Orchards
Coed Glas Primary School
Rhiwbina
TY GLAS AVENUE
Superstore
Inland Revenue Offices
Fitness First Health Club
Factory
PARC TY GLAS IND. EST.
Livingwell Cardiff Premier
Warehouse
CARDIFF BUSINESS PARK
CARDIFF INDUSTRIAL PARK
Depot
Coedycaeau
Rhydypenau
CAERPHILLY ROAD
Birchgrove
Hill Snook Park
Ty-Glas
Warehouses
Playing Fields
HEOL-Y-BONT
HEOL CAERHYS
BEULAH ROAD
FISHGUARD ROAD
EVEREST AVENUE
LLANON ROAD
HEOL HIR
CHERRY ORCHARD RD.
RIDGEWAY
LLYSFAEN
MILLRACE

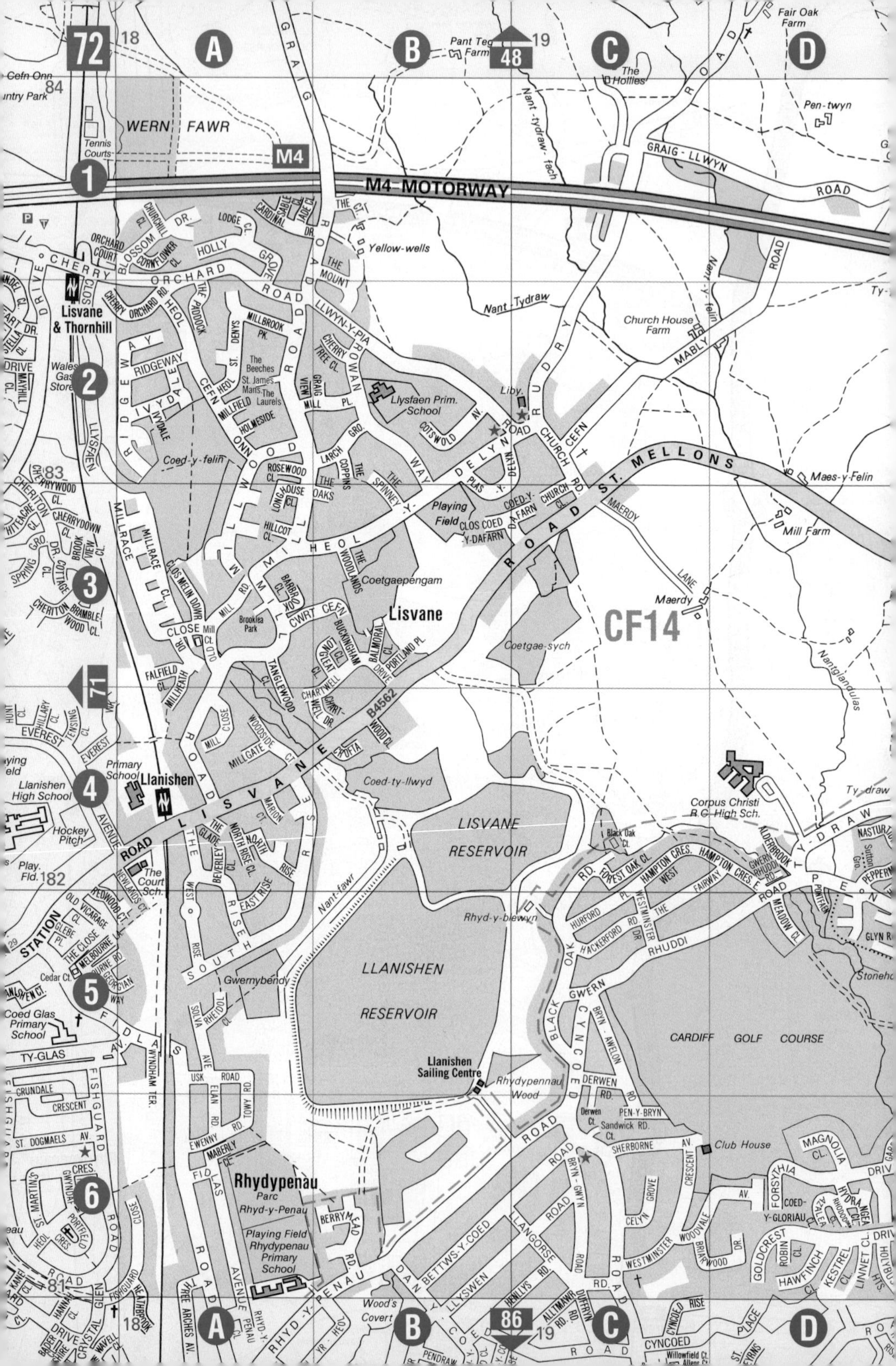

72
18
A
B
C
D
48
19
Pant Teg Farm
The Hollies
Fair Oak Farm
Cefn Onn
84
ountry Park
WERN FAWR
Tennis Courts
M4
M4 MOTORWAY
Nant-tydraw fach
Pen-twyn
GRAIG - LLWYN
ROAD
1
CHURCHILL DR.
BLOSSOM
LODGE CL.
CARDINAL DR.
SABLE CL.
JADE CL.
THE CT.
ORCHARD COURT
CORNFLOWER CL.
HOLLY GROVE
Yellow-wells
THE MOUNT
CHERRY CLOSE
ORCHARD ROAD
Lisvane & Thornhill
CHERRY ORCHARD RD.
HEOL
THE PADDOCK
MILLBROOK PK.
LLWYN-Y-PIA
Nant-Tydraw
Church House Farm
MABLY
Nant-y-felin
RIDGEWAY
Wales Gas Store
2
The Beeches
St. James Mans.
The Laurels
CHERRY TREE CL.
ROWAN
Llysfaen Prim. School
GRAIG VIEW
MILL PL.
Liby.
RUDRY ROAD
CEFN
DENYS
MILLFIELD
HOLMESIDE
IVYDALE
LLYSFAEN
Coed-y-felin
CEFN ONN
LLWYN WOOD
COTSWOLD AV.
LARCH GRO.
COPPINS
THE SPINNEY
DELYN WAY
CHURCH RD.
ST. MELLONS
Maes-y-Felin
83
CHERRYWOOD CL.
CHERITON
WHITEACRE CL.
CHERRYDOWN CL.
ROSEWOOD CL.
LONGHOUSE CL.
THE OAKS
PLAS-Y-DELYN
Playing Field
CLOS COED-Y-DAFARN
COED-Y-DAFARN
CHURCH CL.
MAERDY
Mill Farm
MILLRACE
MILLRACE CL.
HILLCOT CL.
HEOL-Y-
THE WOODLANDS
ROAD
LANE
SPRING GRO.
BROOK VIEW CL.
COTTAGE DR.
3
CLOS MELIN DWR
MILL RD.
BARBROOK CL.
Coetgaepengam
Maerdy
CF14
CHERITON BRAMBLE WOOD CL.
CLOSE
Mill Ct.
Brooklea Park
CWRT CEFN
BUCKINGHAM
Lisvane
BALMORAL CL.
PORTLAND PL.
Coetgae-sych
Nantglandulas
GLEANN CL.
TANGLEWOOD CL.
DRIVE
FALFIELD CL.
MILLHEATH
71
CHARTWELL
CHARTWELL DR.
B4562
HILLARY CL.
TENSING CL.
EVEREST
MILL CLOSE
WOODSIDE CT.
MILLGATE
CROFTA
WOOD CL.
Primary School
Llanishen
LISVANE
Coed-ty-llwyd
Corpus Christi R.C. High Sch.
Ty-draw
Llanishen High School
4
Hockey Pitch
AVENUE
ROAD
MARION CT.
THE GLADE
NORTH RISE CL.
NORTH RISE
LISVANE RESERVOIR
Black Oak Ct.
FOREST OAK CL.
HAMPTON CRES. WEST
HAMPTON CRES. E.
GWERN RHUDDI RD.
ALDERBROOK
TY-DRAW
NASTURTIUM
Play. Fld.
182
The Court Sch.
NEWLANDS CT.
BEVERLEY CL.
WEST RISE
EAST RISE
Nant-fawr
Rhyd-y-blewyn
HURFORD PL.
WESTMINSTER DR.
THE FAIRWAY
HACKERFORD RD.
MEADOW CL.
PONTFAEN
PEPPERMINT
OLD VICARAGE
REDWOOD CT.
GLEBE PL.
STATION
THE CLOSE
MELBOURNE RD.
SOUTH RISE
RHUDDI
GLYN RD
Cedar Ct.
GEORGIAN WAY
5
Gwernybendy
LLANISHEN RESERVOIR
BLACK OAK
GWERN
CYNCOED
BRYN-AWELON
Stonehouse
CARDIFF GOLF COURSE
Coed Glas Primary School
FIDLAS AV.
SOLVA AVE.
RHEIDOL CL.
TY-GLAS
WYNDHAM TER.
CRUNDALE CRESCENT
USK ROAD
ELAN RD.
TOWY RD.
Llanishen Sailing Centre
Rhydypenau Wood
DERWEN RD.
Derwen Ct.
PEN-Y-BRYN
Sandwick RD. Ct.
SHERBORNE AV.
Club House
MAGNOLIA CL.
ST. DOGMAELS AV.
FISHGUARD ROAD
EWENNY RD.
MABERLY CT.
FIDLAS ROAD
Rhydypenau
Parc Rhyd-y-Penau
Playing Field Rhydypenau Primary School
BERRYMEAD RD.
BRYN-GWYN ROAD
CELYN GROVE
CRESCENT
FORSYTHIA
COED-Y-GLORIAU
HYDRANGEA CL.
AZALEA
6
ST. MARTIN'S CRES.
GWYNDAF
PORTFIELD CRES.
HEOL
ROAD
BETTWS-Y-COED
LLANGORSE ROAD
WESTMINSTER CRES.
WOODVALE
BRIARWOOD DR.
GOLDCREST
ROBIN CL.
HAWFINCH
KESTREL CL.
LINNET CL.
81
HANNAH
CRYSTAL GLEN
FISHGUARD CL.
HEATHBROOK
DAN-Y-PENAU
LLYSWEN
PENLLYS RD.
DUFFRYN
RD.
18
THREE ARCHES AV.
AVENUE
RHYD-Y-PENAU
Wood's Covert
86
ALLTMAWR RD.
CYNCOED RISE
PLACE
19
CYNCOED ROAD
Willowfield Ct.
PENDRAW
DRIVE
WAVELL

73
49
87
74
E
F
G
H
1
2
3
4
5
6
CF3
CF23
Cardiff
Pontprennau
Pentwyn
Llanrumney
CEFN MABLEY WOODS
Graig-llwyn
Fort Castle Field
GRAIG-LLWYN ROAD
CEFN-PORTH ROAD
HEOL MAES-Y-BRYN
HEOL-Y-PARC
Llan
Parkwall
M4
M4 MOTORWAY
Junction 30
Nant Glandulas
Malthouse Wood
Malthouse Farm
PARKWALL ROAD
ST. MELLONS ROAD
B4562
Cardiff Gate Service Area
CARDIFF GATE BUSINESS PARK
CARDIFF GATE RETAIL PARK
Superstore
Prennau House
Rhymney Ho.
Regus Ho.
MALTHOUSE AVENUE
MULBERRY DR.
OAK TREE CT.
COPSE WK.
WOODSY CL.
FORESTER WY.
COPPICE RD.
DAMSON PL.
GREENWOOD CL.
BECK CT.
BRIDGE RD.
LINK ROAD
A4232
NORTH PENTWYN LINK
PONTPRENNAU ROAD
HEOL PONTPRENNAU
Llangattock
Bryngolau
CRANBOURNE
TARRAGON WY.
FELBRIGG CR.
WISLEY PL.
CHAMOMILE CL.
AMBERGATE DR.
AMBERLEY CL.
OAKMEAD
ACORN GROVE
CROESCADARN RD.
CROESCADARN CL.
HUNTINGTON DR.
CLOS-Y-FFYNNON
CARDIFF BUPA HOSP.
MALTINGS
PENTWYN ROAD
THE AVENUE INDUSTRIAL PARK
Glebe
Church Farm
St. Edeyrn's Church
CHURCH ROAD
EASTERN AVENUE
A48
New Mill Farm
MILL LANE
COEDEN DAL
GLYN EIDDEW
ST. CLEMENTS CT.
St. Nicholas Ct.
Ty Enfys
PENTWYN BUS. CEN.
WHARFEDALE RD
Factory
PENTWYN DRIVE
WYNCLIFFE RD.
CAXTON PL
St. Bernadette's R C Primary Sch.
The Hollies School
PENTWYN SHOPPING PRECINCT
Hlth. Cen.
Comm. Cen.
BRYNCYN
PENT LEE
WAUN FACH
LLWYN CASTAN
PINWYDDEN
COED-Y-GORES
Glyncoed Jun. & Inf. Schools
THE HAWTHORNS
Bryn Celyn Prim. Sch.
BRYN CELYN ROAD
GLYN COLLEN
PANT GLAS
Playing Fields
Rhymney River
Glan-yr-Afon Jun. & Inf. Schs.
St. Cadoc's RC Prim. School
DICKENS AVENUE
BROWNING CL.
RUSKIN CL.
KIPLING CL.
DRYDEN CL.
LAUREATE CL.
CHESTERTON
Lower Rookery
BURNHAM AVENUE
HONITON ROAD
MALMESMEAD
WILLITON
DURLEIGH CL.
TORRINGTON
PARRACOMBE CL.
Pentwyn Interchange

74
22
23
50
88
A
B
C
D
1
2
3
4
5
6
84
83
82
81
MABLEY PK.
CEFN
Pentreporth
Fairwater Bungalow
Fairwater Farm
Wern Uchaf
Reservoirs
RHYMNEY RIVER
AFON CL.
ROAD
Rhymney Valley Nurseries
Reservoir
Began Farm
Began
Junction 30
M4
M4 MOTORWAY
River
BEGAN ROAD
Maes-y-crochan Farm
NEWPORT
CARDIFF
(CASNEWYDD)
(CAERDYDD)
DRUIDSTONE
St.Julian's Farm
Cardiff Gate Service Area
Rhymney
Brook House
Cardiff
CF3
Pistyll-yr-achddu
Began House
JINDABYNE CL.
Pwll-coch
CARDIFF GATE RETAIL PARK
73
Superstore
PENTWYN
LINK ROAD
BRIDGE RD.
BRIDGE
B4562
Bridge Farm
(Rhymni)
River
Marleigh Lodge
DRUIDSTONE ROAD
A48(M)
A48 (M) MOTORWAY
PONTPRENNAU
DRIVE
NORTH A4232
Llanedern Bridge
Llyn y Corwydd
Junction 29a
St. Mellons Interchange
Recreation Ground
Tennis Court
Glebe
RUPERRA
Ty'r-bont
ROAD
CLOSE
St. Edeyrn's Church
Subs.
Sub.
Church Farm
CHURCH
A48
EASTERN AVENUE
MELROSE CL.
MELVILLE AV.
THE EASTERN BUSINESS PARK
Offices
OLD NEWPORT RD
ROAD
New Mill Farm
MILL LANE
BRONTE
CRES.
AVENUE
ARNOLD
CHAUCER CL.
WALPOLE CL.
THE DELL
BLUEBELL
EASTERN
SILVINE WAY
TY-TO-MAEN CL.
FFORDD
WERN FAWR LANE
HEATHCLIFFE CL.
LYNCROFT
WINCH
HASTINGS CRES.
ALLEN
PARKSTONE
Wern Fawr Cl.
VAINDRE
HERITAGE PK.
HERITAGE PARK
BRONTE CL.
BRONTE CR.
HOUSMAN CL.
OTHERY PL.
BRAYFORD PL.
BUNYAN
AUSTEN CL.
AVENUE
BLUEBELL DR.
Mill Lane
MILL LA.
EVIR WG.
CRES.
St. John's College
NICHOLLS DR.
WILLIAM
CORMORANT CL.
TERN CL.
DR.
Prim. Sch.
Faendre Gardens
MILL
HAZLITT
BOSWELL
BURNHAM
AVENUE
ASHBURTON
OKEHAMPTON AV.
WITHYCOMBE RD
B4562
GOULD CL.
CRES.
B4487
EIDER CT.
OSPREY CL.
EIDER
FULMAR CL.
KINGFISHER CL.
SANDERLING
St. Cadoc's RC Prim. School
MACAULAY AV.
BROWNING CL.
SHAW
HONITON
MALMESMEAD ROAD
SEDGEMOOR
ELGAR
COATES PL.
CHURCH LA.
LLANEWRWG
ALDERWOOD CL.
HAZELWOOD
LIMEWOOD
ASPEN CL.
REDWOOD CL.
BROADLANDS
WILLOWBROOK
CRICKHOWELL
WILLOWBROOK LAB. UNITS
LLANDOGO RD.
St. Mellons
ROAD
CRESCENT
SOMERSET CT.
BURNHAM
WILLITON
ROAD
AVENUE
WEEKES CL.
COURTENAY CL.
Llandaff Sq.
ORCHARD
PK. CL.
PARK
ROAD
WAY
Broadlands Ho.
DISTRICT SHOPPING CENTRE
Crickhowell
ARVANS
BLAINA CL.
CRUMLIN
BALL
DICKENS
CHESTERTON
AVENUE
DURLEIGH CL.
TORRINGTON
WASHFORD
MILVERTON
PORLOCK RD.
PURCELL RD.
SULLIVAN CL.
ELGAR CRES.
NEW PORT RD
CHAPEL ROW
ORCHARD
FERNTREE
Sub.
Oakfield Jun. & Inf. Sch.
Bowl. Grn.
Comm. Cen.
Lib.
ROGERSTONE
RISCA CL.
MALPAS
GOLDSMITH CL.
FIELDING CL.
Lower Rookery
PARRACOMBE
COUNTISBURY
ROAD
Pen-y-Bryn Prim. & St. Mellons Church in Wales Schs.
CHAPEL RW.
OAKLANDS CL.
MAYLARD CL.
Cath-Cobb Wood
BROCKHAMPTON RD.
Oak Pl.
WAKEHURST
BAMPTON RD.
BANWELL PL.
BLACKMOOR
DUNSTER
INSTOW
Lib.
Comm. Cen.
MINEHEAD
AXBRIDGE
OLDHILL
GREENWAY
BROOKFIELD
MILLFIELD CL.
Playing Field
JAMES CT.
Playground
BARN
STAPLE CL.
AVENUE
Ty Coch

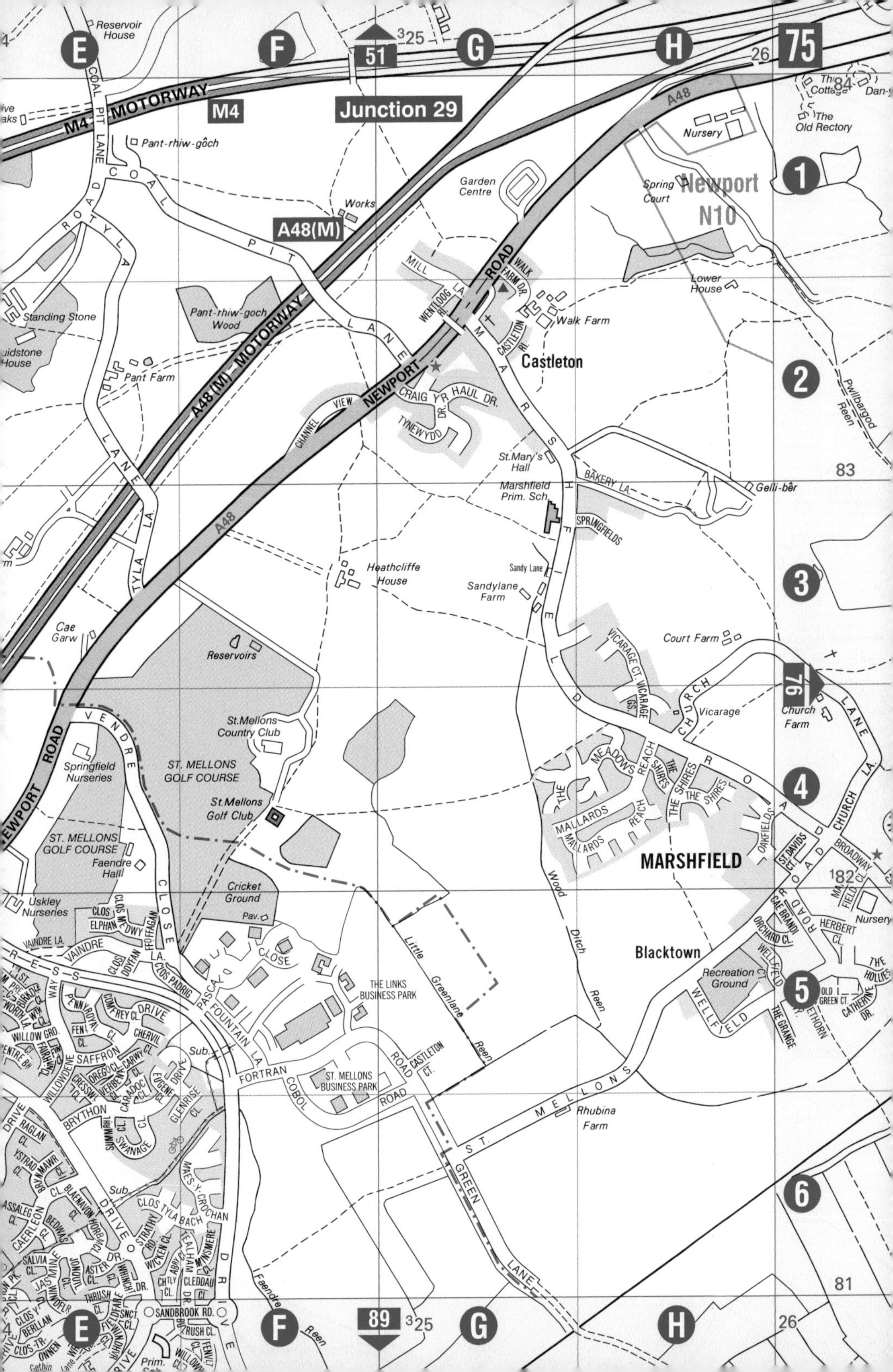

75
51
89
76
E
F
G
H
1
2
3
4
5
6
325
26
84
83
82
81
Junction 29
M4
M4 - MOTORWAY
A48(M)
A48 (M) - MOTORWAY
A48
Reservoir House
Pant-rhiw-gôch
Pant-rhiw-goch Wood
Standing Stone
Pant Farm
Cae Garw
Works
Garden Centre
Nursery
The Cottage
The Old Rectory
Spring Court
Newport N10
Lower House
Walk Farm
Castleton
St.Mary's Hall
Marshfield Prim. Sch.
Gelli-bêr
Heathcliffe House
Sandy Lane
Sandylane Farm
Court Farm
Vicarage
Church Farm
Reservoirs
St.Mellons Country Club
ST. MELLONS GOLF COURSE
St.Mellons Golf Club
Springfield Nurseries
Faendre Hall
Uskley Nurseries
Cricket Ground
Pav.
THE LINKS BUSINESS PARK
ST. MELLONS BUSINESS PARK
Sub.
MARSHFIELD
Blacktown
Recreation Ground
Rhubina Farm
Nursery
Pwllbargod Reen
Wood Ditch Reen
Little Greenlane Reen
Faendre Reen
COAL PIT LANE
ROTYLA ROAD
TYLA LANE
TYLA LA.
NEWPORT ROAD
CHANNEL VIEW
CRAIG YR HAUL DR.
TYNEWYDD DR.
MILL LA.
WENTLOOG RI.
WALK FARM DR.
CASTLETON RI.
MARSHFIELD ROAD
BAKERY LA.
SPRINGFIELDS
VICARAGE CT.
VICARAGE GS.
CHURCH ROAD
CHURCH LANE
CHURCH LA.
BROADWAY
THE MEADOWS
REACH
THE SHIRES
THE MALLARDS
MALLARDS
OAKFIELDS
ST DAVIDS CT.
CAE BRANDI
ORCHARD CL.
WELLFIELD
WELLFIELD CT.
HERBERT CL.
THE HOLLIES
OLD GREEN CT.
CATHERINE DR.
THE GRANGE
ST. MELLONS ROAD
GREEN LANE
VENDRE CLOSE
VAINDRE LA.
VAINDRE CLOSE
CLOS ELPHAN
CLOS MEDWY
FFAGAN
CLOS DOYFAN
CLOS PADRIG
PASCAL CLOSE
FOUNTAIN LA.
FORTRAN ROAD
COBOL ROAD
CASTLETON CT.
WILLOW GRO.
WILLOWDENE
PENNYROYAL CL.
COMFREY CL.
FENNEL CL.
SAFFRON
CHERVIL CL.
OREGANO CL.
CARAWAY
VERBENA CL.
CARADOC
EUGENE CL.
GLENRISE CL.
BRYTHON
SWANAGE
RAGLAN CL.
YSTRAD CL.
BRYNMAWR CL.
BLAENAVON CL.
BASSALEG CL.
CAERLEON CL.
BEDWAS CL.
SALVIA CL.
JASMINE CL.
JONQUIL
ASTER DR.
THRUSH CL.
CLOS TYLA BACH
MAES-Y-CROCHAN
WICKEN CL.
STRATHY RD.
CLEDDAU CL.
SANDBROOK RD.
RUSH CL.
CLOS TRWYN
FIELDFARE DR.

76
52
75
A
B
C
D
1
2
3
4
5
6
26
27
84
83
82
81
A48
The Cottage
Dan-y-graig
The Old Rectory
Nursery
Longhouse
Ty'n-y-brwyn
Works
CHURCH RD.
Nant-y-moor
M4 RELIEF ROAD (Proposed
Club House
The Stud Farm
Maerdy Farm
Cowleaze Reen
Coedkernew
PARC GOLF RANGE
Lower House
Nant y Selsig
Tyn-y-brwyr Reen
Pwllbargod
Reen
Gelli-bêr
PERCOED
LANE
HAWSE LANE
TYMAWR LANE
Drenewydd
Court Farm
CHURCH
Vicarage
Church Farm
CHURCH LANE
CHURCH LA.
MARSHFIELD ROAD
THE SHIRES
OAKFIELDS
ST.DAVIDS CT.
CAMBRIAN DR.
CAMBRIAN WY.
CAMBRIAN GS.
CAMBRIAN CL.
CAMBRIAN GRO.
WOODFIELD CL.
Tymawr Farm
Glandwr Fm.
MARSHFIELD
MARYSFIELD CL.
Nursery
HERBERT CL.
GAE BRANDI
ORCHARD CL.
WELLFIELD CT.
ST. MELLONS
WELLFIELD
Rec. Grd.
THE HOLLIES
PENTWYN TER.
BAKERS CT.
OLD GREEN CT.
CATHERINE DR.
WHITETHORN WY.
THE GRANGE
Blacktown
Cardiff CF3
Penning
Reen
Horsecroft
WENTLOOGE LEVEL
Station Ho.
BROADWAY ROAD
Broadway
Horsecroft
Summerway
Reen
Blackwater
Drains
Greenacre Farm
B4239
Gout Farm
Club Ho.
PETERSTONE GOLF & COUNTRY CLUB
Gout Fawr
PETERSTONE GOLF CL

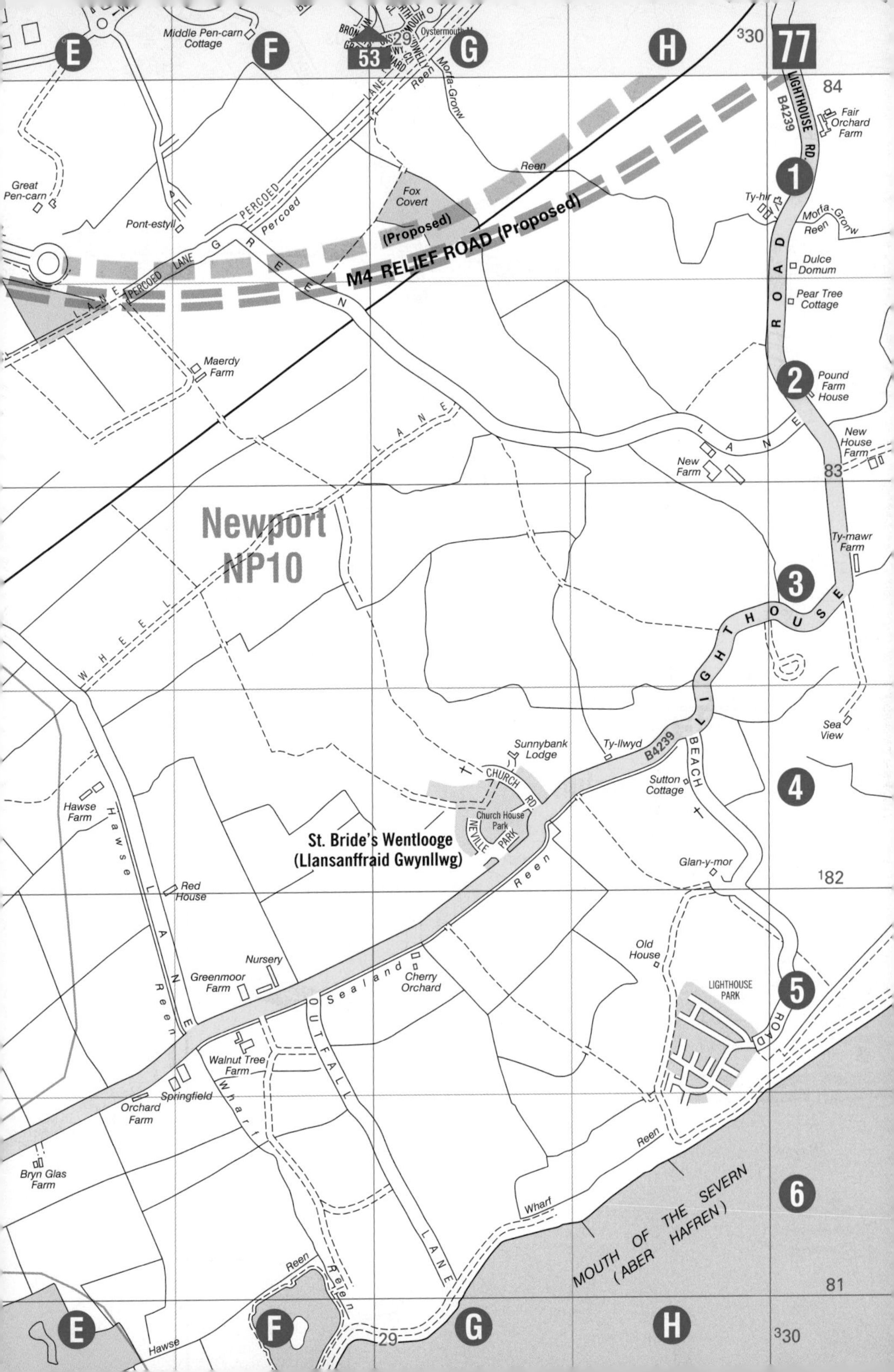

Middle Pen-carn Cottage
Oystermouth M
53
E
F
G
H
330
84
LIGHTHOUSE RD.
B4239
Fair Orchard Farm
Reen
Morfa-Gronw
Great Pen-carn
Pont-estyll
Fox Covert
(Proposed)
M4 RELIEF ROAD (Proposed)
PERCOED LANE
Percoed
GREEN LANE
Ty-hir
Morfa-Gronw
Reen
Dulce Domum
Pear Tree Cottage
ROAD
Maerdy Farm
Pound Farm House
New House Farm
New Farm
83
LANE
Newport NP10
Ty-mawr Farm
WHEEL LANE
LIGHTHOUSE
Sea View
Sunnybank Lodge
Ty-llwyd
B4239
BEACH
CHURCH RD
Sutton Cottage
Hawse Farm
Church House Park
NEVILLE PARK
St. Bride's Wentlooge (Llansanffraid Gwynllwg)
Reen
Glan-y-mor
182
Hawse LANE
Red House
Old House
Nursery
Greenmoor Farm
Sealand
Cherry Orchard
LIGHTHOUSE PARK
ROAD
Reen
OUTFALL LANE
Walnut Tree Farm
Springfield
Orchard Farm
Wharf
Reen
Bryn Glas Farm
Wharf
MOUTH OF THE SEVERN (ABER HAFREN)
Reen
Reen
81
Hawse
29
1
2
3
4
5
6

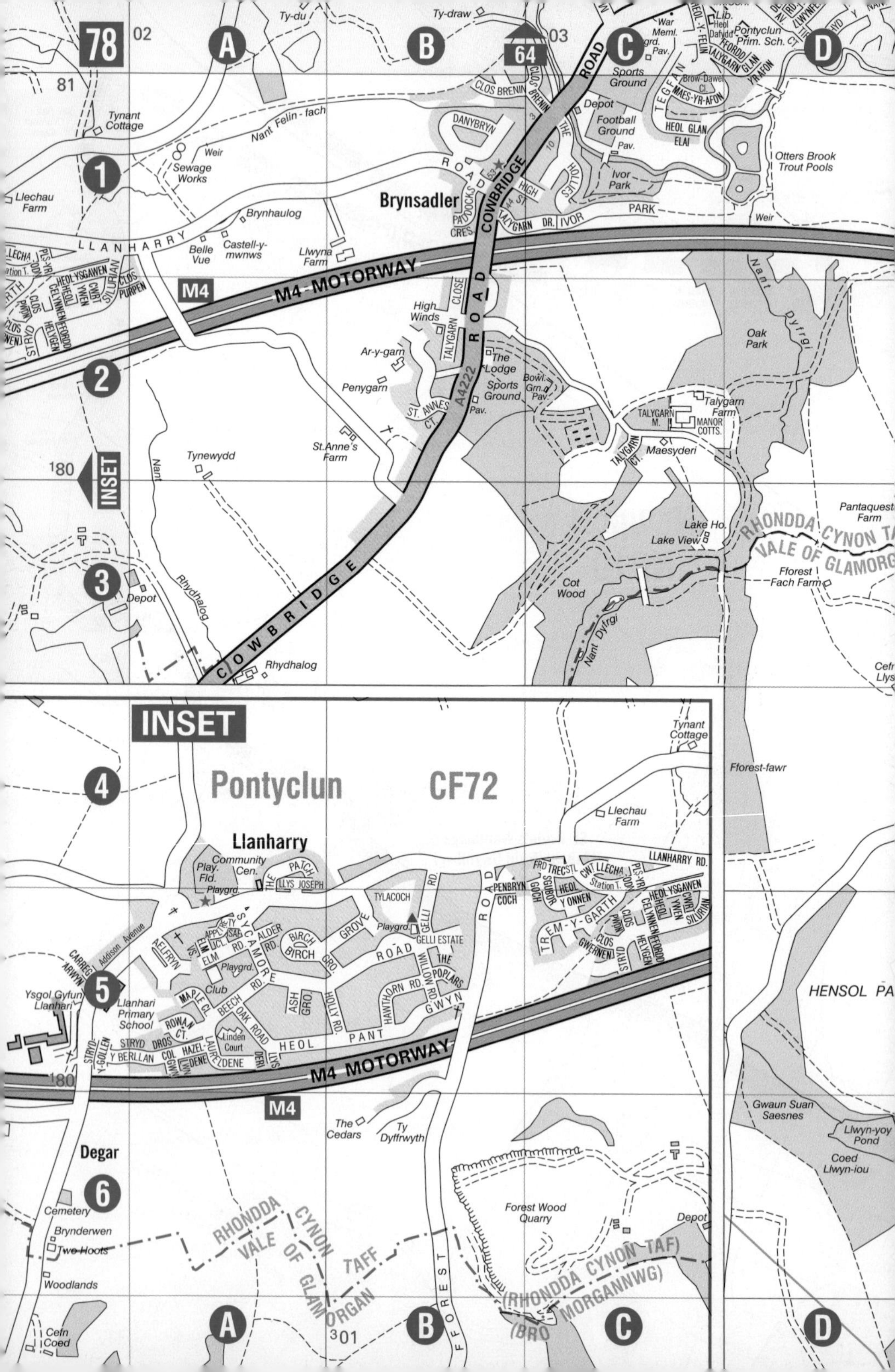
78
02
03
64
A
B
C
D
1
2
3
4
5
6
81
180
301
INSET
Ty-du
Ty-draw
War Meml.
Plgrd.
Pav.
Lib.
Heol Dafydd
Pontyclun Prim. Sch.
HEOL-Y-FELIN
FFORDD TALYGARN
GLAN YRAFON
LLWYNFEN
Sports Ground
Depot
Football Ground
Pav.
Ivor Park
TEGFAN
Brow-Dawel Cl.
MAES-YR-AFON
HEOL GLAN ELAI
Otters Brook Trout Pools
Weir
Tynant Cottage
Nant Felin-fach
Weir
Sewage Works
Llechau Farm
CLOS BRENIN
DANYBRYN
ROAD
COWBRIDGE
HIGH ST.
THE HOLLIES
Brynsadler
PADDOCKS CRES.
TALYGARN DR.
IVOR PARK
Brynhaulog
LLANHARRY
Belle Vue
Castell-y-mwnws
Llwyna Farm
M4 MOTORWAY
M4
CLOSE
High Winds
TALYGARN
Ar-y-garn
Penygarn
A4222
The Lodge
Sports Ground
Bowl. Grn.
Pav.
ST. ANNES CT.
St.Anne's Farm
TALYGARN M.
MANOR COTTS.
Talygarn Farm
TALYGARN CT.
Maesyderi
Oak Park
Nant Dyfrgi
Tynewydd
Nant
Lake Ho.
Lake View
Pantaquest Farm
RHONDDA CYNON TAF
VALE OF GLAMORGAN
Fforest Fach Farm
Depot
Rhydhalog
Cot Wood
Nant Dyfrgi
Rhydhalog
Cefn Llys
INSET
Pontyclun
CF72
Tynant Cottage
Fforest-fawr
Llechau Farm
Llanharry
LLANHARRY RD.
Community Cen.
Play. Fld.
Playgrd.
THE PATCH
LLYS JOSEPH
TYLACOCH
GELLI RD.
PENBRYN COCH
Station T.
HEOL Y ONNEN
TREM-Y-GARTH
HEOL YSGAWEN
CELYNNEN
FFORDD HELYGEN
CLOS GWERNEN
SILURIAN
SYCAMORE
ALDER RD.
BIRCH
GROVE
Playgrd.
GELLI ESTATE
ROAD
THE POPLARS
ELM
AELFRYN
Addison Avenue
CARREG ARWYN
Playgrd.
Club
MAPLE CL.
BEECH RD.
OAK ROAD
ASH GRO.
HOLLY RD.
HAWTHORN RD.
WILLOW RD.
GWYN
PANT
HEOL
Ysgol Gyfun Llanhari
Llanhari Primary School
ROWAN CT.
Linden Court
STRYD DROS
Y BERLLAN
HAZEL DENE
LAUREL DENE
M4 MOTORWAY
HENSOL PA
M4
The Cedars
Ty Dyffrwyth
Degar
Gwaun Suan Saesnes
Llwyn-yoy Pond
Coed Llwyn-iou
Forest Wood Quarry
Depot
Cemetery
Brynderwen
Two Hoots
Woodlands
Cefn Coed
RHONDDA CYNON TAFF
VALE OF GLAMORGAN
FFOREST
(RHONDDA CYNON TAF)
(BRO MORGANNWG)

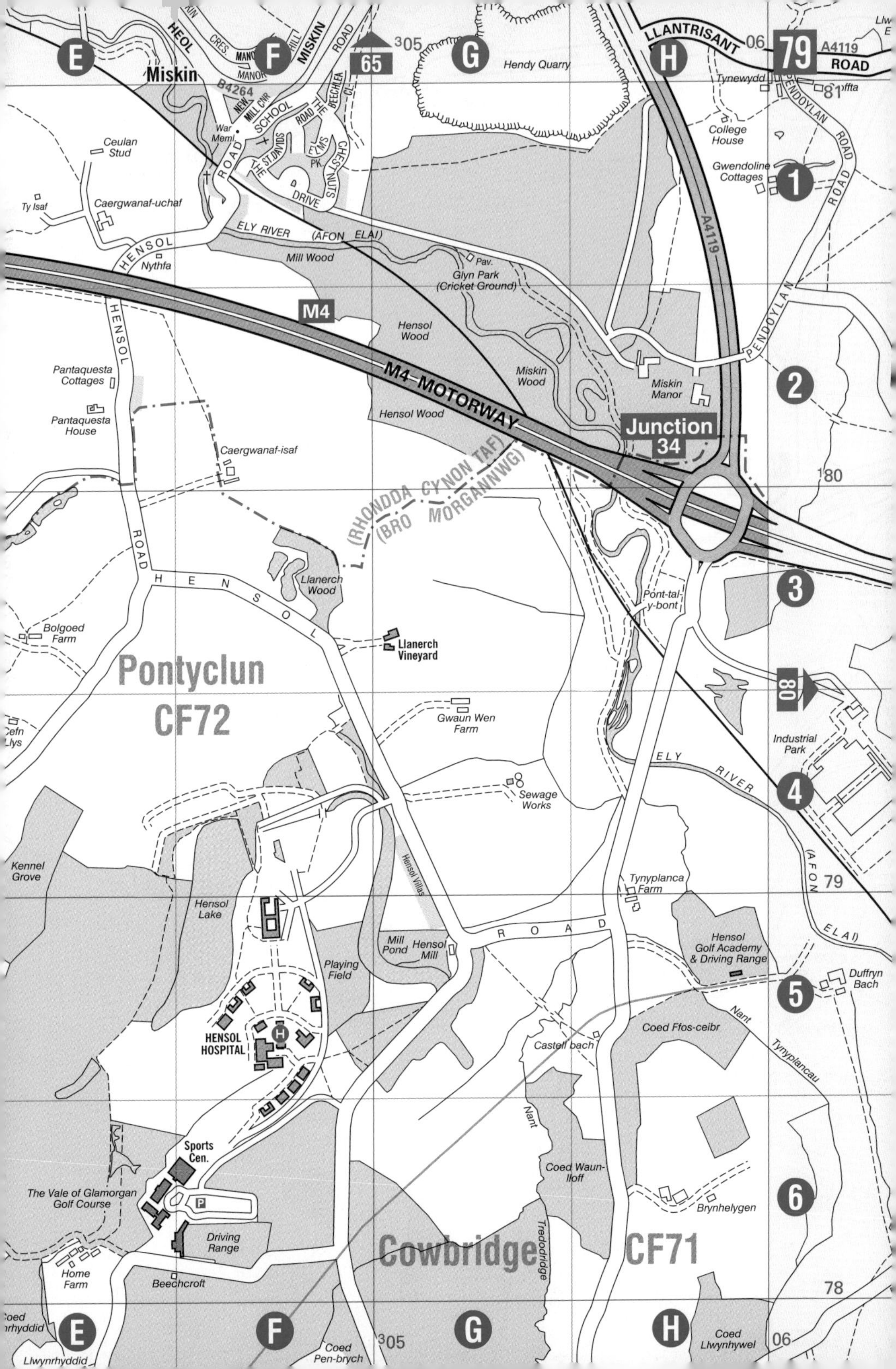
E
F
G
H
65
305
06
79
A4119
ROAD
LLANTRISANT
Hendy Quarry
Miskin
HEOL
MISKIN
ROAD
B4264
NEW
MILL CNR
SCHOOL
ROAD
THE BEECHLEA
CHESTNUTS
DRIVE
War Meml.
Ceulan Stud
Ty Isaf
Caergwanaf-uchaf
HENSOL
Nythfa
ELY RIVER (AFON ELAI)
Mill Wood
Pav.
Glyn Park (Cricket Ground)
Tynewydd
81
PENDOYLAN ROAD
College House
Gwendoline Cottages
1
A4119
M4
M4 MOTORWAY
Hensol Wood
Miskin Wood
Miskin Manor
Pantaquesta Cottages
Pantaquesta House
Hensol Wood
Junction 34
2
80
Caergwanaf-isaf
(RHONDDA CYNON TAF)
(BRO MORGANNWG)
Llanerch Wood
HENSOL
ROAD
3
Pont-tal-y-bont
Bolgoed Farm
Llanerch Vineyard
Pontyclun
CF72
80
Industrial Park
Gwaun Wen Farm
Cefn Llys
ELY RIVER
4
Sewage Works
Kennel Grove
Hensol Villas
Tynyplanca Farm
(AFON ELAI)
79
Hensol Lake
ROAD
Mill Pond
Hensol Mill
Playing Field
Hensol Golf Academy & Driving Range
Duffryn Bach
5
Nant Tynyplancau
HENSOL HOSPITAL
Castell bach
Coed Ffos-ceibr
Nant
Sports Cen.
Coed Waun-lloff
The Vale of Glamorgan Golf Course
P
Brynhelygen
6
Driving Range
Tredodridge
Cowbridge
CF71
Home Farm
Beechcroft
78
Llwynrhyddid
305
Coed Pen-brych
Coed Llwynhywel
06

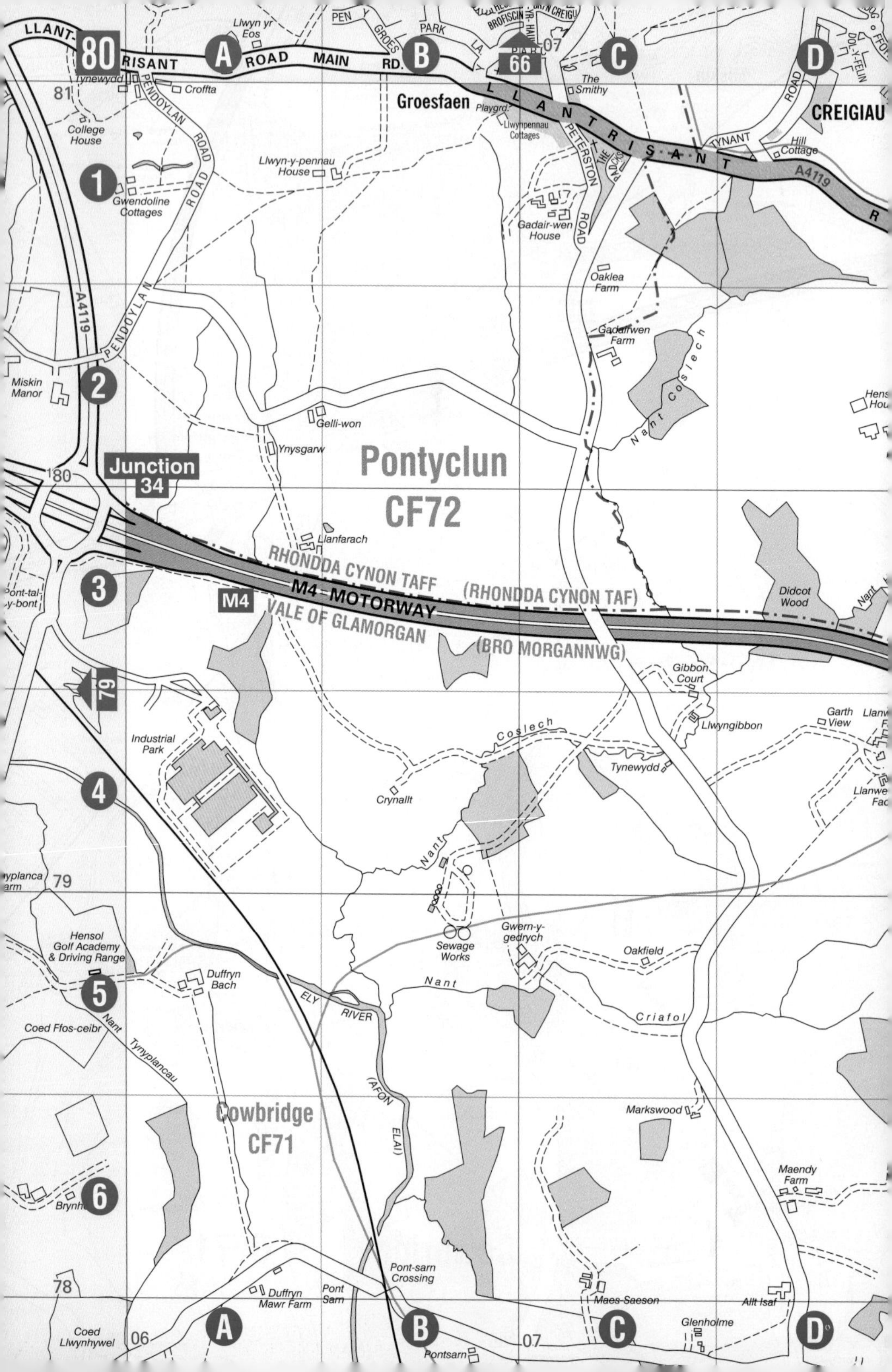

LLANTRISANT ROAD
MAIN RD.
Llwyn yr Eos
PEN Y GROES
PARK LA.
66
The Smithy
Groesfaen
Playgrd.
Llwynpennau Cottages
CREIGIAU
Hill Cottage
TYNANT
A4119
LLANTRISANT R
Tynewydd
Croffta
College House
PENDOYLAN ROAD
Llwyn-y-pennau House
Gwendoline Cottages
PETERSTON ROAD
THE PADDCKS
Gadair-wen House
Oaklea Farm
Gadairwen Farm
Nant Coslech
A4119
PENDOYLAN
Miskin Manor
Gelli-won
Ynysgarw
Pontyclun
CF72
Junction 34
180
Llanfarach
RHONDDA CYNON TAFF
(RHONDDA CYNON TAF)
M4
M4 - MOTORWAY
VALE OF GLAMORGAN
(BRO MORGANNWG)
Didcot Wood
Pont-tal-y-bont
79
Industrial Park
Gibbon Court
Llwyngibbon
Garth View
Coslech
Tynewydd
Crynallt
Nant
79
Sewage Works
Gwern-y-gedrych
Oakfield
Hensol Golf Academy & Driving Range
Duffryn Bach
Nant
Criafol
ELY RIVER
Coed Ffos-ceibr
Nant Tynyplancau
(AFON ELAI)
Cowbridge
CF71
Markswood
Maendy Farm
Pont-sarn Crossing
78
Duffryn Mawr Farm
Pont Sarn
Maes-Saeson
Allt Isaf
Glenholme
Coed Llwynhywel
06
07
Pontsarn
1
2
3
4
5
6
A
B
C
D

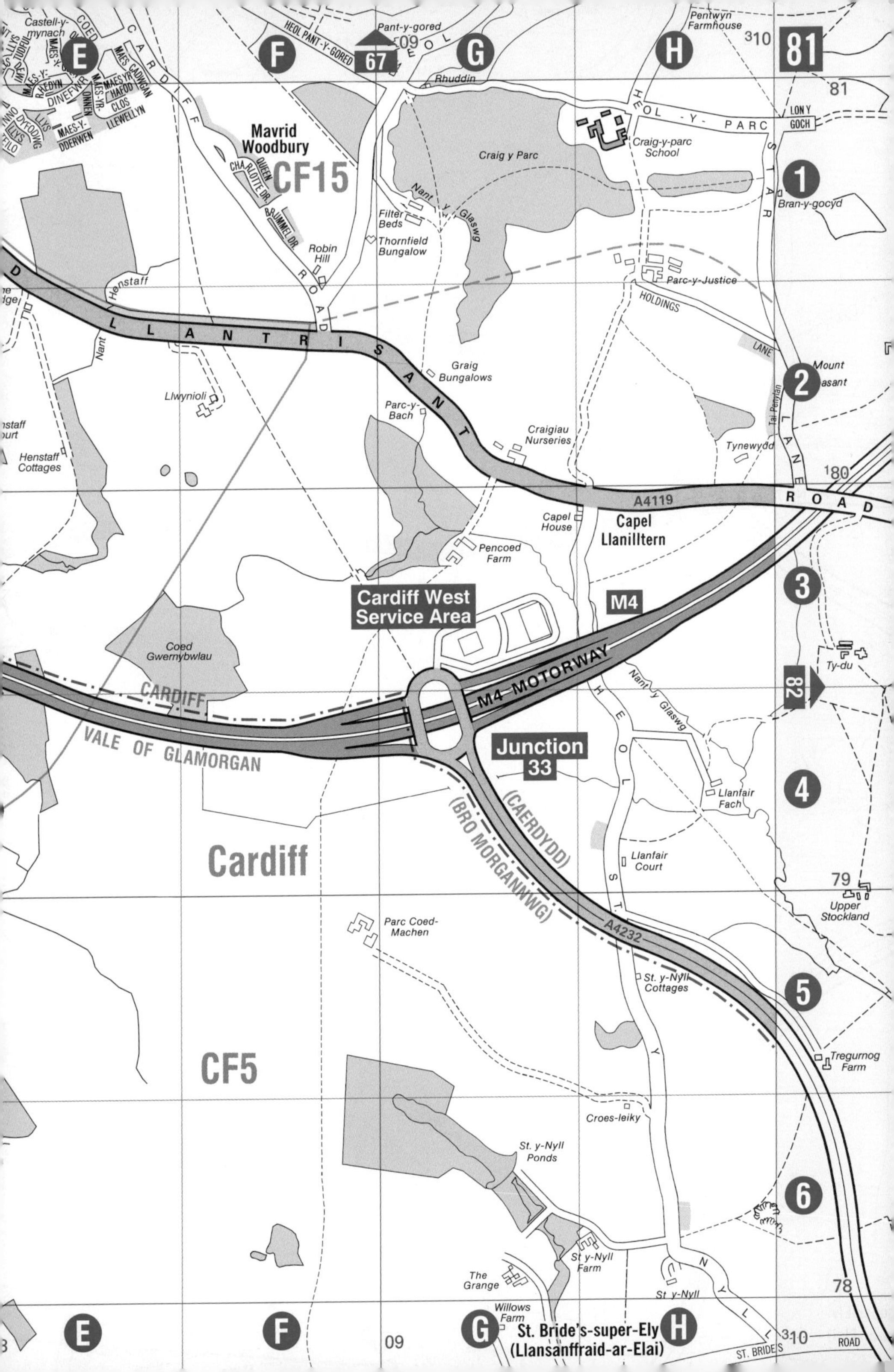
81
67
82
E
F
G
H
1
2
3
4
5
6
Mavrid Woodbury
CF15
Craig y Parc
Craig-y-parc School
Pentwyn Farmhouse
Pant-y-gored
HEOL PANT-Y-GORED
Rhuddin
HEOL-Y-PARC
LON Y GOCH
Bran-y-gocyd
Filter Beds
Thornfield Bungalow
Robin Hill
Parc-y-Justice
HOLDINGS LANE
Henstaff
LLANTRISANT ROAD
Graig Bungalows
Llwynioli
Parc-y-Bach
Craigiau Nurseries
Tynewydd
Henstaff Cottages
A4119
ROAD
Capel House
Capel Llanilltern
Pencoed Farm
Cardiff West Service Area
M4
M4 MOTORWAY
Coed Gwernybwlau
CARDIFF
VALE OF GLAMORGAN
Junction 33
(CAERDYDD)
(BRO MORGANNWG)
Nant y Glaswg
Ty-du
Llanfair Fach
Llanfair Court
Cardiff
Upper Stockland
Parc Coed-Machen
A4232
St. y-Nyll Cottages
CF5
Tregurnog Farm
Croes-leiky
St. y-Nyll Ponds
St y-Nyll Farm
The Grange
St y-Nyll
Willows Farm
St. Bride's-super-Ely (Llansanffraid-ar-Elai)
ST. BRIDE'S ROAD
09
310
180
79
78

Pentwyn Farmhouse
Pant-y-caeau
Llwynda'-ddu
Coedcae Fawr
HEOL - Y - PARC
LON Y GOCH
CHURCH
Bran-y-gocyd
White Lodge
Tylamorris Farm
Coedcae-fach
PANT
Coed Tre Wern
Tylamorris
Goitre fawr
M4 MOTORWAY
M4
HOLDINGS LANE
STAR LANE
Tre-Wern
Mount Pleasant
Tai Penylan
Tynewydd
NANT Y FFYNNON
GARTH RI.
LLEWELYN
GOCH
CAER CEFFYL
ERW HIR
WINDSOR
CLIVE DR.
OLD MILL DR.
WERN MIGNA
NANT Y GWLADYS
PRINCE OF WALES DR.
CAER EFAIL
CAE GARW
BACH
CLOS ST CATWG
FFORDD
GWERN
RHYDLAFAR DR.
ROAD
Gwern-y-cegyrn
LLANTRISANT ROAD
A4119
LLANTRI
Rhydlafr Farm
Goitre-fa
CROFFT-Y-GENAU
Coed-y-trenches
Ty-du
Rhyd-lafar
Nant Dowlais
Crofft-y-genau
Llanfair Fach
CF5
Upper Stockland
Lower Stockland
Nant
Garn
Tregurnog Fm.
Pheasantry
Kennels
Slanney Woods
A4232
ROAD
Mount Pleasant
ST. BRIDES ROAD
PEN
super-Ely
d-ar-Elai)
Tregochas
Sports Ground

68
81
92

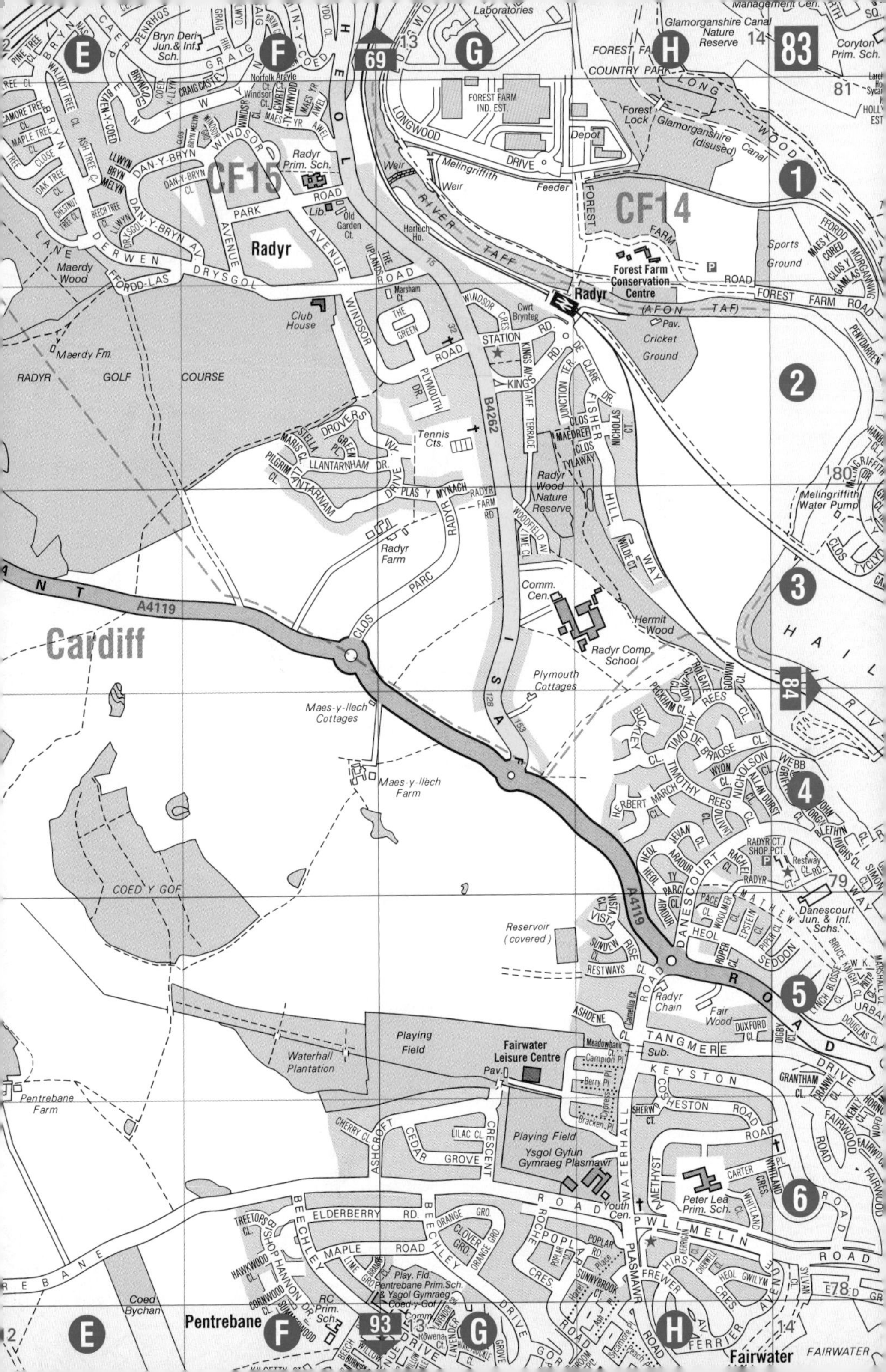
83
69
84
93
E
F
G
H
1
2
3
4
5
6
CF15
CF14
Cardiff
Radyr
Pentrebane
Fairwater
Laboratories
Management Cen.
Glamorganshire Canal Nature Reserve
Coryton Prim. Sch.
FOREST FARM COUNTRY PARK
FOREST FARM IND. EST.
LONGWOOD DRIVE
Forest Lock
Glamorganshire (disused) Canal
Depot
Melingriffith Weir
Feeder
Weir
RIVER TAFF
Forest Farm Conservation Centre
FOREST FARM ROAD
(AFON TAF)
Pav.
Cricket Ground
Sports Ground
Bryn Deri Jun.& Inf. Sch.
Radyr Prim. Sch.
Lib.
Old Garden Ct.
Harlech Ho.
PARK ROAD
AVENUE
DRYSGOL ROAD
DERWEN
FFORDD-LAS
Maerdy Wood
Maerdy Fm.
Club House
RADYR GOLF COURSE
WINDSOR
Marsham Ct.
THE GREEN
PLYMOUTH DR.
STATION RD.
KINGS AV.
KING
Cwrt Brynteg
Tennis Cts.
DROVERS WY.
LLANTARNHAM DR.
PLAS Y MYNACH
RADYR FARM RD
Radyr Farm
CLOS PARC
B4262
A4119
Radyr Wood Nature Reserve
TYLAWAY HILL WAY
Comm. Cen.
Hermit Wood
Radyr Comp. School
Plymouth Cottages
Maes-y-llech Cottages
Maes-y-llech Farm
Melingriffith Water Pump
COED Y GOF
Reservoir (covered)
RESTWAYS CL.
Radyr Chain
Fair Wood
DANESCOURT ROAD
Danescourt Jun. & Inf. Schs.
RADYR CT. SHOP. PCT.
Restway
TANGMERE DRIVE
Playing Field
Fairwater Leisure Centre
Waterhall Plantation
Pentrebane Farm
KEYSTON ROAD
COSHESTON ROAD
WATERHALL
Playing Field
Ysgol Gyfun Gymraeg Plasmawr
Peter Lea Prim. Sch.
Youth Cen.
PWLLMELIN ROAD
ELDERBERRY RD.
MAPLE ROAD
CEDAR GROVE
CRESCENT
ASHCROFT
BEECHLEY DRIVE
Play. Fid.
Pentrebane Prim.Sch. & Ysgol Gymraeg Coed-y-Gof
RC Prim. Sch.
Coed Bychan
PLASMAWR ROAD
FERRIER AV.
FAIRWATER

Glamorganshire Canal Nature Reserve
Coryton
Whitchurch
Rhiwbina
PARC CAEDELYN
WHITCHURCH HOSPITAL (YSBYTY EGLWYS NEWYDD)
VELINDRE HOSPITAL
TEGFAN DAY HOSP.
Velindre Grange
CF15
Radyr Junction
Melingriffith Water Pump
Whitchurch High School (Upper)
Whitchurch High School (Lower)
HAILEY PARK
Llandaff (for Whitchurch)
Llandaff North
Cardiff
Recreation Ground
RADYR COURT
CF5
Radyr Court
Danescourt
Danescourt Jun. & Inf. Schs.
Ysgol Gyfun Gymraeg Glantaf
Youth Centre
Gabalfa Prim. Sch.
Meadowbank School
Rowing Club
Playing Field
BBC Cymru (Wales)
Bishop of Llandaff C in W High Sch.
ROOKWOOD HOSPITAL
Llandaff Cathedral
University of Wales Institute, Cardiff (Llandaff Campus)
Cemetery
Bishops Castle
The Cathedral School
Peter Lea Prim. Sch.
Fairwater
FAIRWATER PARK
Llandaff
Llandaff City Church in Wales Prim. Sch.
A4054
A470
A4119
70
83
94

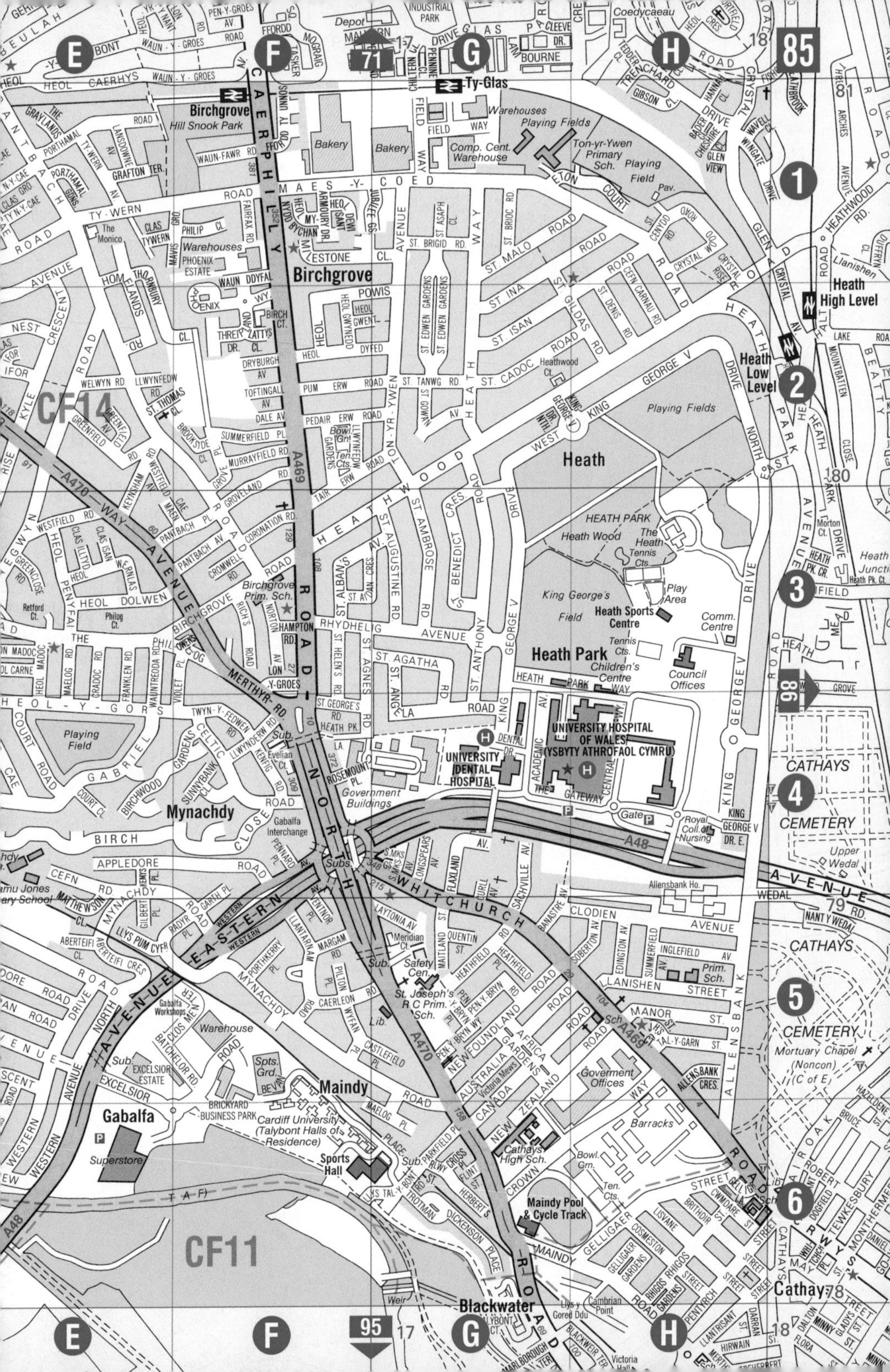

85
E
F
G
H
71
1
2
3
4
5
6
86
95
17
18
Birchgrove
Ty-Glas
Heath High Level
Heath Low Level
CF14
CF11
Birchgrove
Heath
Heath Park
Mynachdy
Gabalfa
Maindy
Blackwater
Cathays
Hill Snook Park
Bakery
Warehouses
Playing Fields
Comp. Cent. Warehouse
Ton-yr-Ywen Primary Sch.
Playing Field
The Monico
Phoenix Estate
HEATH PARK
Heath Wood
The Heath Tennis Cts.
King George's Field
Heath Sports Centre
Play Area
Comm. Centre
Council Offices
Children's Centre
UNIVERSITY HOSPITAL OF WALES (YSBYTY ATHROFAOL CYMRU)
UNIVERSITY DENTAL HOSPITAL
Government Buildings
Gabalfa Interchange
Birchgrove Prim. Sch.
Royal Coll. of Nursing
CATHAYS CEMETERY
Upper Wedal
Allensbank Ho.
Prim. Sch.
Safety Cen.
St. Joseph's R C Prim. Sch.
Gabalfa Workshops
Warehouse
Excelsior Estate
Spts. Grd.
Brickyard Business Park
Cardiff University (Talybont Halls of Residence)
Sports Hall
Superstore
Barracks
Goverment Offices
Cathays High Sch.
Maindy Pool & Cycle Track
Mortuary Chapel (Noncon) (C of E)
Cambrian Point
Llys y Gored Ddu
A469
A470
A48
CAERPHILLY ROAD
NORTH ROAD
WHITCHURCH ROAD
EASTERN AVENUE
WESTERN AVENUE
MERTHYR ROAD
HEATHWOOD ROAD
KING GEORGE V DRIVE
HEATH PARK AVENUE
ALLENSBANK ROAD
MAES-Y-COED ROAD

72
85
96
A
B
C
D
1
2
3
4
5
6
Cyncoed
Cardiff
Pen-y-Lan
Cathays
Roath Park
CF14
CF23
CF24
Heath Low Level
Heath High Level
Playing Field Rhydypenau Primary School
Wood's Covert
Rec. Grd.
Playing Field
Cardiff High School
Llanishen Brook
Roath Park
ROATH PARK LAKE
Landing Stage
Boathouse
Scott Memorial
Lakeside Primary Sch.
Heath Junction
Cemetery
Cathays Cemetery
CATHAYS CEMETERY
Mortuary Chapel (Noncon) (C of E)
Upper Wedal
Comm. Centre
Council Offices
Playing Fields
Play Area
Royal Coll. of Nursing
Prim. Sch.
Springwood Primary School
UWIC Inter Cardiff FC
Athletics Track
Rugby Grd.
Indoor Athletic Stadium
Halls of Residence
University of Wales Institute Cardiff (Cyncoed Campus)
Gymnastic Cen.
Astro Turf
Spts. Cen. for the Disabled
Tennis Cts.
Tennis Centre
Multisports Centre
All Saints C. of W. Prim. Sch.
Ty Wyn Cl. Spec. Sch.
Cardiff Uni. Halls of Residence
Synagogue
Observatory
Playing Field
St. Teilo's C in W High Sch.
St. David's RC Sixth Form Coll.
ROATH PARK Recreation Ground
Roath Brook
Subway
Mosque
WESTERN AVENUE
A48
A469
CELYN AVENUE
LAKE ROAD NORTH
LAKE ROAD WEST
LAKE ROAD EAST
HEATH PARK AVENUE
KING GEORGE V DRIVE
CYNCOED ROAD
CIRCLE WAY
LLANEDEYRN ROAD
WATERLOO ROAD
PEN-Y-LAN ROAD
WHITCHURCH RD.
CRWYS RD.
ALLENSBANK RD.
CEFN-COED ROAD
HIGHFIELD ROAD
WINDERMERE AV.
FAIROAK RD.
WEDAL ROAD
NINIAN ROAD
TY-DRAW RD.
MELROSE AVE.
COLCHESTER AVE.
MARLBOROUGH ROAD
ALBANY ROAD
BLENHEIM ROAD

73
97
88
21
22
78
79
80
81
CF3
Llanrumney
Llanedeyrn
Rumney (Rhymni)
Pentwyn Leisure Centre
Playing Fields
WERN-GOCH PARK
WERN GOCH EAST
Pentwyn Interchange
BRYN CELYN ROAD
HOLLYBUSH ROAD
CYNCOED ROAD
PENTWYN
NORTH CIRCLE
WEST CIRCLE
Lake
Subway
Llanrumney High School
Youth Cen.
Fishpond Wood
COED-Y-GORES
St. Phillip Evans RC Prim. Sch.
Playgrd.
BRYN-Y-NANT
EASTERN AVENUE
ROUND WOOD
Health Cen.
MAELFA Shop. Cen.
Comm. Cen.
Youth Cen.
Llanedeyrn High School
Home for Elderly People
CHAPEL WOOD
Llanedeyrn Primary School
Tennis Courts
University of Wales, Cardiff Playing Fields
Running Track
Rugby Pitch Rumney RUFC (Riverside Park)
Coed-y-Cwar
Rumney Rugby Football Clubhouse
Ysgol Bro Eirwg
Riverside Playing Fields
Lower Gorse
Public Playing Fields
Weir
River Rhymney
Llanedeyrn Interchange
Bryn Hafod Primary Sch.
Eastern Leisure Centre
Playground
Lower Rookery
Rumney Hill Gdns.
Bowl. Grn.
Rumney Jun. & Inf. Schs.
Howardian Nature Reserve
David Lloyd Leisure
SOUTHERN WAY
A48
A4161
A4232
B4487
B4239
NEWPORT ROAD
WENTLOOG ROAD
LLANRUMNEY AVENUE
BALL ROAD
RIDGEWAY
RIDGEWAY ROAD
NEW ROAD
TY-MAWR
CHURCH ROAD
TYR-Y-SARN RD
QUARRY DALE
CAE-GLAS
GLASTONBURY TER.
CHEDDAR CRESCENT
UPHILL ROAD
CLEVEDON ROAD
BRAUNTON CRES.
CROYDE AVENUE
The Howardian Centre
Uni. of Wales Institute, Cardiff (Colchester Av. Campus)
COLCHESTER FACTORY ESTATE
DOMINIONS WAY INDUSTRIAL ESTATE
Megabowl Cardiff
SENLAN INDUSTRIAL ESTATE
Willie Seager Memorial Homes
Superstore
Warehouse
Works
Depot
Factory
Offices
Dairy
TREDELERCH PARK
LAMBY WAY
River Rhymney
Roath Brook
Rumney Bri.
DOWNLANDS WY.
COLCHESTER AVENUE
IPSWICH ROAD
Warehouse Depot

88
22
23
A
B
C
D
1
2
3
4
5
6
74
87
81
80
79
78
Llanrumney
Trowbridge
St. Mellons
Trowbridge Mawr
Rumney (Rhymni)
Wentloog
Newton
Playground
Playing Fields
Playing Field
Depot
Nursery
St. Illtyd's RC High School
Rumney High Sch.
Trowbridge Jun. Sch.
St. John Lloyd R C Primary School
Coleg Glan Hafren (Trowbridge Campus)
Recreation Ground
Pav.
Playgrd.
Club
Greenway Primary School
Comm. Cen.
Rumney Jun. & Inf. Schs.
Oakfield Prim. Sch.
Cath-Cobb Wood
Bowl. Grn.
Comm. Cen.
Lib.
Inf. Sch.
Alexandra Industrial Estate
Spring Meadow Business Park
Capital Business Park
Capital Point
Ringside Bus. Cen.
The Laurels Bus. Park
Mellyn Mair Bus. Cen.
Eastgate Bus. Pk.
Lamby Industrial Park
Wentloog Corp. Industrial Pk.
Warehouse
Longcross Farm
Sea Bank Farm
Maerdy Farm
Ty-to-maen
Newton Willows Farm
Newlands
Pen-pill
Tredelerch Park
Drain
Reen
Rhosog Fach
Pil-du
Pil Melyn
B4487
B4239
Newport Road
Wentloog Road
Wentloog Avenue
Newton Road
Mardy Road
Lamby Way
Parkway
Parkway South
Greenway Road
Trowbridge Road
Hendre Road
Willowbrook Drive
Crickhowell Road
Countisbury Avenue
Ball Road
Burnham Avenue
Ilfracombe Road
Bideford Road
Cardiff Road
Llanstephan Rd.
Harris Av.
Heron Rd.
Abergele Road
Trowbridge Green

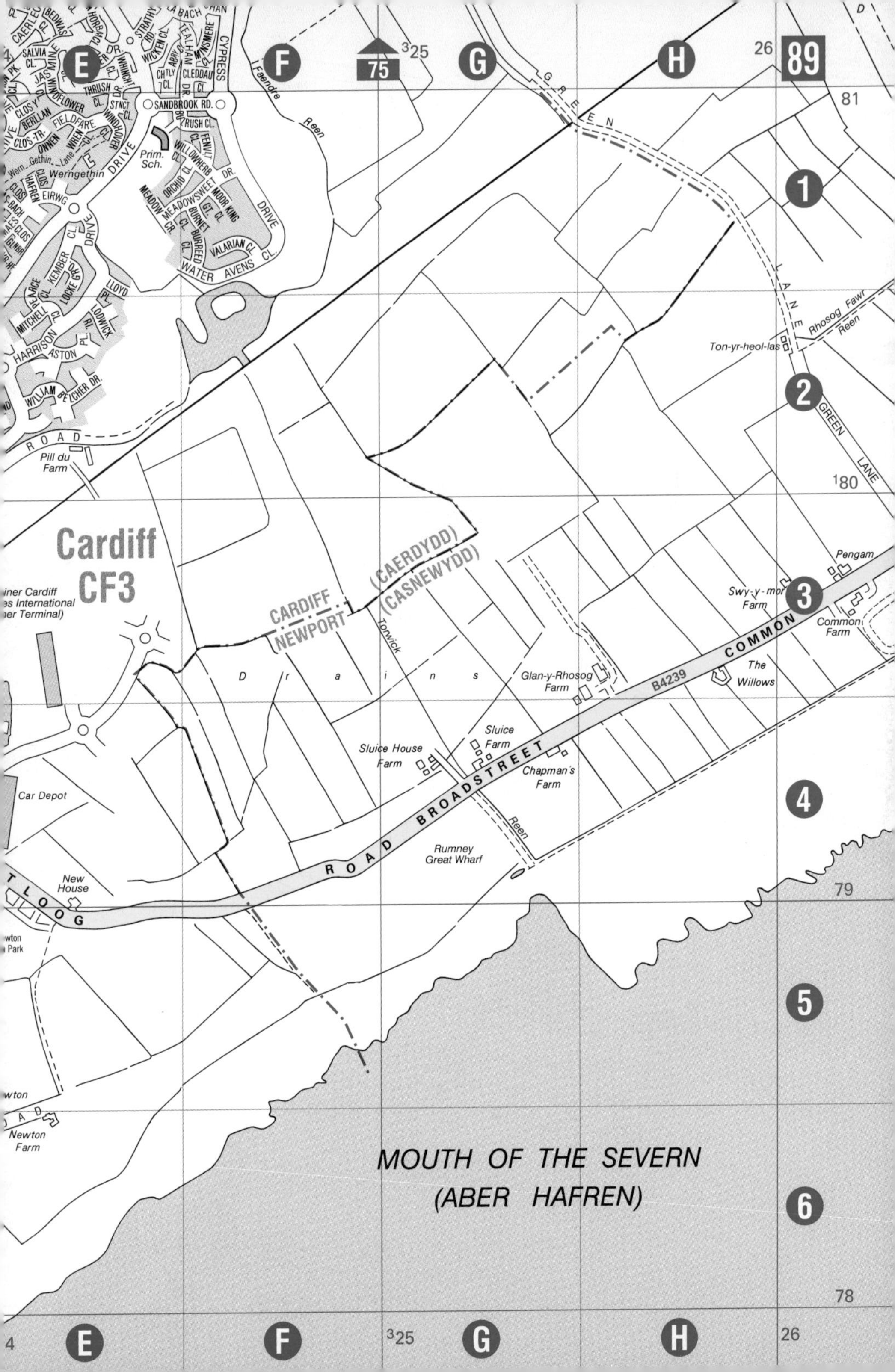
E
F
G
H
75
325
26
81
180
79
78
1
2
3
4
5
6
SANDBROOK RD.
DRIVE
Prim. Sch.
Werngethin
WILLOWHERB
MEADOWSWEET DR.
MOOR KING
WATER AVENS CL.
VALARIAN CL.
KEMBER CL.
LOCKE GR.
MITCHELL CL.
PEARCE
HARRISON
ASTON PL.
LODWICK RL.
LLOYD PL.
WILLIAM BELCHER DR.
ROAD
Pill du Farm
Faendre Reen
GREEN LANE
Rhosog Fawr Reen
Ton-yr-heol-las
Cardiff CF3
CARDIFF (CAERDYDD)
NEWPORT (CASNEWYDD)
Torwick
D r a i n s
Glan-y-Rhosog Farm
Pengam
Swy-y-mor Farm
Common Farm
COMMON
B4239
The Willows
Sluice Farm
Sluice House Farm
Chapman's Farm
ROAD BROADSTREET
Reen
Rumney Great Wharf
Car Depot
New House
TLOOG
Newton Farm
MOUTH OF THE SEVERN
(ABER HAFREN)

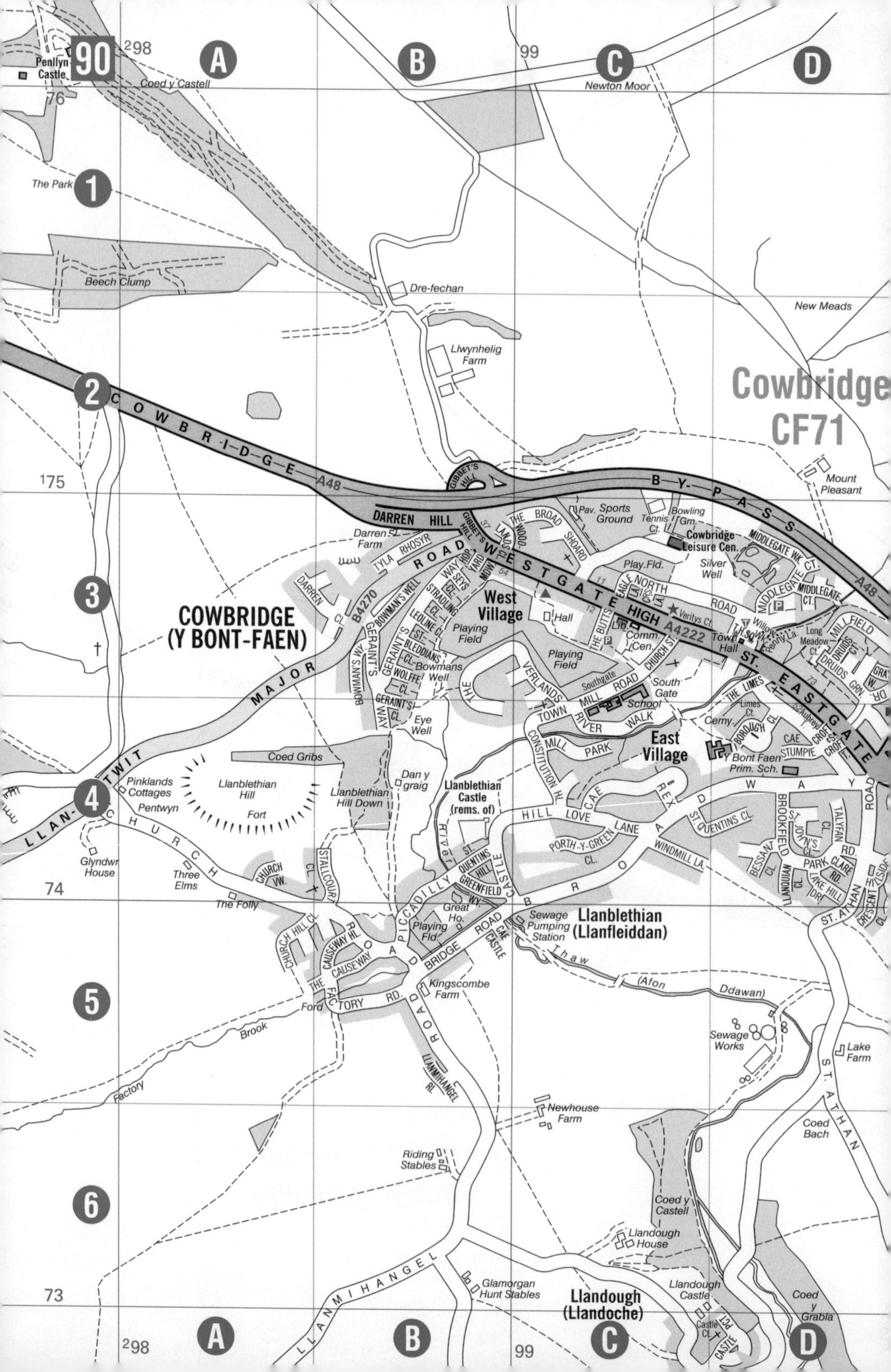

Cowbridge
CF71
COWBRIDGE
(Y BONT-FAEN)
Penllyn Castle
Coed y Castell
Newton Moor
The Park
Beech Clump
Dre-fechan
New Meads
Llwynhelig Farm
COWBRIDGE BY-PASS
A48
Gibbet's Hill
Mount Pleasant
DARREN HILL
Darren Farm
Pav. Sports Ground
Tennis Ct.
Bowling Grn.
Cowbridge Leisure Cen.
Silver Well
Play. Fld.
WESTGATE
HIGH ST.
A4222
EASTGATE
Veritys Ct.
Town Hall
Lib.
Comm. Cen.
Hall
West Village
East Village
Playing Field
Bowmans Well
Eye Well
Southgate
South Gate
School
Cemy.
Y Bont Faen Prim. Sch.
TYLA RHOSYR
DARREN CL.
B4270
MAJOR ROAD
BOWMAN'S WELL
BOWMAN'S WY.
GERAINT'S WAY
GERAINT'S CL.
STRADLING CL.
LEOLINE CL.
ST. BLEDDIANS CL.
WOLFFE CL.
THE BROAD SHOARD
NORTH ROAD
THE BUTTS
CHURCH ST.
THE LIMES
MIDDLEGATE WK.
MIDDLEGATE CT.
MILLFIELD
DRUIDS GRN.
Long Meadow Ct.
Limes Ct.
BOROUGH CL.
CAE STUMPIE
TOWN MILL ROAD
RIVER WALK
MILL PARK
CONSTITUTION HL.
REX
CAE RHYS
LOVE LANE
HILL
PORTH-Y-GREEN CL.
ST QUENTINS CL.
WINDMILL LA.
BROOKFIELD
BESSANT CL.
LLANTWIT MAJOR
COWBRIDGE
LLAN-TWIT
CHURCH
Pinklands Cottages
Pentwyn
Coed Gribs
Llanblethian Hill
Fort
Llanblethian Hill Down
Dan y graig
Llanblethian Castle (rems. of)
Glyndwr House
Three Elms
The Folly
CHURCH VW.
STALLCOURT CL.
CHURCH HILL CL.
CAUSEWAY HL.
THE CAUSEWAY
PICCADILLY
QUENTINS HILL
GREENFIELD WY.
Great Ho.
Playing Fld.
BRIDGE ROAD
CAE CASTLE
CASTLE
Sewage Pumping Station
Llanblethian (Llanfleiddan)
Thaw (Afon Ddawan)
Kingscombe Farm
THE FACTORY RD.
Ford
Factory Brook
LLANMIHANGEL ROAD
LLANMIHANGEL RL.
Sewage Works
Lake Farm
ST. ATHAN ROAD
CRESCENT CL.
Newhouse Farm
Coed Bach
Riding Stables
Coed y Castell
Llandough House
LLANMIHANGEL
Glamorgan Hunt Stables
Llandough (Llandoche)
Llandough Castle
Castle Ct.
Coed y Grabla
298
99
175
74
73
76
A
B
C
D
1
2
3
4
5
6

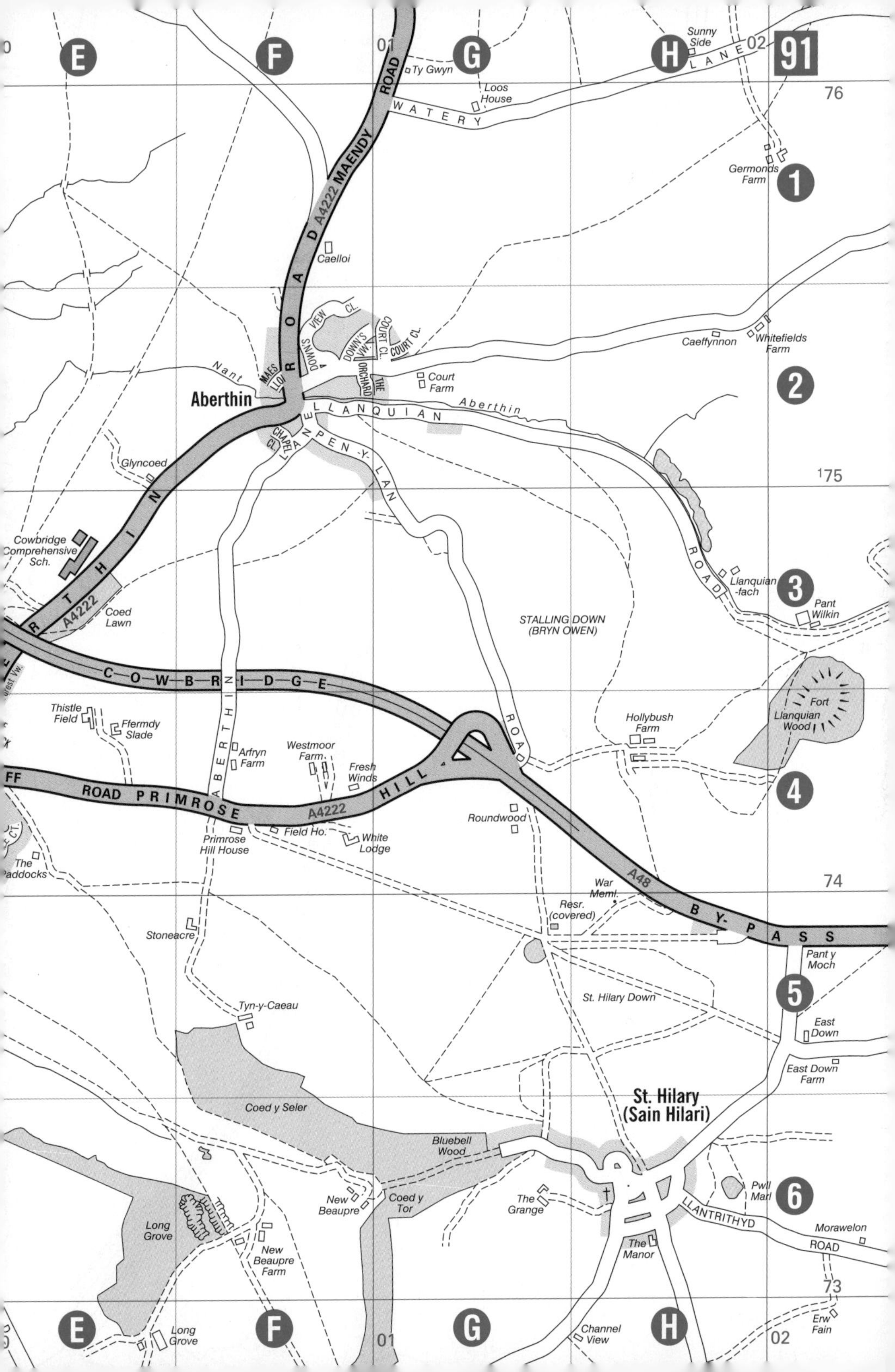

E
F
G
H
01
02
76
75
74
73
1
2
3
4
5
6
Sunny Side
LANE
Ty Gwyn
Loos House
WATERY
MAENDY ROAD
A4222
Germonds Farm
Caelloi
DOWN'S VIEW CL.
COURT CL.
DOWN'S VW.
COURT CL.
MAES LOI
THE ORCHARD
Caeffynnon
Whitefields Farm
Nant
Aberthin
Court Farm
LLANQUIAN
Aberthin
CHAPEL CL.
LLANE PEN-Y-LAN
Glyncoed
ROAD
Llanquian -fach
Pant Wilkin
Cowbridge Comprehensive Sch.
ABERTHIN ROAD
A4222
Coed Lawn
STALLING DOWN (BRYN OWEN)
COWBRIDGE
Thistle Field
Ffermdy Slade
ABERTHIN
Arfryn Farm
Westmoor Farm
Fresh Winds
ROAD
Hollybush Farm
Fort
Llanquian Wood
ROAD PRIMROSE HILL
A4222
Roundwood
Primrose Hill House
Field Ho.
White Lodge
The Paddocks
A48
BY-PASS
War Meml.
Resr. (covered)
Stoneacre
Pant y Moch
St. Hilary Down
Tyn-y-Caeau
East Down
East Down Farm
Coed y Seler
St. Hilary (Sain Hilari)
Bluebell Wood
New Beaupre
Coed y Tor
The Grange
Pwll Marl
LLANTRITHYD
ROAD
Morawelon
Long Grove
New Beaupre Farm
The Manor
Long Grove
Channel View
Erw Fain

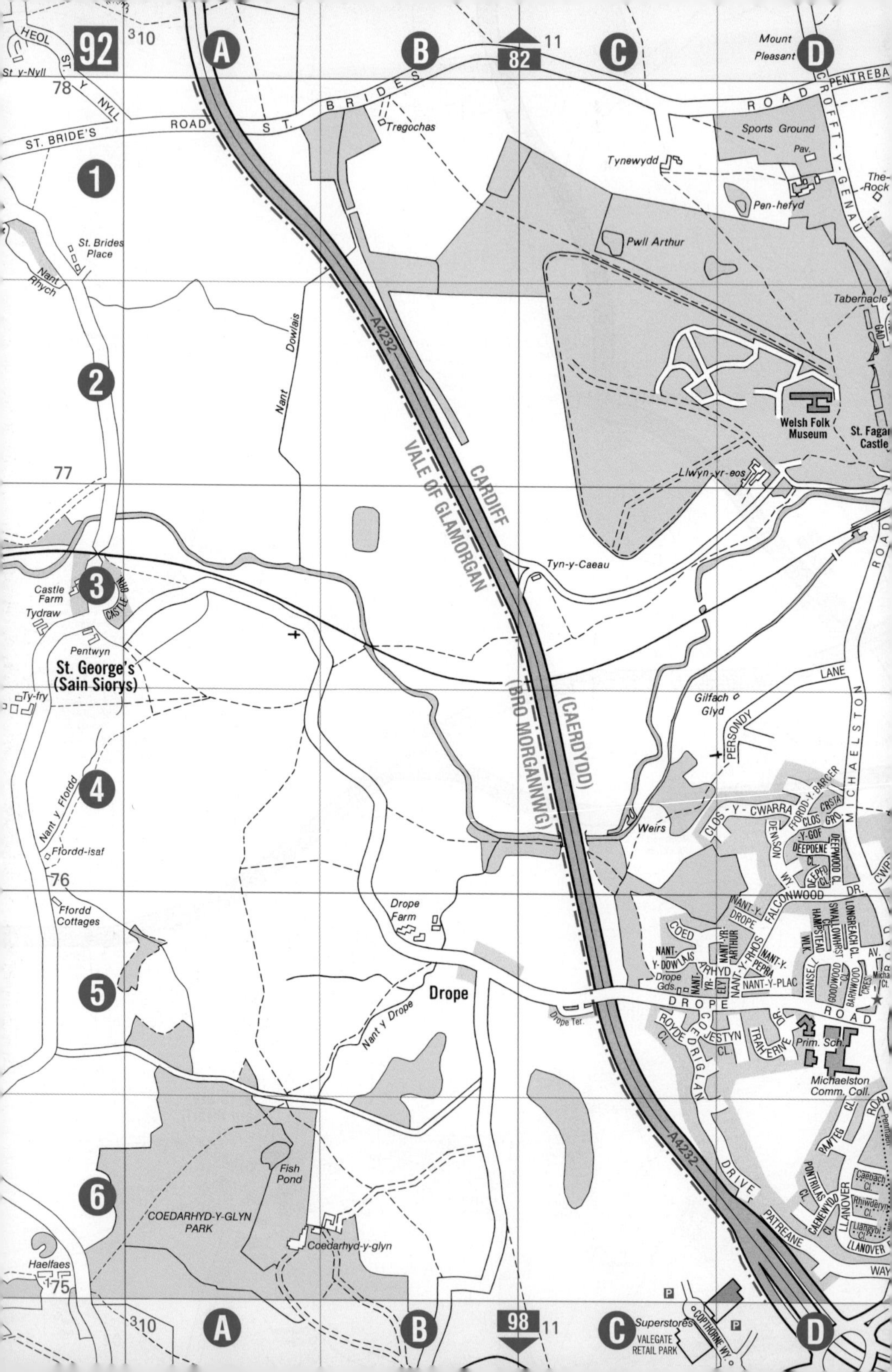
HEOL ST. Y NYLL
St y-Nyll
ST. BRIDE'S ROAD
ST. BRIDES ROAD
Tregochas
Mount Pleasant
CROFFT-Y-GENAU
PENTREBANE
Sports Ground
Pav.
Tynewydd
Pen-hefyd
The-Rock
Castle
Pwll Arthur
St. Brides Place
Nant Rhych
Nant Dowlais
Tabernacle
A4232
Welsh Folk Museum
St. Fagans Castle
VALE OF GLAMORGAN
CARDIFF
Llwyn-yr-eos
Tyn-y-Caeau
Castle Farm
CASTLE GRN
Tydraw
Pentwyn
St. George's (Sain Siorys)
Ty-fry
(BRO MORGANNWG)
(CAERDYDD)
LANE
Gilfach Glyd
PERSONDY
MICHAELSTON
ROAD
Nant y Ffordd
Ffordd-isaf
Weirs
CLOS-Y-CWARRA
FFORDD-Y-BARCER
CLOS CRSTAL
GRO
Y-GOF
DENISON WY.
DEEPDENE CL.
DEEPWOOD CL.
DEEPFD CL.
Ffordd Cottages
Drope Farm
FALCONWOOD DR.
NANT-Y-DROPE
COED
NANT-YR-ARTHUR
NANT-Y-RHOS
NANT-Y-PEPRA
HAMPSTEAD WLK.
SWALLOWHRST CL.
LONGREACH CL.
AV.
NANT-Y-DOWLAIS
ARHYD
NANT-YR-ELY
Drope Gds.
NANT-Y-PLAC
MANSEL
GOODWOOD
BARNWOOD
CRES.
Drope
DROPE ROAD
Drope Ter.
Nant y Drope
ROYDE CL.
COEDRIGLAN
JESTYN CL.
TRAHERNE DR.
Prim. Sch.
Michaelston Comm. Coll.
DRIVE
PANTEG CL.
Caebach Cl.
Rhiwderyn Cl.
Llangybi Cl.
PONTRILAS CL.
CAENEWYDD CL.
LLANOVER
LLANOVER
PATREANE
WAY
Fish Pond
COEDARHYD-Y-GLYN PARK
Coedarhyd-y-glyn
Haelfaes
Superstores
VALEGATE RETAIL PARK
COPTHORNE WY.
A B C D
1 2 3 4 5 6
310 11
78 77 76 175
82
98

93
83
94
99
E
F
G
H
1
2
3
4
5
6
12
13
14
78
77
76
75
Cardiff
CF5
Fairwater
FAIRWATER PARK
Cardiff Ski Centre
Pentrebane
St. Fagans
Michaelston-super-Ely
Ely
Caerau
Play. Fld.
School
Comm. Cen.
RC Prim. Sch.
Sports Ground
Rec. Grd.
Health Cen.
Lib.
Fairwater Primary School
Community Centre
Curling Pond
Resr.
Llanmaes House
Llanmaes Farm
PLYMOUTH GREAT WOOD
Rec. Grd.
Community Hall
Recreation Ground
Herbert Thompson Jun. & Infs. Schs.
Ten. Cts.
Bowl. Grn.
Pav.
Recreation Ground
Windsor Clive Jun. & Inf. Schs.
St. Francis RC Inf. & Jun. Schs.
Comm. Cen.
Vachell Nursery Sch.
Western Leisure Centre
Superstore
Hywel Dda Jun. & Infs. Schs.
Cwrt-yr-Ala Jun. Sch.
Caerau Inf. Sch.
Caerau Nursy. Sch.
Caerau Wood
Castle Ring
St. Mary's Church
Caerau Fort
Warehouse
Western Cemetery
Recreation Ground
ELY DISTRIBUTION
ELY RIVER
(AFON ELAI)
CARDIFF ROAD
ST. FAGANS ROAD
BWLCH ROAD
COWBRIDGE ROAD WEST
A48
A4232
GRAND AVENUE
ARCHER ROAD
PLYMOUTH WOOD ROAD
FRANK ROAD
MILL ROAD
HEOL TRELAI
CARNAU ROAD
BISHOPSTON ROAD
CHURCH ROAD
CWRT-YR-ALA ROAD
HEOL-Y-CASTELL
SNOWDEN ROAD
WILSON ROAD
HIGHMEAD ROAD
VACHELL ROAD
CROSSWAYS ROAD
TY-COCH RD.
RED HOUSE ROAD
LLEWELLYN AVENUE
PETHYBRIDGE ROAD
ILLTYD RD.
STANWAY ROAD
HOWELL ROAD
DEERE ROAD
PARKER ROAD
MACDONALD RD
GREEN FARM ROAD
FARM ROAD
CAERAU LANE
PYLE RD
TIDENHAM ROAD
PANTYDERI CL.
LLANDOW RD.
CAMROSE RD
HAVERFORD WAY
NARBERTH ROAD
AMROTH ROAD
TRESEDER WAY
WAUN-GRON ROAD
PLASMAWR ROAD
POPLAR ROAD
GORSE DRIVE
BEECHLEY DRIVE
MAPLE ROAD
FIRS AVENUE
HEOL ELFED
HEOL GWILYM
DOYLE AVENUE
WELLWRIGHT ROAD
EVERSWELL ROAD
CARTWRIGHT LA.
COED-BYCHAN
GREENWOOD LANE
HOLLY RD.
FERN PLACE
FAIRWAYS CRES.
GLAN ELY CLOSE
CHORLEY CL.
TATEM DR.
OAKWAY
LANDWADE CL.

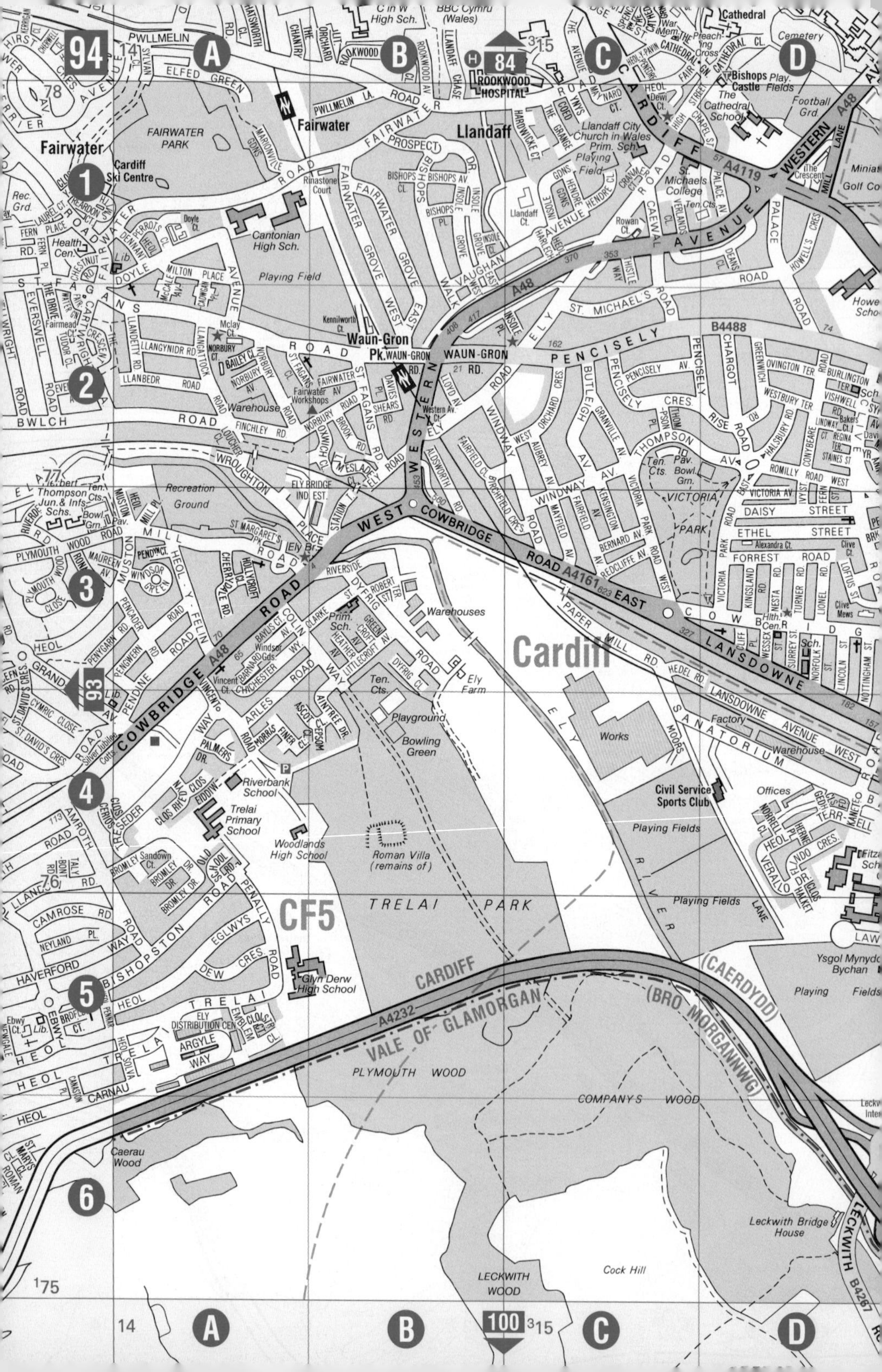

94
A
B
C
D
1
2
3
4
5
6
84
100
93
14
315
175
Fairwater
Llandaff
Cardiff
CF5
Fairwater Park
Cardiff Ski Centre
Cantonian High Sch.
Playing Field
Rookwood Hospital
Cathedral
Cemetery
Bishops Castle
The Cathedral School
Football Grd.
Llandaff City Church in Wales Prim. Sch.
St. Michaels College
Waun-Gron Pk.
Fairwater Workshops
Warehouse
Recreation Ground
Ely Bridge Ind. Est.
Ely Br.
Robert Thompson Jun. & Inf. Schs.
Victoria Park
Warehouses
Ely Farm
Works
Civil Service Sports Club
Playing Fields
Riverbank School
Trelai Primary School
Woodlands High School
Roman Villa (remains of)
Trelai Park
Glyn Derw High School
Ely Distribution Cen.
Plymouth Wood
Company's Wood
Caerau Wood
Leckwith Wood
Cock Hill
Leckwith Bridge House
Ysgol Mynydd Bychan
Cardiff (Caerdydd)
Vale of Glamorgan (Bro Morgannwg)
River Ely
Western Avenue
Cowbridge Road West
Cowbridge Road East
Lansdowne Road
Lansdowne Avenue West
Sanatorium Road
Paper Mill Rd.
Pencisely Road
St. Fagans Road
Waun-Gron Rd.
Fairwater Road
Bwlch Road
Wroughton Pl.
Mill Road
Heol-y-Felin
Bishopston Road
Heol Trelai
Heol Carnau
Leckwith Road
A48
A4161
A4119
A4232
B4488
B4267

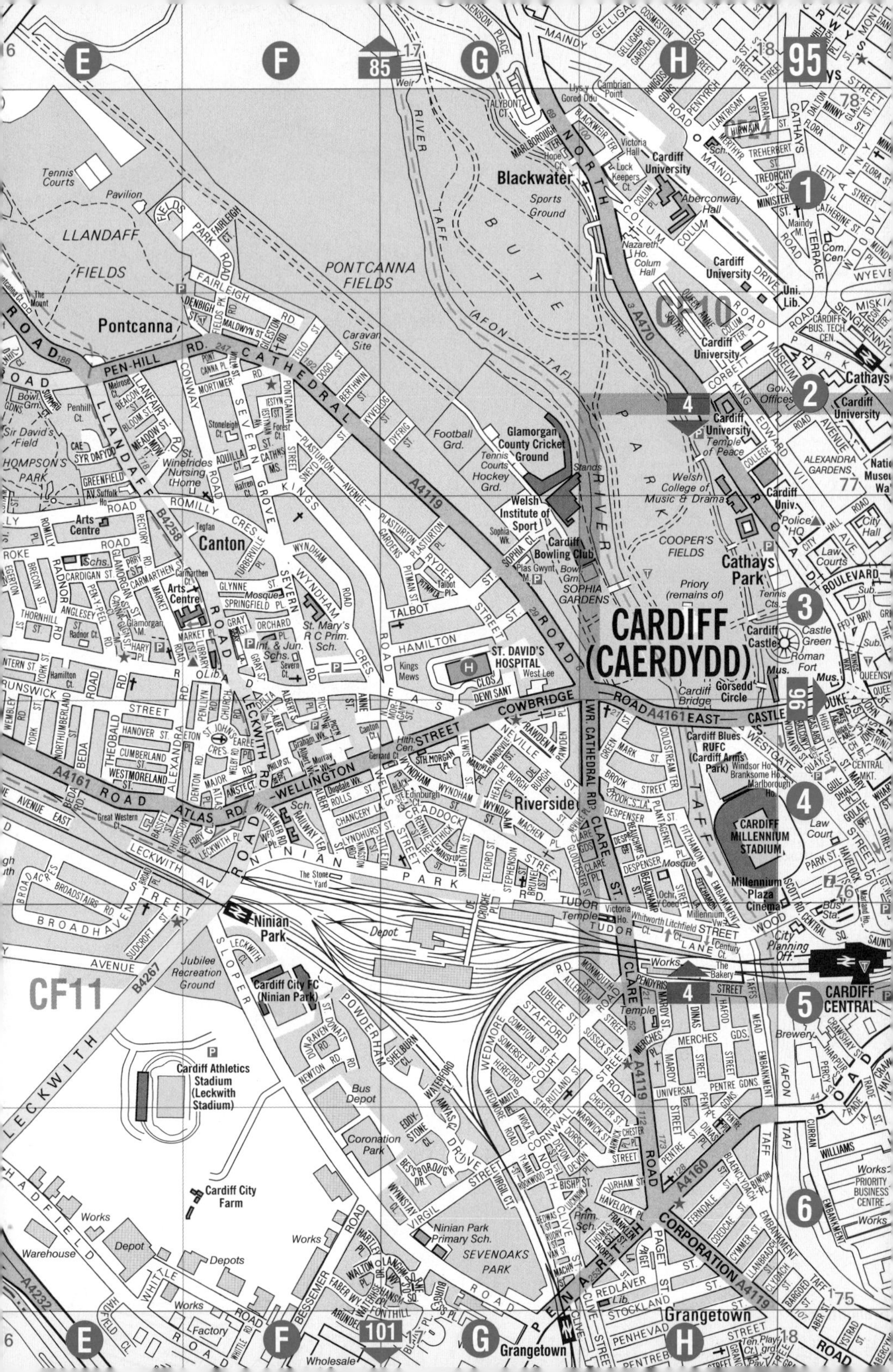

95
E
F
G
H
85
17
18
101
1
2
3
4
5
6
75
76
77
78
CF10
CF11
CARDIFF
(CAERDYDD)
Blackwater
Sports Ground
Pontcanna
PONTCANNA FIELDS
LLANDAFF FIELDS
Tennis Courts
Pavilion
The Mount
Caravan Site
Canton
Riverside
Grangetown
Cathays
Cathays Park
BUTE PARK
RIVER TAFF
(AFON TAF)
Weir
Cardiff University
Aberconway Hall
Nazareth Ho.
Colum Hall
Uni. Lib.
Victoria Hall
Lock Keepers Ct.
Hope Ct.
Llys y Gored Ddu
Cambrian Point
Talybont Ct.
Cardiff Bus. Tech. Cen.
Gov. Offices
Temple of Peace
Welsh College of Music & Drama
COOPER'S FIELDS
Priory (remains of)
Cardiff Castle
Castle Green
Roman Fort
Gorsedd Circle
Cardiff Bridge
Alexandra Gardens
National Museum Wales
City Hall
Law Courts
Police HQ
Cardiff Univ.
Glamorgan County Cricket Ground
Stands
Football Grd.
Tennis Courts
Hockey Grd.
Welsh Institute of Sport
Cardiff Bowling Club
Sophia Gardens
Plas Gwynt
St. David's Hospital
Kings Mews
West Lee
St. Mary's R C Prim. Sch.
Inf. & Jun. Schs.
St. Winefrides Nursing Home
Arts Centre
Tegfan
Mosque
Lib.
Hlth. Cen.
Cardiff Blues RUFC (Cardiff Arms Park)
Windsor Ho.
Branksome Ho.
Marlborough Ho.
CARDIFF MILLENNIUM STADIUM
Millennium Plaza Cinema
Law Court
Bus Sta.
City Planning Off.
CARDIFF CENTRAL
Brewery
Priority Business Centre
Works
Mus.
The Stone Yard
Depot
Temple
The Bakery
Ninian Park
Jubilee Recreation Ground
Cardiff City FC (Ninian Park)
Cardiff Athletics Stadium (Leckwith Stadium)
Cardiff City Farm
Bus Depot
Coronation Park
Ninian Park Primary Sch.
SEVENOAKS PARK
Prim. Sch.
Warehouse
Depots
Factory
Wholesale
A470
A4119
A4161
A4160
B4258
B4267
A4232
CATHEDRAL ROAD
COWBRIDGE ROAD EAST
CASTLE ST.
WESTGATE ST.
NORTH ROAD
KING EDWARD VII AVENUE
CITY HALL ROAD
BOULEVARD DE NANTES
DUKE ST.
WOOD ST.
CENTRAL SQ.
PARK ST.
HAVELOCK ST.
TUDOR ST.
TUDOR LANE
PENARTH ROAD
CORPORATION ROAD
CLARE ROAD
CLARE ST.
LWR. CATHEDRAL RD.
WELLINGTON STREET
LECKWITH ROAD
LECKWITH AV.
SLOPER ROAD
NINIAN PARK ROAD
WYNDHAM CRES.
PLASTURTON AVENUE
KINGS ROAD
SEVERN GROVE
SEVERN ROAD
CONWAY ROAD
PONTCANNA ST.
PEN-HILL RD.
LLANDAFF ROAD
ROMILLY ROAD
ROMILLY CRES.
MARKET RD.
ATLAS RD.
CRADDOCK ST.
NEVILLE ST.
FITZHAMON EMBANKMENT
PENDYRIS ST.
MERCHES GDS.
MARDY ST.
DINAS ST.
CORNWALL ST.
STAFFORD RD.
COURT RD.
WEDMORE RD.
VIRGIL ST.
AMYAS DRIVE
BESSEMER ROAD
HADFIELD ROAD
WHITTLE ROAD
LECKWITH ROAD
BROADHAVEN
BROADSTAIRS RD.
CLIVE ST.
PAGET ST.
STOCKLAND ST.
REDLAVER ST.
PENHEVAD ST.
EMBANKMENT
MUSEUM AVENUE
PARK PLACE
COLUM ROAD
CATHAYS TERRACE
MAINDY ROAD
WOODVILLE ROAD
SENGHENNYDD RD.
FAIRLEIGH RD.
DOGO ST.
BERTHWIN ST.
TEILO ST.

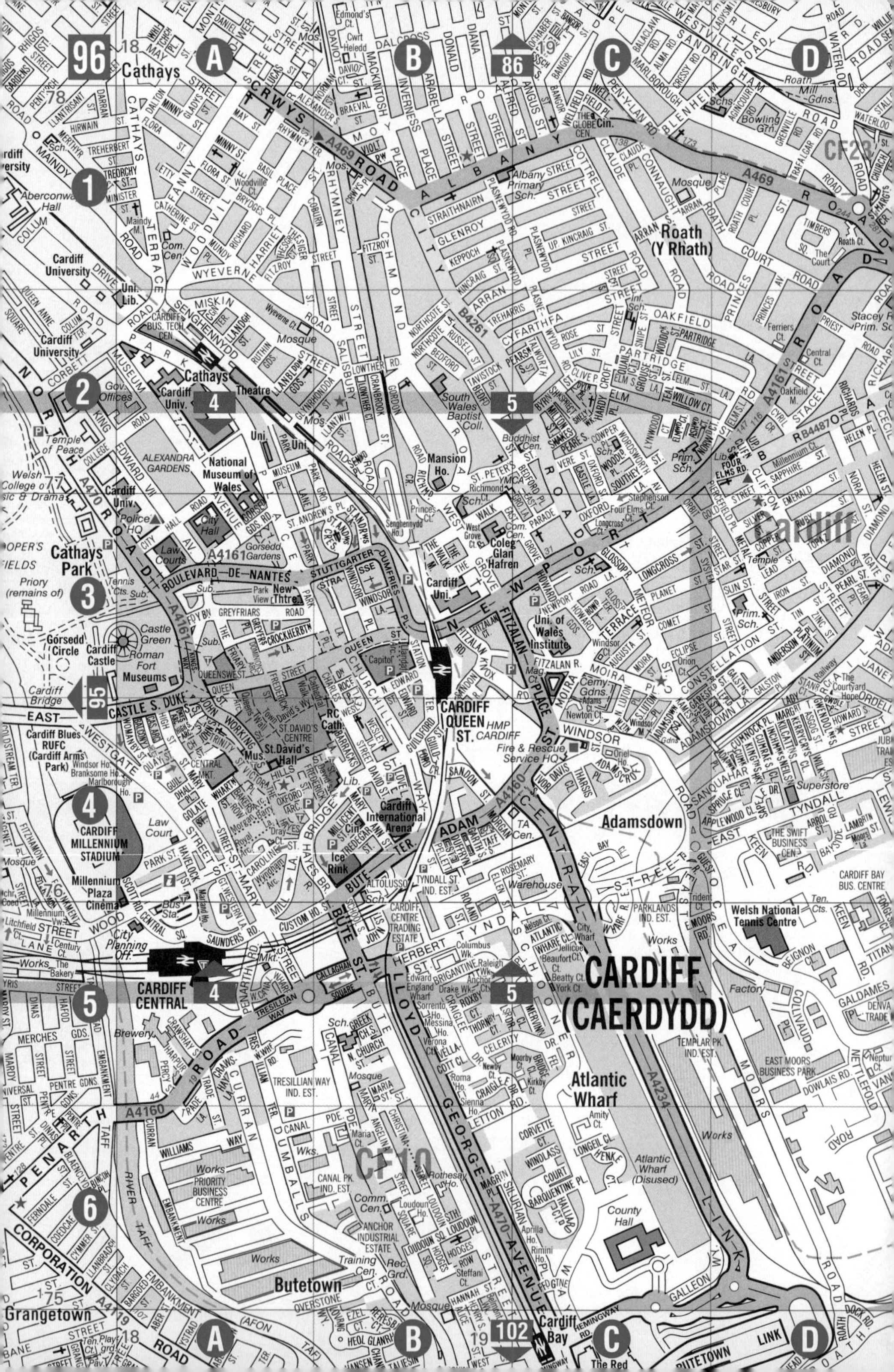
A
B
C
D
86
Cathays
Roath
(Y Rhath)
CF23
CF10
Cathays Park
Cardiff University
Aberconway Hall
Uni. Lib.
Gov. Offices
Temple of Peace
Welsh College of Music & Drama
Alexandra Gardens
National Museum of Wales
City Hall
Law Courts
Gorsedd Gardens
Boulevard-de-Nantes
Priory (remains of)
Gorsedd Circle
Cardiff Castle
Castle Green
Roman Fort
Museums
Cardiff Bridge
95
Cardiff Blues RUFC (Cardiff Arms Park)
Cardiff Millennium Stadium
Millennium Plaza Cinema
St. David's Centre
St. David's Hall
Central Mkt.
RC Cath.
Capitol
Cardiff Queen St.
HMP Cardiff
Fire & Rescue Service HQ
Cardiff International Arena
Ice Rink
Mansion Ho.
South Wales Baptist Coll.
Coleg Glan Hafren
Uni. of Wales Institute
Cemy. Gdns.
Adamsdown
Cardiff Central
4
5
Brewery
City Planning Off.
Cardiff Centre Trading Estate
Tyndall St. Ind. Est.
Parklands Ind. Est.
Cardiff (Caerdydd)
Welsh National Tennis Centre
Cardiff Bay Bus. Centre
The Swift Business Cen.
Superstore
Templar Pk. Ind. Est.
East Moors Business Park
Atlantic Wharf
Atlantic Wharf (Disused)
County Hall
Tresillian Way Ind. Est.
Priority Business Centre
Canal Pk. Ind. Est.
Anchor Industrial Estate
Butetown
Grangetown
Cardiff Bay
102
River Taff
Crwys Road
Albany Road
City Road
Newport Road
Richmond Road
Cathays Terrace
North Road
Penarth Road
Tresillian Way
Bute St.
Lloyd George Avenue
Central Link
Corporation Road
Ocean Way
Moorland
Adamsdown La.
Constellation St.
Tyndall St.
East Moors Rd.
Dumballs Road
Butetown Link
Newport Road
A469
A4161
A470
A4160
A4234
A4119
B4261
B4487
1
2
3
4
5
6
18
19

87
103
CF3
CF24
Pengam
Tremorfa
Splott
PENGAM GREEN
TREMORFA PARK
Little Wharf Saltings
RHYMNEY RIVER (AFON RHYMNI)
Rhymney River Sailing & Angling Club
MOUTH OF THE SEVERN (ABER HAFREN)
Tremorfa Foreshore
Welsh Water Treatment Works
Waste Water Treatment Works
Welsh Water Pumping Station
Caravan Site
Cardiff Heliport
South Point
NEWPORT ROAD A4161
ROVER WAY
A4232
LAMBY WAY
FFORDD PENGAM
EAST BAY LINK ROAD
(Proposed)
SEAWALL ROAD
WILLOWS AVENUE
TWEEDSMUIR ROAD
CLYDESMUIR ROAD
MUIRTON ROAD
MOORLAND ROAD
OCEAN WAY
GLASS AV
ROATH DOCK ROAD
CLIPPER ROAD
FORESHORE RD
TIDE FIELDS ROAD
PORTMANMOOR ROAD
PACIFIC ROAD
TIDAL SIDINGS
Tidal Sidings
Mineral Railway
COLCHESTER FACTORY ESTATE
DOMINIONS WAY INDUSTRIAL ESTATE
ROVER WAY INDUSTRIAL ESTATE
TAYMUIR GREEN IND. EST.
CLYDESMUIR INDUSTRIAL ESTATE
GUARDIAN INDUSTRIAL ESTATE
SEAWALL ROAD INDUSTRIAL ESTATE
PENGAM INDUSTRIAL ESTATE
PORTMANMOOR ROAD INDUSTRIAL ESTATE
PACIFIC BUSINESS PARK
TREMORFA INDUSTRIAL ESTATE
SEAVIEW INDUSTRIAL ESTATE
Pengam Junction
Willows High School
Splott Swim. Pool
Splott Park
Moorland Park
Recreation Ground
Tremorfa Nursery Sch.
St. Alban's RC Prim. Sch.
Baden Powell Prim. Sch.
Superstore
Works
Depot
ROATH DOCK
CARDIFF DOCKS
E
F
G
H
1
2
3
4
5
6
20
21
22
75
76
77
78

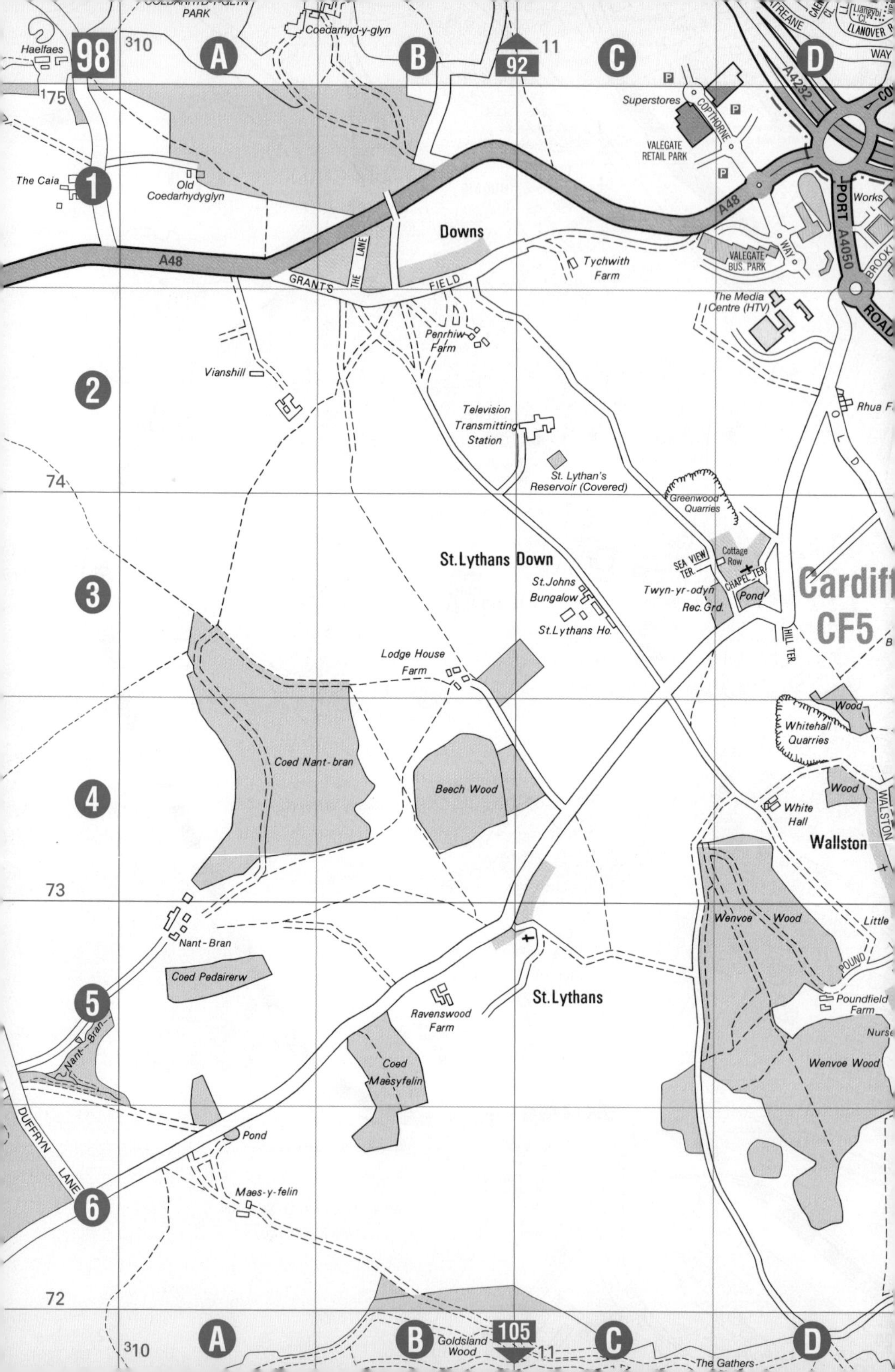

Coedarhyd-y-glyn
PARK
Haelfaes
310
A
B
92
11
C
D
175
Superstores
COPTHORNE
VALEGATE RETAIL PARK
A4232
LLANOVER
WAY
The Caia
1
Old Coedarhydyglyn
A48
Downs
THE LANE
GRANTS FIELD
Tychwith Farm
VALEGATE BUS. PARK
PORT A4050 ROAD
Works
The Media Centre (HTV)
Penrhiw Farm
Vianshill
2
Rhua F
Television Transmitting Station
St. Lythan's Reservoir (Covered)
OLD
74
Greenwood Quarries
3
St.Lythans Down
SEA VIEW TER.
Cottage Row
CHAPEL TER.
St.Johns Bungalow
Twyn-yr-odyn
Rec.Grd.
Pond
Cardiff CF5
St.Lythans Ho.
HILL TER.
Lodge House Farm
Wood
Whitehall Quarries
Coed Nant-bran
4
Beech Wood
Wood
White Hall
WALSTON
Wallston
73
Wenvoe Wood
Little
Nant-Bran
Coed Pedairerw
POUND
5
St.Lythans
Poundfield Farm
Ravenswood Farm
Nant-Bran
Coed Maesyfelin
Wenvoe Wood
DUFFRYN LANE
Pond
6
Maes-y-felin
72
A
B
105
C
D
310
Goldsland Wood
11
The Gathers

99
E
F
G
H
93
106
100
1
2
3
4
5
6
13
14
175
74
73
72
CARDIFF
(CAERDYDD)
VALE OF GLAMORGAN
(BRO MORGANNWG)
A4232
A4050
A48
Culverhouse Cross
Wenvoe
Caerau Wood
Castle Ring
St. Mary's Church
Caerau Fort
CHURCH ROAD
HERITAGE DR.
LAURISTON PK.
LAURISTON CL.
ST. MARYS CT.
CWRT-YR-ALA
HEOL YR ODYN
WOODLANDS PK. DR.
LON-YR-EFAIL
LANE CAERAU
Playing Fields
Mary Immaculate R.C. High School
Spts. Grd.
Pav.
Ten. Cts.
Lawnview
Pen-y-lan Farm
Balas Farm
Balas Farmhouse
Coed y Ffynnon
Tank
Bullcroft
Alps Bungalow
Alps Quarry
Coed y Cymdda
The Lawns
ALPS QUARRY ROAD
Council Offices
Depot
Alps Court
Alps Farm
Wenvoe Quarries
Twyn Bwmbegan
Coed y Cymdda
Cwm-slade
Coed Cwm-slade
Limekiln Wood
Brook
Greave
PORT ROAD
CAERAU
NANT ISAF
Enclosure
EAST
STATION ROAD
The Old Station
Ty Pica Farm
Football Ground
Sewage Works
Pav
Playing Field
Weir
Salmon Leaps
Coed Penllwynog
Penllwynog
Park W
Wrinstone
Wrinstone Farm
MORFA LANE
Beauville Wood
BEAUVILLE LANE
Beauville Farm
Vishwell Farm
ST. ANDREW'S ROAD
VISHWELL RD.
Nursery
Ysguborddegwm
Ysguborgoch Farm
CF64
The Lodge
West Lodge
Culverhouse Cross
Lib.
Play Fld.
Gwenfo C in W Prim. Sch.
WENVOE CL.
SPRINGFIELD CL.
OLD MARKET
VENWOOD CL.
LLANFAIR ROAD
RECTORY CL.
GRANGE CL.
TY-PICA DR.
GWENFO DR.
STATION RD. WEST

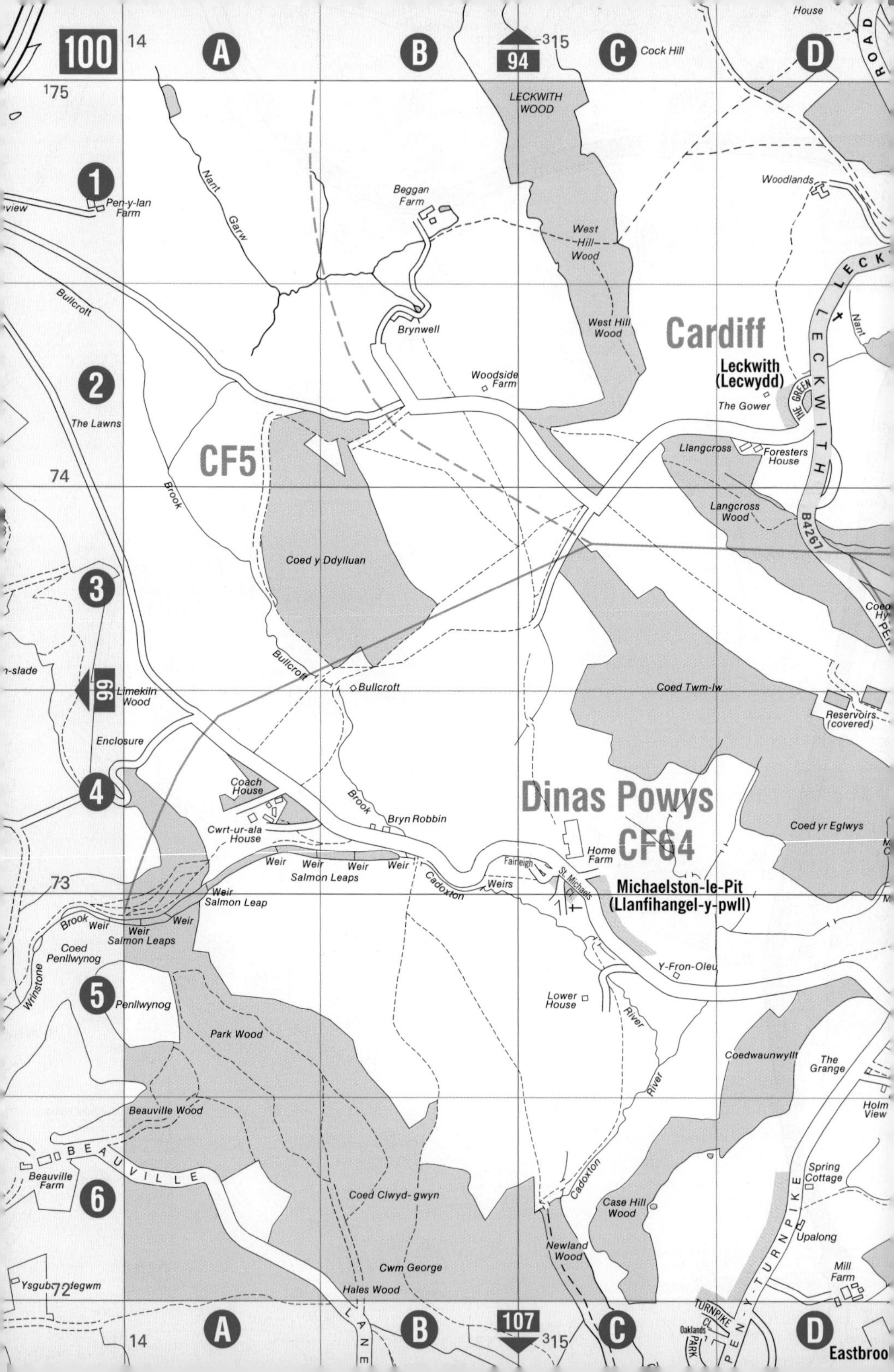

14
A
B
94
315
C
Cock Hill
D
House
ROAD
175
LECKWITH WOOD
1
Pen-y-lan Farm
Nant Garw
Beggan Farm
West Hill Wood
West Hill Wood
Woodlands
Bullcroft
Brynwell
Cardiff
Leckwith (Lecwydd)
LECKWITH
Nant
2
The Lawns
Woodside Farm
THE GREEN
The Gower
CF5
Llangcross
Foresters House
74
Brook
Langcross Wood
B4267
Coed y Ddylluan
3
n-slade
99
Limekiln Wood
Bullcroft
Bullcroft
Coed Twm-Iw
Reservoirs (covered)
Enclosure
4
Coach House
Brook
Bryn Robbin
Dinas Powys
CF64
Cwrt-ur-ala House
Home Farm
Coed yr Eglwys
Weir
Weir
Weir
Weir
Salmon Leaps
Cadoxton
Weirs
Faireigh
St Michaels Cl.
Michaelston-le-Pit (Llanfihangel-y-pwll)
73
Weir
Salmon Leap
Brook
Weir
Weir
Weir
Salmon Leaps
Coed Penllwynog
Wrinstone
Y-Fron-Oleu
5
Penllwynog
Lower House
River
Park Wood
Coedwaunwyllt
The Grange
River
Beauville Wood
Holm View
BEAUVILLE
Beauville Farm
6
Coed Clwyd-gwyn
Cadoxton
Spring Cottage
Case Hill Wood
PEN-Y-TURNPIKE
Upalong
Newland Wood
Cwm George
Mill Farm
Ysgubo 72 degwm
Hales Wood
TURNPIKE CL.
Oaklands PARK
LANE
14
A
B
107
315
C
D
Eastbroo

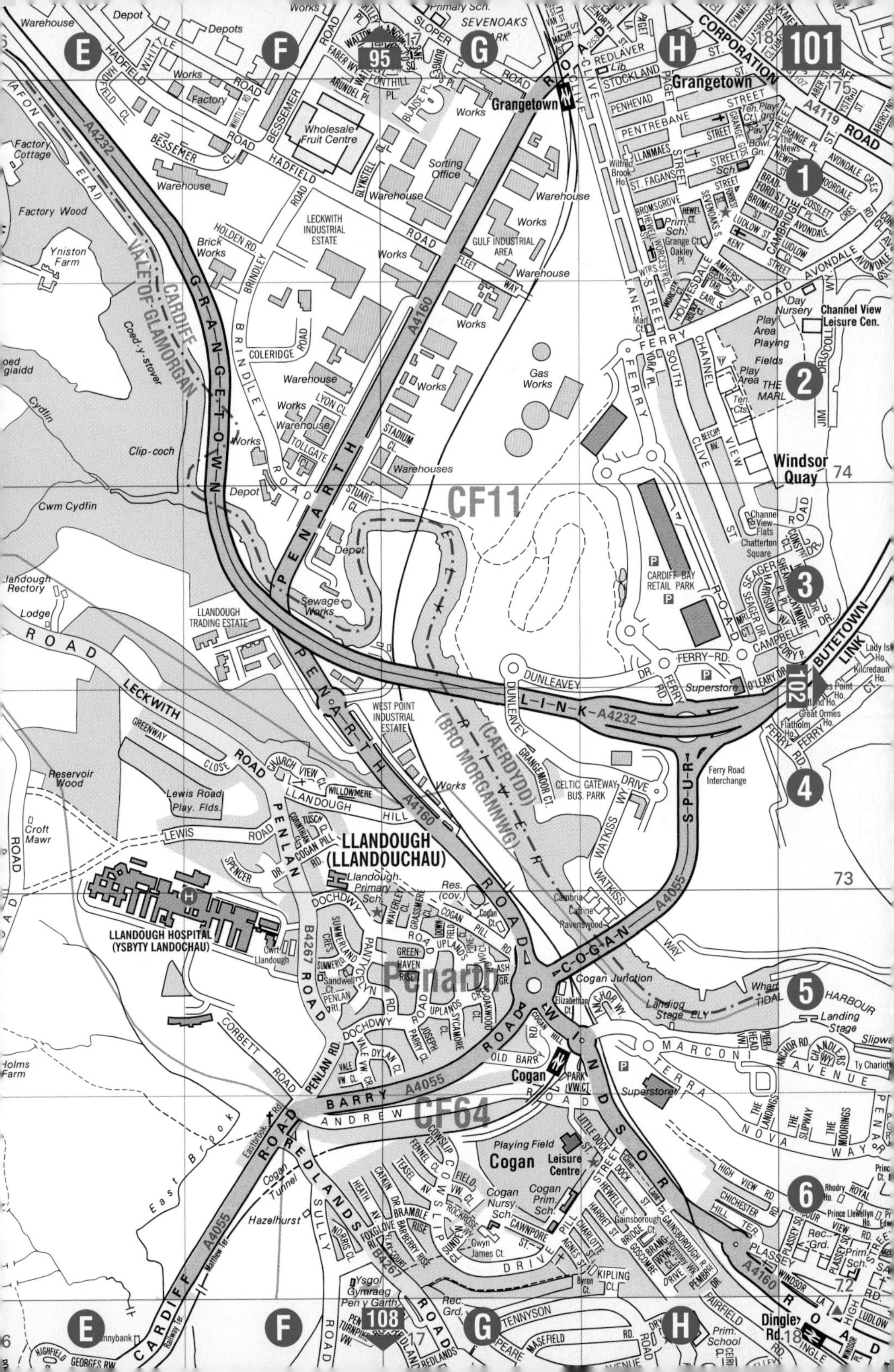

101
95
102
108
E
F
G
H
1
2
3
4
5
6
CF11
CF64
Grangetown
Penarth
LLANDOUGH
(LLANDOUCHAU)
LLANDOUGH HOSPITAL
(YSBYTY LANDOCHAU)
Cogan
Windsor
Quay
Dingle Rd.
CARDIFF BAY
RETAIL PARK
LECKWITH
INDUSTRIAL
ESTATE
GULF INDUSTRIAL
AREA
LLANDOUGH
TRADING ESTATE
WEST POINT
INDUSTRIAL
ESTATE
CELTIC GATEWAY
BUS. PARK
Wholesale
Fruit Centre
Sorting
Office
Gas
Works
Sewage
Works
Channel View
Leisure Cen.
Ferry Road
Interchange
Cogan Junction
Factory Wood
Yniston
Farm
Factory
Cottage
Coed-y-stover
Cydfin
Clip-coch
Cwm Cydfin
Llandough
Rectory
Reservoir
Wood
Lewis Road
Play. Flds.
Croft
Mawr
Holms
Farm
Hazelhurst
Cogan
Tunnel
East Brook
Playing Field
Leisure
Centre
Superstore
Landing
Stage
TIDAL HARBOUR
CARDIFF
VALE OF GLAMORGAN
GRANGETOWN
LINK A4232
PENARTH ROAD
A4160
A4055
A4119
A4267
B4267
RIVER ELY
(CAERDYDD)
(BRO MORGANNWG)
CORPORATION ROAD
LECKWITH ROAD
HADFIELD ROAD
BESSEMER ROAD
FERRY ROAD
CLIVE STREET
DUNLEAVEY DR.
SPUR
COGAN
BARRY ROAD
ANDREW ROAD
CARDIFF ROAD
REDLANDS ROAD
SULLY ROAD
WINDSOR ROAD
MARCONI AVENUE
PENARTH ROAD
NOVA WAY
BUTETOWN LINK

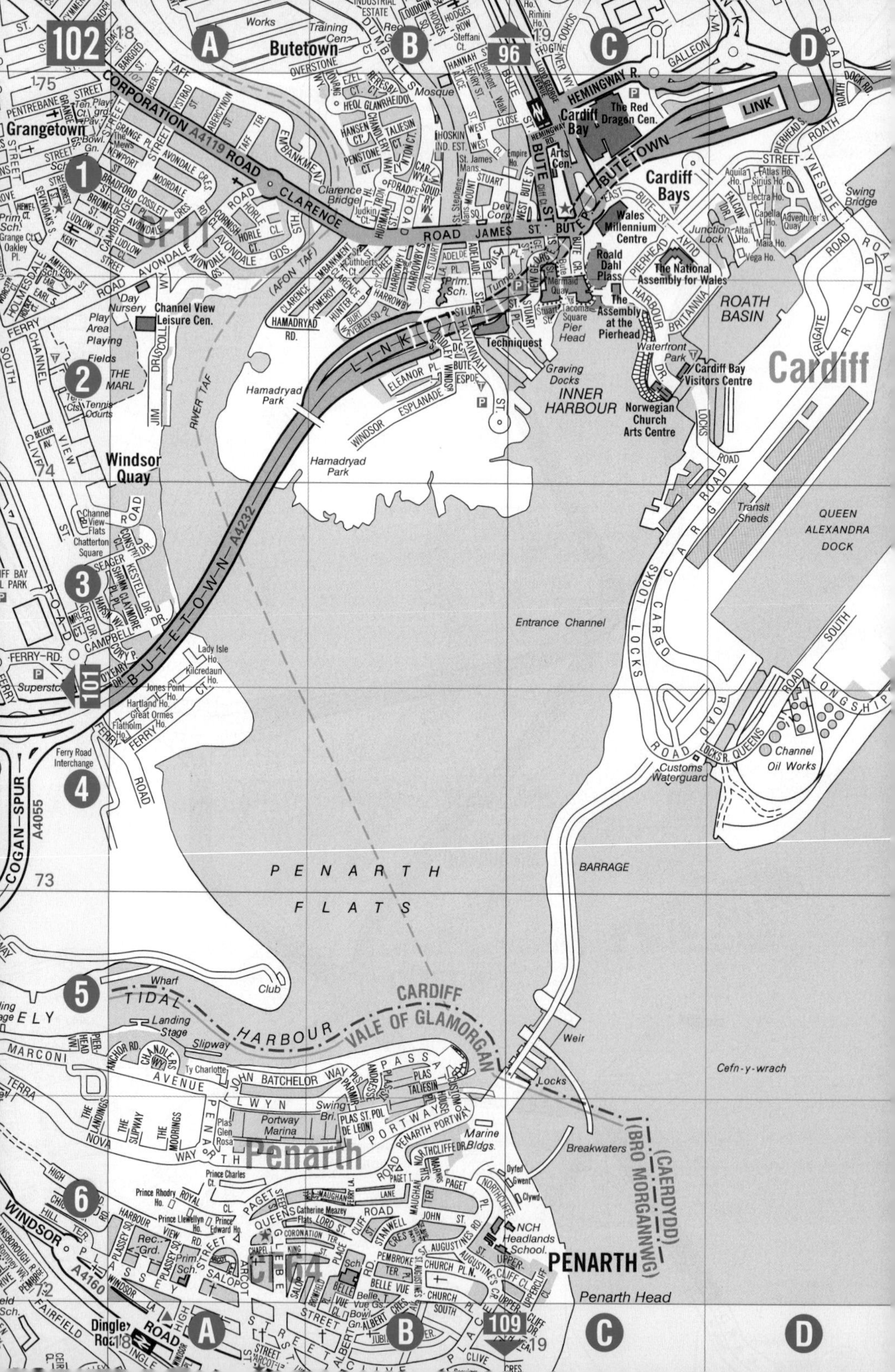

A
B
C
D
1
2
3
4
5
6
96
101
109
Butetown
Grangetown
Works
Training Cen.
Corporation Road
A4119
Clarence Road
James St.
Bute St.
Hemingway R.
Galleon
Link
Butetown Link
The Red Dragon Cen.
Cardiff Bay
Arts Cen.
Cardiff Bays
Wales Millennium Centre
Roald Dahl Plass
The National Assembly for Wales
The Assembly at the Pierhead
Mermaid Quay
Tacoma Square
Pier Head
Techniquest
Graving Docks
INNER HARBOUR
Norwegian Church Arts Centre
Cardiff Bay Visitors Centre
Waterfront Park
ROATH BASIN
Cardiff
Swing Bridge
Junction Lock
Adventurer's Quay
Mosque
Clarence Bridge
Hoskin Ind. Est.
Channel View Leisure Cen.
Day Nursery
Play Area
Playing Fields
THE MARL
Tennis Courts
Windsor Quay
Chatterton Square
Hamadryad Park
River Taf
(Afon Taf)
Butetown Link
A4232
Windsor Esplanade
Ferry Rd.
Superstore
Ferry Road Interchange
Cogan Spur
A4055
Lady Isle Ho.
Kilcredaun Ho.
Jones Point Ho.
Hartland Ho.
Great Ormes Ho.
Flatholm Ho.
Entrance Channel
Transit Sheds
QUEEN ALEXANDRA DOCK
Cargo Road
Locks Road
Queens
Longships
South
Channel Oil Works
Customs Waterguard
BARRAGE
PENARTH FLATS
Wharf
Club
TIDAL HARBOUR
ELY
CARDIFF
VALE OF GLAMORGAN
Landing Stage
Slipway
Marconi
Anchor Rd.
Chandlers Wy.
Ty Charlotte
John Batchelor Way
Avenue
Llwyn
Penarth Portway
Portway Marina
Swing Bri.
Plas St. Pol de Leon
Plas Glen Rosa
The Landings
The Slipway
The Moorings
Nova
Penarth
Marine Bldgs.
Weir
Locks
Breakwaters
Cefn-y-wrach
(CAERDYDD)
(BRO MORGANNWG)
Dyfed
Gwent
Clwyd
NCH Headlands School
PENARTH
Penarth Head
Prince Charles Ct.
Prince Rhodry Ho.
Prince Llewellyn Ho.
Prince Edward Ho.
Royal
Harbour View Rd.
Plassey Sq.
Rec. Grd.
Prim. Sch.
Windsor
A4160
Catherine Meazey Flats
Queens
Glebe Street
Paget
Maughan
Stanwell
Church Pl. N.
Upper Cliff Cl.
Belle Vue
Albert Cres.
CF64
CF11
Dingle Road
Fairfield
73
72
74
75
18
19

E
F
G
H
97
21
22
175
74
73
72
1
2
3
4
5
6
Depot
ROAD
CLIPPER
OLD CLIPPER ROAD
CLIPPER RD.
FORESHORE
CLOS
South Point
Boom
ROATH DOCK
CARDIFF DOCKS
Works
VIKING WAY
ROAD
South Point
OLD CLIPPER RD.
Waste Recycling Centre
ROVER ROAD
Fletcher's Wharf
Oil Storage Terminal
PLACE
LONGSHIPS ROAD
COLDSTORES ROAD
Works
Warehouses
CF10
Timber Depot
CARDIFF FLATS
MOUTH OF THE SEVERN
(ABER HAFREN)
E
F
21
G
H
22

08
A
B
Coed y Graig
DYFFRYN GOLWCH
09
C
Dyffryn Gardens
D
72
Whitton Mawr
Doghill Farm
Moat
Home Farm
Dyffryn
Treoda
1
Ffynnon Whitton-mawr
Little Hamston Farm
Little Hamston
Dyffryn Mill
Whitton Lodge
A4226
2
River Waycock
Goldsland
Great Hamston
71
Moulton Brook
Old Wallace
3
Northcliff Farm
Northcliff Cottage
Grovelands
Lidmore
Lidmore Mill
4
Brynhill
Coed Garw
Ffynnon y Coed
Nant
170
Lidmore Wood
Coed y Capel
Sutton
5
Coed Bach
Barry CF62
Suddon Mawr
Sutton Wood
Sewage Works
Welsh Hawking Centre
6
A4226
Coed Mawr
Ffynnon y Hofel
Middleton Plantation
WAYCOCK ROAD
Barry College
Coed yr Ychen
69
A
B
C
D
08
09
Walters Farm

116

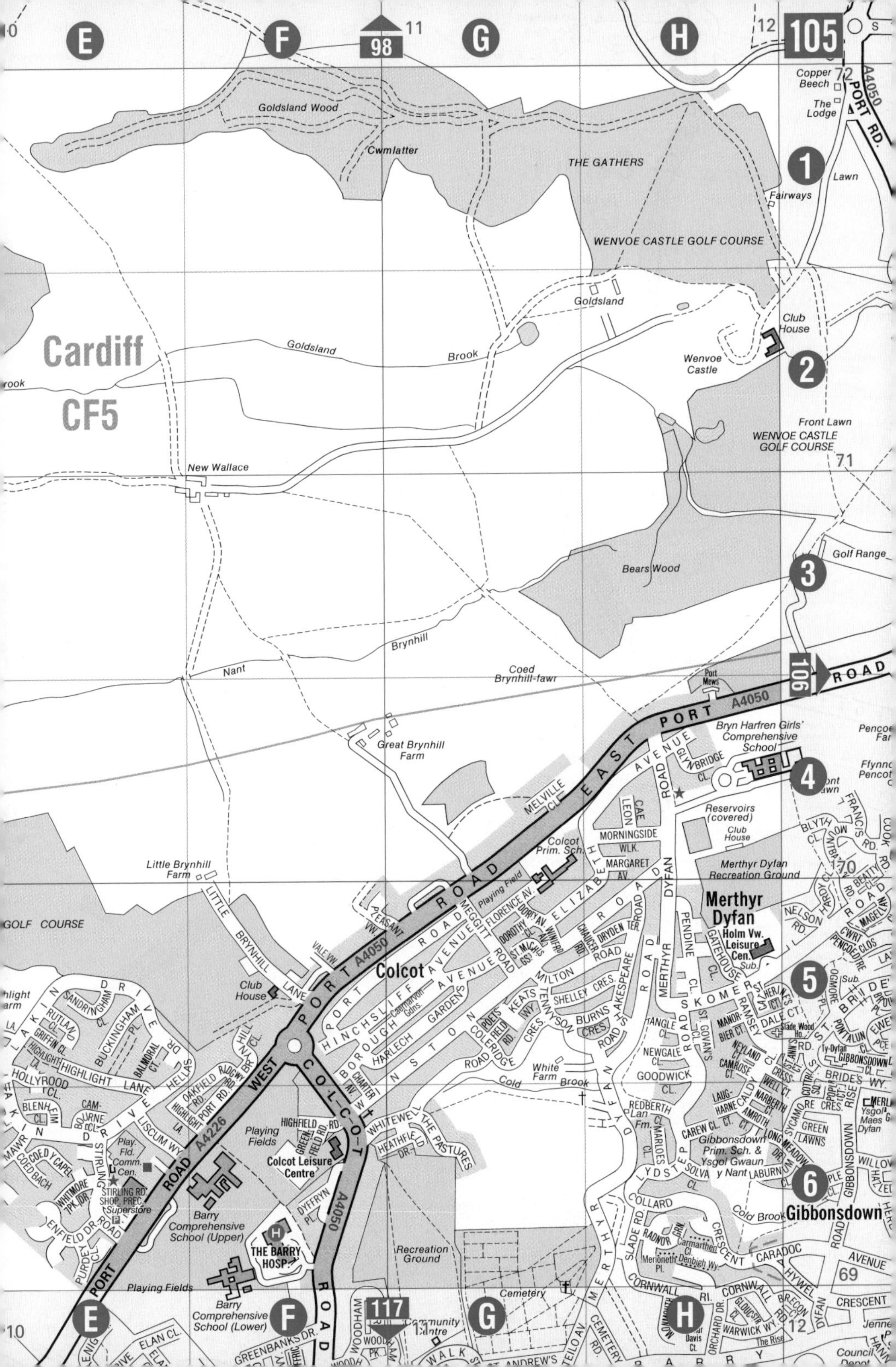
E
F
G
H
98
117
106
Cardiff
CF5
Goldsland Wood
Cwmlatter
THE GATHERS
WENVOE CASTLE GOLF COURSE
Fairways
Copper Beech
The Lodge
Lawn
PORT RD.
A4050
Goldsland
Goldsland
Brook
Club House
Wenvoe Castle
Front Lawn
WENVOE CASTLE GOLF COURSE
New Wallace
Bears Wood
Golf Range
Brynhill
Nant
Coed Brynhill-fawr
Port Mews
PORT ROAD EAST
A4050
Bryn Harfren Girls' Comprehensive School
Great Brynhill Farm
Reservoirs (covered)
Club House
Merthyr Dyfan Recreation Ground
Merthyr Dyfan
Holm Vw. Leisure Cen.
Little Brynhill Farm
GOLF COURSE
Colcot Prim. Sch.
Playing Field
Colcot
Club House
PORT ROAD WEST
A4226
COLCOT ROAD
A4050
Playing Fields
Colcot Leisure Centre
Barry Comprehensive School (Upper)
THE BARRY HOSP.
Recreation Ground
Cemetery
Playing Fields
Barry Comprehensive School (Lower)
Community Centre
Gibbonsdown Prim. Sch. & Ysgol Gwaun y Nant
Gibbonsdown
Cold Brook
Cold Brook
White Farm
Stirling Rd. Shop. Prec.
Superstore
Comm. Cen.
Play. Fld.
Ysgol Maes Dyfan
Ty-Dyfan
Slade Wood Ho.
Lan Fm.
Pencoed Far
Ffynnon Pencoed
CARADOC AVENUE
HYWEL CRESCENT
GIBBONSDOWN ROAD
72
71
70
69
10
11
12
1
2
3
4
5
6

106
A
B
C
D
99
118
105
1
2
3
4
5
6
Cardiff
CF5
CF62
CF63
Barry
St. Andrews Major
(Saint Andras)
PORT ROAD A4050
BARRY DOCKS LINK A4231
Vishwell Farm
ST. ANDREWS RD.
Copper Beech
The Lodge
Nursery
Waun Lawn
Fairways
Garn
Coed Ceaugeirwon
West Lodge
Ysguborgoch Farm
St. Andrew's House
Lodge
Coed Ysgubor-goch
Pentwyn
Nefoedd Fach
Keepers Cottage
Argae Farm
Argae House Stables
Ty-gwyn
Rectory
Ty-draw
Oaklands
ARGAE LANE
Nant yr Argae
Coed yr Argae
Wenvoe Castle
Club House
Front Lawn
WENVOE CASTLE GOLF COURSE
Crow Hill
Windrush
White Oaks
Dingle
Dinglewood Stables
Ger-y-nant Farm
Glendon
Gilberts Cross
EAST WESTRA
Westra Kennels
Gilbert Garden
Bears Wood
Golf Range
Greenyard Farm
Pencoetre Wood
GILBERT LANE
Gilbert Nurseries
Port Mews
Bryn Harfren Girls' Comprehensive School
Pencoedtre Farm
Ffynnon Pencotry
Super-store
Reservoirs (covered)
Club House
Merthyr Dyfan Recreation Ground
Merthyr Dyfan
Holm Vw. Leisure Cen.
Woodfield Farm
Coldbrook - fawr
Cold Brook
St. Richard Gwyn R.C. High Sch.
Playing Field
Parc Clwyd
Eastbourne Ct.
Westbourne Ct.
Stratford Grn.
Cadoxton
Cassy Hill
Gibbonsdown
Ysgol Maes Dyfan
Gibbonsdown Prim. Sch. & Ysgol Gwaun y Nant
Greenacres Prim. Sch.
Palmerstown
Hanover Ct.
Sea View Ter.
Victoria Park
Victoria Bowl. Gn.
Jun. & Inf. Sch.
Nursy. Sch.
Comm. Cen.
Ty Cerrig
PALMERSTON WORKSHOPS
PALMERS VALE BUS. CEN.
Park Prim. Sch.
Council Depot
Liddicoat
Ty Gwenfo
Arthur Davis Ct.
Educ. Cen.
Cold Brook
Carmarthen Cl.
Denbigh Wk.
72
71
170
69
12
13

E
F
G
H
100
119
108
1
2
3
4
5
6
Upalong
Newland
Mill Farm
Hales Wood
BEAUVILLE LANE
Garn-hill
DINAS POWYS GOLF COURSE
DINAS POWYS
Dinas Powys Castle
Castle Wood
Coed Twyncyn
Club Ho.
Quarry (disused)
Coed yr Eglwys
The Croft
Twyncyn
Golden Beeches
Pav.
Bryneithin
St. Andrew's Major Prim. Sch.
Tennis Courts
Bowling Green
Westra
WESTRA ROAD
Westra-fawr
Tanglewood
Playhill
Dinas Powys Common
Southra
The Gables
Nursery Cott.
Dinas Powys CF64
Eastbrook
Ardwyn (Children's Home)
TURNPIKE CL.
Oaklands
PARK RD.
CWM DRIVE
PEN-Y-TURNPIKE RD.
MILLBROOK HEIGHTS
ST. DAVIDS
JESTYN
MILLBROOK RD.
LETTONS WAY
HIGHWALLS AV.
HIGHWALLS AVENUE
HIGHWALLS END
Castlewood Cotts.
HEOL-Y-CAWL
CEFN MOUNT
TWYNCYN
MEREVALE
Kings Ride
BRITWAY ROAD
Britway Cl.
The Square
OLD FARM MS.
THE MOUNT
MOUNT ROAD
SOUTHRA
STATION RD.
MILL RD.
Hall
WESLEY
ELM GROVE
GROVE LA.
GREENFIELD
STACEY RD.
MILL CL.
EDITH RD.
ORCHARD CR.
Hlth. Cen.
Dinas Powys Inf. Sch.
MURCH RD.
A4055
CARDIFF ROAD
PERCLOSE
Library
VALE CT.
Murch Jun. Sch.
Rec. Grd.
Youldon Ho.
Ten. Cts.
Bowl. Grn.
ELM GROVE PL.
FAIROAKS
PEN-Y-WAUN
SUNNYCROFT
SUNNYCROFT LA.
AVENUE
Dinas Powys
ST. AMBROSE CL.
ST. NICHOLAS
ST. GWYNNOS
ST. ILLTYD CL.
ST. DYFRIG CL.
ST. LYTHAN CL.
ST. CADOCS
ST. WINIFDS. CL.
ST. PAULS CL.
WELL WOOD DR.
SYCAMORE CL.
ROBIN HILL
HAWTHORN RISE
GREEN MEADOW CL.
HAZEL GRO.
LONGMEADOW DRIVE
LABURNUM WAY
CHESTNUT CL.
ASHGROVE
KINGS
CROSS COMMON
Cross Common
COMMON ROAD
CROFFTA
DRYLLA
CAE'R PWLL
FRENHINES
NAVOD
CAE GARW
CAE'R
HEOL-Y-
Playing Field
Murch
ESSYLLT ROAD
Playgrd.
THE DRIVE
WINDRIDGE
IVOR PL.
NIGHTINGALE PL.
SIR IVOR PL.
CASTLE CL.
PEMBROKE
HARLECH
CAERNAR-VON CL.
MANOR DR.
BIER CL.
DUNRAVEN CL.
TENBY CL.
RAGLAN
ST. DONATS CL.
CASTLE
BROOKSIDE
CHAMBERLAIN
POWYS DR.
POWYS PL.
POWYS GDS.
CHAPEL CL.
CHAPEL ROW
GEORGES
HIGHFIELD CL.
LEE CL.
DENYS CL.
CELTIC GRN.
EAST-BROOK CL.
St. Cyres Sch. (Dinas Powys)
Dinas Powys Moors
Cadoxton River
Pop Hill
GREEN LANE
Sewage Works
Cog Moors
Biglis Moors
Biglis Farm
Pumping Station
Cold Brook
Pymbylu Moors
Brook
PRIORITY BUS. PK.
TY VERLON INDUSTRIAL ESTATE
SULLY VIEW
VERLON CL.
Depot
A4231
A4055
B4267
SULLY MOORS RD.
Wks.
Cog Moors
NORTH ROAD
EAST
DONNINGTON RD.
Works
Sully Brook
Sully Moors
Penarth CF64
Cog Farm
315
16
72
71
70
69

101
120
107
A
B
C
D
1
2
3
4
5
6
16
17
72
170
69
Eastbrook
CARDIFF ROAD A4055
Dinas Powys Inf. Sch.
Library
Camm's Cnr.
The Parade
Murch
St. Cyres School (Dinas Powys Site)
Dinas Powys
CF64
The Breeches
Glascoed Farm
Hickley Lodge
Old Cogan Hall Farm
Morristown
St. Joseph's RC Prim. Sch.
ST. CYRES PARK
Ashgrove Sch.
Ysgol Erw'r Delyn
Erw'r-delyn
St. Cyres School (Penarth Site)
Redlands Ho.
Ysgol Gymraeg Pen'y Garth
REDLANDS ROAD B4267
Fairfield Prim. Sch.
Victoria Play. Fld.
Health Cen.
Stanwell School
Playing Field
Carmarthen Ho.
Merioneth Ho.
Radnor Ho.
Brecon Ho.
Ty Dewi Sant
Oak Court
St. James Ct.
Recreation Grd.
Rugby Football Grd.
Hadley Ho.
LAVERNOCK ROAD B4267
DINAS ROAD
Penarth Cemetery
Lower Penarth
COMMON ROAD
SULLY ROAD
CROSS COMMON ROAD
Pop Hill
Rose Cottage
Claygate
Woodlands
Downs Farm
Sewage Works
GREEN LANE
Sully Brook
Ford
Cog Bridge
Sully Moors
Cog Farm
Cogan Plantation
COSMESTON LAKES COUNTRY PARK
Downs Wood
GLAMORGANSHIRE GOLF COURSE
Visitors Centre
Medieval Village
Lower Cosmeston Farm

E
F
G
H
102
Headlands School.
Penarth Head
PENARTH
Penarth
CF64
Slipway
Penarth Pier
Marina Pavilion
Penarth Yacht Club
Slipway
The Kymin
Homeside House
Council Offices
Turner Ho.
Alexandra Park
Marie Curie Cen. (Holme Tower)
Miniature Golf Course
Cosmeston
Club House
Linear Park
Railway Walk
MOUTH OF THE SEVERN
(ABER HAFREN)
A4160
STANWELL RD.
PLYMOUTH ROAD
WESTBOURNE ROAD
RAISDALE ROAD
CLIFF PARADE
MARINE PARADE
ESPLANADE
CLIFF WALK
1
2
3
4
5
6
72
71
170
69
320
19

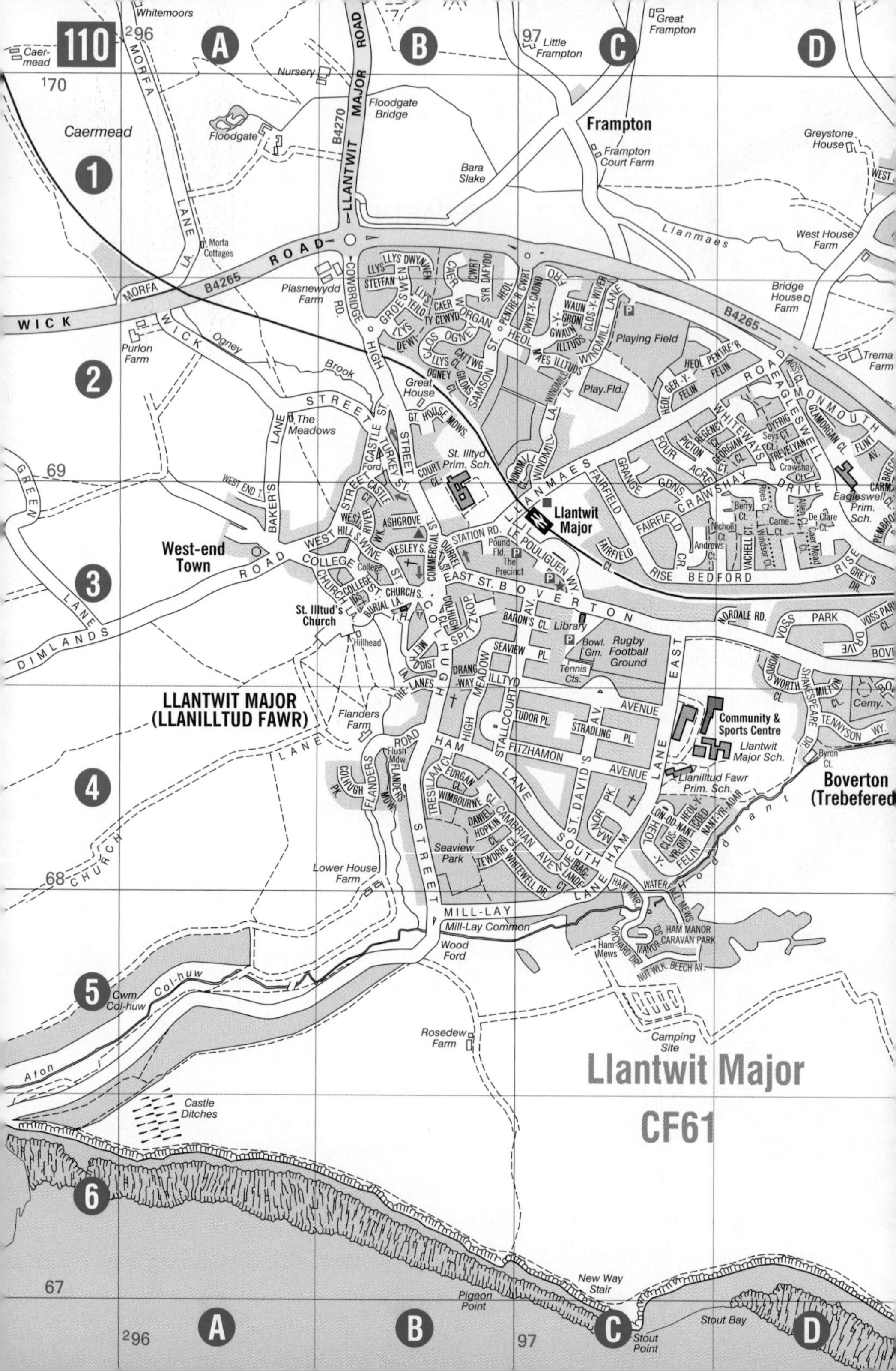
Llantwit Major
CF61
LLANTWIT MAJOR
(LLANILLTUD FAWR)
West-end Town
Frampton
Boverton
(Trebefered
Llantwit Major
St. Illtud's Church
Community & Sports Centre
Llantwit Major Sch.
Llanilltud Fawr Prim. Sch.
Eagleswell Prim. Sch.
St. Illtyd Prim. Sch.
Rugby Football Ground
Caermead
Floodgate
Floodgate Bridge
Bara Slake
Frampton Court Farm
Great Frampton
Little Frampton
Greystone House
West House Farm
Bridge House Farm
Trema Farm
Plasnewydd Farm
Purlon Farm
Morfa Cottages
Nursery
Whitemoors
Great House
The Meadows
Flanders Farm
Lower House Farm
Rosedew Farm
Camping Site
Castle Ditches
Cwm Col-huw
Afon Col-huw
Mill-Lay Common
Wood Ford
Ham Manor Caravan Park
New Way Stair
Pigeon Point
Stout Point
Stout Bay
Seaview Park
Playing Field
Play. Fld.
Library
Tennis Cts.
Bowl. Grn.
Cemy.
Hillhead
T.H.
Pound Fld.
The Precinct
WICK ROAD
B4265
B4270
LLANTWIT MAJOR ROAD
MORFA LANE
DIMLANDS ROAD
CHURCH LANE
GREEN LANE
EAST ST.
BOVERTON ROAD
COLHUGH ST.
HIGH STREET
HAM LANE
SOUTH HAM LANE
FLANDERS ROAD
LLANMAES ROAD
EAGLESWELL ROAD
CRAWSHAY DRIVE
BEDFORD RISE
VOSS PARK DRIVE
ILLTYD AVENUE
FITZHAMON AVENUE
HAM LANE EAST
MILL-LAY
Hoddnant

E
F
G
H
99
300
170
Brook Farm
Gadlys
Llanmaes
Great House Farm
Brook
Splott House
MILLANDS PARK
Millands Farm
Camping Site
Froglands Farm
Old Froglands Brook
Picketston House
Picketston
Picketston Cottage
Barry
CF62
1
2
3
4
5
6
69
68
67
Boverton
ROAD
EAGLE
WREN
PARTRIDGE
WAGTAIL
BULLFINCH
RD.
CURLEW CR.
KINGFISHER
SQUARE
WOODPECKER
SQUARE
BLACKBIRD
MAGPIE RD.
STARLING
RD.
ROOK CL.
CHURCH MDW.
RAF St. Athan
B4265
LLANTWIT RD.
LLANTWIT ROAD
Playing Field
Playing Field
Pav.
Batslays
DENBIGH DR.
CARDIGAN
RADNOR RD.
HEOL MERIONETH
GLAN Y MOR
HARDING CL.
PERCY SMITH RD.
GASKELL CL.
ORCHARD
ORCHARD CL.
BOVERTON
BOVERTON PARK DR.
ROAD
BROOK
REDWOOD CL.
Orchard House
Boverton Place Farm
Nursery
CASTLE CL.
Boverton Mill Farm
112

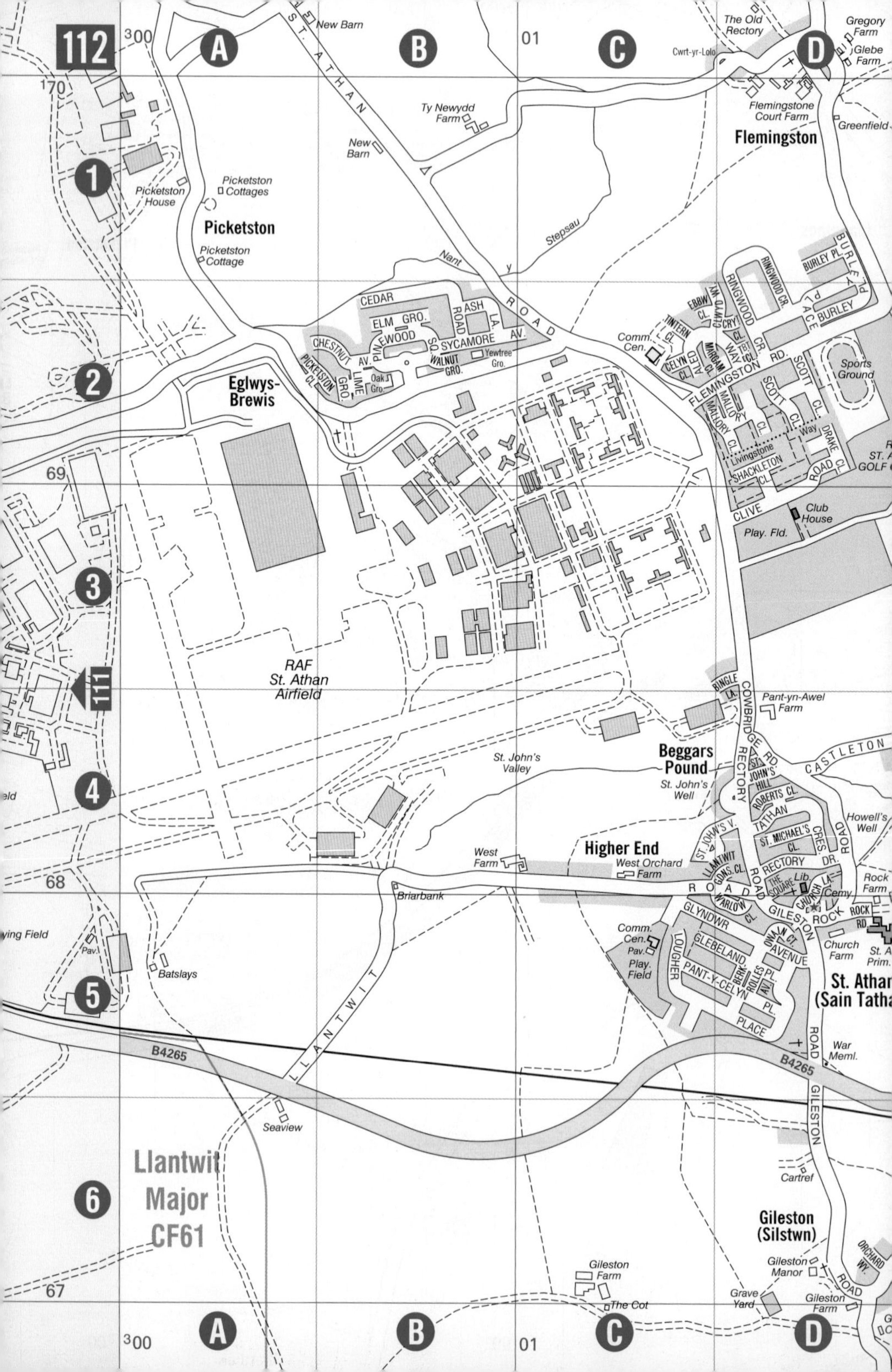
A
B
C
D
300
01
170
69
68
67
1
2
3
4
5
6
111
New Barn
The Old Rectory
Gregory Farm
Glebe Farm
Cwrt-yr-Lolo
Ty Newydd Farm
New Barn
Flemingstone Court Farm
Greenfield
Flemingston
Picketston Cottages
Picketston House
Picketston
Picketston Cottage
ST. ATHAN ROAD
Nant y Stepsau
CEDAR
ELM GRO.
ASH LA.
ROAD
PINEWOOD SQ.
SYCAMORE AV.
CHESTNUT AV.
PICKETSTON CL.
GRO.
LIME GRO.
Oak Gro.
WALNUT GRO.
Yewtree Gro.
Eglwys-Brewis
Comm. Cen.
EBBW CL.
TINTERN CL.
TAWE CL.
CRYT CL.
RINGWOOD CR.
RINGWOOD
BURLEY PL.
BURLEY PLACE
BURLEY
CELYN CL.
ALED
MARGAM
WAY
TBT
FLEMINGSTON RD.
SCOTT
SCOTT CL.
Sports Ground
MALLORY
MALLORY CL.
RY CL.
Livingstone Way
DRAKE CL.
SHACKLETON CL.
ROAD
CLIVE
Club House
Play. Fld.
ST. A GOLF
RAF St. Athan Airfield
BINGLE LA.
Pant-yn-Awel Farm
COWBRIDGE RD.
RECTORY
ST. JOHN'S HILL
CASTLETON
Beggars Pound
St. John's Valley
St. John's Well
ROBERTS CL.
TATHAN
ST. MICHAEL'S CL.
CRES.
ROAD
Howell's Well
ST. JOHN'S V.
LLANTWIT GDNS. CL.
Higher End
West Farm
West Orchard Farm
RECTORY DR.
Rock Farm
ROAD
THE SQUARE
Lib.
CHURCH LA.
Cemy.
Briarbank
WARLOW CL.
GILESTON
ROCK
RD.
GLYNDWR
OWAIN CT.
Comm. Cen.
Pav.
Play. Field
LOUGHER
GLEBELAND
AVENUE
BERK.
ROLLES AV.
PL.
PANT-Y-CELYN
PL.
PLACE
Church Farm
St. A Prim.
St. Athan (Sain Tatha
Pav.
Batslays
ying Field
eld
LLANTWIT
B4265
ROAD
War Meml.
B4265
GILESTON
Seaview
Llantwit Major CF61
Cartref
Gileston (Silstwn)
ORCHARD WY.
Gileston Manor
ROAD
Gileston Farm
The Cot
Grave Yard
Gileston Farm

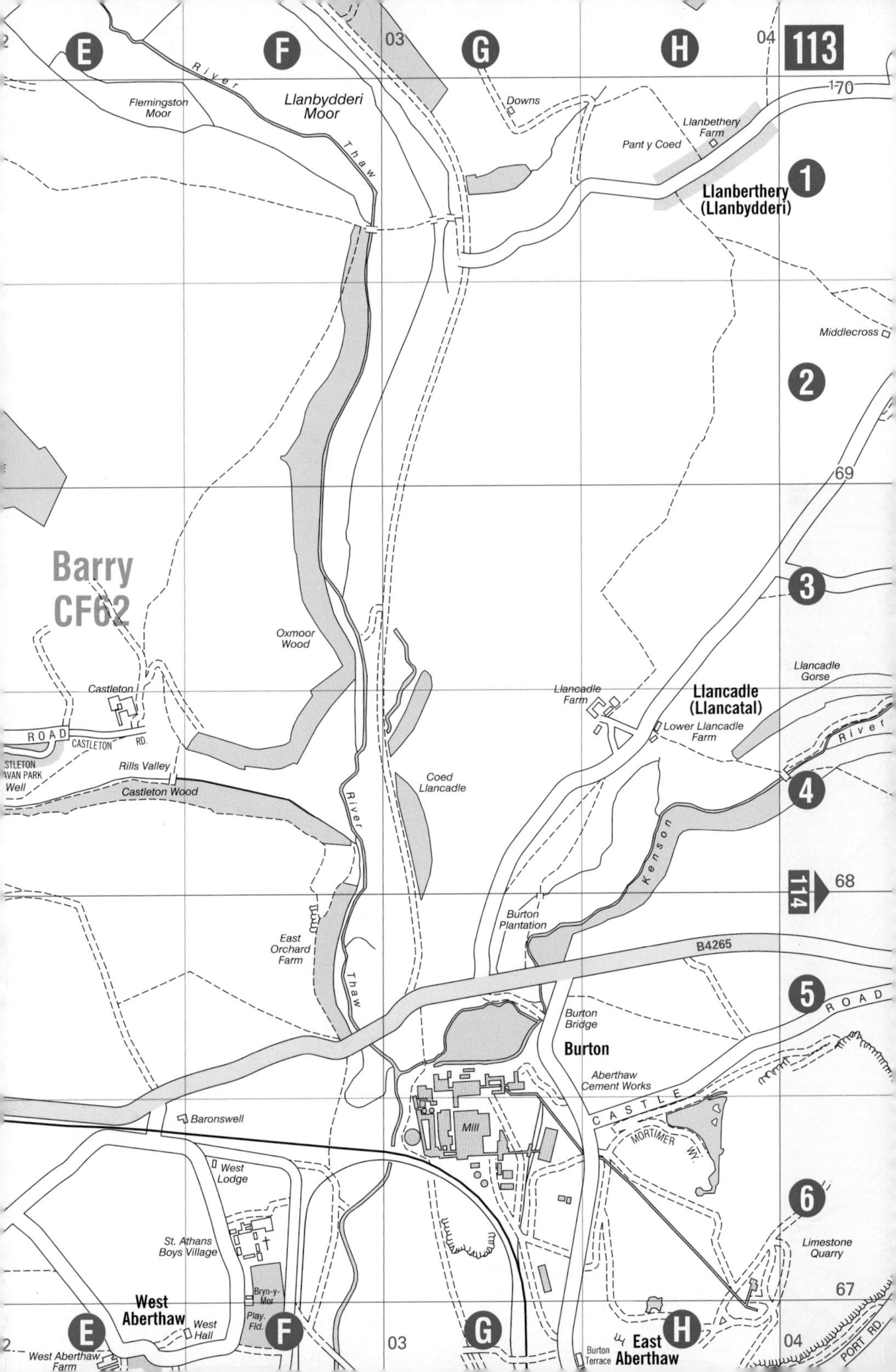
E
F
G
H
03
04
70
69
68
67
1
2
3
4
5
6
River Thaw
Flemingston Moor
Llanbydderi Moor
Downs
Llanbethery Farm
Pant y Coed
Llanberthery (Llanbydderi)
Middlecross
Barry CF62
Oxmoor Wood
Castleton
ROAD
CASTLETON RD.
Rills Valley
Castleton Wood
Well
Coed Llancadle
Llancadle Farm
Llancadle (Llancatal)
Lower Llancadle Farm
Llancadle Gorse
River
River Kenson
114
Burton Plantation
East Orchard Farm
B4265
ROAD
Burton Bridge
Burton
Aberthaw Cement Works
CASTLE
MORTIMER WY.
Mill
Baronswell
West Lodge
St. Athans Boys Village
Bryn-y-Mor
Play. Fld.
West Aberthaw
West Hall
West Aberthaw Farm
Limestone Quarry
Burton Terrace
East Aberthaw
PORT RD.

04
A
B
C
D
305
69
Pen-doines
Penmark
(Pen-marc)
Penmark Farm
Barrenhill
JOHN
CROFT
Cliff Wood
Kenson Wood
KENSON
HILL
Kenson
Penmark Place
Sefton Bungalow
Llancadle Gorse
Llancadle
(Llancatal)
Lower Llancadle Farm
New Wood
River
Kenson
Castle Wood
Ffwl-y-mwn
Brook
Fonmon Castle
Watch Tower
Woodhouse
168
113
B4265
Castle Lodge
ROAD
Rocks Head
CASTLE
Fon-mon Pond
Fonmon
(Ffwl-y-mwn)
Barry
CF62
FONMON
Home Farm
Fonmon Farmhouse
Limestone Quarry
PORT ROAD
Chapel Farm
Nurston
Bird Farm
67
FONMON PARK
BEAUFORT WY.
ADENFIELD
MATTHEW
NURSTON CL.
WAY
FEE
ODYN'S
Font-y-gary
(Ffont-y-gari)
Playground
ST. JOHN'S PL.
NORSEMAN CL.
CELTIC WAY
LA.
SHOWLE ACRE
LLANMEAD
GDS.
ST. STORS
READERS WY.
MEADE
WESLEY AV.
SPEEDWELL DR.
THAW CL.
WHITTAN CL.
Community Cen.
Bowling Grn.
Tennis Cts.
SMEATON CL.
CELTIC
WHARTON CL.
MILBURN CL.
MARINERS WY.
CHANNEL CL.
LON CEFN MARLY
KENSON CL.
FONTYGARY ROAD
Resr. (covered)
Railway Houses
Caravan Park
66
Andrew's Pant
Fontygary Bay Caravan Park
Tidal Ponds
Tidal Pond
Nature Reserve
Font-y-gari
Watch House Beach
Fontygari Cave
1
2
3
4
5
6

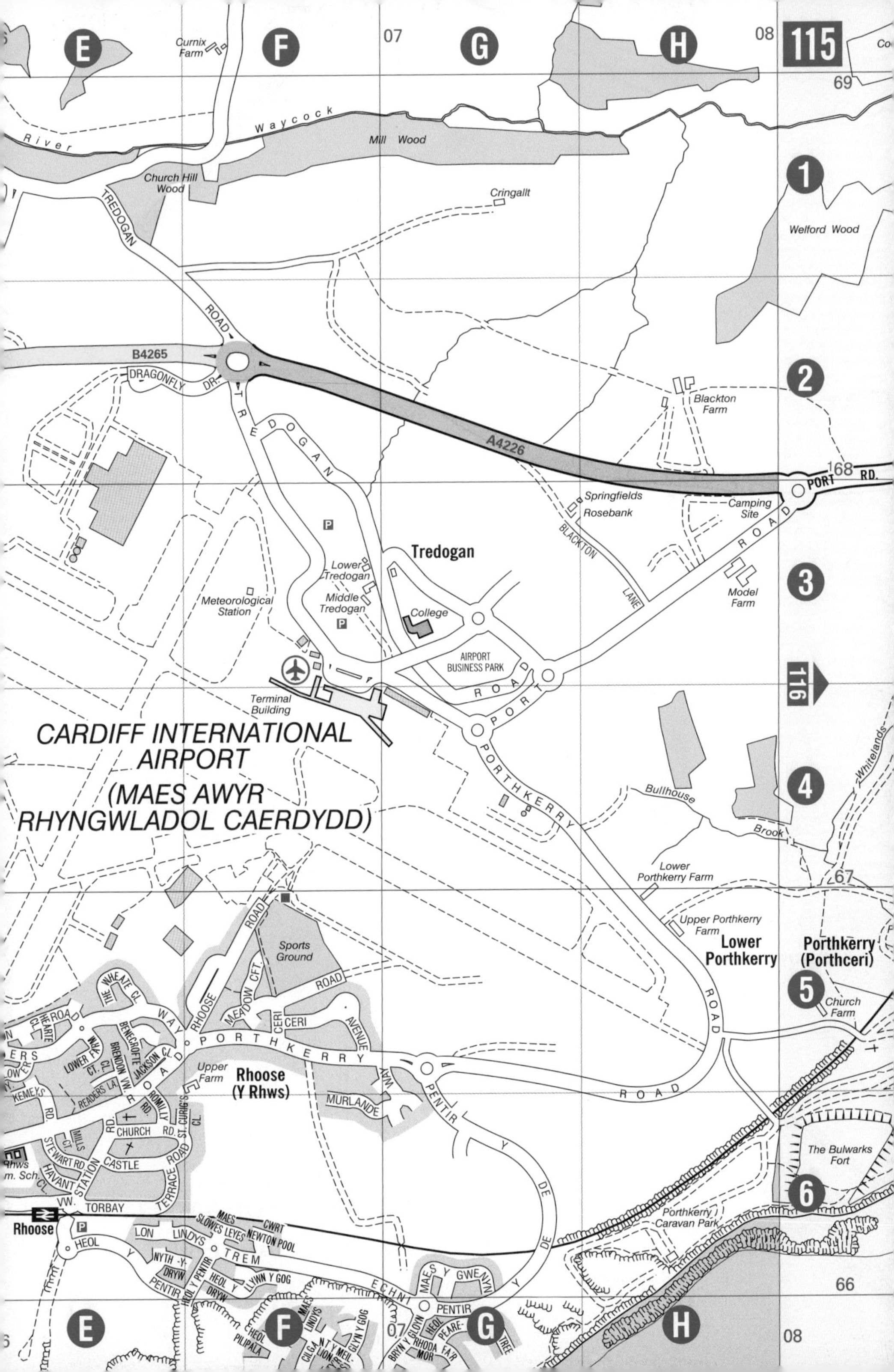

CARDIFF INTERNATIONAL AIRPORT
(MAES AWYR RHYNGWLADOL CAERDYDD)
Tredogan
Rhoose
(Y Rhws)
Lower Porthkerry
Porthkerry
(Porthceri)
Curnix Farm
River Waycock
Mill Wood
Church Hill Wood
Cringallt
Welford Wood
TREDOGAN ROAD
B4265
A4226
DRAGONFLY DR.
Blackton Farm
PORT RD.
Springfields
Rosebank
BLACKTON LANE
Camping Site
Model Farm
Lower Tredogan
Middle Tredogan
College
Meteorological Station
AIRPORT BUSINESS PARK
PORT ROAD
Terminal Building
PORTHKERRY ROAD
Bullhouse Brook
Lower Porthkerry Farm
Upper Porthkerry Farm
Whitelands
Church Farm
Sports Ground
The Bulwarks Fort
Porthkerry Caravan Park
Upper Farm
Rhoose
PENTIR Y DE
116

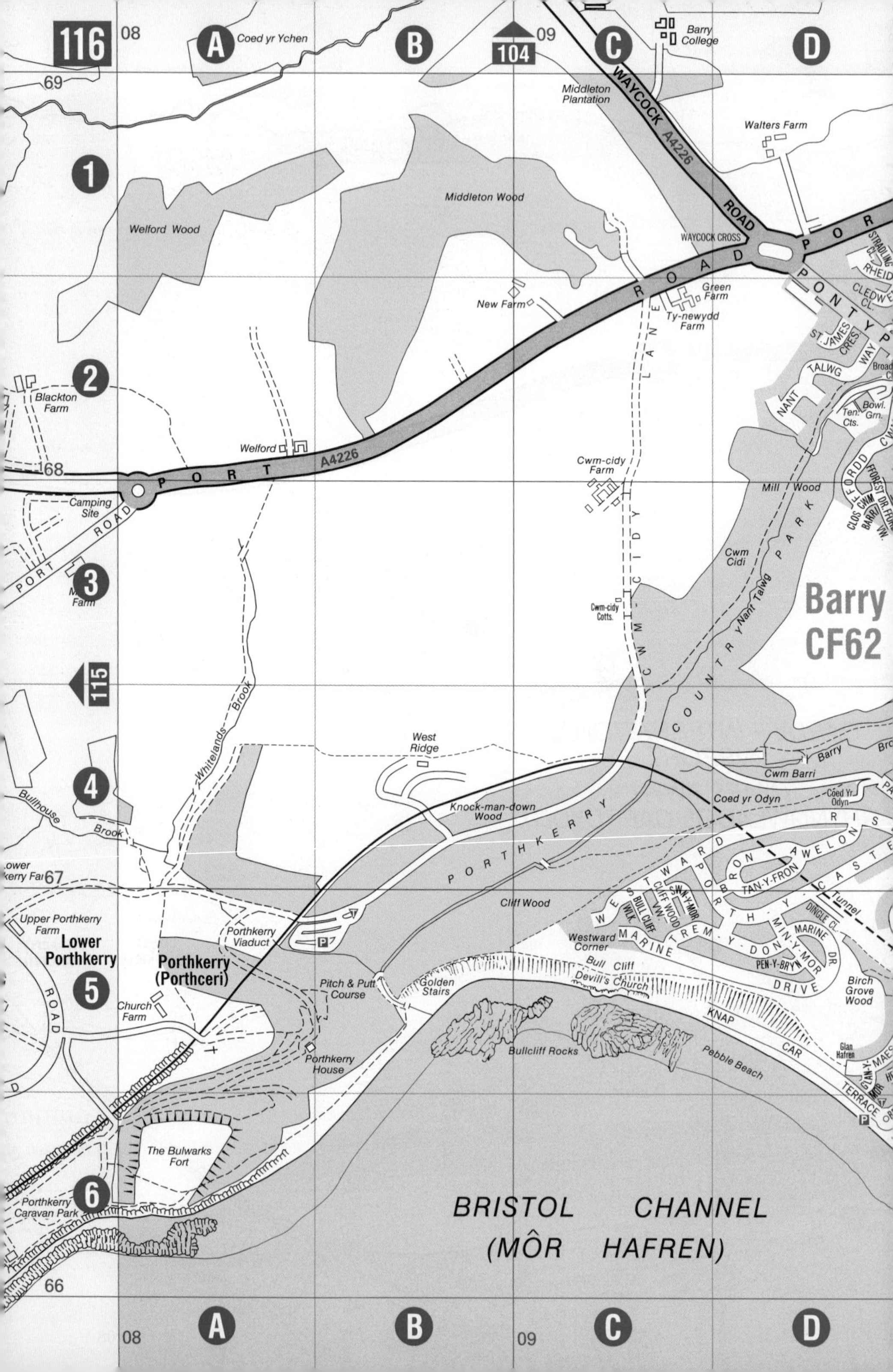
08
09
A
B
C
D
1
2
3
4
5
6
69
168
67
66
104
115
Coed yr Ychen
Barry College
Middleton Plantation
WAYCOCK ROAD A4226
Walters Farm
Welford Wood
Middleton Wood
WAYCOCK CROSS
PORT ROAD A4226
New Farm
Green Farm
Ty-newydd Farm
STRADLING CL.
RHEID
CLEDWEN CL.
PONTYP
ST. JAMES CRES.
TALWG WAY
NANT
Broad Cl.
Bowl. Grn.
Ten. Cts.
Blackton Farm
Welford
Cwm-cidy Farm
Mill Wood
FFORDD CWM
CLOS CWM BARRI
FFOREST DR.
VW.
Camping Site
PORT ROAD
Cwm Cidi
COUNTRY PARK
Nant Talwg
CWM CIDY LANE
Barry CF62
Cwm-cidy Cotts.
Whitelands Brook
West Ridge
Barry
Cwm Barri
Coed yr Odyn
Coed Yr Odyn
Knock-man-down Wood
PORTHKERRY
Bullhouse Brook
Lower Porthkerry Farm
WESTWARD
PORTH-Y-CASTELL
RISE
BRON AWELON
TAN-Y-FRON
Tunnel
BULL CLIFF WLK
CLIFF WOOD VW.
SWN-Y-MOR
Cliff Wood
Upper Porthkerry Farm
Porthkerry Viaduct
Lower Porthkerry
Porthkerry (Porthceri)
Westward Corner
MARINE
TREM-Y-DON
MIN-Y-MOR
DINGLE CL.
MARINE DR.
PEN-Y-BRYN
Bull Cliff
Devil's Church
DRIVE
Birch Grove Wood
Pitch & Putt Course
Golden Stairs
ROAD
Church Farm
Bullcliff Rocks
KNAP CAR TERRACE
Pebble Beach
Glan Hafren
GLAN-Y-MOR
MAES
Porthkerry House
The Bulwarks Fort
Porthkerry Caravan Park
BRISTOL CHANNEL
(MÔR HAFREN)

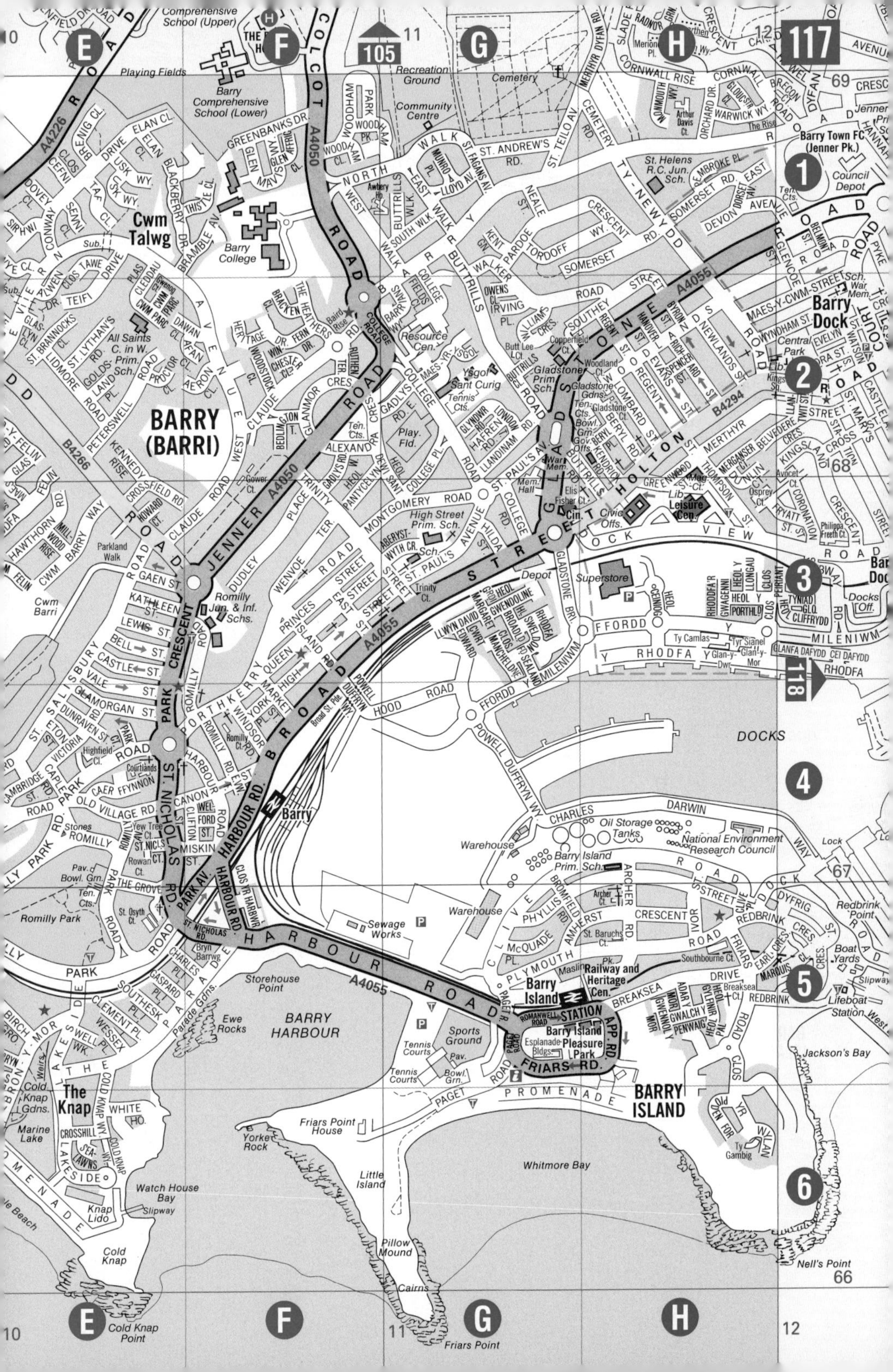

117
105
118
E
F
G
H
1
2
3
4
5
6
10
11
12
69
68
67
66
BARRY (BARRI)
BARRY ISLAND
Barry Dock
Cwm Talwg
Cwm Barri
The Knap
BARRY HARBOUR
DOCKS
Whitmore Bay
Jackson's Bay
Watch House Bay
Cold Knap
Cold Knap Point
Friars Point
Friars Point House
Nell's Point
Little Island
Pillow Mound
Cairns
Yorke Rock
Ewe Rocks
Storehouse Point
Redbrink Point
Boat Yards
Lifeboat Station
Lock
Marine Lake
Knap Lido
Slipway
Cold Knap Gdns.
Romilly Park
Parkland Walk
Playing Fields
Recreation Ground
Cemetery
Community Centre
Comprehensive School (Upper)
Barry Comprehensive School (Lower)
Barry College
Barry Town FC (Jenner Pk.)
Council Depot
St. Helens R.C. Jun. Sch.
All Saints C. in W. Prim. Sch.
Romilly Jun. & Inf. Schs.
High Street Prim. Sch.
Gladstone Prim. Sch.
Ysgol Sant Curig
Barry Island Prim. Sch.
Resource Cen.
Leisure Cen.
Civic Offs.
Superstore
Depot
Docks Off.
Sewage Works
Warehouse
Oil Storage Tanks
National Environment Research Council
Railway and Heritage Cen.
Barry Island Pleasure Park
Sports Ground
Tennis Courts
Esplanade Bldgs.
Barry
Barry Island
A4226
A4050
A4055
B4266
B4294
JENNER ROAD
COLCOT ROAD
BROAD STREET
HOLTON ROAD
GLADSTONE ROAD
HARBOUR ROAD
PARK CRESCENT
ST. NICHOLAS RD.
PAGET ROAD
FRIARS RD.
STATION APP. RD.
PROMENADE
CHARLES DARWIN WAY
POWELL DUFFRYN WY.
FFORDD Y MILENIWM
Y RHODFA
HOOD ROAD
DOCK VIEW ROAD
PLYMOUTH ROAD
CLIVE RD.
AMHERST CRESCENT
BREAKSEA DRIVE
REDBRINK CRES.
ST. ANDREW'S RD.
NORTH WALK
CEMETERY RD.
TY-NEWYDD RD.
SOMERSET RD.
MAES-Y-CWM STREET
CLAUDE ROAD
PORTHKERRY RD.
ROMILLY RD.
OLD VILLAGE RD.
PARK ROAD
THE PARADE
LAKESIDE

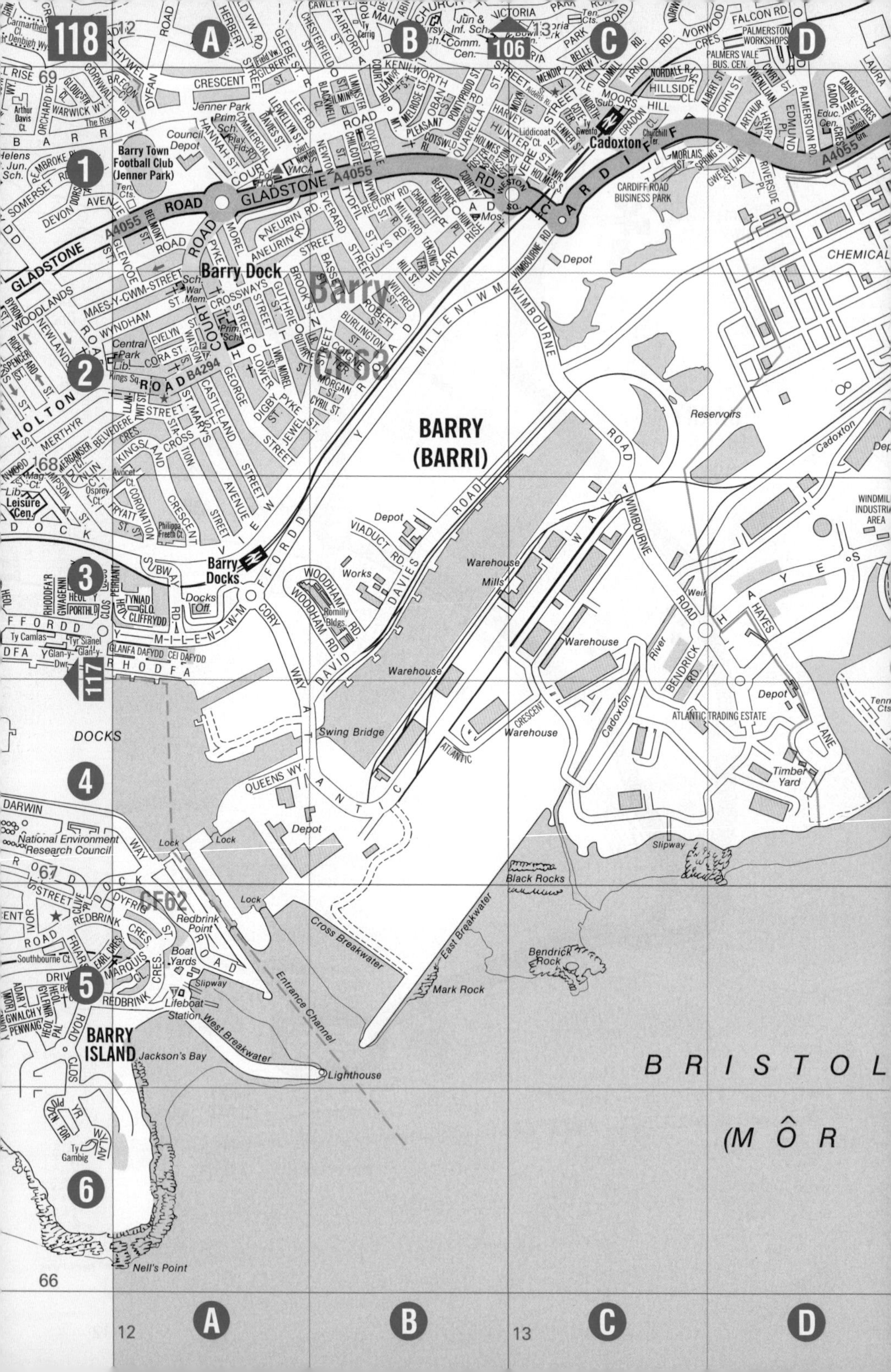

A
B
C
D
1
2
3
4
5
6
106
117
12
13
69
168
67
66
BARRY (BARRI)
Barry
CF63
CF62
Barry Dock
Barry Docks
Cadoxton
BARRY ISLAND
Barry Town Football Club (Jenner Park)
Council Depot
Jenner Park Prim. Sch.
CARDIFF ROAD BUSINESS PARK
Reservoirs
CHEMICAL
WINDMILL INDUSTRIAL AREA
ATLANTIC TRADING ESTATE
Timber Yard
Depot
Warehouse
Mills
Works
Swing Bridge
Lock
Cross Breakwater
East Breakwater
West Breakwater
Entrance Channel
Lighthouse
Jackson's Bay
Nell's Point
Black Rocks
Bendrick Rock
Mark Rock
Slipway
Boat Yards
Lifeboat Station
Redbrink Point
Docks Off.
National Environment Research Council
DOCKS
Leisure Cen.
Central Park
Kings Sq.
Arthur Davis Ct.
Palmerston Workshops
Palmers Vale Bus. Cen.
GLADSTONE ROAD A4055
HOLTON ROAD B4294
A4055
CARDIFF
FFORDD Y MILENIWM
WIMBOURNE ROAD
HAYES ROAD
DAVID DAVIES ROAD
ATLANTIC WAY
CORY WAY
QUEENS WY.
VIADUCT RD.
WOODHAM RD.
DOCK VIEW ROAD
HILLARY RISE
DOCK ROAD
HAYES LANE
BENDRICK RD.
DARWIN WAY
REDBRINK CRES.
Cadoxton River
B R I S T O L
(M Ô R

E
F
G
H
107
315
16
69
Penarth
CF64
Sully Moors
Cog Moors
Cog Farm
SULLY
Sully Brook
Works
Wks.
Depot
VERLON CL.
SULLY
B4267
MOORS
ROAD
NORTH ROAD
EAST
BICESTER RD.
DONNINGTON RD.
BREON
BRYANSTON RD.
ELEVEN ST.
CENTRAL WAY
ROAD
WEST ROAD
FURNACE ST.
COLUMN ST.
TOWER WY.
HORTON WY.
Weir
VALE ENTERPRISE CENTRE
SOUTH ROAD
ROAD
Hall
Recycling Site
Southleigh Community Home
ASHBY ROAD
MEADOW VIEW CT.
The Halt
COG
BASSETT ROAD
KETERINGHAM CL.
ROOKERY CL.
ROOKERY WOOD
DESPENSER
CROFT RD. GDS.
DANIELL CL.
ECKLEY RD.
STRADLING CL.
GLASTONBURY
PORLOCK
SOUTHGATE
DONIFORD CL.
BRIDGEWATER RD.
CONYBEARE ROAD
UPHILL CL.
SLADE CL.
WESTMINSTER DR.
CANNING-TON CL.
LYNTON CL.
GRIMSON CL.
KINGSLEY CL.
DULVERTON DR.
DRIVE
ELWORTHY CL.
ARLINGTON
ARLINGTN RD.
BREAN CL.
MINEHEAD AV.
MINEHEAD
DUNSTER DR.
AVENUE
LYNMOUTH DR.
Sully Prim. Sch.
BURNHAM AV.
SMITHIES
Breaksea Cl.
WESTON AV.
B4267
WIMBORNE CRES.
ROAD
NAVLSEA CT.
ELM CL.
WINSFORD RD.
HIGHBRIDGE CL.
ROAD
168
Lib.
Sports Ground
Bowl. Grn.
Hall
Boat Yard
AVENUE
OYSTER BEND
SOMERSET VW.
CLEVEDON AV.
Bowling Grn.
Sports Gr
Slipway
Slipway
TY HAFAN CHILDREN'S HOSPICE
d-yr-Hayes
Sully Bay
Hayes Point
120
1
2
3
4
5
6
67
66
CHANNEL
HAFREN)
E
F
315
G
H
16

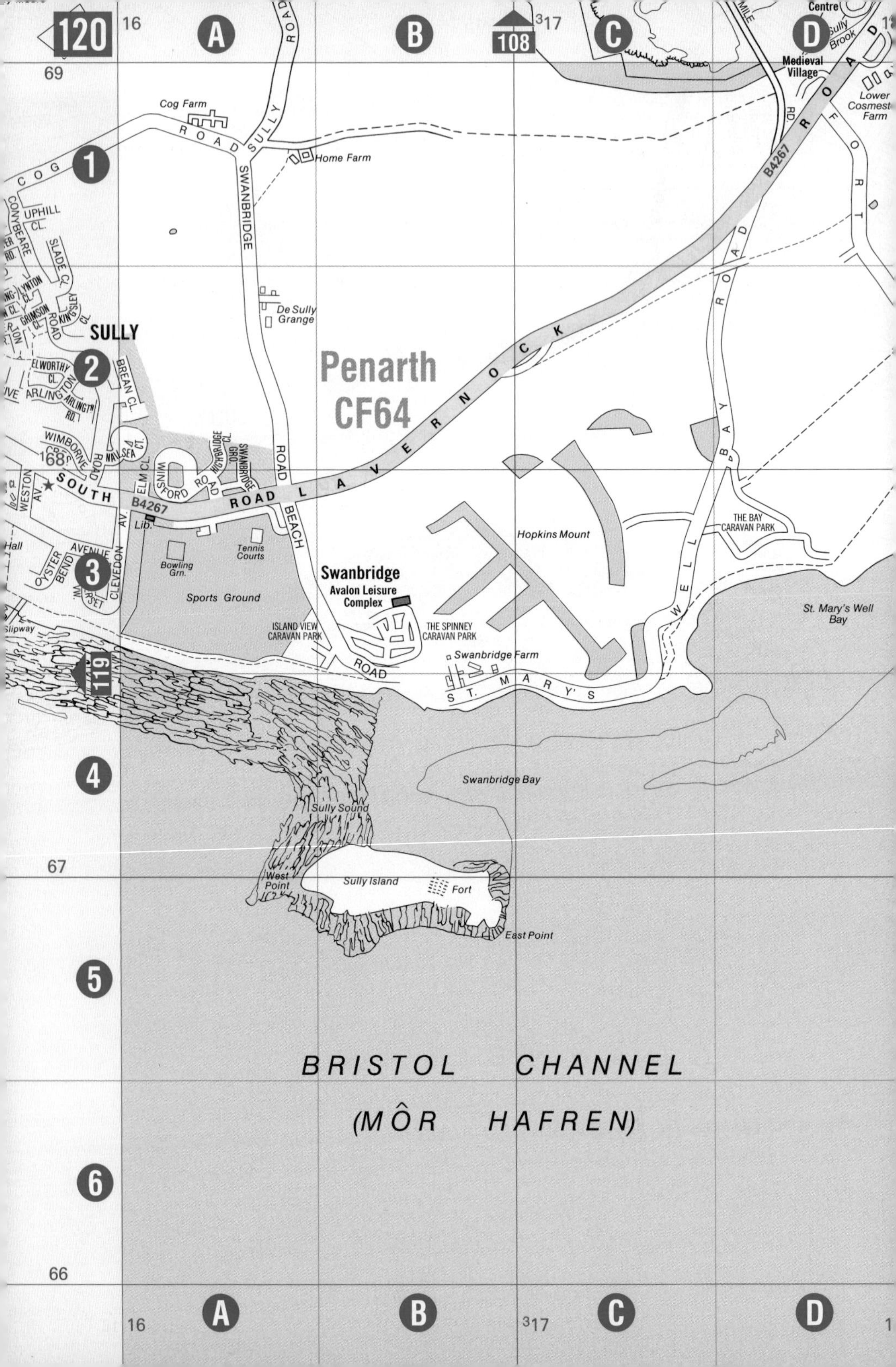

16
A
B
108
317
C
D
69
Centre
Sully Brook
Medieval Village
Lower Cosmeston Farm
Cog Farm
COG ROAD
SULLY ROAD
Home Farm
SWANBRIDGE ROAD
B4267
FORD ROAD
1
CONYBEARE
UPHILL CL.
SLADE CL.
LYNTON CL.
GRIMSON CL.
ROAD
KINGSLEY CL.
SULLY
De Sully Grange
Penarth CF64
LAVERNOCK ROAD
2
ELWORTHY CL.
ARLINGTON
ARLINGTN RD.
BREAN CL.
WIMBORNE CRES.
168
SEA CT.
HIGHBRIDGE CL.
SWANBRIDGE GRO.
WINSFORD ROAD
ELM CL.
WESTON AV.
SOUTH ROAD
B4267
Lib.
BEACH ROAD
BAY ROAD
Hall
AVENUE
OYSTER BEND
3
CLEVEDON AV.
Bowling Grn.
Tennis Courts
Sports Ground
Swanbridge
Avalon Leisure Complex
Hopkins Mount
THE BAY CARAVAN PARK
ST. MARY'S WELL BAY ROAD
St. Mary's Well Bay
Slipway
119
ISLAND VIEW CARAVAN PARK
THE SPINNEY CARAVAN PARK
Swanbridge Farm
ROAD
4
Swanbridge Bay
Sully Sound
67
West Point
Sully Island
Fort
East Point
5
BRISTOL CHANNEL
(MÔR HAFREN)
6
66
A
16
B
317
C
D
1

INDEX

Including Streets, Places & Areas, Hospitals & Hospices, Industrial Estates, Selected Flats & Walkways, Stations and Selected Places of Interest.

HOW TO USE THIS INDEX

1. Each street name is followed by its Postcode District and then by its Locality abbreviation(s) and then by its map reference; e.g. **Aberfawr Rd.** CF83: Abert . . . .2E **27** is in the CF83 Postcode District and the Abertridwr Locality and is to be found in square 2E on page **27**. The page number is shown in bold type.
2. A strict alphabetical order is followed in which Av., Rd., St., etc. (though abbreviated) are read in full and as part of the street name; e.g. **Ash Cl.** appears after **Ashchurch Row** but before **Ashcroft Cres.**
3. Streets and a selection of flats and walkways too small to be shown on the maps, appear in the index with the thoroughfare to which it is connected shown in brackets; e.g. **Alexandra Ct.** *NP20: Newp . . . .1D* ***54*** *(off Alexandra Rd.)*
4. Addresses that are in more than one part are referred to as not continuous.
5. Places and areas are shown in the index in **BLUE TYPE** and the map reference is to the actual map square in which the town centre or area is located and not to the place name shown on the map; e.g. **ABERTRIDWR 2E 27**
6. An example of a selected place of interest is **Bishops Castle 6D 84**
7. An example of a station is **Aber Station (Rail) 1B 46**
8. An example of a hospital or hospice is **BARRY HOSPITAL, THE 6F 105**
9. Map references for entries that appear on large scale pages **4-5** are shown first, with small scale references shown in brackets; e.g. **Adams Ct.** CF24: Card 4G **5** (4C **96**)

MYNEGAI

Yn cynnwys Strydoedd, Lleoedd ac Ardaloedd, Ysbytai a Hosbisys, Stadau Diwydiannol, Fflatiau a Llwybrau Troed dethol, Gorsafoedd a Detholiad o Fannau Diddorol.

SUD I DDEFNYDDIO'R MYNEGAI HWN

1. Dilynir pob enw stryd gan ei Ardal Cod Post ac wedyn gan fyrfodd(au) ei Leoliad ac wedyn gan ei gyfeirnod map; e.e. Mae **Aberfawr Rd.** CF83: Abert . . . .2E **27** yn Ardal Cod Post CF83 a Lleoliad Abertridwr a gellir dod o hyd iddi yn sgwâr 2E ar dudalen **27**. Dangosir Rhif y Dudalen mewn teip trwm.
2. Glynir yn gaeth wrth drefn y wyddor, gyda Av., Rd., St., ayb (er eu bod wedi eu talfyrru) yn cael eu darllen yn llawn ac fel rhan o enw'r stryd; e.e. mae **Ash Cl.** yn ymddangos ar ôl **Ashchurch Row** ond cyn **Ashcroft Cres**
3. Mae strydoedd a detholiad o fflatiau a llwybrau troed sy'n rhy fychan i'w dangos ar y mapiau, yn ymddangos yn y mynegai gyda'r dramwyfa y mae'n gysylltiedig â hi wedi'i dangos mewn cromfachau; e.e. **Alexandra Ct.** *NP20: Newp . . . .1D* ***54*** *(off Alexandra Rd.)*
4. Cyfeirir at gyfeiriadau sydd mewn mwy nag un rhan fel cyfeiriadau nan ydynt yn barhaus.
5. Dangosir ardaloedd a lleoedd yn y mynegai mewn **TEIP GLAS** ac mae'r cyfeirnod map yn cyfeirio at y sgwâr ar y map lle mae lleoliad canol y dref neu'r ardal ac nid at yr enw lle a ddangosir ar y map; e.e. **ABERTRIDWR 2E 27**
6. Enghraifft o fan diddorol dethol yw **Bishops Castle 6D 84**
7. Enghraifft o orsaf yw **Aber Station (Rail) 1B 46**
8. Enghraifft o Ysbyty neu Hosbis yw **BARRY HOSPITAL, THE 6F 105**
9. Mae cyfeirnodau map ar gyfer cofnodion sy'n ymddangos ar dudalennau ar raddfa fawr **4-5** yn cael eu dangos gyntaf, gyda chyfeirnodau map ar raddfa fechan yn cael eu dangos mewn cromfachau; e.e. **Adams Ct.** CF24: Card 4G **5** (4C **96**)

GENERAL ABBREVIATIONS *Talfyriadau Cyffredinol*

App. : Approach
Arc. : Arcade
Av. : Avenue
Bri. : Bridge
Bldg. : Building
Bldgs. : Buildings
Bungs. : Bungalows
Bus. : Business
Cvn. : Caravan
Cen. : Centre
Chu. : Church
Circ. : Circle
Cl. : Close
Comn. : Common
Cnr. : Corner
Cotts. : Cottages
Ct. : Court
Cres. : Crescent
Cft. : Croft
Dr. : Drive
E. : East
Emb. : Embankment
Ent. : Enterprise
Est. : Estate
Fld. : Field
Flds. : Fields
Gdn. : Garden
Gdns. : Gardens
Gth. : Garth
Ga. : Gate
Gt. : Great
Grn. : Green
Gro. : Grove
Hgts. : Heights
Ho. : House
Ho's. : Houses
Ind. : Industrial
Info. : Information
Junc. : Junction
La. : Lane
Lit. : Little
Lwr. : Lower
Mnr. : Manor
Mans. : Mansions
Mkt. : Market
Mdw. : Meadow
Mdws. : Meadows
M. : Mews
Mt. : Mount
Mus. : Museum
Nth. : North
Pde. : Parade
Pk. : Park
Pas. : Passage
Pl. : Place
Pct. : Precinct
Ri. : Rise
Rd. : Road
Rdbt. : Roundabout
Shop. : Shopping
Sth. : South
Sq. : Square
St. : Street
Ter. : Terrace
Trad. : Trading
Up. : Upper
Va. : Vale
Vw. : View
Vs. : Villas
Vis. : Visitors
Wlk. : Walk
W. : West
Yd. : Yard

LOCALITY ABBREVIATIONS *Byrfoddau Lleoliadau*

A'thin : **Aberthin**
Abert : **Abertridwr**
Barry : **Barry**
Bass : **Bassaleg**
B'ly : **Beachley**
Bed : **Beddau**

B'ws : **Bedwas**
Bet : **Bettws**
Bov : **Boverton**
Bul : **Bulwark**
C'ln : **Caerleon**
Caer : **Caerphilly**
C'went : **Caer-went**
Cald : **Caldicot**
Card : **Cardiff**
Cas : **Castleton**
Chep : **Chepstow**
Chu V : **Church Village**
C'fydd : **Cilfynydd**
Coedk : **Coedkernew**
C'bri : **Cowbridge**
Cre : **Creigiau**
C'iog : **Croesyceiliog**
C Inn : **Cross Inn**
C'keys : **Crosskeys**
C'avn : **Cwmavon**
C'brn : **Cwmbran**
C'crn : **Cwmcarn**
Cyn : **Cyncoed**
Din P : **Dinas Powys**
Duf : **Duffryn**
E Isaf : **Efail Isaf**
Ely : **Ely**
F'wtr : **Fairwater**
Glas : **Glascoed**
Glyn : **Glyncoch**
G'mdw : **Greenmeadow**
Grif : **Griffithstown**
Groes F : **Groes-Faen**
Gwae G : **Gwaelod-y-garth**
Heath : **Heath**
H'lys : **Henllys**
Hens : **Hensol**
L'stne : **Langstone**
L'vne : **Lisvane**
Lit M : **Little Mill**
L'thian : **Llanblethian**
L'brad : **Llanbradach**
L'dff : **Llandaff**
Llan N : **Llandaff North**
L'dgh : **Llandough**
L'dyrn : **Llanedeyrn**
Llanf : **Llanfrechfa**
L'harry : **Llanharry**
L'shn : **Llanishen**
L'maes : **Llanmaes**
L'rmy : **Llanrumney**
L'sant : **Llantrisant**
Llan F : **Llantwit Fardre**
Llan M : **Llantwit Major**
L'wrn : **Llanwern**
Llan : **Llanyravon**
Lwr M : **Lower Machen**
Mac : **Machen**
Magor : **Magor**
Malp : **Malpas**
M'fld : **Marshfield**
Math : **Mathern**
Mic P : **Michaelston-le-Pit**
Morg : **Morganstown**
N'grw : **Nantgarw**
New I : **New Inn**
Newp : **Newport**
Oakf : **Oakfield**
P'rth : **Penarth**
P'rch : **Pentyrch**
P'cae : **Penycoedcae**
Pen L : **Pen-y-Lan**
Pet W : **Peterstone Wentlooge**
P'hir : **Ponthir**
Pnwd : **Pontnewydd**
P'nydd : **Pontnewynydd**
Pontp : **Pontprennau**
P'clun : **Pontyclun**
P'pool : **Pontypool**
P'prdd : **Pontypridd**
P'waun : **Pontywaun**
Pskwt : **Portskewett**
Pwllm : **Pwllmeyric**
Rad : **Radyr**
Rhiw : **Rhiwbina**
R'drn : **Rhiwderin**
Rho : **Rhoose**
R'fln : **Rhydyfelin**
Ris : **Risca**
Roger : **Rogerstone**
Rog : **Rogiet**
Rud : **Rudry**
Rum : **Rumney**
St A : **St Athan**
St Brid : **St Bride's-super-Ely**
St Bri : **St Bride's Wentlooge**
St F : **St Fagans**
St G : **St George's-super-Ely**
St H : **St Hilary**
St M : **St Mellons**
St N : **St Nicholas**
Sed : **Sedbury**
Sen : **Senghenydd**
Sud : **Sudbrook**
Sul : **Sully**
Taff W : **Taff's Well**
T Grn : **Talbot Green**
Thorn : **Thornhill**
Tong : **Tongwynlais**
Tont : **Tonteg**
T'fail : **Tonyrefail**
T'rest : **Treforest**
Tret : **Trethomas**
Tut : **Tutshill**
Under : **Underwood**
Undy : **Undy**
Up Bo : **Upper Boat**
Up Cwm : **Upper Cwmbran**
Up R : **Upper Race**
Wen : **Wenvoe**
Whit : **Whitchurch**
Y'bwl : **Ynysybwl**

1st The Queen's Dragoon Guards Regimental Mus. . . . 3C 4 (3A 96)

A

Abbey Cl. CF15: Taff W . . . 1F **69**
Abbey Ct. CF38: Chu V . . . 2E **43**
Abbey Farm La. NP44: Oakf . . . 6B **12**
Abbey Grn. NP44: Oakf . . . 5H **11**
Abbey Gro. NP44: Oakf . . . 1B **20**
Abbey Rd. NP19: Newp . . . 3B **38**
NP44: C'brn . . . 3G **11**
Abbots M. NP20: Newp . . . 6B **36**
Aberaeron Cl. CF63: Barry . . . 5A **106**
Aberbran Rd. CF14: Llan N . . . 5E **85**
Abercynon Rd. CF37: Glyn . . . 1D **14**
Abercynon St. CF11: Card . . . 1A **102**
Aberdaron Rd. CF3: Rum . . . 2B **88**
Aberdore Rd. CF14: Llan N . . . 5E **85**
Aberdovey Cl. CF64: Din P . . . 2A **108**
Aberdovey St. CF24: Card . . . 4E **97**
Aberdulais Cres. CF14: Llan N . . . 5D **84**
Aberdulais Rd. CF14: Llan N . . . 5D **84**
Aberfawr Rd. CF83: Abert . . . 2E **27**
Aberfawr Ter. CF83: Abert . . . 2E **27**
Abergele Cl. CF3: Rum . . . 1C **88**
Abergele Rd. CF3: Rum . . . 2B **88**
Abernethy Cl. CF3: St M . . . 6E **75**
Aberporth Rd. CF14: Llan N . . . 4D **84**
Aber Station (Rail) . . . 1B **46**
Aber St. CF11: Card . . . 1A **102**
Aberteifi Cl. CF14: Llan N . . . 5E **85**
Aberteifi Cres. CF14: Llan N . . . 5E **85**
Aberthaw Av. NP19: Newp . . . 5B **38**
Aberthaw Circ. NP19: Newp . . . 5H **37**
Aberthaw Cl. NP19: Newp . . . 4A **38**
Aberthaw Dr. NP19: Newp . . . 5H **37**
Aberthaw Rd. CF5: Ely . . . 4G **93**
NP19: Newp . . . 4H **37**
ABERTHIN . . . 2F **91**
Aberthin Rd. CF71: A'thin, C'bri . . . 4D **90**
Aberth La. CF71: C'bri . . . 4F **91**
ABERTRIDWR . . . 2E **27**
Aberystwyth Cres. CF62: Barry . . . 3G **117**
Aberystwyth St. CF24: Card . . . 4E **97**
Abingdon St. CF63: Barry . . . 6B **106**
Acacia Av. NP19: Newp . . . 4H **37**
NP26: Undy . . . 3E **59**
Acacia Sq. NP19: Newp . . . 4H **37**
Acacia St. CF37: R'fln . . . 4G **25**
Academic Av. CF14: Heath . . . 4G **85**
Acer Av. CF38: Llan F . . . 6C **42**
Acer Way NP10: Roger . . . 3A **34**
Acorn Cl. CF72: P'clun . . . 6F **65**
NP10: Roger . . . 2B **34**
Acorn Gro. CF23: Pontp . . . 4G **73**
CF38: Chu V . . . 3E **43**
Acorns, The CF14: Thorn . . . 2G **71**
Adams Ct. CF24: Card . . . 4G **5** (4C **96**)
Adamscroft Pl. CF24: Card . . . 4G **5** (4C **96**)
ADAMSDOWN . . . 4H **5** (4C **96**)
Adamsdown La. CF24: Card . . . 4H **5** (4C **96**)
Adamsdown Pl. CF24: Card . . . 4H **5** (4D **96**)
Adamsdown Sq. CF24: Card . . . 4H **5** (4C **96**)
Adam St. CF24: Card . . . 5F **5** (4B **96**)
Adar y Mor CF62: Barry . . . 5H **117**
Addison Av. CF72: L'harry . . . 5A **78**
Addison Cres. CF5: Ely . . . 4G **93**
Addison Way CF83: Mac, Tret . . . 3B **30**
Adelaide Pl. CF10: Card . . . 1B **102**
Adelaide St. CF10: Card . . . 1B **102**
NP20: Newp . . . 2C **36**
Adeline St. CF24: Card . . . 3D **96**
NP20: Newp . . . 1C **54**
Adenfield Way CF62: Rho . . . 5B **114**
Adit Wlk. NP44: Pnwd . . . 6C **8**
(not continuous)
Admiral Ho. CF24: Card . . . 2G **5**
Adrian Boult Grn. NP19: Newp . . . 5A **38**
Adventurer's Quay CF10: Card . . . 1D **102**
Aelfryn CF72: L'harry . . . 5A **78**
Aelybryn CF37: P'prdd . . . 5A **14**
Ael-y-Bryn CF15: P'rch . . . 5H **67**
CF15: Rad . . . 6F **69**
CF23: L'dyrn . . . 3D **86**
CF38: Bed . . . 4A **42**
CF83: Caer . . . 4A **28**
CF83: Tret . . . 3H **29**
Ael-y-Coed CF62: Barry . . . 2D **116**
Aeron Cl. CF62: Barry . . . 2F **117**
Afal Sur CF63: Barry . . . 4B **106**
Afan Cl. CF62: Barry . . . 2F **117**
Afon Cl. CF3: St M . . . 1B **74**
NP4: New I . . . 6G **7**
Afon Ebbw Rd. NP10: Roger . . . 2G **33**
Afon Gdns. NP18: P'hir . . . 2G **21**
Afon Lwyd Cl. NP18: C'ln . . . 4A **22**
Afon Mead NP10: Roger . . . 3H **33**
Afon Ter. NP44: C'iog . . . 6F **9**
Africa Gdns. CF14: Card . . . 5G **85**
Agate St. CF24: Card . . . 3D **96**
Agincourt Rd. CF23: Pen L . . . 1D **96**
Agincourt St. NP20: Newp . . . 2B **36**
Agnes St. CF64: P'rth . . . 6G **101**
Aidens Ri. CF63: Barry . . . 1C **118**
Ailesbury St. NP20: Newp . . . 2C **36**
Ainon Ct. CF24: Card . . . 4E **97**
Aintree Dr. CF5: Ely . . . 4B **94**
Airport Bus. Pk. CF62: Rho . . . 3G **115**
Alanbrooke Av. NP20: Malp . . . 3A **20**
Alan Cl. NP10: Roger . . . 5D **34**
Albany Ct. CF64: P'rth . . . 1F **109**
Albany Ind. Est. NP20: Newp . . . 2C **36**
Albany Rd. CF24: Card . . . 1B **96**
Albany St. NP20: Newp . . . 2C **36**
Albany Trad. Est. NP20: Newp . . . 2C **36**
Alberta Pl. CF64: P'rth . . . 3E **109**
Alberta Rd. CF64: P'rth . . . 3F **109**
Albert Av. NP19: Newp . . . 4E **37**
Albert Ct. NP19: Newp . . . 4E **37**
Albert Cres. CF64: P'rth . . . 1F **109**
Albert Rd. CF37: P'prdd . . . 1B **24**
CF64: P'rth . . . 1F **109**
Albert St. CF11: Card . . . 3F **95**
(Cowbridge Rd. E.)
CF11: Card . . . 4F **95**
(Wellington St.)
CF63: Barry . . . 1C **118**
NP20: Newp . . . 6C **36**
Albert St. La. CF11: Card . . . 4F **95**
Albert Ter. NP20: Newp . . . 5B **36**
Albert Wlk. CF11: Card . . . 4F **95**
Albion Cl. NP20: Newp . . . 1D **54**
Albion Ct. CF37: C'fydd . . . 4F **15**
NP20: Newp . . . 1C **54**
Albion Ho. NP26: Cald . . . 5C **60**
Albion Ind. Est. CF37: C'fydd . . . 1F **15**
Albion Pl. NP4: P'nydd . . . 1A **6**
Albion Rd. NP4: P'pool . . . 4B **6**
Albion Sq. NP16: Chep . . . 2E **63**
Albion St. NP20: Newp . . . 1C **54**
Albion Way NP26: Magor . . . 4C **58**
Alcock Cl. NP19: Newp . . . 6G **37**
Alcove Wood NP16: Chep . . . 2C **62**
Alderbrook CF23: L'vne . . . 4D **72**
Alder Cl. NP4: New I . . . 4H **7**
Alder Gro. CF38: Llan F . . . 6C **42**
NP20: Malp . . . 5B **20**
Alderney St. NP20: Newp . . . 2C **36**
Alder Rd. CF23: Card . . . 5B **86**
CF72: L'harry . . . 5A **78**
Alders, The NP44: Llan . . . 4B **12**
Alderwood Cl. CF3: St M . . . 6C **74**
Aldsworth Rd. CF5: Card, F'wtr . . . 2B **94**
Aldwych Cl. CF14: Thorn . . . 3G **71**

Aled Way CF62: St A .2C **112**
Alexander Ct. CF83: Caer .6E **29**
Alexander St. CF24: Card .1A **96**
Alexandra Ct. CF5: Card .3D **94**
CF64: P'rth .2F **109**
NP20: Newp .1D 54
(off Alexandra Rd.)
Alexandra Cres. CF62: Barry .2F **117**
Alexandra Ind. Est. CF3: Rum .4B **88**
Alexandra La. NP20: Newp .2C **54**
Alexandra Rd. CF5: Card .4E **95**
CF37: T'rest .1D **24**
NP4: Grif .2E **9**
NP16: Bul .4F **63**
NP20: Newp .2C **54**
Alexandra Ter. CF38: Llan F .5C **42**
Alfreda Rd. CF14: Whit .3B **84**
Alfred's Ter. CF15: Taff W .2E **69**
Alfred St. CF24: Card .6B **86**
NP19: Newp .3D **36**
Alianore Rd. NP26: Cald .6C **60**
Alice Cres. NP16: Bul .6G **63**
Alice St. CF10: Card .1B **102**
NP20: Newp .2C **54**
Allan Durst Cl. CF5: L'dff .4H **83**
Allen Cl. CF3: St M .5C **74**
NP20: Bet .6E **19**
Allen Ct. CF71: Bov .3D **110**
Allensbank Cres. CF14: Card .5H **85**
Allensbank Ho. CF14: Card .4H **85**
Allensbank Rd. CF14: Card, Heath .5H **85**
Allens Ct. CF23: Cyn .1C **86**
Allerton St. CF11: Card .6A **4** (5G **95**)
Alltmawr Rd. CF23: Cyn .1C **86**
Allt Wen CF14: Rhiw .5B **70**
ALLT-YR-YN .4H **35**
Allt-yr-yn Av. NP20: Newp .4G **35**
Allt-yr-yn Cl. NP20: Newp .3A **36**
Allt-yr-yn Ct. NP20: Newp .3A **36**
Allt-yr-yn Cres. NP20: Newp .2A **36**
Allt-yr-yn Hgts. NP20: Newp .3H **35**
Allt-yr-yn Nature Reserve .3H **35**
Allt-yr-yn Rd. NP20: Newp .3H **35**
Allt-yr-yn Vw. NP20: Newp .4G **35**
Allt-yr-yn Way NP20: Newp .2A **36**
Allt y Wennol CF23: Pontp .4F **73**
Allt y Wiwer CF38: Chu V .3E **43**
Alma Cl. NP20: Newp .6C **36**
Alma Dr. NP16: Bul .6G **63**
Alma Pl. NP4: Grif .2E **9**
Alma Rd. CF23: Pen L .6C **86**
Alma St. CF83: Mac .2G **31**
NP20: Newp .6C **36**
Alma Ter. CF38: Chu V .3F **43**
Almond Av. NP11: Ris .5F **17**
Almond Cl. CF38: Llan F .5C **42**
Almond Dr. CF23: Pontp .4F **73**
NP20: Malp .4A **20**
Alpha Pl. CF37: P'prdd .5D **14**
Alpha Rd. NP16: Bul .4F **63**
Alpha St. CF37: P'prdd .5D **14**
Alps Quarry Rd. CF5: Wen .3E **99**
Altair Ho. CF10: Card .1D **102**
Althorp Dr. CF64: P'rth .6E **109**
Altolusso CF10: Card .5E **5** (4B **96**)
Alton Ter. *NP4: P'pool .2B 6*
(off Pontypool Western By-Pass)
ALWAY .5B **38**
Alway Cl. NP19: Newp .4B **38**
Alway Cres. NP19: Newp .4A **38**
Alway Pde. NP19: Newp .5B **38**
Alwen Dr. CF14: Thorn .2H **71**
CF62: Barry .2E **117**
Alwyn Cl. NP10: Roger .2C **34**
Amalfi Ho. *CF10: Card .6C 96*
(off Ffordd Garthorne)
Amber Cl. CF23: Pontp .4F **73**
Ambergate Dr. CF23: Pontp .5F **73**
Amberheart Dr. CF14: Thorn .2H **71**
Amberley Cl. CF23: Pontp .5F **73**
Amberwood Cl. CF23: Pontp .4F **73**
Amblecote Cl. CF23: Pontp .4F **73**
Ambleside Av. CF23: Cyn .5A **86**
Ambrooke Cl. CF23: Pontp .4F **73**
Ambrose Wlk. NP4: New I .5G **7**
Ambryn Rd. NP4: New I .5H **7**
American Vs. NP11: Ris .4D **16**
Amesbury Rd. CF23: Pen L .6D **86**
Amethyst Rd. CF5: F'wtr .6H **83**
Amherst Cres. CF62: Barry .5G **117**
Amherst St. CF11: Card .1H **101**
Amity Ct. CF10: Card .6C **96**
Amroth Ct. CF62: Barry .6H **105**
Amroth Rd. CF5: Ely .4H **93**
Amroth Wlk. NP44: G'mdw .3E **11**
Amyas Cl. CF11: Card .6G **95**
Amy Johnson Cl. NP19: Newp .6G **37**
Anchor Ct. CF10: Card .6F **5** (5B **96**)
Anchor Ind. Est. CF10: Card .6B **96**
Anchor Rd. CF64: P'rth .5A **102**
Anchor St. CF15: Taff W .2E **69**
Anchor Way CF64: P'rth .5H **101**
Anderson Cl. NP20: Newp .6A **36**
Anderson Pl. CF24: Card .3D **96**
NP20: Malp .3A **20**
Andover Cl. CF62: Barry .6D **104**
Andrew Rd. CF64: P'rth .6F **101**
Andrews Ct. CF71: Bov .3C **110**
Andrew's Rd. CF14: Llan N .5B **84**
Aneurin Bevan Ct. NP4: P'pool .3C **6**
NP10: Duf .4G **53**
Aneurin Bevan Dr.
CF38: Chu V .3D **42**
Aneurin Rd. CF63: Barry .1A **118**
Angelica Way CF14: Thorn .2F **71**
Angelina St. CF10: Card .6B **96**
Angiddy Cl. NP26: Cald .4D **60**
Angle Cl. CF62: Barry .5H **105**
Angle Pl. CF14: L'shn .4F **71**
Anglesey Cl. CF38: Tont .1G **43**
CF71: Bov .2D **110**
Anglesey Ct. NP18: C'ln .4F **21**
Anglesey St. CF5: Card .3E **95**
Angus St. CF24: Card .6C **86**
Anisa M. NP20: Newp .5C **36**
Annesley Rd. NP19: Newp .3E **37**
Anne St. CF11: Card .4F **95**
Ann St. CF37: C'fydd .2F **15**
Ansari Ct. CF72: L'sant .6D **40**
Anson Ct. CF10: Card .6G **5**
Anson Grn. NP19: Newp .2C **38**
Anstee Ct. CF11: Card .4F **95**
Anthony Dr. NP18: C'ln .4F **21**
Anton Ct. CF14: Whit .2C **84**
Anwyll Cl. NP18: C'ln .3G **21**
Apollo Cl. CF14: Thorn .3G **71**
Apple Av. NP26: Undy .4F **59**
Appledore Rd. CF14: Llan N .4E **85**
Appletree Cl. CF72: L'harry .5A **78**
Applewood Cl. CF24: Card .5H **5** (4D **96**)
Apprentice Cl. NP16: B'ly .6H **63**
Aprilla Ho. CF10: Card .6C **96**
Aquila Ho. CF10: Card .1D **102**
Aquilla Ct. CF11: Card .2F **95**
Arabella St. CF24: Card .6B **86**
Aragon Ho. NP20: Newp .4A **36**
Aragon St. NP20: Newp .2C **36**
Aran Ct. NP44: G'mdw .6B **8**
Arbroath Ct. CF24: Card .2F **97**
Arcade CF37: P'prdd .6C **14**
Arcade, The NP44: C'brn .2H **11**
Archer Ct. CF62: Barry .5H **117**
Archer Cres. CF5: Ely .3H **93**
Archer Pl. CF5: Ely .3G **93**
CF64: P'rth .2E **109**
Archer Rd. CF5: Ely .3F **93**
CF62: Barry .4H **117**
CF64: P'rth .2D **108**
NP44: G'mdw .2D **10**
Archer Ter. CF5: Ely .3H **93**
CF64: P'rth .3E **109**
Arch Hill NP11: P'waun .1A **16**
Archibald St. NP19: Newp .4E **37**
Arcot La. CF64: P'rth .1E **109**
Arcot La. Nth. CF64: P'rth .6A **102**
Arcot St. CF64: P'rth .6A **102**
ARD Bus. Pk. NP4: New I .5F **7**
Arden Way CF63: Barry .6C **106**
Ardwyn CF14: Rhiw .5B **70**
Arfonfab Cres. CF37: R'fln .5H **25**
Argae La. CF63: Barry .5D **106**
CF64: Barry, Din P .2C **106**
Argosy Way NP19: Newp .5E **37**
Argyle Ct. CF15: Rad .6F **69**
Argyle St. NP20: Newp .2C **36**
Argyle Way CF5: Ely .5A **94**
Arles Rd. CF5: Ely .4A **94**
Arlington Cl. NP20: Malp .3A **20**
NP26: Undy .4F **59**
Arlington Ct. NP16: Sed .2H **63**
Arlington Cres. CF3: L'rmy .1A **88**
Arlington Rd. CF64: Sul .2H **119**
Armoury Dr. CF14: Heath .1F **85**
Armstrong Cl. NP19: Newp .5H **37**
Arne Cl. NP19: Newp .4C **38**
Arnold Av. CF3: L'rmy .5A **74**
Arnold Cl. NP20: Newp .1H **53**
Arno Rd. CF63: Barry .1C **118**
Arnside Rd. CF23: Pen L .5C **86**
Arran Cl. CF37: P'cae .3B **24**
NP11: Ris .6G **17**
Arran Pl. CF24: Card .1C **96**
Arran St. CF24: Card .2B **96**
(not continuous)
Arrol St. CF24: Card .4D **96**
Arthur Bliss Rd. NP19: Newp .5A **38**
Arthur Cl. NP20: Newp .1C **54**
Arthur Davis Ct. CF62: Barry .1H **117**
Arthurs Ct. NP26: Pskwt .5F **61**
Arthur St. CF24: Card .2E **97**
CF63: Barry .1D **118**
NP18: C'ln .5A **22**
NP20: Newp .1C **54**
Artillery Pl. NP19: Newp .4C **36**
Arundel Cl. NP44: G'mdw .2C **10**
Arundel Pl. CF11: Card .1F **101**
Arundel Rd. NP19: Newp .4F **37**
Ar-y-Nant CF63: Barry .5A **106**
Ascot Cl. CF5: Ely .4A **94**
Asgog St. CF24: Card .4D **96**
Ashburton Av. CF3: L'rmy .6A **74**
Ashby Rd. CF64: Sul .1G **119**
Ashchurch Cl. CF14: Whit .2C **84**
Ashchurch Row CF14: Whit .2C **84**
Ash Cl. NP16: Bul .5E **63**
Ashcroft Cres. CF5: F'wtr .6F **83**
Ashdene Cl. CF5: F'wtr .5H **83**
Ashdown Cl. CF3: St M .6D **74**
Ashdown Ct. CF37: C'fydd .3F **15**
Ashfield Cl. CF37: Glyn .2C **14**
Ashfield Ct. CF3: St M .6C **74**
Ashford Cl. NP44: C'iog .6H **9**
Ashford Cl. Nth. NP44: C'iog .6H **9**
Ashford Cl. Sth. NP44: C'iog .1B **12**
Ash Grn. NP44: Oakf .5H **11**
Ash Gro. CF5: Ely .1E **99**
CF14: Whit .1C **84**
CF63: Barry .6C **106**
CF64: L'dgh .5G **101**
CF72: L'harry .5A **78**
CF72: P'clun .5B **64**
NP4: C'avn .1D **6**
NP26: Cald .4C **60**
Ashgrove CF37: Glyn .1D **14**
CF64: Din P .3H **107**
CF71: Llan M .3B **110**
CF83: Tret .3H **29**
Ashgrove Cl. NP4: Grif .2D **8**
Ash La. CF62: St A .2B **112**
Ashleigh Ct. NP44: H'lys .4B **10**
Ashley Rd. NP19: Newp .4H **37**
Ashman Cl. CF83: Caer .2H **45**
Ash Pl. CF5: F'wtr .1H **93**
Ash Sq. CF37: R'fln .4G **25**
Ash Tree Cl. CF15: Rad .1E **83**
Ash Wlk. CF72: T Grn .3E **65**
Ashwell NP18: C'ln .1A **38**
Ashwood Ct. CF24: Card .1H **5** (2C **96**)
Aspen Cl. CF3: St M .6C **74**
Aspen Way CF38: Llan F .6C **42**
NP20: Malp .4A **20**
(not continuous)
Asquith St. NP4: Grif .6E **7**
Assembly at the Pierhead, The .2C **102**
Aster Cl. CF3: St M .6E **75**
NP11: Ris .5F **17**
Aston Cres. NP20: Newp .1B **36**
Aston Pl. CF3: St M .2E **89**
Astoria Cl. CF14: Thorn .3G **71**
Athelstan Rd. CF14: Whit .3B **84**
Atlantic Cres. CF63: Barry .4B **118**
Atlantic Pl. CF63: Barry .6C **106**
Atlantic Trad. Est. CF63: Barry .4C **118**
Atlantic Way CF63: Barry .4A **118**
ATLANTIC WHARF .6G **5** (5C **96**)
Atlantic Wharf Cl. CF10: Card .6G **5** (5C **96**)
Atlas Ho. CF10: Card .1D **102**
Atlas Pl. CF5: Card .4F **95**
Atlas Rd. CF5: Card .4F **95**
Attfield Cl. CF23: Pen L .6E **87**
Attlee Ct. CF83: Caer .6E **29**
Aubrey Av. CF5: Card .2C **94**
Aubrey Hames Cl. NP20: Newp .1A **54**
Aubrey Ter. CF71: C'bri .4D **90**
Auckland Rd. NP20: Newp .6F **35**
Augusta Cres. CF64: P'rth .4E **109**
Augustan Cl. NP18: C'ln .4F **21**
Augustan Dr. NP18: C'ln .4F **21**
Augustan Way NP18: C'ln .4F **21**
Augusta Rd. CF64: P'rth .4E **109**
Augusta St. CF24: Card .3H **5** (3C **96**)
Augustus John Cl. NP19: Newp .1G **37**
Aust Cres. NP16: Bul .5E **63**
Austen Cl. CF3: L'rmy .5B **74**
Austin Friars NP20: Newp .4C **36**
Austin Rd. NP4: Grif .2E **9**
Australia Rd. CF14: Card .5G **85**
Avalon Cl. NP4: P'pool .3B **6**

Avalon Dr. NP19: Newp 2F **37**
Avalon Leisure Complex 3B **120**
Avenue, The CF3: Rum 5A **88**
CF5: L'dff 6C **84**
CF14: Whit 3B **84**
CF37: P'prdd 6D **14**
CF83: Tret 3A **30**
NP4: Grif 1E **9**
NP4: New I 4F **7**
NP10: Coedk 4E **53**
*NP20: Newp 6C **36***
(off Clytha Sq.)
NP26: Cald 6B **60**
Avenue Ind. Pk., The CF23: Pontp 5G **73**
Avoca Pl. CF11: Card 6G **95**
Avocet Ct. CF63: Barry 2A **118**
Avon Cl. CF63: Barry 6C **106**
NP20: Bet 5G **19**
NP26: Cald 4C **60**
Avondale Bus. Pk. NP44: Pnwd 5E **9**
Avondale Cl. NP44: Pnwd 5F **9**
Avondale Cres. CF11: Card 1A **102**
NP44: Pnwd 4F **9**
Avondale Gdns. CF11: Card 1A **102**
Avondale Gdns. Sth. CF11: Card 1A **102**
Avondale Rd. CF11: Card 1A **102**
NP4: Grif, Pnwd 3F **9**
NP44: Pnwd 3F **9**
Avondale Way NP44: Pnwd 4F **9**
Avonmuir Rd. CF24: Card 1F **97**
Avon Pl. NP44: Llan 2A **12**
Avonridge CF14: Thorn 3F **71**
Awbery Ho. CF62: Barry 1F **117**
Awelfryn CF37: P'cae 6A **24**
Awel Mor CF23: L'dyrn 4D **86**
Axbridge Cres. CF3: L'rmy 1B **88**
Axminster Rd. CF23: Pen L 1E **97**
Azalea Cl. CF23: L'dyrn 6D **72**
Azalea Rd. NP10: Roger 2G **33**

B

Baber Cl. CF23: Pen L 6E **87**
Back, The NP16: Chep 1F **63**
(not continuous)
Backhall St. NP18: C'ln 5A **22**
Bacon Pl. NP20: Malp 4A **20**
Bacton Ct. CF14: Llan N 5D **84**
Bacton Rd. CF14: Llan N 5D **84**
Baden Rd. CF24: Card 3G **97**
Bader Cl. CF14: L'shn 1H **85**
Badgers Dr. NP16: Chep 2D **62**
Badgers Mdw. NP16: Pwllm 4B **62**
NP18: P'hir 6F **13**
Badgers Mede NP44: G'mdw 2D **10**
Badgers Wlk. NP26: Undy 4E **59**
Badgers Wood Cl. NP10: Bass 1B **52**
Badham Cl. CF83: Caer 2H **45**
Badminton Rd. NP19: Newp 1F **37**
Badminton Vs. NP16: Chep 1F **63**
Bagley Ct. NP44: G'mdw 6B **8**
Bailey Cl. CF5: F'wtr .2A **94**
Bailey's Hay NP16: Math 6B **62**
Baileys Ter. *NP4: P'nydd 1A **6***
(off Hanbury Rd.)
Bailey St. NP20: Newp 4B **36**
Baird Cl. NP20: Malp 4H **19**
Baird Ri. CF62: Barry 2F **117**
Bakers Ct. CF3: M'fld 5A **76**
CF5: Card 2D **94**
Baker's La. CF71: Llan M 3A **110**
Bakers Row CF10: Card 4D **4** (4A **96**)
Bakers Wharf CF37: P'prdd 5D **14**
Bakery, The CF11: Card 6B **4** (5H **95**)
Bakery La. CF3: Cas .2H **75**
Balaclava Rd. CF23: Pen L 6C **86**
Bala Dr. NP10: Roger 2C **34**
Bala Rd. CF14: Llan N 5C **84**
Baldwin Cl. CF5: L'dff 3H **83**
NP20: Newp 1C **54**
Baldwin St. NP20: Newp 1C **54**
Balfe Rd. NP19: Newp 5B **38**
Ball Cl. CF3: L'rmy 6H **73**
Ball La. CF3: L'rmy 1G **87**
Ball Rd. CF3: L'rmy 1H **87**
Balmond Ter. NP4: P'pool 1B **6**
Balmoral Cl. CF14: L'vne 3B **72**
CF37: P'cae 3B **24**
Balmoral Ct. CF62: Barry 5E **105**
Balmoral La. NP19: Newp 5G **37**
Balmoral Rd. NP19: Newp 5G **37**
Baltic Ter. NP44: Oakf 6G **11**
Baltimore Cl. CF23: Pontp 3G **73**
Bampton Rd. CF3: L'rmy 6A **74**
Banastre Av. CF14: Card 5G **85**
Banc yr Afon CF15: Gwae G 2E **69**
Baneswell Courtyard NP20: Newp 5B **36**
Baneswell Rd. NP20: Newp 4B **36**
Bangor Ct. *CF24: Card 6C **86***
(off Bangor La.)
Bangor La. CF24: Card 6C **86**
Bangor St. CF24: Card 6C **86**
Bank La. NP19: Newp 1E **37**
Bankside NP19: Newp 5D **36**
Bankside Cl. CF14: Thorn 2H **71**
Bank Sq. NP16: Chep 2E **63**
Bank St. NP16: Chep .2E **63**
NP19: Newp 1D **36**
Bannatyne's Health Club 6D **36**
Bantock Cl. NP19: Newp 4C **38**
Banwell Ct. NP44: G'mdw 6B **8**
Banwell Pl. CF3: L'rmy 1A **88**
Barberry Ri. CF64: P'rth 6G **101**
Barbirolli Grn. NP19: Newp 5B **38**
Barbrook Cl. CF14: L'vne 3A **72**
Bardsey Cres. CF14: L'shn 4F **71**
Bardsy Cl. NP19: Newp 2F **37**
Bareland St. NP26: Magor 5A **58**
Bargoed St. CF11: Card 6A **96**
Barletta Ho. *CF10: Card 6B **96***
(off Vellacott Cl.)
Barmouth Rd. CF3: Rum 4H **87**
Barnard Av. CF5: Ely .3A **94**
Barnard St. NP19: Newp 3D **36**
Barnard Way CF38: Chu V 3D **42**
Barnets NP44: G'mdw 2D **10**
Barnets Wood NP16: Chep 2C **62**
Barnfield NP18: P'hir 2F **21**
Barnfield Cl. CF23: Pontp 4H **73**
Barnfield Dr. CF15: Morg 5E **69**
Barnfield Pl. NP44: Pnwd 5C **8**
Barnstaple Rd. CF3: L'rmy 1A **88**
Barnwood Cres. CF5: Ely 5D **92**
Baron Cl. CF64: P'rth 2D **108**
Baroness Pl. CF64: P'rth 2D **108**
Baron La. CF64: P'rth 1D **108**
Baron Rd. CF64: P'rth 2D **108**
Baron's Cl. CF71: Llan M 3B **110**
Barons Ct. NP26: Undy 4F **59**
Baron's Ct. Rd. CF23: Pen L 5D **86**
Barquentine Pl. CF10: Card 6C **96**
BARRACK HILL 2B **36**
Barrack Hill NP20: Newp 2A **36**
Barracks La. CF10: Card 4E **5** (4B **96**)
Barrenhill CF62: Rho 1C **114**
BARRI 3F **117**
Barrians Way CF62: Barry 2G **117**
Barrie Gdns. NP20: Newp 1G **53**
Barrington Rd. CF14: Whit 3D **84**
BARRY 3F **117**
BARRY DOCK 1A **118**
Barry Docks Link Rd.
CF63: Barry 3B **106**
Barry Docks Station (Rail) 3A **118**
BARRY HOSPITAL, THE 6F **105**
BARRY ISLAND 5H **117**
Barry Island Pleasure Pk. 5G **117**
Barry Island Station (Rail) 5G **117**
Barry La. CF10: Card 5D **4** (4A **96**)
Barry Leisure Cen. .3H **117**
Barry Rd. CF37: P'prdd 6A **14**
CF62: Barry 1G **117**
CF63: Barry 1G **117**
CF64: L'dgh 6F **101**
Barry Station (Rail) 4F **117**
Barry Town FC 1A **118**
Barry Wlk. NP10: Roger 3C **34**
Barthropp St. NP19: Newp 6G **37**
Bartlett St. CF83: Caer 1D **46**
Bartlett St. Ind. Est. CF83: Caer 1D **46**
Basil Pl. CF24: Card .1A **96**
BASSALEG 1D **52**
Bassaleg Cl. CF3: St M 6E **75**
Bassaleg Rd. NP20: Newp 6E **35**
Bassett Rd. CF64: Sul 2G **119**
Bassetts Fld. CF14: Rhiw, Thorn 2E **71**
Bassett St. CF5: Card 4E **95**
CF37: P'prdd 5D **14**
CF63: Barry 1B **118**
Bastian Cl. CF63: Barry 6B **106**
Batchelor Rd. CF14: Card 5E **85**
NP19: Newp 4F **37**
Bath Grn. NP44: Llanf 3B **12**
Bath St. NP19: Newp .3D **36**
Batten Way CF37: C'fydd 4F **15**
Bay Cvn. Pk., The CF64: Sul 3D **120**
Baylis Ct. CF5: Ely 3A **94**
Baynton Cl. CF5: L'dff 5A **84**
Bayside Rd. CF24: Card 4D **96**
Baytree Cl. NP18: C'ln 5E **21**
Beach La. CF64: P'rth 1F **109**
BEACHLEY 6H **63**
Beachley Rd. NP16: B'ly 4H **63**
NP16: Tut 1F **63**
Beach Rd. CF64: P'rth 1F **109**
CF64: Sul 3A **120**
NP10: St Bri 4H **77**
Beachway CF62: Barry 6D **116**
Beacons Cl. NP10: Roger 2C **34**
Beacon St. CF11: Card 2E **95**
Beale Cl. CF5: L'dff 5A **84**
Beatrice Rd. CF14: Whit 3D **84**
CF63: Barry 1B **118**
Beatty Av. CF23: Cyn .2A **86**
Beatty Cl. CF62: Barry 4A **106**
Beatty Ct. CF10: Card 6G **5** (5C **96**)
Beatty Rd. NP19: Newp 2D **38**
Beauchamp St. CF11: Card 5A **4** (4H **95**)
(not continuous)
Beaufort Cl. NP44: F'wtr 4E **11**
Beaufort Ct. CF10: Card 6G **5** (5C **96**)
CF72: C Inn 3G **65**
Beaufort Pk. NP16: Bul 6F **63**
Beaufort Pk. Way NP16: Bul 6F **63**
Beaufort Pl. NP16: Chep 2E **63**
NP19: Newp 1F **37**
Beaufort Rd. NP19: Newp 1F **37**
Beaufort Sq. CF23: Card 6F **87**
NP16: Chep 2E **63**
Beaufort Ter. NP20: Newp 5B **36**
Beaufort Way CF62: Rho 5C **114**
Beaumaris Cl. CF38: Tont 1F **43**
NP10: R'drn 6A **34**
Beaumaris Dr. NP44: Llan 3A **12**
Beaumaris Rd. CF3: Rum 4H **87**
Beaumont Cl. CF62: Barry 6D **104**
Beaumont Ct. CF64: P'rth 2D **108**
Beauville La. CF64: Din P 6H **99**
Beavers Wlk. NP10: Roger 5D **34**
Beck Ct. CF23: Pontp 3H **73**
Beckgrove Cl. CF24: Card 1G **97**
Beda Rd. CF5: Card 4E **95**
Bedavere Cl. CF14: Thorn 3G **71**
BEDDAU 4H **41**
Beddick NP44: G'mdw 2C **10**
Bedford Cl. NP44: G'mdw 2C **10**
Bedford Pl. CF24: Card 1G **5** (2C **96**)
Bedford Ri. CF71: Bov 3C **110**
Bedford Rd. NP19: Newp 4D **36**
Bedford St. CF24: Card 1F **5** (2B **96**)
(not continuous)
Bedlington Ter. CF62: Barry 2F **117**
BEDWAS 3G **29**
Bedwas Bus. Cen. CF83: B'ws 3F **29**
Bedwas Cen. CF83: B'ws 3G **29**
Bedwas Cl. CF3: St M 6E **75**
Bedwas Ho. Ind. Est. CF83: B'ws 3E **29**
(not continuous)
Bedwas Pl. CF64: P'rth 1D **108**
Bedwas Rd. CF83: Caer 6D **28**
(not continuous)
Bedwas St. CF11: Card 6G **95**
Bedw Rd. CF37: C'fydd 3F **15**
Beecham St. NP19: Newp 4B **38**
Beech Av. CF71: Llan M 5C **110**
Beech Cl. CF83: Caer 2H **45**
NP44: Pnwd 5D **8**
Beech Ct. CF15: Tong 3H **69**
Beechcroft Rd. NP19: Newp 3G **37**
Beechdale Rd. NP19: Newp 4G **37**
Beecher Av. CF11: Card 2H **101**
Beecher Ter. NP11: C'keys 2A **16**
Beeches, The CF14: L'vne 2A **72**
NP20: Newp 6H **35**
NP44: C'brn 3F **11**
Beeches Farm Cvn. Pk. NP26: Undy 3D **58**
Beeches Ind. Est., The CF72: P'clun 4C **64**
Beechfield Av. NP19: Newp 3G **37**
Beech Gro. NP10: Duf 3H **53**
NP16: Bul 3D **62**
Beechgrove CF83: Caer 4E **29**
Beech Ho. CF14: Whit 6A **70**
Beeching Way *CF38: Tont 1E **43***
(off Brecon Way)
Beechlea Cl. CF72: P'clun 1F **79**
Beechleigh Cl. NP44: G'mdw 2B **10**
Beechley Dr. CF5: F'wtr 6F **83**
Beech Rd. CF5: F'wtr .1F **93**
CF72: L'harry 5A **78**
NP4: Grif 2D **8**
NP26: Cald 4B **60**
Beech Tree Cl. CF15: Rad 1E **83**
Beech Trees Ter. NP4: P'nydd 1A **6**
Beech Vs. CF37: P'prdd 6B **14**
BEECHWOOD 4G **37**
Beech Wood NP16: Chep 2C **62**
Beechwood Cres. NP19: Newp 4G **37**

Beechwood Dr. CF38: Llan F 5C 42
CF64: P'rth 3C 108
Beechwood Hgts. CF38: Llan F 5C 42
Beechwood Rd. CF15: Taff W 1F 69
NP19: Newp 4G 37
Beechwood St. CF37: R'fln 4H 25
BEGAN 2B 74
Began Rd. CF3: St M 2B 74
BEGGARS POUND 4C 112
Beidr Ioewg CF63: Barry 5C 106
Beignon Cl. CF24: Card 5D 96
Beili Bach CF3: Rum 4G 87
Belgrave Cl. CF14: Thorn 2G 71
Belgrave Ct. NP4: P'nydd 1A 6
Belgrave Ter. CF37: P'prdd 4E 15
Belle Vw. Ter. CF63: Barry 6C 106
Belle Vue Cl. CF64: P'rth 6B 102
Bellevue Cl. NP44: C'brn 3G 11
Belle Vue Cres. CF14: Llan N 4B 84
Belle Vue La. NP20: Newp 6B 36
Bellevue Rd. NP44: C'brn 4G 11
Belle Vue Ter. CF37: T'rest 2E 25
CF64: P'rth 6B 102
NP20: Newp 1C 54
Bellevue Ter. NP44: H'lys 4A 10
Bellin Cl. NP18: C'ln 4G 21
Bell St. CF62: Barry 3E 117
Belmont Hill NP18: C'ln 1A 38
Belmont St. CF63: Barry 1A 118
Belmont Wlk. CF10: Card 6B 96
Belvedere Cres. CF63: Barry 2H 117
Belvedere Ter. NP11: Ris 4D 16
NP20: Newp 2B 36
Belvoir Ct. CF72: C Inn 3G 65
Benbow Rd. NP19: Newp 2C 38
Bencroft La. NP26: Rog, Undy 1F 59
Bendrick Rd. CF63: Barry 3C 118
Benecrofte CF62: Rho 5E 115
Ben Jonson Way NP20: Newp 1G 53
Bennetts Ter. CF83: Caer 5E 29
Benson Av. NP10: Roger 4D 34
(not continuous)
Bentley Cl. NP10: Roger 2C 34
Beresford Ct. CF24: Card 1E 97
Beresford Rd. CF24: Card 1E 97
NP19: Newp 4D 36
Beresford Rd. La. CF24: Card 1E 97
Berkeley Ct. NP44: G'mdw 6B 8
Berkeley Cres. NP4: Grif 3E 9
Berkeley Sq. CF5: Ely 1E 99
Berkley Cl. NP10: Bass 6B 34
Berkley Dr. CF64: P'rth 2F 109
Berkley Rd. NP10: Bass 6B 34
Berkrolles Av. CF62: St A 5D 112
BERLLAN-GOLLEN 1D 48
Bernard Av. CF5: Card 3C 94
Berry Ct. CF71: Llan M 3D 110
Berrymead Rd. CF23: Cyn 6B 72
Berry Pl. CF5: F'wtr 5H 83
Bertha St. CF37: T'rest 4E 25
Berthin NP44: G'mdw 2D 10
Berthlwyd CF15: P'rch 4A 68
Berthwin St. CF11: Card 2F 95
Bertram St. CF24: Card 2D 96
Berw Rd. CF37: P'prdd 5C 14
Beryl Pl. CF62: Barry 2H 117
Beryl Rd. CF62: Barry 2H 117
Bessant Cl. CF71: C'bri, L'thian 4D 90
Bessborough Dr. CF11: Card 6G 95
Bessemer Cl. CF11: Card 1E 101
NP20: Malp 3H 19
Bessemer Rd. CF11: Card 1F 101
Bethania Row CF3: St M 1B 88
Bethel La. NP44: Up Cwm 5B 8
Bethel Pl. CF14: L'shn 4F 71
Bethel St. CF37: P'prdd 1B 24
Bethesda Cl. NP10: Roger 3C 34
Bethesda Pl. NP10: Roger 3B 34
Betjeman Av. NP26: Cald 6B 60
BETTWS 5F 19
Bettws Cen. NP20: Bet 5F 19
Bettws Cl. NP20: Bet 6H 19
Bettws Hill NP20: Bet 6E 19
Bettws La. NP20: Bet, Newp 6H 19
Bettws Leisure Cen. 6H 19
Bettws-y-Coed Rd. CF23: Cyn 6B 72
Betwyns *NP44: F'wtr* 4E 11
(off Henllys Way)
Beulah Rd. CF14: Rhiw 6E 71
Bevan Cl. CF83: Tret 3H 29
Bevan Pl. CF14: Card 5F 85
Bevan Ri. CF83: Tret 3H 29
Bevans' La. NP44: Pnwd 3D 8
Beverley Cl. CF14: L'shn 4A 72
Beverley St. CF63: Barry 6B 106
Bicester Rd. CF64: Sul 1E 119
Bideford Cl. NP20: Newp 2A 54
Bideford Rd. CF3: L'rmy 2A 88
NP20: Newp 2H 53
Bighams Row NP4: P'pool 5B 6
Bigstone Cl. NP16: Tut 1G 63
Bigstone Gro. NP16: Tut 1G 63
Bilston St. NP19: Newp 5F 37
Bingle La. CF62: St A 3D 112
Birbeck Rd. NP26: Cald 5B 60
Birch Cl. NP26: Undy 4E 59
Birch Ct. CF14: Heath 2F 85
CF15: Tong 3H 69
Birch Cres. CF38: Llan F 6C 42
Birches, The NP44: Pnwd 6C 8
Birchfield Cl. CF38: Tont 2G 43
Birchfield Cres. CF5: Card 2B 94
BIRCHGROVE 1F 85
Birch Gro. CF38: Chu V 2F 43
CF62: Barry 5E 117
CF72: L'harry 5A 78
CF83: Caer 4E 29
NP11: Ris 5E 17
NP44: H'lys 5C 10
Birchgrove CF37: T'rest 1C 24
CF83: Tret 3H 29
NP10: Roger 3B 34
Birchgrove Cl. NP20: Malp 5B 20
Birchgrove Rd. CF14: Heath, Whit 3F 85
Birchgrove Station (Rail) 1F 85
Birch Hill CF15: Tong 4G 69
NP20: Malp 4B 20
Birch La. CF64: P'rth 4E 109
Birchley CF37: T'rest 3D 24
Birch Rd. CF5: F'wtr 1H 93
Birch Tree NP10: Bass 1D 52
Birch Wlk. CF5: F'wtr 1H 93
Birchwood Av. CF37: T'rest 4E 25
Birchwood Gdns. CF14: Whit 4E 85
CF83: B'ws 3F 29
Birchwood La. CF23: Pen L 4B 86
Birchwood Rd. CF23: Pen L 4B 86
Birdsfield Cotts. *CF37: P'prdd* 1B 24
(off Grover St.)
Birds Ind. Est. NP11: Ris 1E 33
Birdwood Gdns. NP16: Math 6C 62
Birkdale Cl. CF3: St M 5E 75
Bishop Cl. NP26: C'went 1B 60
Bishop Hannon Dr. CF5: F'wtr 6F 83
Bishops Av. CF5: L'dff 1B 94
Bishops Castle 6D 84
Bishops Cl. CF5: L'dff 1B 94
CF14: Whit 3C 84
NP16: Bul 6F 63
Bishops Ct. CF14: Whit 3C 84
Bishops Ga. CF14: Whit 3C 84
Bishops Mead NP16: Math 6B 62
Bishops Pl. CF5: L'dff 1B 94
CF14: Whit 3C 84
Bishops Rd. CF14: Whit 3C 84
Bishopston Rd. CF5: Ely 5H 93
Bishop St. CF11: Card 6G 95
NP19: Newp 3D 36
Bishops Wlk. CF5: L'dff 1B 94
BISHPOOL 4B 38
Bishpool Av. NP19: Newp 3B 38
Bishpool Cl. NP19: Newp 3B 38
Bishpool Ct. NP19: Newp 3B 38
Bishpool Gdns. NP19: Newp 3B 38
Bishpool Gro. NP19: Newp 3B 38
Bishpool La. NP19: Newp 3B 38
Bishpool Pl. NP19: Newp 3B 38
Bishpool Ri. NP19: Newp 3B 38
Bishpool Vw. NP19: Newp 3B 38
Bishpool Way NP19: Newp 3B 38
Bishton Rd. NP18: L'wrn 4F 39
Bishton St. NP19: Newp 4E 37
Bisley Cl. CF24: Card 2H 97
Bittern Way CF64: P'rth 5E 109
Blackberry Dr. CF62: Barry 1E 117
Blackberry Way CF23: Pontp 4G 73
Black Bird Cl. NP10: Roger 6E 35
Black Bird Rd. CF62: St A 3F 111
Blackbird Rd. NP26: Cald 6D 60
Blackbirds Cl. NP44: Oakf 2A 20
Blackbirds Way CF3: St M 5B 74
Blackett Av. NP20: Malp 4A 20
Blackmoor Pl. CF3: L'rmy 1A 88
Black Oak Ct. CF23: Cyn 4C 72
Black Oak Rd. CF23: Cyn 5C 72
Black Prince Rd. CF83: Caer 1H 45
Black Rd. CF37: P'cae, Chu V, T'rest 4B 24
CF38: Chu V 4B 24
Black Rock Rd. NP26: Pskwt 5H 61
Blacksmiths Way NP10: Coedk 5C 52
Blackstone St. CF11: Card 4G 95
Blackthorn Gro. NP18: C'ln 5E 21
Blackton La. CF62: Rho 3G 115
BLACKTOWN 5H 75
Blackvein Rd. NP11: C'keys, Ris 5A 16
Black Wall NP26: Magor 6C 58
BLACKWATER 1G 95
Blackwater Cl. NP20: Bet 5F 19
Blackweir Ter. CF10: Card 1H 95
Blackwell Cl. CF63: Barry 1B 118
Blaenavon Cl. CF3: St M 6E 75
Blaenclydach Pl. CF11: Card 6H 95
Blaenclydach St. CF11: Card 6H 95
Blaendare Rd. NP4: P'pool 4D 6
NP4: P'pool, Up R 5B 6
(not continuous)
Blaen Ifor CF83: Caer 3A 28
Blaenwern NP44: Pnwd 5F 9
Blaen-y-Coed CF14: Rhiw 5E 71
CF15: Rad 1E 83
Blaen-y-Cwm Vw. NP44: H'lys 4B 10
Blaen-y-Pant Av. NP20: Newp 1A 36
Blaen-y-Pant Cres. NP20: Newp 6A 20
Blaen-y-Pant Pl. NP20: Newp 1A 36
Blagdon Cl. CF3: L'rmy 2H 87
Blaina Cl. CF3: St M 6D 74
Blaise Pl. CF11: Card 1G 101
Blake Ct. CF10: Card 6G 5
Blake Rd. NP19: Newp 6H 37
Blanche Cl. NP10: Duf 5H 53
Blanche St. CF24: Card 2E 97
CF37: P'prdd 5C 14
Blandings Ct. CF23: Cyn 1C 86
Blandon Way CF14: Whit 3C 84
Blanthorn Ct. CF14: Whit 1B 84
Blenheim Av. NP26: Magor 4C 58
Blenheim Cl. CF62: Barry 6E 105
NP26: Magor 4C 58
Blenheim Ct. NP26: Magor 4C 58
NP44: G'mdw 3E 11
Blenheim Dr. NP26: Magor 4C 58
Blenheim Gdns. NP26: Magor 4C 58
Blenheim Pk. NP26: Magor 4C 58
Blenheim Rd. CF23: Pen L 1C 96
NP19: Newp 4G 37
NP44: G'mdw 3E 11
Blenheim Sq. Shops NP44: G'mdw 3E 11
Bleriot Cl. NP19: Newp 6G 37
Blethin Cl. CF5: L'dff 4A 84
Blewitt St. NP20: Newp 5B 36
Blodwen Rd. NP4: New I 5G 7
Blodwen Way NP4: New I 5G 7
Blodyn y Gog CF63: Barry 5C 106
Bloomfield Cl. NP19: Newp 3B 38
Bloom St. CF11: Card 2E 95
Blosse Rd. CF14: Llan N 5C 84
Blossom Cl. NP18: L'stne 1F 39
Blossom Dr. CF14: L'vne 1A 72
Bluebell Ct. NP44: F'wtr 3B 10
Bluebell Dr. CF3: L'rmy, St M 5B 74
NP16: Bul 5F 63
Bluebell Way NP10: Roger 2H 33
Blue Ho. Rd. CF14: L'shn 4G 71
Blyth Cl. CF62: Barry 4A 106
Boddington Ter. *NP18: C'ln* 5A 22
(off Cross St.)
Bodnant Cl. CF3: St M 1D 88
Bodwenarth Rd. CF37: C'fydd 3F 15
Boleyn Wlk. CF23: Pen L 5C 86
Bolt Cl. NP20: Newp 6D 36
Bolton Rd. NP20: Newp 5A 36
Bolton St. NP20: Newp 3B 36
Bolts Row NP19: Newp 4H 37
Bolt St. NP20: Newp 6D 36
Boncath Rd. CF14: Llan N 5C 84
Bond St. NP19: Newp 3C 36
Bonvilston Rd. CF37: P'prdd 5D 14
Bonvilston Ter. CF37: P'prdd 5D 14
Booker St. CF24: Card 2E 97
Boon Cl. CF63: Barry 6A 106
Borage Cl. CF23: Pontp 4E 73
Borough Av. CF62: Barry 5F 105
Borough Cl. CF71: C'bri 4D 90
Borrowdale Cl. CF23: Pen L 5C 86
Borth Rd. CF3: Rum 2B 88
Boswell Cl. CF3: L'rmy 5H 73
NP20: Newp 1H 53
Bosworth Dr. NP20: Newp 2A 36
Boulevard de Nantes CF10: Card 2C 4 (3A 96)
BOVERTON 4E 111
Boverton Brook CF71: Bov 4D 110
Boverton Brook Shops *CF71: Bov* 4E 111
(off Boverton Rd.)
Boverton Ct. CF71: Bov 3D 110
Boverton Pk. CF71: Bov 4E 111
Boverton Pk. Dr. CF71: Bov 4E 111
Boverton Rd. CF71: Bov, Llan M 3C 110
Boverton St. CF23: Card 6B 86

Bovil Vw. CF83: Mac 2G **31**
Bowdens La. NP26: Magor 1B **58**
Bowen Pl. *NP20: Newp 6C 36*
(off Francis Dr.)
Bowleaze NP44: G'mdw 2D **10**
Bowley Ct. CF24: Card 4E **97**
Bowlplex 2D **44**
Bowls Cl. CF83: Caer 4H **27**
Bowls La. CF83: Caer 2H **27**
(not continuous)
Bowls Ter. CF83: Caer 4A **28**
Bowman's Way CF71: C'bri 3B **90**
Bowmans Well CF71: C'bri 3B **90**
Bow St. CF5: Ely 1E **99**
Boxer Ind. Est. NP18: C'ln 3H **21**
Boxtree Cl. NP18: C'ln 5E **21**
Boyle Cl. NP20: Malp 5H **19**
Brachdy Cl. CF3: Rum 5H **87**
Brachdy La. CF3: Rum 5H **87**
Brachdy Rd. CF3: Rum 5H **87**
Bracken Pl. CF5: F'wtr 6H **83**
Bradenham Pl. CF64: P'rth 1E **109**
Brades, The NP18: C'ln 4H **21**
Bradford Pl. CF64: P'rth 1F **109**
Bradford St. CF11: Card 1H **101**
CF83: Caer 1C **46**
Bradley St. CF24: Card 2E **97**
Braeval St. CF24: Card 1B **96**
Bramble Av. CF62: Barry 1F **117**
Bramble Cl. CF5: F'wtr 6F **83**
Bramble Ri. CF64: P'rth 6G **101**
Bramblewood Cl. CF14: Thorn 3H **71**
Brambling Dr. CF14: Thorn 2G **71**
Bramley Cl. NP18: L'stne 1G **39**
Bramshill Dr. CF23: Pontp 4H **73**
Brandreth Gdns. CF23: Pen L 5C **86**
Brandreth Rd. CF23: Pen L 4B **86**
Brangwyn Av. NP44: Oakf 5H **11**
Brangwyn Cl. CF64: P'rth 6H **101**
Brangwyn Cres. NP19: Newp 2F **37**
Branksome Ho. CF10: Card 4B **4** (4H **95**)
Branwen Cl. CF5: Ely 6E **93**
Brassknocker St. NP26: Magor 4D **58**
Braunton Av. CF3: L'rmy 1H **87**
Braunton Cres. CF3: L'rmy 1H **87**
Brayford Pl. CF3: L'rmy 5A **74**
Breaksea Cl. CF64: Sul 3H **119**
Breaksea Ct. CF62: Barry 5H **117**
Breaksea Dr. CF62: Barry 5H **117**
Brean Cl. CF64: Sul 2A **120**
Brechfa Cl. NP18: P'hir 6E **13**
Brecon Beacons National Pk. 1F **7**
Brecon Ct. CF62: Barry 1A **118**
NP18: C'ln 4F **21**
Brecon Ho. CF64: P'rth 3D **108**
Brecon Rd. NP19: Newp 2F **37**
Brecon St. CF5: Card 3E **95**
CF71: Bov 2D **110**
Brecon Wlk. NP44: C'brn 2G **11**
Brecon Way CF38: Tont 1E **43**
Bredon Cl. NP11: Ris 6G **17**
Brendon Cl. CF3: L'rmy 1A **88**
Brendon Ct. CF83: Caer 1E **47**
Brendon Vw. CF62: Rho 5E **115**
Brenig Cl. CF14: Thorn 2H **71**
CF62: Barry 1E **117**
Brentwood Ct. CF14: L'shn 4G **71**
Breon Rd. CF64: Sul 1E **119**
Brian Cl. NP19: Newp 3E **39**
Brianne Dr. CF14: Thorn 2H **71**
Briar Cl. CF5: F'wtr 1G **93**
NP26: Undy 4D **58**
Briarmeadow Dr. CF14: Thorn 2G **71**
Briars, The NP26: Magor 4C **58**
Briar Way CF38: Tont 2G **43**
Briarwood Dr. CF23: Cyn 6C **72**
Brickyard Bus. Pk. CF14: Card 6F **85**
Bridewell Gdns. NP26: Undy 5F **59**
Bridgefield St. CF83: Abert 1E **27**
Bridgeman Ct. CF64: P'rth 2F **109**
Bridgeman Rd. CF64: P'rth 2F **109**
Bridge Rd. CF3: St M 2H **73**
CF5: L'dff 5B **84**
CF14: Llan N 5B **84**
CF37: Up Bo 1B **44**
CF71: L'thian 5B **90**
Bridge St. CF5: L'dff 6C **84**
CF10: Card 5D **4** (4B **96**)
CF37: P'prdd 6C **14**
CF37: T'rest 2E **25**
CF63: Barry 6B **106**
CF64: P'rth 6H **101**
NP4: Grif 6E **7**
NP11: Ris 5D **16**
NP16: Chep 1E **63**
NP20: Newp 4B **36**
Bridget Dr. NP16: Sed 3G **63**
Bridge Ter. CF3: Lwr M 4E **51**
Bridgewater Rd. CF64: Sul 1H **119**
Bridgwater Rd. CF3: L'rmy 1A **88**
Brierley Cl. NP11: Ris 6G **17**
Briers Ga. NP44: H'lys 5A **10**
Brigantine Cl. NP10: Duf 5H **53**
Brigantine Dr. NP10: Duf 5H **53**
Brigantine Gro. NP10: Duf 5H **53**
Brigantine Pl. CF10: Card 6F **5** (5B **96**)
Brigantine Way NP10: Duf 5H **53**
Brigham Ct. CF83: Caer 5G **27**
Bright St. NP11: C'keys 3A **16**
Brindley Rd. CF11: Card 1F **101**
Bristol St. NP19: Newp 3D **36**
Bristol Ter. CF15: Gwae G 1D **68**
Bristol Vw. Cl. NP44: G'mdw 1C **10**
Britannia Quay CF10: Card 2C **102**
Brithdir St. CF24: Card 6H **85**
British Legion Dr. CF3: Rum 3H **87**
Briton Cl. NP16: Bul 6G **63**
Brittania Cl. NP11: Ris 6E **17**
Britten Cl. NP19: Newp 5B **38**
Britten Rd. CF64: P'rth 4D **108**
Britway Ct. CF64: Din P 2G **107**
Britway Rd. CF64: Din P 2G **107**
Broadacres CF11: Card 4E **95**
Broadcommon Cl. NP19: Newp 6A **38**
Broad Ct. CF62: Barry 2D **116**
Broadfield Ct. CF5: Ely 5H **93**
Broadhaven CF11: Card 5E **95**
Broadlands Ct. CF3: St M 6C **74**
NP26: Undy 4E **59**
Broadlands Ho. CF3: St M 6C **74**
Broadmead Pk. NP19: Newp 6A **38**
Broad Pl. CF11: Card 4E **95**
Broad Quay Rd. NP19: Newp 3E **55**
Broad Shoard, The CF71: C'bri 3C **90**
Broadstairs Rd. CF11: Card 4E **95**
Broad St. CF11: Card 4D **94**
CF62: Barry 4F **117**
NP4: Grif 6E **7**
NP20: Newp 1D **54**
Broadstreet Comn. CF3: Pet W 4G **89**
NP18: L'wrn, Newp 4B **56**
Broad St. Pde. CF62: Barry 4F **117**
Broad Vw. NP44: Pnwd 6C **8**
Broadwalk NP18: C'ln 5H **21**
Broadwater Rd. NP19: Newp 2A **56**
Broadway CF3: Pet W 5B **76**
CF24: Card 2D **96**
CF37: P'prdd, T'rest 1C **24**
CF71: C'bri, L'thian 4C **90**
NP4: P'pool 2B **6**
NP18: C'ln 6H **21**
Broadweir Rd. NP44: C'brn 3G **11**
Broadwell Cl. CF3: St M 1D **88**
Broadwell Ct. NP18: C'ln 5H **21**
Broadwood Cl. NP19: Newp 4C **38**
Bro Athro CF3: Rum 3B **88**
Brocastle Rd. CF14: Whit 1D **84**
Brockhampton Rd. CF3: St M 6D **74**
Brockhill Ri. CF64: P'rth 5E **109**
Brockhill Way CF64: P'rth 5E **109**
Brock St. CF63: Barry 6B **106**
Brodeg CF15: P'rch 5A **68**
Bromfield Pl. CF64: P'rth 6B **102**
Bromfield Rd. CF62: Barry 5G **117**
Bromfield St. CF11: Card 1H **101**
Bromley Dr. CF5: Ely 4A **94**
Bromsgrove St. CF11: Card 1H **101**
Bron Awelon CF62: Barry 4D **116**
Bron Felin CF14: Thorn 3F **71**
Bron Haul CF15: P'rch 5A **68**
Bronhaul CF72: T Grn 3E **65**
Bronllwyn CF15: P'rch 5H **67**
Bronllys Gro. NP10: Coedk 6F **53**
Bronllys Pl. NP44: C'iog 6G **9**
Bronmynnyd CF83: Abert 3E **27**
Bron Rhiw CF83: Mac 2F **31**
Bronrhiw Av. CF83: Caer 2D **46**
Bronrhiw Fach CF83: Caer 2D **46**
Bronte Cl. CF3: L'rmy 5A **74**
Bronte Cres. CF3: L'rmy 5A **74**
Bronte Gro. NP20: Newp 1G **53**
Bronwydd Av. CF23: Pen L 5C **86**
Bronwydd Cl. CF23: Pen L 5C **86**
Bronwydd Rd. CF24: Card 1G **97**
Bron-y-Mor CF62: Barry 5E **117**
Brook Ct. *CF5: F'wtr 2B 94*
(off St Fagans Rd.)
Brookdale Ct. CF38: Chu V 3F **43**
Brook Fld. CF71: C'bri 4D **90**
Brookfield CF37: Y'bwl 1A **14**
Brookfield Av. CF63: Barry 5C **106**
Brookfield Cl. NP19: Newp 6H **37**
Brookfield Dr. CF3: St M 1C **88**
Brookfield La. CF37: P'prdd 4E **15**
Brookland Ho. NP44: Pnwd 6E **9**
Brookland Rd. NP11: Ris 6E **17**
Brooklands NP11: C'crn 1A **16**
Brooklands Ter. CF5: Ely 1D **98**
Brookland Ter. NP44: Pnwd 5E **9**
Brooklea NP18: C'ln 3G **21**
Brooklea Pk. CF14: L'vne 3A **72**
Brooklyn Cl. CF14: Rhiw 4C **70**
Brook Rd. CF5: F'wtr 2B **94**
CF14: Whit 3D **84**
Brookside CF38: Tont 2G **43**
CF64: Din P 2H **107**
NP20: Bet 5G **19**
NP26: Cald 3C **60**
NP44: G'mdw 3E **11**
Brookside Cl. CF14: Heath 2F **85**
CF37: C'fydd 3F **15**
CF83: Caer 5H **27**
Brookside Cres. CF83: Caer 6E **29**
Brook St. CF11: Card 4A **4** (4H **95**)
CF37: T'rest 3E **25**
CF63: Barry 2A **118**
CF83: Abert 1E **27**
NP44: Pnwd 4E **9**
Brook St. La. CF11: Card 5A **4** (4H **95**)
Brook Ter. CF38: Chu V 2F **43**
Brookvale Dr. CF14: Thorn 2G **71**
Brookview Cl. CF14: Thorn 3H **71**
Brookway CF38: Tont 2G **43**
Broom Cl. NP10: Roger 3A **34**
Broome Path NP44: G'mdw 3E **11**
Broomfield Cl. CF38: Tont 2G **43**
Broomfield St. CF83: Caer 1D **46**
Broom Pl. CF5: F'wtr 1H **93**
Broughton Pl. CF63: Barry 5A **106**
Brow-Dawel Cl. CF72: P'clun 1C **78**
Brown Cl. NP19: Newp 6G **37**
Brown Ct. CF3: St M 2D **88**
Browning Cl. CF3: L'rmy 6H **73**
NP20: Newp 1H **53**
Bro-y-Fan CF83: Caer 4E **29**
Bruce Knight Cl. CF5: L'dff 5A **84**
Bruce St. CF24: Card 6A **86**
Brummel Dr. CF15: Cre 1F **81**
Brundall Cres. CF5: Ely 6E **93**
Brunel Av. NP10: Roger 3D **34**
Brunel Cl. CF63: Barry 5D **106**
Brunel Rd. NP16: Bul 4E **63**
NP44: F'wtr 3C **10**
Brunel St. CF11: Card 5A **4** (4G **95**)
NP20: Newp 2D **54**
(not continuous)
Brunswick St. CF5: Card 3E **95**
Bruton Pl. CF5: L'dff 6C **84**
Bryanston Rd. CF64: Sul 1E **119**
Brydges Pl. CF24: Card 1A **96**
Bryn, The CF83: Tret 2H **29**
NP20: Bet 5G **19**
Bryn Aber CF83: Abert 1E **27**
Bryn Aber Ter. CF83: Abert 1E **27**
Bryn Adar CF14: Rhiw 5B **70**
Brynamlwg CF72: P'clun 5E **65**
BRYNAU 6E **29**
Bryn Aur CF37: Glyn 1D **14**
Brynau Rd. CF15: Taff W 1F **69**
CF83: Caer 6D **28**
Bryn Awel CF37: Glyn 1D **14**
CF83: B'ws 3H **29**
Brynawel CF83: Caer 3H **27**
Bryn-Awelon Rd. CF23: Cyn 5C **72**
Bryn Bach CF14: Rhiw 5D **70**
Brynbala Way CF3: Rum 2C **88**
Bryn Barrwg CF62: Barry 5F **117**
Bryn Bevan NP20: Newp 6B **20**
Bryn Calch CF15: Morg 5E **69**
Bryn Canol CF83: B'ws 3G **29**
Bryn Castell CF15: Rad 6F **69**
Bryn Celyn CF23: L'dyrn 6F **73**
Bryncelyn Pl. NP44: Pnwd 6D **8**
Bryn Celyn Rd. CF23: L'dyrn 1F **87**
NP44: Pnwd 6C **8**
Bryn Cl. CF83: Tret 3H **29**
Bryncoch CF15: Taff W 1E **69**
Bryncoed CF15: Rad 6E **69**
Bryncoed Ter. CF83: Abert 1E **27**
Bryn Creigiau CF72: Groes F 6C **66**
Bryncyn CF23: L'dyrn 5F **73**
Bryn Derw CF38: Bed 4A **42**
Bryn Derwen CF15: Rad 6E **69**
CF83: Caer 3B **28**
Brynderwen CF37: C'fydd 2F **15**
Brynderwen Cl. CF23: Cyn 3C **86**
Brynderwen Ct. NP19: Newp 3E **37**
Brynderwen Gro. NP19: Newp 3E **37**

Brynderwen Rd. CF37: C'fydd 2F 15
NP19: Newp 3E 37
Bryn Dewi Sant CF72: P'clun 5E 65
Bryn-Dolwen CF83: B'ws 2G 29
Bryn Eglwys CF37: P'prdd 6A 14
NP44: C'iog 6G 9
Brynfab Rd. CF37: R'fln 5H 25
Brynfedw CF23: L'dyrn 2E 87
CF83: B'ws 2G 29
Bryn Garw NP44: C'iog 6G 9
Bryngelli Ter. CF83: Abert 1E 27
BRYNGLAS 6A 20
Bryn Glas CF14: Thorn 3E 71
CF83: B'ws 2G 29
Brynglas CF83: Caer 3A 28
NP44: F'wtr 5E 11
Brynglas Av. NP20: Newp 6C 20
Brynglas Cl. NP20: Newp 6B 20
Brynglas Ct. NP20: Newp 6B 20
Brynglas Cres. NP20: Newp 1B 36
Brynglas Dr. NP20: Newp 6B 20
Brynglas Rd. NP20: Newp 2B 36
Brynglas Tunnels & Malpas Rd. Relief Rd.
NP20: Oakf 3A 20
NP44: C'ln, Oakf 3A 20
Bryn Goleu CF83: B'ws 2G 29
Bryngoleu CF83: Rud 6B 30
Bryn Golwg CF15: Rad 6F 69
Bryn Gomer NP44: C'iog 5G 9
BRYNGWYN 2C 46
Bryngwyn CF83: Caer 2B 46
Bryngwyn Rd. NP4: P'pool 3B 6
NP20: Newp 5H 35
Bryn-Gwyn Rd. CF23: Cyn 6C 72
Bryn-Gwyn St. CF83: B'ws 2F 29
Brynhafod Rd. CF83: Abert 1E 27
Bryn Haidd CF23: L'dyrn 6F 73
Brynhedydd NP10: Bass, R'drn 6A 34
Bryn Heol CF83: B'ws 3G 29
Bryn Heulog CF14: Whit 2B 84
CF83: Caer 4A 28
NP4: Grif, P'pool 5D 6
Brynheulog CF23: L'dyrn 6F 73
Bryn Heulog Ter. CF83: Mac 1F 31
Brynhill CF23: Cyn 1C 86
Brynhill Cl. CF62: Barry 5F 105
Bryn Hyfryd CF15: Rad 6F 69
Brynhyfryd CF38: Bed 4A 42
CF83: B'ws 2F 29
CF83: Caer 4A 28
NP44: C'iog 5G 9
Brynhyfryd Av. NP20: Newp 5B 36
Brynhyfryd Pl. CF37: T'rest 2D 24
Brynhyfryd Rd. NP20: Newp 5A 36
Brynhyfryd Ter. CF37: P'prdd 6B 14
CF83: Mac 2F 31
Bryn-Hyfryd Ter. NP11: Ris 5D 16
Bryn Ifor CF83: Caer 4H 27
Bryn Ilan CF37: R'fln 1F 25
Bryn Llus CF37: P'prdd 2C 24
Brynmawr Cl. CF3: St M 6E 75
Bryn Milwr NP44: F'wtr 5E 11
Bryn Nant CF83: Caer 3H 27
Bryn Olwg CF37: P'prdd 5E 15
Brynonnen Ct. NP44: H'lys 5B 10
Bryn Owain CF83: Caer 3A 28
Bryn Pinwydden CF23: L'dyrn 5E 73
Bryn Rhedyn CF37: Glyn 1D 14
CF38: Tont 1F 43
NP44: Llanf 5B 12
Bryn-Rhedyn CF83: Caer 5F 29
Bryn Rhosyn CF15: Rad 6E 69
BRYNSADLER 1B 78
Bryn Siriol CF15: P'rch 5H 67
CF83: Caer 4H 27
Bryntail Rd. CF37: P'prdd, R'fln 1G 25
BRYNTEG 6H 41
Bryn Teg CF83: Caer 4A 28
Brynteg CF14: Rhiw 4C 70
CF83: B'ws 2G 29
Brynteg Cl. CF23: Cyn 3C 86
Brynteg Ct. CF38: Bed 6A 42
Brynteg La. CF38: Bed 6H 41
CF72: Bed 6H 41
Bryn Ter. CF38: Llan F 4D 42
NP4: P'nydd 1A 6
Bryntirion CF14: Rhiw 5E 71
CF83: B'ws 2G 29
CF83: Caer 4A 28
BRYNWERN 3B 6
Brynwern NP4: P'pool 3B 6
Bryn-y-Fran Av. CF83: Tret 3H 29
Bryn y Gloyn CF62: Rho 6G 115
Bryn-y-Mor CF62: St A 6F 113
Bryn-y-Nant CF23: L'dyrn 2F 87
Bryn-yr-Eglwys CF15: P'rch 5A 68
Bryn-yr-Ysgol CF83: Caer 3H 27
Brython Dr. CF3: St M 6E 75
Buccaneer Cl. NP10: Duf 5H 53
Buccaneer Gro. NP10: Duf 5G 53
Buccaneer Way NP10: Duf 5H 53
Buchanan Way NP10: Coedk 5D 52
Buchan Cl. NP20: Newp 1H 53
Buckingham Cl. CF14: L'vne 3B 72
Buckingham Cres.
NP19: Newp 3F 37
Buckingham Pl. CF62: Barry 5E 105
NP19: Newp 3F 37
Buckle Wood NP16: Chep 2C 62
Buckley Cl. CF5: L'dff 4H 83
Budden Cres. NP26: Cald 4C 60
Builth Cl. NP10: Coedk 6F 53
Bull Cliff Wlk. CF62: Barry 5C 116
Bullfinch Rd. CF62: St A 3G 111
Bull Ring CF72: L'sant 1F 65
Bulmore Rd. NP18: C'ln 1A 38
Bulrush Cl. CF3: St M 1F 89
BULWARK 4E 63
Bulwark Av. NP16: Bul 4F 63
Bulwark Ind. Est. NP16: Bul 4E 63
Bulwark Rd. NP16: Bul 3E 63
Bunyan Cl. CF3: L'rmy 5B 74
Burberry Cl. NP10: Roger 2H 33
Burges Ho. CF24: Card 1H 5
Burgesse Cres. CF72: L'sant 3F 65
Burgess Pl. CF11: Card 6G 95
Burial La. CF71: Llan M 3B 110
Burleigh Rd. NP20: Newp 5A 36
Burley Pl. CF62: St A 1D 112
Burlington St. CF63: Barry 2B 118
Burlington Ter. CF5: Card 2D 94
Burnaby St. CF24: Card 3E 97
Burne Jones Cl. CF5: L'dff 5A 84
Burnfort Rd. NP20: Newp 6G 35
Burnham Av. CF3: L'rmy 6A 74
CF64: Sul 3H 119
Burnham Ct. CF3: L'rmy 1A 88
Burns Cl. CF83: Mac 3C 30
NP20: Newp 2G 53
Burns Cres. CF62: Barry 5H 105
NP26: Cald 6B 60
Burnside Ct. CF5: F'wtr 1F 93
Burns La. NP44: G'mdw 3F 11
Burn's Way CF37: P'cae 4B 24
Burnt Barn Rd. NP16: Bul 5E 63
Burreed Cl. CF3: St M 1F 89
BURTON 5G 113
Burton Homes NP20: Newp 6B 36
NP26: C'went 1B 60
Burton Rd. NP19: Newp 1F 37
Burton Ter. CF62: Rho 6H 113
Burt Pl. CF10: Card 1B 102
Burt St. CF10: Card 2B 102
Burwell Cl. CF23: Pontp 4H 73
Bush La. NP4: P'pool 3B 6
(not continuous)
Bushy Pk. NP4: P'pool 2A 6
Bute Cres. CF10: Card 1C 102
Bute Esplanade CF10: Card 2B 102
Bute La. CF64: P'rth 1E 109
Bute Pl. CF10: Card 1C 102
Bute St. CF10: Card 6E 5 (5B 96)
(not continuous)
CF15: Tong 4G 69
Bute Ter. CF10: Card 5E 5 (4B 96)
BUTETOWN 6B 96
Butetown History & Arts Cen. 1C 102
Butetown Link CF10: Card 3A 102
CF11: Card 3A 102
Butetown Link Rd. CF10: Card 1C 102
Butleigh Av. CF5: Card 2C 94
Butterbur Pl. CF5: Ely 4E 93
Buttercup Cl. NP10: Roger 2H 33
Buttercup Ct. NP44: F'wtr 4B 10
Butterfield Dr. CF23: Pontp 4E 73
Butterfly Cl. CF38: Chu V 3F 43
Buttermere Way NP19: Newp 1F 37
Butterworth Cl. NP19: Newp 4C 38
Buttington Hill NP16: Sed, B'ly 3H 63
Buttington Rd. NP16: Sed 3G 63
Buttington Ter. NP16: B'ly 4H 63
Butt Lee Ct. CF62: Barry 2G 117
Buttrills Cl. CF62: Barry 2G 117
Buttrills Rd. CF62: Barry 1G 117
Buttrills Wlk. CF62: Barry 1G 117
Butts, The CF71: C'bri 3C 90
Buxton Cl. NP20: Newp 2H 53
Buxton Ct. CF83: Caer 6E 29
Bwlch Rd. CF5: F'wtr 2H 93
Byrd Cres. CF64: P'rth 4C 108
Byrde Cl. NP19: Newp 4A 38
Byron Av. CF38: Bed 6A 42
Byron Ct. CF64: P'rth 6H 101
CF71: Llan M 4D 110
Byron Pl. CF64: P'rth 1D 108
NP26: Cald 6B 60
NP44: G'mdw 3F 11
Byron Rd. NP20: Newp 6H 35
Byron St. CF24: Card 1G 5 (2C 96)
CF62: Barry 2H 117
Bythway Rd. NP4: C'avn 1C 6
Byways NP44: G'mdw 2D 10

C

Caban Cl. NP10: Roger 2D 34
Cader Idris Cl. NP11: Ris 6G 17
Cadman Cl. CF24: Card 2G 97
Cadnant Cl. CF14: L'shn 4F 71
Cadoc Cl. NP26: C'went 1B 60
Cadoc Cres. CF63: Barry 1D 118
Cadoc Rd. NP44: Pnwd 5C 8
Cadoxton Station (Rail) 1C 118
Cadvan Rd. CF5: Ely 3F 93
Cadwgan Pl. CF5: F'wtr 2A 94
Cae Bach CF83: Mac 2E 31
Caebach Cl. CF5: Ely 6D 92
Cae Bedw CF83: Caer 2B 28
Cae Brandi CF3: M'fld 5A 76
Cae-Bryn CF83: Abert 1E 27
Cae Brynton Rd. NP20: Newp 1H 53
Cae Cadno CF38: Chu V 2D 42
Cae Calch CF83: Caer 3A 28
Cae Canol CF64: P'rth 4C 108
Cae Caradog CF83: Caer 3G 27
Cae Castle CF71: L'thian 5B 90
Cae Croes Heol CF83: Caer 2H 45
Caedelyn Rd. CF14: Whit 1C 84
Cae Derwen NP44: C'brn 4F 11
Cae Du Mawr CF83: Caer 3A 28
Cae Fardre CF38: Chu V, Tont 1F 43
Cae Ffynnon CF38: Chu V 1E 43
CF83: Caer 3A 28
Cae Garw CF14: Thorn 3F 71
CF38: Llan F 6B 42
CF64: Din P 3G 107
Cae Garw Bach CF5: St F 3C 82
Cae Gethin CF83: Caer 2A 28
Cae Glas CF63: Barry 6B 106
CF83: Caer 4A 28
Cae-Glas Av. CF3: Rum 4H 87
Cae-Glas Rd. CF3: Rum 4H 87
Cae Gwyn CF64: P'rth 3C 108
Caegwyn Rd. CF14: Heath, Whit 3E 85
Cae Leon CF62: Barry 4H 105
Caelewis CF15: Tong 4H 69
Cae Llwyd CF83: Caer 4D 28
Cae Maen CF14: Heath 3F 85
Cae Marchog CF83: Caer 3B 28
Cae Mawr Av. NP26: Cald 5C 60
Cae Mawr Gro. NP26: Cald 5C 60
Cae Mawr Rd. CF14: Rhiw 6E 71
NP26: Cald 5C 60
Cae Meillion CF83: Caer 2A 46
Caenant CF37: R'fln 3F 25
Cae Nant Gledyr CF83: Caer 6H 27
Cae Nant Gogh CF83: Caer 2H 45
Caenant Rd. CF83: Caer 5C 28
Caenewydd Cl. CF5: Ely 6D 92
Caepalish *NP4: P'nydd* 1A 6
(off Pentrepiod Rd.)
Caepalish Pl. *NP4: P'nydd* 1A 6
(off Pentrepiod Rd.)
Cae Pandy CF83: Caer 4D 28
Cae Pant CF83: Caer 3B 28
Cae Pen-y-Graig CF83: Caer 2A 28
Cae Perllan Rd. NP20: Newp 1A 54
CAERAU 5G 93
Caerau Castle 6H 93
Caerau Ct. CF5: Ely 5G 93
CF72: C Inn 2H 65
Caerau Ct. Rd. CF5: Ely 5G 93
Caerau Cres. NP20: Newp 5A 36
Caerau Fort 1G 99
Caerau La. CF5: Ely 6F 93
CF5: Ely, Wen 3E 99
CF15: P'rch 5B 68
Caerau Pk. Cres. CF5: Ely 5G 93
Caerau Pk. Pl. CF5: Ely 5G 93
Caerau Pk. Rd. CF5: Ely 5G 93
Caerau Rd. CF5: Ely 5G 93
NP20: Newp 5A 36
Caerbragdy CF83: Caer 6D 28
Caer Cady Cl. CF23: Cyn 3C 86
Caer Castell Pl. CF3: Rum 2A 88
Caer Ceffyl CF5: St F 2C 82
CAERDYDD 3E 5 (4A 96)

Caer Efail CF5: St F 3C 82
Cae Rex CF71: L'thian 4C 90
Cae'r Fferm CF83: Caer 6A 28
CAERFFILI 1D 46
Caer Ffynnon CF62: Barry 4E 117
Cae'r Gerddi CF38: Chu V 2E 43
Caer Graig CF15: Rad 6E 69
Cae Rhedyn NP44: C'iog 1B 12
Cae Rhos CF83: Caer 4D 28
CAERLEON 5H 21
Caerleon Cl. CF3: St M 6E 75
Caerleon Ct. CF83: Caer 5G 27
Caerleon Rd. CF14: Card 5F 85
CF64: Din P 2A 108
NP18: C'ln 3D 36
NP18: P'hir 1F 21
NP19: Newp 3D 36
NP44: Llanf 3B 12
(not continuous)
Caerleon Roman Baths & Mus. 5H 21
Caerleon Way NP16: Bul 5F 63
CAERLLION 5H 21
Caer Mead Cl. CF71: Bov 3D 110
Caernarvon Cl. CF64: Din P 2A 108
NP44: Llan 2A 12
Caernarvon Ct. CF83: Caer 5H 27
Caernarvon Cres. NP44: Llan 2A 12
Caernarvon Dr. NP10: R'drn 6A 34
Caernarvon Gdns. CF62: Barry 5G 105
Caernarvon Way CF3: Rum 2B 88
Cae'r Odyn CF64: Din P 3G 107
CAERPHILLY 1D 46
Caerphilly Bus. Pk. CF83: Caer 1E 47
Caerphilly By-Pass CF83: Caer 2H 45
Caerphilly Castle 6D 28
Caerphilly Cl. CF64: Din P 1A 108
NP10: R'drn 6A 34
CAERPHILLY DISTRICT MINERS HOSPITAL 2B 46
Caerphilly Leisure Cen. 5D 28
CAERPHILLY PARC ESTATE 4D 28
Caerphilly Rd. CF14: Heath, L'shn, Rhiw 6F 71
CF15: N'grw 4D 44
(not continuous)
CF83: Sen 1D 26
NP10: Bass, R'drn 6A 34
(not continuous)
Caerphilly Station (Rail) 1D 46
Caerphilly Vis. Cen. *1D 46*
(off Castle St.)
Caer ty Clwyd CF71: Llan M 2B 110
Caer Wenallt CF14: Rhiw 5B 70
CAER-WENT 1A 60
Caerwent Gdns. NP26: C'went 1B 60
Caerwent La. NP16: Bul 6F 63
Caerwent Rd. CF5: Ely 4E 93
NP4: C'avn 1D 6
NP44: C'iog 4F 9
Caer Worgan CF71: Llan M 1B 110
Cae Samson CF5: Ely 5G 93
Caesar Cres. NP18: C'ln 4G 21
Cae Stumpie CF71: C'bri 4D 90
Cae Syr Dafydd CF5: Card 2E 95
Cae Tymawr CF14: Whit 3A 84
Cae Uwchllyn CF83: Caer 2A 46
Caewal Rd. CF5: L'dff 1C 94
Cae Yorath CF14: Whit 2D 84
Cae-yr-Ebol NP44: Pnwd 6E 9
Cae Ysgubor CF83: Caer 2A 28
Caird St. NP16: Chep 3E 63
Cairnmuir Rd. CF24: Card 2F 97
Calderton Rd. CF38: Bed 5A 42
CALDICOT 5D 60
Caldicot By-Pass NP26: Cald 6C 60
Caldicot Castle 4E 61
Caldicot Castle Country Pk. 4E 61
Caldicot Ct. CF83: Caer 5H 27
Caldicot Rd. CF5: Ely 5H 93
NP26: C'went, Cald 2B 60
NP26: Pskwt 5E 61
NP26: Rog 5A 60
Caldicot Station (Rail) 6B 60
Caldicot St. NP19: Newp 5F 37
Caldicott Cl. CF38: Bed 6A 42
Caldicot Way NP44: Pnwd 5F 9
Caldwell Cl. CF38: Bed 6A 42
Caldy Cl. CF62: Barry 6H 105
NP19: Newp 2F 37
Caldy Ct. CF14: Llan N 4C 84
Caldy Rd. CF14: Llan N 4C 84
Caledfryn Way CF83: Caer 3H 27
Callaghan Ct. CF24: Card 3E 97
Callaghan Sq. CF10: Card 6E 5 (5B 96)
Cambourne Av. CF14: Whit 2B 84
Cambourne Cl. CF62: Barry 6E 105
Cambria CF11: Card 5H 101
Cambria Cl. NP18: C'ln 5A 22
Cambrian Av. CF71: Llan M 4B 110
Cambrian Cen. NP20: Newp 4B 36
Cambrian Cl. CF3: M'fld 4A 76
Cambrian Cres. *CF3: M'fld 4A 76*
(off Cambrian Way)
Cambrian Dr. CF3: M'fld 4A 76
Cambrian Gdns. CF3: M'fld 4A 76
Cambrian Gro. CF3: M'fld 4A 76
Cambrian Ind. Est. (East Side)
CF72: P'clun 5C 64
Cambrian Ind. Est. (West Side)
CF72: P'clun 5C 64
Cambrian Pl. CF37: T'rest 2E 25
Cambrian Point CF24: Card 6H 85
Cambrian Residential Cvn. Pk. CF5: Ely 1E 99
Cambrian Rd. NP20: Newp 4B 36
Cambrian Way CF3: M'fld 4A 76
Cambria Rd. CF5: Ely 6F 93
Cambria St. NP4: Grif 1E 9
Cambridge Ct. NP18: C'ln 3E 21
Cambridge Rd. NP19: Newp 4D 36
Cambridge St. CF11: Card 1A 102
CF62: Barry 4E 117
Cam Ct. NP44: G'mdw 6A 8
Camellia Ct. CF5: F'wtr 5H 83
Camellia Dr. NP10: Roger 2H 33
Camelot Ct. NP18: C'ln 5A 22
Camelot Pl. NP19: Newp 3D 36
Camelot Way CF14: Thorn 3F 71
Cameron St. CF24: Card 2E 97
Camm's Cnr. CF64: Din P 2A 108
Campanula Dr. NP10: Roger 2H 33
Campbell Dr. CF11: Card 3H 101
Campbell St. NP4: P'pool 2A 6
Camperdown Rd. NP19: Newp 6G 37
Camperly Cl. CF38: Bed 6A 42
Campion Cl. NP20: Newp 3A 36
NP44: H'lys 5C 10
Campion Pl. CF5: F'wtr 5H 83
Camp Rd. NP16: Bul 4F 63
NP26: Sud 6H 61
Campton Pl. CF38: Bed 6B 42
Camrose Ct. CF62: Barry 5H 105
Camrose Rd. CF5: Ely 5H 93
Camrose Wlk. NP44: G'mdw 3E 11
Canada Rd. CF14: Card 6G 85
Canal Cl. NP4: Grif 1E 9
Canal Cotts. CF37: P'prdd 5D 14
Canal Pde. CF10: Card 6E 5 (5B 96)
NP20: Newp 5C 36
(not continuous)
Canal Pk. Ind. Est. CF10: Card 6B 96
Canal St. NP20: Newp 2B 36
Canal Ter. NP20: Newp 6D 36
Canaston Pl. CF5: Ely 5H 93
Canberra Cl. NP44: C'brn, G'mdw 3F 11
Canberra Cres. NP20: Newp 5F 35
Candwr La. NP18: P'hir 5G 13
Candwr Pk. NP18: P'hir 6F 13
Candwr Rd. NP18: P'hir 1G 21
Cannington Av. CF3: L'rmy 2A 88
Cannington Cl. CF64: Sul 2H 119
Cannon La. NP26: C'went 1B 60
Canon St. CF62: Barry 4F 117
NP19: Newp 3D 36
Canopus Cl. CF3: St M 1B 88
Canterbury Cl. NP20: Newp 3C 36
Canterbury Way NP26: Pskwt 5G 61
CANTON 3E 95
Canton Ct. CF11: Card 4F 95
Cantref Cl. CF14: Thorn 2H 71
NP10: Roger 2C 34
Capel Ct. NP4: P'nydd 1A 6
Capel Cres. NP20: Newp 6B 36
Capel Edeyrn CF23: Pontp 5H 73
Capelgwilym Rd. CF14: Thorn 1E 71
Capella Ho. CF10: Card 1D 102
CAPEL LLANILLTERN 3H 81
Capel St. NP4: P'pool 3C 6
NP20: Newp 1C 54
Capital Bus. Pk. CF3: Rum 5B 88
Capital Point CF3: Rum 5B 88
Capitol CF10: Card 3E 5 (3B 96)
Caple Rd. CF62: Barry 4E 117
Caradoc Av. CF63: Barry 6H 105
Caradoc Cl. CF3: St M 6E 75
NP18: C'ln 4G 21
Caradoc Rd. NP44: C'brn 1G 11
Caraway Cl. CF3: St M 5E 75
CARDIFF 3E 5 (4A 96)
Cardiff Arms Pk. 4B 4 (4H 95)
Cardiff Athletics Stadium 5F 95
Cardiff Bay Bus. Cen. CF24: Card 4D 96
Cardiff Bay Retail Pk. CF11: Card 3H 101
CARDIFF BAYS 1C 102
Cardiff Bay Station (Rail) 1C 102
Cardiff Bay Vis. Cen. 2C 102
Cardiff Blues RUFC 4B 4 (4H 95)
Cardiff Bowling Club 2A 4 (3G 95)
CARDIFF BUPA HOSPITAL, THE 4F 73
Cardiff Bus. Pk. CF14: L'shn 6H 71
Cardiff Bus. Technology Cen. CF10: Card 2A 96
Cardiff Castle 3C 4 (3H 95)
Cardiff Central Station (Rail) 6C 4 (5A 96)
Cardiff Cen. Trad. Est. CF10: Card 6E 5 (5B 96)
Cardiff City Farm 6F 95
Cardiff City FC 5F 95
Cardiff Ga. Bus. Pk. CF23: Pontp 3G 73
Cardiff Ga. Retail Pk. CF23: Pontp 3H 73
CARDIFF HELIPORT 6F 97
Cardiff Ind. Pk. CF14: L'shn 6G 71
CARDIFF INTERNATIONAL AIRPORT 4E 115
Cardiff International Arena 5E 5 (4B 96)
Cardiff Millennium Stadium 5B 4 (4H 95)
Cardiff Queen Street Station (Rail) 3F 5 (3B 96)
Cardiff RC Cathedral 4E 5 (4B 96)
Cardiff Rd. CF5: L'dff 6C 84
CF5: St F 2E 93
CF15: Cre 6E 67
CF15: N'grw, Taff W 3D 44
CF37: R'fln, Up Bo 2E 25
CF63: Barry, Din P 1C 118
CF64: Din P, P'rth 6F 107
CF71: C'bri 4D 90
CF72: L'sant 2F 65
CF72: P'clun 5G 65
CF83: Caer 1D 46
NP10: Coedk 5E 53
NP20: Newp 3F 53
Cardiff Rd. Bus. Pk. CF63: Barry 1C 118
Cardiff Ski Cen. 1A 94
Cardiff University
Colum Rd. 1H 95
Museum Av. 1D 4 (2A 96)
Parade, The 3F 5 (3B 96)
Cardiff University Sports Hall 6F 85
Cardigan Cl. CF38: Tont 2F 43
CF64: Din P 2A 108
NP44: C'iog 5F 9
Cardigan Ct. NP18: C'ln 4F 21
Cardigan Cres. CF71: Bov 3E 111
NP44: C'iog 5F 9
Cardigan Ho. CF64: P'rth 2D 108
Cardigan Pl. NP19: Newp 3F 37
Cardigan Rd. CF64: Din P 2A 108
Cardigan St. CF5: Card 3E 95
Cardinal Dr. CF14: L'vne 1A 72
Carew Cl. CF62: Barry 6H 105
Carey Rd. NP19: Newp 4G 37
Carfax Path NP44: F'wtr 4D 10
Cargill Cl. CF38: Bed 6B 42
Cargo Rd. CF10: Card 3C 102
Carisbrooke Rd. NP19: Newp 4F 37
Carisbrooke Way CF23: Pen L 4C 86
Carling Pl. CF5: Ely 6E 93
Carlisle St. CF24: Card 3E 97
NP20: Newp 1D 54
Carlotta Way CF10: Card 1B 102
Carlton Cl. CF14: Thorn 2G 71
Carlton Ct. NP4: P'nydd 1A 6
Carlton Cres. CF38: Bed 6A 42
Carlton Pl. NP11: C'keys 2A 16
Carlton Rd. NP19: Newp 2E 37
Carlton Ter. NP11: C'keys 2A 16
NP18: C'ln 6A 22
Carmarthen Cl. CF62: Barry 6H 105
CF71: Bov 3D 110
Carmarthen Ct. CF5: Card 3F 95
CF83: Caer 5H 27
Carmarthen Dr. CF38: Tont 1F 43
Carmarthen Ho. CF64: P'rth 3D 108
Carmarthen Rd. CF64: Din P 2A 108
Carmarthen St. CF5: Card 3E 95
Carmel Ct. CF23: Pen L 5C 86
Carn Celyn CF38: Bed 6A 42
Carne Ct. CF71: Bov 3D 110
Carnegie Dr. CF23: Cyn 2B 86
Carn-yr-Ebol CF63: Barry 4B 106
Caroline Rd. NP4: New I 5G 7
Caroline St. CF10: Card 5D 4 (4A 96)
NP20: Newp 5C 36
Caroline Way NP4: New I 5G 7
Carpenters Arms La. NP20: Newp 4C 36
Ca'r Pwll CF64: Din P 3G 107
Carreg Arwyn CF72: L'harry 5A 78
Carshalton Rd. CF38: Bed 6A 42
Carter Pl. CF5: F'wtr 6H 83
Cartref Melys NP19: Newp 6G 37
Cartwright Ct. CF24: Card 6B 86
Cartwright Grn. NP20: Malp 5A 20
Cartwright La. CF5: F'wtr 2H 93

Carys Cl. CF5: Ely . . . 1E **99**
CF64: P'rth . . . 4C **108**
CAS-GWENT . . . 2E **63**
CASNEWYDD . . . 4C **36**
Caspian Cl. CF3: St M . . . 1D **88**
Castan Rd. CF72: P'clun . . . 6D **64**
Castellau Rd. CF38: Bed . . . 3G **41**
Castell Coch . . . 3G **69**
Castell Coch Dr. NP10: Coedk . . . 6G **53**
Castell Coch Vw. CF15: Tong . . . 4G **69**
Castell Meredith CF83: Caer . . . 4E **29**
Castell Morgraig CF83: Caer . . . 4E **29**
Castell Morgraig (remains of) . . . 6D **46**
CASTELL-Y-BWCH . . . 2C **18**
Castell-y-Fan CF83: Caer . . . 4E **29**
Castell-y-Mynach Rd. CF38: Bed . . . 4H **41**
Castertown Pill NP26: Cald . . . 6E **61**
Castle Arc. CF10: Card . . . 4C **4**
Castle Arc. Balcony CF10: Card . . . 4C **4** (4A **96**)
Castle Av. CF3: Rum . . . 5F **87**
CF64: P'rth . . . 4D **108**
CF83: Caer . . . 4C **28**
Castle Cl. CF15: Cre . . . 5E **67**
CF64: Din P . . . 2A **108**
CF71: Bov . . . 4E **111**
NP10: Roger . . . 5D **34**
(not continuous)
NP11: P'waun . . . 1A **16**
Castle Ct. CF38: Chu V . . . 2F **43**
CF71: Llan M . . . 3B **110**
CF71: L'thian . . . 6C **90**
NP11: P'waun . . . 1A **16**
NP26: Pskwt . . . 5F **61**
(Gray Hill Vw.)
NP26: Pskwt . . . 6E **61**
(Symondscliff Way)
NP44: H'lys . . . 5B **10**
Castle Ct. Shop. Cen. CF83: Caer . . . 6D **28**
Castle Cres. CF3: Rum . . . 5F **87**
Castle Dr. CF64: Din P . . . 2A **108**
Castlefield Pl. CF14: Card . . . 5G **85**
Castleford Cl. CF38: Bed . . . 5A **42**
Castleford Gdns. NP16: Tut . . . 1F **63**
Castleford Hill NP16: Tut . . . 1E **63**
Castle Gdns. NP16: Chep . . . 1D **62**
NP26: Cald . . . 4C **60**
Castle Grn. CF5: St G . . . 3A **92**
Castle Hill CF5: St F . . . 2D **92**
CF71: L'thian . . . 4B **90**
Castle Ivor St. CF37: P'prdd . . . 6A **14**
Castleland St. CF63: Barry . . . 2A **118**
Castle La. CF24: Card . . . 1G **5** (2C **96**)
NP11: P'waun . . . 1A **16**
NP18: C'ln . . . 5A **22**
Castle Lea NP26: Cald . . . 5D **60**
Castle Lodge Cl. NP26: Cald . . . 5E **61**
Castle Lodge Cres. NP26: Cald . . . 5E **61**
Castle M. *CF71: L'thian . . . 5C 90*
(off Bridge St.)
NP18: C'ln . . . 5A **22**
Castle Mound . . . 5A **22**
CASTLE PARK . . . 6D **28**
Castle Pk. Cl. NP20: Newp . . . 6F **35**
Castle Pk. Rd. NP20: Newp . . . 6F **35**
Castle Pct. CF71: L'thian . . . 6D **90**
Castle Ri. CF3: Rum . . . 5G **87**
Castle Rd. CF15: Tong . . . 3G **69**
CF62: Rho . . . 6H **113**
(Mortimer Way)
CF62: Rho . . . 6E **115**
(Station Rd.)
Castle St. CF10: Card . . . 4B **4** (4H **95**)
CF15: Taff W . . . 2E **69**
CF37: T'rest . . . 2E **25**
CF62: Barry . . . 3E **117**
CF71: Llan M . . . 2B **110**
CF72: L'sant . . . 2F **65**
CF83: Caer . . . 6D **28**
NP18: C'ln . . . 6A **22**
NP20: Newp . . . 1D **54**
CASTLETON . . . 2G **75**
Castleton Cvn. Pk. CF62: St A . . . 4E **113**
Castleton Ct. CF3: St M . . . 5G **75**
Castleton Ri. CF3: Cas . . . 2G **75**
Castleton Rd. CF62: St A . . . 4D **112**
Castle Vw. CF15: Tong . . . 5H **69**
CF83: Caer . . . 3B **28**
NP16: Tut . . . 1G **63**
Castle Way NP26: Pskwt . . . 5E **61**
Castle Wood NP16: Chep . . . 2C **62**
Castlewood Cotts. CF64: Din P . . . 2G **107**
Cas Troggi NP26: Cald . . . 4C **60**
Caswell Rd. CF3: Rum . . . 4H **87**
Caswell Way NP19: Newp . . . 3G **55**
Catalpa Cl. NP20: Malp . . . 4B **20**
CATHAYS . . . 6A **86**
CATHAYS PARK . . . 1C **4** (3A **96**)
Cathays Station (Rail) . . . 1C **4** (2A **96**)
Cathays Ter. CF24: Card . . . 6A **86**
Cath Cob Cl. CF3: St M . . . 1C **88**
Cathedral Cl. CF5: L'dff . . . 6D **84**
Cathedral Ct. CF5: L'dff . . . 6C **84**
NP20: Newp . . . 5B **36**
Cathedral Grn., The CF5: L'dff . . . 6C **84**
Cathedral Rd. CF11: Card . . . 3A **4** (2F **95**)
Cathedral Vw. CF14: Llan N . . . 5D **84**
Cathedral Wlk. CF10: Card . . . 3D **4** (3A **96**)
Catherine Cl. NP10: Duf . . . 6H **53**
Catherine Dr. CF3: M'fld . . . 5A **76**
CF15: Tong . . . 3H **69**
Catherine Meazy Flats CF64: P'rth . . . 6B **102**
Catherine St. CF24: Card . . . 1A **96**
CF37: P'prdd . . . 6C **14**
Catkin Dr. CF64: P'rth . . . 6G **101**
Catrine CF11: Card . . . 5H **101**
CAT'S ASH . . . 5G **23**
Catsash Rd. NP18: C'ln, L'stne . . . 2B **38**
Cat's La. CF83: B'ws . . . 2G **29**
Cattwg Cl. CF71: Llan M . . . 2B **110**
Causeway, The CF71: L'thian . . . 5B **90**
NP26: Undy . . . 5F **59**
Causeway Hill CF71: L'thian . . . 5B **90**
Cavendish Cl. CF14: Thorn . . . 3G **71**
Cavendish Pl. CF38: Bed . . . 5A **42**
Cawley Pl. CF63: Barry . . . 6B **106**
Cawnpore St. CF64: P'rth . . . 6G **101**
CAXDOXTON . . . 6B **106**
Caxton Pl. CF23: L'dyrn . . . 5G **73**
NP20: Newp . . . 4B **36**
Caynham Av. CF64: P'rth . . . 5E **109**
Cecil Ct. CF24: Card . . . 2D **96**
Cecil La. NP10: Roger . . . 5D **34**
Cecil Sharp Rd. NP19: Newp . . . 4D **38**
Cecil St. CF24: Card . . . 2D **96**
Cedar Cl. NP16: Bul . . . 5E **63**
Cedar Ct. CF14: L'shn . . . 5H **71**
Cedar Cres. CF38: Tont . . . 2G **43**
Cedar Gro. CF5: F'wtr . . . 6G **83**
Cedar Ho. CF14: Whit . . . 1A **84**
Cedar La. CF37: R'fln . . . 4H **25**
Cedar Rd. CF62: St A . . . 2B **112**
NP19: Newp . . . 4D **36**
Cedar Wlk. NP44: Up Cwm . . . 6B **8**
Cedar Way CF64: P'rth . . . 2C **108**
Cedar Wood Cl. NP10: Roger . . . 2H **33**
Cedar Wood Dr. NP10: Roger . . . 2H **33**
Cefn Bychan CF15: P'rch . . . 4A **68**
Cefn Carnau Rd. CF14: Heath . . . 1H **85**
Cefn Cl. CF37: Glyn . . . 1C **14**
NP10: Roger . . . 4D **34**
NP44: C'iog . . . 5G **9**
Cefn Coch CF15: Rad . . . 6E **69**
Cefn Coed CF15: N'grw . . . 3D **44**
Cefn-Coed Av. CF23: Cyn . . . 3B **86**
Cefn-Coed Cres. CF23: Cyn . . . 4C **86**
Cefn-Coed Gdns. CF23: Cyn . . . 4B **86**
Cefn-Coed Rd. CF23: Cyn . . . 4B **86**
Cefn Ct. NP10: Roger . . . 4D **34**
Cefn Dr. NP10: Roger . . . 4D **34**
Cefn Graig CF14: Rhiw . . . 5D **70**
Cefn Ilan CF83: Abert . . . 2D **26**
Cefn La. CF37: Glyn . . . 2B **14**
Cefn Llan CF15: P'rch . . . 5A **68**
Cefn Mably Farm . . . 6C **50**
Cefn Mably Pk. CF3: Lwr M . . . 1A **74**
Cefn Mably Rd. CF14: L'vne . . . 2C **72**
Cefn Milwr NP44: F'wtr . . . 5F **11**
Cefn Mt. CF64: Din P . . . 2G **107**
Cefn Nant CF14: Rhiw . . . 4D **70**
Cefn Onn Mdws. CF14: Thorn . . . 1H **71**
Cefn Penuel CF15: P'rch . . . 5H **67**
Cefn-Porth Rd. CF14: Rud . . . 4E **49**
Cefn Ri. NP10: Roger . . . 3C **34**
Cefn Rd. CF14: Llan N . . . 4E **85**
NP10: Roger . . . 3B **34**
Cefn Wlk. NP10: Roger . . . 4D **34**
Cefn-y-Lon CF83: Caer . . . 3H **27**
CEFNYRHENDY . . . 5E **65**
Cei Dafydd CF63: Barry . . . 3A **118**
Ceiriog Cl. CF63: Barry . . . 5A **106**
CF64: P'rth . . . 1D **108**
Ceiriog Cres. CF37: R'fln . . . 3F **25**
Ceiriog Dr. CF14: Rhiw . . . 5C **70**
CF83: Caer . . . 5C **28**
Celandine Ct. NP16: Bul . . . 5F **63**
NP44: F'wtr . . . 3B **10**
Celandine Rd. CF5: Ely . . . 4E **93**
Celerity Dr. CF10: Card . . . 5B **96**
Celtic Cl. NP26: Undy . . . 4E **59**
Celtic Gateway Bus. Pk. CF11: Card . . . 4G **101**
Celtic Grn. CF64: Din P . . . 1H **107**
CELTIC LAKES . . . 5E **53**
Celtic Manor Golf Course . . . 6E **23**
Celtic Rd. CF14: Whit . . . 4F **85**
Celtic Springs NP10: Coedk . . . 5D **52**
Celtic Way CF62: Rho . . . 6C **114**
CF83: B'ws . . . 3G **29**
NP10: Coedk . . . 5D **52**
Celyn Av. CF23: Cyn . . . 2B **86**
CF83: Caer . . . 5C **28**
Celyn Cl. CF62: St A . . . 2C **112**
Celyn Ct. NP44: Pnwd . . . 5C **8**
Celynen Gro. NP20: Newp . . . 3H **53**
Celyn Gro. CF23: Cyn . . . 6C **72**
CF83: Caer . . . 5C **28**
Cemaes Cres. CF3: Rum . . . 2C **88**
Cemetery La. NP20: Newp . . . 5B **36**
Cemetery Rd. CF15: Taff W . . . 2F **69**
CF37: R'fln . . . 2F **25**
CF62: Barry . . . 1H **117**
Cenfedd St. NP19: Newp . . . 2D **36**
Cennin Pedr CF63: Barry . . . 4B **106**
Centenary Ct. CF38: Bed . . . 5B **42**
Central Av. NP19: Newp . . . 1B **56**
Central Bldgs. *CF83: Tret . . . 3A 30*
(off Newport Rd.)
Central Ct. CF24: Card . . . 2D **96**
Central Link CF10: Card . . . 5G **5** (4C **96**)
Central Mkt. CF10: Card . . . 4D **4** (4A **96**)
Central M. NP4: P'pool . . . 3C **6**
Central Sq. CF10: Card . . . 6C **4** (5A **96**)
CF37: P'prdd . . . 5D 14
(off Ralph St.)
Central St. CF83: Caer, L'brad . . . 2B **28**
Central Way CF14: Heath . . . 4H **85**
CF64: Sul . . . 1E **119**
NP44: Pnwd . . . 6C **8**
Centre Ct. CF37: Up Bo . . . 3C **44**
Centurion Cl. CF5: Ely . . . 6H **93**
Centurion Ga. NP18: C'ln . . . 5A **22**
Centurions Ct. NP26: C'went . . . 1C **60**
Century Ct. CF11: Card . . . 6B **4** (5H **95**)
Cerdin Av. CF72: P'clun . . . 6D **64**
Ceredig Ct. NP44: Llan . . . 3B **12**
Ceri Av. CF62: Rho . . . 5F **115**
Ceridwen Ter. *CF72: L'sant . . . 2F 65*
(off Heol-y-Beila)
Ceri Rd. CF62: Rho . . . 5F **115**
Chadwick Cl. NP20: Malp . . . 5A **20**
Chaffinch Way NP10: Duf . . . 4H **53**
Chalfont Cl. CF38: Bed . . . 5B **42**
Chalvington Cl. CF38: Bed . . . 5A **42**
Chamberlain Rd. CF14: Llan N . . . 4B **84**
Chamberlain Row CF64: Din P . . . 1A **108**
Chamomile Cl. CF23: Pontp . . . 4E **73**
Chancery La. CF11: Card . . . 4F **95**
Chandlers Reach CF38: Llan F . . . 6C **42**
Chandlers Way CF64: P'rth . . . 5A **102**
Chandlery Way CF10: Card . . . 1B **102**
Channel Cl. CF62: Rho . . . 6D **114**
Channel Vw. CF3: Cas . . . 2F **75**
CF64: P'rth . . . 4F **109**
NP4: P'pool . . . 1D **6**
NP10: Bass . . . 6B **34**
NP11: Ris . . . 6F **17**
NP16: Bul . . . 4E **63**
NP44: Pnwd . . . 6C **8**
Channel Vw. Flats CF11: Card . . . 3H **101**
Channel View Recreation Cen. . . . 2A **102**
Channel Vw. Rd. CF11: Card . . . 2H **101**
Chantry, The CF5: L'dff . . . 6A **84**
Chantry Ri. CF64: P'rth . . . 4E **109**
Chapel Cl. CF64: Din P . . . 1A **108**
CF71: A'thin . . . 2F **91**
NP16: Pwllm . . . 5B **62**
NP20: Newp . . . 6C **36**
Chapel Ct. CF83: Tret . . . 2A **30**
Chapel La. CF64: P'rth . . . 6A **102**
NP16: Math, Pwllm . . . 6B **62**
NP44: C'iog, Pnwd . . . 4F **9**
Chapel M. *CF15: Tong . . . 4G 69*
(off Railway Ter.)
Chapel Rd. CF15: Morg . . . 5F **69**
NP4: P'nydd . . . 1A **6**
NP18: L'wrn, Newp . . . 4E **57**
Chapel Row CF3: St M . . . 6B **74**
CF64: Din P . . . 1A **108**
Chapel Row La. CF3: St M . . . 6B **74**
Chapel St. CF5: L'dff . . . 1C **94**
CF37: P'prdd . . . 6C **14**
CF37: R'fln . . . 4F **25**
NP44: Pnwd . . . 1G **11**
Chapel Ter. CF5: Wen . . . 3D **98**
NP4: P'nydd . . . 1A **6**
NP10: R'drn . . . 5A **34**
NP26: Magor . . . 5D **58**
Chapel Wood CF23: L'dyrn . . . 3E **87**
Chapman Cl. NP20: Malp . . . 4A **20**

Chapman Ct. NP20: Newp 5H **35**
Chapter Art Cen. 3E **95**
Chard Av. CF3: L'rmy 2H **87**
Chard Ct. CF3: L'rmy 2H **87**
Chargot Rd. CF5: Card 2D **94**
Charles Darwin Way CF62: Barry 4G **117**
Charles Pl. CF62: Barry 5E **117**
Charles St. CF10: Card 3E **5** (3B **96**)
CF37: P'prdd 6A **14**
CF83: Caer 6D **28**
NP4: Grif 6E **7**
NP10: Roger 5C **34**
NP20: Newp 5C **36**
(not continuous)
NP44: Pnwd 5E **9**
CHARLESVILLE 1A **6**
Charlesville NP4: P'nydd 1A **6**
Charlock Cl. CF14: Thorn 2E **71**
Charlotte Dr. NP20: Newp 6C **36**
Charlotte Pl. CF63: Barry 1B **118**
Charlotte Sq. CF14: Rhiw 6E **71**
Charlotte St. CF64: P'rth 6H **101**
NP20: Newp 6C **36**
Charlotte Wlk. *NP20: Newp 6C* ***36***
(off Alma St.)
Charnwood Dr. CF23: Pontp 4G **73**
Charnwood Rd. NP19: Newp 1D **36**
Charston NP44: G'mdw 2D **10**
Charter Av. CF62: Barry 5F **105**
Charteris Cl. CF64: P'rth 5E **109**
Charteris Cres. CF5: Ely 3H **93**
Charteris Rd. CF5: Ely 3H **93**
Chartist Ct. NP11: Ris 6F **17**
Chartist Dr. NP10: Roger 4C **34**
Chartist Rd. CF72: L'sant 2E **65**
Chartists Way NP16: Bul 5E **63**
Chartley Cl. CF3: St M 6E **75**
Chartwell Ct. CF15: P'rch 4A **68**
Chartwell Dr. CF14: L'vne 4B **72**
CHATHAM 2G **31**
Chatham CF83: Mac 2G **31**
Chatham Pl. *CF83: Mac 2H* ***31***
(off Chatham St.)
Chatham St. CF83: Mac 2H **31**
Chatsworth Rd. CF5: F'wtr 6A **84**
Chatterton Sq. CF11: Card 3H **101**
Chaucer Cl. CF3: L'rmy 5A **74**
CF64: P'rth 1D **108**
NP26: Cald 6B **60**
Chaucer Ct. NP19: Newp 4F **37**
Chaucer Rd. CF62: Barry 5H **105**
NP19: Newp 4F **37**
Cheam Pl. CF14: L'shn 5H **71**
Cheddar Cres. CF3: L'rmy 2H **87**
Cheeseman's Trad. Est. NP26: Rog 5A **60**
Chelmer Cl. NP20: Bet 6E **19**
Chelmer Wlk. NP20: Bet 6E **19**
Chelston Pl. NP20: Newp 2B **36**
CHEPSTOW 2E **63**
Chepstow & District Leisure Cen. 1D **62**
Chepstow Castle 1E **63**
Chepstow Cl. CF5: Ely 5H **93**
NP44: C'iog 5G **9**
CHEPSTOW COMMUNITY HOSPITAL 2D **62**
Chepstow Ct. CF83: Caer 5H **27**
Chepstow Mus. 1F **63**
Chepstow Ri. NP44: C'iog 5G **9**
Chepstow Rd. NP18: L'stne 1E **39**
NP18: Newp 2C **38**
NP19: Newp 4D **36**
NP26: Cald 5D **60**
Chepstow Station (Rail) 2F **63**
Cheriton Dr. CF14: Thorn 3H **71**
Cheriton Gro. CF38: Tont 2H **43**
Cheriton Path NP44: F'wtr 3D **10**
Cherry Cl. CF5: F'wtr 6F **83**
CF64: Din P 3A **108**
CF64: P'rth 5E **109**
Cherrydale Rd. CF5: Ely 3A **94**
Cherrydown Cl. CF14: Thorn 3H **71**
Cherry Orchard Rd. CF14: L'vne, Thorn 1G **71**
Cherry Tree Cl. CF14: L'vne 2B **72**
CF83: B'ws 2E **29**
NP18: C'ln 4H **21**
NP18: L'stne 1F **39**
NP20: Malp 4B **20**
NP44: C'iog 6H **9**
Cherry Tree Wlk. CF72: T Grn 3E **65**
Cherrywood Cl. CF14: Thorn 2H **71**
Chervil Cl. CF3: St M 5E **75**
Cherwell Cl. CF5: F'wtr 6H **83**
Cherwell Rd. CF64: P'rth 3D **108**
Cherwell Wlk. NP20: Bet 5E **19**
Cheshire Cl. CF14: L'shn 1H **85**
Chester Cl. CF3: St M 1D **88**
NP4: New I 4H **7**
Chester Ct. CF83: Caer 4H **27**
Chesterfield St. CF63: Barry 6A **106**
Chester Pl. CF11: Card 6H **95**
Chester St. CF11: Card 5H **95**
Chesterton Rd. CF3: L'rmy 6H **73**
Chestnut Av. CF62: St A 2B **112**
Chestnut Cl. CF64: Din P 3H **107**
CF83: Mac 2G **31**
NP4: New I 4H **7**
NP26: Magor 4D **58**
Chestnut Dr. NP26: Rog 5A **60**
Chestnut Gro. NP18: C'ln 5E **21**
NP44: Up Cwm 6B **8**
Chestnut Rd. CF5: F'wtr 1H **93**
Chestnuts, The CF72: P'clun 1F **79**
Chestnut St. CF37: R'fln 4G **25**
Chestnut Tree Cl. CF15: Rad 1E **83**
Chestnut Way CF64: P'rth 2D **108**
Cheviot Cl. CF14: L'shn 6G **71**
NP11: Ris 5G **17**
Chichester Cl. NP19: Newp 6F **21**
Chichester Rd. CF64: P'rth 6H **101**
Chichester Way CF5: Ely 3A **94**
Chick La. NP20: Newp 6H **35**
Chilcote St. CF63: Barry 1B **118**
Chiltern Cl. CF14: L'shn 6G **71**
NP11: Ris 6H **17**
NP19: Newp 3A **38**
Chorley Cl. CF5: F'wtr 2G **93**
CHRISTCHURCH 2B **38**
Christchurch Hill NP18: C'ln 2B **38**
Christchurch Rd. NP18: C'ln, Newp 3A **38**
NP19: Newp 3E **37**
Christina Cres. NP10: Roger 5E **35**
Christina St. CF10: Card 6B **96**
Chumleigh Cl. CF3: Rum 3G **87**
Church Av. CF64: P'rth 1F **109**
Church Cl. CF14: L'vne 3C **72**
CF38: Llan F 5D **42**
NP4: C'avn 1C **6**
NP4: New I 1G **9**
NP20: Newp 5E **35**
NP26: Cald 4D **60**
NP44: C'iog 6G **9**
Church Ct. NP19: Newp 1G **37**
Church Cres. NP10: Bass 6C **34**
NP10: Coedk 6C **52**
Church Farm Cl. NP20: Bet 6G **19**
Churchfield Av. NP26: Cald 4C **60**
Churchfields CF63: Barry 5B **106**
Church Hill Cl. CF71: L'thian 5A **90**
Chu. House Pk. NP10: St Bri 4G **77**
Churchill Cl. CF14: L'vne 1A **72**
CHURCHILL PARK 4C **28**
Churchill Ter. CF63: Barry 1C **118**
Churchill Way CF10: Card 3E **5** (3B **96**)
Church La. CF3: M'fld 4H **75**
CF3: St M 6B **74**
(not continuous)
CF15: N'grw 4E **45**
CF62: St A 5D **112**
(not continuous)
CF71: Llan M 4A **110**
(Llantwit Major)
CF71: Llan M 3B **110**
(West-end Town)
NP4: C'avn, P'nydd 1B **6**
NP4: New I 6H **7**
NP10: Coedk 1C **76**
NP26: Undy 5F **59**
Churchmead NP10: Bass 1D **52**
Church Mdw. CF62: St A 3F **111**
Church Pl. Nth. CF64: P'rth 6B **102**
Church Pl. Sth. CF64: P'rth 6B **102**
Church Ri. CF5: Wen 5E **99**
NP26: Undy 5G **59**
Church Rd. CF3: Rum 4G **87**
CF3: St M 5H **73**
CF5: Card 4F **95**
CF5: Ely 6G **93**
CF5: St F 5A **68**
CF14: L'vne 2C **72**
CF14: Whit 3B **84**
CF15: P'rch 5A **68**
CF23: L'dyrn, Pontp 5G **73**
CF37: P'prdd 5D **14**
CF38: Tont 1E **43**
CF62: Rho 6E **115**
CF63: Barry 6B **106**
CF64: P'rth 1F **109**
CF71: L'thian 4A **90**
CF83: Abert 2D **26**
NP10: Coedk 6C **52**
NP10: St Bri 4G **77**
NP11: Ris 4D **16**
NP16: Chep 1F **63**
Church Rd. NP19: Newp 3D **36**
NP26: Cald 3D **60**
NP26: Undy 4F **59**
NP44: Llanf 5D **12**
NP44: Pnwd 6D **8**
Church Rd. Ter. NP11: Ris 4D **16**
Church Row NP16: Chep 1F **63**
NP26: Sud 6H **61**
Church St. CF10: Card 4C **4** (4A **96**)
CF15: Taff W 2E **69**
CF37: P'prdd 6C **14**
CF71: C'bri 3C **90**
CF71: Llan M 3B **110**
CF72: L'sant 2F **65**
CF83: B'ws 3G **29**
CF83: Mac 2G **31**
NP10: Roger 3B **34**
NP18: C'ln 5H **21**
NP20: Newp 1D **54**
(not continuous)
Church Ter. CF23: Pen L 1D **96**
CF63: Barry 6C **106**
NP4: P'nydd 1A **6**
Church Vw. CF37: P'prdd 1A **24**
CF71: L'thian 4A **90**
NP10: Bass 1D **52**
Church Vw. Cl. CF64: L'dgh 4F **101**
CHURCH VILLAGE 3E **43**
Churchward Dr. NP19: Newp 6H **37**
Churchwood NP4: Grif 1E **9**
Churchwood Cl. NP4: P'pool 2C **6**
Church Wood Rd. NP44: Pnwd 6D **8**
Cidermill Cl. NP16: Bul 6F **63**
Cilfedw CF15: Rad 6F **69**
CILFYNYDD 2F **15**
Cilfynydd Rd. CF37: C'fydd 3F **15**
Cilgant y Meillion CF62: Rho 6F **115**
Cilgerran Ct. NP44: Llan 2B **12**
Cilgerran Cres. CF14: L'shn 5F **71**
Cil Hendy CF72: P'clun 6E **65**
Cineworld Cinema
Cardiff 5E **5** (4B **96**)
Newport 1B **56**
Circle, The NP44: C'brn 4F **11**
Circle Way E. CF23: L'dyrn 1E **87**
Circle Way W.
CF23: Cyn, L'dyrn, Pen L 3D **86**
CF23: L'dyrn 2D **86**
City Hall Rd. CF10: Card 2C **4** (3A **96**)
City Link CF24: Card 1E **97**
City Lofts *CF24: Card 1B* ***96***
(off Crwys Rd.)
City Rd. CF24: Card 1G **5** (1B **96**)
City Wharf CF10: Card 6G **5** (5C **96**)
Civil Service Sports Club 4C **94**
Claerwen Dr. CF23: Cyn 2B **86**
Clairwain NP4: New I 6G **7**
Clarbeston Rd. CF14: Llan N 5C **84**
Clare Drew Way NP44: C'iog 6H **9**
Clare Gdns. CF11: Card 5A **4** (4H **95**)
Claremont NP20: Malp 3B **20**
Claremont Av. CF3: Rum 3H **87**
Claremont Cres. CF3: Rum 3H **87**
Clarence Cnr. NP4: P'pool 3C **6**
Clarence Emb. CF10: Card 2A **102**
Clarence Pl. CF10: Card 1B **102**
NP4: P'pool 4C **6**
NP11: Ris 5D **16**
NP19: Newp 4C **36**
Clarence Rd. CF10: Card 1A **102**
CF11: Card 1A **102**
NP4: P'pool 4C **6**
Clarence St. NP4: P'pool 3C **6**
NP20: Newp 1D **54**
Clarendon CF23: Cyn 1D **86**
Clarendon Cl. NP16: Bul 6G **63**
Clarendon Rd. CF23: Pen L 4D **86**
Clare Pl. CF11: Card 5A **4** (4H **95**)
Clare Rd. CF11: Card 6A **4** (5H **95**)
CF71: C'bri 4D **90**
Clare St. CF11: Card 5A **4** (4H **95**)
Clark Av. NP44: Pnwd 5D **8**
Clarke St. CF5: Ely 3B **94**
Clas Dyfrig CF14: Whit 4D **84**
Clas Gabriel CF14: Whit 4D **84**
Clas Ifor CF14: Heath 2E **85**
Clas Illtyd CF14: Whit 3E **85**
Clas Isan CF14: Whit 3E **85**
Clas Odyn CF14: Whit 2D **84**
Clas Teilo CF14: Whit 4D **84**
Clas-Ty-Gelli CF37: Glyn 1D **14**
Clas Tynewydd CF14: Whit 3D **84**
Clas Ty'n-y-Cae CF14: Rhiw 1E **85**
Clas Tywern CF14: Heath 1E **85**
Clas Yorath CF14: Whit 2D **84**
Claude Pl. CF24: Card 1C **96**

Claude Rd. CF24: Card . . . 1C **96**
CF62: Barry . . . 2F **117**
CF83: Caer . . . 1C **46**
Claude Rd. W. CF62: Barry . . . 3E **117**
Claverton Cl. CF38: Bed . . . 5B **42**
Claverton Way CF23: Pontp . . . 4E **73**
Claymore Pl. CF11: Card . . . 3A **102**
Clayton Cres. CF37: Glyn . . . 2C **14**
Clayton St. NP19: Newp . . . 3D **36**
Clearwater Rd. NP19: Newp . . . 3B **56**
Clearwater Way CF23: Cyn . . . 2B **86**
Clearwell Ct. NP10: Bass . . . 6A **34**
Cleddau Cl. CF3: St M . . . 6F **75**
Cledwen Cl. CF62: Barry . . . 2D **116**
Cleeve Dr. CF14: L'shn . . . 6G **71**
Clement Atlee Dr. NP19: Newp . . . 3B **38**
Clement Pl. CF62: Barry . . . 5E **117**
Cleppa Pk. NP10: Coedk . . . 4E **53**
Cleppa Pk. Ind. Est. NP10: Coedk . . . 4E **53**
Clevedon Av. CF64: Sul . . . 3H **119**
Clevedon Cl. NP19: Newp . . . 3F **37**
Clevedon Rd. CF3: L'rmy . . . 1H **87**
NP19: Newp . . . 4F **37**
Cleveland Dr. NP11: Ris . . . 6G **17**
Clewer Ct. NP20: Newp . . . 5H **35**
Clewer Ct. M. NP20: Newp . . . 5H **35**
Cliff Ct. CF10: Card . . . 1C **102**
Cliff Hill CF64: P'rth . . . 3F **109**
Cliff Pde. CF64: P'rth . . . 3F **109**
Cliff Pl. CF5: Card . . . 3D **94**
Cliff Rd. CF64: P'rth . . . 3F **109**
Cliffside CF64: P'rth . . . 4F **109**
Cliff St. CF64: P'rth . . . 6B **102**
Cliff Ter. CF37: T'rest . . . 1D **24**
Cliff Vw. NP16: Sed . . . 3H **63**
Cliff Wlk. CF64: P'rth . . . 4F **109**
(Channel Vw.)
CF64: P'rth . . . 6F **109**
(Whitecliffe Dr.)
Cliff Wood Vw. CF62: Barry . . . 5C **116**
Clifton Pl. NP20: Newp . . . 5B **36**
Clifton Rd. NP20: Newp . . . 5B **36**
Clifton Sq. NP4: Grif . . . 6E **7**
Clifton St. CF24: Card . . . 1H **5** (2D **96**)
CF62: Barry . . . 4F **117**
CF83: Caer . . . 1D **46**
NP10: Roger . . . 1H **33**
Clinton Rd. CF64: P'rth . . . 2E **109**
Clipper Cl. NP19: Newp . . . 6F **21**
Clipper Rd. CF10: Card . . . 6F **97**
Clist Rd. NP20: Bet . . . 5E **19**
Clist Wlk. NP20: Bet . . . 5E **19**
Clive Ct. CF5: Card . . . 3D **94**
Clive Cres. CF64: P'rth . . . 1F **109**
Clive La. CF11: Card . . . 1G **101**
CF64: P'rth . . . 6H **101**
Clive M. CF5: Card . . . 3D **94**
Clive Pl. CF24: Card . . . 1G **5** (2C **96**)
CF62: Barry . . . 5H **117**
CF64: P'rth . . . 1F **109**
Clive Rd. CF5: Card . . . 2D **94**
CF62: Barry . . . 5G **117**
CF62: St A . . . 3D **112**
Clive St. CF11: Card . . . 6H **95**
CF83: Caer . . . 1C **46**
Clodien Av. CF14: Card . . . 5H **85**
Cloister Ct. CF5: Ely . . . 5A **94**
Clomendy Rd. NP44: C'brn . . . 3G **11**
(Cwmbran)
NP44: C'brn . . . 1E **11**
(Forge Hammer)
Clonakilty Way CF23: Pontp . . . 3G **73**
Clos Aled NP26: Cald . . . 4D **60**
Clos Alwen NP26: Cald . . . 3D **60**
Clos Alyn CF23: Pontp . . . 4F **73**
Clos Aneurin CF37: R'fln . . . 5H **25**
Clos Avro CF24: Card . . . 2H **97**
Clos Berriew CF14: Llan N . . . 4D **84**
Clos Brenin CF72: P'clun . . . 6C **64**
Clos Bron Iestyn CF37: P'prdd . . . 6A **14**
Clos Brynderi CF14: Rhiw . . . 6E **71**
Clos Bryn Melyn CF15: Rad . . . 1F **83**
Clos Cadw Gan CF38: Bed . . . 6H **41**
Clos Cae'r Wern CF83: Caer . . . 3A **46**
Clos Cae Wal CF15: Tong . . . 4G **69**
Clos Caewal CF15: P'rch . . . 4A **68**
Clos Camlas CF37: P'prdd . . . 5D **14**
Clos Caradog CF38: Llan F . . . 3D **42**
Clos Cas-Bach CF3: St M . . . 1E **89**
Clos Cefn Bychan CF15: P'rch . . . 4B **68**
Clos Cefn Glas CF38: Llan F . . . 6B **42**
Clos Cefni CF62: Barry . . . 1E **117**
Clos Cemaes CF14: Llan N . . . 4D **84**
Clos Cerios CF5: Ely . . . 4H **93**
Clos Chappell CF3: St M . . . 2D **88**
Clos Coed Hir CF14: Whit . . . 1B **84**
Clos Coed-y-Dafarn CF14: L'vne . . . 3B **72**
Clos Collwyn CF38: Llan F . . . 6B **42**
Clos Cornel CF14: Whit . . . 3D **84**
Clos Corris CF14: Llan N . . . 4D **84**
Clos Cradog CF64: P'rth . . . 4C **108**
(not continuous)
Clos Creyr CF38: Chu V, Llan F . . . 2D **42**
Clos Cromwell CF14: Rhiw . . . 4E **71**
Clos Culver CF5: Ely . . . 6F **93**
Clos Cwm Barri CF62: Barry . . . 3D **116**
Clos Cwm Creunant CF23: Pontp . . . 4F **73**
Clos Cwm Du CF23: Pontp . . . 4F **73**
Clos Cwm Garw CF83: Caer . . . 6H **27**
Clos Cyncoed CF83: Caer . . . 3H **27**
Clos Darren Las CF15: Cre . . . 6E **67**
Clos Ddyfan CF3: St M . . . 5E **75**
Clos Derwen CF23: Pen L . . . 5B **86**
Clos Dewi Sant CF11: Card . . . 3G **95**
Clos Dol Heulog CF23: Pontp . . . 4F **73**
Clos Dwyerw CF83: Caer . . . 2A **46**
Clos Dyfnaint CF3: St M . . . 1E **89**
Clos Dyfodwg CF38: Llan F . . . 6B **42**
Close, The CF14: L'shn . . . 5H **71**
NP26: Cald . . . 5B **60**
NP26: Pskwt . . . 5F **61**
NP44: Oakf . . . 5H **11**
Clos Edno CF23: Pen L . . . 4C **86**
Clos Eiddiw CF5: Ely . . . 4A **94**
Clos Elphan CF3: St M . . . 5E **75**
Clos Enfys CF83: Caer . . . 2A **46**
Clos Fach CF14: Rhiw . . . 5E **71**
Clos Gedrych CF11: Card . . . 4D **94**
Clos Glanaber CF3: St M . . . 1E **89**
Clos Glas Llwch CF3: St M . . . 2D **88**
Clos Guto CF83: Caer . . . 5F **29**
Clos Gwastir CF83: Caer . . . 2A **46**
Clos Gwaun Gledyr CF83: Caer . . . 6H **27**
Clos Gwent CF38: Bed . . . 6H **41**
Clos Gwernen CF72: L'harry . . . 5C **78**
Clos Gwernydd CF83: Caer . . . 5H **27**
Clos Gwlad-yr-Haf CF3: St M . . . 1E **89**
Clos Gwy CF23: Pontp . . . 4F **73**
Clos Gwynedd CF38: Bed . . . 6H **41**
Clos Gwynle CF83: Caer . . . 2H **45**
Clos Hafodyrynys CF3: St M . . . 1D **88**
Clos Hafren CF3: St M . . . 1E **89**
Clos Halket CF11: Card . . . 4D **94**
Clos Hector CF24: Card . . . 2H **97**
Clos Hendre CF14: Rhiw . . . 5F **71**
Clos Hereford CF72: L'sant . . . 2F **65**
Clos Heulwen CF15: Taff W . . . 5E **45**
Clos Lancaster CF72: L'sant . . . 3F **65**
Clos Leland CF72: L'sant . . . 3F **65**
Clos Lindsay CF5: Ely . . . 6F **93**
Clos Llanfair CF5: Wen . . . 5E **99**
Clos Llangefni CF38: Bed . . . 5H **41**
Clos Llawhaden CF63: Barry . . . 5A **106**
Clos Llewellyn CF15: Cre . . . 1E **81**
Clos Llysfaen CF14: L'vne . . . 2H **71**
Clos Mabon CF14: Rhiw . . . 5D **70**
Clos Maedref CF15: Rad . . . 2H **83**
Clos Maerun CF3: St M . . . 1D **88**
Clos Maes Brag CF83: Caer . . . 6D **28**
Clos Maes Mawr CF83: Caer . . . 3B **28**
Clos Maes-y-Mor CF3: St M . . . 2D **88**
Clos Mair CF23: Pen L . . . 4B **86**
Clos Mancheldowne CF62: Barry . . . 3G **117**
Clos Manmoel CF3: St M . . . 1D **88**
Clos Marian CF10: Card . . . 6F **97**
Clos Medwy CF3: St M . . . 5E **75**
Clos Meifod CF14: Llan N . . . 4D **84**
Clos Melin Ddwr CF14: L'vne . . . 3A **72**
Clos Menter CF14: Card . . . 5F **85**
Clos Morgan Gruffydd CF83: Abert . . . 2D **26**
Clos Myddlyn CF38: Bed . . . 6H **41**
Clos Nant Coslech CF23: Pontp . . . 4E **73**
Clos Nant Ddu CF23: Pontp . . . 4F **73**
Clos Nanteos CF23: Pontp . . . 5H **73**
Clos Nant Glaswg CF23: Pontp . . . 4E **73**
Clos Nant Mwlan CF23: Pontp . . . 3F **73**
Clos Nant y Cor CF23: Pontp . . . 4F **73**
Clos Nant y Cwm CF23: Pontp . . . 4F **73**
Clos Nant yr Aber CF83: Caer . . . 5B **28**
Clos Newydd CF14: Whit . . . 3B **84**
Clos Ogney CF71: Llan M . . . 2B **110**
Clos Padrig CF3: St M . . . 5E **75**
Clos Pandy CF83: B'ws . . . 3F **29**
Clos Pant Glas CF83: Tret . . . 3H **29**
Clos Pantycosyn CF3: St M . . . 1D **88**
Clos Parc Radyr CF15: Rad . . . 3F **83**
Clos Peiriant CF63: Barry . . . 3H **117**
Clos Pen y Clawdd CF3: St M . . . 1D **88**
Clos Pinwydden CF72: L'harry . . . 5C **78**
Clos Powys CF38: Bed . . . 5H **41**
Clos Pupren CF72: L'harry . . . 5C **78**
Clos Rhedyn CF5: Ely . . . 4A **94**
Clos Rheidol NP26: Cald . . . 3D **60**
Clos Rhiannon CF14: Thorn . . . 3F **71**
Clos St Catwg CF5: St F . . . 2C **82**
Clos Springfield CF72: T Grn . . . 3D **64**
Clos Synod CF14: Llan N . . . 4D **84**
Clos Taf CF5: L'dff . . . 5B **84**
Clos Tawe CF62: Barry . . . 1E **117**
Clos Tecwyn CF23: Pen L . . . 4B **86**
Clos Ton Mawr CF14: Rhiw . . . 4E **71**
Clos Trefeddyg CF83: Mac . . . 3F **31**
Clos Tregare CF3: St M . . . 1D **88**
Clos Treoda CF14: Whit . . . 2D **84**
Clos-tr-Onnen CF3: St M . . . 1E **89**
Clos ty Bronna CF5: F'wtr . . . 2G **93**
Clos Tyclyd CF14: Whit . . . 3A **84**
Clos Tyla Bach CF3: St M . . . 6E **75**
Clos Tylaway CF15: Rad . . . 2H **83**
Clos Tyniad Glo CF63: Barry . . . 3H **117**
Clos Tyrywen CF83: B'ws . . . 3E **29**
*Clos Waun Fach CF83: Caer . . . 2H **45***
(off Heol Tyddyn)
Clos William CF14: Rhiw . . . 4E **71**
Clos William Price CF37: R'fln . . . 1F **25**
Clos y Berllan CF3: St M . . . 1E **89**
Clos y Betws CF3: St M . . . 1D **88**
Clos-y-Blaidd CF14: Thorn . . . 2F **71**
Clos-y-Broch CF14: Thorn . . . 2G **71**
Clos-y-Cadno CF14: Thorn . . . 2F **71**
Clos-y-Carlwm CF14: Thorn . . . 2F **71**
Clos-y-Carw CF38: Llan F . . . 5B **42**
Clos-y-Cedr CF83: Caer . . . 3C **28**
Clos-y-Ceinach CF14: Thorn . . . 2G **71**
Clos y Coed CF38: Chu V . . . 3E **43**
Clos-y-Culfor CF3: St M . . . 1D **88**
Clos-y-Cwarra CF5: Ely . . . 4C **92**
Clos y Dolydd CF38: Bed . . . 6A **42**
Clos-y-Draenog CF14: Thorn . . . 2G **71**
Clos y Dryw CF14: Thorn . . . 2G **71**
Clos-y-Dyfrgi CF14: Thorn . . . 2F **71**
Clos-y-Ffynnon CF23: Pontp . . . 4F **73**
Clos y Fran CF14: Thorn . . . 1G **71**
Clos y Gamlas CF14: Whit . . . 1A **84**
Clos y Gelyn CF23: L'dyrn . . . 6F **73**
Clos-y-Gof CF5: Ely . . . 4D **92**
Clos y Graig CF14: Rhiw . . . 4D **70**
Clos-y-Gwadd CF14: Thorn . . . 2F **71**
Clos y Gwalch CF14: Thorn . . . 1G **71**
Clos y Gwyddfid CF15: Morg . . . 5E **69**
Clos y Hebog CF14: Thorn . . . 1G **71**
Clos y Mynydd CF15: Morg . . . 6E **69**
Clos-y-Nant CF5: F'wtr . . . 1H **93**
Clos Ynysddu CF72: P'clun . . . 5C **64**
Clos-y-Pant CF83: Caer . . . 3A **46**
Clos yr Aer CF14: Rhiw . . . 5E **71**
Clos yr Alarch CF14: Thorn . . . 1G **71**
Clos yr Arad CF83: Caer . . . 2H **45**
Clos-yr-Ardd CF14: Rhiw . . . 6D **70**
Clos-yr-Bryn CF14: Rhiw . . . 4C **70**
Clos yr Eos CF14: Thorn . . . 1G **71**
Clos-yr-Gornant CF3: St M . . . 1E **89**
Clos yr Hafod CF14: Rhiw . . . 5E **71**
Clos yr Harbwr CF62: Barry . . . 5F **117**
Clos-y-Rhiw CF5: Ely . . . 6F **93**
Clos-yr-Onnen CF71: Llan M . . . 4C **110**
Clos yr Wenallt CF14: Rhiw . . . 4C **70**
Clos yr Wylan CF62: Barry . . . 5H **117**
Clos Ysbyty CF83: Caer . . . 2B **46**
Clos Ysgallen CF15: Morg . . . 5E **69**
Clos Ystum Taf CF14: Whit . . . 3A **84**
Clos y Wern CF14: Rhiw . . . 5E **71**
Clos-y-Wiver CF71: Llan M . . . 2C **110**
Clos-y-Wiwer CF14: Thorn . . . 2G **71**
Clovelly Cres. CF3: L'rmy . . . 2G **87**
Clover Ct. NP44: F'wtr . . . 4B **10**
Clover Gro. CF5: F'wtr . . . 6G **83**
Club Rd. NP4: P'pool . . . 3A **6**
Clun Av. CF72: P'clun . . . 5D **64**
Clun Cres. CF72: P'clun . . . 5D **64**
Clun Ter. CF24: Card . . . 5A **86**
Clwyd CF64: P'rth . . . 6C **102**
Clwyd Way CF62: St A . . . 2D **112**
Clydach Cl. CF37: Glyn . . . 2D **14**
NP20: Bet . . . 6G **19**
Clydach St. CF11: Card . . . 6H **95**
Clydesmuir Ind. Est. CF24: Card . . . 1F **97**
Clydesmuir Rd. CF24: Card . . . 2F **97**
Clyde St. CF24: Card . . . 4H **5** (4C **96**)
NP11: Ris . . . 6E **17**
Clyffard Cres. NP20: Newp . . . 5A **36**
Clyffes NP44: G'mdw . . . 2D **10**
Clyro Pl. CF14: Llan N . . . 4C **84**
Clytha Cres. NP20: Newp . . . 6C **36**
CLYTHA PARK . . . 5A **36**
Clytha Pk. Rd. NP20: Newp . . . 4A **36**
Clytha Sq. NP20: Newp . . . 6C **36**
Coal Pit La. CF3: Cas, Lwr M . . . 6E **51**

Coaster Pl. CF10: Card 6F **97**
Coates Pl. CF3: L'rmy 6B **74**
Coates Rd. CF64: P'rth 4D **108**
Cobb Cres. NP26: Cald 6C **60**
Cobden Pl. NP11: C'keys 3A **16**
Cobden St. NP11: C'keys 3A **16**
Cobol Rd. CF3: St M 5F **75**
Coburn St. CF24: Card 1E **5** (1B **96**)
Coch-y-North Rd. NP4: P'nydd, P'pool 3A **6**
Cocker Av. NP44: C'brn 4F **11**
Coed Arhyd CF5: Ely 5C **92**
Coed Arian CF14: Llan N 4D **84**
Coed Bach CF62: Barry 6E **105**
Coed Cae CF83: Caer 5E **29**
NP44: Pnwd 6C **8**
Coedcae La. CF72: P'clun 5B **64**
Coedcae La. Ind. Est. CF72: P'clun 4B **64**
Coedcae Pl. NP4: P'pool 3B **6**
Coedcae Rd. CF83: Abert 2E **27**
Coedcae St. CF11: Card 6H **95**
Coedcae Ter. NP4: P'pool 3B **6**
Coed Camlas NP4: New I 4F **7**
Coed Ceirios CF14: Rhiw 6D **70**
Coed Cochwyn Av. CF14: L'shn 4G **71**
Coed Criafol CF63: Barry 4B **106**
Coed Edeyrn CF23: L'dyrn 3D **86**
Coeden Dal CF23: L'dyrn 5E **73**
COED EVA 5D **10**
Coedeva Mill NP44: C'brn 5E **11**
Coed Garw NP44: C'iog 5G **9**
Coed Gethin CF83: Caer 3B **28**
Coed Glas NP44: C'brn 4F **11**
Coed Glas Rd. CF14: L'shn 5F **71**
Coed Isaf Rd. CF37: P'prdd 1A **24**
COEDKERNEW 4F **53**
Coed Leddyn CF83: Caer 3B **28**
Coed Lee NP44: C'brn 4E **11**
Coed Main CF83: Caer 5F **29**
Coed Mawr CF62: Barry 6E **105**
Coed Mieri CF72: P'clun 5C **64**
COED-PEN-MAEN 5C **14**
Coedpenmaen Cl. CF37: P'prdd 6D **14**
Coedpenmaen Rd. CF37: P'prdd 5D **14**
Coed Pwll CF83: Caer 5E **29**
Coedriglan Dr. CF5: Ely 5C **92**
Coed-y-Brain Ct. CF83: L'brad 1B **28**
Coed-y-Brain Rd. CF83: L'brad 1B **28**
Coed y Brenin CF37: P'prdd 1A **24**
Coed-y-Caerau La. NP18: L'stne 5G **23**
Coed-y-Canddo Rd. NP4: New I 4F **7**
Coed y Capel CF62: Barry 6E **105**
Coed-y-Dafarn CF14: L'vne 3C **72**
Coed y Dyffryn CF38: Chu V 3E **43**
Coed-y-Felin CF62: Barry 2E **117**
Coed-y-Gloriau CF23: L'dyrn 6D **72**
Coed-y-Gores CF23: L'dyrn 1E **87**
(not continuous)
Coedygric Rd. NP4: Grif 5E **7**
Coed-y-Lan Rd. CF37: Glyn 2D **14**
Coed-y-Llinos CF83: Caer 6A **28**
Coed-y-Llyn CF15: Rad 1E **83**
CF23: Cyn 3B **86**
Coed y Pandy CF83: B'ws 3F **29**
Coed-y-Pica CF83: Abert 3E **27**
Coed-yr-Eos CF83: Caer 6A **28**
Coed yr Esgob CF72: L'sant 1E **65**
Coed-yr-Odyn CF62: Barry 4D **116**
Coed yr Ynn CF14: Rhiw 5E **71**
Coed y Wenallt CF14: Rhiw 4D **70**
Coed-y-Wennol CF83: Caer 1A **46**
COGAN 6H **101**
Cogan Ct. CF64: L'dgh 5G **101**
Cogan Hill CF64: P'rth 5G **101**
Cogan Pill Rd. CF64: L'dgh 4F **101**
(not continuous)
Cogan Spur CF11: Card 5H **101**
CF64: Card 5H **101**
Cogan Station (Rail) 5G **101**
Cogan Ter. CF24: Card 2A **96**
Coggins Cl. CF83: Caer 2H **45**
Cog Rd. CF64: Sul 2G **119**
Coigne Ter. CF63: Barry 2B **118**
Coity Cl. CF3: St M 6E **75**
Colborne Wlk. CF11: Card 4F **95**
Colbourne Rd. CF38: Bed 5A **42**
Colchester Av. CF23: Pen L 6D **86**
Colchester Ct. CF23: Pen L 6D **86**
Colchester Factory Est. CF23: Pen L 6E **87**
COLCOT 5F **105**
Colcot Leisure Cen. 6F **105**
Colcot Rd. CF62: Barry 5F **105**
Cold Bath Rd. NP18: C'ln 5H **21**
Coldbrook Rd. E. CF63: Barry 6C **106**
Coldbrook Rd. W. CF63: Barry 6B **106**
Cold Knap Way CF62: Barry 5E **117**
(not continuous)
COLDRA 2D **38**
Coldra, The NP18: Newp 2C **38**
Coldra Rd. NP20: Newp 6A **36**
Coldra Woods Dr. NP18: C'ln 1C **38**
Coldstores Rd. CF10: Card 2E **103**
Coldstream Cl. NP44: C'iog 6G **9**
Coldstream Ter. CF11: Card 4A **4** (4H **95**)
Cole Ct. CF83: Caer 5F **29**
Coleford Dr. CF3: St M 1D **88**
Coleford Path NP44: G'mdw 2E **11**
Coleg Glan Hafren (City Cen. Campus) 2F **5** (3B **96**)
Coleridge Av. CF64: P'rth 1D **108**
Coleridge Cres. CF62: Barry 5G **105**
Coleridge Gdns. CF83: Mac 3C **30**
Coleridge Grn. NP44: G'mdw 3E **11**
Coleridge Rd. CF11: Card 2F **101**
NP19: Newp 4G **37**
Colhugh Cl. CF71: Llan M 3B **110**
Colhugh Pk. CF71: Llan M 4B **110**
Colhugh St. CF71: Llan M 3B **110**
Colin Way CF5: Ely 3A **94**
Collard Cres. CF62: Barry 6H **105**
College Cl. CF14: Whit 3D **84**
College Cres. NP18: C'ln 5H **21**
College Flds. Cl. CF62: Barry 2G **117**
College Gdns. CF71: Llan M 3B **110**
College Glade NP18: C'ln 3G **21**
College Pl. CF62: Barry 3G **117**
College Rd. CF10: Card 1B **4** (2H **95**)
CF14: Llan N, Whit 5C **84**
CF14: Whit 3D **84**
CF62: Barry 2F **117**
(not continuous)
NP4: P'pool 2C **6**
NP18: C'ln 4H **21**
College St. CF71: Llan M 3B **110**
College Ter. CF71: Llan M 3B **110**
NP4: P'nydd 1A **6**
Collier St. NP19: Newp 3D **36**
Colliery Rd. CF83: B'ws, Tret 2G **29**
Collingwood Av. NP19: Newp 5G **37**
Collingwood Cl. NP16: Bul 5G **63**
NP19: Newp 5G **37**
Collingwood Cres. NP19: Newp 5G **37**
Collingwood Rd. NP19: Newp 5G **37**
Collins Cl. NP20: Newp 1G **53**
Collins Ter. CF37: T'rest 3E **25**
Collivaud Pl. CF24: Card 5D **96**
Collwyn St. CF39: T'fail 3A **40**
Colne St. NP19: Newp 4D **36**
Colston Av. NP19: Newp 6F **37**
Colston Ct. NP19: Newp 6G **37**
Colston Pl. NP19: Newp 6G **37**
Colts Foot Cl. NP20: Newp 4A **36**
Columbus Cl. CF62: Barry 5A **106**
Columbus Ho. NP18: L'stne 6E **23**
Columbus Wlk. CF10: Card 6F **5** (5B **96**)
Colum Dr. CF10: Card 1H **95**
Column St. CF64: Sul 1E **119**
Colum Pl. CF10: Card 1H **95**
Colum Rd. CF10: Card 1H **95**
Colum Ter. CF10: Card 2H **95**
Colwill Rd. CF14: Llan N 5D **84**
Colwinstone Cl. CF14: Llan N 4C **84**
Colwinstone St. CF14: Llan N 4C **84**
Colwyn Rd. CF3: Rum 3H **87**
Comet St. CF24: Card 3H **5** (3C **96**)
Comfrey Cl. CF3: St M 5E **75**
NP20: Newp 3A **36**
Commercial Rd. CF63: Barry 1A **118**
CF83: Mac 3H **31**
(Royal Oak)
CF83: Mac 2F **31**
(Wesley Hill)
NP20: Newp 6C **36**
Commercial St. CF38: Bed 4A **42**
CF71: Llan M 3B **110**
CF72: L'sant 2F **65**
NP4: Grif 6E **7**
NP4: P'pool 2C **6**
NP11: Ris 6D **16**
NP20: Newp 4C **36**
(not continuous)
NP44: C'brn 3G **11**
NP44: Pnwd 6E **9**
Commercial St. Cvn. Site
NP11: Ris 1E **33**
Commercial Wharf NP20: Newp 1E **55**
Common App. CF38: Bed 5A **42**
Common Rd. CF37: P'prdd 6D **14**
(not continuous)
COMMON-Y-COED 1E **59**
Compass Rd. CF10: Card 2D **102**
Compton Cl. NP10: Roger 3D **34**
Compton St. CF11: Card 5G **95**
Congress Theatre *1G* **11**
(off Gwent Sq.)
Conifer Cl. NP18: C'ln 5E **21**
Conifer Ct. CF5: F'wtr 1F **93**
Coniston Cl. NP19: Newp 1E **37**
Connaught Rd. CF24: Card 1C **96**
Constable Dr. NP19: Newp 1F **37**
Constables Cl. NP20: Newp 1D **54**
Constance St. NP19: Newp 2D **36**
Constant Cl. CF11: Card 3A **102**
Constellation St. CF24: Card 3H **5** (3C **96**)
Constitution Hill CF71: C'bri 4C **90**
Conway Cl. CF37: Glyn 2C **14**
CF64: Din P 2A **108**
NP44: C'brn 1G **11**
Conway Ct. CF83: Caer 5H **27**
NP19: Newp 5G **37**
Conway Cres. CF38: Tont 1F **43**
Conway Cft. NP19: Newp 5G **37**
Conway Dr. CF62: Barry 1E **117**
Conway Rd. CF11: Card 2F **95**
NP4: P'pool 2B **6**
NP19: Newp 4F **37**
Conway Sac NP19: Newp 5G **37**
Conway Ter. NP44: C'iog 6F **9**
Conybeare Rd. CF5: Card 2D **94**
CF64: Sul 1H **119**
Cook Rd. CF62: Barry 4A **106**
Coolgreany Cl. NP20: Malp 6A **20**
Coolgreany Cres. NP20: Malp 6A **20**
Coomassie St. NP20: Newp 2D **54**
Coopers Ct. CF10: Card 5D **4**
Coopers La. CF71: C'bri 3C **90**
Coopers Pl. CF83: Caer 2H **45**
Coopers Way CF72: C Inn 2H **65**
Copleston Rd. CF14: Llan N 5C **84**
Copper Beech Cl. NP18: C'ln 5E **21**
Copperfield Ct. CF62: Barry 2G **117**
Copperfield Dr. CF14: Thorn 3H **71**
Copper St. CF24: Card 2H **5** (3D **96**)
Coppice, The CF38: Tont 1G **43**
CF72: P'clun 5F **65**
Coppice Rd. CF23: Pontp 3H **73**
Coppins, The CF14: L'vne 2B **72**
NP20: Malp 4B **20**
Copse Wlk. CF23: Pontp 3G **73**
Copthorne Way CF5: Ely 1C **98**
Cora St. CF63: Barry 2A **118**
Corbett Cres. CF83: Caer 2D **46**
Corbett Gro. CF83: Caer 2A **46**
Corbett Rd. CF10: Card 1B **4** (2H **95**)
CF64: L'dgh 5F **101**
Corbetts La. CF83: Caer 3C **28**
Corelli St. NP19: Newp 3D **36**
Coriander Cl. NP20: Newp 3A **36**
Corinthian Cl. CF64: L'dgh 4F **101**
Cork Dr. CF23: Pontp 3G **73**
Cork Rd. NP20: Newp 2D **54**
Cormorant Cl. CF3: St M 5D **74**
Cormorant Way NP10: Duf 5H **53**
Cornbrook Rd. NP20: Bet 4F **19**
Cornelly Cl. CF14: Llan N 4C **84**
Cornelly St. CF14: Llan N 4C **84**
Cornerswell La. CF64: P'rth 2D **108**
Cornerswell Pl. CF64: P'rth 1C **108**
Cornerswell Rd. CF64: P'rth 2D **108**
Cornfield Cl. CF14: L'shn 4F **71**
Cornfield Ri. CF83: B'ws 3F **29**
Cornflower Cl. CF14: L'vne 1A **72**
NP10: Roger 3A **34**
Corn Glas CF63: Barry 5C **106**
Cornish Cl. CF11: Card 1A **102**
Corn Stairs Hill CF37: P'prdd 6D **14**
Corn St. NP20: Newp 4C **36**
Cornwall Ri. CF62: Barry 6H **105**
Cornwall Rd. CF62: Barry 1H **117**
NP19: Newp 3E **37**
Cornwall St. CF11: Card 6G **95**
Cornwood Cl. CF5: F'wtr 6F **83**
Coronation Pl. NP11: P'waun 1A **16**
Coronation Rd. CF14: Heath 3F **85**
Coronation St. CF63: Barry 3A **118**
CF83: Tret 3A **30**
NP11: Ris 6E **17**
Coronation Ter. CF37: P'prdd 4E **15**
CF64: P'rth 6A **102**
NP4: P'nydd 1A **6**
(off Hanbury Rd.)
Corporation Rd. CF11: Card 6H **95**
NP19: Newp 4D **36**
Corris NP44: C'iog 5F **9**
Corvette Ct. CF10: Card 6C **96**
Corwen Cres. CF14: Llan N 4C **84**
Cory Pk. NP44: Oakf 1B **20**
Cory Pl. CF11: Card 3A **102**
CORYTON 6B **70**

Coryton Cl. CF14: Whit 6B 70
Coryton Cres. CF14: Whit 6A 70
Coryton Dr. CF14: Whit 6A 70
Coryton Interchange CF14: Tong 5A 70
Coryton Ri. CF14: Whit 6A 70
Coryton Station (Rail) 1B 84
Cory Way CF63: Barry 3A 118
Cosheston Rd. CF5: F'wtr 5H 83
COSMESTON 5E 109
Cosmeston Dr. CF64: P'rth 6E 109
Cosmeston Lakes Country Pk. 5C 108
Cosmeston Lakes Country Pk. Vis. Cen. 6D 108
Cosmeston St. CF24: Card 6H 85
Cosslett Pl. CF11: Card 1A 102
Cot Farm Circ. NP19: Newp 3D 38
Cot Farm Cl. NP19: Newp 3D 38
Cot Farm Gdns. NP19: Newp 3D 38
Cot Farm Wlk. NP19: Newp 3D 38
Cot Hill NP18: L'wrn 3E 39
Cotman Cl. NP19: Newp 2G 37
Cotswold Av. CF14: L'vne 2B 72
Cotswold Cl. NP19: Newp 3A 38
Cotswold Ri. CF63: Barry 1B 118
Cotswold Way NP11: Ris 6G 17
NP19: Newp 3A 38
Cottage Cl. CF14: Thorn 3H 71
Cottage Row CF5: Wen 3D 98
Cottesmore Way CF72: C Inn 3G 65
Cottrell Rd. CF14: Whit 3D 84
CF24: Card 1C 96
Cottrell Sq. CF63: Barry 6A 106
Coulson Cl. NP20: Newp 6C 36
Countess Pl. CF64: P'rth 2D 108
Countisbury Av. CF3: L'rmy 1A 88
COUNTY HOSPITAL 5E 7
County Vw. CF37: R'fln 5A 26
Court, The CF14: L'vne 1B 72
CF24: Card 1D 96
Court Cl. CF14: Whit 4E 85
CF71: A'thin 2G 91
CF71: Llan M 2B 110
Court Cres. NP10: Bass 1D 52
Courtenay Cl. CF3: St M 6B 74
Courtenay Rd. CF24: Card 3E 97
CF63: Barry 1B 118
Court Farm Cl. NP44: Oakf 5A 12
Court Farm Rd. NP44: Oakf 5A 12
Courtfield Cl. NP10: Roger 3A 34
Court Gdns. NP10: Roger 3A 34
Court Ho. NP26: Cald 5D 60
Court Ho. Cl. NP26: Cald 5D 60
Court Ho. St. CF37: P'prdd 1C 24
Courtis Rd. CF5: Ely 4F 93
Courtlands CF62: Barry 4E 117
Courtlands, The NP44: G'mdw 2D 10
Court Mdw. NP18: L'stne 1G 39
Court Newton CF63: Barry 1A 118
Courtney St. NP19: Newp 3D 36
Court Rd. CF11: Card 6A 4 (5G 95)
CF14: Whit 4E 85
CF63: Barry 2A 118
(Holton Rd.)
CF63: Barry 6B 106
(Kenilworth Rd.)
CF83: Caer 4B 28
NP44: C'brn, Oakf 4H 11
Court Rd. Ind. Est. NP44: Oakf 4H 11
Court Vw. NP18: L'stne 1G 39
Courtyard, The CF24: Card 3D 96
NP10: Coedk 5F 53
Courtybella Gdns. NP20: Newp 1C 54
Courtybella Ter. NP20: Newp 1C 54
Court-y-Bella Ter. NP20: Newp 1B 54
Coveny St. CF24: Card 3E 97
Coverjack Rd. NP19: Newp 5D 36
Covert Wlk. NP44: F'wtr 4D 10
COWBRIDGE 3D 90
Cowbridge By-pass CF71: C'bri 2A 90
Cowbridge Leisure Cen. 3C 90
Cowbridge Rd. CF62: St A 4D 112
CF71: Llan M 1B 110
CF72: P'clun 3A 78
CF72: T Grn 4D 64
(not continuous)
Cowbridge Rd. E. CF5: Card 3B 94
CF10: Card 4A 4 (4G 95)
CF11: Card 4A 4 (4G 95)
Cowbridge Rd. W. CF5: Ely, F'wtr 6E 93
Cowbridge St. CF63: Barry 6B 106
Cowleaze NP26: Magor 4D 58
Cowper Cl. CF64: P'rth 1D 108
NP20: Newp 1G 53
Cowper Pl. CF24: Card 1G 5 (2C 96)
Cowshed La. NP10: Bass 1C 52
Cowslip Cl. CF23: Pontp 4G 73
Cowslip Dr. CF64: P'rth 6G 101
Coychurch Ri. CF63: Barry 5A 106
Craddock St. CF11: Card 5A 4 (4G 95)
Cradoc Rd. CF14: Whit 3E 85
Cragside Cl. CF3: St M 1D 88
Craig Castell CF15: Rad 1F 83
Craig-Ceiliog La. NP10: H'lys 3C 18
NP44: H'lys 3C 18
Craiglee Dr. CF10: Card 6F 5 (5B 96)
Craigmuir Rd. CF24: Card 2F 97
CRAIGYFEDW 2F 27
Craig-yr-Allt CF14: Rhiw 4D 70
Craig yr Haul Dr. CF3: Cas 2G 75
Cranbourne Way CF23: Pontp 4E 73
Cranbrook St. CF24: Card 1E 5 (2B 96)
Crane St. NP4: P'pool 3C 6
Cranleigh Ri. CF3: Rum 3G 87
Cranmer Ct. CF5: L'dff 1C 94
Cranwell Cl. CF5: F'wtr 5A 84
Craven Wlk. CF64: P'rth 5E 109
Crawford Cl. CF38: Bed 5B 42
Crawford Dr. CF23: Pontp 4G 73
Crawford St. NP19: Newp 3D 36
Crawford Trad. Est. NP19: Newp 2D 36
Crawley Cl. CF14: Thorn 2G 71
Crawshay Ct. CF71: Llan M 2D 110
Crawshay Dr. CF71: Llan M 3C 110
Crawshay La. CF10: Card 5A 96
Crawshay St. CF10: Card 5A 96
Crediton Rd. CF3: L'rmy 1A 88
CREIGIAU 6E 67
Crescent, The CF5: F'wtr 2H 93
CF5: L'dff 1D 94
CF62: Barry 2D 116
CF83: B'ws 3G 29
CF83: Caer 6A 28
CF83: Mac 3F 31
NP44: C'brn 4F 11
Crescent Ct. NP19: Newp 3F 37
Crescent Rd. CF83: Caer 6C 28
NP11: Ris 4C 16
NP19: Newp 3F 37
Cresent Cl. CF71: C'bri 5D 90
Cressfield Dr. CF23: Pontp 4H 73
Cresswell Cl. CF3: St M 5E 75
Cresswell Ct. CF62: Barry 5H 105
Cresswell Wlk. NP44: G'mdw 2E 11
Cressy Rd. CF23: Pen L 6C 86
Cresta Gro. CF5: Ely 4D 92
Criccieth Ct. CF64: Din P 1B 108
Criccieth Rd. CF3: Rum 3A 88
CRICK 1E 61
Crickhowell Rd. CF3: Rum, St M 1C 88
Crickhowell Wlk. CF3: St M 6D 74
Crick Rd. NP26: C'went, Pskwt 1E 61
NP26: Pskwt 5G 61
CRINDAU 1B 36
Crindau Ind. Est. NP20: Newp 1C 36
Crindau Rd. NP20: Newp 1B 36
Crockett Pl. CF37: P'prdd 5A 14
Crockherbtown La. CF10: Card 3D 4 (3A 96)
Crocus Cl. NP10: Roger 3H 33
Croescadarn Cl. CF23: Pontp 4G 73
Croescadarn Rd. CF23: Pontp 4F 73
(Huntington Dr.)
CF23: Pontp 3F 73
(St Mellons Rd., not continuous)
Croescade Rd. CF38: Llan F 4B 42
Croeswen NP44: Oakf 5H 11
CROESYCEILIOG 1A 12
Croesyceiliog By-Pass NP44: C'iog 5H 9
CROES-Y-MWYALCH 2A 20
Croffta CF64: Din P 3G 107
Crofft-y-Genau Rd. CF5: St F 3C 82
Crofta CF14: L'vne 4B 72
Croft Gdns. CF64: Sul 2G 119
Croft John CF62: Rho 1D 114
Crofton Mede NP44: F'wtr 4D 10
Crofts Cnr. NP44: G'mdw 2D 10
Croft St. CF24: Card 1G 5 (1C 96)
CF71: C'bri 4D 90
Croft Ter. CF71: C'bri 4D 90
Cromwell Pl. NP44: Pnwd 6E 9
Cromwell Rd. CF14: Heath 3F 85
NP11: Ris 3B 16
NP16: Bul 5E 63
NP19: Newp 5F 37
Cromwell Rd. Bungs. NP11: Ris 3B 16
Crossbrook St. CF37: P'prdd 6C 14
Cross Common Rd. CF64: Din P 3H 107
CF64: P'rth 3H 107
Crossfield Rd. CF62: Barry 3E 117
Crosshill CF62: Barry 6E 117
CROSS INN 3G 65
Cross Inn Rd. CF72: L'sant 2F 65
CROSS KEYS 3A 16
Crosskeys RUFC 2A 16
Crosskeys Station (Rail) 3A 16
Cross La. NP20: Newp 5C 36
Cross Pl. CF14: Card 6G 85
Cross Roads CF38: Bed 4H 41
Cross St. CF15: Tong 4G 69
CF37: C'fydd 2F 15
CF37: P'prdd 5D 14
CF63: Barry 2A 118
CF83: Abert 2E 27
CF83: B'ws 3G 29
NP18: C'ln 5A 22
Crossway NP26: Rog 6A 60
CROSSWAY GREEN 1D 62
Crossways Cl. NP26: Undy 5F 59
Crossways Pk. CF83: Caer 4E 29
Crossways Rd. CF5: Ely 4G 93
Crossways St. CF37: P'prdd 5D 14
CF63: Barry 2A 118
Crosswells Way CF5: Ely 4E 93
Crouch Cl. NP20: Bet 6F 19
Crown Arc. NP20: Newp 4C 36
(off Market St.)
Crown Cl. NP18: C'ln 5A 22
NP44: Pnwd 5D 8
Crown Hill CF38: Llan F 5C 42
Crown Hill Dr. CF38: Llan F 5C 42
Crown La. NP19: Newp 4E 37
Crown Ri. NP44: Llanf 3B 12
Crown Rd. NP44: Llanf 5B 12
Crown St. NP19: Newp 3E 37
Crown Wlk. CF83: Mac 2H 31
Crown Way CF14: Card 6G 85
Croyde Av. CF3: L'rmy 1A 88
Croydon Cl. NP19: Newp 1E 37
Croydon Ct. NP19: Newp 1E 37
Crumlin Dr. CF3: St M 6D 74
Crumlin Rd. NP4: P'nydd, P'pool 4A 6
Crumlin St. NP4: P'pool 3B 6
Crundale Cres. CF14: L'shn 5H 71
Crwys Cres. CF37: Up Bo 5A 26
Crwys La. CF63: Barry 5B 106
Crwys Pl. CF24: Card 1B 96
Crwys Rd. CF24: Card 6A 86
Crynant Cl. CF62: St A 2D 112
Crystal Av. CF23: Heath 1A 86
Crystal Glen CF14: L'shn 1H 85
Crystal Ri. CF14: Heath 1H 85
Crystal Wood Dr. CF72: P'clun 5E 65
Crystal Wood Rd. CF14: Heath 1H 85
Cuckoofield Cl. CF15: Morg 5E 69
Cudd y Coed CF63: Barry 5C 106
Cules Ter. CF15: Taff W 6D 44
Culver Cl. CF64: P'rth 4C 108
CULVERHOUSE CROSS 1E 99
Cumberland Rd. NP19: Newp 1E 37
Cumberland St. CF5: Card 4E 95
Cumnock Pl. CF24: Card 4H 5 (4D 96)
Cumnock Ter. CF24: Card 4H 5 (4D 96)
Cumrae St. CF24: Card 4D 96
Cunningham Cl. CF23: Cyn 3A 86
Cunningham Rd. NP19: Newp 2C 38
Curie Cl. NP20: Malp 4A 20
Curlew Av. NP26: Cald 6D 60
Curlew Cl. CF14: Whit 1C 84
NP19: Newp 2C 56
Curlew Cres. CF62: St A 3F 111
Curll Av. CF14: Card 4G 85
Curran Emb. CF10: Card 6A 96
Curran Rd. CF10: Card 5A 96
Curzon Ct. NP19: Newp 5B 38
Custom Ho. Pl. CF64: P'rth 5B 102
Custom Ho. St. CF10: Card 6D 4 (5A 96)
Cutter Cl. NP19: Newp 6F 21
Cwlwm Cariad CF63: Barry 4B 106
Cwm Barry Way CF62: Barry 3E 117
CWMBRAN 1G 11
Cwmbran Dr. NP44: C'brn, Oakf, Pnwd 1G 11
Cwmbran FC 4H 11
Cwmbran Retail Pk. NP44: C'brn 2F 11
Cwmbran Stadium 4H 11
Cwmbran Station (Rail) 1H 11
CWMBRÂN 1G 11
CWMCARN 1A 16
Cwmcarn Cl. CF3: St M 6D 74
Cwmcarn Forest Dr. NP11: C'crn, P'waun 1A 16
NP11: C'keys 1C 16
Cwm-cidy Cotts. CF62: Barry 3C 116
Cwm-Cidy La. CF62: Barry 3C 116
Cwm Cwddy Dr. NP10: Bass, R'drn 6A 34
Cwm Cwddy La. NP10: Bass 1A 52
Cwmdare St. CF24: Card 6H 85
Cwm Dr. CF64: Din P 1G 107
Cwm Dylan Cl. NP10: Bass 1A 52
Cwm Farm Cl. NP4: P'pool 4C 6
Cwm Fedw CF83: Mac 1G 31
CWM FIELDS 4C 6

Cwm Gwynlais CF15: Tong 5H **69**
Cwm La. NP10: Roger 2D **34**
Cwm-Nant Flds. NP44: C'brn 3F **11**
Cwmnant Vs. NP44: C'brn 3F **11**
Cwm Nofydd CF14: Rhiw 5D **70**
Cwmnofydd La. CF83: Mac 3E **31**
Cwm Parc CF62: Barry 2E **117**
Cwmsor Cl. NP4: New I 5H **7**
CWM TALWG 1E **117**
Cwm-y-Nant NP11: Ris 1E **33**
Cwmynyscoy Rd. NP4: P'pool 5C **6**
Cwrdy Cl. NP4: Grif 1D **8**
Cwrdy La. NP4: Grif, Up R 1C **8**
Cwrdy Rd. NP4: Grif 1D **8**
Cwrdy Wlk. NP4: Grif 1D **8**
Cwrt Aethen CF63: Barry 4B **106**
Cwrt Bala CF3: Rum 2C **88**
Cwrt Bleddyn NP44: C'brn 4F **11**
Cwrt Boston CF23: Card 6G **87**
Cwrt Brynteg CF15: Rad 2G **83**
Cwrt Cefn CF14: L'vne 3A **72**
Cwrt Coed-y-Brenin CF38: Chu V 3E **43**
Cwrt Coles CF23: Card 6G **87**
Cwrt Deri CF14: Rhiw 5D **70**
Cwrt Dowlas NP44: C'brn 5G **11**
NP44: C'brn, Oakf 6G **11**
Cwrt Draw Llyn CF83: Caer 3B **46**
Cwrt Dyfed CF63: Barry 5C **106**
Cwrt Edward CF62: Barry 3G **117**
Cwrt Eglwys Newydd CF14: Whit 2C **84**
Cwrt Eirlys CF62: Barry 4A **106**
CF63: Barry 4A **106**
Cwrt Faenor CF38: Bed 6H **41**
Cwrt Glas CF14: L'shn 5G **71**
Cwrtglas NP44: C'iog 1A **12**
Cwrt Glyndwr CF37: T'rest 3D **24**
Cwrt Golwg Sianel NP11: Ris 6F **17**
Cwrt Griffin CF83: Rud 1C **48**
Cwrt Gwenillian CF63: Barry 1D **118**
Cwrt Heledd CF24: Card 6B **86**
Cwrt Llandough CF64: L'dgh 5F **101**
Cwrt Llanfabon CF83: Caer 4B **28**
Cwrt Llechau CF72: L'harry 4C **78**
Cwrt Morgan NP26: C'went 1C **60**
Cwrt Nant y Felin CF83: Caer 2H **45**
Cwrt Newton Pool CF62: Rho 6F **115**
Cwrt Pencoeotre CF62: Barry 5A **106**
Cwrt Pensarn CF3: Rum 2C **88**
Cwrt Pentre Bach CF3: St M 5E **75**
Cwrt Pentwyn CF38: Llan F 4B **42**
Cwrt Roberts CF5: Ely 6E **93**
Cwrt St Cyres CF64: P'rth 1C **108**
Cwrt Severn NP26: Cald 6B **60**
Cwrt-Ty-Fferm CF83: L'brad 1B **28**
Cwrt Ty Mawr CF64: P'rth 3C **108**
CF83: Caer 1F **47**
Cwrt Ty-Mynydd CF15: Rad 1F **83**
Cwrt-y-Cadno CF5: Ely 4D **92**
CF71: Llan M 2C **110**
Cwrt y Castell CF83: Caer 6D **28**
Cwrt Y Ffowndri CF37: T'rest 2E **25**
Cwrt y Gth. CF38: Bed 6A **42**
Cwrt-y-Goedwig CF38: Llan F 4B **42**
Cwrt y Melin *CF11: Card 4F 95*
(off Leckwith Pl.)
Cwrt-yr-Ala Av. CF5: Ely 6F **93**
Cwrt-yr-Ala Rd. CF5: Ely, Mic P 6F **93**
Cwrt yr Ardal CF3: Rum 2C **88**
Cwrt-yr-Lolo CF62: St A 1C **112**
Cwrt-yr-Ysgol NP11: Ris 4D **16**
Cwrt-y-Vil Rd. CF64: P'rth 2E **109**
Cwrt-y-Vil Rd. (Lwr.) CF64: P'rth 3E **109**
Cwrt y Waun CF38: Bed 6A **42**
Cwrt Ywen CF72: L'harry 5C **78**
Cyfarthfa St. CF24: Card 2C **96**
Cymmer St. CF11: Card 6H **95**
Cymric Cl. CF5: Ely 4H **93**
Cynan Cl. CF38: Bed 5A **42**
CF63: Barry 5B **106**
CYNCOED 1C **86**
Cyncoed Av. CF23: Cyn 1C **86**
Cyncoed Cres. CF23: Cyn 1D **86**
Cyncoed Flats CF23: Cyn 3C **86**
Cyncoed Gdns. CF23: Pen L 4C **86**
Cyncoed Pl. CF23: Cyn 1C **86**
Cyncoed Ri. CF23: Cyn 1C **86**
Cyncoed Rd. CF23: Cyn 5C **72**
CF23: Pen L 4C **86**
Cynon Vw. CF37: C'fydd 4F **15**
Cyntwell Av. CF5: Ely 6F **93**
Cyntwell Cres. CF5: Ely 6F **93**
Cyntwell Pl. CF5: Ely 5F **93**
Cypress Cl. NP18: C'ln 5E **21**
Cypress Dr. CF3: St M 5D **74**
Cypress Pl. CF5: F'wtr 6H **83**
Cypress St. CF37: R'fln 4G **25**
Cyrch-y-Gwas Rd. CF37: T'rest 2E **25**
Cyril Cres. CF24: Card 2D **96**
Cyril St. CF63: Barry 2B **118**
NP19: Newp 5D **36**

D

Daffodil Ct. NP44: F'wtr 3B **10**
Daffodil La. NP10: Roger 2H **33**
Dafydd Pl. CF63: Barry 5A **106**
Daisy St. CF5: Card 3D **94**
Daisy Vw. NP4: P'pool 4D **6**
Dalcross St. CF24: Card 6B **86**
Dale Av. CF14: Heath 2F **85**
Dale Ct. CF62: Barry 5H **105**
Dale Path NP44: F'wtr 3D **10**
Dale Rd. NP19: Newp 3B **38**
Dalmuir Rd. CF24: Card 2F **97**
Dalton St. CF24: Card 1A **96**
Damson Pl. CF23: Pontp 2H **73**
Dan Caerlan CF72: L'sant 1G **65**
Dancarga Dr. NP26: Cald 5C **60**
Dancing Cl. NP26: Undy 3D **58**
Dancing Hill NP26: Undy 4D **58**
Danes Cl. NP16: Chep 2D **62**
Danescourt Station (Rail) 5A **84**
Danescourt Way CF5: L'dff 5H **83**
Danes Hill NP16: Sed 3H **63**
Daniel Hopkin Cl. CF71: Llan M 4B **110**
Daniell Cl. CF64: Sul 2G **119**
Daniel Pl. NP20: Newp 6C **36**
Daniel St. CF24: Card 6A **86**
CF63: Barry 6A **106**
NP20: Newp 6C **36**
Dannog y Coed CF63: Barry 4B **106**
Dan-y-Bank Cotts. CF15: Tong 4F **69**
Danybryn CF72: P'clun 1B **78**
Dan-y-Bryn Av. CF15: Rad 1E **83**
Dan-y-Bryn Cl. CF15: Rad 1E **83**
Danybryn Vs. CF37: T'rest 2D **24**
Danycoed CF83: Caer 2D **46**
Dan-y-Coedcae Rd. CF37: P'prdd 2B **24**
Dan-y-Coed Cl. CF23: Cyn 1B **86**
Dan-y-Coed Ri. CF23: Cyn 1B **86**
Dan-y-Coed Rd. CF23: Cyn 6B **72**
Dan-y-Der CF83: B'ws 2E **29**
Dan-y-Felin CF72: L'sant 2E **65**
DANYGRAIG 5D **16**
Dan y Graig NP11: Ris 5D **16**
Danygraig CF83: Mac 3B **30**
NP44: C'iog 4G **9**
Dan-y-Graig CF14: Rhiw 5B **70**
CF83: Abert 2E **27**
Dan y Graig Bungs. NP11: Ris 6C **16**
Danygraig Cres. CF72: T Grn 2E **65**
Danygraig Dr. CF72: T Grn 2E **65**
Dan y Graig Hgts. CF72: L'sant 2E **65**
Dan-y-Graig Rd. NP11: Ris 5D **16**
Danygraig St. CF37: P'prdd 2B **24**
Danylan Rd. CF37: P'prdd 6A **14**
Dan-y-Meio CF83: Abert 2D **26**
Dan y Myndd CF14: Thorn 2E **71**
Dan-yr-Allt Cl. CF37: R'fln 4H **25**
Dan yr Ardd CF83: Caer 2A **46**
Dan-yr-Heol CF23: Cyn 1A **86**
Darby Cl. NP10: Roger 3D **34**
Darby Rd. CF24: Card 5G **97**
Daren Ddu Rd. CF37: Y'bwl, P'prdd 1A **14**
Darent Cl. NP20: Bet 6E **19**
Darent Rd. NP20: Bet 6E **19**
Darent Wlk. NP20: Bet 6E **19**
Darlington Ct. NP19: Newp 1D **36**
Darran Rd. NP11: C'keys, Ris 2D **16**
Darran St. CF24: Card 1H **95**
Darren Cl. CF71: C'bri 3A **90**
CF83: Caer 4F **29**
Darren Hill CF71: C'bri 3B **90**
Darren Pk. CF37: P'prdd 4D **14**
Darren Vw. Ct. CF37: P'prdd 4E **15**
Dartington Dr. CF23: Pontp 4E **73**
Dart Rd. NP20: Bet 6G **19**
Darwin Dr. NP20: Malp 5A **20**
Darwyn Las CF83: B'ws 2E **29**
David Cl. NP20: Newp 2C **54**
David Davies Rd. CF63: Barry 3B **118**
David Lloyd Leisure 5F **87**
David's Ct. CF72: P'clun 5D **64**
David St. CF10: Card 4E **5** (4B **96**)
CF63: Barry 5C **106**
David Wlk. *NP10: Roger 5D 34*
(off Ebenezer Dr.)
Davies Dr. CF83: Caer 3B **28**
Davies Pl. CF5: F'wtr 2B **94**
Davies Sq. *NP20: Newp 6C 36*
(off Charlotte Dr.)
Davies St. CF63: Barry 1A **118**
Daviot Ct. CF24: Card 6B **86**
Daviot St. CF24: Card 6B **86**
Davis Cl. NP4: P'pool 2B **6**
Davis Ct. *NP16: Chep 1E 63*
(off Bridge St.)
Davis's Ter. CF14: Whit 2D **84**
Davis St. CF24: Card 4G **5** (4C **96**)
Davnic Cl. CF63: Barry 1B **118**
Davy Cl. NP20: Malp 4A **20**
Dawan Cl. CF62: Barry 2E **117**
Dawson Cl. NP19: Newp 3D **38**
Dean Ct. NP44: H'lys 5B **10**
Deanery Gdns. NP20: Newp 5B **36**
Deans Cl. CF5: L'dff 1D **94**
CF37: R'fln 3F **25**
Deans Gdns. NP16: Chep 1D **62**
Deans Hill NP16: Chep 2D **62**
Dean St. NP19: Newp 3D **36**
De-Barri St. CF37: R'fln 5F **25**
De Bawdrip Rd. CF23: Card 1F **97**
De Braose Cl. CF5: L'dff 4H **83**
De Burgh Pl. CF11: Card 4A **4** (4G **95**)
De Burgh St. CF11: Card 4A **4** (4G **95**)
De Clare Ct. CF71: Bov 3D **110**
CF83: Caer 4C **28**
De Clare Dr. CF15: Rad 2H **83**
Decoypool La. NP18: L'wrn 4E **57**
De Croche Pl. CF11: Card 5G **95**
Deemuir Rd. CF24: Card 2F **97**
Deemuir Sq. CF24: Card 1F **97**
Deepdale Cl. CF23: Pen L 4B **86**
Deepdene Cl. CF5: Ely 4D **92**
Deepfield Cl. CF5: Ely 4D **92**
DEEPWEIR 6E **61**
Deepweir NP26: Cald 6E **61**
Deepweir Dr. NP26: Cald 5E **61**
Deepweir Gdns. NP26: Cald 6E **61**
Deepwood Cl. CF5: Ely 4D **92**
Deerbrook NP44: G'mdw 3D **10**
Deere Cl. CF5: Ely 5F **93**
Deere Pl. CF5: Ely 5F **93**
Deere Rd. CF5: Ely 5E **93**
CF38: Llan F 5C **42**
Deer Pk. La. NP20: Bass 6E **35**
Deganwy Cl. CF14: L'shn 4G **71**
DEGAR 6A **78**
De Havilland Rd. CF24: Card 2G **97**
Dehewydd La. CF38: Llan F 4D **42**
Delfryn CF72: P'clun 6E **65**
Delius Cl. NP10: Roger 3C **34**
NP19: Newp 4A **38**
Dell, The CF3: St M 5B **74**
CF38: Tont 6F **25**
Dell Vw. NP16: Chep 2E **63**
Delphinium Rd. NP10: Roger 2H **33**
Delta St. CF11: Card 4F **95**
Denbigh Cl. CF38: Tont 1F **43**
Denbigh Ct. CF64: P'rth 2D **108**
CF83: Caer 5G **27**
Denbigh Dr. CF71: Bov 3E **111**
NP16: Bul 5G **63**
Denbigh Rd. CF64: Din P 1A **108**
NP19: Newp 1E **37**
Denbigh St. CF11: Card 2F **95**
Denbigh Way CF62: Barry 6H **105**
Dene Ct. NP4: P'nydd 1A **6**
Denison Way CF5: Ely 4D **92**
Denmark Dr. NP16: Sed 3H **63**
Denny Vw. NP26: Cald 6E **61**
Den Roche Pl. CF10: Card 3E **5** (3B **96**)
DENSCOMBE 1B **46**
Denstone Ct. CF23: Pen L 4C **86**
Dental Dr. CF14: Heath 4G **85**
Denton Rd. CF5: Card 4F **95**
Dents Cl. NP19: Newp 4B **38**
Dents Hill NP19: Newp 4B **38**
Denvale Trade Pk. CF24: Card 5D **96**
Denys Cl. CF64: Din P 1H **107**
Derby Gro. NP19: Newp 1H **55**
Deri Cl. CF23: Pen L 6E **87**
Dering Rd. CF23: Pontp 4H **73**
Deri Rd. CF23: Pen L 1D **96**
Derwen Ct. CF23: Cyn 6C **72**
Derwendeg Av. CF37: Glyn 2D **14**
Derwen Rd. CF23: Cyn 5C **72**
CF72: P'clun 6D **64**
Derwent Cl. CF14: Thorn 3G **71**
Derwent Ct. NP20: Bet 6E **19**
Deryn Ct. CF23: L'dyrn 5F **73**
Despenser Av. CF72: L'sant 3F **65**
Despenser Gdns. CF11: Card 5A **4** (4H **95**)
Despenser Pl. CF11: Card 5A **4** (4H **95**)
Despenser Rd. CF64: Sul 2G **119**
Despenser St. CF11: Card 5A **4** (4H **95**)
Dessmuir Rd. CF24: Card 2F **97**

Devon Av. CF63: Barry 1H **117**
Devon Ct. NP18: C'ln 4G **21**
Devon Pl. CF11: Card 6G **95**
NP20: Newp 4B **36**
Devon St. CF11: Card 6G **95**
Dewberry Gro. NP10: Roger 1H **33**
Dew Cres. CF5: Ely 5A **94**
Dewi Ct. CF5: L'dff 1C **94**
Dewinton Ter. CF83: L'brad 1B **28**
DEWI SANT HOSPITAL 1C **24**
Dewi St. CF37: P'prdd 4E **15**
Dewsland Pk. Rd. NP20: Newp 5B **36**
Dewston Cl. NP26: Cald 5B **60**
Dewston Gdns. NP26: Cald 5B **60**
Dewstow Rd. NP26: C'went, Cald 3A **60**
Dewstow St. NP19: Newp 5F **37**
Diamond Cl. CF83: Caer 5B **28**
Diamond St. CF24: Card 3D **96**
(not continuous)
Diana La. CF24: Card 6B **86**
Diana St. CF24: Card 6B **86**
Dibdin Cl. NP19: Newp 4D **38**
Dickens Av. CF3: L'rmy 6H **73**
Dickens Ct. CF83: Mac 3C **30**
Dickens Dr. NP20: Newp 1G **53**
(not continuous)
Digby Cl. CF5: F'wtr 5A **84**
Digby St. CF63: Barry 2A **118**
Dimlands Rd. CF71: Llan M 3A **110**
Dinas Path NP44: F'wtr 3D **10**
Dinas Pl. CF11: Card 6H **95**
DINAS POWYS 2G **107**
Dinas Powys Castle 1G **107**
Dinas Powys Station (Rail) 3G **107**
Dinas Rd. CF64: P'rth 3C **108**
Dinas St. CF11: Card 6B **4** (5H **95**)
Dinch Hill NP26: Undy 4D **58**
Dingle, The CF64: P'rth 2F **109**
Dingle Cl. CF62: Barry 5D **116**
Dingle La. CF64: P'rth 1E **109**
NP44: Pnwd 5C **8**
Dingle Rd. CF64: P'rth 1E **109**
NP4: P'pool 4D **6**
Dingle Road Station (Rail) 1E **109**
Discovery Pk. NP20: Newp 3B **36**
Distillery Rd. La. *CF37: P'prdd 5A **14***
(off Margaret St.)
District Shop. Cen. CF3: St M 6C **74**
CF14: Thorn 3G **71**
Ditchling Ct. CF64: P'rth 3E **109**
Dixon Pl. NP11: Ris 5E **17**
Dobbins Rd. CF63: Barry 5D **106**
Dochdwy Rd. CF64: L'dgh 5F **101**
Dock Rd. CF62: Barry 5H **117**
Dock St. CF64: P'rth 6H **101**
Docks Way NP20: Newp 3G **53**
Dock Vw. Rd. CF63: Barry 3H **117**
Dockwell Ter. NP18: L'wrn 5F **39**
Doddington Pl. CF37: P'prdd 5E **15**
Doe Cl. CF23: Pen L 6E **87**
Dogfield St. CF24: Card 6A **86**
Dogo St. CF11: Card 2F **95**
Dol Fran CF83: Caer 5F **29**
Dolgellau Av. CF38: Tont 1F **43**
Dolgoch Cl. CF3: Rum 2B **88**
Dol Gwartheg CF64: P'rth 3C **108**
Doloman Theatre 5C **36**
Dolphin Ct. *NP20: Newp 6C **36***
(off Commercial Rd.)
Dolphin St. NP20: Newp 6D **36**
(not continuous)
Dolwen Rd. CF14: Llan N 5C **84**
Dolyfelin CF83: B'ws 2E **29**
Dol-y-Felin CF15: Cre 6D **66**
Dol-y-Felin St. CF83: Caer 6C **28**
Dol-y-Llan CF72: P'clun 5F **65**
Dol-y-Pandy CF83: B'ws 2E **29**
Dol-y-Paun CF83: Caer 1A **46**
Dol-yr-Eos CF83: Caer 5E **29**
Dombey Cl. CF14: Thorn 3H **71**
Dominions Arc. CF10: Card 3D **4** (3A **96**)
Dominions Way CF24: Pen L 1E **97**
Dominions Way Ind. Est. CF24: Pen L 1E **97**
Donald St. CF24: Card 6B **86**
Don Cl. NP20: Bet 6F **19**
Doniford Cl. CF64: Sul 1H **119**
Donnington Rd. CF64: Sul 1E **119**
Dorallt Cl. NP44: H'lys 4A **10**
Dorallt Way NP44: H'lys 5A **10**
Dorchester Av. CF23: Pen L 5D **86**
Dorleigh Ct. NP44: G'mdw 6B **8**
Dorothy Av. CF62: Barry 5G **105**
Dorothy Cl. CF62: Barry 5G **105**
Dorothy St. CF37: P'prdd 5D **14**
Dorset Av. CF63: Barry 1H **117**
Dorset Cl. NP19: Newp 1H **55**
Dorset Cres. NP19: Newp 1H **55**
Dorset St. CF11: Card 6G **95**
Dorstone Wlk. NP44: Llan 2A **12**
Dos Rd. NP20: Newp 2B **36**
Douglas Cl. CF5: L'dff 5A **84**
Dovedale Cl. CF23: Pen L 4B **86**
Dovedale St. CF63: Barry 1B **118**
Dovey Cl. CF3: Rum 2B **88**
CF62: Barry 1E **117**
Dowlais Arc. *CF10: Card 1C **102***
(off W. Bute St.)
Dowlais Rd. CF24: Card 5D **96**
Dowland Cl. NP19: Newp 4B **38**
Downfield Cl. CF64: L'dgh 5G **101**
Downing St. NP19: Newp 6G **37**
Downland Rd. CF64: P'rth 4C **108**
Downlands Way CF3: Rum 5G **87**
DOWNS 1B **98**
Down's Vw. CF71: A'thin 2F **91**
Down's Vw. Cl. CF71: A'thin 2F **91**
Downton Grange CF3: Rum 5A **88**
Downton Ri. CF3: Rum 5H **87**
Downton Rd. CF3: Rum 5H **87**
Doyle Av. CF5: F'wtr 1A **94**
Doyle Ct. CF5: F'wtr 1A **94**
DRAETHEN 6A **32**
Dragonfly Dr. CF62: Rho 2E **115**
Drake Cl. CF62: St A 2D **112**
NP19: Newp 3C **38**
Drake Wlk. CF10: Card 6F **5** (5B **96**)
Drangway CF71: Llan M 3B **110**
Dranllwyn Cl. CF83: Mac 2F **31**
Dranllwyn La. CF83: Mac 2F **31**
Drawlings Cl. CF3: St M 5B **74**
Dray Ct. CF10: Card 5D **4** (4A **96**)
Drayton Ct. NP44: G'mdw 2E **11**
Drinkwater Cl. NP20: Newp 1H **53**
Drinkwater Gdns. NP20: Newp 1H **53**
Drinkwater Ri. NP20: Newp 1H **53**
Drinkwater Vw. NP20: Newp 1H **53**
Drive, The CF5: F'wtr 2H **93**
CF64: Din P 2A **108**
CF72: P'clun 1F **79**
DROPE 5B **92**
Drope Rd. CF5: Ely 5C **92**
Drope Ter. CF5: St G 5C **92**
Dros Col CF72: L'harry 5A **78**
Dros-y-Mor CF64: P'rth 3F **109**
Dros-y-Morfa CF3: Rum 5A **88**
Drovers M. NP20: Newp 6C **36**
Drovers Way CF15: Rad 2F **83**
Druids Cl. CF83: Caer 1A **46**
Druids Grn. CF71: C'bri 3D **90**
Druidstone Rd. CF3: Cas, St M 3D **74**
CF3: St M 4C **74**
Drum Tower Vw. CF83: Caer 1H **45**
Drury Cl. CF14: Thorn 3G **71**
Dr William Price Bus. Cen.
CF37: T'rest 3E **25**
Drybrook Cl. CF3: St M 1D **88**
NP44: C'brn 2H **11**
Dryburgh Av. CF14: Heath 2F **85**
Dryden Cl. CF3: L'rmy 6H **73**
Dryden Rd. CF64: P'rth 1D **108**
Dryden Ter. CF62: Barry 5H **105**
Drylla CF64: Din P 3G **107**
Drysgol Rd. CF15: Rad 1F **83**
Dubricius Gdns. NP26: Undy 4F **59**
Duckpool Rd. NP19: Newp 3E **37**
Dudley Ct. CF10: Card 2B **102**
Dudley Pl. CF62: Barry 3F **117**
Dudley St. CF10: Card 2B **102**
NP19: Newp 5E **37**
DUFFRYN 4G **53**
Duffryn Av. CF23: Cyn 2B **86**
Duffryn Bach Ter. CF38: Chu V 4F **43**
Duffryn Cl. CF23: Cyn 1A **86**
NP10: Bass 6C **34**
Duffryn Dr. NP10: Duf 4G **53**
Duffryn Est. NP10: Duf 3G **53**
Duffryn Ffwd CF15: N'grw 3E **45**
Duffryn La. CF5: Ely 6A **98**
Duffryn Rd. CF23: Cyn 1C **86**
CF37: R'fln 4F **25**
Duffryn St. CF10: Card 5F **5** (4B **96**)
Duffryn Ter. *CF38: Chu V 3F **43***
(off Main Rd.)
Duffryn Way NP10: Duf 5G **53**
Dugdale Wlk. CF11: Card 4F **95**
Duke St. CF10: Card 4C **4** (4A **96**)
CF37: T'rest 3D **24**
NP20: Newp 6D **36**
Duke St. Arc. CF10: Card 4C **4** (4A **96**)
Dulverton Av. CF3: L'rmy 6A **74**
Dulverton Dr. CF64: Sul 2H **119**
Dulwich Gdns. CF5: Card 2D **94**
Dumballs Rd. CF10: Card 6A **96**
Dumfries Pl. CF10: Card 2E **5** (3B **96**)
NP20: Newp 5C **36**
Dummer Cl. CF3: St M 1D **88**
Dunbar Cl. CF23: Pontp 4G **73**
Duncan Cl. CF3: St M 1B **88**
Dungarvan Dr. CF23: Pontp 4G **73**
Dunkery Cl. CF3: L'rmy 2H **87**
Dunleavey Dr. CF11: Card 3G **101**
Dunlin Av. NP26: Cald 6C **60**
Dunlin Ct. CF63: Barry 3H **117**
Dunnet Gdns. NP4: New I 6H **7**
Dunn Sq. *NP20: Newp 6C **36***
(off Francis Dr.)
Dunraven Cl. CF64: Din P 2A **108**
Dunraven Ct. CF83: Caer 5G **27**
Dunraven Cres. CF72: T Grn 3C **64**
Dunraven Dr. NP10: Coedk 6F **53**
Dunraven Ho. CF10: Card 4B **4**
Dunraven Rd. CF11: Card 5F **95**
NP44: Llan 3B **12**
Dunraven St. CF62: Barry 4E **117**
Dunsmuir Rd. CF24: Card 3F **97**
Dunstable Rd. NP19: Newp 4C **38**
Dunster Dr. CF64: Sul 2G **119**
Dunster Rd. CF3: L'rmy 1B **88**
Durand Rd. NP26: Cald 6C **60**
Durham La. NP19: Newp 2D **36**
(not continuous)
Durham Rd. NP19: Newp 2D **36**
Durham St. CF11: Card 6H **95**
Durleigh Cl. CF3: L'rmy 6A **74**
Durlston Cl. CF14: Llan N 4B **84**
Durrel St. CF71: Llan M 3B **110**
Duxford Cl. CF5: F'wtr 5H **83**
Dyfan Rd. CF63: Barry 1A **118**
Dyfed CF64: P'rth 6C **102**
Dyfed Dr. CF83: Caer 4B **28**
DYFFRYN 1D **104**
Dyffryn Av. CF37: R'fln 3G **25**
Dyffryn Cres. CF37: R'fln 3G **25**
Dyffryn Gdns. 1D **104**
Dyffryn Gdns. CF37: R'fln 3G **25**
Dyffryn La. NP10: Coedk 5D **52**
Dyffryn Pl. CF62: Barry 6F **105**
Dyffryn Rd. CF37: R'fln 4G **25**
Dyfnallt Rd. CF63: Barry 5A **106**
Dyfrig Cl. CF5: Ely 3B **94**
Dyfrig Ct. CF71: Bov 2D **110**
Dyfrig Rd. CF5: Ely 3B **94**
Dyfrig St. CF11: Card 2G **95**
CF62: Barry 5A **118**
Dyhewydd Isaf CF38: Llan F 4D **42**
Dylan Av. CF38: Bed 6A **42**
Dylan Cl. CF64: L'dgh 5G **101**
Dylan Cres. CF63: Barry 5B **106**
Dylan Dr. CF83: Caer 4C **28**
Dylan Pl. CF24: Card 1G **5** (2C **96**)
Dynea Cl. CF37: R'fln 4H **25**
Dynea Rd. CF37: R'fln, Up Bo 3H **25**
Dynevor Cl. NP44: Llan 2B **12**
Dynevor Rd. CF23: Pen L 4D **86**
Dyserth Rd. CF64: P'rth 2D **108**

E

Eagle Cl. NP26: Cald 6D **60**
Eagle La. CF71: C'bri 3C **90**
Eagle Rd. CF62: St A 3F **111**
Eagleswell Rd. CF71: Bov 2D **110**
Earl Cres. CF62: Barry 5H **117**
Earl Cunningham Ct.
CF10: Card 6G **5**
Earle Pl. CF5: Card 4F **95**
Earl La. CF11: Card 2H **101**
Earl Rd. CF64: P'rth 2D **108**
Earl's Ct. Pl. CF23: Pen L 6D **86**
Earl's Ct. Rd. CF23: Pen L 5D **86**
Earlsmede NP44: G'mdw 2D **10**
Earl St. CF11: Card 2H **101**
Earlswood Rd. CF14: L'shn 6G **71**
EAST ABERTHAW 6H **113**
East Av. CF83: B'ws 3G **29**
CF83: Caer 5B **28**
NP4: Grif 2E **9**
E. Bank Rd. NP19: Newp 3E **55**
E. Bay Cl. CF10: Card 5G **5** (4C **96**)
E. Bay Link Rd. CF24: Card 6F **97**
Eastbourne Ct. CF63: Barry 5C **106**
EASTBROOK 1H **107**
Eastbrook Cl. CF64: Din P 1H **107**
Eastbrook Rd. CF64: P'rth 6F **101**
Eastbrook Station (Rail) 1A **108**
E. Bute St. CF10: Card 1C **102**
E. Dock Rd. NP20: Newp 6D **36**

Eastern Av. CF3: Pontp, St M . . . 6G 73
CF14: Card, Cyn, Llan N . . . 5F 85
CF23: L'dyrn, Pen L . . . 5D 86
Eastern Bus. Pk., The CF3: St M . . . 5C 74
Eastern Cl. CF3: St M . . . 5B 74
Eastern Leisure Cen. . . . 3H 87
Eastfield Cl. NP18: C'ln . . . 3G 21
Eastfield Ct. CF72: L'sant . . . 3G 65
Eastfield Dr. NP18: C'ln . . . 3G 21
Eastfield M. NP18: C'ln . . . 3G 21
Eastfield Rd. NP18: C'ln . . . 3G 21
Eastfield Vw. NP18: C'ln . . . 3G 21
Eastfield Way NP18: C'ln . . . 3G 21
Eastgate CF71: C'bri . . . 3D 90
Eastgate Bus. Pk. CF3: Rum . . . 6A 88
Eastgate Cres. NP26: C'went . . . 1B 60
Eastgate M. *CF71: C'bri . . . 4D 90*
(off Eastgate)
East Gro. CF24: Card . . . 2G 5 (3B 96)
East Gro. La. CF24: Card . . . 2G 5 (3C 96)
East Gro. Rd. NP19: Newp . . . 4H 37
E. Lynne Gdns. NP18: C'ln . . . 4A 22
E. Market St. NP20: Newp . . . 6D 36
(not continuous)
Eastmoor Rd. NP19: Newp . . . 6A 38
E. Moors Bus. Pk. CF24: Card . . . 5D 96
E. Moors Rd. CF10: Card . . . 4C 96
CF24: Card . . . 5H 5 (4C 96)
East Rise CF14: L'shn . . . 5A 72
East Rd. CF64: Sul . . . 1F 119
NP44: Oakf . . . 5H 11
East Roedin NP44: F'wtr . . . 5E 11
East St. CF37: P'prdd . . . 5D 14
CF62: Barry . . . 3F 117
CF71: Llan M . . . 3B 110
NP20: Newp . . . 4B 36
E. Tyndall St. CF24: Card . . . 5H 5 (4D 96)
E. Usk Rd. NP19: Newp . . . 3C 36
East Vw. CF83: Caer . . . 1D 46
NP4: Grif . . . 1E 9
NP4: P'pool . . . 3B 6
East Vw. Ter. CF62: Barry . . . 4F 117
EAST VILLAGE . . . 4C 90
East Wlk. CF62: Barry . . . 1G 117
Eastway Rd. NP20: Newp . . . 2D 54
Ebbw Cl. CF62: St A . . . 2C 112
Ebbw Ct. NP11: C'keys . . . 3A 16
Ebbw Rd. NP26: Cald . . . 4C 60
Ebbw St. NP11: Ris . . . 5D 16
Ebenezer Dr. NP10: Roger . . . 5C 34
Ebenezer St. CF37: R'fln . . . 3F 25
Ebenezer Ter. NP20: Newp . . . 5C 36
Ebley Gdns. NP26: Cald . . . 6E 61
Ebwy Ct. CF5: Ely . . . 5H 93
Eckley Rd. CF64: Sul . . . 2G 119
Eclipse St. CF24: Card . . . 3H 5 (3C 96)
Eddystone Cl. CF11: Card . . . 6G 95
Edgcort NP44: F'wtr . . . 4D 10
Edgehill NP44: Llanf . . . 4B 12
Edgehill Av. CF14: L'shn . . . 4E 71
Edinburgh Cl. NP44: G'mdw . . . 2C 10
Edinburgh Ct. CF11: Card . . . 4G 95
Edington Av. CF14: Card . . . 5H 85
Edison Ridge NP20: Malp . . . 4A 20
Edith Rd. CF64: Din P . . . 2H 107
Edlogan Sq. NP44: C'iog . . . 5G 9
Edlogan Way NP44: C'brn . . . 1H 11
Edmond Rd. NP16: Sed . . . 2H 63
Edmonds Ct. CF24: Card . . . 6B 86
Edmund Pl. CF63: Barry . . . 1D 118
Edney Vw. NP10: Duf . . . 4H 53
Edward VII Av. NP20: Newp . . . 5H 35
Edward VII Cres. NP20: Newp . . . 4A 36
Edward VII La. NP20: Newp . . . 4H 35
Edward Clarke Cl. CF5: L'dff . . . 5A 84
Edward England Wharf CF10: Card . . . 6F 5 (5B 96)
Edward German Cres. NP19: Newp . . . 4C 38
Edwardian Way CF72: P'clun . . . 6F 65
Edward La. NP20: Newp . . . 5B 36
(not continuous)
Edward Nicholl Ct. CF23: Pen L . . . 5D 86
Edward St. CF10: Card . . . 3E 5 (3B 96)
CF63: Barry . . . 6B 106
NP4: Grif . . . 6E 7
NP4: P'pool . . . 2B 6
Edward Ter. CF83: Abert . . . 1E 27
Edward Thomas Cl. CF83: Rud . . . 5B 30
Edwin Ind. Est. NP20: Newp . . . 2B 36
Edwin St. NP10: Roger . . . 5C 34
NP20: Newp . . . 2C 36
EFAIL ISAF . . . 6E 43
Egerton M. CF5: Card . . . 3E 95
Egerton St. CF5: Card . . . 3E 95
Egham St. CF5: Card . . . 3E 95
Eglwys Av. CF37: R'fln . . . 4G 25
EGLWYS-BREWIS . . . 2A 112
Eglwysilan Rd. CF15: N'grw, Caer . . . 2B 26
CF37: P'prdd, R'fln . . . 5G 15
CF83: Abert, N'grw . . . 2B 26
Eglwysilan Way CF83: Abert . . . 2D 26
Egremont Rd. CF23: Pen L . . . 4B 86
Egypt St. CF37: T'rest . . . 1D 24
Eider Cl. CF3: St M . . . 5C 74
Eifion Cl. CF63: Barry . . . 5A 106
Eisteddfod Wlk. NP19: Newp . . . 3B 38
Eithinen Ber CF63: Barry . . . 4B 106
Elaine Cl. CF14: Thorn . . . 3G 71
Elaine Cres. NP19: Newp . . . 2F 37
Elan Cl. CF62: Barry . . . 1E 117
NP20: Bet . . . 6G 19
Elan Rd. CF14: L'shn . . . 5A 72
Elan Wlk. NP44: G'mdw . . . 3E 11
Elan Way NP26: Cald . . . 4D 60
Elderberry Rd. CF5: F'wtr . . . 6F 83
Elder Cl. NP18: C'ln . . . 5F 21
Elder Wood Cl. CF23: Pen L . . . 4E 87
Eleanor Pl. CF10: Card . . . 2B 102
Electra Ho. CF10: Card . . . 1D 102
Eleven St. CF64: Sul . . . 1E 119
Elfed Av. CF64: P'rth . . . 2C 108
Elfed Grn. CF5: F'wtr . . . 6A 84
Elfed Way CF63: Barry . . . 5B 106
Elford Rd. CF5: Ely . . . 4G 93
Elgar Av. NP19: Newp . . . 4A 38
Elgar Circ. NP19: Newp . . . 4B 38
Elgar Cl. NP19: Newp . . . 4B 38
Elgar Cres. CF3: L'rmy . . . 6B 74
Elgar Rd. CF64: P'rth . . . 4D 108
Elizabethan Ct. CF64: P'rth . . . 5G 101
Elizabeth Av. CF62: Barry . . . 5G 105
Elled Rd. NP4: P'nydd, P'pool . . . 1A 6
Ellen St. CF10: Card . . . 5F 5 (4B 96)
Ellesmere Ct. CF3: St M . . . 1B 88
Ellipse, The NP4: Grif . . . 2D 8
Ellis CF72: L'sant . . . 6C 40
Ellis Fisher Ct. CF62: Barry . . . 3G 117
Ellwood Cl. CF3: St M . . . 1D 88
Ellwood Path NP44: G'mdw . . . 2D 10
Elm Av. NP26: Undy . . . 5E 59
Elm Cl. CF64: Sul . . . 3A 120
Elmdale NP16: Chep . . . 1E 63
Elm Dr. NP11: Ris . . . 5E 17
Elmfield Cl. CF3: St M . . . 1C 88
Elm Gro. CF62: St A . . . 2B 112
CF63: Barry . . . 5C 106
CF83: Caer . . . 4E 29
NP4: Grif . . . 2E 9
NP20: Malp . . . 5B 20
Elmgrove CF83: Tret . . . 3H 29
Elmgrove Cl. CF37: Glyn . . . 2C 14
Elm Gro. La. CF64: Din P . . . 2G 107
Elm Gro. Pl. CF64: Din P . . . 2H 107
Elm Gro. Rd. CF64: Din P . . . 2G 107
Elmgrove Rd. CF14: Whit . . . 3A 84
Elm Ho. CF14: Whit . . . 1A 84
Elm Rd. CF72: L'harry . . . 5A 78
NP26: Cald . . . 4B 60
Elms, The NP26: Undy . . . 4F 59
Elms Hill NP26: Undy . . . 4F 59
Elms Pk. CF72: P'clun . . . 1F 79
Elm St. CF24: Card . . . 1H 5 (2C 96)
CF37: R'fln . . . 4G 25
Elm St. La. CF24: Card . . . 1H 5 (2C 96)
Elmwood Ct. CF24: Card . . . 1H 5 (2C 96)
Elworthy Cl. CF64: Sul . . . 2H 119
Elwyn St. CF39: T'fail . . . 3A 40
ELY . . . 4H 93
Ely Brewery Workshops *CF5: F'wtr . . . 3B 94*
(off Wroughton Pl.)
Ely Bri. Ind. Est. CF5: F'wtr . . . 2A 94
Ely Distribution Cen. CF5: Ely . . . 5A 94
Ely Rd. CF5: F'wtr, L'dff . . . 2B 94
Elysia St. NP19: Newp . . . 2D 36
Ely St. CF72: P'clun . . . 5D 64
Ely Valley Ind. Est. CF72: P'clun . . . 5C 64
Ely Valley Rd. CF39: T'fail . . . 2A 40
(not continuous)
CF72: L'sant, T Grn . . . 4A 40
Emanuel Cl. CF83: Caer . . . 2H 45
Emblem Cl. CF5: Ely . . . 5A 94
Emerald St. CF24: Card . . . 3D 96
Emerson Dr. CF5: Ely . . . 1F 99
Emlyn Dr. CF83: Caer . . . 5C 28
Emlyn Sq. NP20: Newp . . . 5C 36
Emlyn St. NP20: Newp . . . 5C 36
Emlyn Wlk. NP20: Newp . . . 5C 36
Empire Ho. CF10: Card . . . 1C 102
Emsworth Ct. CF23: Cyn . . . 1C 86
Enbourne Dr. CF23: Pontp . . . 4F 73
Endyngs NP44: F'wtr . . . 4D 10
ENERGLYN . . . 4B 28
Energlyn Cl. CF83: Caer . . . 5B 28
Energlyn Ct. *CF83: Caer . . . 5B 28*
(off Energlyn Cl.)
Energlyn Cres. CF83: Caer . . . 4B 28
Energlyn Row CF83: Caer . . . 3B 28
Energlyn Ter. CF83: Caer . . . 4A 28
Enfield Dr. CF62: Barry . . . 6E 105
Ennerdale Cl. CF23: Pen L . . . 5B 86
Ennerdale Ct. NP19: Newp . . . 1F 37
Enterprise Pk. Ind. Est. NP20: Newp . . . 6D 36
Enterprise Way NP20: Newp . . . 6D 36
Enville Cl. NP20: Newp . . . 5G 35
Enville Rd. NP20: Newp . . . 5G 35
Eppynt Cl. NP11: Ris . . . 5G 17
Epsom Cl. CF5: Ely . . . 4B 94
Epstein Cl. CF5: L'dff . . . 5H 83
Erederick St. CF10: Card . . . 3D 4 (3A 96)
Eric Coates Cl. NP19: Newp . . . 5B 38
Eric Coates Wlk. *NP18: Newp . . . 5B 38*
(off Eric Coates Cl.)
Erris Ct. CF37: P'prdd . . . 4D 14
Erskine Ct. CF24: Card . . . 2E 97
Erw Fach CF38: Chu V . . . 2D 42
Erw Hir CF5: St F . . . 2C 82
CF72: L'sant . . . 2F 65
Erw Las CF14: Whit . . . 3C 84
Erw'r Delyn Cl. CF64: P'rth . . . 1B 108
Erw Wen CF14: Rhiw . . . 5D 70
Erw Wen Cotts. CF15: P'rch . . . 4A 68
Eschol Cl. NP19: Newp . . . 6H 37
Eschol Ct. NP19: Newp . . . 6H 37
Esgid Mair CF63: Barry . . . 4C 106
Eskdale Cl. CF23: Pen L . . . 4B 86
Esperanto Way NP19: Newp . . . 2E 55
Esplanade CF64: P'rth . . . 2F 109
Esplanade Bldgs. CF62: Barry . . . 5G 117
Essex Ct. NP18: C'ln . . . 4G 21
Essex St. NP19: Newp . . . 5E 37
Essich St. CF24: Card . . . 6C 86
Estate Rd. NP4: P'nydd . . . 1A 6
Estuary Rd. NP19: Newp . . . 2A 56
Estuary Vw. NP26: Cald . . . 6E 61
Ethel St. CF5: Card . . . 3D 94
Eton Ct. CF14: Heath . . . 1G 85
Eton Pl. CF5: Card . . . 4F 95
Eton Rd. NP19: Newp . . . 4D 36
Eton St. CF62: Barry . . . 4E 117
Eugene Cl. CF3: St M . . . 5E 75
Eurgan Cl. CF71: Llan M . . . 4B 110
Eurwg Cres. CF3: St M . . . 5B 74
Evansfield Rd. CF14: Llan N . . . 4B 84
Evans Sq. CF37: P'prdd . . . 4E 15
Evans St. CF62: Barry . . . 2H 117
NP20: Newp . . . 3C 36
Evelian Ct. CF14: Whit . . . 4F 85
Evelyn St. CF63: Barry . . . 2A 118
Evenlode Av. CF64: P'rth . . . 3D 108
Evenwood Cl. CF23: Pontp . . . 4F 73
Everard St. CF63: Barry . . . 1B 118
Everard Way CF23: Cyn . . . 3B 86
Everest Av. CF14: L'shn . . . 4H 71
Everest Wlk. CF14: L'shn . . . 4H 71
Everswell Av. CF5: F'wtr . . . 2H 93
Everswell Rd. CF5: F'wtr . . . 2H 93
Evesham Ct. NP20: Newp . . . 2A 36
Eve's Well Ct. NP19: Newp . . . 4E 37
Eveswell La. NP19: Newp . . . 4F 37
Eveswell Pk. Rd. NP19: Newp . . . 3F 37
Eveswell St. NP19: Newp . . . 4F 37
Evtol Ind. Est. *NP20: Newp . . . 1D 54*
(off Portland St.)
Ewbank Cl. CF63: Barry . . . 5C 106
Ewenny Cl. CF63: Barry . . . 5A 106
Ewenny Rd. CF14: L'shn . . . 6A 72
Excalibur Dr. CF14: Thorn . . . 3F 71
Excelsior Cl. NP19: Newp . . . 5E 37
Excelsior Est. CF14: Card . . . 5E 85
Excelsior Rd. CF14: Card . . . 5E 85
Exchange Ct. NP11: Ris . . . 4D 16
Exchange Rd. NP11: Ris . . . 4D 16
Exe Rd. NP20: Bet . . . 5F 19
Exeter Cl. NP44: G'mdw . . . 2C 10
Exeter Rd. NP19: Newp . . . 3E 37
Exeter St. NP19: Newp . . . 4E 37
Exford Cres. CF3: L'rmy . . . 2G 87
Exmouth Pl. NP16: Chep . . . 1F 63
Eyre St. CF24: Card . . . 3E 97
Ezel Ct. CF10: Card . . . 1B 102

F

Faber Way CF11: Card . . . 6F 95
Factory Cotts. NP11: Ris . . . 6F 17
Factory La. CF37: P'prdd . . . 1B 24
Factory Rd. CF71: L'thian . . . 5B 90
NP20: Newp . . . 3B 36

Fairacre Cl. CF14: Thorn 3G 71
Fairbrook Cl. CF14: Rhiw 5D 70
Fairfax Rd. CF14: Heath 1F 85
NP19: Newp 5G 37
Fairfield NP4: P'pool 2A 6
Fairfield Av. CF5: Card 3C 94
Fairfield Cl. CF5: Card 2B 94
CF37: R'fln 5G 25
CF71: Llan M 3C 110
NP18: C'ln 4F 21
NP26: Cald 5B 60
Fairfield Cres. CF71: Llan M 3C 110
Fairfield Ind. Est. CF15: Gwae G 3F 69
Fairfield La. CF37: R'fln 5G 25
Fairfield Ri. CF71: Llan M 2C 110
Fairfield Rd. CF64: P'rth 1D 108
NP16: Bul 4E 63
NP18: C'ln 4F 21
Fairford St. CF63: Barry 6B 106
Fairhaven Cl. CF3: St M 5E 75
Fairhill NP44: F'wtr, G'mdw 3D 10
Fairhill Dr. CF38: Tont 2G 43
Fairhill Wlk. NP44: F'wtr 3D 10
(Fairwater Cl., not continuous)
NP44: F'wtr 3C 10
(Oaksford)
Fairland Cl. CF72: L'sant 2G 65
Fairleigh CF64: Mic P 4B 100
Fairleigh Ct. CF11: Card 1F 95
Fairleigh Rd. CF11: Card 1F 95
Fairmead Ct. CF5: F'wtr 2H 93
Fair Mdw. CF15: P'rch 4A 68
Fairmound Pl. CF38: Tont 2G 43
Fairoak Av. NP19: Newp 3E 37
Fairoak Ct. CF23: Pen L 5B 86
NP19: Newp 3E 37
Fair Oak Gro. NP10: Bass 1B 52
Fairoak La. NP44: C'iog 1A 12
Fairoak M. CF24: Card 5A 86
NP19: Newp 3E 37
Fairoak Rd. CF23: Card 5B 86
CF24: Card 6A 86
Fairoaks CF64: Din P 2H 107
Fairoak Ter. NP19: Newp 4E 37
Fairthorn Cl. CF14: Thorn 2G 71
Fair Vw. NP16: Bul 3D 62
Fairview CF38: Bed 5A 42
Fairview Av. NP11: Ris 5E 17
Fair Vw. Cl. CF72: P'clun 6D 64
Fairview Cl. CF3: St M 5E 75
Fairview Ct. CF23: L'dyrn 6D 72
NP4: P'nydd 1A 6
FAIRWATER
Cardiff **6H 83**
Cwmbran **4D 10**
Fairwater Av. CF5: F'wtr 2B 94
Fairwater Cl. CF3: Lwr M 6E 51
NP44: F'wtr 3D 10
Fairwater Grn. CF5: F'wtr 2H 93
Fairwater Gro. E. CF5: L'dff 1B 94
Fairwater Gro. W. CF5: L'dff 1B 94
Fairwater Leisure Cen.
Radyr Court **5G 83**
St Dials **3C 10**
Fairwater Rd. CF5: F'wtr 1H 93
CF5: L'dff 1B 94
Fairwater Sq. Shops NP44: F'wtr 3C 10
Fairwater Station (Rail) **1A 94**
Fairwater Way NP44: F'wtr 4D 10
Fairwater Workshops CF5: F'wtr 2A 94
Fairway, The CF23: Cyn 5C 72
NP4: New I 5H 7
Fairway Cl. NP10: Roger 2C 34
Fairway Dr. CF83: Caer 3B 28
Fairways Cres. CF5: F'wtr 2G 93
Fairways Vw. CF72: T Grn 2C 64
Fairwood Cl. CF5: F'wtr 6A 84
Fairwood Rd. CF5: F'wtr 6A 84
Falcon Cl. NP26: Cald 6D 60
Falcon Dr. CF10: Card 1D 102
Falcon Gro. CF64: P'rth 6E 109
Falcon Rd. CF63: Barry 6D 106
Falconwood Dr. CF5: Ely 5D 92
Falfield Cl. CF14: L'shn 3A 72
Fallowfield Dr. NP19: Newp 6A 38
Fallowfields NP44: F'wtr 4D 10
Fan Heulog CF37: Glyn 1D 14
Fanheulog CF72: T Grn 3D 64
Fanny St. CF24: Card 1A 96
Faraday Cl. NP20: Malp 5H 19
Fardre Ct. CF38: Chu V 1E 43
Fardre Cres. CF38: Chu V 2F 43
Farlays NP44: F'wtr 4C 10
Farlow Wlk. NP44: G'mdw 3E 11
(not continuous)
Farm Cl. CF83: Abert 2E 27
Farm Dr. CF23: Cyn 3B 86
Farm Hill NP4: C'avn 1B 6
Farmhouse Way CF5: Ely 6F 93
Farm La. NP19: Newp 2E 37
NP44: C'brn 1H 11
Farmleigh CF3: Rum 4H 87
Farm Rd. CF83: Caer 6E 29
NP4: P'pool 4C 6
Farmville Rd. CF24: Card 3E 97
Farmwood Cl. NP19: Newp 4H 37
Farnaby Cl. NP19: Newp 4B 38
Farriers Ga. NP10: Bass 1D 52
Farthings, The CF23: Pontp 4F 73
Faulkner Rd. NP20: Newp 4B 36
Fedw Wood NP16: Chep 2C 62
Feering St. NP19: Newp 5E 37
Felbridge Cl. CF10: Card 5C 96
Felbrigg Cres. CF23: Pontp 4E 73
Felin Fach CF14: Whit 4D 84
Felin Wen CF14: Rhiw 6E 71
Felnex Ind. Est. NP19: Newp 3E 55
Felsted Cl. CF23: Pontp 4F 73
Fennel Cl. CF3: St M 5E 75
CF64: P'rth 6G 101
Fenner Brockway Cl. NP19: Newp 2B 38
Fenviolet Cl. CF3: St M 1F 89
Fernbank NP44: G'mdw 3D 10
Fern Cl. NP16: Bul 5F 63
Ferndale St. CF11: Card 6H 95
Fern Dr. CF62: Barry 2F 117
Ferney Cres. NP26: Cald 5A 60
Ferneycross NP26: Cald 5B 60
FERNLEA **4D 16**
Fernlea NP11: Ris 4E 17
Fernleigh Rd. NP26: Cald 5B 60
Fern Pl. CF5: F'wtr 1H 93
Fern Ri. NP20: Malp 4B 20
Fernside NP19: Newp 6H 37
Fern St. CF5: Card 3D 94
Ferntree Dr. CF3: St M 6C 74
Ferny Ct. CF23: Pen L 5D 86
Ferrier Av. CF5: F'wtr 1H 93
Ferriers Ct. CF24: Card 2D 96
Ferry Ct. CF11: Card 4A 102
Ferry La. CF64: P'rth 6B 102
Ferry Rd. CF11: Card 2H 101
Ferry Rd. Interchange CF11: Card 4H 101
Ferry Way NP16: B'ly 6H 63
Fescue Pl. CF5: Ely 4E 93
Festiniog Rd. CF14: Llan N 5C 84
Festival Cres. NP4: New I 5H 7
Fetty Pl. NP44: C'brn 4F 11
Fferm-y-Graig *CF62: St A* *5D 112*
(off Rock Rd.)
FFONT-Y-GARI **5C 114**
Ffordd Bleddyn CF15: Taff W 1E 69
Ffordd Bodlyn CF23: Pen L 4C 86
Ffordd Brynhyfryd CF3: St M 5C 74
Ffordd Catraeth CF37: C'fydd 4F 15
Ffordd Cefn-yr-Hendy CF72: P'clun 5E 65
Ffordd Celyn CF14: Whit 3D 84
Ffordd Cwellyn CF23: Pen L 4B 86
Ffordd Cwm Cidi CF62: Barry 3D 116
Ffordd Daniel Lewis CF3: St M 2D 88
Ffordd Deg CF83: Caer 2D 46
Ffordd Dinefwr CF15: Cre 6D 66
Ffordd Elin CF63: Barry 6D 106
Ffordd Erw CF83: Caer 3A 46
Ffordd Eynon Evans CF83: Caer 3H 27
Ffordd Ffagan CF3: St M 5E 75
Ffordd Garthorne CF10: Card 6C 96
Ffordd Gerdinan CF38: Tont 1G 43
Ffordd Glas-y-Dorlan CF38: Llan F 6B 42
Ffordd Gower Davies CF37: Y'bwl 1A 14
Ffordd Gwern CF5: St F 2C 82
Ffordd Gwynfth CF63: Barry 5C 106
Ffordd Gwynno CF38: Llan F 6B 42
Ffordd Helygen CF72: L'harry 5C 78
Ffordd Kanetone CF11: Card 4D 94
Ffordd Las CF83: Abert 1E 27
Ffordd-Las CF15: Rad 1E 83
Ffordd Mograig CF14: L'shn 6F 71
Ffordd Morgannwg CF14: Whit 1A 84
Ffordd Pengam CF24: Card 1G 97
Ffordd Penrhos CF83: Caer 6H 27
Ffordd Radcliffe CF10: Card 1B 102
Ffordd Sealand CF62: Barry 3G 117
Ffordd Taliesin CF37: C'fydd 3F 15
Ffordd Talygarn CF72: P'clun 6D 64
Ffordd Traws Cwm CF83: Caer 2A 46
Ffordd Trecastell CF72: L'harry 4C 78
Ffordd Treforgan CF15: Morg 5E 69
Ffordd Tryweryn CF37: C'fydd 4F 15
Ffordd Ty Unnos CF14: Heath 1F 85
Ffordd-y-Barcer CF5: Ely 4D 92
Ffordd y Bedol CF37: Glyn 1D 14
Ffordd y Berllan CF15: Morg 6E 69
Ffordd y Brenin CF10: Card 3C 4 (3A 96)
Ffordd-y-Capel CF38: E Isaf 6F 43
Ffordd-y-Gollen CF38: Tont 1F 43
Ffordd y Mileniwm CF63: Barry 3A 118
Ffordd yr Afon CF15: Gwae G 2E 69
Ffordd-yr-Ywen CF38: Tont 1G 43
Fford Traws Cwm CF83: Caer 2H 45
Fford y Mileniwm CF62: Barry 4G 117
CF63: Barry 3H 117
Fforest Dr. CF62: Barry 3D 116
Fforest Glade NP19: Newp 3F 37
Fforest Rd. CF72: L'harry 6B 78
Fforest Uchaf Farm **4D 24**
Fforest Vw. CF62: Barry 3D 116
Ffos-y-Fran NP10: Bass 1B 52
FFWL-Y-MWN **3B 114**
Ffwrwm Art & Crafts Cen. *6A 22*
(off High St.)
Ffwrwm Rd. CF83: Mac 2F 31
Ffynnonbwla Rd. CF15: N'grw 4C 26
CF37: Up Bo 4C 26
FFYNNON TAF **2E 69**
Fidlas Av. CF14: Cyn 6A 72
Fidlas Rd. CF14: Cyn, L'shn 5H 71
Fieldfare Dr. CF3: St M 1E 89
Fielding Cl. CF3: L'rmy 6H 73
Fieldings *NP44: F'wtr* *4D 10*
(off Fairwater Way)
Fields Av. NP44: Pnwd 5D 8
Fields Pk. Av. NP20: Newp 4H 35
Fields Pk. Ct. NP20: Newp 4A 36
Fields Pk. Cres. NP20: Newp 4A 36
Fields Pk. Gdns. NP20: Newp 4H 35
Fields Pk. La. NP20: Newp 4H 35
Fields Pk. Rd. CF11: Card 1E 95
NP20: Newp 5H 35
Fields Pk. Ter. NP11: C'keys 2A 16
Fields Rd. NP11: Ris 1F 33
NP20: Newp 4A 36
NP44: Oakf 4G 11
Field Ter. CF15: P'rch 4A 68
Field Vw. CF63: Barry 6A 106
Field Vw. Cl. CF64: P'rth 6G 101
Field Vw. Rd. CF63: Barry 6A 106
NP44: C'iog 6G 9
Field Way CF14: Heath 1G 85
Fifth St. NP19: Newp 4G 55
Filey Rd. NP19: Newp 2D 36
Finchley Rd. CF5: F'wtr 2A 94
Finnimore Ct. CF14: Llan N 4B 84
Firbank Av. NP19: Newp 3G 37
Firbank Cres. NP19: Newp 3G 37
Firbanks Way CF72: T Grn 2C 64
Firs, The NP20: Malp 5C 20
Firs Av. CF5: F'wtr 1F 93
Firs Rd. NP26: Cald 4B 60
First Av. CF83: Caer 6A 28
Firstbrook Cl. CF23: Pen L 6E 87
First St. NP19: Newp 3G 55
Firtree Cl. CF5: F'wtr 1G 93
NP18: C'ln 5E 21
Firwood Cl. CF14: Whit 3B 84
Fisher Cl. NP19: Newp 2D 38
Fisher Hill CF15: Rad 2H 83
Fishermans Wlk. NP16: Bul 5F 63
Fishguard Cl. CF14: L'shn 6A 72
Fishguard Rd. CF14: L'shn 6H 71
Fish La. CF37: P'prdd 1C 24
Fishpond Rd. CF3: L'rmy 1H 87
Fitness First Health Club **6F 71**
Fitzalan Ct. CF24: Card 3F 5 (3B 96)
Fitzalan Pl. CF24: Card 3G 5 (3B 96)
Fitzalan Rd. CF24: Card 3G 5 (3C 96)
(Fitzalan Pl.)
CF24: Card 3F 5 (3B 96)
(Newport Rd.)
Fitzhamon Av. CF71: Llan M 4B 110
Fitzhamon Emb. CF11: Card 5B 4 (4H 95)
Fitzhamon La. CF11: Card 5B 4 (4H 95)
Fitzosborn Cl. NP16: Chep 3D 62
Fitzroy St. CF24: Card 1A 96
(not continuous)
Fitzwalter Rd. NP26: Cald 6C 60
Fitzwilliam Cl. CF72: C Inn 3G 65
Five Ho's. NP4: Up R 5B 6
FIVE LOCKS **5C 8**
Five Locks Cl. NP44: Pnwd 4D 8
Five Locks Rd. NP44: Pnwd 5D 8
Five Oaks La. NP44: C'iog 6G 9
Flanders Mdw. CF71: Llan M 4B 110
Flanders Rd. CF71: Llan M 4B 110
Flatholm Ho. CF11: Card 4A 102
Flavius Cl. NP18: C'ln 4F 21
Flax Ct. CF64: P'rth 6G 101
Flaxland Av. CF14: Card 4G 85

Fleet Way CF11: Card 1G **101**
Fleetwood Cl. NP19: Newp 5F **37**
Fleming Cl. NP20: Malp 5A **20**
FLEMINGSTON 1D **112**
Flemingston Rd. CF62: St A 2C **112**
Fleming Wlk. CF38: Chu V 3D **42**
Flindo Cres. CF11: Card 4D **94**
Flint Av. CF71: Bov 2D **110**
Flint Cl. NP19: Newp 2G **37**
Flint Ct. *NP18: C'ln 4G 21*
(off Roman Way)
Flint St. CF14: Card 6G **85**
Flora St. CF24: Card 1A **96**
Florence Av. CF62: Barry 5G **105**
Florence Gro. CF83: Caer 1C **46**
Florence Pl. NP4: Grif 1E **9**
Florence St. CF24: Card 2E **97**
Florentia St. CF24: Card 6A **86**
Flush Mdw. CF71: Llan M 4B **110**
Foel Vw. Cl. CF38: Llan F 4B **42**
Folly La. NP4: C'avn 1C **6**
(not continuous)
Folly Rd. NP4: C'avn 1C **6**
Folly Vw. NP4: P'pool 2D **6**
FONMON 3B **114**
Fonmon Castle 2B **114**
Fonmon Cres. CF5: Ely 4H **93**
Fonmon Pk. Rd. CF62: Rho 5B **114**
Fonmon Rd. CF62: Rho 4B **114**
Fonthill Pl. CF11: Card 1F **101**
Fontigary Rd. CF3: Rum 4A **88**
FONT-Y-GARY 5C **114**
Fontygary Rd. CF62: Rho 6C **114**
Ford Rd. CF37: P'prdd 6A **14**
CF37: Up Bo 1B **44**
Ford St. NP20: Newp 4B **36**
Fordwell CF5: L'dff 6C **84**
Foreland Rd. CF14: Whit 2C **84**
Foreshore Rd. CF10: Card 6F **97**
Forest Cl. NP19: Newp 3F **37**
NP44: F'wtr 5D **10**
Forest Ct. CF11: Card 2F **95**
CF37: T'rest 2E **25**
Forestet Way CF23: Pontp 3G **73**
Forest Farm Conservation Cen. 1H **83**
Forest Farm Country Pk. 6H **69**
Forest Farm Ind. Est. CF14: Whit 1G **83**
Forest Farm Rd. CF14: Whit 1H **83**
Forest Gro. CF37: T'rest 4E **25**
Forest Hills Dr. CF72: T Grn 3C **64**
Forest Oak Cl. CF23: Cyn 4C **72**
Forest Rd. CF37: T'rest 3E **25**
CF38: Bed 5A **42**
Forest Vw. CF5: F'wtr 2G **93**
CF72: T Grn 3E **65**
NP44: H'lys 5A **10**
Forest Vw. Bus. Pk. CF72: L'sant 5E **41**
Forest Wlk. CF72: T Grn 3C **64**
Forge Cl. NP18: C'ln 4H **21**
FORGE HAMMER 1F **11**
Forge Hammer Ind. Est. NP44: C'brn 1F **11**
Forge La. NP10: Bass 1D **52**
Forge M. NP10: Bass 6D **34**
Forge Pl. CF5: Ely 5F **93**
Forge Rd. CF83: Mac 2G **31**
NP10: Bass, Coedk 1D **52**
Forge Row *NP4: P'nydd 1A 6*
(off Hanbury Rd.)
Forgeside NP44: C'brn 1G **11**
Forgeside Cl. CF24: Card 5D **96**
Forio Ho. *CF10: Card 1C 102*
(off Ffordd Garthorne)
Forrest Rd. CF5: Card 3D **94**
CF64: P'rth 4E **109**
Forrest St. CF11: Card 1H **101**
Forsythia Cl. NP11: Ris 6G **17**
Forsythia Dr. CF23: L'dyrn 6D **72**
Fortlee *NP20: Newp 6G 35*
(off Gaer Rd.)
Fortran Rd. CF3: St M 5F **75**
Fort Rd. CF64: Sul 1D **120**
Fort St. CF24: Card 2E **97**
Fort Vw. NP10: Bass 6C **34**
Fosse Cl. NP19: Newp 1A **56**
Fosse La. NP18: C'ln 5H **21**
Fosse Rd. NP19: Newp 6A **38**
Foster Dr. CF23: Pen L 6E **87**
Foster St. CF63: Barry 1B **118**
Fothergill St. CF37: T'rest 2E **25**
Foundry Cl. CF5: Card 4F **95**
Foundry Pl. CF37: P'prdd 5D **14**
Foundry Rd. CF37: P'prdd 6A **14**
Fountain La. CF3: St M 5F **75**
Fountain Rd. NP4: P'pool 4E **7**
Fountain Way NP16: Bul 6F **63**
Four Acre CF71: Llan M 2C **110**
Fouracres Cl. CF63: Barry 6C **106**
Four Elms Ct. CF24: Card 2H **5** (3C **96**)
Four Elms Rd. CF24: Card 1H **5** (2D **96**)
FOURTEEN LOCKS 3D **34**
Fourteen Locks Canal Cen. 3D **34**
Fourth St. NP19: Newp 3G **55**
Fowler St. NP4: P'pool 1A **6**
Foxberry Cl. CF23: Pontp 4H **73**
Foxglove Cl. CF5: Ely 5F **93**
Foxglove Ri. CF64: P'rth 6F **101**
FOX HILL 4G **33**
Fox La. CF24: Card 2D **96**
Fox Russell Cl. CF14: Llan N 4C **84**
Fox St. CF24: Card 2E **97**
Foxwood Cl. NP10: Bass 6B **34**
Foxwood Ct. NP10: Bass 6B **34**
FRAMPTON 1C **110**
Francis Cl. *NP20: Newp 6C 36*
(off Francis St.)
Francis Dr. NP20: Newp 6C **36**
Francis Rd. CF62: Barry 4A **106**
Francis St. CF37: R'fln 5G **25**
CF83: Abert 2D **26**
NP11: Ris 6E **17**
NP20: Newp 6C **36**
Francis Ter. CF37: P'prdd 4E **15**
Franklen Rd. CF14: Whit 3E **85**
Franklen St. CF11: Card 6H **95**
Frank Rd. CF5: Ely 3G **93**
Frank St. NP19: Newp 3C **36**
Fraternal Pde. *CF37: P'prdd 6C 14*
(off Taff St.)
Fred Edwards Cl. NP19: Newp 4D **38**
Frederick M. NP20: Newp 6D **36**
Frederick St. CF10: Card 4E **5** (4A **96**)
NP20: Newp 1D **54**
Fremington Pl. CF3: L'rmy 2A **88**
Freshmoor Rd. CF24: Card 4E **97**
Freshwater Rd. NP19: Newp 2B **56**
Frewer Av. CF5: F'wtr 6H **83**
Friars Ct. NP20: Newp 6B **36**
Friars Cres. NP20: Newp 5B **36**
Friars Fld. NP20: Newp 6B **36**
Friars Gdn. NP44: Llan 4B **12**
Friars Rd. CF62: Barry 5G **117**
(Paget Rd.)
CF62: Barry 5H **117**
(Plymouth Rd.)
NP20: Newp 6B **36**
Friars St. NP20: Newp 5C **36**
Friary, The CF10: Card 3D **4** (3A **96**)
Frigate Rd. CF10: Card 2D **102**
Frobisher Rd. NP19: Newp 6H **37**
Frome Wlk. NP20: Bet 5E **19**
Fronheulog CF37: P'prdd 5A **14**
Fron Ter. CF37: P'prdd 5D **14**
Fryatt St. CF63: Barry 3A **118**
Fryth Wood NP16: Chep 2C **62**
Fulmar Cl. CF3: St M 5D **74**
CF64: P'rth 6E **109**
Furnace St. CF64: Sul 1E **119**
Furness Cl. CF5: Ely 5E **93**
Fuscia Way NP10: Roger 3H **33**

G

GABALFA 6E **85**
Gabalfa Av. CF14: Llan N 5C **84**
Gabalfa Interchange
CF14: Llan N 4F **85**
Gabalfa Rd. CF14: Llan N 5C **84**
Gabalfa Workshops CF14: Card 5E **85**
Gables, The CF64: Din P 3G **107**
NP16: Chep 1F **63**
Gadlys Rd. E. CF62: Barry 2G **117**
Gadlys Rd. W. CF62: Barry 3F **117**
Gaen St. CF62: Barry 3E **117**
GAER 2H **53**
Gaer La. NP20: Newp 6A **36**
Gaer Pk. Av. NP20: Newp 1G **53**
Gaer Pk. Dr. NP20: Newp 1G **53**
Gaer Pk. Hill NP20: Newp 6G **35**
Gaer Pk. La. NP20: Newp 6G **35**
Gaer Pk. Pde. NP20: Newp 1G **53**
Gaer Pk. Rd. NP20: Newp 1G **53**
Gaer Rd. NP20: Newp 6G **35**
(not continuous)
Gaer St. NP20: Newp 1A **54**
Gaer Va. NP20: Newp 2H **53**
Gaerwen Cl. CF14: L'shn 5F **71**
Gainsborough Cl. NP44: Oakf 5A **12**
Gainsborough Ct. CF64: P'rth 6H **101**
Gainsborough Dr. NP19: Newp 1F **37**
Gainsborough Rd. CF64: P'rth 6H **101**
Galahad Cl. CF14: Thorn 4E **71**
Galaxy Globe Cinema *1C 96*
(off Albany Rd.)
Galdames Pl. CF24: Card 5D **96**
Gallagher Retail Pk. CF83: Caer 3E **29**
Gallamuir Rd. CF24: Card 2F **97**
Galston Pl. CF24: Card 3H **5** (3D **96**)
Galston St. CF24: Card 3H **5** (3D **96**)
Gdn. City Way NP16: Chep 2E **63**
Gardenia Cl. CF23: L'dyrn 6D **72**
Gardens, The NP26: Magor 4C **58**
Garden Suburbs NP11: P'waun 1A **16**
Garden Village CF83: Caer 5D **28**
Gardner Cl. CF37: Glyn 2D **14**
Garesfield St. CF24: Card 4H **5** (4C **96**)
Gareth Cl. CF14: Thorn 3F **71**
Garrick Dr. CF14: Thorn 3G **71**
GARTH 6B **34**
Garthalan Dr. NP26: Rog 6B **60**
Garth Av. CF37: Glyn 2C **14**
Garth Cl. CF15: Morg 5F **69**
CF83: Rud 6B **30**
NP10: Bass 6C **34**
Garth Est. CF83: Abert 2C **26**
Garthfields Cotts. NP10: Bass 6B **34**
Garth Hill CF15: Gwae G, P'rch 3H **67**
NP10: Bass 6B **34**
Garth La. CF83: Rud 6B **30**
Garth Lwyd CF83: Caer 4F **29**
Garth Maelwg CF72: T Grn 3D **64**
Gartholwg CF15: Gwae G 6D **44**
GARTH PLACE 6B **30**
Garth Pl. CF14: Llan N 5F **85**
Garth Ri. CF5: St F 2C **82**
Garth Rd. NP44: C'brn 4F **11**
Garth St. CF10: Card 5F **5** (4B **96**)
CF15: Taff W 2E **69**
CF39: T'fail 3A **40**
Garth Ter. NP10: Bass 1B **52**
Garth Vw. CF15: N'grw 3E **45**
CF15: Taff W 6D **44**
CF38: Bed 5A **42**
CF38: Chu V 3F 43
(off Main Rd.)
CF83: B'ws 2F **29**
Garth Vs. CF83: Abert 2D **26**
Garvey Cl. NP16: Bul 6F **63**
Garw, The NP44: C'iog 6H **9**
Garw Row NP44: C'iog 6H **9**
Garw Wood Dr. NP44: C'iog 5G **9**
Gaskell Cl. CF71: Bov 3E **111**
Gaskell St. NP19: Newp 6F **37**
Gaspard Pl. CF62: Barry 5E **117**
Gas Rd. CF37: P'prdd 6C **14**
Gatehouse Cl. CF62: Barry 5H **105**
Gateside Cl. CF23: Pontp 3G **73**
Gateway, The CF14: Heath 4G **85**
GATLAS 1A **22**
Gatlas La. NP18: C'ln, P'hir 5H **13**
Gaudi Wlk. NP10: Roger 3C **34**
Gaulden Gro. CF23: Pontp 4E **73**
Gawain Cl. CF14: Thorn 3F **71**
Gaynors *NP44: F'wtr 4D 10*
(off Pace Rd.)
Gelli Av. NP11: Ris 6E **17**
Gelli Cl. NP11: Ris 5E **17**
Gelli Cres. NP11: Ris 5E **17**
Gelli Dawel CF83: Caer 5B **28**
Gellidawel Rd. CF37: R'fln 3G **25**
Gelli Deg CF14: Rhiw 5D **70**
CF83: Caer 4B **28**
Gellideg Rd. CF37: P'prdd 1A **24**
Gelli Est. CF72: L'harry 5B **78**
Gelli Fawr Ct. NP44: H'lys 5B **10**
Gelli Frongoch CF23: Pontp 4F **73**
Gelligaer Gdns. CF24: Card 6H **85**
Gelligaer La. CF14: Card 6H **85**
Gelligaer St. CF24: Card 6H **85**
Gelli Hirion CF37: R'fln 5A **26**
Gelli Hirion Ind. Est. CF37: Up Bo 5A **26**
Gelli'r Felin CF83: Caer 5B **28**
Gelli Rd. CF72: L'harry 5B **78**
Gelli Ter. CF83: Sen 1E **27**
Gelli-Unig Pl. NP11: P'waun 1A **16**
Gelli-Unig Rd. NP11: P'waun 1A **16**
Gelli-Unig Ter. NP11: P'waun 1A **16**
Gelliwastad Gro. CF37: P'prdd 6C **14**
Gelliwastad Rd. CF37: P'prdd 6C **14**
Gelliwasted Ct. *CF37: P'prdd 6C 14*
(off Library Rd.)
Gelliwion Rd. CF37: P'prdd 2A **24**
Gelliwion Woods CF37: P'prdd 1A **24**
Gelynis Ter. CF15: Morg 5F **69**
Gelynis Ter. Nth. CF15: Morg 5F **69**
Gelynog Ct. CF38: Bed 3H **41**
Gelyn-y-Cler CF63: Barry 4B **106**
Geoffrey Ashe Ct. CF71: C'bri 4E **91**

George Cl. CF15: Taff W 2E **69**
George Lansbury Dr. NP19: Newp 2C **38**
Georges Row CF64: Din P 1A **108**
George St. CF10: Card 1C **102**
CF63: Barry 2A **118**
CF72: L'sant 2F **65**
NP4: P'nydd 1A **6**
NP4: P'pool 2B **6**
(not continuous)
NP19: Newp 5D **36**
NP20: Newp 6C **36**
NP44: Pnwd 1G **11**
Georgetown CF15: Gwae G 2D **68**
Georgian Cl. CF71: Llan M 2D **110**
Georgian Way CF14: L'shn 5H **71**
CF72: P'clun 6F **65**
Geraint Cl. CF14: Thorn 3F **71**
Geraint Pl. CF63: Barry 6A **106**
Geraint's Cl. CF71: C'bri 4B **90**
Geraint's Way CF71: C'bri 3B **90**
Gerbera Dr. NP10: Roger 2H **33**
Gerddi Margaret CF62: Barry 3G **117**
Gerddi Taf CF5: L'dff 4A **84**
Gerddi ty Celyn CF14: Whit 6B **70**
Gernant CF14: Rhiw 6E **71**
Gerrard Ct. CF11: Card 4F **95**
Gerry Galvin Ct. CF24: Card 2E **97**
Ger y Afon CF37: Glyn 1D **14**
Gibbet's Hill CF71: C'bri 2B **90**
Gibbon Cl. NP19: Newp 5A **38**
GIBBONSDOWN **6A 106**
Gibbonsdown Cl. CF63: Barry 5A **106**
Gibbonsdown Ri. CF63: Barry 6A **106**
Gibbs Rd. NP19: Newp 4G **37**
Gibraltar Way NP16: B'ly 6H **63**
Gibson Cl. CF14: L'shn 1H **85**
Gifford Cl. NP44: C'brn 4F **11**
Gilbert Cl. NP19: Newp 5B **38**
Gilbert La. E. CF63: Barry 4C **106**
CF64: Din P 4C **106**
Gilbert La. W. CF63: Barry 4B **106**
Gilbert Pl. CF14: Llan N 5E **85**
Gilbert St. CF63: Barry 1A **118**
Gildas Cl. CF71: Llan M 2B **110**
GILESTON **6D 112**
Gileston Rd. CF11: Card 2F **95**
CF62: St A 5D **112**
Gileston Wlk. NP44: G'mdw 3E **11**
Gilian Rd. CF5: L'dff 6B **84**
Gilwern Cres. CF14: L'shn 4G **71**
Gilwern Farm Cl. NP18: P'hir 6F **13**
Gilwern Pl. CF14: L'shn 4G **71**
NP44: Pnwd 6D **8**
Glade, The CF14: L'shn 4A **72**
Glade Cl. NP44: F'wtr 5C **10**
Glades, The CF64: P'rth 2F **109**
Gladeside Cl. CF14: Thorn 2G **71**
Gladstone Bri. CF62: Barry 3G **117**
Gladstone Ct. CF62: Barry 2H **117**
Gladstone Pl. NP4: Grif 3E **9**
Gladstone Rd. CF62: Barry 3G **117**
CF63: Barry 3G **117**
Gladstone St. NP11: C'keys 3A **16**
Gladys St. CF24: Card 1A **96**
Glamorgan Cl. CF71: Bov 2D **110**
Glamorgan County Cricket Ground . . . **1A 4 (2G 95)**
Glamorgan M. CF5: Card 3E **95**
Glamorganshire Canal Nature Reserve **6H 69**
Glamorgan St. CF5: Card 3E **95**
CF62: Barry 4E **117**
Glamorgan St. M. CF5: Card 3E **95**
Glamorgan Va. Retail Pk. CF72: T Grn 3F **65**
Glamorgan Wanderers RUFC **4E 93**
Glan Creigiau CF72: Groes F 6C **66**
Glandovey Gro. CF3: Rum 1C **88**
Glandwr Pl. CF14: Whit 3D **84**
Glan Ely Cl. CF5: F'wtr 2G **93**
Glanfa Dafydd CF63: Barry 3A **118**
Glanfelin Flats CF37: R'fln 5G **25**
Glan Ffrwd CF83: Caer 3H **27**
Glan Hafren CF62: Barry 5D **116**
Glanmor Ct. NP19: Newp 4H **37**
Glanmor Cres. CF62: Barry 2F **117**
NP19: Newp 4H **37**
Glanmor Pk. Av. NP19: Newp 4H **37**
Glanmuir Rd. CF24: Card 1G **97**
Glan Nant Cl. CF83: Caer 2C **46**
Glan Rhyd CF83: Caer 5B **28**
NP44: F'wtr 5C **10**
Glanrhyd CF14: Rhiw 6E **71**
Glan Rhymni CF23: Card 6G **87**
Glantorvaen Rd. NP4: P'pool 3C **6**
Glanwern Av. NP19: Newp 3A **38**
Glanwern Cl. NP19: Newp 3A **38**
Glanwern Dr. NP19: Newp 3A **38**
Glanwern Gro. NP19: Newp 3A **38**
Glanwern Ho. NP4: P'pool 3B **6**
Glanwern Ri. NP19: Newp 3A **38**
Glanwern Ter. NP4: P'pool 3B **6**
Glan-y-Dwr CF63: Barry 3H **117**
Glan-y-Ffordd CF15: Taff W 5E **45**
GLAN-Y-ILYN **6E 45**
Glan-y-llyn Ind. Est.
CF15: Taff W 6E **45**
Glan y Mor CF71: Bov 3E **111**
Glan-y-Mor CF62: Barry 5D **116**
CF63: Barry 3H **117**
Glan-y-Mor Rd. CF3: Rum 2C **88**
Glan y Nant CF37: R'fln 5A **26**
Glan-y-Nant Cl. NP44: C'brn 4F **11**
Glan-y-Nant Rd. CF14: Whit 2D **84**
Glan-y-Nant Ter. CF14: Whit 2D **84**
Glan yr Afon CF72: P'clun 6D **64**
Glanyrafon CF15: Gwae G 1D **68**
Glan-yr-Afon CF83: Mac 3F **31**
Glan-yr-Ely CF72: L'sant 6C **40**
Glas Canol CF14: Whit 4D **84**
Glascoed Rd. NP4: New I 5H **7**
Glas Cwm CF37: Glyn 1D **14**
Glas Efail CF14: Rhiw 6F **71**
Glas Heulog CF14: Whit 3D **84**
GLASLLWCH **5E 35**
Glasllwch Cres. NP20: Newp 5E **35**
Glasllwch La. NP20: Newp 6E **35**
Glasllwch Vw. NP20: Newp 6E **35**
Glaslyn Cl. CF62: Barry 2E **117**
Glaslyn Ct. NP44: C'iog 6F **9**
Glass Av. CF24: Card 6E **97**
Glass Works Cotts. NP20: Newp 1C **36**
Glastonbury Cl. NP20: Newp 3C **36**
Glastonbury Rd. CF64: Sul 1H **119**
Glastonbury Ter. CF3: L'rmy 2H **87**
Glas y Llwyn CF63: Barry 4C **106**
Glas-y-Pant CF14: Whit 1B **84**
Glebe Gdns. NP10: Bass 1D **52**
Glebeland Pl. CF62: St A 5C **112**
Glebelands Stadium **1D 36**
Glebe Pl. CF14: L'shn 5H **71**
Glebe Rd. CF83: Tret 3A **30**
Glebe St. CF63: Barry 6A **106**
CF64: P'rth 6A **102**
CF83: B'ws 3G **29**
NP19: Newp 4E **37**
Glen, The NP18: L'stne 6H **23**
Glen Affric Cl. CF62: Barry 1F **117**
Glenbrook Dr. CF63: Barry 5D **106**
Glencoe St. CF63: Barry 1A **118**
Glencourt NP4: Grif 2E **9**
Glendale Av. CF14: L'shn 4G **71**
Glendower Ct. CF14: Whit 2B **84**
Glenfields Est. CF83: Caer 6A **28**
Glengariff Ct. NP4: Grif 1D **8**
Glen Mavis Way CF62: Barry 1F **117**
Glenmount Way CF14: Thorn 3F **71**
Glenrise Cl. CF3: St M 6E **75**
Glenroy NP4: Up R 6A **6**
Glenroy St. CF24: Card 1B **96**
GLENSIDE **4A 16**
Glenside NP44: Pnwd 5D **8**
Glenside Ct. CF23: Pen L 5C **86**
Glen Usk Vw. NP18: C'ln 3G **21**
Glen Vw. CF14: L'shn 1H **85**
NP16: Math 6B **62**
NP44: C'brn 1F **11**
Glenwood CF23: L'dyrn 1D **86**
Globe Cen., The CF24: Card 1C **96**
Glos Gwyn-y-Mor CF3: St M 1D **88**
Glossop Rd. CF24: Card 2H **5** (3C **96**)
Glossop Ter. CF24: Card 3H **5** (3C **96**)
Gloster Pl. NP19: Newp 3D **36**
Gloster's Pde. NP4: New I 6H **7**
Gloster St. NP19: Newp 3D **36**
Gloucester Cl. CF62: Barry 1H **117**
NP44: Llan 2B **12**
Gloucester Ct. *NP18: C'ln* *4G* ***21***
(off Caradoc Cl.)
Gloucester St. CF11: Card 5A **4** (4G **95**)
Glynbridge Cl. CF62: Barry 4H **105**
GLYNCOCH **2D 14**
Glyncoch Ter. CF37: Glyn 2E **15**
Glyn Coed Rd. CF23: L'dyrn 6E **73**
Glyn Collen CF23: L'dyrn 6G **73**
Glyn Derw CF83: Caer 5C **28**
Glyndwr Av. CF62: St A 5C **112**
Glyn-Dwr Av. CF37: R'fln 3F **25**
Glyndwr Rd. CF5: Ely 3F **93**
CF62: Barry 2G **117**
CF64: P'rth 2C **108**
NP44: C'brn 1H **11**
Glyn Eiddew CF23: L'dyrn 5F **73**
Glynne St. CF11: Card 3F **95**
Glynrhondda St. CF24: Card 1D **4** (2A **96**)
Glyn Rhosyn CF23: L'dyrn 5D **72**
Glyn Rhymni CF3: Rum 5A **88**
Glyn Simon Cl. CF5: L'dff 4A **84**
Glynstell Cl. CF11: Card 1F **101**
GLYNTAFF **2F 25**
Glyntaff Cl. CF37: R'fln 3G **25**
Glyntaff Crematorium CF37: R'fln 2F **25**
Glyntaff Housing Est. CF37: R'fln 3G **25**
Glyntaff Rd. CF37: R'fln 1F **25**
Glyntirion NP44: C'brn 4F **11**
Glyn Vw. *NP4: P'pool* *4A* ***6***
(off Crumlin Rd.)
Glyn y Gog CF62: Rho 6F **115**
Godfrey Rd. NP20: Newp 4A **36**
NP44: Pnwd 6D **8**
Godwin Cl. CF5: L'dff 3H **83**
Golate Ct. CF10: Card 5C **4**
Golate St. CF10: Card 5C **4** (4A **96**)
Gold Cliff Ct. NP44: C'brn 2H **11**
Goldcliff Rd. NP18: Newp 6B **56**
Goldcrest Dr. CF23: L'dyrn 6D **72**
Goldcroft Comn. NP18: C'ln 5H **21**
Goldcroft Ct. NP18: C'ln 5H **21**
Golden Mile Vw. NP20: Bass 1E **53**
Goldfinch Cl. NP26: Cald 6C **60**
(not continuous)
Goldsland Pl. CF62: Barry 2E **117**
Goldsmith Cl. CF3: L'rmy 6H **73**
NP20: Newp 1G **53**
Gold St. CF24: Card 2H **5** (3C **96**)
Gold Tops NP20: Newp 4B **36**
Golf Rd. NP4: New I 5G **7**
Golwg y Coed CF83: Caer 4H **27**
Golwg-yr-Eglwys CF83: B'ws 3F **29**
Golygfa'r Eglwys CF37: P'prdd 6A **14**
GOLYNOS **6A 18**
Goodrich Av. CF83: Caer 1E **47**
Goodrich Ct. NP44: Llan 3B **12**
Goodrich Cres. NP20: Newp 2B **36**
Goodrich Gro. NP10: Coedk 6G **53**
Goodrich La. NP20: Newp 2B **36**
Goodrich St. CF83: Caer 1D **46**
Goodwick Cl. CF62: Barry 5H **105**
Goodwick Rd. CF3: Rum 4A **88**
Goodwood Cl. CF5: Ely 5D **92**
Goossens Cl. NP19: Newp 3D **38**
Gordings NP44: G'mdw 2D **10**
Gordon Rd. CF24: Card 1E **5** (2B **96**)
Gordon St. NP19: Newp 4E **37**
Gore St. NP19: Newp 2D **36**
Gorsedd Circle **3B 4**
Gorsedd Gdns. Rd.
CF10: Card 2D **4** (3A **96**)
Gorse Pl. CF5: F'wtr 1G **93**
Goscombe Dr. CF64: P'rth 6H **101**
Gough Rd. CF5: Ely 4G **93**
Gould Cl. CF3: St M 6B **74**
Govilon Pl. NP44: Pnwd 6D **8**
Gowan Ct. CF14: Thorn 2F **71**
Gower Ct. CF62: Barry 2F **117**
Gower Davies Ct. CF37: Y'bwl 1A **14**
Gower Grn. NP44: C'iog 5G **9**
Gower St. CF24: Card 6A **86**
Goya Cl. NP19: Newp 2G **37**
Gradon Cl. CF63: Barry 1C **118**
Grafton Cl. CF23: Pen L 4D **86**
Grafton Dr. CF72: C Inn 3G **65**
Grafton La. NP19: Newp 4D **36**
Grafton Rd. NP19: Newp 4C **36**
Grafton Ter. CF14: Rhiw 1E **85**
Graham Bell Cl. NP20: Malp 3H **19**
Graham Cl. CF23: Pen L 5E **87**
Graham Ct. CF83: Caer 6E **29**
Grahamstown Gro. NP16: Sed 2G **63**
Grahamstown Rd. NP16: Sed 2H **63**
Graham St. NP20: Newp 5B **36**
Graham Wlk. CF11: Card 4F **95**
GRAIG **2B 24**
Graig Av. CF37: P'prdd 2B **24**
Graig Cl. NP10: Bass 6C **34**
Graig Fach CF37: R'fln 2F **25**
Graig Hir CF15: Rad 6F **69**
Graig-Llwyn Rd. CF14: L'vne, Pontp 1C **72**
Graig Lwyd CF15: Rad 6F **69**
Graig Pk. Av. NP20: Malp 5A **20**
Graig Pk. Circ. NP20: Malp 6A **20**
Graig Pk. Hill NP20: Malp 6B **20**
Graig Pk. La. NP20: Malp 6B **20**
Graig Pk. Pde. NP20: Malp 6B **20**
Graig Pk. Rd. NP20: Malp 6A **20**
Graig Pk. Vs. NP20: Malp 6A **20**
Graig Rd. CF14: L'vne 6A **48**
NP44: G'mdw, Up Cwm 1C **10**
Graigside CF15: N'grw 5E **45**
Graig St. CF37: P'prdd 1C **24**
Graig Ter. CF37: P'prdd 1C **24**

Graig Vw. CF14: L'vne 2B **72**
CF15: N'grw 3F **45**
CF83: Mac 2H **31**
NP11: Ris 6D **16**
NP44: Up Cwm 5B **8**
Graig Wen CF15: Morg 5F **69**
Graigwen Cres. CF83: Abert 2F **27**
(not continuous)
Graigwen Parc CF37: P'prdd 4A **14**
Graigwen Pl. CF37: P'prdd 6B **14**
Graigwen Rd. CF37: P'prdd 4A **14**
Graig Wood Cl. NP20: Malp 6A **20**
Graig-y-Fedw CF83: Abert 2F **27**
Graig y Fforest CF37: T'rest 4E **25**
CF38: Tont, T'rest 4E **25**
GRAIG-Y-RHACCA 3C **30**
Graig-y-Rhacca CF83: Mac 2D **30**
Graig-yr-Helfa Rd. CF37: P'prdd, R'fln 1E **25**
Graig yr Hesg Pl. CF37: P'prdd 4D **14**
Graig yr Hesg Rd. CF37: P'prdd 4D **14**
Graig-yr-Wylan CF83: Caer 1A **46**
Grand, The CF10: Card 4B **4**
Grand Av. CF5: Ely 5E **93**
Grange, The CF3: M'fld 5A **76**
CF5: L'dff 1C **94**
CF64: P'rth 2D **108**
CF83: Caer 6B **28**
Grange Av. CF5: Wen 5E **99**
Grange Cl. CF5: Wen 4E **99**
CF83: Caer 6B **28**
Grange Ct. NP4: P'nydd 1A **6**
NP20: Newp 5A **36**
Grange Gdns. CF11: Card 1H **101**
CF71: Llan M 2C **110**
Grange Ind. Est. NP44: C'brn 3H **11**
Grange La. NP44: C'brn 1G **11**
Grangemoor Ct. CF11: Card 4G **101**
Grange Path NP44: Llanf 4B **12**
Grange Pl. CF11: Card 1A **102**
Grange Rd. NP26: Undy 3D **58**
NP44: C'brn 1H **11**
(not continuous)
GRANGETOWN 1H **101**
Grangetown Link CF11: Card 2F **101**
Grangetown Station (Rail) 1G **101**
Grangewood Cl. CF23: Pontp 4H **73**
Granston Ho. NP44: F'wtr 3D **10**
Granston Sq. NP44: F'wtr 3D **10**
Grantham Cl. CF5: F'wtr 5A **84**
Grant's Cl. CF15: Tong 5G **69**
Grant's Fld. CF5: St N 1A **98**
Granville Av. CF5: Card 2C **94**
Granville Cl. NP10: Roger 5E **35**
Granville La. NP20: Newp 5D **36**
Granville Sq. NP20: Newp 5D **36**
Granville St. NP20: Newp 5D **36**
Granville Ter. NP16: Tut 1F **63**
Grasmere Av. CF23: Cyn 4A **86**
Grasmere Way NP16: Bul 6G **63**
Grassmere Cl. CF64: L'dgh 5G **101**
Gray Hill Vw. NP26: Pskwt 5F **61**
Graylands, The CF14: Rhiw 1E **85**
Gray La. CF11: Card 3F **95**
Grays Gdns. CF83: Mac 3C **30**
(not continuous)
Gray St. CF11: Card 3F **95**
(not continuous)
Grays Wlk. CF71: C'bri 3D **90**
Gt. Burnet Cl. CF3: St M 1F **89**
Greater Gwent Crematorium NP44: C'iog 4H **9**
Great Ho. Mdws. CF71: Llan M 2B **110**
Gt. Oaks Pk. NP10: Roger 2B **34**
Gt. Oaks Vw. NP10: Roger 3B **34**
Gt. Ormes Ho. CF11: Card 4A **102**
Gt. Thomas Cl. CF62: Rho 5D **114**
Gt. Western Ct. CF5: Card 4E **95**
Gt. Western La. CF10: Card 5D **4** (4A **96**)
Greave Cl. CF5: Wen 4E **99**
Greek Chu. St. CF10: Card 5B **96**
Green, The CF11: Mic P 2D **100**
CF15: Rad 2G **83**
Green Acre CF15: Cre 6E **67**
NP44: C'brn 4F **11**
Greenacre Dr. CF23: Pontp 3H **73**
CF83: B'ws 2F **29**
Greenacre Gdns. CF83: Tret 3H **29**
Greenacres CF63: Barry 6D **106**
Greenacres Pk. NP18: Newp 4D **56**
Green Av. NP26: Cald 5C **60**
Greenbanks Dr. CF62: Barry 1F **117**
Greenclose Rd. CF14: Whit 3E **85**
Green Ct. NP26: Cald 5B **60**
Greencourt NP44: C'iog 5G **9**
Greencroft Av. CF5: Ely 3B **94**
Greendale Pl. CF15: Tong 5H **69**
Greene Cl. NP19: Newp 4D **38**
Grn. Farm Cl. CF5: Ely 5E **93**
Grn. Farm La. CF5: Ely 6E **93**
Grn. Farm Rd. CF5: Ely 5E **93**
Greenfield NP18: C'ln 4F **21**
NP26: Cald 5C **60**
Greenfield Av. CF5: Card 2E **95**
CF14: Heath 2E **85**
CF37: Glyn 2C **14**
CF64: Din P 1G **107**
Greenfield Cl. NP44: Pnwd 5D **8**
Greenfield Pl. CF83: Abert 2C **26**
Greenfield Rd. CF14: Heath 2E **85**
CF62: Barry 6F **105**
NP10: Roger 5D **34**
Greenfield Stones NP10: Roger 5D **34**
Greenfield Way CF71: L'thian 4B **90**
Greenforge Way NP44: C'brn 2E **11**
Greenhaven Ri. CF64: L'dgh 5G **101**
Greenhill Cl. NP4: Grif 2E **9**
Greenhill Rd. NP4: Grif 1E **9**
NP44: C'brn 1F **11**
Greenland Cres. CF5: F'wtr 1G **93**
Greenland Rd. NP4: C'avn 1B **6**
Greenlands Rd. CF72: L'sant 2G **65**
Green La. CF3: Pet W, St M 6G **75**
CF63: Barry 5C **106**
CF64: Din P 5G **107**
CF71: Llan M 3A **110**
NP10: St Bri 1F **77**
NP26: Cald 5C **60**
Green Lawns CF62: Barry 6A **106**
Greenlawns CF23: Pen L 5C **86**
GREENMEADOW 2C **10**
Greenmeadow CF83: Mac 4D **30**
Greenmeadow Av. NP19: Newp 6A **38**
Greenmeadow Cl. CF37: Glyn 2D **14**
CF64: Din P 3H **107**
NP44: C'brn 3F **11**
Greenmeadow Community Farm 1D **10**
Greenmeadow Ct. CF72: L'sant 3G **65**
Greenmeadow Dr. CF15: Tong 4H **69**
NP11: C'keys 3B **16**
Greenmeadow Rd. NP19: Newp 6A **38**
Greenmeadows CF3: Rum 2C **88**
Greenmeadow Sq. *NP44: C'brn* *3F 11*
(off Greenmeadow Way)
Greenmeadow Way NP44: C'brn, G'mdw 2E **11**
Grn. Moor La. NP26: Magor 4B **58**
(not continuous)
Greenock Rd. CF3: Rum 1B **88**
Green Pk. CF72: P'clun 4B **64**
CF72: T Grn 3E **65**
Green Pl. CF15: Rad 2F **83**
Green Row CF83: Mac 3F **31**
Greenside CF71: C'bri 4D **90**
Green St. CF11: Card 4A **4** (4H **95**)
NP16: Chep 3E **63**
Greenway CF83: B'ws 3E **29**
Greenway Av. CF3: Rum 4A **88**
Greenway Cl. CF64: L'dgh 4E **101**
NP4: Grif 1D **8**
Greenway Ct. CF63: Barry 5D **106**
Greenway Dr. NP4: Grif 1D **8**
Greenway Rd. CF3: Rum, St M 4A **88**
Greenways, The NP26: Magor 4C **58**
Greenway Wlk. NP4: Grif 1D **8**
Greenway Workshops CF83: B'ws 3F **29**
Greenwich Rd. CF5: Card 2D **94**
NP20: Newp 2A **54**
Green Willows NP44: Oakf 5H **11**
Greenwood Av. NP44: Pnwd, Up Cwm 5B **8**
Greenwood Cl. CF23: Pontp 3H **73**
Greenwood Ct. CF83: Caer 6E **29**
Greenwood Dr. CF38: Llan F 4B **42**
NP44: H'lys 5A **10**
Greenwood La. CF5: St F 2E **93**
Greenwood Rd. CF5: L'dff 6B **84**
Greenwood St. CF63: Barry 3H **117**
Grenadier Dr. NP18: L'stne 1G **39**
Grennbay Rd. CF24: Card 3G **97**
Grenville Rd. CF23: Pen L 1D **96**
Grenville Ter. NP26: Rog 6A **60**
Gresford Cl. CF3: St M 1B **88**
Greyfriars Pl. CF10: Card 3D **4** (3A **96**)
Greyfriars Rd. CF10: Card 3D **4** (3A **96**)
Greyhound La. CF72: L'sant 2F **65**
Grey's Dr. CF71: Bov 3D **110**
Greys Rd. NP4: P'pool 5C **6**
Grey Waters NP44: Llan 2A **12**
Griffin, The NP10: Bass 1C **52**
Griffin Cl. CF62: Barry 5E **105**
Griffin St. NP20: Newp 4C **36**
GRIFFITHSTOWN 6E **7**
Griffithstown Railway Mus. 1E **9**
Grimson Cl. CF64: Sul 2H **119**
Grindle Wlk. NP10: Roger 3C **34**
Grisedale Cl. CF23: Pen L 5B **86**
Groes Cl. NP10: Roger 2C **34**
GROESFAEN 1C **80**
Groesllanfro Gdns. NP10: Roger 2C **34**
Groes Lon CF14: Rhiw 5D **70**
Groes Rd. NP10: Roger 3C **34**
(Cefn Rd.)
NP10: Roger 2C **34**
(Ruskin Av.)
Groeswen CF71: Llan M 2B **110**
Groeswen Dr. CF83: Caer 5H **27**
Groeswen Riding Stables 1A **30**
Groeswen Rd. CF15: Caer 1E **45**
CF83: Caer 1E **45**
Gron Ffordd CF14: Rhiw 4D **70**
Grongaer Ter. CF37: P'prdd 1B **24**
Grosmont NP44: C'iog 5G **9**
Grosmont Rd. NP4: New I 5H **7**
Grosmont Way NP10: Coedk 6F **53**
Grosvenor Pl. NP4: Grif 2E **9**
Grosvenor Rd. NP10: Bass 6B **34**
Grosvenor St. CF5: Card 4D **94**
Grouse St. CF24: Card 1H **5** (2C **96**)
Grove, The CF3: Rum 4A **88**
CF37: Glyn 1D **14**
CF62: Barry 4E **117**
NP20: Newp *6C 36*
(off Clytha Sq.)
Grove Est. CF83: Tret 2A **30**
NP4: P'nydd 1A **6**
Grove Gdns. NP26: Cald 5D **60**
Groveland Rd. CF14: Heath 3F **85**
Grove La. NP20: Newp 6C **36**
Grove Pk. NP44: Pnwd 5E **9**
Grove Pk. Av. NP44: Pnwd 5E **9**
Grove Pk. Dr. NP20: Malp 5B **20**
Grove Pk. Rdbt. NP20: Newp 6C **20**
Grove Pl. CF14: Heath 2F **85**
CF64: P'rth 1E **109**
NP4: Grif 1E **9**
Grove Pl. La. CF64: P'rth 1E **109**
Grove Rd. NP4: P'nydd 1A **6**
NP11: Ris 4C **16**
Grovers Cl. CF37: Glyn 1D **14**
Grover St. CF37: P'prdd 1B **24**
Groves Rd. NP20: Newp 5E **35**
Grove Ter. CF64: P'rth 1E **109**
NP4: P'nydd 1A **6**
Grove Way CF3: Rum 4H **87**
Gruffyd Dr. CF83: Caer 4C **28**
Guardian Ind. Est. CF24: Card 2F **97**
Guenever Cl. CF14: Thorn 3E **71**
Guest Rd. CF24: Card 5D **96**
(Ocean Way)
CF24: Card 5H **5** (4C **96**)
(Tyndall St.)
Guildford Cres. CF10: Card 4F **5** (4B **96**)
Guildford St. CF10: Card 4F **5** (4B **96**)
Guildhall Pl. CF10: Card 5C **4** (4A **96**)
Gulf Ind. Area CF11: Card 1G **101**
Guthrie St. CF63: Barry 2A **118**
Guy's Rd. CF63: Barry 1B **118**
Gwaelod y Foel CF38: Llan F 3D **42**
GWAELOD-Y-GARTH 1D **68**
Gwaelod-y-Garth Rd. CF37: Up Bo 1A **44**
Gwalch y Penwaig CF62: Barry 5H **117**
Gwalia Gro. CF37: R'fln 3F **25**
Gwaun Cl. CF14: Whit 3A **84**
Gwaun Hyfryd CF83: Caer 5F **29**
Gwaun Illtuds CF71: Llan M 2C **110**
Gwaunmiskin Rd. CF38: Bed 4H **41**
Gwaun Newydd CF83: Caer 5F **29**
Gwaun Rd. CF37: R'fln 3F **25**
Gwaunruperra Cl. CF72: L'sant 1F **65**
Gwaunruperra Rd. CF72: L'sant 1F **65**
Gwaun y Cwrt CF83: Caer 2H **45**
Gwbert Cl. CF3: Rum 2C **88**
Gwendoline Pl. CF24: Card 4D **96**
Gwendoline Rd. NP11: Ris 6D **16**
Gwendoline St. CF24: Card 4D **96**
Gwenfo Dr. CF5: Wen 4E **99**
Gwenllian St. CF63: Barry 1D **118**
Gwenllian Ter. CF37: T'rest 5F **25**
Gwennol y Mor CF62: Barry 5H **117**
Gwennyth St. CF24: Card 6A **86**
Gwenog Ct. CF62: Barry 2E **117**
Gwent CF64: P'rth 6C **102**
Gwentlands Cl. NP16: Bul 3E **63**
Gwent Rd. CF5: Ely 5F **93**
CF37: Up Bo 2C **44**
Gwent Sq. NP44: C'brn 1G **11**
Gwent St. NP4: P'pool 3B **6**
Gwern Heulog CF39: T'fail 1A **40**
Gwern Rhuddi Rd. CF23: Cyn 5C **72**
(not continuous)
Gwili Rd. CF37: Up Bo 6B **26**

Gwilym Pl. CF63: Barry .5A **106**
Gwilym St. CF37: R'fln .5F **25**
Gwladys Pl. NP18: C'ln .4G **21**
GWNDY .4F **59**
Gwy Ct. NP16: Chep .1F **63**
Gwynant Cres. CF23: Cyn .2B **86**
Gwyn Dr. CF83: Caer .5C **28**
Gwyndy Rd. NP26: Undy .4E **59**
Gwyn James Ct. CF64: P'rth .6G **101**
Gwynllyw NP44: Pnwd .5C **8**
Gwyn St. CF37: T'rest .4E **25**
Gyfeillon Rd. CF37: P'prdd .5A **14**
Gypsy La. CF15: Caer .6G **27**

H

Habershon St. CF24: Card .4E **97**
Hackerford Rd. CF23: Cyn .5C **72**
Haden St. NP4: P'pool .3B **6**
Hadfield Cl. CF11: Card .6E **95**
Hadfield Rd. CF11: Card .6E **95**
Hadley Ho. CF64: P'rth .4D **108**
Hadrian Cl. NP18: C'ln .4G **21**
Hafan Heulog CF37: Glyn .1D **14**
Hafan-Werdd CF83: Caer .4F **29**
Hafod CF72: L'sant .6C **40**
Hafod Cl. NP18: P'hir .1F **21**
Hafod Ct. Rd. NP44: G'mdw .6A **8**
Hafod Cwrt NP20: Newp .6A **36**
Hafod Gdns. NP18: P'hir .1F **21**
Hafod La. CF37: P'prdd .5A **14**
Hafod M. NP18: P'hir .1F **21**
Hafod Rd. NP18: P'hir .1F **21**
Hafod St. CF11: Card .6B **4** (5H **95**)
Hafod-y-Bryn NP11: Ris .6E **17**
Hafren Ct. CF11: Card .2F **95**
Hafren Rd. CF62: Barry .2G **117**
NP44: G'mdw .1C **10**
Haig Pl. CF5: Ely .6E **93**
Hailey Ct. CF14: Llan N .4B **84**
Haines Cl. CF83: Caer .2A **46**
Haisbro Av. NP19: Newp .1E **37**
Haldane Ct. CF83: Caer .6F **29**
Haldane Pl. NP20: Malp .5A **20**
Haldens, The NP44: F'wtr .4D **10**
Hale Wood NP16: Chep .2C **62**
Half Acre La. NP18: L'wrn .6H **57**
Halifax Cl. CF24: Card .2G **97**
Halle Cl. NP19: Newp .4E **39**
Halliard Ct. CF10: Card .6C **96**
Halls Rd. NP11: C'keys, P'waun .1A **16**
Halls Rd. Ter. NP11: C'keys .2A **16**
Halsbury Rd. CF5: Card .2D **94**
Halstead St. NP19: Newp .5E **37**
Halt, The CF64: Sul .2G **119**
Halton Cl. CF64: P'rth .5E **109**
Hamadryad Rd. CF10: Card .2A **102**
Hamilton Ct. CF5: Card .3E **95**
Hamilton St. CF11: Card .3G **95**
NP19: Newp .6F **37**
Ham La. E. CF71: Llan M .4C **110**
Ham La. Sth CF71: Llan M .4B **110**
Ham Mnr. CF71: Llan M .4C **110**
Ham Mnr. Cvn. Pk.
CF71: Llan M .5C **110**
Ham M. CF71: Llan M .5C **110**
Hammond Dr. NP19: Newp .5F **37**
Hammond Way CF23: Pen L .6E **87**
Hampden Ct. NP19: Newp .6G **37**
Hampden Rd. NP19: Newp .6G **37**
Hampshire Av. NP19: Newp .1H **55**
Hampshire Cl. NP19: Newp .1H **55**
Hampshire Cres. NP19: Newp .1H **55**
Hampstead Wlk. CF5: Ely .5D **92**
Hampton Ct. Rd. CF23: Pen L .5D **86**
Hampton Cres. E. CF23: Cyn .4D **72**
Hampton Cres. W. CF23: Cyn .4C **72**
Hampton Rd. CF14: Heath .3F **85**
Hanbury Cl. CF14: Whit .2A **84**
NP18: C'ln .6A **22**
NP44: C'brn .1G **11**
Hanbury Gdns. NP4: P'nydd .1A **6**
Hanbury Rd. NP4: P'nydd .1A **6**
NP4: P'pool .3C **6**
Handel Cl. CF64: P'rth .4D **108**
NP19: Newp .4D **38**
Hand Farm Rd. NP4: New I .4F **7**
Handley Rd. CF24: Card .2G **97**
Handsworth St. NP19: Newp .5F **37**
Hanfield Pk. NP44: C'iog .1A **12**
Hanley Path NP44: G'mdw .3E **11**
Hannah Cl. CF14: L'shn .1H **85**
Hannah St. CF10: Card .6B **96**
CF63: Barry .1A **118**
Hanover Cl. NP16: Chep .1D **62**
Hanover Ct. CF14: Whit .1B **84**
CF63: Barry .6D **106**
NP16: Sed .2G **63**
Hanover St. CF5: Card .4E **95**
CF62: Barry .2H **117**
Hansen Ct. CF10: Card .1B **102**
Hansom Pl. CF11: Card .6G **95**
Harbour Dr. CF10: Card .2C **102**
Harbour Rd. CF62: Barry .4F **117**
Harbour Vw. Rd. CF64: P'rth .6A **102**
Harding Av. NP20: Malp .4A **20**
Harding Cl. CF71: Bov .3E **111**
HARDWICK .3E **63**
Hardwick Av. NP16: Chep .3E **63**
Hardwicke Ct. CF5: L'dff .1C **94**
Hardwick Hill NP16: Chep .3D **62**
Hardwick Hill La. NP16: Chep .3E **63**
Hardwick Ter. NP16: Chep .2E **63**
(not continuous)
Hardy Cl. CF62: Barry .5A **106**
NP20: Newp .2G **53**
Hardy Ct. NP4: P'nydd .1A **6**
Hardy Pl. CF24: Card .1G **5** (2C **96**)
Harefield Cl. CF23: Pontp .4H **73**
Harford Cl. CF14: Whit .2A **84**
Hargreaves Dr. NP20: Malp .4A **20**
Harlech Cl. CF64: Din P .2A **108**
NP44: C'iog .5G **9**
Harlech Ct. CF14: Whit .1C **84**
CF83: Caer .5H **27**
Harlech Dr. CF64: Din P .1A **108**
NP10: R'drn .6A **34**
Harlech Gdns. CF62: Barry .5F **105**
Harlech Ho. CF15: Rad .1G **83**
Harlech Retail Pk. NP20: Newp .1A **54**
Harlech Rd. CF3: Rum .4A **88**
Harlequin Ct. NP20: Newp .3B **36**
Harlequin Dr. NP20: Newp .3B **36**
Harlequin Rdbt. NP20: Newp .3C **36**
Harlequins Ct. CF24: Pen L .1E **97**
Harold St. CF24: Card .2E **97**
NP44: Pnwd .6E **9**
Harold Wlk. *NP10: Roger .5D 34*
(off Ebenezer Dr.)
Harpur St. CF10: Card .5A **96**
Harriet St. CF24: Card .1A **96**
CF64: P'rth .6H **101**
Harrington Ct. CF5: Ely .6F **93**
Harris Av. CF3: Rum .3A **88**
Harrismith Rd. CF23: Pen L .6C **86**
Harrison Dr. CF3: St M .2D **88**
Harrison Way CF11: Card .3H **101**
Harrogate Rd. NP19: Newp .1E **37**
Harrowby La. CF10: Card .2B **102**
Harrowby Pl. CF10: Card .2B **102**
Harrowby St. CF10: Card .1B **102**
Harrow Cl. NP18: C'ln .3F **21**
Harrow Rd. NP19: Newp .4D **36**
Hart Gdns. *NP20: Newp .6C 36*
(off Alma St.)
Hartland Ho. CF11: Card .4A **102**
Hartland Rd. CF3: L'rmy .2G **87**
Hartley Pl. CF11: Card .6F **95**
Hart Pl. CF23: Card .1F **97**
Hartridge Farm Rd. NP18: Newp .5C **38**
Hartshorn Ct. CF83: Caer .6F **29**
Harvard Rd. CF83: Abert .2D **26**
Harvey Cl. NP20: Malp .5A **20**
Harvey Pl. CF5: Card .3E **95**
Harvey St. CF63: Barry .1B **118**
(not continuous)
Hassocks Lea NP44: F'wtr .4D **10**
Hastings Av. CF64: P'rth .1C **108**
Hastings Cl. CF64: P'rth .1C **108**
Hastings Cres. CF3: St M .5B **74**
Hastings Pl. CF64: P'rth .1C **108**
Hathaway Pl. CF63: Barry .5C **106**
Hathaway St. NP19: Newp .5F **37**
Hatherleigh NP19: Newp .4H **37**
Hatherleigh Rd. CF3: Rum .3G **87**
Haul Fryn CF14: Rhiw .5B **70**
Havannah St. CF10: Card .2B **102**
Havant Cl. CF62: Rho .6E **115**
Havelock Pl. CF11: Card .6H **95**
Havelock St. CF10: Card .5C **4** (4A **96**)
NP20: Newp .5B **36**
Havenwood Dr. CF14: Thorn .2G **71**
Haverford Way CF5: Ely .5H **93**
Hawarden Grn. NP44: Llan .3B **12**
Hawarden Rd. NP19: Newp .4G **37**
(not continuous)
Hawfinch Cl. CF23: L'dyrn .6D **72**
Hawke Cl. NP19: Newp .2C **38**
Hawker Cl. CF24: Card .2G **97**
Hawkes Ridge NP44: F'wtr .3B **10**
Hawkins Cres. NP19: Newp .2C **38**
Hawksmoor Cl. NP10: Roger .3D **34**
Hawksworth Gro. NP19: Newp .5H **37**
Hawkwood Cl. CF5: F'wtr .6F **83**
Hawse La. NP10: M'fld, St Bri .3D **76**
HAWTHORN .5G **25**
Hawthorn Av. CF64: P'rth .2C **108**
Hawthorn Cl. CF64: Din P .3H **107**
NP18: Under .3H **39**
NP26: Undy .3D **58**
Hawthorn Cres. CF37: R'fln .5H **25**
Hawthorne Av. NP19: Newp .5G **37**
Hawthorne Cl. NP16: Bul .6E **63**
Hawthorne Fosse NP19: Newp .5H **37**
Hawthorne Sq. NP19: Newp .5G **37**
Hawthorn Gdns. NP18: C'ln .4A **22**
Hawthorn Leisure Cen. .5G **25**
Hawthorn Pl. NP11: P'waun .1A **16**
Hawthorn Rd. CF37: R'fln .5H **25**
CF62: Barry .3E **117**
CF72: L'harry .5B **78**
NP4: Grif .2D **8**
Hawthorn Rd. E. CF14: Llan N .4B **84**
Hawthorn Rd. W. CF14: Llan N .4B **84**
Hawthorns, The CF23: L'dyrn .6E **73**
NP18: C'ln .4A **22**
NP44: Up Cwm .5B **8**
Hayes, The CF10: Card .4D **4** (4A **96**)
Hayes Bri. Rd. CF10: Card .5D **4** (4A **96**)
Hayes La. CF64: Barry .3D **118**
Hayes Rd. CF64: Barry, Sul .3D **118**
Hayling Cl. NP19: Newp .2F **37**
Haynes Ct. NP20: Newp .1D **54**
Hayswayn NP44: F'wtr .4D **10**
Hazel Av. NP26: Cald .4B **60**
Hazel Cl. NP4: New I .4H **7**
Hazeldene CF72: L'harry .5A **78**
Hazeldene Av. CF24: Card .5A **86**
Hazel Gro. CF64: Din P .3H **107**
CF83: Caer .4E **29**
CF83: Tret .2H **29**
Hazelhurst Ct. CF14: Llan N .4B **84**
Hazelhurst Rd. CF14: Llan N .4B **84**
Hazell Dr. NP10: Coedk .5D **52**
Hazel Pl. CF5: F'wtr .6H **83**
Hazel Rd. CF64: P'rth .3D **108**
Hazel Tree Cl. CF15: Rad .1E **83**
Hazel Wlk. NP18: C'ln .5F **21**
NP44: C'iog .5G **9**
Hazelwood Dr. CF3: St M .6C **74**
Hazledene Cl. CF63: Barry .6A **106**
Hazlitt Cl. CF3: L'rmy .5H **73**
NP20: Newp .2G **53**
Headland, The NP16: Bul .6G **63**
Hearte Cl. CF62: Rho .5E **115**
HEATH .2A **86**
Heath Av. CF64: P'rth .6F **101**
Heathbrook CF14: L'shn .6A **72**
Heathcliffe Cl. CF3: St M .5B **74**
Heath Cl. NP19: Newp .1A **56**
Heath Cres. CF37: P'prdd .6B **14**
Heather Av. CF5: Ely .3B **94**
Heather Cl. NP16: Bul .5F **63**
Heather Ct. NP44: F'wtr .4B **10**
Heather Rd. NP19: Newp .1E **37**
Heathers, The CF62: Barry .2F **117**
Heather Vw. Rd. CF37: P'prdd .5E **15**
Heather Way CF5: F'wtr .1H **93**
Heathfield Dr. CF62: Barry .6G **105**
Heathfield Pl. CF14: Card .5G **85**
Heathfield Rd. CF14: Card .5G **85**
Heath Halt Rd. CF23: Cyn, Heath .2A **86**
Heath High Level Station (Rail) .2A **86**
Heathland Vs. CF37: T'rest .2E **25**
Heath Low Level Station (Rail) .2A **86**
Heath Mead CF14: Heath .3A **86**
HEATH PARK .3F **85**
Heath Pk. Av. CF14: Heath .2H **85**
Heath Pk. Ct. CF14: Heath .3A **86**
Heath Pk. Cres. CF14: Heath .3A **86**
Heath Pk. Dr. CF14: Heath .2A **86**
Heath Pk. La. CF14: Heath .2A **86**
(Heath Pk. Av.)
CF14: Heath .4F **85**
(St Agnes Rd.)
Heath Pk. Way CF14: Heath .3G **85**
Heath Sports Cen. .3H **85**
Heath St. CF11: Card .4G **95**
Heath Ter. CF37: P'prdd .6B **14**
Heath Way CF14: Heath .2G **85**
Heathwood Ct. CF14: Heath .2G **85**
Heathwood Gro. CF14: Heath .3A **86**
Heathwood Rd. CF14: Cyn .1A **86**
CF14: Heath .3F **85**
Hebbles La. CF63: Barry .6C **106**
Heddfan Nth. CF23: L'dyrn .6F **73**
Heddfan Sth. CF23: L'dyrn .6F **73**

Hedel Rd. CF11: Card . . . 3C **94**
Heidenheim Dr. NP20: Newp . . . 2B **36**
Helen Pl. CF24: Card . . . 2D **96**
Helen St. CF24: Card . . . 2D **96**
Helford Sq. NP20: Bet . . . 5F **19**
Hellas Dr. CF62: Barry . . . 5E **105**
Helpstone Ter. NP4: P'pool . . . 2A **6**
Hemingway Rd. CF10: Card . . . 1C **102**
Hendre CF83: Caer . . . 2A **28**
Hendre Cl. CF5: L'dff . . . 1C **94**
Hendre Ct. NP44: H'lys . . . 5B **10**
Hendredenny Dr. CF83: Caer . . . 5G **27**
HENDREDENNY PARK . . . 5H **27**
Hendre Farm Ct. NP19: Newp . . . 3D **38**
Hendre Farm Dr. NP19: Newp . . . 3D **38**
Hendre Farm Gdns. NP19: Newp . . . 4C **38**
Hendre Gdns. CF5: L'dff . . . 1C **94**
Hendre Rd. CF3: Rum, St M . . . 1B **88**
CF83: Abert . . . 2C **26**
Hendrick Dr. NP16: Sed . . . 2G **63**
HENDY . . . 6F **65**
Hendy St. CF23: Card . . . 6B **86**
Henfron CF83: Caer . . . 3A **28**
Hengoed Cl. CF5: Ely . . . 5G **93**
Henke Ct. CF10: Card . . . 6C **96**
HENLLYS . . . 5B **10**
Henllys La. NP10: H'lys . . . 5C **18**
NP20: Bet . . . 5C **18**
NP44: H'lys . . . 5A **10**
Henllys Rd. CF23: Cyn . . . 1B **86**
HENLLYS VALE . . . 2D **18**
Henllys Village Rd. NP44: H'lys . . . 5B **10**
Henllys Way NP44: C'brn . . . 4G **11**
NP44: F'wtr, H'lys . . . 5B **10**
Henry Morgan Cl. NP10: Duf . . . 5H **53**
Henry St. CF10: Card . . . 6B **96**
CF37: P'prdd . . . 5A **14**
CF63: Barry . . . 1D **118**
Henry Wood Cl. NP19: Newp . . . 5A **38**
Henry Wood Wlk. NP19: Newp . . . 5A **38**
Hensol Cl. NP10: Roger . . . 3D **34**
NP44: Llan . . . 2A **12**
HENSOL HOSPITAL . . . 5F **79**
Hensol Rd. CF72: Hens, P'clun . . . 1E **79**
(not continuous)
Hensol Vs. CF72: Hens . . . 4G **79**
Henson St. NP19: Newp . . . 5F **37**
Henwysg Cl. CF37: P'prdd . . . 5A **14**
Heol Aer CF14: Rhiw . . . 5E **71**
Heol Amlwch CF14: Llan N . . . 4D **84**
Heol Aneurin CF83: Caer . . . 3H **27**
Heol Appryce CF38: Bed . . . 5A **42**
Heol Aradur CF5: L'dff . . . 4H **83**
Heol Barri CF83: Caer . . . 4B **28**
Heol Berllan CF83: Caer . . . 4D **28**
Heol Berry CF15: Gwae G . . . 2D **68**
Heol Beulah CF83: L'brad . . . 1B **28**
Heol Beuno NP4: New I . . . 4G **7**
Heol Billingsley CF15: N'grw . . . 3C **44**
Heol Blakemore CF14: Whit . . . 2B **84**
Heol Booker CF14: Whit . . . 2A **84**
Heol Briwnant CF14: Rhiw . . . 4D **70**
Heol Broadland CF62: Barry . . . 3G **117**
Heol Brofiscin CF72: Groes F . . . 6B **66**
Heol Bro Wen CF83: Caer . . . 5D **28**
Heol Bryn Glas CF38: Llan F . . . 4D **42**
Heol Brynglas CF14: Rhiw . . . 5C **70**
Heol Bryn Heulog CF38: Llan F . . . 3D **42**
Heol Brynhyfryd CF38: Llan F . . . 4B **42**
Heol Brynmoor John CF38: Chu V . . . 2D **42**
Heol Cae Bach CF83: Caer . . . 3D **28**
Heol Cae Celynnen CF83: Caer . . . 3D **28**
Heol Cae Fan Heulog CF83: Caer . . . 4D **28**
Heol Cae Gwyn CF83: Caer . . . 2A **46**
Heol Cae Maen CF83: Caer . . . 4D **28**
Heol Caerhys CF14: Rhiw . . . 1E **85**
Heol Caerlan CF38: Bed . . . 5H **41**
Heol Camddwr CF23: Pontp . . . 4H **73**
Heol Carnau CF5: Ely . . . 6H **93**
Heol Carne CF14: Whit . . . 3E **85**
Heol Cattwg CF14: Whit . . . 4D **84**
Heol Cawrdaf CF38: Bed . . . 5A **42**
Heol Cefn Onn CF14: L'vne . . . 2A **72**
Heol Cefn-yr Hendy CF72: P'clun . . . 6E **65**
Heol Celyn CF38: Chu V, Tont . . . 2F **43**
Heol Celynen CF37: Glyn . . . 1D **14**
Heol Celynnen CF72: L'harry . . . 5C **78**
Heol Ceniog CF63: Barry . . . 3H **117**
Heol Chappell CF14: Whit . . . 2B **84**
Heol Chudleigh CF3: St M . . . 2D **88**
Heol Cliffrydd CF63: Barry . . . 3A **118**
Heol Clwyddau CF38: Bed . . . 6A **42**
Heol Clyd CF83: Caer . . . 4H **27**
Heol Coed Cae CF14: Whit . . . 3D **84**
Heol Collen CF5: Ely . . . 1E **99**
Heol Coroniad CF38: Bed . . . 4A **42**
Heol Corswigen CF63: Barry . . . 5B **106**
Heol Creigiau CF15: Cre . . . 4D **66**
CF38: E Isaf . . . 6D **42**
Heol Crochendy CF15: N'grw . . . 2C **44**
Heol Cronfa CF37: C'fydd . . . 3F **15**
Heol Cwarrel Clark CF83: Caer . . . 2H **27**
Heol Cwm Ifor CF83: Caer . . . 3H **27**
Heol Dafydd CF72: P'clun . . . 6C **64**
Heol Danyrodyn CF15: P'rch . . . 4A **68**
Heol Dderwen CF38: Tont . . . 1G **43**
Heol Ddeusant CF38: Bed . . . 5H **41**
Heol Ddu CF72: L'sant . . . 2C **40**
Heol Deg CF38: Tont . . . 2F **43**
Heol Deiniol NP4: New I . . . 4G **7**
Heol Dennant CF5: F'wtr . . . 1A **94**
Heol Derlwyn CF14: Rhiw . . . 5D **70**
Heol Derwen NP4: New I . . . 4G **7**
Heol Deva CF5: Ely . . . 6G **93**
Heol Dewi Sant CF14: Heath . . . 1F **85**
CF62: Barry . . . 2G **117**
Heol Dolwen CF14: Whit . . . 3E **85**
Heol Don CF14: Whit . . . 2B **84**
Heol Dowlais CF38: E Isaf . . . 6D **42**
Heol Draenen Wen CF5: Ely . . . 1E **99**
Heol Draw CF38: Chu V . . . 2E **43**
Heol Dyfed CF14: Heath . . . 2F **85**
CF38: Bed . . . 6H **41**
Heol Dyfodwg CF72: L'sant . . . 1F **65**
Heol Dyhewydd CF38: Llan F . . . 4B **42**
Heol Ebwy CF5: Ely . . . 5H **93**
Heol Edwards CF15: N'grw . . . 3E **45**
Heol Eglwys CF5: Ely . . . 5A **94**
Heol Erwin CF14: Rhiw . . . 4E **71**
Heol Erw-y-Rhos CF83: Caer . . . 4D **28**
Heol Esgyn CF23: Cyn . . . 1A **86**
Heol Fach CF15: N'grw . . . 3E **45**
CF83: Caer . . . 5A **28**
Heol Faenor CF38: Bed . . . 6H **41**
Heol Fair CF5: L'dff . . . 1C **94**
Heol Fawr CF83: Caer . . . 3H **27**
Heol Fer CF83: Caer . . . 3A **28**
Heol Ffrwd Philip CF38: E Isaf . . . 6F **43**
Heol Ffynnon Wen CF14: Rhiw . . . 5B **70**
Heol Fioled CF63: Barry . . . 4B **106**
Heol Gabriel CF14: Whit . . . 4D **84**
Heol Gam CF15: P'rch . . . 4H **67**
Heol Ganol CF83: Caer . . . 6B **28**
Heol Gelynog CF38: Bed . . . 5A **42**
Heol Ger-y-Felin CF71: Llan M . . . 2C **110**
Heol Glandulais CF23: Pontp . . . 4F **73**
Heol Glan Elai CF72: P'clun . . . 1C **78**
Heol Glanrheidol CF10: Card . . . 1B **102**
Heol Glaslyn CF23: Pontp . . . 4H **73**
NP26: Cald . . . 3D **60**
Heol Gledyr CF83: Caer . . . 1C **46**
Heol Glyn CF83: Caer . . . 4B **28**
Heol Goch CF15: Gwae G, P'rch . . . 4A **68**
Heol Graig Wen CF83: Caer . . . 4H **27**
Heol Groeswen CF37: Up Bo . . . 6B **26**
Heol Gwaun Rhos CF83: Caer . . . 4D **28**
Heol Gwendoline CF62: Barry . . . 3G **117**
Heol Gwent CF14: Heath . . . 2F **85**
Heol Gwerthyd CF63: Barry . . . 4A **106**
Heol Gwilym CF5: F'wtr . . . 6H **83**
Heol Gwrgan CF14: Whit . . . 2D **84**
CF38: Bed . . . 5H **41**
Heol Gwyndaf CF14: L'shn . . . 6H **71**
Heol Gwynedd CF14: Heath . . . 2F **85**
Heol Gwynno CF72: L'sant . . . 1F **65**
Heol Gylfinir CF62: Barry . . . 5H **117**
Heol Harlech CF5: L'dff . . . 1C **94**
Heol Hendre CF14: Rhiw . . . 5E **71**
Heol Hendy CF72: P'clun . . . 6E **65**
Heol Hensol CF38: Bed . . . 5A **42**
Heol Hir CF14: L'shn, Thorn . . . 3H **71**
CF14: Thorn . . . 6G **47**
(not continuous)
Heol Homfray CF5: Ely . . . 6E **93**
Heol Ida CF38: Bed . . . 4A **42**
Heol Iestyn CF14: Whit . . . 2D **84**
Heol Ifor CF14: Heath . . . 2E **85**
Heol Illtyd CF72: L'sant . . . 1F **65**
Heol Isaf CF14: Rhiw . . . 4D **70**
CF15: Rad . . . 6F **69**
CF38: Llan F . . . 6B **42**
NP4: New I . . . 4G **7**
Heol Isaf Hendy CF72: P'clun . . . 6E **65**
Heol Iscoed CF14: Rhiw . . . 5E **71**
CF38: E Isaf . . . 6E **43**
Heol Johnson CF72: T Grn . . . 3D **64**
Heol Las CF72: L'sant . . . 1E **65**
CF83: Caer . . . 2A **28**
Heol Leubren CF63: Barry . . . 4A **106**
Heol Lewis CF14: Rhiw . . . 4E **71**
CF83: Caer . . . 4F **29**
Heol Llangan CF14: Rhiw . . . 1D **84**
Heol Llanishen Fach CF14: Rhiw . . . 5D **70**
Heol Llinos CF14: Thorn . . . 1G **71**
Heol Lodwig CF38: Chu V . . . 3E **43**
Heol Mabon CF14: Rhiw . . . 5D **70**
Heol Maddoc NP4: New I . . . 4G **7**
Heol Madoc CF14: Whit . . . 3E **85**
Heol Maerdy CF83: Caer . . . 5F **29**
Heol Maes Eirwg CF3: St M . . . 1D **88**
Heol Mathew CF14: Whit . . . 2B **84**
Heol Merioneth CF71: Bov . . . 3E **111**
Heol Merlin CF14: L'shn . . . 6H **71**
Heol Miaren CF63: Barry . . . 5C **106**
Heol Miles CF72: T Grn . . . 3D **64**
Heol Miskin CF72: P'clun . . . 5D **64**
Heol Moor CF62: Barry . . . 3D **116**
Heol Muston CF5: Ely . . . 3H **93**
Heol Mwyrdy CF38: Bed . . . 5H **41**
Heol Mynydd CF37: C'fydd . . . 3F **15**
CF38: Tont . . . 2G **43**
Heol Mynydd Bychan CF14: Heath . . . 1F **85**
Heol Nant CF37: C'fydd . . . 3F **15**
CF38: Tont, Chu V . . . 2F **43**
Heol Nant Castan CF14: Rhiw . . . 4D **70**
Heol Nest CF14: Heath . . . 2D **84**
Heol Newydd CF3: Rum . . . 3B **88**
NP44: Up Cwm . . . 5C **8**
Heol Padarn NP4: New I . . . 4G **7**
Heol Pal CF62: Barry . . . 5H **117**
Heol Pant Gwyn CF72: L'harry . . . 5A **78**
Heol Pantycelyn CF14: Whit . . . 1B **84**
CF62: Barry . . . 3F **117**
Heol Pantyderi CF5: Ely . . . 5G **93**
Heol Pant-y-Gored CF15: Cre, P'rch . . . 6E **67**
Heol Pant-y-Rhyn CF14: Whit . . . 6B **70**
Heol Pardoe CF15: N'grw . . . 2D **44**
Heol Pearetree CF62: Rho . . . 6G **115**
Heol Pencarreg CF14: Llan N . . . 5D **84**
Heol Penlan CF14: Whit . . . 3A **84**
Heol Penllwyn CF15: P'rch . . . 4H **67**
Heol Pennar CF5: Ely . . . 5H **93**
Heol Pentre'r Cwrt CF71: Llan M . . . 2B **110**
Heol Pentre'r Felin CF71: Llan M . . . 2C **110**
Heol Pentwyn CF14: Whit . . . 6B **70**
Heol-Pen-y-Bryn CF83: Tong . . . 6A **46**
Heol Penyfai CF14: Whit . . . 3E **85**
Heol Pen-y-Foel CF37: Glyn . . . 1D **14**
Heol Pen-y-Parc CF37: Glyn . . . 1D **14**
CF72: L'sant . . . 2F **65**
Heol Peredur CF14: Thorn . . . 3F **71**
Heol Pilipala CF62: Rho . . . 6F **115**
Heol Pontprennau CF23: Pontp . . . 4F **73**
(not continuous)
Heol Pont-y-Cwcw NP10: St Bri . . . 6A **54**
Heol Powis CF14: Heath . . . 2F **85**
Heol Poyston CF5: Ely . . . 6G **93**
Heol Pwllypant CF83: Caer . . . 4B **28**
Heol Pwllyplaca CF3: St M . . . 1D **88**
Heol Rhayader CF14: Whit . . . 3A **84**
Heol Rhos CF83: Caer . . . 6H **27**
Heol Rhosyn CF38: Llan F . . . 6B **42**
Heol St Denys CF14: L'vne . . . 2A **72**
Heol Salem CF38: Chu V, Tont . . . 2F **43**
Heol Seddon CF5: L'dff . . . 5H **83**
Heol Serth CF83: Caer . . . 3H **27**
Heol Seward CF38: Bed . . . 6H **41**
Heol Sirhwi CF62: Barry . . . 1E **117**
Heol Solva CF5: Ely . . . 5A **94**
Heol Sticil-y-Beddau CF72: L'sant . . . 2F **65**
Heol Stradling CF14: Whit . . . 2D **84**
Heol St. CF5: St F . . . 4H **81**
Heol Syr Lewis CF15: Morg . . . 5F **69**
Heol Teifi NP26: Cald . . . 4D **60**
Heol Teilo NP4: New I . . . 4G **7**
Heol Terrell CF11: Card . . . 4D **94**
Heol Thomas CF83: Caer . . . 1B **46**
Heol Tir Bach CF83: Caer . . . 3H **27**
Heol Tir Coch CF38: E Isaf . . . 6E **43**
Heol Tir Gibbon CF83: Caer . . . 4A **28**
Heol Towy NP26: Cald . . . 3D **60**
Heol Trecastell CF83: Caer . . . 1B **46**
Heol Tredwen CF10: Card . . . 1B **102**
Heol Treferig CF38: Bed . . . 5A **42**
Heol Trefgarne CF5: Ely . . . 6G **93**
Heol Tre Forys CF64: P'rth . . . 3C **108**
Heol Trelai CF5: Ely . . . 6F **93**
(not continuous)
Heol Trenewydd CF5: Ely . . . 6G **93**
Heol Trostre CF3: St M . . . 2D **88**
Heol Ty Crwn CF83: Caer . . . 4D **28**
Heol Tyddyn CF83: Caer . . . 2H **45**
Heol ty Ffynnon CF23: Pontp . . . 4F **73**
Heol Ty Maen CF37: Up Bo . . . 1B **44**
Heol Ty Merchant CF83: Caer . . . 4D **28**
Heol Ty'n-y-Cae CF14: Rhiw . . . 1D **84**
Heol Ty'n y Coed CF14: Rhiw . . . 5E **71**
Heol Uchaf CF14: Rhiw . . . 4D **70**

Heol Undeb CF38: Bed 5H **41**
Heol Urban CF5: L'dff 5A **84**
Heol Waun Fawr CF83: Caer 2A **46**
Heol Waun Waelod CF83: Caer 3B **46**
Heol Waun y Nant CF14: Whit 4D **84**
Heol Wen CF14: Rhiw 6D **70**
Heol Wernlas CF14: Whit 3E **85**
Heol y Barcud CF14: Thorn 1G **71**
Heol y Beddau CF83: Caer 1B **46**
Heol-y-Beddau CF38: Bed 4A **42**
Heol-y-Beila CF72: L'sant 2F **65**
Heol-y-Berllan CF5: Ely 5G **93**
Heol y Berth CF83: Caer 3A **46**
Heol-y-Bont CF14: Rhiw 6E **71**
Heol y Brenin CF64: P'rth 3C **108**
Heol-y-Bryn CF14: Rhiw 6C **70**
CF15: P'rch 4H **67**
CF37: R'fln 3H **25**
CF62: Barry 5D **116**
CF72: P'clun 6E **65**
Heol-y-Bwnsi CF15: N'grw 6B **26**
CF37: Up Bo 6B **26**
Heol-y-Cadno CF14: Thorn 2F **71**
Heol-y-Carnau CF83: Caer 4D **28**
Heol-y-Carw CF14: Thorn 2G **71**
Heol-y-Castell CF5: Ely 6G **93**
Heol-y-Cawl CF64: Din P 2G **107**
Heol y Clun CF38: Bed 5H **41**
Heol y Coed CF38: Bed 5H **41**
Heol-y-Coed CF14: Rhiw 5C **70**
CF15: N'grw 3E **45**
CF71: Llan M 4C **110**
CF72: P'clun 5D **64**
Heol y Cwm CF15: Morg 6D **68**
Heol-y-Cwm CF83: Caer 2B **46**
Heol-y-Dderwen CF15: N'grw 3F **45**
Heol-y-Ddol CF83: Caer 4D **28**
Heol-y-Delyn CF14: L'vne 3B **72**
Heol-y-Deri CF14: Rhiw 5D **70**
CF37: P'prdd 5A **14**
Heol-y-Dreflan CF83: Caer 4D **28**
Heol y Dryw CF62: Rho 6F **115**
Heol-y-Fedwen CF38: Tont 1G **43**
Heol-y-Felin CF5: Ely 3A **94**
CF14: Rhiw 5D **70**
CF71: Llan M 4C **110**
CF72: P'clun 6C **64**
CF83: Caer 6B **28**
Heol-y-Fforest CF14: Tong 3H **69**
CF15: Tong 3H **69**
Heol-y-Ffynnon CF38: E Isaf 5F **43**
Heol-y-Foel CF38: Llan F 3D **42**
Heol-y-Forlan CF14: Whit 1C **84**
Heol-y-Frenhines CF64: Din P 3G **107**
Heol-y-Fro CF38: Chu V 2E **43**
CF71: Llan M 2C **110**
Heol-y-Gaer CF5: Ely 6G **93**
CF62: Barry 5D **116**
Heol y Gamlas CF15: N'grw 2C **44**
Heol y Gth. CF83: Rud 6B **30**
Heol y Goedwig CF38: Chu V 3E **43**
Heol-y-Gogledd CF83: Caer 3A **28**
Heol-y-Gors CF14: Whit 4E **85**
CF15: N'grw 3F **45**
CF83: Caer 4D **28**
Heol-y-Graig CF72: L'sant 2F **65**
Heol y Gyfraith CF72: T Grn 3E **65**
Heol y Llongau CF63: Barry 3H **117**
Heol-y-Maes CF38: Llan F 4D **42**
Heol-y-Nant CF14: Rhiw 1D **84**
CF15: Gwae G 2D **68**
CF63: Barry 6A **106**
CF83: Caer 6B **28**
Heol Ynys Ddu CF83: Caer 2A **46**
Heol y Onnen CF72: L'harry 5C **78**
Heol-y-Parc CF14: Pontp 1G **73**
CF15: P'rch 6H **67**
CF38: E Isaf 5F **43**
CF83: Caer 6B **28**
Heol-y-Pavin CF5: L'dff 6C **84**
Heol y Pentir CF62: Rho 6E **115**
Heol-y-Pentre CF15: P'rch 4A **68**
Heol-y-Pia CF83: Caer 6A **28**
Heol y Porthladd CF63: Barry 3H **117**
Heol y Pwca NP44: Pnwd 5C **8**
Heol y Pwll CF15: N'grw 3D **44**
Heol-yr-Efail CF14: Rhiw 6E **71**
Heol-yr-Haul CF72: Groes F 6C **66**
Heol y Rhosog CF3: Rum 5B **88**
Heol yr Odyn CF5: Ely 6F **93**
CF15: N'grw 3D **44**
Heol-yr-Onen CF83: Caer 6B **28**
Heol yr Orsaf CF72: P'clun 6C **64**
Heol-yr-Ynys
CF15: Gwae G, Tong 3F **69**
Heol-yr-Ysbyty CF83: Caer 2A **46**
Heol yr Ysgol CF83: Tret 3A **30**
Heol-y-Sarn CF72: L'sant 1F **65**
Heol Ysgawen CF72: L'harry 5C **78**
Heol Ysgubor CF83: Caer 2A **46**
Heol-y-Waun CF14: Whit 4D **84**
Heol-y-Wenallt CF83: Rhiw 1C **70**
Heol y Wern CF14: Rhiw 5E **71**
Heol-y-Wern CF83: Caer 4D **28**
Herbert Av. NP11: Ris, Roger 1G **33**
Herbert Cl. CF3: M'fld 5A **76**
Herbert Dr. CF83: Caer 4B **28**
Herbert March Cl. CF5: L'dff 4H **83**
Herbert Rd. NP19: Newp 3D **36**
NP26: Cald 4C **60**
Herbert St. CF10: Card 6E **5** (5B **96**)
CF14: Card 6G **85**
CF63: Barry 6A **106**
NP20: Newp 6C **36**
Herbert Ter. CF64: P'rth 1E **109**
Herbert Wlk. NP20: Newp 6C **36**
Hereford Ct. NP18: C'ln 4G **21**
Hereford St. CF11: Card 5G **95**
NP19: Newp 4D **36**
Heritage Ct. NP44: Oakf 6B **12**
Heritage Dr. CF5: Ely 1G **99**
CF62: Barry 2F **117**
Heritage Pk. CF3: St M 5D **74**
Hermon Hill CF15: Tong 4G **69**
Herne Pl. CF11: Card 4D **94**
Heron Rd. CF3: Rum 4A **88**
NP26: Cald 6D **60**
Heronston Cl. NP26: Undy 4F **59**
Herons Way CF83: Caer 2A **46**
Heron Way NP10: Duf 4H **53**
Herrick Pl. CF83: Mac 2D **30**
Hertford Pl. NP19: Newp 3F **37**
Heston Cl. NP26: Pskwt 5H **61**
Hewell Ct. CF11: Card 1H **101**
Hewell St. CF11: Card 1H **101**
CF64: P'rth 6H **101**
Hibiscus Ct. CF38: Llan F 6C **42**
Hickman Rd. CF64: P'rth 1E **109**
Hickory Ct. CF24: Card 4H **5** (4D **96**)
Highbank CF23: Pontp 3H **73**
High Banks NP19: Newp 1E **37**
High Beech La. NP16: Bul 4D **62**
NP16: Chep 4D **62**
(not continuous)
Highbridge Cl. CF64: Sul 2A **120**
Highbury Pl. CF5: Ely 5F **93**
Highbury Rd. CF5: Ely 4G **93**
High Cl. NP44: Llanf 4B **12**
High Cnr. CF15: P'rch 4A **68**
Highcroft Rd. NP20: Newp 3A **36**
High Cft. Wlk. CF3: L'rmy 2H **87**
HIGH CROSS 5D **34**
High Cross Cl. NP10: Roger 5D **34**
High Cross Dr. NP10: Roger 4D **34**
High Cross La. NP10: Roger 6E **35**
(not continuous)
Highcross Rd. NP10: Roger 4D **34**
NP20: Roger 4D **34**
Highdale Cl. CF72: L'sant 3G **65**
HIGHER END 4C **112**
Highfield NP26: C'went 1B **60**
Highfield Cl. CF38: Tont 2G **43**
CF62: Barry 4E **117**
CF64: Din P 1A **108**
NP11: Ris 5D **16**
NP18: C'ln 3F **21**
NP44: Llanf 5B **12**
Highfield Ct. NP10: Bass 6C **34**
Highfield Gdns. NP10: Bass 6B **34**
Highfield La. NP10: Bass 6B **34**
Highfield Rd. CF14: Heath 3A **86**
CF23: Cyn 3A **86**
CF62: Barry 6F **105**
NP10: Bass 6C **34**
NP18: C'ln 4F **21**
NP20: Newp 6G **35**
Highfields CF5: L'dff 5B **84**
Highfield Ter. CF37: P'prdd 6B **14**
High Fld. Way NP18: C'ln 3F **21**
Highland Gro. NP44: Pnwd 5E **9**
Highlands CF3: Rum 5G **87**
Highlight La. CF62: Barry 5D **104**
(not continuous)
High Mdw. CF71: Llan M 4B **110**
Highmead Rd. CF5: Ely 4H **93**
High St. CF5: L'dff 1C **94**
CF10: Card 4C **4** (4A **96**)
CF37: P'prdd 1C **24**
CF62: Barry 3F **117**
CF64: P'rth 1E **109**
CF71: C'bri 3C **90**
CF71: Llan M 2B **110**
High St. CF72: L'sant 2F **65**
(not continuous)
CF72: P'clun 1B **78**
CF83: Abert 1E **27**
CF83: Tret 2A **30**
NP4: Grif 6E **7**
NP4: P'pool 3B **6**
NP11: C'keys, P'waun 2A **16**
NP16: Chep 2E **63**
NP18: C'ln 5H **21**
NP20: Newp 4C **36**
High St. Arc. CF10: Card 4C **4** (4A **96**)
High Trees NP11: Ris 5F **17**
High Vw. NP16: Chep 2E **63**
High Vw. Rd. CF64: P'rth 6H **101**
High Vw. Way CF37: Glyn 2D **14**
Highwalls Av. CF64: Din P 1F **107**
Highwalls End CF64: Din P 1G **107**
Highwalls Rd. CF64: Din P 2G **107**
High Way, The NP4: New I, P'pool 4F **7**
Highway, The NP44: C'iog 5H **9**
NP44: Oakf 4H **11**
Hilda St. CF37: T'rest 4E **25**
CF62: Barry 3G **117**
Hiles Rd. CF5: Ely 4G **93**
Hilla Rd. NP20: Newp 5A **36**
Hillary Cl. CF14: L'shn 4H **71**
Hillary Ri. CF63: Barry 1B **118**
NP11: P'waun 1A **16**
Hill Barn Vw. NP26: Pskwt 5H **61**
(not continuous)
Hill Cl. NP4: P'pool 3A **6**
Hillcot Cl. CF14: L'vne 3A **72**
Hillcrest NP4: New I 5H **7**
NP18: C'ln 3F **21**
Hillcrest Cl. CF14: Thorn 2H **71**
Hillcrest Rd. NP4: New I 4F **7**
Hill Dr. CF38: Llan F 4D **42**
Hillfort Cl. CF5: Ely 6H **93**
Hillhead CF71: Llan M 3B **110**
Hillrise CF23: L'dyrn 2D **86**
Hillside CF83: Caer 2D **46**
NP11: Ris 6E **17**
(not continuous)
Hillside Av. CF83: Abert 2C **26**
Hillside Cl. CF63: Barry 1C **118**
Hillside Ct. CF23: Pen L 5C **86**
CF38: Llan F 5C **42**
NP44: Pnwd 6D **8**
Hillside Cres. NP10: Roger 5D **34**
Hillside Dr. CF71: C'bri 4D **90**
NP4: P'pool 5C **6**
Hillside Pk. Est. CF15: Taff W 6E **45**
Hillside Rd. NP4: Grif 6D **6**
Hillside Ter. CF37: P'prdd 5C **14**
CF83: B'ws 3G **29**
Hillside Vw. CF37: P'prdd 5B **14**
Hill-Snook Rd. CF5: Ely 4G **93**
Hills St. CF10: Card 4D **4** (4A **96**)
Hill St. CF63: Barry 1B **118**
CF64: P'rth 6B **102**
NP4: Grif 6E **7**
NP4: P'nydd 1A **6**
NP11: Ris 6E **17**
NP20: Newp 5C **36**
NP44: Oakf 4G **11**
Hill Ter. CF5: Wen 3D **98**
CF64: P'rth 6H **101**
Hill Top NP44: C'brn 3F **11**
Hilltop NP16: Chep 3D **62**
Hilltop Av. CF37: C'fydd 4F **15**
Hilltop Cres. CF37: P'prdd 6E **15**
Hilltop Grn. NP44: Pnwd 6C **8**
Hill Vw. CF5: F'wtr 1G **93**
(not continuous)
CF38: Bed 5A **42**
Hillview NP20: Newp 6H **35**
Hillview Cres. NP19: Newp 6H **37**
Hilton Pl. CF14: Llan N 4B **84**
Hinchsliff Av. CF62: Barry 5F **105**
Hind Cl. CF24: Card 2H **97**
Hinter Path *NP44: F'wtr 4D 10*
(off Jule Rd.)
Hinton St. CF24: Card 4E **97**
Hiraethog Rd. CF37: Up Bo 6B **26**
Hirst Cres. CF5: F'wtr 6H **83**
Hirwain St. CF24: Card 1H **95**
Hitchen Hollow NP16: B'ly 6H **63**
HMP Cardiff CF24: Card 4F **5**
Hobart Cl. NP20: Newp 5G **35**
Hocker Hill St. NP16: Chep 1E **63**
Hodges Cl. NP26: Pskwt 5H **61**
Hodges Row CF10: Card 6B **96**
Hodges Sq. CF10: Card 6B **96**
Hogarth Cl. NP19: Newp 2F **37**
NP44: Oakf 5A **12**

Holbein Rd. NP19: Newp 2G **37**
Holden Rd. CF11: Card 1F **101**
Holdings La. CF5: P'rch 2H **81**
Holgate Cl. CF5: L'dff 3H **83**
Holland Cl. NP10: Roger 2C **34**
Holland Way CF63: Barry 6A **106**
Hollies, The CF3: M'fld 5A **76**
CF72: P'clun 1C **78**
Hollington Dr. CF23: Pontp 4G **73**
Hollins Cl. NP16: Chep 1F **63**
HOLLYBUSH 5E **11**
Hollybush NP44: C'brn 4F **11**
Hollybush Av. NP20: Malp 5A **20**
Hollybush Cl. CF38: Tont 2G **43**
NP20: Malp 5A **20**
NP44: C'brn 4E **11**
Hollybush Est. CF14: Whit 1A **84**
Hollybush Hgts. CF23: L'dyrn 6D **72**
Hollybush Ri. CF23: Cyn 1D **86**
Hollybush Rd. CF23: Cyn 1C **86**
CF23: L'dyrn 1E **87**
Hollybush Ter. CF38: Tont 2G **43**
NP4: P'nydd 1A **6**
Hollybush Vw. NP44: F'wtr 5F **11**
Hollybush Vs. CF38: Chu V, Tont 2F **43**
Hollybush Wlk. NP10: Bass 6C **34**
Hollybush Way NP44: C'brn, F'wtr, Oakf 5D **10**
Holly Cl. NP16: Bul 5E **63**
Holly Ct. *CF62: Barry* *4E 117*
(off St Nicholas Cl.)
Hollycroft Cl. CF5: Ely 3A **94**
Holly Gro. CF14: L'vne 1A **72**
Hollyhock Cl. NP10: Roger 3A **34**
Holly La. CF37: P'prdd 5E **15**
Holly Lodge Cl. NP44: C'iog 5H **9**
Holly Lodge Gdns. NP44: C'iog 5H **9**
Holly Lodge Grn. NP44: C'iog 5H **9**
Holly Lodge Rd. NP44: C'iog 5G **9**
Holly Rd. CF5: F'wtr 1H **93**
CF72: L'harry 5B **78**
NP11: Ris 5E **17**
Hollyrood Cl. CF62: Barry 5E **105**
Holly St. CF37: R'fln 4G **25**
Holly Ter. CF14: Llan N 5C **84**
Holmdale NP44: G'mdw 3D **10**
Holmesdale Ct. CF11: Card 2H **101**
Holmesdale St. CF11: Card 2H **101**
Holmeside CF14: L'vne 2A **72**
Holmes St. CF63: Barry 1B **118**
Holmsdale Pl. CF64: P'rth 2F **109**
Holmsview Cl. CF3: Rum 3A **88**
Holmview Ct. CF3: Rum 2A **88**
Holm View Leisure Cen. 5H **105**
Holmwood Cl. CF23: Cyn 3C **86**
Holst Cl. NP19: Newp 3E **39**
Holton Rd. CF63: Barry 3H **117**
Holyhead Ct. CF83: Caer 5G **27**
Holyoake Ter. NP4: P'nydd 1A **6**
Holywell Rd. CF38: Tont 1G **43**
Home Farm Cl. NP18: C'ln 5F **21**
Home Farm Cres. NP18: C'ln 5F **21**
Home Farm Grn. NP18: C'ln 5F **21**
Homelands Rd. CF14: Heath 1E **85**
Homeside Ho. CF64: P'rth 1F **109**
Honddu Cl. NP26: Cald 4C **60**
Honeysuckle Cl. CF5: F'wtr 1G **93**
NP10: Roger 6D **34**
Honiton Rd. CF3: L'rmy 6A **74**
Hood Rd. CF62: Barry 4G **117**
NP19: Newp 2D **38**
Hope Ct. CF10: Card 1G **95**
Hopefield NP20: Newp 2B **36**
Hope Ter. CF24: Card 3D **96**
Hopewell Cl. NP16: Bul 6G **63**
Hop Gdn., The NP16: Bul 6F **63**
HOPKINSTOWN 6A **14**
Hopkinstown Rd. CF37: P'prdd 5A **14**
Hopkins Wlk. NP19: Newp 4D **38**
Hopyard Mdw. CF71: C'bri 3B **90**
Horace Ter. CF83: L'brad 1B **28**
Horle Cl. CF11: Card 1A **102**
Hornbeam Cl. CF3: St M 6E **75**
NP18: C'ln 5E **21**
Hornbeam Wlk. NP10: Bass 6B **34**
Hornchurch Cl. CF5: L'dff 6A **84**
Horrocks Cl. NP20: Malp 3A **20**
Horton Way CF64: Sul 1E **119**
Horwood Cl. CF24: Card 2E **97**
Hoskin Ind. Est. CF10: Card 1B **102**
Hoskins St. NP20: Newp 2C **36**
Hospital Rd. CF37: P'prdd 6E **15**
NP4: P'nydd 1A **6**
Hotham Cl. CF23: Pontp 4G **73**
Houlston Ct. CF24: Card 2F **97**
Housman Cl. CF3: L'rmy 5A **74**
Hove Av. NP19: Newp 2G **37**
Howard Cl. NP19: Newp 3C **38**
Howard Ct. CF10: Card 6G **5**
CF62: Barry 3E **117**
Howard Dr. CF83: Caer 4C **28**
Howard Gdns. CF24: Card 3G **5** (3C **96**)
Howardian Cl. CF23: Pen L 6E **87**
Howardian Nature Reserve 4F **87**
Howard Pl. CF24: Card 2G **5** (3C **96**)
Howard St. CF24: Card 4D **96**
Howard Ter. CF24: Card 3G **5** (3C **96**)
Howe Circ. NP19: Newp 2C **38**
Howell Rd. CF5: Ely 4G **93**
Howell's Cres. CF5: L'dff 1D **94**
Howells Row *NP16: Chep* *1F 63*
(off Bridge St.)
Howell St. CF37: C'fydd 2F **15**
Hoyley Stadium 2C **56**
Hubert Ri. NP10: Roger 5D **34**
Hubert Rd. NP19: Newp 2E **37**
Hughes Cres. NP16: Chep 3E **63**
Hughs Cl. CF5: L'dff 4A **84**
Hugon Cl. CF23: Pen L 6E **87**
Humber Cl. NP20: Bet 6G **19**
Humber Rd. NP20: Bet 6F **19**
Hunt Cl. CF14: L'shn 4H **71**
Hunter Cl. NP10: Roger 3C **34**
Hunters Ridge CF23: Cyn 3B **86**
NP26: Undy 4E **59**
Hunter St. CF10: Card 2B **102**
CF63: Barry 1B **118**
Huntfield Rd. NP16: Chep 1D **62**
Huntingdon Cl. NP44: G'mdw 2C **10**
Huntington Dr. CF23: Pontp 4F **73**
Hunt Pl. CF63: Barry 1B **118**
Huntsmead Cl. CF14: Thorn 2G **71**
Hurford Cres. CF37: P'prdd 6B **14**
Hurford Pl. CF23: Cyn 5C **72**
Hurford St. CF37: P'prdd 1A **24**
Hurman St. CF10: Card 1B **102**
Huron Cres. CF23: Cyn 3B **86**
Huxley Grn. NP20: Malp 5A **20**
Hydrangea Cl. CF23: L'dyrn 6D **72**
NP10: Roger 6D **34**
Hyssop Cl. CF23: Pontp 4D **72**
Hywel Cres. CF63: Barry 6A **106**

I

Idencroft Cl. CF23: Pontp 4G **73**
Iestynian Av. CF11: Card 2F **95**
Iestyn St. CF11: Card 2F **95**
Ifor Hael Rd. NP10: Roger 3B **34**
Ifor Jones Ct. CF23: L'dyrn 2D **86**
Ifton Av. NP26: Rog 6A **60**
Ifton Ind. Pk. NP26: Rog 5A **60**
Ifton La. NP26: Rog 5A **60**
Ifton Pl. NP19: Newp 6G **37**
Ifton Quarry Ind. Est. NP26: Rog 5A **60**
Ifton Rd. NP26: Rog 5A **60**
Ifton St. NP19: Newp 6G **37**
Ifton Ter. NP26: Rog 6A **60**
Ilan Av. CF37: R'fln 3F **25**
Ilan Rd. CF83: Abert 2D **26**
Ilchester Rd. CF3: L'rmy 1A **88**
Ilex Cl. CF14: L'shn 5H **71**
Ilfracombe Cres. CF3: L'rmy 2A **88**
Illtyd Av. CF71: Llan M 3B **110**
Illtyd Rd. CF5: Ely 3F **93**
Illtyd St. CF37: P'prdd 2B **24**
Ilminster Cl. CF63: Barry 1B **118**
Ilminster St. CF63: Barry 1B **118**
Ilton Rd. CF23: Pen L 6D **86**
Imperial Bldgs. Row *CF5: L'dff* *1C 94*
(off Heol Fair)
Imperial Ho. NP10: Coedk 5F **53**
Imperial Pk. Ind. Est. NP10: Coedk 5F **53**
Imperial Way NP10: Coedk, Duf 5F **53**
Inchmarnock St. CF24: Card 4D **96**
Indoor Bowls Cen. 1D **36**
Inglefield Av. CF14: Card 5H **85**
Ingles *NP44: F'wtr* *4D 10*
(off Henllys Way)
Inner Loop Rd. NP16: B'ly 4H **63**
Insole Cl. CF5: L'dff 1B **94**
Insole Gdns. CF5: L'dff 1C **94**
Insole Gro. E. CF5: L'dff 1B **94**
Insole Gro. W. CF5: L'dff 1B **94**
Insole Pl. CF5: L'dff 2C **94**
Insole Ter. CF72: L'sant 2F **65**
Instow Pl. CF3: L'rmy 1B **88**
Inverness Pl. CF24: Card 6B **86**
Iolo Pl. CF63: Barry 6B **106**
Ipswich Rd. CF23: Pen L 6E **87**
Ireland Cl. CF3: St M 2E **89**
Ireton Cl. CF23: Pontp 4G **73**
Iris Rd. NP10: Roger 3H **33**
Iron Bri. Rd. CF15: Tong 5G **69**
Iron St. CF24: Card 3D **96**
Irving Pl. CF62: Barry 2G **117**
Isaf Rd. NP11: Ris 6F **17**
Isca Cl. NP44: C'brn 1H **11**
Isca Ct. NP18: C'ln 4H **21**
Isca M. NP18: C'ln 5A **22**
Isca Rd. NP18: C'ln 6A **22**
Isca (Roman Fortress) 6H **21**
Island Rd. CF62: Barry 3F **117**
Island Vw. Cvn. Pk. CF64: Sul 3A **120**
Islwyn Ct. NP11: Ris 6F **17**
Islwyn Dr. CF83: Caer 5C **28**
Islwyn Way CF63: Barry 5A **106**
Islwyn Workshops NP11: Ris 1E **33**
Is-y-Coed CF5: Wen 5D **98**
Itchen Cl. NP20: Bet 4F **19**
Itchen Rd. NP20: Bet 4F **19**
Itton Rd. NP16: Chep 1C **62**
Ivor John Wlk. NP18: C'ln 3G **21**
Ivor Pk. CF72: P'clun 1C **78**
Ivor St. CF24: Card 4G **5** (4C **96**)
CF62: Barry 5H **117**
NP20: Newp 5C **36**
Ivydale CF14: L'vne 2A **72**
Ivy Rd. NP20: Newp 5A **36**
Ivy St. CF5: Card 3D **94**
CF64: P'rth 1E **109**
Ivy Ter. CF37: P'prdd 5A **14**

J

Jackson Cl. CF62: Rho 5E **115**
Jackson Ct. NP19: Newp 3E **37**
Jackson Pl. NP19: Newp 3E **37**
Jackson Rd. CF5: Ely 4F **93**
Jack's Pill Ind. Est. NP20: Newp 6D **36**
Jacrow Sq. CF5: Ely 5G **93**
Jade Cl. CF14: L'vne 1A **72**
Jamaica Circ. NP10: Duf 4F **53**
Jamaica Cl. NP10: Coedk 4F **53**
Jamaica Gdns. NP10: Duf 4G **53**
Jamaica Gro. NP10: Duf 4G **53**
Jamaica Wlk. *NP10: Duf* *4G 53*
James Ct. CF3: St M 1D **88**
CF23: Cyn 2B **86**
James Pl. CF37: T'rest 2E **25**
James St. CF10: Card 1B **102**
CF37: T'rest 2E **25**
CF63: Barry 1D **118**
CF83: Tret 2A **30**
NP4: P'pool 2C **6**
NP10: Roger 5C **34**
NP20: Newp 1D **54**
Jane Austen Cl. NP20: Newp 2G **53**
Jane Cl. NP10: Duf 6H **53**
Janet St. CF24: Card 3D **96**
CF37: R'fln 4F **25**
Japonica Cl. NP20: Malp 4B **20**
Jasmine Cl. NP10: Roger 2H **33**
Jasmine Dr. CF3: St M 6E **75**
Jasper Cl. CF5: L'dff 5A **84**
Jaycroft Cl. CF23: Pontp 4G **73**
Jeans Cl. NP20: Malp 4A **20**
Jeddo Cl. NP20: Newp 1C **54**
Jeddo St. NP20: Newp 1C **54**
Jeffrey St. NP19: Newp 4E **37**
Jellicoe Cl. NP19: Newp 2D **38**
Jellicoe Ct. CF10: Card 6G **5** (5C **96**)
Jellicoe Gdns. CF23: Cyn 2A **86**
Jenkins St. CF37: P'prdd 6A **14**
NP19: Newp 6F **37**
Jenkin St. CF63: Barry 6B **106**
Jenkinsville *CF64: P'rth* *1F 109*
(off Clive Pl.)
Jenkins Way CF3: St M 2D **88**
Jenner Pk. 1A **118**
Jenner Rd. CF62: Barry 3F **117**
Jenner St. CF63: Barry 1C **118**
Jenner Wlk. CF38: Chu V 2E **43**
Jerries La. CF83: B'ws 2F **29**
Jerusalem Cl. NP4: New I 6H **7**
Jerusalem La. NP4: Glas, New I 6H **7**
Jervis Wlk. NP19: Newp 3C **38**
Jesmond Dene CF15: Taff W 1F **69**
Jessop Cl. NP10: Roger 3D **34**
Jessop Rd. NP10: Roger 3D **34**
Jestyn Cl. CF5: Ely 5C **92**
CF64: Din P 1H **107**
Jevan Cl. CF5: L'dff 4H **83**
Jewell La. NP20: Newp 1B **36**
Jewel St. CF63: Barry 2A **118**
Jim Driscoll Way CF11: Card 2A **102**
Jindabyne Cl. CF3: St M 3D **74**

John Baker Cl. NP44: Oakf .5H **11**
John Batchelor Way CF64: P'rth .5A **102**
John Bull Cl. NP19: Newp .3C **38**
John Fld. Wlk. *NP19: Newp .5B 38*
(off Ringland Circ.)
John Frost Sq. NP20: Newp .5C **36**
John Ireland Cl. NP19: Newp .4B **38**
John Morgan Cl. CF5: L'dff .4A **84**
John Pl. CF37: T'rest .3E **25**
Johnsey Trad. Est. NP19: Newp .6E **37**
Johns La. CF14: Llan N .5C **84**
Johnston Cl. NP10: Roger .3C **34**
Johnston Rd. CF14: L'shn .4F **71**
John St. CF10: Card .6E **5** (5B **96**)
CF37: T'rest .3E **25**
CF63: Barry .1D **118**
CF64: P'rth .6B **102**
NP4: P'pool .3C **6**
NP20: Newp .6D **36**
Jolyons Ct. NP26: Cald .5D **60**
Jones Ct. CF10: Card .4C **4** (4A **96**)
Jones Pl. CF37: P'prdd .5E **15**
Jones Point Ho. CF11: Card .4A **102**
Jones St. CF37: C'fydd .1F **15**
NP20: Newp .5B **36**
Jonquil Cl. CF3: St M .6E **75**
Joseph Parry Cl. CF64: L'dgh .5G **101**
Jovian Villa *NP18: C'ln .4F 21*
(off Roman Way)
Joyce Cl. NP20: Newp .1G **53**
Jubilee Gdns. CF14: Heath .1G **85**
CF63: Barry .6D **106**
Jubilee La. CF64: P'rth .1F **109**
Jubilee St. CF11: Card .6A **4** (5G **95**)
Jubilee Ter. NP4: P'pool .1A **6**
Jubilee Trad. Est. CF24: Card .4D **96**
Jubilee Way NP26: Cald .5C **60**
Judkin Ct. CF10: Card .1B **102**
Jule Rd. NP44: F'wtr .4D **10**
Julius Cl. NP18: C'ln .4F **21**
Junction Cottage Mus. .4E **7**
Junction Ind. Est. CF72: P'clun .6C **64**
Junction Rd. NP19: Newp .3D **36**
Junction Ter. CF15: Rad .2G **83**
Juniper Cres. NP44: H'lys .5C **10**
Juno Villa *NP18: C'ln .4G 21*
(off Flavius Cl.)
Justin Cl. CF23: Cyn .3C **86**

K

Kames Pl. CF24: Card .4H **5** (4C **96**)
Kane Cl. CF14: L'shn .6H **71**
Kathleen St. CF62: Barry .3E **117**
Kear Ct. *NP20: Newp .5C 36*
(off Commercial St.)
Kear St. NP20: Newp .5C **36**
Keats Cl. NP20: Newp .1G **53**
NP44: C'brn .3F **11**
Keats Rd. NP26: Cald .5B **60**
Keats Way CF62: Barry .5G **105**
Keble Ct. CF83: Mac .2D **30**
Keene Av. NP10: Roger .6E **35**
Keene St. NP19: Newp .5F **37**
Keen Rd. CF24: Card .5H **5** (4D **96**)
(not continuous)
Kelly Rd. NP19: Newp .2G **37**
Kelston Cl. CF14: Whit .2B **84**
Kelston Pl. CF14: Whit .2B **84**
Kelston Rd. CF14: Whit .2B **84**
Kelvedon St. NP19: Newp .5E **37**
Kelvin Cl. NP20: Malp .5H **19**
Kelvin Rd. CF23: Card .6B **86**
Kember Cl. CF3: St M .1E **89**
Kemeys Fawr Cl. NP4: Grif .2D **8**
Kemeys Rd. CF62: Rho .5E **115**
Kemys Pl. CF14: Llan N .4E **85**
Kemys St. NP4: Grif .1E **9**
Kemys Wlk. NP44: C'brn .4F **11**
Kendall Sq. NP16: Chep .1F **63**
Kendrick Rd. CF62: Barry .2H **117**
Kenfig Pl. NP44: Llan .2A **12**
Kenfig Rd. CF14: Whit .4F **85**
Kenilworth Ho. CF10: Card .4B **4**
Kenilworth Pl. NP44: C'brn .3E **11**
Kenilworth Rd. CF63: Barry .6B **106**
NP19: Newp .4G **37**
Kenley Cl. CF5: F'wtr .6A **84**
Kenmare M. CF23: Pontp .3F **73**
Kenmuir Rd. CF24: Card .2F **97**
Kennedy Cl. CF38: Bed .4A **42**
Kennedy Ri. CF62: Barry .2E **117**
Kennerleigh Rd. CF3: Rum .3G **87**
Kenneth Treasure Ct. CF3: St M .6B **74**
Kennilworth Ct. CF5: F'wtr .2B **94**
Kennington Cl. CF14: Thorn .3G **71**
Kensington Av. CF5: Card .3C **94**
Kensington Gdns. NP19: Newp .3F **37**
Kensington Gro. NP19: Newp .4F **37**
Kensington Pk. NP26: Magor .4B **58**
Kensington Pl. NP19: Newp .4F **37**
Kenson Cl. CF62: Rho .6C **114**
Kenson Hill CF62: Rho .1C **114**
Kent Cl. NP10: Roger .2C **34**
Kent Ct. *NP18: C'ln .4G 21*
(off Roman Way)
Kent Grn. CF62: Barry .1G **117**
Kent St. CF11: Card .1H **101**
Kenwood Rd. CF5: Ely .4F **93**
Kenwyn Ter. CF37: P'prdd .4D **14**
Kenyon Rd. CF24: Card .2G **97**
Keppoch St. CF24: Card .1B **96**
Kerrigan Cl. CF5: F'wtr .6H **83**
Kerrycroy St. CF24: Card .4D **96**
Kestell Dr. CF11: Card .3A **102**
Kestrel Cl. CF23: L'dyrn .6D **72**
NP26: Cald .6C **60**
Kestrel Way CF64: P'rth .5E **109**
NP10: Duf .4G **53**
Keswick Av. CF23: Cyn .4A **86**
Keteringham Cl. CF64: Sul .2G **119**
Kewstoke Av. CF3: L'rmy .2H **87**
Kewstoke Cl. CF3: L'rmy .2H **87**
Kewstoke Pl. CF3: L'rmy .2H **87**
Keyes Av. CF23: Cyn .2A **86**
Keyes Ct. CF10: Card .6G **5**
Keynsham Av. NP20: Newp .6C **36**
Keynsham Rd. CF14: Heath .3E **85**
Keyston Rd. CF5: F'wtr .5H **83**
Kidwelly Cl. NP10: St Bri .6G **53**
NP44: Llan .3A **12**
(not continuous)
Kidwelly Ct. CF83: Caer .5H **27**
Kidwelly Rd. NP44: Llan .3A **12**
Kidz Playground .6A **26**
Kier Hardie Cres. NP19: Newp .3B **38**
Kier Hardie Dr. NP19: Newp .2B **38**
Kilcattan St. CF24: Card .4D **96**
Kilcredaun Ho. CF11: Card .3A **102**
Kilgetty Cl. CF5: Ely .5G **93**
Kilgetty Ct. CF5: F'wtr .1F **93**
Kiln Way NP26: Undy .4E **59**
Kimberley Rd. CF23: Pen L .6C **86**
Kimberley Ter. CF14: L'shn .5H **71**
NP20: Newp .1A **36**
Kincraig St. CF24: Card .1B **96**
King Alfreds Rd. NP16: Sed .3G **63**
Kingarth St. CF24: Card .4H **5** (4D **96**)
King Edward VII Av. CF10: Card .1B **4** (2H **95**)
King Edward Av. CF83: Caer .1D **46**
Kingfisher Cl. CF3: St M .6D **74**
NP26: Cald .6D **60**
Kingfisher Pl. NP10: Duf .3G **53**
Kingfisher Sq. CF62: St A .3F **111**
King George V Dr. E. CF14: Heath .4H **85**
(not continuous)
King George V Dr. Nth.
CF14: Heath .2G **85**
King George V Dr. W. CF14: Heath .4G **85**
King La. NP20: Newp .6C **36**
Kings Acre CF38: Llan F .5C **42**
Kingsacre NP20: Newp .4H **35**
Kings Av. CF15: Rad .2G **83**
Kings Cl. CF83: Abert .2E **27**
Kings Ct. CF64: Din P .3H **107**
Kingsdale Ct. NP20: Newp .6A **36**
Kingshill Ct. NP20: Newp .5B **36**
Kingsland Cres. CF63: Barry .2A **118**
Kingsland Rd. CF5: Card .3D **94**
CF14: Whit .3B **84**
Kingsland Ter. CF37: T'rest .2E **25**
Kingsland Wlk. NP44: G'mdw .2D **10**
Kingslea *NP44: F'wtr .4D 10*
(off Jule Rd.)
Kingsley Cl. CF64: Sul .2H **119**
Kingsmark La. NP16: Chep .1C **62**
Kings M. CF11: Card .3G **95**
Kingsmill La. NP20: Newp .5B **36**
Kingsmill Ter. NP20: Newp .5B **36**
Kings Pde. NP20: Newp .6D **36**
(not continuous)
Kings Ride CF64: Din P .2F **107**
Kings Rd. CF11: Card .2F **95**
CF15: Rad .2G **83**
Kings Sq. CF63: Barry .2A **118**
Kingston Rd. CF11: Card .4F **95**
NP19: Newp .4E **37**
King St. CF15: Taff W .2E **69**
CF37: T'rest .3E **25**
CF64: P'rth .6A **102**
CF83: Abert .2E **27**
King St. NP4: P'pool .2B **6**
NP20: Newp .5C **36**
Kingsvale *NP20: Newp .5C 36*
(off King St.)
Kingsway CF10: Card .3C **4** (3A **96**)
NP20: Newp .4C **36**
Kingsway Cen. NP20: Newp .5C **36**
King Wood Cl. CF23: Pen L .4E **87**
Kinnock Ct. NP44: C'iog .5G **9**
Kinsale Cl. CF23: Pontp .3G **73**
Kipling Cl. CF3: L'rmy .6H **73**
CF64: P'rth .6H **101**
Kipling Hill NP20: Newp .1G **53**
Kipling Rd. NP26: Cald .5B **60**
Kirby Daniel Ct. NP20: Newp .6C **36**
Kirby La. NP20: Newp .6C **36**
Kirkby Ct. CF10: Card .5C **96**
Kirkhouse St. CF37: P'prdd .1B **24**
Kirkwall Ct. CF24: Card .2F **97**
Kirrlach Cl. NP26: Cald .5B **60**
Kirton Cl. CF5: L'dff .6A **84**
Kitchener Rd. CF11: Card .4F **95**
Kitty Hawk Dr. NP19: Newp .6G **37**
KNAP, THE .6E **117**
Knap Car Ter. CF62: Barry .5D **116**
Knight Cl. *NP20: Newp .6C 36*
(off Francis Dr.)
Knighton Ct. NP18: C'ln .5H **21**
Knights Wlk. CF83: Caer .1H **45**
Knightswell Cl. CF5: Ely .1E **99**
Knightswell Rd. CF5: Ely .6E **93**
Knole Cl. CF23: Pontp .4G **73**
KNOLLBURY .3D **58**
Knowbury Av. CF64: P'rth .5F **109**
Knox Rd. CF24: Card .3F **5** (3B **96**)
Kyle Av. CF14: Heath .2D **84**
Kyle Cres. CF14: Heath .2E **85**
Kymin Rd. CF64: P'rth .1F **109**
Kymin Ter. CF64: P'rth .1F **109**
Kyveilog St. CF11: Card .2F **95**

L

Laburnum Bush La. NP19: Newp .6A **38**
Laburnum Cl. CF62: Barry .6H **105**
NP10: Roger .2A **34**
NP26: Undy .3E **59**
Laburnum Ct. *CF37: R'fln .4H 25*
(off Poplar Rd.)
Laburnum Dr. NP4: New I .4H **7**
NP19: Newp .5H **37**
NP44: H'lys .5C **10**
Laburnum Gro. NP26: Pskwt .5H **61**
Laburnum Pl. CF5: F'wtr .1H **93**
Laburnum Ter. CF37: R'fln .4H **25**
NP26: Pskwt .5H **61**
Laburnum Way CF64: Din P .3H **107**
CF64: P'rth .2C **108**
NP16: Bul .4E **63**
Ladybench NP44: F'wtr .4D **10**
Ladyhill Grn. NP19: Newp .5A **38**
Ladyhill Rd. NP19: Newp .5A **38**
Lady Isle Ho. CF11: Card .3A **102**
Lady Margaret Ct. CF23: Pen L .6D **86**
NP16: Bul .6F **63**
Lady Margaret Ter. CF24: Card .4D **96**
Lady Mary Rd. CF23: Pen L .5B **86**
Ladysmith Rd. CF23: Pen L .6D **86**
Ladywell NP44: Pnwd .6E **9**
Lake Hill Dr. CF71: C'bri .4D **90**
Lakelands Ct. *CF23: Cyn .1A 86*
(off Rhyd-y-Penau Rd.)
Lake Rd. NP19: Newp .2A **56**
Lake Rd. E. CF23: Cyn .2B **86**
Lake Rd. Nth. CF23: Cyn .2A **86**
Lake Rd. W. CF23: Cyn .2A **86**
Lakeside CF62: Barry .5E **117**
Lakeside Cl. NP44: Oakf .1A **20**
Lakeside Dr. CF23: Cyn .2B **86**
NP10: Coedk .5D **52**
Lakeview NP44: Oakf .1A **20**
Lakeview Cl. CF23: Cyn .3B **86**
Lakin Dr. CF62: Barry .5E **105**
Laleston Cl. CF5: Ely .5G **93**
CF63: Barry .5A **106**
Lamb Cl. NP20: Newp .2G **53**
Lambert Cl. NP20: Newp .2B **36**
Lamberton St. CF24: Card .4D **96**
Lambert St. NP20: Newp .2B **36**
Lamb La. NP18: P'hir .6E **13**
Lambourne Cres. CF14: L'shn .6G **71**
NP20: Bet .6F **19**
Lambourne Wlk. NP20: Bet .6F **19**
Lambourne Way NP20: Bet .5F **19**
Lamby Ind. Pk. CF3: Rum .6B **88**

Lamby Way CF3: Rum 1G 97
CF23: Card 1G 97
Lamby Way Workshops CF3: Rum 5A 88
Lancaster Dr. CF38: Llan F 4D 42
Lancaster Rd. NP4: New I 1G 9
Lancaster Way NP16: Chep 2D 62
Lancers Way NP10: Duf 4H 53
Lan Cl. CF37: P'prdd 5B 14
Landau Cl. NP26: Undy 4E 59
Landings, The CF64: P'rth 6H 101
Landmark Pl. CF10: Card 4E 5
Landraw Ct. CF37: P'prdd 6A 14
Landraw Rd. CF37: P'prdd 6A 14
Landseer Cl. NP19: Newp 2G 37
Landwade Cl. CF5: F'wtr 2G 93
Lane, The CF5: St N 1B 98
Lanelay Cl. CF72: T Grn 3C 64
Lanelay Ct. CF72: T Grn 3C 64
Lanelay Cres. CF37: P'prdd 6B 14
Lanelay Ind. Est. CF72: P'clun 4C 64
Lanelay Pk. CF72: T Grn 3C 64
Lanelay Rd. CF72: T Grn 3C 64
Lanelay Ter. CF37: P'prdd 6B 14
Lanes, The CF71: Llan M 3B 110
Langdale Cl. CF23: Pen L 5C 86
Langditch La. NP19: Newp 6B 38
Langham Way CF11: Card 6G 95
Langland Rd. CF3: Rum 4A 88
Langlands Rd. CF63: Barry 5C 106
Langland Way NP19: Newp 2G 55
Langley Cl. NP26: Magor 3C 58
Langport Av. CF3: L'rmy 1B 88
LANGSTONE
Cat's Ash 6H 23
Ringland 1G 39
Langstone Bus. Village NP18: L'stne 1E 39
Langstone Cotts. NP18: L'stne 1E 39
Langstone Ct. NP44: C'brn 4E 11
Langstone Ct. Rd. NP18: L'stne 3F 39
Langstone La. NP18: L'stne, L'wrn 4F 39
LANGSTONE PARK 1F 39
Lanhydrock Cl. CF3: St M 1D 88
Lanpark Rd. CF37: P'prdd 5C 14
Lansbury Cl. CF83: Caer 4B 28
LANSBURY PARK 5F 29
Lansdale Dr. CF38: Tont 2G 43
Lansdowne NP4: Grif 2E 9
Lansdowne Av. CF14: Rhiw 1E 85
Lansdowne Av. E. CF11: Card 4D 94
Lansdowne Av. W. CF11: Card 4D 94
Lansdowne Gdns. NP44: Oakf 2A 20
Lansdowne Rd. CF5: Card 3D 94
NP18: C'ln 5H 21
NP20: Newp 1H 53
Lantrisant Ind. Est. CF72: L'sant 5D 40
Lanwern Rd. CF37: P'prdd 1B 24
Lanwood Rd. CF37: P'prdd 5B 14
Lapwing Av. NP26: Cald 6D 60
Lapwing Cl. CF64: P'rth 6E 109
Larch Cl. NP4: New I 5G 7
Larch Ct. CF15: Tong 4H 69
NP20: Malp 4A 20
Larch Dr. CF72: C Inn 3H 65
Larch Gro. CF14: L'vne 2B 72
CF83: Caer 4E 29
NP18: Under 3H 39
NP20: Malp 4A 20
Larch Ho. CF14: Whit 1A 84
Larchwood CF5: Wen 5D 98
Larkfield Av. NP16: Bul 3E 63
Larkfield Cl. NP18: C'ln 3F 21
Larkfield Pk. NP16: Chep 3D 62
Larkhill Cl. NP16: Bul 3E 63
Larkwood Av. CF64: P'rth 3E 109
Lascelles Dr. CF23: Pontp 4H 73
Latch Sq. *NP20: Newp 6C 36*
(off Alma St.)
Latteys Cl. CF14: Heath 2F 85
Laugharne Av. CF3: Rum 4A 88
Laugharne Ct. CF62: Barry 6H 105
Laugharne Rd. CF3: Rum 4A 88
Launcelot Cres. CF14: Thorn 3F 71
Laundry Rd. CF37: P'prdd 6B 14
Laural Wlk. NP44: Up Cwm 5C 8
Laura St. CF37: T'rest 1D 24
CF63: Barry 6D 106
Laureate Cl. CF3: L'rmy 6H 73
Laurel Av. CF37: R'fln 5H 25
Laurel Cl. NP26: Undy 3E 59
Laurel Ct. CF5: F'wtr 1H 93
CF62: Barry 4E 117
(off St Nicholas Cl.)
CF83: B'ws 3G 29
Laurel Cres. NP20: Malp 5B 20
NP26: Undy 4F 59
(not continuous)
Laureldene CF72: L'harry 5A 78
Laurel Dr. NP10: Bass 6D 34
Laurel Grn. NP44: Up Cwm 5B 8
Laurel Rd. NP10: Bass 6B 34
Laurels, The CF14: L'vne 2A 72
Laurels Bus. Pk., The CF3: Rum 5B 88
Lauriston Cl. CF5: Ely 1G 99
Lauriston Pk. CF5: Ely 1G 99
Lavender Gro. CF5: F'wtr 1G 93
Lavender Way NP10: Roger 2H 33
LAVERNOCK 1D 120
Lavernock Rd. CF64: P'rth 3D 108
CF64: Sul 2B 120
Lavery Cl. NP19: Newp 2G 37
Lawns, The NP26: Magor 4C 58
Lawn Ter. CF37: T'rest 2E 25
LAWRENCE HILL 3H 37
Lawrence Hill NP19: Newp 4H 37
(not continuous)
Lawrence Hill Av. NP19: Newp 4H 37
Lawrence St. CF83: Caer 6D 28
Lawrenny Av. CF11: Card 5D 94
Laybourne Cl. NP44: Pnwd 1G 11
Laytonia Av. CF14: Card 5G 85
Leach Rd. NP20: Bet 4E 19
Lea Cl. NP20: Bet 5F 19
NP26: Undy 3D 58
Leacroft Pl. CF23: Pontp 4E 73
Leadon Ct. NP44: G'mdw 1C 10
Lead St. CF24: Card 3D 96
Leamington Rd. CF14: Rhiw 1D 84
Leas, The NP44: Pnwd 6C 8
LECKWITH 2D 100
Leckwith Av. CF11: Card 4E 95
Leckwith Cl. CF11: Card 5F 95
Leckwith Ct. CF5: Ely 5G 93
Leckwith Ind. Est. CF11: Card 1F 101
Leckwith Pl. CF11: Card 4F 95
Leckwith Rd. CF11: Card 4F 95
CF11: L'dgh, Mic P 2D 100
CF64: L'dgh 4E 101
CF64: Mic P 2D 100
Leckwith Rd. Interchange CF11: Card 6D 94
Leckwith Stadium 5F 95
LECWYDD 2D 100
Ledbrooke Cl. NP44: C'brn 4E 11
Ledbury Dr. NP20: Newp 3C 36
LEECHPOOL 3H 61
Leechpool NP26: Pskwt 2H 61
Lee Cl. CF23: L'dyrn 3D 86
CF64: Din P 1H 107
Lee Ct. CF14: Rhiw 4E 71
Lee Rd. CF63: Barry 1A 118
Lee St. CF37: P'prdd 6B 14
Lee Way NP19: Newp 1A 56
Leeway Ct. NP19: Newp 2A 56
Lee Way Ind. Est. NP19: Newp 3A 56
Leicester Dr. NP44: G'mdw 2C 10
Leicester Rd. NP19: Newp 3E 37
Leigh Cl. CF71: Bov 3D 110
Leigh Rd. NP4: C'avn, P'nydd 1B 6
Leighton Ct. NP44: G'mdw 3E 11
Lennard St. NP19: Newp 5E 37
Lennox Grn. CF63: Barry 1D 118
Leoline Cl. CF71: C'bri 3B 90
Leon Av. CF15: Taff W 2E 69
Le Pouliguen Way CF71: Llan M 3C 110
Leslie Grn Ct. NP10: Duf 3H 53
Leslie Ter. NP10: Roger 5D 34
Letterston Rd. CF3: Rum 3A 88
Letton Rd. CF10: Card 6B 96
Lettons Way CF64: Din P 1G 107
Letty St. CF24: Card 1A 96
Leven Cl. CF23: Cyn 2B 86
Lewis Cl. NP20: Newp 6C 36
Lewis Dr. CF83: Caer 4B 28
Lewis Rd. CF24: Card 4D 96
CF64: L'dgh 4E 101
Lewis St. CF11: Card 4G 95
CF37: P'prdd 1C 24
CF37: T'rest 2E 25
CF38: Chu V 3E 43
CF62: Barry 3E 117
CF72: P'clun 5D 64
CF83: Mac 2G 31
Lewis Ter. CF37: P'prdd 5C 14
CF83: L'brad 1B 28
(off De Winton Ter.)
NP4: P'nydd 1A 6
Lewis Vw. NP10: Roger 4D 34
Lewis Way NP16: Bul 6F 63
Lewis Wood NP4: P'nydd 1A 6
Leydene Cl. NP11: Ris 4D 16
Leyshon Cl. CF15: Taff W 6D 44
Leyshon St. CF37: P'prdd 2B 24
Libeneth Rd. NP19: Newp 5G 37
Library Cl. CF37: R'fln 4G 25
Library Rd. CF37: P'prdd 6C 14
Library St. CF5: Card 3F 95
Liddell Cl. CF23: Pontp 4H 73
Liddicoat Ct. CF63: Barry 1C 118
Lidmore Rd. CF62: Barry 2E 117
Lighthouse Pk. NP10: St Bri 5H 77
Lighthouse Rd. NP10: Duf, St Bri 3H 53 & 1A 77
Lilac Cl. CF5: F'wtr 6G 83
Lilac Dr. CF38: Llan F 5C 42
Lilac Gro. NP10: Roger 2H 33
Lilburne Cl. CF23: Pontp 4G 73
Lilburne Dr. NP19: Newp 5F 37
Lili Mai CF63: Barry 4B 106
Lilleshall St. NP19: Newp 6E 37
Lily St. CF24: Card 2C 96
Lily Way NP10: Roger 3A 34
Limebourne Ct. CF14: Whit 4C 84
Lime Cl. CF15: Rad 3G 83
NP20: Newp 1C 54
Lime Cres. NP19: Newp 5H 37
Lime Gro. CF5: F'wtr 6F 83
CF62: St A 2B 112
Limes, The CF71: C'bri 3D 90
NP26: Undy 4D 58
Limes Ct. CF71: C'bri 4D 90
Limeslade Cl. CF5: F'wtr 2B 94
Lime St. CF37: R'fln 4G 25
Limewood Cl. CF3: St M 6C 74
Lincoln Cl. NP19: Newp 3F 37
Lincoln Ct. CF23: L'dyrn 2D 86
NP18: C'ln 4G 21
(off Caradoc Cl.)
Lincoln St. CF5: Card 3D 94
Lindbergh Cl. NP19: Newp 6G 37
Linden Av. CF23: Pen L 6C 86
Linden Cl. NP16: Bul 5E 63
Linden Ct. CF72: L'harry 5A 78
Linden Gro. CF3: Rum 3H 87
CF83: Caer 4E 29
Linden Rd. NP19: Newp 4G 37
Lindway Ct. CF5: Card 2D 94
Lingholm Cl. CF3: St M 6D 74
Link Rd. NP4: New I 5G 7
Links Bus. Pk., The CF3: St M 5F 75
Linley Cl. NP19: Newp 3E 39
Linnet Cl. CF23: L'dyrn 6D 72
Linnet Rd. NP26: Cald 6C 60
Linton St. NP20: Newp 1D 54
Lionel Rd. CF5: Card 3D 94
Lionel Ter. CF37: R'fln 4F 25
Liscombe St. NP19: Newp 5G 37
Liscum Way CF62: Barry 6E 105
Lisnagarvey Ct. CF14: Rhiw 5B 70
Lister Cl. CF38: Chu V 2D 42
Lister Grn. NP20: Malp 5A 20
LISVANE 2B 72
Lisvane & Thornhill Station (Rail) 2H 71
Lisvane Rd. CF14: L'vne, L'shn 4A 72
Lisvane St. CF24: Card 6H 85
LISWERRY 6A 38
Liswerry Cl. NP44: Llan 3B 12
(not continuous)
Liswerry Dr. NP44: Llan 2B 12
Liswerry Pk. Dr. NP19: Newp 5A 38
Liswerry Rd. NP19: Newp 6H 37
(not continuous)
Litchfield Ct. CF11: Card 6B 4 (5H 95)
Lit. Brynhill La. CF62: Barry 5F 105
Littlecroft Av. CF5: Ely 3B 94
Littledene NP44: G'mdw 2D 10
Lit. Dock St. CF64: P'rth 6H 101
Lit. Frederick St. CF10: Card 4E 5
Little Mill CF14: Whit 4C 84
Lit. Moors Hill CF63: Barry 1C 118
Little Orchard CF5: L'dff 6B 84
CF64: Din P 2A 108
Littleton St. CF11: Card 4G 95
Livale Cl. NP20: Bet 5G 19
Livale Ct. NP20: Bet 5G 19
Livale Rd. NP20: Bet 5G 19
Livale Wlk. NP20: Bet 5G 19
Liverpool St. NP19: Newp 3E 37
Livingstone Pl. NP19: Newp 4E 37
Livingstone Way CF62: St A 2D 112
(not continuous)
Livingwell Cardiff Premier 6G 71
Livorno Ho. *CF10: Card 6C 96*
(off Ffordd Garthorne)
Llanarth Cl. CF83: Mac 2H 31
Llanarth Sq. NP11: Ris 6E 17
Llanarth St. CF83: Mac 3H 31
NP20: Newp 5C 36
Llanbedr Rd. CF5: F'wtr 2A 94
Llanberis Cl. CF38: Tont 1E 43
NP10: R'drn 6A 34

LLANBERTHERY 1H 113
Llanbleddian Gdns. CF24: Card 1D 4 (2A 96)
LLANBLETHIAN 5C 90
Llanblethian Castle 4B 90
LLANBRADACH 1B 28
Llanbradach Station (Rail) 1B 28
Llanbradach St. CF11: Card 6H 95
CF37: P'prdd 6B 14
LLANBYDDERI 1H 113
LLANCADLE 4H 113
Llancaiach Rd. CF14: Whit 3D 84
LLANCATAL 4H 113
LLANDAFF 1B 94
Llandaff Arc. CF10: Card 3E 5 (3B 96)
Llandaff Cathedral 6D 84
Llandaff Chase CF5: L'dff 6B 84
Llandaff Cl. CF64: P'rth 3E 109
Llandaff Ct. CF5: L'dff 1C 94
Llandaff (for Whitchurch) Station (Rail) 3B 84
Llandaff Grn. NP44: C'brn 1G 11
LLANDAFF NORTH 4B 84
Llandaff Pl. CF5: L'dff 2E 95
Llandaff Rd. CF11: Card 2E 95
Llandaff Sq. CF3: St M 6B 74
Llandaff St. NP20: Newp 6A 36
Llandegefedd Way NP4: New I 6G 7
Llandegfedd Cl. CF14: Thorn 2H 71
NP10: Roger 2D 34
LLANDEGVETH 1H 13
Llandegveth Cl. NP44: C'iog 5H 9
Llandennis Av. CF23: Cyn 1B 86
Llandennis Ct. CF23: Cyn 1C 86
Llandennis Grn. CF23: Cyn 1B 86
Llandennis Rd. CF23: Cyn 1A 86
Llandenny Rd. NP26: Magor 5B 58
Llandenny Wlk. NP44: C'brn 2G 11
Llanderfel Ct. NP44: G'mdw 1C 10
Llandetty Rd. CF5: F'wtr 2A 94
LLANDEVENNY 5A 58
Llandilo Cl. CF64: Din P 2A 108
Llandinam Cres. CF14: Llan N 6D 84
Llandinam Rd. CF62: Barry 2G 117
LLANDOCH 4F 101
LLANDOCHE 6D 90
Llandogo Rd. CF3: St M 6D 74
LLANDOUCHAU 4F 101
LLANDOUGH
Cogan 4F 101
Cowbridge 6D 90
Llandough Hill CF64: L'dgh 4F 101
LLANDOUGH HOSPITAL (YSBYTY LLANDOCHAU) 5F 101
Llandough St. CF24: Card 2A 96
Llandough Trad. Est. CF11: Card 3F 101
Llandovery Cl. CF5: Ely 5G 93
Llandowlais St. NP44: C'brn, Oakf 4G 11
Llandow Rd. CF5: Ely 5H 93
Llandraw Woods CF37: P'prdd 6A 14
Llandudno Rd. CF3: Rum 3A 88
Llandyfrig Cl. CF64: Din P 2A 108
LLANEDEYRN 2E 87
Llanedeyrn Cl. CF23: Pen L 4D 86
Llanedeyrn Dr. CF23: L'dyrn 1E 87
Llanedeyrn Interchange CF23: Pen L 4F 87
Llanedeyrn Rd. CF23: Pen L 5D 86
Llanerch Goed CF38: Llan F 2D 42
Llanerch Path NP44: G'mdw 3D 10
Llanerch Vineyard 3G 79
Llanewrwg Way CF3: St M 6C 74
Llanfabon Ct. CF37: C'fydd 3F 15
Llanfabon Dr. CF83: B'ws, Tret 2H 29
Llanfair Rd. CF11: Card 2E 95
CF37: P'prdd 1B 24
Llanfedw Cl. CF83: Caer 4G 29
LLANFIHANGEL NEAR ROGIET 3H 59
LLANFIHANGEL-Y-PWLL 4C 100
LLANFLEIDDAN 5C 90
LLANFRECHFA 5D 12
LLANFRECHFA GRANGE HOSPITAL 3C 12
Llanfrechfa Way NP44: C'brn, Llan 3H 11
Llangattock Ct. NP44: C'iog 6H 9
Llangattock Rd. CF5: F'wtr 2A 94
Llangefni Pl. CF14: L'shn 4G 71
Llangorse Dr. NP10: Roger 2D 34
Llangorse Path NP44: Llan 4A 12
Llangorse Rd. CF23: Cyn 6C 72
NP44: Llan 3A 12
Llangranog Pl. CF14: L'shn 4F 71
Llangranog Rd. CF14: L'shn 4F 71
Llangwm Pl. CF3: Rum 3A 88
Llangybi Cl. CF5: Ely 6D 92
Llangynidr Rd. CF5: F'wtr 2A 94
LLANHARRY 5A 78
Llanharry Rd. CF72: L'harry, P'clun 4C 78
LLANHENNOCK 1C 22
Llanidloes Rd. CF14: Llan N 5D 84
LLANILLTUD FAERDREF 5D 42
LLANILLTUD FAWR 3B 110
Llanina Gro. CF3: Rum 2C 88
LLANISHEN 4F 71
Llanishen Ct. CF14: L'shn 5H 71
Llanishen Leisure Cen. 5G 71
Llanishen Sailing Cen. 5B 72
Llanishen Station (Rail) 4A 72
Llanishen St. CF14: Card 5H 85
LLANMAES 1E 111
Llanmaes Rd. CF71: Llan M 3C 110
Llanmaes St. CF11: Card 1H 101
Llanmead Gdns. CF62: Rho 5D 114
Llanmihangel Ri. CF71: L'thian 5B 90
Llanmihangel Rd. CF71: L'thian 6A 90
Llanmorlais Rd. CF14: Llan N 6E 85
Llanon NP44: C'iog 5F 9
Llanon Rd. CF14: L'shn 4G 71
Llanover Cl. NP20: Malp 6A 20
Llanover Hall Arts Cen. 3E 95
Llanover Rd. CF5: Ely 6D 92
CF37: P'prdd 5D 14
Llanover St. CF37: P'prdd 6D 14
CF63: Barry 1B 118
Llanquian Cl. CF71: C'bri 4D 90
Llanquian Rd. CF71: A'thin 2F 91
LLANRUMNEY 1A 88
Llanrumney Av. CF3: L'rmy 3H 87
LLANSANFFRAID-AR-ELAI 6H 81
LLANSANFFRAID GWYNLLWG 4G 77
Llansannor Dr. CF10: Card 6F 5 (5B 96)
Llanstephan Rd. CF3: Rum 4A 88
LLANTARNAM 6B 12
Llantarnam By-Pass NP44: Llanf, Oakf 2B 20
Llantarnam Cl. NP44: C'brn 3H 11
(not continuous)
Llantarnam Gdns. NP44: Oakf 6B 12
Llantarnam Grange Arts Cen. 1H 11
Llantarnam Ind. Est. NP44: Oakf 6A 12
Llantarnam Ind. Pk. NP44: Oakf 6H 11
Llantarnam Leisure Cen. 6A 12
Llantarnam Pk. Way NP44: Oakf 6H 11
Llantarnam Rd. CF14: Card 5F 85
NP44: C'brn, Oakf 3H 11
Llantarnham Dr. CF15: Rad 2F 83
Llanthewy Cl. NP44: C'iog 6H 9
Llanthewy Rd. NP20: Newp 5A 36
Llanthony Cl. NP26: Cald 4D 60
LLANTRISANT 2F 65
Llantrisant Bus. Pk. CF72: L'sant 4E 41
Llantrisant Castle 2F 65
Llantrisant Leisure Cen. 2F 65
Llantrisant Ri. CF5: L'dff 5B 84
Llantrisant Rd. CF5: F'wtr, St F 3C 82
CF5: P'rch 2E 81
CF37: P'cae, P'prdd 5A 24
CF38: Bed 4H 41
CF38: Bed, Chu V, Llan F 1A 66
CF72: Bed, Chu V, Llan F 1A 66
CF72: C Inn 2H 65
CF72: Groes F 6H 65
CF72: P'clun 6D 64
Llantrisant St. CF24: Card 1H 95
Llantrithyd Rd. CF71: St H 6H 91
LLANTWIT FARDRE 5D 42
Llantwit Fardre Sports Cen. 2F 43
Llantwit Fardre Sports Club 2F 43
Llantwit Gdns. Cl. CF62: St A 4D 112
LLANTWIT MAJOR 3B 110
Llantwit Major Leisure Cen. 4D 110
Llantwit Major Rd. CF71: C'bri 4A 90
CF71: Llan M 1B 110
Llantwit Major Station (Rail) 3C 110
Llantwit Rd. CF37: T'rest, Tont 3E 25
CF62: St A 4F 111
(Boverton, not continuous)
CF62: St A 5A 112
(Higher End)
Llantwit St. CF24: Card 1E 5 (2B 96)
Llant Witt St. CF63: Barry 2A 118
Llanvair Rd. NP19: Newp 3D 36
LLANVIHANGEL PONTYMOEL 2G 7
LLANWERN 4F 39
Llanwern Rd. CF5: Ely 5G 93
NP19: Newp 2C 38
NP26: Magor 6A 58
Llanwern St. NP19: Newp 4E 37
Llanwonno Cl. CF37: P'prdd 5A 14
(not continuous)
Llanwonno Rd. CF37: P'prdd 5A 14
LLANYRAFON 3A 12
Llanyrafon Farm Mus. 3A 12
Llanyrafon Mill 3A 12
Llan-yr-Avon Sq. NP44: Llan 3A 12
Llan-yr-Avon Way NP44: C'iog, Llan 3A 12
Llest Ter. CF38: Llan F 5C 42
Llew A Dor Ct. *NP18: C'ln 5A 22*
(off Tram Rd.)
Llewellin St. NP19: Newp 4G 37
Llewellyn Av. CF5: Ely 3F 93
Llewellyn Dr. CF83: Caer 5C 28
Llewellyn Gro. NP20: Malp 4A 20
Llewellyn St. CF63: Barry 1A 118
Llewelyn Goch CF5: St F 2C 82
Llewelyn St. CF37: P'prdd 5A 14
Lloft Deri CF14: Rhiw 6E 71
Lloyd Av. CF5: L'dff 2B 94
CF62: Barry 1G 117
Lloyd George Av. CF10: Card 6E 5 (5B 96)
Lloyd Pl. CF3: St M 1E 89
Lloyd St. NP19: Newp 6G 37
Llwyd Coed CF14: Rhiw 4B 70
Llwyd-y-Berth CF83: Caer 1A 46
Llwyn Bryn Melyn CF15: Rad 1E 83
Llwyn Castan CF23: L'dyrn 6E 73
Llwyn Celyn NP44: C'brn 4F 11
Llwyncrwn Rd. CF38: Bed 5H 41
Llwyn David CF62: Barry 3G 117
Llwyn Deri Cl. NP10: Bass 1A 52
Llwynderi Rd. NP20: Newp 5A 36
Llwynderw Rd. CF14: Whit 4F 85
Llwyn Drysgol CF15: Rad 1E 83
Llwyn Eithan CF83: Caer 4F 29
Llwynfedw Gdns. CF14: Heath 2F 85
(not continuous)
Llwynfedw Rd. CF14: Heath 2E 85
Llwynfen Rd. CF72: P'clun 6D 64
Llwyn Grug CF14: Rhiw 5E 71
Llwyn Gwyn CF72: L'harry 5A 78
Llwynmadoc St. CF37: P'prdd 6B 14
Llwyn Mallt CF15: Tong 5H 69
Llwyn On NP18: P'hir 1G 21
Llwynon NP11: Ris 5E 17
Llwyn-on Cl. CF83: Caer 5B 28
Llwyn Onn CF14: Rhiw 5B 70
CF72: P'clun 5C 64
NP44: C'iog 1B 12
Llwyn-on St. CF83: Caer 5B 28
Llwyn Passat CF64: P'rth 6A 102
Llwynpennau Cotts. CF72: Groes F 1B 80
Llwyn Rhosyn CF14: Rhiw 5E 71
Llwyn-y-Grant Pl. CF23: Pen L 5D 86
Llwyn-y-Grant Rd. CF23: Pen L 5D 86
Llwyn-y-Grant Ter. CF23: Pen L 5D 86
Llwyn-y-Pia Rd. CF14: L'vne 2B 72
Llyn Berwyn Cl. NP10: Roger 3D 34
Llyn Celyn Cl. NP10: Roger 2D 34
Llyn Cl. CF23: Cyn 2B 86
Llyn Pandy CF83: B'ws 3F 29
Llys Cambria CF83: L'brad 1B 28
Llys Caradog CF15: Cre 6D 66
Llys Catwg CF72: T Grn 3E 65
Llys Celyn *CF38: Tont 2G 43*
(off Cedar Cres.)
Llys Coed CF37: Glyn 1D 14
CF62: Barry 3E 117
Llys Coed Derw CF38: Llan F 3D 42
Llys Corrwg CF37: R'fln 4H 25
Llys Deri CF72: L'harry 5A 78
Llys Derwen CF37: Glyn 1D 14
CF72: L'sant 3F 65
Llys Dewi CF15: Cre 6E 67
CF71: Llan M 2B 110
Llys Dwynwen CF71: Llan M 1B 110
Llys Dyfodwg CF15: Cre 1E 81
Llys Dyfrig CF15: Cre 1D 80
Llys Fach CF38: Chu V 3F 43
Llys Gth. CF38: Llan F, Chu V 2D 42
Llys Gwent CF63: Barry 5C 106
Llys Gwynno CF15: Cre 1D 80
Llys Gwyrdd NP44: H'lys 6C 10
Llys Hafen CF15: Taff W 2E 69
Llys Hanner Erw CF83: Caer 4D 28
Llys Illtyd CF15: Cre 6D 66
Llys Joseph CF72: L'harry 4A 78
Llys Llywelyn CF38: Llan F 3D 42
Llys Maelwg CF72: T Grn 3E 65
Llys Nant Pandy CF83: Caer 5C 28
Llys Nant yr Aber CF83: Caer 5B 28
Llys Pegasus CF14: L'shn 5G 71
Llys Pum Cyfair CF14: Llan N 5E 85
Llys Steffan CF71: Llan M 2B 110
Llys Tal-y-Bont Rd. CF14: Card 6G 85
Llys Teilo CF15: Cre 1E 81
CF71: Llan M 2B 110
CF72: T Grn 3E 65
Llys Tripp CF15: Gwae G 2E 69
Llys Tudful CF15: Cre 6E 67
Llys Ty Gwyn CF37: P'prdd 5E 15
Llyswen CF83: Mac 2F 31
Llyswen Rd. CF23: Cyn 1B 86
Llyswen Wlk. NP44: Llan 4A 12

Llys-y-Celyn CF83: Caer 4E 29
Llys-y-Fedwen CF83: Caer 5E 29
Llys y Fran CF38: Chu V 3E 43
Llys y Gored Ddu CF10: Card 1G 95
Llywelyn Rd. NP44: C'brn 1G 11
Llywn y Gog CF62: Rho 6F 115
Lobelia Cl. NP10: Roger 3A 34
Lochaber St. CF24: Card 6C 86
Locke Gro. CF3: St M 1E 89
Locke St. NP20: Newp 4B 36
Lock Keepers Ct. CF10: Card 1H 95
Locks Rd. CF10: Card 3C 102
Lock Ter. CF37: P'prdd 5D 14
Lodden Cl. NP20: Bet 5G 19
Lodge Av. NP18: C'ln 4G 21
Lodge Cl. CF14: L'vne 1A 72
Lodge Hill NP18: C'ln 4F 21
NP18: L'wrn 4F 39
Lodge Rd. NP18: C'ln 5E 21
Lodge Way NP26: Pskwt 5F 61
Lodge Wood NP4: New I, P'pool 4E 7
Lodwick Ri. CF3: St M 2E 89
Loftus St. CF5: Card 3D 94
Lombard St. CF62: Barry 2H 117
Lomond Cres. CF23: Cyn 2C 86
Loncae Porth CF14: Rhiw 4E 71
Lon Cefn Mably CF62: Rho 6D 114
London St. NP19: Newp 4E 37
Lon Elai CF72: P'clun 5D 64
Lon Fach CF14: Rhiw 6D 70
CF83: Caer 1B 46
Lon Fawr CF83: Caer 1B 46
Lon Fferm Felin CF62: Barry 3D 116
Long Acre NP44: F'wtr 4D 10
Longacre Cl. CF63: Barry 5D 106
CF72: L'sant 3G 65
Lon Ganol CF14: Rhiw 6D 70
Longbridge NP18: P'hir 1F 21
Longbridge Ct. *NP11: Ris 4D 16*
(off St Mary St.)
Longcroft Rd. NP26: Cald 5C 60
Longcross Ct. CF24: Card 2G 5 (3C 96)
Longcross St. CF24: Card 2H 5 (3C 96)
Longditch Rd. NP19: Newp 2B 56
Longeil Cl. CF10: Card 6C 96
Longfellow Cl. NP26: Rog 5B 60
Longfellow Ct. NP26: Cald 6B 60
Longfellow Gdns. CF83: Mac 2C 30
Longfellow Pl. NP26: Cald 6B 60
Longfellow Rd. NP26: Cald 5B 60
Long Hollow NP44: C'brn 1G 11
Longhouse Cl. CF14: L'vne 3A 72
Longhouse Gro. NP44: H'lys 5B 10
Longleat Cl. CF14: L'vne 3B 72
Long Mdw. Ct. CF71: C'bri 3D 90
Longmeadow Ct. NP19: Newp 6A 38
Long Mdw. Dr. CF62: Barry 6H 105
Longmeadow Dr. CF64: Din P 3H 107
Longreach Cl. CF5: Ely 5D 92
Long Row *CF37: T'rest 3E 25*
(off Park St.)
NP4: Up R 5B 6
Longships Rd. CF10: Card 1F 103
Longspears Av. CF14: Card 4G 85
Longtown Gro. NP10: Coedk 6G 53
Longwood Dr. CF14: Whit 6G 69
Lon Hafren CF83: Caer 2B 46
Lon Helyg NP44: C'iog 1B 12
Lon Helygen CF37: Glyn 1D 14
Lon Heulog CF37: R'fln 5G 25
Lon Isa CF14: Rhiw 6D 70
Lon Isaf CF83: Caer 1B 46
Lon Lindys CF62: Rho 6E 115
Lon Madoc CF14: Whit 3E 85
Lon Nant NP44: Pnwd 6F 9
Lon-Od-Nant CF71: Llan M 4C 110
Lon Owain CF5: Ely 6F 93
Lon Penllyn CF14: Rhiw 1D 84
Lon Robin Goch CF83: Caer 6A 28
Lonsdale Rd. CF23: Pen L 4E 87
Lon Ty'n-y-cae CF14: Rhiw 1E 85
Lon Ucha CF14: Rhiw 6D 70
Lon Uchaf CF83: Caer 1B 46
Lon Werdd CF5: Ely 4E 93
Lon Werdd Cl. CF5: Ely 4E 93
Lon-y-Barri CF83: Caer 4B 28
(not continuous)
Lon y Cadno CF38: Chu V 4E 43
Lon-y-Castell CF5: Ely 6G 93
Lon-y-Celyn CF14: Whit 1B 84
Lon-y-Dail CF14: Rhiw 6D 70
Lon-y-Dderwen CF14: Rhiw 6D 70
Lon-y-Ddraenen CF83: Caer 1B 46
Lon-y-Deri CF14: Rhiw 6D 70
CF83: Caer 1B 46
Lon-y-Ffin CF5: Ely 4E 93
Lon-y-Fran CF83: Caer 6A 28
Lon-y-Fro CF15: P'rch 5A 68
Lon-y-Garwa CF83: Caer 3B 46
Lon y Goch CF15: P'rch 1A 82
Lon-y-Gors CF83: Caer 1A 46
Lon-y-Groes CF14: Heath 3F 85
Lon-y-Llyn CF83: Caer 1B 46
Lon-y-Mynydd CF14: Rhiw 6E 71
Lon y Nant CF14: Rhiw 6E 71
Lon-y-Parc CF14: Heath 2D 84
Lon-yr-Awel CF72: P'clun 5E 65
Lon-yr-Efail CF5: Ely 6F 93
Lon-y-Rhedyn CF83: Caer 1A 46
(not continuous)
Lon-y-Rheydyn CF83: Caer 1B 46
Lon-y-Rhyd CF14: Rhiw 6D 70
Lon yr Odyn CF83: Caer 6E 29
Lon yr Ysgol CF83: B'ws 3F 29
Lon-Ysgubor CF14: Rhiw 5D 70
Lon y Tresglen CF83: Caer 6A 28
Lon y Twyn CF83: Caer 1D 46
Lon-y-Waun CF83: Caer 1A 46
Lon-y-Wern CF83: Caer 1B 46
Lon-y-Winci CF14: Rhiw 5D 70
Loop Rd. NP16: B'ly 4H 63
Lord Eldon Dr. NP16: Bul 6F 63
Lord St. CF64: P'rth 6B 102
NP19: Newp 3D 36
Lothian Cres. CF23: Pen L 4D 86
Loucher Cl. CF5: F'wtr 2A 94
Loudoun Ho. CF10: Card 6B 96
Loudoun Sq. CF10: Card 6B 96
Lougher Pl. CF62: St A 5C 112
Louisa Pl. CF10: Card 1B 102
Lovage Cl. CF23: Pontp 5E 73
Love La. CF10: Card 4E 5 (4B 96)
CF71: L'thian 4C 90
Loveluck Ct. *CF71: Llan M 3B 110*
(off Spitzcop)
Lovering Way CF10: Card 1B 102
Lowdon Ter. CF62: Barry 2G 117
Lower Acre CF5: Ely 6F 93
Lwr. Alma Ter. CF37: T'rest 1D 24
Lower Bri. St. NP4: P'pool 3C 6
Lwr. Cathedral Rd. CF11: Card 4A 4 (4H 95)
Lwr. Church St. NP16: Chep 1F 63
Lowerdale Dr. CF72: L'sant 3G 65
Lwr. Dock St. NP20: Newp 5C 36
Lwr. Farm Ct. CF62: Rho 5E 115
Lwr. Glyn Gwyn St. CF83: Tret 3A 30
Lwr. Guthrie St. CF63: Barry 2A 118
Lwr. Holmes St. CF63: Barry 1C 118
LOWER MACHEN 4B 32
Lwr. Morel St. CF63: Barry 2A 118
LOWER NEW INN 6G 7
LOWER OCHRWYTH 1E 33
Lwr. Park Gdns. NP4: P'pool 2C 6
Lwr. Park Ter. NP4: P'pool 3C 6
LOWER PENARTH 4D 108
LOWER PORTKERRY 5H 115
Lwr. Pyke St. CF63: Barry 2A 118
Lwr. Rhymney Valley Relief Rd.
CF83: Caer, L'brad 2B 28
Lwr. Taff Vw. CF37: P'prdd 4E 15
Lwr. Wyndham Ter. NP11: Ris 6F 17
Lowfield Dr. CF14: Thorn 3F 71
Lowland Dr. CF38: Tont 2G 43
LOWLANDS 5D 8
Lowlands Cres. NP44: Pnwd 5D 8
Lowlands Rd. NP44: Pnwd 5E 9
Lowndes Cl. NP10: Bass 6B 34
Lowther Ct. CF24: Card 1E 5 (2B 96)
Lowther Rd. CF24: Card 1E 5 (2B 96)
Lucas Cl. CF63: Barry 5C 106
Lucas St. CF24: Card 6A 86
NP20: Newp 3B 36
Lucerne Dr. CF14: Thorn 3F 71
Lucknow St. CF11: Card 6G 95
Ludlow Cl. CF11: Card 1A 102
NP19: Newp 5F 37
NP44: Llan 4B 12
(not continuous)
Ludlow La. CF64: P'rth 1E 109
Ludlow St. CF11: Card 1H 101
CF64: P'rth 1E 109
CF83: Caer 1C 46
Lulworth Rd. NP18: C'ln 6A 22
Lundy Cl. CF14: L'shn 5G 71
Lundy Dr. NP19: Newp 3F 37
Lupin Gro. NP10: Roger 3A 34
Lwynpia Cotts. CF15: Morg 5F 69
Lydford Cl. CF14: Rhiw 1D 84
Lydstep Cres. CF14: Llan N 6D 84
Lydstep Flats CF14: Llan N 5D 84
Lydstep Rd. CF62: Barry 6H 105
Lydwood Cl. CF83: Mac 2G 31
Lynch Blosse Cl. CF5: L'dff 5A 84
Lyncroft NP44: G'mdw 2D 10
Lyncroft Cl. CF3: St M 5B 74
Lyndhurst Av. NP20: Newp 1H 53
Lyndhurst St. CF11: Card 4F 95
Lyndon Way NP10: Roger 4D 34
Lyne Rd. NP11: Ris 6E 17
NP20: Newp 2C 36
Lynmouth Cres. CF3: Rum 4G 87
Lynmouth Dr. CF64: Sul 3G 119
Lyn Pac Trad. Est. NP44: Pnwd 5E 9
Lynton Cl. CF3: L'rmy 3H 87
CF64: Sul 2H 119
Lynton Ct. CF10: Card 1B 102
Lynton Pl. CF3: L'rmy 3G 87
Lynton Ter. CF3: L'rmy 3G 87
Lynwood Ct. CF24: Card 1H 5 (2C 96)
Lyon Cl. CF11: Card 2F 101
Lyric Way CF14: Thorn 3G 71
Lysander Ct. CF24: Card 2G 97
Lytham Gro. CF3: St M 5E 75

M

Maberly Cl. CF14: Cyn 6A 72
Macaulay Av. CF3: L'rmy 6H 73
Macauley Gdns. NP20: Newp 2G 53
McCale Av. CF5: F'wtr 2A 94
McCarthy's Ct. NP20: Newp 5C 36
Macdonald Cl. CF5: Ely 5E 93
Macdonald Pl. CF5: Ely 5E 93
Macdonald Rd. CF5: Ely 5E 93
MACHEN 2F 31
Machen Cl. CF3: St M 6D 74
NP11: Ris 6F 17
Machen Pl. CF11: Card 5A 4 (4G 95)
Machen St. CF11: Card 6G 95
CF64: P'rth 1D 108
NP11: Ris 5D 16
Mackintosh Pl. CF24: Card 6B 86
Mackintosh Rd. CF37: P'prdd 6D 14
McLay Ct. CF5: F'wtr 2A 94
McQuade Pl. CF62: Barry 5G 117
Madoc Cl. CF64: Din P 2A 108
Madocke Rd. NP16: Sed 3G 63
Madoc Rd. CF24: Card 3F 97
Madoc St. CF37: P'prdd 1C 24
Maelfa CF23: L'dyrn 3E 87
Maelog Cl. CF72: P'clun 5D 64
Maelog Pl. CF14: Card 6G 85
Maelog Rd. CF14: Whit 3E 85
Maendy Pl. NP44: Pnwd 5C 8
Maendy Rd. CF37: P'cae, Chu V, T'rest 3B 24
CF38: Chu V 3B 24
CF71: A'thin 1F 91
Maendy Sq. NP44: Pnwd 6C 8
Maendy Way NP44: C'brn, Pnwd, Up Cwm 5C 8
Maendy Wood Ri. NP44: Pnwd 6C 8
Maerdy Cl. NP20: Newp 2H 53
Maerdy La. CF14: L'vne 3C 72
MAES AWYR CAERDYDD-CYMRU 4E 115
Maes Briallu CF83: Caer 5F 29
Maes Brith y Garn CF23: Pontp 4F 73
Maes Cadwgan CF15: Cre 6E 67
Maes Cefn Mabley CF72: L'sant 1F 65
Maes Coed Rd. CF37: P'prdd 1B 24
Maesderwen Cres. NP4: P'pool 4D 6
Maesderwen Ri. NP4: P'pool 4D 6
Maesderwen Rd. NP4: P'pool 4D 6
Maes Ganol CF37: R'fln 5A 26
MAES-GLAS 3H 53
Maes Glas CF14: Whit 4C 84
CF37: Glyn 1D 14
CF62: Barry 3E 117
CF83: Caer 1E 47
Maesglas Av. NP20: Newp 2H 53
Maesglas Cl. NP20: Newp 3H 53
Maesglas Cres. NP20: Newp 2H 53
(not continuous)
Maesglas Gro. NP20: Newp 3H 53
Maesglas Ind. Est. NP20: Newp 2A 54
Maesglas Retail Pk. NP20: Newp 2C 54
(Docks Way)
NP20: Newp 2B 54
(Port Rd.)
Maesglas Rd. NP20: Newp 2H 53
(not continuous)
Maesglas St. NP20: Newp 3H 53
Maes Gwyn CF83: Caer 1D 46
Maesgwyn NP44: Pnwd 5D 8
Maes Hir CF83: Caer 4B 28
Maes Illtuds CF71: Llan M 2C 110
Maes Lindys CF62: Rho 6F 115
Maes Lloi CF71: A'thin 2F 91
Maes Maelwg CF38: Bed 5H 41

Maes Sarn CF72: L'sant 1F **65**
Maes Slowes Leyes CF62: Rho 6F **115**
Maesteg Cres. CF38: Tont 2G **43**
Maesteg Gdns. CF38: Tont 2G **43**
Maesteg Gro. CF38: Tont 2G **43**
Maes Trane CF38: Bed 5A **42**
Maes Trisant CF72: T Grn 3E **65**
(not continuous)
Maes Uchaf CF37: R'fln 5A **26**
Maes Watford CF83: Caer 3B **46**
Maes y Briallu CF15: Morg 6E **69**
Maes y Bryn CF15: Rad 6F **69**
CF23: Pontp 5G **73**
Maes-y-Bryn Rd. CF3: Pontp 1G **73**
Maes-y-Celyn NP4: P'pool 5D **6**
MAESYCOED 1A **24**
Maes-y-Coed CF62: Barry 5D **116**
Maesycoed Rd. CF37: P'prdd 6B **14**
Maes-y-Coed Rd. CF14: Heath 1F **85**
Maes y Cored CF14: Whit 1A **84**
Maes-y-Crochan CF3: St M 6F **75**
Maes y Crofft CF15: Morg 6E **69**
Maes-y-Cwm-St CF63: Barry 2H **117**
Maes-y-Dderwen CF15: Cre 1E **81**
Maes-y-Deri CF14: Rhiw 6D **70**
CF37: P'prdd 5A **14**
Maes y Draenog CF15: Tong 3H **69**
Maes-y-Drudwen CF83: Caer 1A **46**
Maes y Felin CF37: R'fln 5A **26**
Maes-y-Felin CF14: Rhiw 1D **84**
CF83: Caer 6D **28**
Maes y Fioled CF15: Morg 6E **69**
Maes y Gad CF5: St F 2D **92**
Maes-y-Gollen CF15: Cre 6E **67**
Maes y Grug CF38: Chu V 2E **43**
Maes y Gwair CF15: Morg 6D **68**
Maes y Gwenyn CF62: Rho 6G **115**
Maes-y-Nant CF15: Cre 6D **66**
Maes y Pandy CF83: B'ws 2E **29**
Maes y Parc CF14: Rhiw 1D **84**
Maes-yr-Afon CF72: P'clun 1C **78**
CF83: Caer 4F **29**
Maes yr Annedd CF5: Card 2D **94**
Maes yr Awel CF15: Rad 1F **83**
CF37: R'fln 5A **26**
Maes yr Haf CF14: Rhiw 5B **70**
Maes yr Hafod CF15: Cre 6E **67**
Maes yr Haul Cotts. *CF72: C Inn 3G 65*
(off Taff Cotts.)
Maes yr Hedydd CF23: Pontp 3F **73**
Maes-y-Rhedyn CF15: Cre 1E **81**
CF72: T Grn 3D **64**
Maes y Rhiw Ct. NP44: G'mdw 2C **10**
Maes yr Odyn CF15: Morg 6E **69**
Maes-yr-Onnen CF15: Cre 1E **81**
Maes yr Orchis CF15: Morg 6E **69**
Maes-yr-Ysgol CF62: Barry 2G **117**
Maes-y-Sarn CF15: P'rch 4H **67**
Maes-y-Siglen CF83: Caer 6A **28**
Maes y Wennol CF23: Pontp 4F **73**
Maes-y-Wennol CF72: P'clun 5F **65**
Mafeking Rd. CF23: Pen L 6C **86**
Magellan Cl. CF62: Barry 5A **106**
Magna Porta Gdns. NP44: Oakf 1B **20**
Magnolia Cl. CF23: L'dyrn 6D **72**
NP16: Bul 5F **63**
NP20: Malp 4B **20**
Magnolia Way CF38: Llan F 5C **42**
MAGOR 4D **58**
Magor Rd. NP18: L'stne 6H **23**
NP18: Under 2A **58**
NP26: Under 2A **58**
Magor St. NP19: Newp 6F **37**
Magpie Rd. CF62: St A 3F **111**
Magretion Pl. CF10: Card 6B **96**
Maia Ho. CF10: Card 1D **102**
Maillard's Haven CF64: P'rth 4F **109**
Main Av. CF23: Pen L 6E **87**
CF37: N'grw, Up Bo 1B **44**
MAINDEE 4E **37**
Maindee Pde. NP19: Newp 3E **37**
Maindee Swimming Pool 4E **37**
Maindee Ter. NP44: Pnwd 6D **8**
MAINDY 5F **85**
Maindy Ct. CF38: Chu V 2E **43**
Maindy Cycle Track 6G **85**
Maindy M. CF24: Card 1A **96**
Maindy Pool 6G **85**
Maindy Rd. CF24: Card 6G **85**
Main Rd. CF15: Gwae G, Taff W 6D **44**
CF38: Chu V, Tont 3E **43**
CF72: C Inn 3G **65**
CF72: Groes F 6B **66**
NP26: Pskwt 5G **61**
NP26: Undy 4D **58**
Main St. CF63: Barry 6B **106**
Maitland Pl. CF11: Card 5G **95**
Maitland St. CF14: Card 5G **85**
Major Cl. NP44: F'wtr 3B **10**
Major Rd. CF5: Card 4F **95**
Malcolm Sargeant Cl. NP18: Newp 5B **38**
Maldwyn St. CF11: Card 2F **95**
Malefant St. CF24: Card 6A **86**
Mall, The NP44: C'brn 2H **11**
Mallard Av. NP26: Cald 6C **60**
Mallard Cl. CF3: St M 6C **74**
Mallards Reach CF3: M'fld 4G **75**
Mallard Way CF64: P'rth 6E **109**
NP10: Duf 5G **53**
Mallory Cl. CF62: St A 2D **112**
Malmesbury Cl. NP20: Newp 3C **36**
Malmesmead Rd. CF3: L'rmy 6A **74**
MALPAS 4A **20**
Malpas Cl. CF3: St M 6D **74**
Malpas Junc. NP20: Newp 2A **36**
Malpas La. NP20: Newp 1B **36**
Malpas Rd. NP20: Malp, Newp 3A **20**
(not continuous)
Malpas St. NP44: C'brn 3G **11**
Malpas Vs. NP20: Malp 4A **20**
Malthouse, The CF10: Card 5D **4**
Malthouse Av. CF23: Pontp 3G **73**
Malthouse La. NP4: P'pool 2B **6**
Malthouse Rd. NP18: C'ln 2E **21**
NP44: C'ln, Oakf 2A **20**
Maltings, The CF23: Pontp 4F **73**
CF24: Card 4E **97**
Malus Av. CF38: Llan F 6C **42**
Malvern Cl. NP11: Ris 6H **17**
NP19: Newp 1G **37**
Malvern Dr. CF14: L'shn 6F **71**
Malvern Rd. NP19: Newp 4D **36**
Malvern Ter. NP11: Ris 6E **17**
Manchester St. NP19: Newp 3D **36**
Mandeville Pl. CF11: Card 4G **95**
Mandeville St. CF11: Card 4G **95**
Manitoba Cl. CF23: Cyn 2C **86**
Manley Rd. NP20: Newp 5A **36**
Manod Rd. CF14: Llan N 5C **84**
Manor, The NP44: Oakf 2A **20**
Manorbier Cl. CF38: Tont 1F **43**
CF64: Din P 2A **108**
Manorbier Ct. CF62: Barry 5H **105**
Manorbier Cres. CF3: Rum 3A **88**
Manorbier Dr. NP44: Llan 2A **12**
Manor Chase CF38: Bed 6A **42**
NP26: Undy 4F **59**
Manor Cl. CF14: Heath 2D **84**
NP11: Ris 6F **17**
Manor Cotts. CF72: P'clun 2C **78**
Manor Ct. CF38: Chu V 2E **43**
NP11: Ris 5F **17**
NP26: Rog 6A **60**
Manor Ga. NP44: G'mdw 2D **10**
Manor Hill CF72: P'clun 6F **65**
Manor Pk. CF71: Llan M 4C **110**
NP10: Duf 5H **53**
Manor Ri. CF14: Whit 3E **85**
Manor Rd. NP11: Ris 6F **17**
Manor Sq. CF71: Llan M 5C **110**
Manor St. CF14: Card 5H **85**
Manor Way CF14: Heath, Whit 2E **85**
NP11: Ris 6F **17**
NP16: Chep 2E 63
(off Dell Vw.)
NP26: Pskwt 5G **61**
Manor Wood NP16: Chep 2C **62**
Mansell Av. CF5: Ely 5D **92**
Mansel St. NP19: Newp 4G **37**
Mansfield St. CF11: Card 4G **95**
Mansion House 1F **5** (2B **96**)
Manston Cl. CF5: L'dff 6A **84**
Maple Av. NP11: Ris 5F **17**
NP16: Bul 4D **62**
Maple Cl. CF62: Barry 6A **106**
CF72: L'harry 5A **78**
NP18: Under 3H **39**
NP26: Cald 4C **60**
Maple Cres. NP4: Grif 2D **8**
Maple Gdns. NP11: Ris 1G **33**
Maple Rd. CF5: F'wtr 6F **83**
CF64: P'rth 2C **108**
NP4: Grif 1D **8**
Maple Rd. Sth. NP4: Grif 2D **8**
Maple St. CF37: R'fln 4G **25**
Maple Tree Cl. CF15: Rad 1E **83**
Maplewood Av. CF14: Llan N 4B **84**
Marchwood Cl. CF3: Rum 2A **88**
Marconi Av. CF64: P'rth 5H **101**
Marconi Cl. NP20: Malp 5H **19**
Marcross Rd. CF5: Ely 5E **93**
Mardy CF72: L'sant 6C **40**
Mardy Cl. CF83: Caer 6E **29**
Mardy Cres. CF83: Caer 6E **29**
Mardy Rd. CF3: Rum 5A **88**
(New Rd.)
CF3: Rum 6B **88**
(Wentloog Av.)
Mardy St. CF11: Card 6A **4** (5H **95**)
(not continuous)
Margam Cl. CF62: St A 2C **112**
Margam Rd. CF14: Card 5F **85**
Margaret Av. CF62: Barry 4H **105**
NP19: Newp 2D **36**
Margaret St. CF37: P'prdd 5A **14**
Margretts Way NP26: Cald 4C **60**
Marguerites Way CF5: Ely 4E **93**
Maria Ct. CF10: Card 6B **96**
Maria St. CF10: Card 5B **96**
MARIE CURIE CENTRE (HOLME TOWER) 2F **109**
Marigold Cl. NP10: Roger 3H **33**
Marina Ct. NP19: Newp 6E **21**
Marine Dr. CF62: Barry 5C **116**
Marine Pde. CF64: P'rth 3F **109**
Mariner's Hgts. CF64: P'rth 6B **102**
Mariners Reach NP16: Bul 6G **63**
Mariners Way CF62: Rho 6D **114**
Mariner Way NP19: Newp 2E **55**
Marine Ter. NP26: Sud 6H **61**
Marion Ct. CF14: L'shn 4A **72**
Marion Pl. NP20: Newp 1D **54**
Marion St. CF24: Card 3E **97**
NP20: Newp 1C **54**
Marionville Gdns. CF5: F'wtr 1A **94**
Maritime Ct. CF83: B'ws 3E **29**
Maritime Ind. Est. CF37: P'prdd 2A **24**
Maritime St. CF37: P'prdd 1B **24**
Maritime Ter. CF37: P'prdd 1B **24**
Market, The CF37: P'prdd 6C **14**
Market Arc. *NP4: P'pool 3C 6*
(off Crane St.)
NP20: Newp 4C **36**
Market Pl. CF5: Card 3F **95**
Market Rd. CF5: Card 3E **95**
Market St. CF15: Tong 4G **69**
CF37: P'prdd 6C **14**
CF62: Barry 4F **117**
CF83: Caer 1D **46**
NP4: P'pool 3C **6**
NP20: Newp 4C **36**
Mark St. CF11: Card 4A **4** (4H **95**)
Marland Ho. CF10: Card 5C **4** (4A **96**)
Marlborough Cl. CF38: Llan F 5D **42**
CF63: Barry 6C **106**
Marlborough Ho. CF10: Card 4B **4** (4H **95**)
Marlborough Rd. CF23: Pen L 6C **86**
NP19: Newp 4D **36**
NP44: G'mdw 2C **10**
Marlborough Ter. CF10: Card 1G **95**
Marl Ct. CF11: Card 2H **101**
NP44: G'mdw 6B **8**
Marle Cl. CF23: L'dyrn 5F **73**
Marloes Cl. CF62: Barry 6H **105**
Marloes Path NP44: G'mdw 2D **10**
Marloes Rd. CF5: Ely 4F **93**
Marlow Cl. NP10: Roger 3D **34**
Marlowe Gdns. NP20: Newp 2G **53**
Marquis Cl. CF62: Barry 5A **118**
Marryat Wlk. NP20: Newp 2G **53**
Marshall Cl. CF5: L'dff 5A **84**
Marsham Ct. CF15: Rad 2G **83**
MARSHFIELD 4A **76**
Marshfield Rd. CF3: Cas, M'fld 2G **75**
Marshfield St. NP19: Newp 6F **37**
Marsh Rd. NP16: Bul 5F **63**
Marston Ct. NP20: Newp 2A **36**
Marston Path NP44: G'mdw 3E **11**
Marten Rd. NP16: Bul 4E **63**
Martindale Rd. NP4: Grif 1E **9**
Martin Rd. CF24: Card 5G **97**
Martins, The NP16: Tut 1G **63**
Martins Rd. NP26: C'went 1B **60**
Mary Ann St. CF10: Card 5E **5** (4B **96**)
Maryland Rd. NP11: Ris 6E **17**
Maryport Rd. CF23: Pen L 5B **86**
Mary Price Ct. *CF24: Card 4E 97*
(off Aberystwyth St.)
Marysfield Cl. CF3: M'fld 5A **76**
Mary St. CF14: Llan N 5B **84**
CF37: C'fydd 2F **15**
CF83: Tret 3A **30**
Masefield Rd. CF64: P'rth 1C **108**
NP26: Cald 6B **60**
Masefield Va. NP20: Newp 1G **53**
Masefield Way CF37: R'fln 3G **25**
Mathern Cres. NP16: Math 6B **62**
Mathern Rd. NP16: Bul, Math 6C **62**
Mathern Way NP16: Bul 4E **63**

Mathew Wlk. CF5: L'dff . . . 5H **83**
Mathias Cl. CF23: Pen L . . . 6E **87**
Matthew Rd. CF62: Rho . . . 5C **114**
Matthewson Cl. CF14: Llan N . . . 5E **85**
Matthew Ter. CF64: Din P . . . 6F **101**
NP4: P'nydd . . . 1A 6
(off Chapel Rd.)
Matthysens Way CF3: St M . . . 2D **88**
Maugham Cl. NP20: Newp . . . 2H **53**
Maughan La. CF64: P'rth . . . 6B **102**
Maughan Ter. CF64: P'rth . . . 6B **102**
Maureen Av. CF5: Ely . . . 3H **93**
Mavis Gro. CF14: Heath . . . 1E **85**
MAVRID WOODBURY . . . 1F **81**
Maxton Ct. CF83: Caer . . . 6E **29**
Maxwell Rd. CF3: Rum . . . 3H **87**
Mayfair CF5: Ely . . . 1E **99**
Mayfair Dr. CF14: Thorn . . . 2G **71**
Mayfield Av. CF5: Card . . . 3C **94**
Mayfield Pl. CF72: L'sant . . . 3G **65**
Mayfield Rd. CF37: P'prdd . . . 5B **14**
Mayflower Av. CF14: L'shn . . . 4F **71**
Mayflower Way CF62: Rho . . . 5E **115**
Mayhill Cl. CF14: Thorn . . . 2H **71**
Maynard Ct. CF5: L'dff . . . 1C **94**
Maynes NP44: F'wtr . . . 4D **10**
May St. CF24: Card . . . 6A **86**
(not continuous)
NP19: Newp . . . 4E **37**
Mead La. NP44: C'brn . . . 1G **11**
Meadow, The NP26: Magor . . . 4C **58**
Meadowbank Ct. CF5: F'wtr . . . 5H **83**
Meadowbrook Av. NP44: Pnwd . . . 5D **8**
Meadow Cl. CF23: Cyn . . . 5D **72**
NP4: Grif . . . 3E **9**
NP11: Ris . . . 3B **16**
Meadow Cres. CF38: Tont . . . 2G **43**
CF83: Caer . . . 1D **46**
NP11: Ris . . . 1G **33**
Meadow Cft. CF62: Rho . . . 5F **115**
Meadowfield Way CF15: Morg . . . 6E **69**
Meadowgate Cl. CF14: Whit . . . 6B **70**
Meadow Hill CF38: Chu V . . . 3D **42**
Meadowland Dr. NP10: Roger . . . 2G **33**
Meadow La. CF64: P'rth . . . 4D **108**
NP44: C'iog . . . 6H **9**
Meadowlark Cl. CF3: St M . . . 6C **74**
Meadow Ri. NP26: Undy . . . 3D **58**
(not continuous)
Meadows, The CF3: M'fld . . . 4G **75**
NP11: Ris . . . 3B **16**
Meadowside CF64: P'rth . . . 2B **108**
Meadows Rd. NP19: Newp . . . 4A **56**
Meadow St. CF11: Card . . . 2E **95**
CF37: T'rest . . . 3E **25**
Meadowsweet Dr. CF3: St M . . . 1E **89**
Meadow Va. CF63: Barry . . . 5C **106**
Meadow Vw. CF63: Barry . . . 5D **106**
CF83: B'ws . . . 2E **29**
Meadow Vw. Ct. CF64: Sul . . . 2G **119**
Meadow Wlk. NP16: Chep . . . 2D **62**
Meadow Way CF83: Caer . . . 2H **45**
Meads Cl. NP19: Newp . . . 1A **56**
Meads Ct. NP16: Bul . . . 4E **63**
Meadvale Rd. CF3: St M . . . 1B **88**
Medart Pl. NP11: C'keys, Ris . . . 3B **16**
Medart St. NP11: C'keys . . . 3B **16**
Medieval Village . . . 6D **108**
Medlock Cl. NP20: Bet . . . 5G **19**
Medlock Cres. NP20: Bet . . . 4F **19**
Medlock Wlk. NP20: Bet . . . 4G **19**
Medway Cl. NP20: Bet . . . 4F **19**
Medway Ct. NP20: Bet . . . 4F **19**
Medway Rd. NP20: Bet . . . 5E **19**
Megabowl
Cardiff . . . 6F **87**
Newport . . . 1B **56**
Meggitt Rd. CF62: Barry . . . 5G **105**
Meirion Cl. CF63: Barry . . . 5B **106**
Meirion Pl. CF24: Card . . . 3F **97**
Meirwen Dr. CF5: Ely . . . 1E **99**
Melbourne Ct. CF14: Whit . . . 1D **84**
NP44: G'mdw . . . 2F **11**
Melbourne La. CF14: L'shn . . . 5H **71**
Melbourne Rd. CF14: L'shn . . . 5H **71**
Melbourne Way NP20: Newp . . . 6F **35**
Melfort Gdns. NP20: Newp . . . 6H **35**
Melfort Rd. NP20: Newp . . . 6H **35**
Meliden La. CF64: P'rth . . . 2D **108**
Meliden Rd. CF64: P'rth . . . 2D **108**
Melin Dwr CF3: Lwr M . . . 6A **32**
Melingriffith Dr. CF14: Whit . . . 2A **84**
Melin Gwlan CF83: Caer . . . 5B **28**
Mellon St. NP20: Newp . . . 5C **36**
Mellyn Mair Bus. Cen. CF3: Rum . . . 5A **88**
Melrose Av. CF23: Pen L . . . 6D **86**
Melrose Cl. CF3: St M . . . 5D **74**
Melrose Ct. CF11: Card . . . 2E **95**
Melrose Gdns. CF23: Pen L . . . 6D **86**
Melrose St. CF63: Barry . . . 1B **118**
Melville Av. CF3: St M . . . 5C **74**
Melville Cl. CF62: Barry . . . 4G **105**
Melville Ter. CF83: Caer . . . 5D **28**
Melyn y Gors CF63: Barry . . . 5C **106**
Menai Cl. CF38: Tont . . . 1E **43**
Menai Way CF3: Rum . . . 1B **88**
MENDALGIEF . . . 2C **54**
Mendalgief Retail Pk. NP20: Newp . . . 2B **54**
Mendalgief Rd. NP20: Newp . . . 1B **54**
Mendip Cl. NP11: Ris . . . 6H **17**
NP19: Newp . . . 3A **38**
Mendip Rd. CF3: L'rmy . . . 2G **87**
Mendip Vw. CF63: Barry . . . 1C **118**
Meon Cl. NP20: Bet . . . 5H **19**
Merchants Hill
NP4: P'nydd, P'pool . . . 1A **6**
Merchants Hill Cl. NP4: P'nydd . . . 1A **6**
Merches Gdns. CF11: Card . . . 6B **4** (5H **95**)
Merches Pl. CF11: Card . . . 5H **95**
Mercian Way NP16: Sed . . . 3G **63**
Mercia Rd. CF24: Card . . . 3F **97**
Meredith Cl. NP20: Newp . . . 1H **53**
Meredith Rd. CF24: Card . . . 3F **97**
Mere Path NP44: G'mdw . . . 2D **10**
Merevale CF64: Din P . . . 2F **107**
Merganser Ct. CF63: Barry . . . 2H **117**
Meridian Ct. CF14: Card . . . 5G **85**
Merioneth Ho. CF64: P'rth . . . 3D **108**
Merioneth Pl. CF62: Barry . . . 6H **105**
Merlin Cl. CF14: Thorn . . . 3G **71**
CF37: P'prdd . . . 6B 14
(off Pwll-Gwaun Rd.)
CF64: P'rth . . . 5E **109**
Merlin Cres. NP19: Newp . . . 2F **37**
Merlin Pl. CF63: Barry . . . 6A **106**
Mermaid Quay CF10: Card . . . 2C **102**
Merrett Ct. CF24: Card . . . 2G **97**
Merriotts Pl. NP19: Newp . . . 4E **37**
Mersey Wlk. NP20: Bet . . . 6E **19**
MERTHYR DYFAN . . . 5H **105**
Merthyr Dyfan Rd. CF62: Barry . . . 6H **105**
(not continuous)
Merthyr Dylan Rd. CF62: Barry . . . 5H **105**
Merthyr Rd. CF14: Tong . . . 4G **69**
CF14: Whit . . . 3D **84**
(Penlline Rd.)
CF14: Whit . . . 3F **85**
(Philog, The)
CF15: Tong . . . 4G **69**
CF37: P'prdd . . . 6D **14**
Merthyr St. CF24: Card . . . 1H **95**
CF63: Barry . . . 2H **117**
CF72: P'clun . . . 5D **64**
Mervinian Cl. CF10: Card . . . 6G **5** (5C **96**)
Mervyn Rd. CF14: Whit . . . 3D **84**
CF24: Card . . . 3F **97**
Mervyn St. CF37: R'fln . . . 4F **25**
Messina Ho. CF10: Card . . . 6F **5** (5B **96**)
Metal St. CF24: Card . . . 2H **5** (3D **96**)
Meteor St. CF24: Card . . . 3H **5** (3C **96**)
Methodist La. CF71: Llan M . . . 3B **110**
Methuen Rd. NP19: Newp . . . 4D **36**
Metroplex Cinema . . . 4B **36**
Mews, The CF11: Card . . . 1A **102**
NP11: C'crn . . . 1A **16**
NP20: Newp . . . 4H **35**
Meyrick Rd. CF5: Ely . . . 5E **93**
Meyricks NP44: F'wtr . . . 5D **10**
Michaelmas Cl. NP10: Roger . . . 3A **34**
Michaelston Cl. CF63: Barry . . . 5B **106**
Michaelston Ct. CF5: Ely . . . 5D **92**
MICHAELSTON-LE-PIT . . . 4C **100**
Michaelston Rd. CF5: Ely . . . 6D **92**
MICHAELSTON-SUPER-ELY . . . 4D **92**
MICHAELSTON-Y-FEDW . . . 5E **51**
Michael Way NP4: P'pool . . . 2B **6**
Michelston Ct. CF5: Ely . . . 5G **93**
Middlegate Ct. CF71: C'bri . . . 3D **90**
Middlegate Wlk. CF71: C'bri . . . 3D **90**
Middle St. CF37: P'prdd . . . 5D **14**
NP16: Chep . . . 2E **63**
Middleton Dr. CF23: Pontp . . . 4E **73**
Middle Way NP16: Bul . . . 5F **63**
Midway Pk. CF37: Up Bo . . . 6B **26**
Milburn Cl. CF62: Rho . . . 6D **114**
Mildred Cl. CF38: Bed . . . 4A **42**
Mildred St. CF38: Bed . . . 4A **42**
Mile Rd. CF64: P'rth . . . 4C **108**
Miles Ct. CF15: Taff W . . . 2E **69**
Milestone Cl. CF14: Heath . . . 1F **85**
Milford Cl. CF38: Tont . . . 1F **43**
Millands Pk. CF62: L'maes . . . 2F **111**
Millbrook Cl. CF64: Din P . . . 1H **107**
Millbrook Ct. NP26: Undy . . . 4D **58**
Millbrook Hgts. CF64: Din P . . . 1H **107**
Millbrook Pk. CF14: L'vne . . . 2A **72**
Millbrook Rd. CF64: Din P . . . 1H **107**
Mill Cl. CF14: L'shn . . . 4A **72**
CF64: Din P . . . 2G **107**
CF83: Caer . . . 5B **28**
Mill Comn. NP26: Undy . . . 4D **58**
Mill Ct. CF14: L'vne . . . 3A **72**
Millennium Ct. CF24: Card . . . 2D **96**
Millennium Plaza . . . 5B **4** (4H **95**)
Millennium Vw. CF11: Card . . . 6B **4** (5H **95**)
Millers Ride NP44: Llan . . . 2A **12**
Millfield CF14: L'vne . . . 2A **72**
CF72: P'clun . . . 6C **64**
Millfield Cl. CF3: St M . . . 1C **88**
Millfield Dr. CF71: C'bri . . . 3D **90**
Millfield Pk. NP26: Undy . . . 3D **58**
Millgate CF14: L'vne . . . 4A **72**
Mill Heath NP20: Bet . . . 4G **19**
Millheath Dr. CF14: L'vne, L'shn . . . 4A **72**
Mill Ho. Ct. NP44: F'wtr . . . 5E **11**
Millicent St. CF10: Card . . . 5E **5** (4B **96**)
Mill La. CF3: Cas . . . 1G **75**
CF3: L'rmy, St M . . . 5H **73**
CF3: St M . . . 5B **74**
CF5: L'dff . . . 1D **94**
CF10: Card . . . 6D **4** (5A **96**)
NP16: Chep . . . 2F **63**
NP26: Cald . . . 6C **60**
NP44: Llan . . . 3B **12**
Mill-Lay La. CF71: Llan M . . . 5B **110**
Mill Pde. NP20: Newp . . . 2D **54**
(not continuous)
Mill Pk. CF71: C'bri . . . 4C **90**
Mill Pl. CF5: Ely . . . 3A **94**
CF14: L'vne . . . 2B **72**
Millrace Cl. CF14: L'vne . . . 3A **72**
Mill Reen NP26: Undy . . . 4D **58**
Mill Rd. CF5: Ely . . . 3A **94**
CF14: L'vne, L'shn . . . 3A **72**
CF15: Tong . . . 4G **69**
CF64: Din P . . . 2G **107**
CF83: Caer . . . 5C **28**
NP4: P'nydd . . . 1A **6**
Mills Ct. CF62: Rho . . . 6E **115**
Mill St. CF37: P'prdd . . . 6B **14**
(not continuous)
NP11: Ris . . . 1F **33**
NP18: C'ln . . . 5H **21**
NP20: Newp . . . 4B **36**
Mill Ter. NP11: Ris . . . 6F **17**
Millwood CF14: L'vne . . . 3A **72**
Millwood Ri. CF62: Barry . . . 3E **117**
Milman St. NP20: Newp . . . 2C **54**
Milner St. NP19: Newp . . . 6F **37**
Milton Cl. CF38: Bed . . . 5A **42**
CF71: Llan M . . . 4D **110**
NP44: C'brn . . . 3F **11**
Milton Ct. NP19: Newp . . . 3D **38**
Milton Hill NP18: L'wrn . . . 4F **39**
Milton Pl. CF5: F'wtr . . . 1A **94**
CF83: Mac . . . 2C **30**
Milton Rd. CF62: Barry . . . 5G **105**
CF64: P'rth . . . 1D **108**
NP19: Newp . . . 4F **37**
Milton St. CF24: Card . . . 1G **5** (2C **96**)
Milverton Rd. CF3: L'rmy . . . 6A **74**
Milward Rd. CF63: Barry . . . 1B **118**
Minafon CF14: Rhiw . . . 4D **70**
Minavon CF14: Whit . . . 2D **84**
Minehead Av. CF64: Sul . . . 2G **119**
Minehead Rd. CF3: L'rmy . . . 1A **88**
Minister St. CF24: Card . . . 1H **95**
Minny St. CF24: Card . . . 1A **96**
(not continuous)
Minories *NP44: F'wtr . . . 4D 10*
(off Rede Rd.)
Minori Ho. *CF10: Card . . . 6C 96*
(off Ffordd Garthorne)
Minsmere Cl. CF3: St M . . . 6F **75**
Minster Cl. CF63: Barry . . . 5B **106**
Minster Rd. CF23: Pen L . . . 1E **97**
Min-y-Coed CF15: Rad . . . 6F **69**
Min-y-Mor CF62: Barry . . . 5D **116**
Min-y-Nant CF14: Rhiw . . . 6D **70**
Min yr Afon CF83: Mac . . . 2G **31**
MISKIN . . . 1F **79**
Miskin Ct. NP26: Undy . . . 4F **59**
Miskin Cres. CF72: P'clun . . . 6F **65**
Miskin Grn. NP44: Llan . . . 2A **12**
Miskin St. CF24: Card . . . 1E **5** (2A **96**)
CF62: Barry . . . 4F **117**
Mitchell Cl. CF3: St M . . . 2E **89**
Mitchell Rd. NP44: Llanf . . . 4B **12**

Mitchell Ter. CF37: P'prdd, T'rest 1D **24**
NP4: P'nydd 1A **6**
Mitel Bus. Pk. NP26: Pskwt 5F **61**
Miterdale Cl. CF23: Pen L 4B **86**
Mithras Way NP18: C'ln 3G **21**
Mitre Ct. CF5: L'dff 6C **84**
Mitre Pl. CF5: L'dff 6C **84**
Model Cotts. NP16: Math 6C **62**
Model House Craft & Design Cen. *2F 65*
(off Bull Ring)
Moel Fryn CF83: Caer 4H **27**
Moira Pl. CF24: Card 3G **5** (3C **96**)
Moira St. CF24: Card 3H **5** (3C **96**)
Moira Ter. CF24: Card 4G **5** (3C **96**)
Mole Cl. NP20: Bet 5E **19**
Molescombe NP44: F'wtr 4D **10**
Mona Cl. NP44: Pnwd 6F **9**
Mona Pl. CF24: Card 2F **97**
Monet Cres. NP19: Newp 2G **37**
Monico, The CF14: Heath 1E **85**
Monks Cl. NP26: Cald 4C **60**
Monk's Ditch NP18: L'wrn 3F **57**
Monkstone Cl. CF64: P'rth 4C **108**
Monkstone Ri. CF3: Rum 2A **88**
Monkton Cl. CF5: F'wtr 2G **93**
Monmouth Cl. CF38: Tont 1F **43**
NP4: New I 6G **7**
Monmouth Ct. CF83: Caer 5H **27**
NP20: Newp 6H **35**
Monmouth Cres. Cl. NP4: New I 1G **9**
Monmouth Dr. NP19: Newp 1G **37**
Monmouth Ho. CF64: P'rth 3D **108**
NP44: C'brn 2G **11**
Monmouth St. CF11: Card 6A **4** (5H **95**)
Monmouth Wlk. NP44: C'brn 2G **11**
Monmouth Way CF62: Barry 1H **117**
CF71: Bov 2D **110**
Monnow Ct. NP44: G'mdw 1C **10**
Monnow Wlk. NP20: Bet 5E **19**
Monnow Way NP20: Bet 5E **19**
Mons Cl. NP20: Newp 3A **36**
Montgomery Rd. CF62: Barry 3F **117**
NP20: Malp 3A **20**
Montgomery St. CF24: Card 6C **86**
Monthermer Rd. CF24: Card 6A **86**
Montreal Cl. NP20: Newp 6F **35**
Montresor Ct. NP44: Oakf 6B **12**
Moorby Ct. CF10: Card 5C **96**
Moordale Rd. CF11: Card 1A **102**
Moore Cl. CF5: Ely 4F **93**
Moore Cres. NP19: Newp 3D **38**
Moore Rd. CF5: Ely 4F **93**
Moorings, The CF64: P'rth 6A **102**
NP4: P'pool 4E **7**
NP19: Newp 1E **37**
Moor King Cl. CF3: St M 1F **89**
Moorland Av. NP19: Newp 6A **38**
Moorland Cres. CF38: Bed 4A **42**
Moorland Gdns. NP19: Newp 6A **38**
Moorland Hgts. CF37: P'prdd 1E **25**
Moorland Pk. NP19: Newp 6A **38**
Moorland Pl. CF24: Card 3F **97**
Moorland Rd. CF24: Card 2E **97**
(not continuous)
Moorlands Vw. NP26: Cald 6E **61**
Moors La. CF11: Card 4C **94**
CF24: Card 4D **96**
Moor St. NP16: Chep 2E **63**
Morden La. NP19: Newp 2E **37**
Morden Rd. NP19: Newp 2E **37**
Morel Ct. CF11: Card 3H **101**
Morel St. CF63: Barry 1A **118**
Moreton St. NP4: P'pool 3B **6**
Morfa Cotts. CF71: Llan M 1A **110**
Morfa Cres. CF3: Rum 2C **88**
Morfa La. CF5: Wen 5E **99**
CF71: Llan M 1A **110**
Morgan Arc. CF10: Card 5D **4** (4A **96**)
Morgan Jones Flats CF83: Caer 6C **28**
MORGANSTOWN 5F **69**
Morgan St. CF10: Card 5F **5** (4B **96**)
CF37: P'prdd 6C **14**
CF63: Barry 2B **118**
CF83: Caer 5C **28**
NP19: Newp 3D **36**
Morgan Way NP10: Duf 5G **53**
Morgraig Av. NP10: Coedk, Duf 6G **53**
Moriah Hill NP11: Ris 5E **17**
Morien Cres. CF37: R'fln 3F **25**
Morlais Ct. CF83: Caer 5H **27**
Morlais St. CF23: Card 6B **86**
CF63: Barry 1C **118**
Morley Cl. NP19: Newp 4B **38**
Morningside Wlk. CF62: Barry 4H **105**
MORNINGTON MEADOWS 4G **29**
Morris Av. CF14: L'shn 4F **71**
Morris Finer Cl. CF5: Ely 4A **94**
Morris St. NP19: Newp 5D **36**
MORRISTOWN 2C **108**
Mortimer Rd. CF11: Card 2F **95**
Mortimer Way CF62: Rho 6H **113**
Morton Ct. CF14: Heath 3A **86**
Morton Way NP20: Newp 1H **53**
Moseley Ter. NP44: Pnwd 4E **9**
Moss Rd. NP44: G'mdw 2D **10**
Mostyn Rd. CF5: Ely 5E **93**
Mound Rd. CF37: P'prdd 1A **24**
Mount, The CF5: L'dff 2E **95**
CF14: L'vne 1B **72**
CF64: Din P 2G **107**
Mountain La. NP4: Grif 6D **6**
Mountain Rd. CF15: P'rch 3H **67**
CF83: B'ws 1F **29**
CF83: Caer 1D **46**
NP4: Up Cwm, Up R 5A **8**
NP11: Ris 4G **17**
NP44: Up Cwm 5A **8**
Mountain Vw. CF37: R'fln 3F **25**
CF83: Abert 2F **27**
CF83: Caer 3C **28**
CF83: Mac 2F **31**
NP4: P'nydd 1A 6
(off Mountain Vw. Rd.)
Mountain Vw. Rd. NP4: P'nydd 1A **6**
Mount Ballan NP26: Pskwt 2E **61**
Mountbatten Cl. CF23: Cyn 2A **86**
NP19: Newp 2D **38**
Mountbatten Rd. CF62: Barry 4A **106**
Mount Bax NP19: Newp 4A **38**
Mountford Cl. NP10: Roger 2C **34**
Mountjoy Av. CF64: P'rth 1C **108**
Mountjoy Cl. CF64: P'rth 1D **108**
Mountjoy Cres. CF64: P'rth 1D **108**
Mountjoy La. CF64: P'rth 2C **108**
Mountjoy Pl. CF64: P'rth 1C **108**
NP20: Newp 6C **36**
Mountjoy Rd. NP20: Newp 6C **36**
Mountjoy St. NP20: Newp 6C **36**
MOUNTON 3A **62**
Mounton Cl. NP16: Chep 3D **62**
Mounton Dr. NP16: Chep 3D **62**
Mounton Rd. NP16: Chep 3B **62**
MOUNT PLEASANT 1A **6**
Mt. Pleasant CF63: Barry 1B **118**
NP16: Chep 2E **63**
NP20: Malp 4A **20**
Mt. Pleasant Av. CF3: L'rmy 1A **88**
Mt. Pleasant Cl. NP44: Pnwd 6D **8**
Mt. Pleasant La. CF3: L'rmy 1A **88**
Mt. Pleasant Rd. NP4: P'nydd 1A **6**
NP11: Ris 5E **17**
NP44: Pnwd 5D **8**
Mt. Pleasant Ter. NP11: P'waun 1A **16**
Mount Rd. CF64: Din P 2G **107**
NP4: C'avn 1D **6**
NP11: Ris 5E **17**
Mountside NP11: Ris 6H **17**
Mt. Stuart Sq. CF10: Card 1B **102**
Mount Way NP16: Chep 1D **62**
(not continuous)
Moxon Rd. NP20: Malp 6A **20**
Moxon St. CF63: Barry 1C **118**
Moyle Gro. NP18: P'hir 1F **21**
Moy Rd. CF15: Taff W 1E **69**
CF24: Card 1B **96**
Moy Rd. Ind. Est. CF15: Taff W 1E **69**
Muirton Rd. CF24: Card 3F **97**
Mulberry Cl. CF38: Llan F 6C **42**
NP10: Roger 2A **34**
Mulberry Ct. *CF62: Barry 4E 117*
(off St Nicholas Ct.)
Mulberry Dr. CF23: Pontp 2G **73**
Mulcaster Av. NP19: Newp 1H **55**
Mullins Av. CF3: Rum 2B **88**
Mundy Pl. CF24: Card 1A **96**
Muni Art Cen. 6C **14**
Munnings Dr. NP19: Newp 2G **37**
Munro Pl. CF62: Barry 1G **117**
MURCH 3H **107**
Murch Cres. CF64: Din P 2A **108**
Murch Rd. CF64: Din P 2H **107**
Mur Gwyn CF14: Rhiw 5E **71**
Murlande Way CF62: Rho 6F **115**
Murrayfield Rd. CF14: Heath 2F **85**
Murray Wlk. CF11: Card 4F **95**
Murrel Cl. CF5: Ely 6E **93**
Murrells Cl. CF38: Llan F 5D **42**
Museum Av. CF10: Card 1C **4** (2A **96**)
Museum Ct. NP4: Grif 1E **9**
Mus. of Magical Machines 4D **4** (4A **96**)
Museum Pl. CF10: Card 1D **4** (2A **96**)
Museum St. NP18: C'ln 5H **21**
MWYNDY 5G **65**
Mwyndy Ter. CF72: Groes F 5G **65**
Mylo Griffiths Cl. CF5: L'dff 4A **84**
MYNACHDY 4F **85**
Mynachdy Rd. CF14: Card 5F **85**
CF14: Llan N 5E **85**
Mynydd Ct. NP4: P'pool 5C **6**
Mynydd Maen Rd. NP44: Pnwd, Up Cwm 5C **8**
Mynydd Vw. NP4: P'pool 5B **6**
Myra Hess Cl. NP19: Newp 3D **38**
Myrtle Cl. CF64: P'rth 2C **108**
NP10: Roger 6D **34**
Myrtle Cotts. NP18: C'ln 5A **22**
Myrtle Dr. NP10: Roger 5D **34**
Myrtle Gro. CF63: Barry 6C **106**
NP19: Newp 4H **37**
Myrtle Pl. NP16: Chep 1F **63**
Myrtles, The NP16: Tut 1G **63**

N

Nailsea Ct. CF64: Sul 2H **119**
Nant Celyn Cl. NP44: Pnwd 5C **8**
Nant Coch Dr. NP20: Newp 5G **35**
Nant Coch Ri. NP20: Newp 5G **35**
Nant Ddu CF83: Caer 1C **46**
Nant Dyfed CF38: Bed 6H **41**
Nant-Fawr Cl. CF23: Cyn 1B **86**
Nant-Fawr Cres. CF23: Cyn 1B **86**
Nant-Fawr Rd. CF23: Cyn 1B **86**
NANTGARW 4D **44**
Nantgarw China Works Mus. 3E **45**
Nantgarw Rd. CF83: Caer 2H **45**
Nant Isaf CF5: Wen 4E **99**
Nantsor Rd. NP18: P'hir 2H **13**
Nant Talwg Way CF62: Barry 2D **116**
Nant Walla CF14: Rhiw 5E **71**
Nant y Coed CF37: P'prdd 5A **14**
Nant-y-Dall Av. CF37: R'fln 5F **25**
Nant-y-Dowlais CF5: Ely 5C **92**
Nant-y-Drope CF5: Ely 5D **92**
Nant y Felin CF38: E Isaf 6E **43**
Nant y Ffynnon CF5: St F 3B **82**
Nant y Garn NP11: Ris 3C **16**
Nant y Gth. CF15: Gwae G 2D **68**
Nant y Gwladys CF5: St F 2C **82**
Nant-y-Hwyad CF83: Caer 6A **28**
Nant-y-Milwr Cl. NP44: H'lys 6B **10**
Nant-y-Moor Cl. NP10: Coedk 5C **52**
Nant-y-Mynydd CF37: Glyn 1D **14**
Nant-y-Pepra CF5: Ely 5D **92**
Nant-y-Plac CF5: Ely 5D **92**
Nant-yr-Adar CF71: Llan M 4C **110**
Nant-yr-Arthur CF5: Ely 5D **92**
Nant-yr-Ely CF5: Ely 5C **92**
Nant-y-Rhos CF5: Ely 5D **92**
Nant y Wedal CF14: Card 5A **86**
Napier St. CF83: Mac 2F **31**
Narberth Cl. NP10: Coedk 6G **53**
Narberth Ct. CF62: Barry 6H **105**
CF83: Caer 5G **27**
Narberth Cres. NP44: Llan 2B **12**
Narberth Rd. CF5: Ely 5H **93**
Narcissus Gro. NP10: Roger 3A **34**
Naseby Cl. CF23: Pontp 4F **73**
NASH 6A **56**
Nash Cl. NP10: Roger 3D **34**
Nash Dr. NP19: Newp 1H **55**
Nash Gro. NP19: Newp 6H **37**
(not continuous)
Nash Mead NP19: Newp 3A **56**
Nash Rd. NP18: Newp 4B **56**
NP19: Newp 6H **37**
Nasturtium Way CF23: Pontp 4D **72**
National Assembly for Wales, The 1C **102**
National Indoor Athletic Stadium 3D **86**
National Mus. of Wales 1D **4** (2A **96**)
Navigation Rd. NP11: Ris 4D **16**
Navigation St. CF83: Tret 2A **30**
Neale St. CF62: Barry 1G **117**
Neath Ct. NP44: G'mdw 1C **10**
Neath St. CF24: Card 4E **97**
Neddern Ct. NP26: Cald 4C **60**
Neddern Way NP26: Cald 3C **60**
Neerings NP44: F'wtr 3C **10**
Neilson Cl. CF24: Card 4D **96**
Nelson Ct. CF10: Card 6G **5** (5C **96**)
Nelson Dr. NP19: Newp 3C **38**
Nelson Ho. *CF10: Card 6B 96*
(off Loudoun Sq.)
Nelson Rd. CF62: Barry 5A **106**
Nelson St. NP16: Chep 2E **63**
(not continuous)
Neptune Ct. CF24: Card 5D **96**
Nesta Rd. CF5: Card 3D **94**

Neston Rd. NP19: Newp 3B 38
Nethercourt NP44: G'mdw 2D 10
Netherwent Vw. NP26: Magor 3C 58
Nettlefold Rd. CF24: Card 5D 96
Neuadda Cl. NP10: Bass 1B 52
Nevern Wlk. NP44: Llan 3B 12
Neville Pk. NP10: St Bri 4G 77
Neville Pl. CF11: Card 5A 4 (4G 95)
Neville St. CF11: Card 4A 4 (4G 95)
Nevin Cres. CF3: Rum 3A 88
Newbarn Path NP44: Llanf 4B 12
Newborough Av. CF14: L'shn 5G 71
Newbridge Ct. CF37: P'prdd 5D 14
Newbridge Rd. CF72: L'sant 1F 65
Newby Ct. CF10: Card 5B 96
Newchurch Ct. NP44: G'mdw 2E 11
New Cotts. NP19: Newp 3C 36
Newent Rd. CF3: St M 1D 88
New Forest Vw. CF71: C'bri 4E 91
Newfoundland Rd. CF14: Card 5G 85
Newgale Cl. CF62: Barry 5H 105
Newgale Pl. CF5: Ely 5H 93
Newgale Row NP44: C'brn 2H 11
New George St. CF10: Card 2C 102
New Ho. Ct. CF63: Barry 6B 106
Newhouse Farm Ind. Est. NP16: Math 6F 63
New Ho's. CF37: P'cae 5A 24
NEW INN 5G 7
New Inn Cen. CF37: P'prdd 6C 14
Newlands Ct. CF14: L'shn 4A 72
Newlands Rd. CF3: Rum 4D 88
Newlands St. CF62: Barry 2H 117
Newman Cl. NP19: Newp 4D 38
Newman Rd. NP4: C'avn 1B 6
New Mill Cnr. CF72: P'clun 1F 79
New Mill Gdns. CF72: P'clun 5F 65
Newminster Rd. CF23: Pen L 1E 97
Newnham Pl. NP44: C'brn 2G 11
New Pk. Rd. NP11: Ris 4B 16
New Pk. Ter. CF37: T'rest 2E 25
New Pastures NP20: Newp 1A 54
NEWPORT 4C 36
Newport Arc. *NP20: Newp* *4B 36*
(off High St.)
Newport Athletic Club Ground 4C 36
Newport Castle 4C 36
Newport FC 1H 55
Newport Gwent Dragons RUFC 4D 36
Newport Ind. Est. NP19: Newp 2B 56
Newport International Sports Village 2H 55
Newport Leisure Cen. 5C 36
Newport Mus. & Art Gallery 5C 36
Newport Provisions Market 4B 36
Newport Retail Pk. NP19: Newp 1B 56
Newport Rd. CF3: Cas 2G 75
CF3: L'rmy, Rum 5G 87
CF3: St M 4E 75
CF23: Pen L 1E 97
CF24: Card 3F 5 (3B 96)
CF24: Pen L 1E 97
CF83: B'ws, Mac, Tret 4F 29
NP4: New I 2G 9
NP11: Ris 1F 33
NP16: Chep, Pwllm 6A 62
NP20: Oakf 3A 20
NP26: Cald 5B 60
NP26: Magor 3B 58
NP44: C'iog 5H 9
NP44: Oakf, Llan, Llanf 1B 20
Newport Rd. La. CF24: Card 3G 5 (3C 96)
Newport Stadium 1H 55
Newport Station (Rail) 4B 36
Newport St. CF11: Card 1A 102
Newport Tennis Cen. 2G 55
New Quay Rd. NP19: Newp 3E 55
New Rd. CF3: Rum 5G 87
CF37: Y'bwl 1A 14
NP4: Grif, New I 6E 7
NP18: C'ln 6A 22
NP26: Cald 5B 60
New Row CF83: Mac 3F 31
NP44: H'lys 4A 10
New Ruperra St. NP20: Newp 6C 36
New St. CF83: Caer 3B 28
NP20: Newp 1D 54
NP44: Pnwd 6E 9
New Theatre 2D 4 (3A 96)
NEWTON 6D 88
Newton Ct. CF24: Card 4G 5 (4C 96)
NEWTON GREEN 6B 62
Newton Ind. Est. NP11: C'keys 4A 16
Newton Rd. CF3: Rum 4C 88
(not continuous)
CF11: Card 5F 95
Newton St. CF63: Barry 1B 118
Newton Way NP20: Malp 5H 19
Newton Wynd NP44: F'wtr 4D 10
NEWTOWN 5D 42
Newtown Ind. Est. CF38: Llan F 4D 42
Newydd Ct. CF15: Tong 5G 69
New Zealand Rd. CF14: Card 6G 85
(not continuous)
Neyland Cl. CF38: Tont 1F 43
Neyland Ct. CF62: Barry 5H 105
Neyland Path NP44: F'wtr 3D 10
Neyland Pl. CF5: Ely 5H 93
Niagara St. CF37: T'rest 1D 24
Nicholas Ct. CF15: Rad 2H 83
Nicholas St. NP4: P'pool 3C 6
Nicholl Ct. CF71: Bov 3D 110
Nicholson Webb Cl. CF5: L'dff 4H 83
Nidd Cl. NP20: Bet 6E 19
Nidd Wlk. *NP20: Bet* *6E 19*
(off Ogmore Cres.)
Nightingale Cl. NP26: Cald 6D 60
Nightingale Ct. NP10: Duf 4G 53
Nightingale Gdns. CF38: Chu V 2D 42
Nightingale Pl. CF64: Din P 2A 108
Nightingale's Bush CF37: P'prdd 1E 25
Nightingale Ter. NP4: P'nydd 1A 6
Nile Rd. CF37: T'rest 1D 24
Ninian Pk. 5F 95
Ninian Pk. Rd. CF11: Card 5A 4 (4F 95)
Ninian Park Station (Rail) 5F 95
Ninian Rd. CF23: Card 5B 86
Nolton Pl. NP44: C'brn 4E 11
Nora St. CF24: Card 2D 96
Norbury Av. CF5: F'wtr 2A 94
Norbury Ct. CF5: F'wtr 2A 94
Norbury Rd. CF5: F'wtr 2A 94
Nordale Ri. CF63: Barry 1C 118
Nordale Rd. CF71: Llan M 3D 110
Norfolk Cl. NP44: G'mdw 2C 10
Norfolk Ct. CF15: Rad 6F 69
Norfolk Rd. NP19: Newp 3F 37
Norfolk St. CF5: Card 3D 94
Norman Ct. NP26: Cald 5C 60
Normandy Way NP16: Chep 1D 62
Norman Rd. CF14: Whit 3D 84
Norman St. CF24: Card 1B 96
NP18: C'ln 5H 21
Norman Ter. NP18: C'ln 5H 21
Norman Way NP26: Pskwt 6F 61
Norrell Cl. CF11: Card 4D 94
Norris Cl. CF64: P'rth 6F 101
Norseman Cl. CF62: Rho 5C 114
Norse Way NP16: Sed 3H 63
Northam Av. CF3: L'rmy 2G 87
Nth. Church St. CF10: Card 5B 96
Northcliffe CF64: P'rth 6B 102
Northcliffe Dr. CF64: P'rth 6B 102
Nth. Clive St. CF11: Card 6G 95
Northcote La. CF24: Card 2B 96
Northcote St. CF24: Card 2B 96
Northcote Ter. CF63: Barry 1C 118
North Ct. NP4: P'nydd 1A 6
Nth. Edward St. CF10: Card 3E 5 (3B 96)
Northern Av. CF14: Heath, Whit 2D 84
CF14: Whit 5A 70
Northfield Cl. NP18: C'ln 3F 21
Northfield Rd. NP18: C'ln 3G 21
Nth. Lake Dr. NP10: Coedk 6E 53
Northlands CF3: Rum 5H 87
Nth. Luton Pl. CF24: Card 4H 5 (4C 96)
Nth. Morgan St. CF11: Card 4G 95
North Pk. Rd. CF24: Card 3E 97
Nth. Pentwyn Link Rd. CF23: Pontp, St M 5H 73
North Ri. CF14: L'shn 4A 72
North Rd. CF14: Card, Whit 1B 4 (4F 85)
CF64: Sul 1E 119
CF71: C'bri 3C 90
NP4: P'pool 3B 6
NP11: C'crn, P'waun 1A 16
NP44: C'iog 6G 9
North St. CF11: Card 6H 95
CF37: P'prdd 5D 14
NP20: Newp 4B 36
Northumberland Rd. NP19: Newp 3F 37
Northumberland St. CF5: Card 4E 95
North Vw. CF15: Taff W 1F 69
North Vw. Ter. CF83: Caer 6D 28
NORTHVILLE 1H 11
North Wlk. CF62: Barry 1F 117
NP44: C'brn 1G 11
Norton Av. CF14: Heath 3F 85
Norwegian Church Arts Cen. 2C 102
Norwich Rd. CF23: Pen L 6F 87
Norwood CF14: Thorn 3H 71
Norwood Ct. CF24: Card 1H 5 (2C 96)
Norwood Cres. CF63: Barry 6C 106
Nottage Rd. CF5: Ely 5G 93
Nottingham St. CF5: Card 3D 94
Novello Wlk. NP19: Newp 4C 38
Nuns Cres. CF37: P'prdd 5B 14
Nurseries, The NP18: L'stne 1H 39
Nursery Cotts. CF64: Din P 3F 107
Nursery Ri. CF83: B'ws 2E 29
Nurston Cl. CF62: Rho 5C 114
Nut Wlk. CF71: Llan M 5C 110
Nyth-y-Dryw CF62: Rho 6E 115
Nyth y Eos *CF62: Rho* *6G 115*
(off Bryn y Gloyn)

O

Oak Bluff NP16: Pwllm 4C 62
Oak Cl. CF72: T Grn 3E 65
NP16: Bul 5E 63
NP26: Undy 4D 58
Oak Ct. CF15: Tong 3H 69
CF64: P'rth 3C 108
NP4: P'nydd 1A 6
Oakdale Cl. NP18: C'ln 5F 21
Oakdale Path NP44: G'mdw 3E 11
Oakdale Pl. NP4: P'nydd 1A 6
Oakdene Cl. CF23: Cyn 3C 86
OAKFIELD 5H 11
Oakfield NP18: C'ln 4F 21
Oakfield Av. NP16: Chep 1D 62
Oakfield Cres. CF38: Tont 2H 43
Oakfield Gdns. CF83: Mac 3H 31
NP20: Newp 5A 36
Oakfield M. CF24: Card 2D 96
NP44: Oakf 4H 11
Oakfield Rd. CF62: Barry 6F 105
NP20: Newp 5H 35
NP44: Oakf 4H 11
Oakfields CF3: M'fld 4H 75
Oakfield St. CF24: Card 2C 96
Oakford Cl. CF23: Pontp 4E 73
Oak Gro. CF62: St A 2B 112
Oak Ho. CF14: Whit 6A 70
Oakland Cres. CF37: C'fydd 3F 15
Oaklands CF64: Din P 1G 107
CF72: P'clun 5F 65
NP18: P'hir 1E 21
Oaklands Cl. CF3: St M 6C 74
Oaklands Pk. NP26: Pskwt 5G 61
Oaklands Pk. Dr. NP10: R'drn 6A 34
Oaklands Rd. NP4: Grif 2D 8
NP19: Newp 4F 37
Oaklands Vw. NP44: G'mdw 2C 10
Oakland Ter. CF37: C'fydd 3F 15
NP44: C'brn, Oakf 5G 11
Oak La. CF83: Mac 3H 31
Oakleafe Dr. CF23: Pontp 5E 73
Oakleigh Ct. NP44: H'lys 5B 10
Oakley Cl. NP26: Cald 4B 60
Oakley Pl. CF11: Card 1H 101
Oakley St. NP19: Newp 6F 37
Oakley Way NP26: Cald 4B 60
Oakmead Cl. CF23: Pontp 4E 73
Oakmeadow Ct. CF3: St M 6D 74
Oakmeadow Dr. CF3: St M 1D 88
Oakridge E. CF14: Thorn 2H 71
Oakridge W. CF14: Thorn 3G 71
Oak Rd. CF72: L'harry 5A 78
NP10: Roger 3B 34
Oaks, The CF14: L'vne 3B 72
CF38: Llan F 3D 42
CF83: Mac 3H 31
NP44: C'iog 6H 9
Oaks Cl. NP20: Newp 1A 54
Oaksford NP44: F'wtr 3C 10
Oak St. CF37: R'fln 3G 25
NP19: Newp 1D 36
NP44: C'brn 3G 11
Oak St. Cl. CF37: R'fln 3G 25
Oak Ter. NP11: C'keys 2A 16
Oak Tree Cl. CF15: Rad 1E 83
NP4: New I 4G 7
Oak Tree Ct. CF23: Pontp 2G 73
NP19: Newp 4H 37
NP44: Oakf 4G 11
Oak Tree Dr. NP10: Roger 2H 33
Oakway CF5: F'wtr 2G 93
Oak Wood Av. CF23: Pen L 5E 87
Oakwood Cl. CF64: L'dgh 5G 101
Oakwood St. CF37: T'rest 4E 25
Oban St. CF63: Barry 1B 118
Ocean Bldgs. *CF10: Card* *1C 102*
(off Bute Cres.)
Ocean Rd. CF24: Card 5E 97
Ocean Way CF24: Card 5H 5 (4D 96)
Ochr y Coed CF11: Card 5A 4 (4H 95)
Octagon, The NP16: Bul 5F 63
Octavius Cl. NP10: Duf 6G 53

Odeon Cinema
Cardiff 1C 102
Odet Ct. CF14: Whit 6A 70
O'Donnell Rd. CF63: Barry 6A 106
Odyn's Fee CF62: Rho 5C 114
Offas Cl. NP16: Sed 3G 63
Offway NP44: F'wtr 5E 11
Ogmore Ct. CF83: Caer 5H 27
Ogmore Cres. NP20: Bet 6E 19
Ogmore Pl. CF63: Barry 5A 106
NP44: Llan 3B 12
Ogmore Rd. CF5: Ely 5G 93
Ogwen Dr. CF23: Cyn 1B 86
Okehampton Av. CF3: L'rmy 5A 74
Old Bakery Ct. CF15: P'rch 4A 68
Old Barn NP19: Newp 1F 37
Old Barn Ct. NP26: Undy 4F 59
Old Barn Est. NP19: Newp 1F 37
Old Barry Rd. CF64: P'rth 5G 101
Old Brewery Quarter, The CF10: Card 5D 4
Old Bri. Ct. NP44: G'mdw 6A 8
Old Bulwark Rd. NP16: Bul 3E 63
Oldbury Rd. NP44: C'brn 3G 11
Old Cardiff Rd. NP20: Newp 2H 53
Old Chepstow Rd. NP18: L'stne 1G 39
Old Church Rd. CF14: Whit 2C 84
Old Clipper Rd. CF10: Card 1E 103
(not continuous)
Old Est. Yd. NP4: P'pool 4E 7
Old Farm La. CF15: Cre 6E 67
Old Farm M. CF64: Din P 2G 107
Old Farm Shop. Cen., The NP16: Bul 6F 63
Old Fld. Rd. CF14: Tong 5A 70
OLD FURNACE 4A 6
Old Furnace Rd. CF83: Caer 5A 28
Old Garden Ct. CF15: Rad 1F 83
Old Grn. Ct. CF3: M'fld 5A 76
Old Grn. Rdbt. NP20: Newp 4C 36
Old Hall Cl. NP10: Duf 4H 53
Old Hill NP18: C'ln 1A 38
Old Hill, The NP16: Tut 1F 63
Oldhill CF3: St M 1B 88
Old Hill Cres. NP18: C'ln 2B 38
Old Langstone Ct. Rd. NP18: L'stne 1F 39
Old Malt Ho. CF64: Din P 2G 107
Old Mkt. CF5: Wen 5E 99
Old Mill Dr. CF5: St F 2C 82
Old Mill Rd. CF14: L'vne 3A 72
Oldmill Rd. CF63: Barry 1C 118
Old Nantgawr Rd. CF15: N'grw 3E 45
Old Newport Rd. CF3: St M 5D 74
Old Oak Cl. NP16: Bul 5F 63
Old Parish Rd. CF37: Y'bwl 1A 14
Old Pk. Ter. CF37: T'rest 2E 25
OLD PENYGARN 1C 6
Old Pill Farm Ind. Est. NP26: Cald 6E 61
Old Port Rd. CF5: Wen 2D 98
Old Roman Rd. NP18: L'stne 5G 23
Old Row NP26: Sud 6H 61
NP44: H'lys 4A 10
Old School Ct. NP11: C'keys 2A 16
Old School Pl. NP4: P'nydd 1A 6
Old School Rd. CF5: Ely 4A 94
Old Shirenewton Rd. NP26: C'went 1E 61
Old Station Yd. CF83: B'ws 2F 29
Old Stone La. NP26: Undy 4E 59
Old Vicarage Cl. CF14: L'shn 5H 71
Old Village Rd. CF62: Barry 4E 117
Oldwell Ct. CF23: Pen L 5C 86
Old Well La. NP26: Undy 5F 59
O'Leary Dr. CF11: Card 3H 101
Oliphant Circ. NP20: Malp 4H 19
Oliver Rd. NP19: Newp 5G 37
Oliver St. CF37: P'prdd 6A 14
Oliver Ter. CF37: T'rest 3E 25
Ollivant Cl. CF5: L'dff 4H 83
Olway Cl. NP44: Llan 4A 12
(not continuous)
Olympic Gymnastic Training Cen. 3C 86
Ombersley La. NP20: Newp 5H 35
Ombersley Rd. NP20: Newp 5H 35
O'Neal Av. NP19: Newp 3G 55
Ontario Way CF23: Cyn 2C 86
Open Hearth Cl. NP4: Grif 1E 9
Orange Gro. CF5: F'wtr 6G 83
Orangery Wlk. NP10: Duf 4H 53
Orbit St. CF24: Card 2H 5 (3C 96)
Orchard, The CF71: A'thin 2F 91
NP18: P'hir 1F 21
Orchard Av. NP16: Bul 5E 63
Orchard Castle CF14: Thorn 3F 71
Orchard Cl. CF3: M'fld 5H 75
CF5: Wen 4E 99
CF71: Bov 4F 111
NP10: Bass 6B 34
NP26: Cald 6C 60
Orchard Ct. CF14: L'vne 1H 71
NP19: Newp 2D 36
Orchard Cres. CF64: Din P 2H 107
Orchard Dr. CF14: Whit 2C 84
CF37: Glyn 2C 14
CF62: Barry 1H 117
CF71: Llan M 5C 110
Orchard Farm Cl. NP16: Sed 3H 63
Orchard Gdns. NP16: Chep 1F 63
NP26: Pskwt 5G 61
Orchard Gro. CF15: Morg 5F 69
Orchard La. NP19: Newp 2E 37
NP44: C'brn 6E 9
Orchard Lodge CF71: Bov 3E 111
Orchard M. NP19: Newp 2D 36
Orchard Pk. CF3: St M 6B 74
Orchard Pk. Cl. CF3: St M 6C 74
Orchard Pl. CF11: Card 3F 95
NP44: C'brn 3F 11
Orchard Ri. CF64: P'rth 1C 108
NP16: Pwllm 5B 62
Orchard Rd. NP18: C'ln 3G 21
Orchards, The CF14: L'shn 5H 71
Orchard St. NP19: Newp 2D 36
Orchard Way CF62: St A 6D 112
Orchid Cl. CF3: St M 1E 89
Orchid Ct. NP44: F'wtr 4C 10
Orchid Dr. NP26: Cald 6E 61
Orchid Mdw. NP16: Pwllm 5B 62
Ordell St. CF24: Card 3D 96
Oregano Cl. CF3: St M 5E 75
Oriel Ho. CF24: Card 4H 5 (4C 96)
Oriel Rd. NP19: Newp 4E 37
Orion Ct. CF24: Card 3H 5 (3C 96)
Ormerod Rd. NP16: Sed 3H 63
Ormonde Cl. CF23: Pen L 4E 87
Osborne Rd. NP4: P'nydd, P'pool 1B 6
Osborne Sq. CF11: Card 6G 95
Osbourne Cl. NP19: Newp 4E 37
Osprey Cl. CF3: St M 5C 74
CF64: P'rth 6E 109
Osprey Ct. CF63: Barry 3H 117
Osprey Dr. NP26: Cald 6D 60
Oswald Rd. NP20: Newp 1C 54
(not continuous)
Oswestry Cl. CF3: Rum 4A 88
Othery Pl. CF3: L'rmy 5A 74
Otter Cl. NP20: Bet 5E 19
Outfall La. NP10: St Bri 5F 77
Overstone Ct. CF10: Card 6A 96
Ovington Ter. CF5: Card 2D 94
Owain Cl. CF23: Cyn 3C 86
CF64: P'rth 2C 108
Owain Ct. CF62: St A 5D 112
Owen Cl. NP18: C'ln 3G 21
Owens Cl. CF62: Barry 2G 117
Owen's Ct. CF14: Whit 3F 85
Owen St. CF37: R'fln 5G 25
Oxford Arc. CF10: Card 5D 4 (4A 96)
Oxford Cl. NP18: C'ln 3F 21
Oxford La. CF24: Card 2G 5 (3C 96)
Oxford St. CF15: N'grw 3C 44
CF24: Card 1G 5 (2C 96)
CF37: T'rest 3E 25
CF62: Barry 4E 117
NP4: Grif 6E 7
NP16: Chep 2E 63
NP19: Newp 4E 37
Oxtens NP44: F'wtr 5D 10
Oxwich Cl. CF5: F'wtr 2B 94
Oxwich Rd. NP19: Newp 2F 55
Oyster Bend CF64: Sul 3H 119
Oystermouth M. NP10: St Bri 6G 53
Oystermouth Way NP10: Coedk 6G 53

P

Pace Cl. CF5: L'dff 5H 83
Pace Rd. NP44: F'wtr 4D 10
Pacific Bus. Pk. CF24: Card 5F 97
Pacific Rd. CF24: Card 4F 97
Padarn Cl. CF23: Cyn 2B 86
Padarn Pl. NP44: Pnwd 6E 9
Paddock, The CF14: L'vne 2A 72
CF23: Pen L 5C 86
CF71: C'bri 4E 91
NP16: Bul 4D 62
Paddock Cl. NP44: Pnwd 6D 8
Paddock Pl. CF63: Barry 6B 106
Paddock Ri. NP44: Llan 4B 12
Paddocks, The CF38: Chu V 2D 42
(not continuous)
CF64: P'rth 4E 109
CF72: Groes F 1C 80
NP18: C'ln 4F 21
Paddocks, The NP18: L'stne 1H 39
NP26: Undy 4F 59
NP44: Llan 4B 12
Paddocks Cres. CF72: P'clun 1B 78
Page Dr. CF23: Card 6G 87
Paget La. CF11: Card 6H 95
Paget Pl. CF64: P'rth 6B 102
Paget Rd. CF62: Barry 5G 117
(not continuous)
CF64: P'rth 6A 102
Paget St. CF11: Card 6H 95
Paget Ter. CF64: P'rth 6B 102
Palace Av. CF5: L'dff 1D 94
Palace Ct. CF23: Cyn 1C 86
Palace Rd. CF5: L'dff 1D 94
Palalwyf Av. CF72: P'clun 6D 64
Pallot Way CF23: Card 1F 97
Palm Cl. NP4: New I 4H 7
Palmers Dr. CF5: Ely 4A 94
Palmerston Rd. CF63: Barry 1D 118
Palmerston Workshops
CF63: Barry 6D 106
PALMERSTOWN 6D 106
Palmer St. CF63: Barry 5D 106
Palmers Vale Bus. Cen. CF63: Barry 6D 106
Palm Sq. NP19: Newp 5G 37
Palmyra Pl. NP20: Newp 5C 36
Pandy NP44: G'mdw 2E 11
Pandy La. CF83: Mac 2G 31
Pandy-Mawr Rd. CF83: B'ws 1D 28
Pandy Pk. 2A 16
Pandy Rd. CF83: B'ws 2C 28
Pandy Vw. NP11: C'keys 2A 16
Pant Bach CF15: P'rch 5A 68
Pantbach Av. CF14: Heath 3F 85
Pantbach Pl. CF14: Heath 3E 85
Pantbach Rd. CF14: Heath, Rhiw 1E 85
Pant Du Rd. CF37: C'fydd 1F 15
PANTEG 6H 7
Panteg CF15: P'rch 5A 68
Panteg Cl. CF5: Ely 6D 92
Panteg Ind. Est. NP4: Grif 1E 9
Panteg Way NP4: New I 6F 7
Pant Glas CF23: L'dyrn 6G 73
Pantglas CF15: P'rch 5A 68
Pant-Glas Ct. NP10: Bass 1B 52
Pant Glas Ind. Est. CF83: B'ws 4H 29
Pant Glas Rd. NP44: Oakf 1F 19
Pant Gwyn Cl. NP44: H'lys 5B 10
Pantgwynlais CF15: Tong 4H 69
Pant La. *NP20: Newp 1B 36*
(off Pant Rd.)
Pant Llygodfa CF83: Caer 2A 46
PANTMAWR 5B 70
Pantmawr Ct. CF14: Rhiw 5B 70
Pantmawr Rd. CF14: Rhiw 6B 70
CF14: Whit 6B 70
Pant Pl. CF15: Taff W 6D 44
Pant Rd. NP20: Newp 1B 36
Pant Tawel La. CF15: Rad 1D 82
Pant-y-Celyn CF62: St A 5C 112
Pantycelyn Dr. CF83: Caer 4B 28
Pantycelyn Rd. CF64: L'dgh 5F 101
Pant y Dderwen CF72: T Grn 4C 64
Pant-y-Deri Cl. CF5: Ely 5G 93
PANTYGRAIG-WEN 5A 14
Pantygraigwen Rd. CF37: P'prdd 5A 14
Pant-yr-Eos NP44: Pnwd 1F 11
Pant-yr-Heol Cl. NP44: H'lys 6B 10
Pant yr Wyn CF23: Pen L 5B 86
Paper Mill Rd. CF11: Card 3C 94
Parade, The CF14: Whit 3B 84
CF24: Card 2F 5 (3B 96)
CF37: P'prdd 5D 14
CF38: Chu V 3E 43
CF62: Barry 5E 117
CF64: Din P 2A 108
NP44: C'brn 2G 11
Parc Av. CF83: Caer 4E 29
NP44: Pnwd 5D 8
Parc Castell-y-Mynach CF15: Cre 5E 67
(not continuous)
Parc Cefn Onn Country Pk. 6H 47
Parc Cenedlaethol Bannau Brycheiniog 1F 7
Parc Clwyd CF63: Barry 5C 106
Parc Hafod CF14: Whit 1B 84
Parc Ifor Hen CF72: P'clun 6G 65
Parc Manwerthu Tonysgyboriau
CF72: T Grn 3E 65
Parc Nant Celyn CF38: E Isaf 4G 43
Parc Nantgarw CF15: N'grw 3D 44
Parc Pontypandy CF83: Caer 3D 28
Parc-ty-Glas CF14: L'shn 5G 71
Parc ty Glas Ind. Est. CF14: L'shn 6G 71
Parc y Brain Rd. NP10: Roger 1D 34
NP20: Bet 1D 34

Parc-y-Bryn CF15: Cre 5D **66**
CF38: Llan F 3D **42**
Parc-y-Coed CF15: Cre 6E **67**
Parc-y-Felin CF15: Cre 6D **66**
Parc-y-Felin St. CF83: Caer 5D **28**
Parc-y-Fro CF15: Cre 5E **67**
Parc-y-Nant CF15: N'grw 4E **45**
Pardoe Cres. CF62: Barry 1G **117**
Pardoe Thomas Cl. *NP20: Newp 6C 36*
(off Francis St.)
Parfitt St. NP19: Newp 6H **37**
Parfitt Ter. NP44: Pnwd 6D **8**
Parish Rd. CF38: Bed 4A **42**
Park Av. CF5: Ely 1E **99**
CF14: Whit 1B **84**
CF62: Barry 5F **117**
CF83: B'ws 3G **29**
NP10: Roger 3B **34**
NP20: Newp 2G **53**
Park Cl. CF37: T'rest 3D **24**
NP20: Newp 2G **53**
NP44: H'lys 5B **10**
Park Ct. CF62: Barry 4E **117**
NP4: P'pool 2C **6**
NP26: Undy 4F **59**
Park Cres. CF14: Whit 1B **84**
CF37: T'rest 2E **25**
CF62: Barry 4E **117**
CF72: P'clun 6C **64**
NP4: P'pool 2D **6**
NP20: Newp 2G **53**
Park Dr. NP20: Newp 2H **53**
Park End NP18: L'stne 6G **23**
Park End Ct. CF23: Cyn 1A **86**
NP18: L'stne 1G **39**
Park End La. CF23: Cyn 1A **86**
Parker Pl. CF5: Ely 5F **93**
Parker Rd. CF5: Ely 5F **93**
Parke's La. NP4: P'pool 4A **6**
Parkfield Pl. CF14: Card 6G **85**
NP20: Newp 4A **36**
Park Gdns. NP4: P'pool 2C **6**
NP20: Newp 2G **53**
Park Gro. CF10: Card 1E **5** (2B **96**)
Park Ho. Flats NP4: P'pool 2C **6**
Parklands NP18: L'wrn 5G **57**
Parklands Cl. NP10: Roger 6E **35**
NP16: Math 6B **62**
NP44: Pnwd 6E **9**
Parklands Ind. Est. CF24: Card 6H **5** (5C **96**)
Parkland Wlk. CF62: Barry 3E **117**
Park La. CF10: Card 1D **4** (2A **96**)
CF14: Whit 1B **84**
CF15: Taff W 1D **68**
CF72: Groes F 6B **66**
CF83: Caer 1C **46**
Parklawn Cl. NP44: Pnwd 5E **9**
Park Pl. CF10: Card 1D **4** (2A **96**)
CF37: C'fydd 1F **15**
NP11: C'keys 2A **16**
NP11: Ris 6E **17**
Park Prospect CF37: P'prdd 5B **14**
Park Rd. CF14: Whit 1B **84**
CF15: Rad 1F **83**
CF62: Barry 4D **116**
CF64: Din P 1G **107**
CF64: P'rth 2F **109**
CF71: C'bri 4D **90**
NP4: P'pool 2C **6**
(not continuous)
NP11: Ris 6D **16**
NP26: Cald 5B **60**
Park Rd. Ind. Est. NP11: Ris 6E **17**
Parkside NP44: C'brn 3G **11**
Parkside Ct. NP4: P'nydd 1A **6**
Park Side La. CF37: P'prdd 6C **14**
Park Sq. NP20: Newp 5C **36**
Parkstone Av. CF3: St M 5C **74**
Park St. CF10: Card 5C **4** (4A **96**)
CF37: T'rest 2E **25**
NP4: Grif 6E **7**
NP11: C'keys 2A **16**
Park Ter. NP4: P'nydd 1A **6**
Parkvale Vw. CF72: L'sant 3G **65**
Park Vw. CF10: Card 3D **4** (3A **96**)
CF72: L'sant 2F **65**
NP4: P'pool 4D **6**
NP10: Bass 6E **35**
NP11: C'keys 2A **16**
NP16: Chep 1C **62**
NP16: Sed 2H **63**
NP44: Pnwd 5E **9**
Park Vw. Ct. CF14: Whit 1C **84**
CF64: P'rth 5G **101**
Park Vw. Gdns. NP10: Bass 6D **34**
Park Vw. Ter. NP4: P'nydd 1A **6**
Parkwall Rd. CF14: Pontp 3F **73**
Parkway CF3: Rum 5B **88**
Parkway Sth. CF3: Rum 5C **88**
Park Wood Cl. NP18: C'ln 4E **21**
Park Wood Dr. NP10: Bass 1A **52**
Parracombe Cl. CF3: L'rmy 6A **74**
Parracombe Cres. CF3: L'rmy 1H **87**
Parret Cl. NP20: Bet 5H **19**
Parret Rd. NP20: Bet 5H **19**
Parret Wlk. NP20: Bet 5H **19**
Parry Dr. NP19: Newp 4A **38**
Parry St. CF5: Card 3E **95**
Partridge La. CF24: Card 1H **5** (2C **96**)
Partridge Rd. CF24: Card 1H **5** (2C **96**)
CF62: St A 3G **111**
Partridge Way NP10: Duf 3G **53**
(not continuous)
Pascal Cl. CF3: St M 5F **75**
Pascall Ct. CF24: Card 1G **5**
Pasteur Gro. CF38: Chu V 2D **42**
Pastures, The CF62: Barry 6G **105**
NP44: Llan 2B **12**
Patch, The CF72: L'harry 4A **78**
Patchway Cres. CF3: Rum 3G **87**
Patmore Cl. CF15: Taff W 1D **68**
Patreane Way CF5: Ely 6D **92**
Patterdale Cl. CF23: Pen L 5B **86**
Patti Cl. NP19: Newp 3D **38**
Pauls End Ct. NP20: Newp 5C **36**
Pavaland Cl. CF3: St M 1D **88**
Pavia Ct. CF37: P'prdd 6C **14**
Paxton Wlk. NP10: Roger 2C **34**
Peach Pl. CF5: F'wtr 1H **93**
Pearce Cl. CF3: St M 2E **89**
Pearce Ct. CF63: Barry 5A **106**
Pearl Pl. CF24: Card 3D **96**
Pearl St. CF24: Card 3D **96**
(not continuous)
Pearson Cres. CF37: Glyn 2C **14**
Pearson St. CF24: Card 1G **5** (2C **96**)
Pear Tree Cl. NP18: C'ln 5E **21**
Pear Tree Cotts. NP19: Newp 6H **37**
Pear Tree La. NP19: Newp 6H **37**
Peckham Cl. CF5: L'dff 4H **83**
Pedair Erw Rd. CF14: Heath 2F **85**
Pellett St. CF10: Card 5F **5** (4B **96**)
Pembrey Path NP44: G'mdw 2E **11**
Pembridge Dr. CF64: P'rth 6H **101**
Pembroke Cl. CF38: Tont 1F **43**
CF64: Din P 2A **108**
NP26: Undy 4F **59**
Pembroke Ct. CF83: Caer 5G **27**
NP26: Undy 4F **59**
Pembroke Cres. CF72: L'sant 6C **40**
Pembroke Gro. NP19: Newp 1G **55**
Pembroke M. CF5: Card 3D **94**
Pembroke Pl. CF62: Barry 1H **117**
CF71: Bov 3D **110**
NP44: Llan 2B **12**
Pembroke Rd. CF5: Card 3E **95**
NP16: Bul 5E **63**
Pembroke Ter. CF64: P'rth 6B **102**
Penally Rd. CF5: Ely 5A **94**
PENARTH 1E **109**
Penarth Ct. NP44: Llan 4B **12**
(not continuous)
PENARTH HEAD 6B **102**
Penarth Head La. CF64: P'rth 1F **109**
Penarth Leisure Cen. 6G **101**
Penarth Pier 2G **109**
Penarth Portway CF64: P'rth 6A **102**
Penarth Rd. CF10: Card 6D **4** (5A **96**)
CF11: Card 3F **101**
CF64: Card 3F **101**
Penarth Station (Rail) 2E **109**
Penbedw NP44: C'iog 1B **12**
Penbryn Coch CF72: L'harry 4B **78**
Pen Bryn Hendy CF72: P'clun 6E **65**
Penbury Ct. CF15: Morg 5F **69**
Pencader Rd. CF5: Ely 3A **94**
Pencarn Av. NP10: Coedk 5E **53**
Pencarn La. NP10: Coedk, Duf 5E **53**
(not continuous)
Pencarn Way NP10: Coedk, Duf 4E **53**
Pencerrig St. CF37: P'prdd 6B **14**
Pencisely Av. CF5: Card 2C **94**
Pencisely Cres. CF5: Card 2C **94**
Pencisely Ri. CF5: Card 2C **94**
Pencisely Rd. CF5: L'dff 2C **94**
Pen Clawdd CF83: Caer 4F **29**
Pencoed Av. CF37: P'prdd 6E **15**
Pencoed Pl. NP44: C'iog 5F **9**
Pencoedtre Rd. CF63: Barry 4A **106**
(not continuous)
Penda Pl. NP16: Sed 2H **63**
Pendine Cl. CF62: Barry 5H **105**
Pendine Rd. CF5: Ely 4A **94**
Pendine Wlk. NP44: G'mdw 3E **11**
Pendoylan Cl. CF63: Barry 5B **106**
Pendoylan Ct. CF5: Ely 3A **94**
Pendoylan Rd. CF72: Groes F 1A **80**
Pendoylan Wlk. NP44: C'brn 3E **11**
Pendragon Cl. CF14: Thorn 3F **71**
Pendraw Pl. CF23: Cyn 1B **86**
Pendwyallt Rd. CF14: Whit 6A **70**
Pendyris St. CF11: Card 6A **4** (5H **95**)
Penedre CF5: L'dff 6C **84**
Penffordd CF15: P'rch 5A **68**
Penford Ct. CF24: Card 1G **5** (2C **96**)
PENGAM 1F **97**
Pengam Ind. Est. CF24: Card 3H **97**
Pengam Rd. CF24: Card 1F **97**
Pengwern Rd. CF5: Ely 3A **94**
Pen Hendy CF72: P'clun 6E **65**
Penheol Ely Rd. CF37: P'prdd 5E **15**
Penhevad St. CF11: Card 1H **101**
Penhill Cl. CF5: L'dff 2E **95**
Penhill Ct. CF5: Card 2E **95**
Penhill Rd. CF11: Card 2E **95**
Penhow M. NP10: Coedk 6G **53**
Penkin Cl. NP19: Newp 5B **38**
Penkin Hill NP19: Newp 4B **38**
Penlan Ri. CF64: L'dgh 5F **101**
Penlan Rd. CF64: L'dgh 4F **101**
Pen Lasgan CF3: Rum 1D **88**
Penlline Ct. CF14: Whit 2C **84**
Penlline Rd. CF14: Whit 2C **84**
Penlline St. CF24: Card 1F **5** (2B **96**)
Penllwyn La. CF83: Mac 2D **30**
Penllwyn Wlk. CF83: Mac 2C **30**
Penllyn Av. NP20: Newp 5H **35**
NP44: Pnwd 5E **9**
Penllyn Castle 1A **90**
Penllyn La. NP20: Newp 5H **35**
Penllyn Rd. CF5: Card 4F **95**
Penmaen Wlk. CF5: Ely 6D **92**
Penmaes CF15: P'rch 5A **68**
Penmaes Rd. NP44: G'mdw 2B **10**
PEN MARC 1D **114**
PENMARK 1D **114**
Penmark Grn. CF5: Ely 4E **93**
Penmark Rd. CF5: Ely 5E **93**
Pennant Cres. CF23: Cyn 1C **86**
Pennard Cl. NP10: Coedk 6G **53**
Pennard Pl. CF14: Llan N 4F **85**
Pennine Cl. CF14: L'shn 6G **71**
NP11: Ris 6H **17**
Pennsylvania CF23: L'dyrn 2D **86**
(not continuous)
Penny Cres. NP20: Malp 4H **19**
Pennyfarthing La. NP26: Undy 4D **58**
Pennyfields NP44: G'mdw 2D **10**
Penny La. CF71: C'bri 3D **90**
Pennyroyal Cl. CF3: St M 5E **75**
PENRHIW 5E **17**
Penrhiw La. CF83: Mac 1G **31**
Penrhiw Rd. CF37: P'prdd 2B **24**
NP11: Ris 5E **17**
Penrhos CF15: Rad 6E **69**
Penrhos Cres. CF3: Rum 3A **88**
Penrhyn Cl. CF3: Rum 2C **88**
Penrice Grn. NP44: Llan 3B **12**
Pensarn Rd. CF3: Rum 2C **88**
Pensarn Way NP44: H'lys 5B **10**
Pensidan Vw. NP10: Bass 1B **52**
Penstone Ct. CF10: Card 1B **102**
Penterry Pk. NP16: Chep 2D **62**
Pentir y De CF62: Rho 6G **115**
Pentland Cl. CF14: L'shn 6F **71**
NP11: Ris 6H **17**
Pent Lee CF23: L'dyrn 6E **73**
Pentonville NP20: Newp 4B **36**
PENTREBACH 1E **25**
Pentrebach Rd. CF37: P'prdd, R'fln 1E **25**
PENTREBANE 1G **93**
Pentrebane Rd. CF5: F'wtr, St F 6D **82**
Pentrebane St. CF11: Card 1H **101**
CF83: Caer 1C **46**
Pentre Cl. NP44: F'wtr 5D **10**
Pentre Gdns. CF11: Card 5H **95**
Pentre La. NP44: Bet, H'lys, Oakf 2C **18**
Pentrepiod Rd. NP4: P'nydd 1A **6**
Pentre Pl. CF11: Card 6H **95**
Pentre-Poeth Cl. NP10: Bass 1A **52**
Pentre-Poeth Rd. NP10: Bass 1B **52**
Pentre St. CF11: Card 6H **95**
Pentre Tai Rd. NP10: R'drn 3H **33**
PENTWYN 6F **73**
Pentwyn CF15: Rad 1E **83**
CF83: Caer 3A **28**
Pentwyn Bus. Cen. CF23: L'dyrn 5F **73**
Pentwyn Cl. NP16: Pwllm 4B **62**

Pentwyn Ct. CF14: Whit 1C **84**
Pentwyn Dr. CF23: L'dyrn 1E **87**
Pentwyngwyn Rd. CF83: Rud 5B **30**
Pentwyn Interchange CF23: L'dyrn 1G **87**
Pentwyn Isaf CF83: Caer 3B **28**
Pen-Twyn La. NP20: Bet 4G **19**
Pentwyn Leisure Cen. 1F **87**
Pentwyn Rd. CF23: L'dyrn 6F **73**
CF23: L'dyrn, Pontp 4D **72**
Pentwyn Shop. Pct. CF23: L'dyrn 6F **73**
Pentwyn Ter. CF3: M'fld 5A **76**
PENTYRCH 5H **67**
Pentyrch St. CF24: Card 1H **95**
Penuel La. CF37: P'prdd 6C **14**
Penuel Rd. CF15: P'rch 5H **67**
Pen-y-Bryn CF37: Glyn 2D **14**
CF62: Barry 5D **116**
CF63: Barry 6D **106**
CF83: Caer 3H **27**
NP4: P'pool 2D **6**
Pen-y-Bryn Cl. NP20: Bet 5G **19**
Pen-y-Bryn Pl. CF14: Card 5G **85**
Pen-y-Bryn Rd. CF14: Card 5G **85**
CF23: Cyn 6C **72**
Pen-y-Bryn Way CF14: Card 5G **85**
Pen-y-Cae CF83: Caer 4F **29**
Pen-y-Cefn CF14: Thorn 3F **71**
Pen y Coed Cae Rd. CF37: Bed, P'cae 4H **41**
CF38: Bed 4H **41**
Pen-y-Cwm CF15: P'rch 4A **68**
Pen-y-Darren Cl. CF37: P'prdd 5C **14**
Penydarren Dr. CF14: Whit 2A **84**
Pen-y-dre CF14: Rhiw, Whit 1C **84**
CF83: Caer 2A **28**
Penyffordd CF83: Caer 5B **28**
PENYGARN 2D **6**
Penygarn Rd. CF5: Ely 3H **93**
NP4: C'avn, P'pool 1C **6**
PENYGAWSI 3F **65**
Penyglog Rd. NP18: P'hir 1G **13**
Penygraig CF14: Rhiw 4D **70**
Pen-y-Graig Ter. NP4: P'pool 4C **6**
Pen y Groes CF72: Groes F 6B **66**
Pen-y-Groes CF83: Caer 3A **28**
Pen-y-Groes Av. CF14: Rhiw 6F **71**
Pen-y-Groes Gro. NP10: Bass 1A **52**
Pen-y-Groes Rd. CF14: Rhiw 6E **71**
PEN-Y-LAN 4C **86**
Penylan Cl. NP4: New I 5H **7**
NP10: Bass 6C **34**
Penylan Ct. CF23: Pen L 4C **86**
NP44: F'wtr 5D **10**
Pen-y-Lan Oval CF23: Pen L 4C **86**
Pen-y-Lan Pl. CF23: Pen L 6C **86**
Penylan Rd. CF37: P'prdd 1B **24**
NP19: Newp 4G **37**
NP44: F'wtr 4C **10**
Pen-y-Lan Rd. CF23: Card, Pen L 6C **86**
CF71: A'thin, C'bri 2F **91**
NP10: Bass 4A **52**
Pen-y-Lan Ter. CF23: Pen L 5D **86**
Pen-y-Llan La. NP4: Lit M, New I 1H **7**
Pen-y-Mynydd CF37: Glyn 1D **14**
Penyparc NP44: Pnwd 5D **8**
Pen-y-Parc CF38: Bed 4H **41**
Pen-y-Peel Rd. CF5: Card 3E **95**
Pen-yr-Allt CF83: Caer 3B **46**
Pen-yr-Eglwys CF38: Chu V, Llan F 3D **42**
PENYRHEOL
Caerphilly 4A **28**
Pontypool 6C **6**
Penyrheol Rd. NP4: P'pool, Up R 5C **6**
Pen-y-Turnpike Rd. CF64: Din P, Mic P 3D **100**
Penyturnpike Vw. CF64: P'rth 1B **108**
Penywain La. NP4: P'pool 3A **6**
Pen-y-Wain La. CF24: Card 6A **86**
Pen-y-Wain Pl. CF24: Card 6B **86**
Penywain Rd. NP4: P'pool 2A **6**
Pen-y-Wain Rd. CF24: Card 6B **86**
Penywain St. NP4: P'pool 2B **6**
Penywain Ter. NP4: P'pool 2B **6**
Penywaun CF38: E Isaf 6F **43**
Pen-y-Waun CF15: P'rch 4H **67**
CF64: Din P 2H **107**
Pen-y-Waun Cl. NP44: C'brn 3F **11**
Penywaun Rd. NP44: F'wtr 4E **11**
(not continuous)
Pen-y-Waun Rd. NP44: G'mdw 3F **11**
(not continuous)
Peppermint Dr. CF23: Pontp 4D **72**
Pepys Cres. CF3: L'rmy 1H **87**
Pepys Gro. NP20: Newp 1G **53**
Percival Cl. CF14: Thorn 3F **71**
Perclose CF64: Din P 2H **107**
Percoed La. NP10: Coedk, St Bri 2D **76**
(not continuous)
Percy Smith Rd. CF71: Bov 3E **111**
Percy St. CF10: Card 5A **96**
Peregrine Ct. NP26: Undy 4E **59**
Perrots Cl. CF5: F'wtr 1A **94**
Perry Ct. NP44: G'mdw 1C **10**
Persondy La. CF5: Ely 4D **92**
Perthy Cl. NP44: F'wtr 5D **10**
Peterston Rd. CF72: Groes F 1C **80**
Peterswell Rd. CF62: Barry 2E **117**
Petherton M. CF5: L'dff 6B **84**
Petherton Pl. CF3: L'rmy 1A **88**
Pethybridge Rd. CF5: Ely 3F **93**
Petrel Cl. CF64: P'rth 5E **109**
Pettingale Rd. NP44: C'iog 5H **9**
Petunia Wlk. NP10: Roger 2H **33**
Philadelphia Cl. CF63: Barry 6D **106**
Philanthropic Cotts. *NP44: H'lys 5B* ***10***
(off Dorallt Way)
Philip Cl. CF14: Heath 1F **85**
Philippa Freeth Ct. CF63: Barry 3A **118**
Philip St. CF11: Card 4F **95**
Phillip Ct. NP19: Newp 4E **37**
Phillips Grn. NP10: Roger 5D **34**
Phillip St. CF37: P'prdd 2B **24**
NP11: Ris 5D **16**
NP19: Newp 4E **37**
Philog, The CF14: Whit 3E **85**
Philog Ct. CF14: Whit 3E **85**
Phoenix Dr. NP16: Bul 6G **63**
Phoenix Est. CF14: Heath 1F **85**
Phoenix Way CF14: Heath 2F **85**
Phyllis St. CF62: Barry 5G **117**
Piccadilly CF71: L'thian 5B **90**
Piccadilly Sq. CF83: Caer 6D **28**
Picked La. NP18: Newp 4H **55**
Pickerston Cl. CF62: St A 2A **112**
PICKETSTON 1A **112**
Pickwick Cl. CF14: Thorn 3H **71**
Picton Ct. CF71: Llan M 2C **110**
Picton Pl. CF11: Card 4F **95**
Picton Rd. CF62: Rho 5E **115**
Picton St. NP4: Grif 6E **7**
Picton Wlk. CF11: Card 4F **95**
NP44: F'wtr 3D **10**
Picwic Grn. *NP44: G'mdw 3D* ***10***
(off Byways)
Piercefield Av. NP16: Chep 1C **62**
Piercefield Pl. CF24: Card 1H **5** (2D **96**)
Pierhead St. CF10: Card 1C **102**
Pierhead Vw. CF64: P'rth 5H **101**
Pilgrim Cl. CF15: Rad 2F **83**
PILL, THE 6F **61**
Pill Farm Est. NP26: Pskwt 6F **61**
PILLGWENLLY 6C **36**
Pillgwenlly Millennium Cen. 1C **54**
Pillmawr Circ. NP20: Malp 5B **20**
Pillmawr Rd. NP18: C'ln 5B **20**
NP20: Malp 5B **20**
Pill Row NP26: Pskwt 5E **61**
Pill St. CF64: P'rth 6G **101**
Pill Way NP26: Pskwt 5F **61**
Pilton Pl. CF14: Card 5F **85**
Pilton Va. NP20: Malp 4B **20**
Pine Cl. NP11: Ris 5E **17**
Pine Ct. CF15: Tong 4H **69**
CF38: Llan F 6C **42**
CF72: T Grn 2C **64**
Pinecrest Dr. CF14: Thorn 2H **71**
Pine Gdns. NP4: P'pool 3A **6**
Pine Gro. NP10: Duf 3H **53**
Pinehurst Rd. CF5: F'wtr 1G **93**
Pines, The CF14: Whit 2C **84**
Pine Tree Cl. CF15: Rad 6E **69**
Pine Tree Rd. NP4: New I 5G **7**
Pinewood Av. CF37: R'fln 4H **25**
Pinewood Cl. CF64: L'dgh 5G **101**
NP20: Malp 5B **20**
Pine Wood Cres. CF23: Pen L 4E **87**
Pinewood Hill CF72: T Grn 3C **64**
Pinewood Sq. CF62: St A 2B **112**
Pinewood Vw. CF37: Glyn 1C **14**
Pinnell Pl. *NP20: Newp 6C* ***36***
(off Coulson Cl.)
Pioden For CF62: Barry 6H **117**
Piper Cl. CF5: L'dff 5H **83**
NP19: Newp 1G **37**
Pipkin Cl. CF23: Pontp 4F **73**
Pitman La. CF11: Card 3G **95**
Pitman St. CF11: Card 3G **95**
Pitmedden Cl. CF3: St M 6D **74**
Place de Cormeilles NP16: Chep 2E **63**
Plane St. CF37: R'fln 4G **25**
Plane Tree Cl. NP18: C'ln 5F **21**
Planet St. CF24: Card 3H **5** (3C **96**)
Plantagenet St. CF11: Card 5A **4** (4H **95**)
Plantation, The NP26: Undy 4D **58**
Plantation Dr. NP44: C'iog 1B **12**
Plas Bryn Gomer NP44: C'iog 5G **9**
Plas Cae Llwyd CF83: L'brad 1B **28**
Plas Carmel CF37: P'prdd 6B **14**
Plas Cleddau CF62: Barry 2E **117**
Plas Craig NP44: C'brn 1H **11**
Plas Cwrt NP44: Oakf 5H **11**
Plas Derwen NP44: C'iog 1B **12**
Plas Ebbw NP44: C'brn 1G **11**
Plas Essyllt CF64: Din P 3H **107**
Plas Glen Rosa CF64: P'rth 6A **102**
Plas Grug CF83: Caer 2B **46**
Plas Gwernen CF63: Barry 5B **106**
Plas Gwynt M. CF11: Card 2A **4** (3G **95**)
Plas Islwyn NP44: C'brn 1G **11**
Plasmawr Rd. CF5: F'wtr 6H **83**
Plas Melin CF14: Whit 3B **84**
Plas Nant CF83: Abert 2E **27**
Plas Newydd CF14: Whit 3C **84**
Plasnewydd Pl. CF24: Card 1C **96**
Plasnewydd Rd. CF24: Card 1G **5** (1B **96**)
(not continuous)
Plasnewydd Sq. CF24: Card 1B **96**
Plas Pamir CF64: P'rth 5B **102**
Plas Phillips CF83: Caer 6B **28**
Plas St Andresse CF64: P'rth 5B **102**
Plas St Pol de Leon CF64: P'rth 6B **102**
Plassey Sq. CF64: P'rth 6A **102**
Plassey St. CF64: P'rth 6H **101**
Plas Taliesin CF64: P'rth 5B **102**
Plas Thomas CF83: Caer 1B **46**
Plas Treoda CF14: Whit 3D **84**
Plas Trosnant NP44: C'brn 6E **9**
Plasturton Av. CF11: Card 2F **95**
Plasturton Gdns. CF11: Card 3G **95**
Plasturton Pl. CF11: Card 3G **95**
Plas Twyn NP44: C'brn 6F **9**
Plas Ty-Coch NP44: Oakf 5H **11**
Plas y Biswell CF3: St M 2D **88**
Plas y Coed CF23: Cyn 4B **86**
Plas-y-Delyn CF14: L'vne 2B **72**
Plas-y-Fedwen CF37: Glyn 1D **14**
Plas-y-Llan CF14: Whit 2C **84**
Plas y Mynach CF15: Rad 3G **83**
Plas yr Eglwys *CF37: P'prdd 5D* ***14***
(off Dorothy St.)
Plas-yr-Odyn CF72: L'harry 4C **78**
Platinum St. CF24: Card 3D **96**
Playford Cres. NP19: Newp 3D **38**
Pleasant Pl. CF83: Caer 4A **28**
Pleasant Vw. CF37: P'prdd 5D **14**
CF38: Bed 5A **42**
CF62: Barry 5F **105**
Plover Cl. NP19: Newp 2C **56**
Plover Cres. NP26: Cald 6D **60**
Plover Way CF64: P'rth 5E **109**
Plum Tree La. NP26: Cald 6C **60**
Plymouth Dr. CF15: Rad 2G **83**
Plymouth Rd. CF37: P'prdd 6A **14**
CF62: Barry 5G **117**
CF64: P'rth 2F **109**
Plymouth Wood Cl. CF5: Ely 3H **93**
Plymouth Wood Cres. CF5: Ely 3G **93**
Plymouth Wood Rd. CF5: Ely 3H **93**
Plym Wlk. NP20: Bet 5G **19**
Poets Cl. CF37: R'fln 3G **25**
Poets Fld. Rd. CF62: Barry 5G **105**
Pollard Cl. NP18: C'ln 5E **21**
Polo Ground Ind. Est. NP4: New I 5F **7**
(High Way, The)
NP4: New I 6F **7**
(Pont-y-Felin Rd.)
Pomeroy St. CF10: Card 2B **102**
Pommergelli Rd. CF14: Llan N 3B **84**
Pontalun Cl. CF63: Barry 5A **106**
Pont Ap Hywell NP4: P'pool 2C **6**
PONTCANNA 2F **95**
Pontcanna Ct. CF5: L'dff 1E **95**
Pontcanna Pl. CF11: Card 2F **95**
Pontcanna St. CF11: Card 2F **95**
Pontfaen CF23: L'dyrn 5D **72**
Pontfaen Rd. NP19: Newp 6A **38**
PONTHIR 1F **21**
Ponthir Rd. NP18: C'ln, P'hir 2G **21**
PONTNEWYDD 6E **9**
Pontnewydd Wlk. NP44: C'brn 6E **9**
PONTNEWYNYDD 1A **6**
Pontnewynydd Small Bus. Cen.
NP4: P'nydd 1A **6**
Pont-Pentre Cvn. Pk. *CF37: Up Bo 6A* ***26***
(off Crwys Cres.)
PONTPRENNAU 4F **73**
PONTRHYDYRUN 5G **9**
Pontrhydyrun Rd. NP44: Pnwd 4E **9**
Pontrilas Cl. CF5: Ely 6D **92**
Pontshonnorton Rd. CF37: P'prdd, C'fydd 4E **15**

PONT SIÔN NORTON 4E 15
PONTYCLUN 6D 64
Pontyclun Station (Rail) 6C 64
PONT-Y-FELIN 1G 9
Pontyfelin Av. NP4: New I 6F 7
Pont-y-Felin La. NP4: New I 1G 9
Pont-y-Felin Rd. NP4: New I 6F 7
Pontygwindy Ind. Est. CF83: Caer 3C 28
Pontygwindy Rd. CF83: Caer 3C 28
Pontymason Cl. NP10: Roger 2A 34
Pontymason Ct. NP10: Roger 2A 34
Pontymason La. NP10: Roger 6H 17
NP11: Ris, Roger 6H 17
Pontymason Ri. NP10: Roger 2A 34
PONTYMISTER 6D 16
Pontymister Ind. Est. NP11: Ris 1E 33
PONTYMOEL 4D 6
Pontypandy Ind. Est. CF83: Caer 3C 28
Pontypandy La. CF83: Caer 4C 28
(not continuous)
Ponty Pandy Vw. CF83: Caer 4C 28
PONTYPOOL 2C 6
Pontypool & New Inn Station (Rail) 4G 7
Pontypool Leisure Cen. 3D 6
Pontypool Mus. 2C 6
Pontypool Nth. Ind. Est. NP4: P'nydd 1A 6
Pontypool Pk. 3D 6
Pontypool RFC 3D 6
Pontypool Ski & Leisure Cen. 2D 6
Pontypool Western By-Pass
NP4: P'nydd, P'pool 1B 6
PONTYPRIDD 1C 24
PONTYPRIDD COTTAGE HOSPITAL (Y BWTHYN) 6E 15
Pontypridd Cricket Club 1D 24
Pontypridd Mus. 6C 14
Pontypridd Rd. CF62: Barry 2D 116
Pontypridd RUFC 1D 24
Pontypridd Rugby Football Ground 6B 14
(off Maes Coed Rd.)
Pontypridd Station (Rail) 1C 24
Pontypridd St. CF63: Barry 1B 118
PONTYPWL 2C 6
PONTYWAUN 1A 16
Pool La. NP19: Newp 2E 37
(not continuous)
Poplar Av. NP4: New I 4G 7
Poplar Cl. CF5: F'wtr 6G 83
NP26: Rog 6A 60
Poplar Ct. CF62: Barry 6A 106
NP18: C'ln 4F 21
Poplar Ho. CF14: Whit 1A 84
Poplar Rd. CF5: F'wtr 6G 83
CF37: R'fln 4G 25
CF83: Caer 1E 47
NP19: Newp 4H 37
NP44: C'iog 6G 9
Poplars, The CF72: L'harry 5B 78
NP11: Ris 4B 16
NP16: Chep 1E 63
Poppyfield Cl. CF3: St M 1C 88
Poppy Pl. NP10: Roger 2H 33
Porcher Av. CF37: Glyn 2C 14
Porfa Ballas *CF62: Rho 6G 115*
(off Rhoda Fa'r Mor)
Porlock Dr. CF64: Sul 2H 119
Porlock Rd. CF3: L'rmy 6B 74
Porset Cl. CF83: Caer 6E 29
Porset Dr. CF83: Caer 6D 28
Porset Pk. CF83: Caer 5E 29
Porset Row CF83: Caer 4F 29
Portfield Cres. CF14: L'shn 6H 71
Porthamal Gdns. CF14: Rhiw 1E 85
Porthamal Rd. CF14: Rhiw 1E 85
Porthcawl Rd. CF5: Ely 5G 93
PORTHCERI 5A 116
PORTHKERRY 5A 116
Porthkerry Country Pk. 4B 116
Porthkerry Pl. CF14: Card 5F 85
Porthkerry Rd. CF62: Barry 4F 117
CF62: Rho 4G 115
Porth Mawr Rd. NP44: C'brn 1G 11
Porth-y-Castell CF62: Barry 4C 116
Porth-y-Green CF71: L'thian 4C 90
Portland Cl. CF64: P'rth 3F 109
Portland Pl. CF14: L'vne 3B 72
Portland St. NP20: Newp 1D 54
Portland Way NP20: Newp 1D 54
Port Madoc Rd. CF3: Rum 2C 88
Portmanmoor Rd. CF24: Card 4E 97
(not continuous)
Portmanmoor Rd. Ind. Est.
CF24: Card 5E 97
Portmanmoor Rd. La. CF24: Card 4E 97
Port M. CF62: Barry 4H 105
Port Reeve Cl. CF72: L'sant 3F 65
Port Rd. CF5: Ely, Wen 1D 98
CF62: Barry 6F 105
(Highlight La.)
CF62: Barry 5F 105
(Hinchsliff Av.)
CF62: Barry 4H 105
(Port Rd. E.)
CF62: Rho 5A 114
(Burton Ter.)
CF62: Rho 4G 115
(Waycock Cross)
CF63: Barry 4H 105
NP20: Newp 2B 54
Port Rd. E. CF62: Barry 5F 105
Port Rd. W. CF62: Barry 1D 116
PORTSKEWETT 5G 61
Portskewett St. NP19: Newp 6F 37
Port Wall 2E 63
Portwall Rd. NP16: Chep 2E 63
Postern *NP44: F'wtr 4E 11*
(off Henllys Way)
Post Office Row CF15: Gwae G 6D 44
NP26: Sud 6H 61
Post Office Ter. NP18: P'hir 1F 21
Potters Cft. NP16: B'ly 6H 63
Potter St. NP20: Newp 1D 54
Pottery Rd. NP20: Newp 1D 54
Pottery Ter. NP20: Newp 1C 54
Pound Fld. CF71: Llan M 3B 110
Pound Hill NP10: Bass, Coedk 4A 52
Pound La. CF5: Wen 5D 98
NP26: C'went 1A 60
Powderham Dr. CF11: Card 5F 95
Powell Duffryn Way
CF62: Barry 4F 117
(Broad St.)
CF62: Barry 4G 117
(Fford y Mileniwm)
Powell's Pl. NP20: Newp 5C 36
Power St. NP20: Newp 3B 36
Powis Cl. NP10: Coedk 6F 53
Powis Vw. CF63: Barry 6C 106
Powys Cl. CF64: Din P 1A 108
Powys Dr. CF64: Din P 1H 107
Powys Gdns. CF64: Din P 1A 108
Powys Pl. CF37: R'fln 3F 25
CF64: Din P 1A 108
Powys Rd. CF37: Up Bo 2B 44
CF64: P'rth 3D 108
Precinct, The CF38: Tont 2G 43
CF71: Llan M 3B 110
Prendergast Pl. CF5: Ely 6H 93
Prennau Ho. CF23: Pontp 3G 73
Presceli Cl. NP11: Ris 5G 17
Prescoch La. NP4: P'pool 5D 6
Prestatyn Rd. CF3: Rum 2B 88
Presteigne Av. CF38: Tont 1F 43
Presteigne Wlk. NP44: C'brn 3E 11
Preston Av. NP20: Newp 5H 35
Preston Cl. NP16: Bul 6F 63
Preswylfa St. CF5: Card 2D 94
Price Av. CF63: Barry 6B 106
Price Cl. NP20: Newp 1C 54
Priestley Cl. NP20: Newp 2H 53
Priest Rd. CF24: Card 2D 96
Primrose Cl. CF3: Rum 5H 87
CF71: C'bri 4E 91
Primrose Ct. NP44: F'wtr 4B 10
Primrose Hill CF71: C'bri 4E 91
Primrose Way NP10: Roger 2H 33
Prince Charles Ct. CF64: P'rth 6A 102
Prince Edward Ho. CF64: P'rth 6A 102
Prince Leopold St. CF24: Card 3H 5 (3D 96)
Prince Llewellyn Ho.
CF64: P'rth 6A 102
Prince of Wales Dr. CF5: St F 2C 82
Prince Rhodry Ho. CF64: P'rth 6A 102
Princes Av. CF24: Card 2D 96
CF83: Caer 2D 46
Princes Ct. CF24: Card 2F 5 (3B 96)
Princes Ri. CF83: Caer 2D 46
Princess St. CF37: T'rest 2D 24
Princes St. CF24: Card 2D 96
CF62: Barry 3F 117
Prince St. NP4: P'pool 2B 6
NP19: Newp 3D 36
Prince's Wlk. NP4: New I 5H 7
Priority Bus. Cen. CF10: Card 6A 96
Priority Bus. Pk. CF63: Barry 6E 107
Priory, The NP16: Chep 2F 63
Priory Cl. CF37: P'prdd 4B 14
NP16: Chep 1D 62
NP18: C'ln 4E 21
NP26: Cald 4C 60
Priory Ct. NP26: Magor 5D 58
Priory Cres. NP18: L'stne 1F 39
Priory Dr. NP18: L'stne 1E 39
Priory Gdns. CF63: Barry 5B 106
NP18: L'stne 6F 23
NP26: Magor 5C 58
Priory Gro. NP18: L'stne 1F 39
Priory (remains of) 3B 4 (3H 95)
Priory St. NP11: Ris 6E 17
Priory Vw. NP18: L'stne 1F 39
Priory Way NP18: L'stne 6F 23
Pritchard Cl. CF5: L'dff 5A 84
Probert Pl. NP19: Newp 4E 37
Proctor Cl. CF62: Barry 2E 117
Promenade CF62: Barry 6G 117
(Barry Island)
CF62: Barry 6E 117
(Knap, The)
Prospect Cres. NP26: Cald 5D 60
Prospect Dr. CF5: L'dff 1B 94
Prospect Pl. NP4: New I 6G 7
NP44: C'brn 3F 11
Prospect St. NP20: Newp 2B 36
Prosser La. NP20: Newp 5H 35
Providence Pl. CF14: Whit 6B 70
Prysg Field Roman Barracks 5H 21
(in Roman Legionary Mus.)
Pugsley St. NP20: Newp 3C 36
Pum Erw Rd. CF14: Heath 2F 85
Pump St. NP20: Newp 4B 36
Purbeck St. CF5: Card 3E 95
Purcell Rd. CF3: L'rmy 6B 74
CF64: P'rth 4D 108
Purcell Sq. NP19: Newp 4A 38
Purdey Cl. CF62: Barry 6E 105
Pwhelli Ct. CF3: Rum 3A 88
PWLL-GWAUN 6B 14
Pwll-Gwaun Rd. CF37: P'prdd 6B 14
Pwllhelyg CF15: Tong 5H 69
Pwll Mawr Av. CF3: Rum 4A 88
Pwll-Mawr Ct. CF3: Rum 5A 88
Pwllmelin La. CF5: L'dff 1B 94
Pwllmelin Rd. CF5: F'wtr, L'dff 6H 83
PWLLMEURIG 5B 62
PWLLMEYRIC 5B 62
Pwllmeyric Cl. NP16: Pwllm 5B 62
Pwll-Pen Ct. NP18: L'wrn 5D 38
PWLLYPANT 3C 28
PYE CORNER 4B 56
Pye Cnr. NP10: Roger 6E 35
Pyke St. CF63: Barry 1A 118
Pyle Rd. CF5: Ely 5G 93
Pyra Ct. *CF62: Barry 4E 117*
(off St Nicholas Cl.)
Pytchley Cl. CF72: C Inn 3G 65

Q

QED Cen., The CF37: Up Bo 2B 44
Quail Ct. CF24: Card 1H 5 (2C 96)
Quantock Cl. NP11: Ris 6G 17
Quantock Dr. NP19: Newp 3A 38
Quarella St. CF63: Barry 1B 118
Quarry Cl. CF5: F'wtr 1G 93
Quarry Cres. CF5: F'wtr 2G 93
Quarry Dale CF3: Rum 5H 87
Quarry Hill Cl. CF37: P'prdd 6A 14
Quarry La. CF15: N'grw 4E 45
Quarry Ri. NP26: Undy 3D 58
Quarry Rd. CF37: P'prdd 6A 14
Quarry St. CF15: N'grw 3D 44
Quasar Cen. 5H 117
(off Station App. Rd.)
Quay St. CF10: Card 4C 4 (4A 96)
Quebec Cl. NP20: Newp 6F 35
Queen Anne Sq. CF10: Card 1B 4 (2H 95)
Queen Arc. CF10: Card 3D 4 (4A 96)
Queen Charlotte Dr. CF15: Cre 1F 81
Queensberry Rd. CF23: Pen L 4D 86
Queen's Cl. NP20: Newp 3B 36
Queen's Cft. NP20: Newp 3B 36
Queens Dr. CF5: Ely 1E 99
CF38: Llan F 5D 42
Queens Gdns. NP26: Magor 4C 58
Queen's Hill NP20: Newp 3B 36
Queen's Hill Cres.
NP20: Newp 3B 36
Queens Rd. CF64: P'rth 6A 102
NP16: Bul 4E 63
Queens Rd. Sth. CF10: Card 4D 102
Queen St. CF10: Card 3D 4 (3A 96)
CF15: Tong 4G 69
CF37: T'rest 2E 25
CF62: Barry 3F 117
NP4: Grif 6E 7
NP4: P'pool 2B 6
NP20: Newp 6C 36

Queens Way CF63: Barry 4A **118**
NP18: L'wrn 2H **57**
NP19: L'wrn, Newp 2B **56**
Queensway CF15: N'grw 4E **45**
NP20: Newp 4B **36**
Queensway Mdws. NP19: Newp 1A **56**
Queensway Mdws. Ind. Est. NP19: Newp 2A **56**
Queenswest CF10: Card 3D **4** (3A **96**)
Queenwood CF23: Pen L 4E **87**
Queenwood Cl. CF23: Pen L 4C **86**
Quentin St. CF14: Card 5G **85**
Quilter Cl. NP19: Newp 5B **38**

R

Rachel Cl. CF5: L'dff 4H **83**
Rachel Sq. NP10: Duf 5G **53**
Radnor Ct. CF5: Card 3E **95**
Radnor Dr. CF38: Tont 1F **43**
Radnor Grn. CF62: Barry 6H **105**
Radnor Ho. CF64: P'rth 3D **108**
Radnor Rd. CF5: Card 3E **95**
CF71: Bov 3E **111**
NP19: Newp 3E **37**
Radnor Way NP44: C'brn 3G **11**
RADYR 2G **83**
RADYR COURT 4A **84**
Radyr Ct. Cl. CF5: L'dff 5B **84**
Radyr Ct. Ri. CF5: L'dff 5B **84**
Radyr Ct. Rd. CF5: L'dff 4H **83**
(not continuous)
Radyr Ct. Shop. Pct. CF5: L'dff 4H **83**
Radyr Farm Rd. CF15: Rad 3G **83**
Radyr Golf Course 2E **83**
Radyr Pl. CF14: Llan N 5F **85**
Radyr Rd. CF14: Llan N 4B **84**
Radyr Station (Rail) 2G **83**
Radyr Wood Nature Reserve 2G **83**
Raglan Cl. CF3: St M 6E **75**
CF64: Din P 2A **108**
Raglan Ct. CF83: Caer 5H **27**
NP20: Newp 6C **36**
NP44: C'iog 5F **9**
Raglande Ct. CF71: Llan M 4C **110**
Raglan Ho. CF10: Card 4B **4**
Raglan M. NP10: Coedk 6G **53**
Raglan St. NP11: Ris 4C **16**
Raglan Way NP16: Bul 5F **63**
Ragnall Cl. CF14: Thorn 2G **71**
Railway Cres. CF24: Card 3D **96**
Railway St. CF14: Card 6G **85**
CF24: Card 3D **96**
NP11: Ris 4D **16**
NP20: Newp 4B **36**
Railway Ter. CF11: Card 4F **95**
CF15: Tong 4G **69**
CF64: Din P 1A **108**
CF64: P'rth 1E **109**
CF72: P'clun 6D **64**
CF83: Caer 1D **46**
NP4: Grif 3E **9**
Railway Vw. NP26: Cald 6E **61**
Raisdale Rd. CF64: P'rth 3E **109**
Raisedale Gdns. CF64: P'rth 3F **109**
Raldan Cl. CF63: Barry 5B **106**
Raleigh Wlk. CF10: Card 6F **5** (5B **96**)
Ralph St. CF37: P'prdd 5D **14**
Rambler Cl. CF14: Thorn 2H **71**
Ramp, The NP26: Undy 5E **59**
Ramsey Cl. NP19: Newp 2F **37**
Ramsey Rd. CF62: Barry 5H **105**
Ramsey Wlk. NP19: Newp 2F **37**
NP44: Pnwd 6C **8**
Ramsons Way CF5: Ely 4E **93**
Rankine Cl. NP20: Malp 5H **19**
Rannoch Dr. CF23: Cyn 2C **86**
Raphael Cl. NP19: Newp 2G **37**
Ravensbrook CF15: Morg 5E **69**
Ravenscourt NP44: G'mdw 2D **10**
Ravens Ct. Cl. CF23: Pen L 5D **86**
Ravenshoe Rd. CF63: Barry 6D **106**
Ravenswood CF11: Card 5H **101**
Ravenswood Ct. NP11: Ris 4C **16**
Raven Way CF64: P'rth 6E **109**
Rawden M. CF11: Card 4A **4** (4G **95**)
Rawden Pl. CF11: Card 4A **4** (4G **95**)
Raymond Ter. CF37: T'rest 3E **25**
Readers La. CF62: Rho 5E **115**
Readers Way CF62: Rho 5D **114**
Reardon Smith Ct. CF5: F'wtr 1H **93**
Rectory Cl. CF5: Wen 6E **99**
CF83: Caer 2C **46**
Rectory Ct. CF64: P'rth 1F **109**
CF71: L'maes 1D **110**
Rectory Dr. CF62: St A 4D **112**
Rectory Gdns. CF83: Mac 2G **31**
NP26: Undy 4F **59**
Rectory Rd. CF5: Card 3E **95**
CF62: St A 4D **112**
CF63: Barry 1B **118**
CF64: P'rth 1F **109**
CF83: B'ws 2G **29**
CF83: Caer 1C **46**
Rectory Rd. La. CF64: P'rth 1F **109**
Redberth Cl. CF62: Barry 6H **105**
Redbrink Ct. CF5: Ely 3G **93**
Redbrink Cres. CF62: Barry 5H **117**
Redbrook Av. CF83: Tret 3A **30**
Redbrook Ct. CF83: Caer 2C **46**
Redbrook La. CF83: Mac 3B **30**
Redbrook Rd. NP20: Newp 4G **35**
Redbrook Way NP44: C'brn 2H **11**
Redcliffe Av. CF5: Card 3C **94**
Reddings, The NP16: Bul 5F **63**
Red Dragon Cen., The 1C **102**
Rede Rd. NP44: F'wtr 4D **10**
Red Ho. Cl. CF5: Ely 3G **93**
Red Ho. Cres. CF5: Ely 4G **93**
Red Ho. Pl. CF5: Ely 3H **93**
Red Ho. Rd. CF5: Ely 3G **93**
Redlands, The NP19: Newp 5A **38**
Redlands Av. CF64: P'rth 1C **108**
Redlands Ho. CF64: P'rth 1C **108**
Redlands Rd. CF64: P'rth 6F **101**
Redland St. NP20: Newp 2B **36**
Redlaver St. CF11: Card 6H **95**
Redmeadow Cres. NP26: Cald 6E **61**
Redvers St. NP19: Newp 5F **37**
Redwell Ct. CF23: Pen L 5C **86**
Redwick Ct. NP44: C'brn 3H **11**
Redwick Rd. NP26: Magor 5C **58**
Redwood Cl. CF3: St M 6C **74**
CF71: Bov 4E **111**
NP16: Bul 5E **63**
NP18: C'ln 5E **21**
Redwood Ct. CF14: L'shn 5H **71**
Redwood Dr. CF38: Llan F 5C **42**
Reene Ct. NP19: Newp 6G **37**
Rees Cl. NP20: Malp 4A **20**
Rees Ct. CF71: Llan M 3D **110**
Rees Ter. *CF37: T'rest 3E 25*
(off Meadow St.)
Reevesland Ind. Est. NP19: Newp 3G **55**
Regency Cl. CF71: Llan M 2C **110**
Regent Av. CF5: Ely 1E **99**
Regent Gdns. CF14: Whit 1C **84**
Regent St. CF62: Barry 2H **117**
(not continuous)
Regent Way NP16: Chep 2E **63**
Reginald Ter. NP10: Roger 5D **34**
Regina Ter. CF5: Card 2D **94**
Regus Ho. CF23: Pontp 3G **73**
Reigate Cl. CF14: Thorn 2G **71**
Relf Rd. CF3: Rum 3A **88**
Rembrandt Way NP19: Newp 1F **37**
Rennie St. CF11: Card 4G **95**
Renoir Rd. NP19: Newp 2G **37**
Reresby Ct. CF10: Card 1B **102**
Reservoir Cl. NP10: Roger 5D **34**
Restway Ct. CF5: L'dff 4A **84**
Restways Cl. CF5: F'wtr 5H **83**
Restway Wall NP16: Chep 2E **63**
Retford Ct. CF14: Whit 3E **85**
Retreat, The CF23: Pen L 5D **86**
Reynolds Cl. NP19: Newp 2F **37**
Rheidol Cl. CF14: L'shn 5A **72**
Rheidol Dr. CF62: Barry 1D **116**
Rhigos Gdns. CF24: Card 6H **85**
Rhigos St. CF24: Card 6H **85**
RHISGA 4D **16**
RHIWBINA 6E **71**
Rhiwbina Garden Village CF14: Rhiw 6D **70**
Rhiwbina Hill CF14: Rhiw, Tong 3B **70**
CF83: Tong 6A **46**
Rhiwbina Station (Rail) 1D **84**
RHIWDERIN 6A **34**
Rhiwderyn Cl. CF5: Ely 6D **92**
Rhiw Fach CF83: Caer 4A **28**
Rhiw Felin CF37: R'fln 3G **25**
Rhiwlas CF14: Thorn 3E **71**
Rhiw Melin NP44: Up Cwm 5B **8**
Rhiwr Ddar CF15: Taff W 6E **45**
Rhiwr Ddar Ho. CF15: Taff W 1E **69**
Rhiwsaeson Rd. CF72: C Inn 3H **65**
Rhoda Fa'r Mor CF62: Rho 6G **115**
Rhoddfa'r Gwagenni CF63: Barry 3H **117**
Rhodfa Felin CF62: Barry 3E **117**
Rhodfa Marics CF72: L'sant 1D **64**
Rhodfa Sweldon CF62: Barry 3G **117**
Rhododendron Cl. CF23: L'dyrn 6D **72**
Rhodri Pl. NP44: Llan 3B **12**
Rhondda Rd. CF37: P'prdd 6B **14**
RHOOSE 5F **115**
Rhoose Rd. CF62: Rho 5F **115**
Rhoose Station (Rail) 6E **115**
Rhos, The CF83: Caer 5E **29**
Rhos Ddu CF64: P'rth 3C **108**
Rhos Helyg CF83: Caer 5F **29**
Rhos Llan CF14: Rhiw 6E **71**
Rhos Llantwit CF83: Caer 5E **29**
Rhossilli Av. CF3: Rum 3A **88**
Rhossilli Rd. CF3: Rum 3A **88**
Rhos St. CF83: Caer 4C **28**
Rhuddlan Cl. NP10: R'drn 6A **34**
Rhuddlan Ct. CF83: Caer 4G **27**
Rhuddlan Way CF64: Din P 1A **108**
Rhydhelig Av. CF14: Heath 3F **85**
Rhydlafar Dr. CF5: St F 3C **82**
RHYDYFELIN 4G **25**
Rhyd-y-Gwern Cl. CF83: Caer 4F **29**
Rhyd y Gwern Isaf CF83: Mac 2G **31**
Rhyd-y-Gwern La. CF83: Mac 3F **31**
Rhyd y Nant CF72: P'clun 6D **64**
RHYDYPENAU 6H **71**
Rhyd-y-Penau Cl. CF14: Cyn 1A **86**
Rhyd-y-Penau Rd. CF23: Cyn 1A **86**
Rhyd-yr-Helyg CF15: N'grw 3D **44**
Rhyl Rd. CF3: Rum 3A **88**
Rhymney Ct. NP44: G'mdw 1C **10**
Rhymney Ho. CF23: Pontp 3G **73**
Rhymney River Bri. Rd.
CF23: Pen L 6F **87**
Rhymney River Sailing & Angling Club 2H **97**
Rhymney St. CF24: Card 1B **96**
Rhymney Ter. CF24: Card 1A **96**
CF83: Caer 1C **46**
RHYMNI 5A **88**
Rialto Ct. CF14: Whit 2D **84**
Ribble Sq. NP20: Bet 5G **19**
Ribble Wlk. NP20: Bet 5G **19**
Richard Lewis Cl. CF5: L'dff 5A **84**
Richards Pl. CF24: Card 2D **96**
Richards Ter. CF24: Card 2D **96**
CF37: P'prdd 5D **14**
Richard St. CF24: Card 1A **96**
CF37: C'fydd 2F **15**
CF62: Barry 2H **117**
Richmond Cl. CF83: L'brad 1B **28**
NP44: Pnwd 6E **9**
Richmond Ct. CF24: Card 1F **5** (2B **96**)
Richmond Cres. CF24: Card 1F **5** (2B **96**)
Richmond Pl. NP44: Pnwd 6E **9**
Richmond Rd. CF24: Card 1F **5** (1B **96**)
NP4: Grif 3E **9**
NP19: Newp 2E **37**
NP44: Pnwd 5E **9**
Richmond St. NP44: Pnwd 6E **9**
Rich's Rd. CF14: Heath 3F **85**
Rickards St. CF37: P'prdd 1C **24**
Rickards Ter. CF37: P'prdd 1C **24**
RIDGEWAY 4H **35**
Ridgeway CF14: L'vne 2A **72**
CF83: Mac 3B **30**
NP20: Newp 5F **35**
Ridgeway Av. NP20: Newp 4G **35**
Ridgeway Cl. CF37: P'prdd 5B **14**
NP20: Newp 4H **35**
Ridgeway Ct. NP20: Newp 4G **35**
Ridgeway Cres. NP20: Newp 5G **35**
Ridgeway Dr. NP20: Newp 5G **35**
Ridgeway Gdns. NP20: Newp 4H **35**
Ridgeway Gro. NP20: Newp 5G **35**
Ridgeway Hill NP20: Newp 4H **35**
Ridgeway Pk. Rd. NP20: Newp 4G **35**
Ridgeway Pl. CF38: Tont 2G **43**
NP20: Newp 4G **35**
Ridgeway Reach NP20: Newp 4H **35**
Ridgeway Ri. NP20: Newp 4H **35**
Ridgeway Rd. CF3: L'rmy, Rum 3G **87**
CF62: Barry 5F **105**
Ridgeway Vw. NP20: Newp 4H **35**
Ridgeway Vs. NP20: Newp 4H **35**
Ridgeway Wlk. NP20: Newp 4H **35**
Ridings, The CF38: Tont 2G **43**
Rifleman St. NP11: Ris 5D **16**
Riflemans Way NP16: Chep 2E **63**
Rimini Ho. CF10: Card 6C **96**
Rinastone Ct. CF5: F'wtr 1B **94**
RINGLAND 3D **38**
Ringland Cen. NP19: Newp 3D **38**
Ringland Circ. NP19: Newp 4B **38**
Ringland Way NP18: Newp 5B **38**
Ringside Bus. Cen. CF3: Rum 5B **88**
Ringwood Av. NP19: Newp 3A **38**
Ringwood Cres. CF62: St A 1D **112**
Ringwood Hill NP19: Newp 4A **38**
Ringwood Pl. NP19: Newp 4B **38**

RISCA 4D 16
Risca & Pontymister Station (Rail) 6E 17
Risca Cl. CF3: St M 6D 74
RISCA DAY HOSPITAL 4C 16
Risca Leisure Cen. 6H 17
Risca Rd. NP10: Roger 1H 33
NP11: C'keys 2A 16
NP20: Newp 5F 35
Rise, The CF14: L'shn 4A 72
CF37: Up Bo 6A 26
CF38: Tont 1F 43
CF62: Barry 1H 117
NP44: Pnwd 6C 8
Riverdale CF5: Ely 3H 93
Riverfront, The 4C 36
River Glade CF15: Gwae G, Taff W 1D 68
Rivermead Way NP10: Roger 2H 33
Riversdale CF5: L'dff 5B 84
River's Edge CF72: P'clun 6C 64
RIVERSIDE 5A 4 (4G 95)
Riverside NP4: P'pool 1B 6
NP16: Chep 1F 63
(off The Back)
NP19: Newp 3C 36
Riverside Ct. NP4: P'pool 2C 6
Riverside Ind. Pk. CF37: Up Bo 2B 44
Riverside Pk. CF83: B'ws 2E 29
Riverside Pl. CF63: Barry 1D 118
Riverside St. CF15: Taff W 6D 44
Riverside Ter. CF5: Ely 3B 94
CF83: Mac 3F 31
Riversmead NP44: Llan 3A 12
River St. CF37: T'rest 2E 25
River Vw. CF14: Llan N 5C 84
(Gabalfa Rd.)
CF14: Llan N 6D 84
(Western Av. Nth.)
NP16: Chep 1F 63
(St Ann St.)
NP16: Chep 2E 63
(School Hill)
River Vw. Ct. CF5: L'dff 5B 84
River Wlk. CF71: C'bri 4C 90
CF71: Llan M 3B 110
Road D NP10: Roger 4B 34
Roald Dahl Plass 1C 102
ROATH 1C 96
Roath Ct. CF24: Card 1D 96
NP44: Llan 2A 12
Roath Ct. Pl. CF24: Card 1D 96
Roath Ct. Rd. CF24: Card 1C 96
Roath Dock Rd. CF10: Card 1D 102
ROATH PARK 4B 86
Robbins La. NP20: Newp 5C 36
Robert Pl. NP20: Newp 1C 54
Roberts Cl. CF62: St A 4D 112
NP10: Roger 2C 34
Robertson Way NP20: Malp 3A 20
Robert St. CF5: Ely 3B 94
CF24: Card 6A 86
CF63: Barry 2B 118
Robin Cl. CF23: L'dyrn 6D 72
Robin Hill CF64: Din P 3H 107
Robins La. CF63: Barry 6B 106
Robinswood Cl. CF64: P'rth 3E 109
Robinswood Cres. CF64: P'rth 3E 109
Rochdale Ter. NP4: P'nydd 1A 6
Roche Cres. CF5: F'wtr 6G 83
Rochester Rd. NP19: Newp 4F 37
Rock Cl. CF62: St A 4F 111
Rock Cotts. CF37: P'prdd 5A 14
Rockery Cl. CF64: Sul 2G 119
Rockfield Cres. NP26: Undy 4F 59
Rockfield Gro. NP26: Undy 3F 59
Rockfield Ho. NP4: P'pool 2B 6
Rockfield La. NP26: Undy 3F 59
Rockfield Ri. NP26: Undy 4F 59
Rockfield St. NP19: Newp 2D 36
Rockfield Vw. NP26: Undy 3E 59
Rockfield Way NP26: Undy 3F 59
Rockhill Rd. NP4: P'pool 3D 6
Rockingstone Ter. CF37: P'prdd 1E 25
Rock Rd. CF62: St A 5D 112
Rockrose Way CF64: P'rth 6G 101
Rock Villa La. NP16: Tut 1F 63
Rockwood Rd. CF15: Taff W 1F 69
NP16: Chep 3E 63
Roden Ct. CF24: Card 1H 5
Roding Cl. NP20: Bet 6F 19
Rodney Parade 4D 36
Rodney Pde. NP19: Newp 4C 36
Rodney Rd. NP19: Newp 4C 36
Rogart Ter. CF37: P'prdd 3D 14
Rogersmoor Cl. CF64: P'rth 3E 109
ROGERSTONE 4C 34
Rogerstone Cl. CF3: St M 6D 74
Rogerstone Station (Rail) 2A 34
ROGIET 6A 60
Rogiet Rd. NP26: Rog 5A 60
Roland St. CF10: Card 6F 5 (5B 96)
Rolls Cl. NP44: F'wtr 3C 10
Rolls St. CF11: Card 4F 95
Rolls Wlk. NP10: Roger 3C 34
Roma Ho. CF10: Card 5B 96
Roman Amphitheatre 6H 21
Roman Cl. CF5: Ely 6H 93
Roman Gates NP18: C'ln 5H 21
Roman Legionary Mus. 5H 21
Roman Reach NP18: C'ln 5E 21
Roman Way NP18: C'ln 4F 21
Romanwell Rd. CF62: Barry 5G 117
Romilly Av. CF62: Barry 4E 117
Romilly Bldgs. CF63: Barry 3B 118
Romilly Ct. CF62: Barry 4F 117
Romilly Cres. CF11: Card 3F 95
Romilly Pk. Rd. CF62: Barry 5D 116
Romilly Pl. CF5: Card 3E 95
Romilly Rd. CF5: Card 3E 95
CF62: Barry 4F 117
(not continuous)
CF62: Rho 6E 115
Romilly Rd. W. CF5: Card 2D 94
Romney Cl. NP19: Newp 2G 37
Romney Wlk. CF64: P'rth 6H 101
Rompney Ter. CF3: Rum 5H 87
Romsley Ct. NP44: G'mdw 3E 11
Ronald Pl. CF5: Ely 3H 93
Ronald Rd. NP19: Newp 3E 37
Rookery Wood CF64: Sul 2G 119
Rookwood Av. CF5: L'dff 6B 84
Rookwood Cl. CF5: L'dff 6B 84
ROOKWOOD HOSPITAL 6B 84
Rookwood St. CF11: Card 6G 95
Roper Cl. CF5: L'dff 5H 83
Rosamund Cl. NP10: Duf 6H 53
Rosary, The NP4: C'avn 1C 6
Roseberry Pl. CF64: P'rth 2D 108
Roseberry St. NP4: Grif 6E 7
Rose Cotts. CF37: P'prdd 6B 14
Rose Ct. NP44: F'wtr 3B 10
Rosecroft Dr. NP18: L'stne 1G 39
Rosedale Cl. CF5: F'wtr 1G 93
Rosegarden, The NP20: Newp 4H 35
Rose Gdns. NP44: C'iog 1B 12
Rosemary La. NP4: P'pool 2C 6
Rosemary St. CF10: Card 5F 5 (4C 96)
Rosemead NP44: G'mdw 2B 10
Rosemont Av. NP11: Ris 5E 17
Rosemount Pl. CF14: Heath 4F 85
Rosendale Ct. NP19: Newp 4F 37
Rose St. CF24: Card 2C 96
NP20: Newp 3B 36
Rose Ter. *NP4: P'nydd 1A 6*
(off Chapel Rd.)
Rose Wlk. NP10: Roger 2H 33
Rosewood Cl. CF14: L'vne 2A 72
Ross Cl. CF37: P'cae 3B 24
Rosser St. CF37: P'prdd 1B 24
NP4: P'pool 2A 6
Rosset Cl. CF3: St M 1C 88
Rossetti Cl. CF5: L'dff 4A 84
Ross La. NP20: Newp 2B 36
Rosslyn Rd. NP19: Newp 4F 37
Ross St. NP20: Newp 1B 36
Rother Cl. NP20: Bet 4F 19
Rothesay Rd. NP19: Newp 4F 37
Rougemont Gro. NP16: Bul 6F 63
Roundabout Ct. CF83: B'ws 3D 28
Roundel Cl. CF14: Thorn 1H 71
Round Wood CF23: L'dyrn 2E 87
Round Wood Cl. CF23: Pen L 4E 87
Routs Vw. NP18: L'wrn 4F 39
Rover Way CF10: Card 1F 103
CF24: Card, Pen L 1F 97
Rover Way Ind. Est. CF24: Card 1F 97
Row, The CF3: Lwr M 6A 32
Rowan Cl. CF37: P'cae 3B 24
CF64: P'rth 4E 109
NP26: Undy 3E 59
Rowan Ct. CF5: L'dff 1C 94
CF62: Barry 4E 117
CF72: L'harry 5A 78
Rowan Cres. NP4: Grif 1D 8
Rowan Dr. NP16: Bul 5E 63
Rowan Gro. *CF62: St A 2B 112*
(off Sycamore Av.)
Rowan Rd. NP11: Ris 5F 17
Rowan Tree La. CF72: P'clun 5F 65
Rowan Way CF14: L'vne 2B 72
NP20: Malp 4B 20
Rowena Ct. CF5: F'wtr 1G 93
Rowland Dr. CF83: Caer 2A 46
Rowsby Ct. CF23: Pontp 4F 73
Roxburgh Gdn. Ct. CF64: P'rth 2F 109
Roxby Ct. CF10: Card 6F 5 (5B 96)
Royal Arc. CF10: Card 5D 4 (4A 96)
Royal Bldgs. CF64: P'rth 2E 109
Royal Cl. CF64: P'rth 6A 102
ROYAL GLAMORGAN HOSPITAL 6D 40
ROYAL GWENT HOSPITAL 6B 36
Royal Oak CF83: Mac 3H 31
Royal Oak Cl. CF83: Mac 2H 31
Royal Oak Dr. NP18: Newp 2C 38
Royal Oak Grn. NP44: C'iog 1B 12
Royal Oak Hill NP18: C'ln, Newp 1C 38
Royal Stuart La. CF10: Card 2B 102
Royce Wlk. NP10: Roger 3C 34
Royde Cl. CF5: Ely 5C 92
Royston Cres. NP19: Newp 5H 37
Rubens Cl. NP19: Newp 2F 37
Ruby St. CF24: Card 3D 96
RUDRY 1C 48
Rudry Cl. CF83: Caer 4G 29
Rudry Rd. CF14: L'vne 2C 72
CF83: Caer 4F 29
CF83: Rud 2C 72
Rudry St. CF11: Card 6G 95
CF64: P'rth 1D 108
NP19: Newp 3C 36
Ruffett's Cl. NP16: Chep 2D 62
Rugby Rd. NP19: Newp 4D 36
RUMNEY 5A 88
Rumney Wlk. NP44: Llan 2B 12
Runcorn Cl. CF3: St M 5B 74
CF63: Barry 6D 106
Runway Rd. CF24: Card 2G 97
Ruperra Castle 2A 50
Ruperra Cl. CF3: St M 4B 74
NP10: Bass 6D 34
Ruperra La. NP20: Newp 6C 36
Ruperra St. CF72: L'sant 1F 65
NP20: Newp 6C 36
Rupert Brooke Dr. NP20: Newp 1H 53
Rushbrook NP44: G'mdw 2D 10
Rushbrook Cl. CF14: Whit 3A 84
Rush Wall NP26: Magor 6A 58
Ruskin Av. NP10: Roger 2C 34
Ruskin Cl. CF3: L'rmy 6H 73
NP44: F'wtr 3C 10
Ruskin Ri. NP20: Newp 1G 53
Russel Cl. NP4: New I 5H 7
Russell Cl. NP10: Bass 6B 34
Russell Dr. NP20: Malp 4A 20
Russell Dr. Gdns. NP20: Malp 5A 20
Russell St. CF24: Card 1F 5 (2B 96)
NP44: Pnwd 6E 9
Russet Cl. NP18: L'stne 1G 39
Ruthen Ter. CF62: Barry 2F 117
Rutherford Hill NP20: Malp 4A 20
Ruthin Gdns. CF24: Card 1D 4 (2A 96)
Ruthin Way CF38: Tont 1F 43
Ruth Rd. NP4: New I 4F 7
Rutland Cl. CF62: Barry 5E 105
Rutland Pl. NP20: Newp 6C 36
Rutland St. CF11: Card 5G 95
Ryder St. CF11: Card 3G 95

S

Sable Cl. CF14: L'vne 1A 72
Sachville Av. CF14: Card 5G 85
Saffron Ct. NP44: F'wtr 4B 10
Saffron Dr. CF3: St M 5E 75
SAIN HILARI 6H 91
SAIN SIORYS 3A 92
St Agatha Rd. CF14: Heath 3G 85
St Agnes Ct. CF24: Card 2E 97
St Agnes Rd. CF14: Heath 3F 85
St Aidan Cres. CF14: Heath 3F 85
St Alban's Av. CF14: Heath 3F 85
St Ambrose Cl. CF64: Din P 3G 107
St Ambrose Rd. CF14: Heath 3G 85
SAINT ANDRAS 1C 106
St Andrew's Av. NP16: Bul 3E 63
St Andrews Cl. CF38: Llan F 5D 42
NP44: Pnwd 4F 9
St Andrews Ct. CF37: P'prdd 1C 24
St Andrew's Cres. CF10: Card 2E 5 (3B 96)
St Andrew's La. CF10: Card 2E 5 (3B 96)
ST ANDREWS MAJOR 1C 106
St Andrew's Pl. CF10: Card 2D 4 (3A 96)
St Andrews Rd. CF5: Wen 6E 99
CF37: P'cae 3B 24
CF62: Barry 1G 117
CF64: Din P 6E 99
St Angela Rd. CF14: Heath 3G 85
St Anne's Av. CF64: P'rth 3D 108

St Anne's Cl. NP10: Roger 5D **34**
NP44: Pnwd 6E **9**
St Annes Ct. CF72: P'clun 2B **78**
St Annes Cres. NP19: Newp 2E **37**
NP26: Undy 4F **59**
St Annes Dr. CF38: Llan F 5D **42**
St Annes Gdns. CF83: Abert 2E **27**
ST ANNE'S HOSPICE 4B **20**
St Ann's Ct. CF62: Barry 5A **106**
St Ann St. NP16: Chep 1F **63**
St Anthony Rd. CF14: Heath 3G **85**
St Anthony's Cl. NP4: Grif 1D **8**
St Arvans Cres. CF3: St M 6D **74**
St Arvans Rd. NP44: C'brn 2H **11**
St Asaph Cl. CF14: Heath 1G **85**
St Asaph's Way CF83: Caer 2C **46**
SAIN TATHAN 5D **112**
ST ATHAN 5D **112**
St Athan Rd. CF62: St A 1A **112**
CF71: C'bri, L'thian 5D **90**
St Athan's Ct. CF83: Caer 1B **46**
St Augustine Rd. CF14: Heath 3G **85**
NP4: Grif 1D **8**
St Augustine's Cres. CF64: P'rth 6B **102**
St Augustine's Path CF64: P'rth 6B **102**
St Augustine's Pl. CF64: P'rth 6B **102**
St Augustines Rd. CF64: P'rth 6B **102**
St Baruch Cl. CF64: Din P 3G **107**
St Baruchs Ct. CF62: Barry 5H **117**
St Basil's Cres. NP10: Bass 6C **34**
St Benedict Ct. NP10: Bass 1C **52**
St Benedict Cres. CF14: Heath 3G **85**
St Benedicts Cl. NP4: Grif 1D **8**
St Bleddians Cl. CF71: C'bri 3B **90**
St Brannocks Cl. CF62: Barry 2E **117**
St Briavels M. NP10: Coedk 6G **53**
St Brides Cl. NP26: Magor 3C **58**
NP44: Llan 3A **12**
(not continuous)
St Brides Ct. CF5: Ely 5G **93**
St Brides Cres. NP20: Newp 3H **53**
St Brides Gdns. NP20: Newp 3H **53**
St Brides Mnr. CF38: Llan F 6D **42**
St Brides Rd. CF5: St Brid, St F 6H **81** & 1A **92**
NP26: Magor 2C **58**
ST BRIDES-SUPER-ELY 6H **81**
St Bride's Way CF63: Barry 5A **106**
ST BRIDE'S WENTLOOGE 4G **77**
St Brigid Rd. CF14: Heath 1G **85**
St Brioc Rd. CF14: Heath 1G **85**
St Cadoc Rd. CF14: Heath 2G **85**
St Cadocs Av. CF64: Din P 3G **107**
St Cadoc's Cl. NP18: C'ln 4G **21**
ST CADOC'S HOSPITAL 5G **21**
St Cadoc's Ri. CF63: Barry 5D **106**
St Cadoc's Rd. NP4: C'avn 1D **6**
St Canna Cl. CF5: Card 3E **95**
St Catherines Cl. CF83: B'ws 3F **29**
St Catherine's Ct. CF62: Barry 5H **105**
NP11: C'keys 3A **16**
St Catherines M. CF11: Card 2F **95**
St Cecilia Ct. NP20: Newp 4A **36**
St Cenydd Cl. CF83: Caer 5A **28**
St Cenydd Leisure Cen. 5H **27**
St Cenydd Rd. CF14: Heath 1H **85**
CF83: Caer 5A **28**
St Christophers Cl. CF83: B'ws 3F **29**
St Christopher's Dr. CF83: Caer 1B **46**
St Clair Ct. *CF10: Card* *1C **102***
(off W. Bute St.)
St Clears Cl. CF83: Caer 1C **46**
St Clements Ct. CF23: L'dyrn 5E **73**
St Curig's Cl. CF62: Rho 6E **115**
St Cuthberts Ct. CF10: Card 1B **102**
St Cyres Cl. CF64: P'rth 1C **108**
St Cyres Rd. CF64: P'rth 2C **108**
St Davids Av. CF38: Chu V 3E **43**
CF64: Din P 1H **107**
CF71: Llan M 4C **110**
St David's Cen. CF10: Card 4D **4** (4A **96**)
St David's Cl. CF37: N'grw 3C **44**
NP4: P'pool 2C **6**
NP16: Bul 3E **63**
St Davids Ct. CF3: M'fld 4A **76**
NP26: Magor 4C **58**
St Davids Cres. CF5: Ely 4H **93**
CF62: St A *4D **112***
(off Cowbridge Rd.)
CF64: P'rth 2B **108**
NP20: Newp 2G **53**
St David's Dr. CF83: Mac 3B **30**
ST DAVID'S FOUNDATION HOSPICE 4F **37**
St David's Hall 4D **4** (4A **96**)
ST DAVIDS HOSPITAL 3G **95**
St David's Link CF10: Card 4E **5** (4B **96**)
St Davids Pl. CF72: L'sant 1G **65**
St Davids Rd. CF14: Whit 3C **84**
CF72: P'clun 1F **79**
NP44: C'brn, Pnwd 6F **9**
St David's Way CF10: Card 4D **4** (4A **96**)
CF83: Caer 2B **46**
St Denis Rd. CF14: Heath 2H **85**
ST DIALS 2E **11**
St Dials Ct. NP44: C'brn 3G **11**
St Dials Rd. NP44: C'brn, G'mdw 2D **10**
(not continuous)
St Dogmaels Av. CF14: L'shn 6H **71**
St Dominics Retreat NP4: P'pool 3B **6**
St Donats Cl. CF64: Din P 2H **107**
St Donats Ct. CF5: Ely 5G **93**
CF83: Caer 1B **46**
St Donats Pl. NP44: Llan 3B **12**
St Donats Rd. CF11: Card 5F **95**
St Dyfrig Cl. CF64: Din P 3H **107**
St Dyfrig Rd. CF64: P'rth 3C **108**
St Edeyrns Cl. CF23: Cyn 1D **86**
St Edeyrn's Rd. CF23: Cyn 1C **86**
St Edward St. NP20: Newp 5B **36**
St Edwen Gdns. CF14: Heath 2G **85**
St Ewens Rd. NP16: Bul 4E **63**
ST FAGANS 2E **93**
St Fagans Av. CF62: Barry 1G **117**
St Fagans Castle 2D **92**
St Fagans Cl. CF5: F'wtr 2A **94**
St Fagans Ct. CF5: Ely 5D **92**
St Fagans Dr. CF5: St F 1E **93**
St Fagans Ri. CF5: F'wtr 1G **93**
St Fagans Rd. CF5: F'wtr 2G **93**
St Fagans St. CF11: Card 1H **101**
CF83: Caer 1C **46**
St Francis Ct. CF24: Card 4F **97**
St Francis Rd. CF14: Whit 2C **84**
St Garmon Rd. CF64: P'rth 3C **108**
St George Rd. NP16: Bul 3E **63**
ST GEORGE'S 3A **92**
St George's Cres. NP19: Newp 2F **37**
St George's Rd. CF14: Heath 4F **85**
St Georges Way NP16: B'ly 6H **63**
St Gildas Rd. CF14: Heath 2G **85**
St Govan's Cl. CF62: Barry 5H **105**
St Gowan Av. CF14: Heath 2G **85**
St Gwynnos Cl. CF64: Din P 2G **107**
St Helen's Ct. CF83: Caer 1B **46**
St Helen's Rd. CF14: Heath 3F **85**
ST HILARY 6H **91**
St Hilary Ct. CF5: Ely 5H **93**
St Hilda's Rd. NP4: Grif 1E **9**
St Ilan's Way CF83: Caer 2C **46**
St Illtud's Church 3A **110**
St Illtyd Cl. CF64: Din P 2H **107**
St Illtyd Rd. CF38: Chu V 1E **43**
St Ina Rd. CF14: Heath 2G **85**
St Isan Rd. CF14: Heath 2G **85**
St James Cl. CF83: Caer 4G **29**
St James Ct. CF64: P'rth 3C **108**
St James Cres. CF62: Barry 2D **116**
St James' Fld. NP4: P'pool 3C **6**
St James Mans. CF10: Card 1B **102**
CF14: L'vne 2A **72**
St James M. *CF11: Card* *2F **95***
(off Severn Gro.)
St Johns Cl. CF71: C'bri 4D **90**
NP4: P'pool 2A **6**
St Johns Ct. *CF62: Barry* *5H **117***
(off Friars Rd.)
NP10: Roger 3B **34**
St John's Cres. CF5: Card 4F **95**
CF14: Whit 1C **84**
NP4: P'pool 2A **6**
NP10: Roger 3B **34**
St Johns Gdns. NP16: Chep 1D **62**
St John's Hill CF62: St A 4D **112**
St John's M. *CF5: Card* *4F **95***
(off St John's Cres.)
St John's Pl. CF14: Whit 1C **84**
CF62: Rho 5C **114**
St John's Rd. NP19: Newp 4F **37**
St John St. CF10: Card 4C **4** (4A **96**)
St John's Vw. CF62: St A 4C **112**
St Joseph Pl. NP44: Oakf 1B **20**
St Josephs Cl. NP26: Undy 4F **59**
St Joseph's Ct. CF14: Card 5H **85**
ST JOSEPH'S HOSPITAL 3B **20**
St Julian Cl. CF63: Barry 6C **106**
ST JULIANS 2F **37**
St Julian's Av. NP19: Newp 2E **37**
St Julians Ct. CF83: Caer 1B **46**
NP19: Newp 2E **37**
St Julian's Rd. NP19: Newp 2E **37**
St Julian St. NP20: Newp 5B **36**
St Kingsmark Av. NP16: Chep 1D **62**
St Lawrence La. NP16: Chep 3C **62**
St Lawrence Pk. NP16: Chep 2C **62**
St Lawrence Rd. NP16: Chep 3D **62**
(Newport Rd.)
NP16: Chep 1C **62**
(Welsh St.)
St Luke's Av. CF37: R'fln 5G **25**
CF64: P'rth 3C **108**
St Lukes Rd. NP4: P'nydd 1A **6**
St Lythan Cl. CF64: Din P 3G **107**
St Lythan Ct. CF5: Ely 5G **93**
ST LYTHANS 5C **98**
ST LYTHANS DOWN 3C **98**
St Lythan's Rd. CF62: Barry 2E **117**
St Malo Rd. CF14: Heath 1G **85**
St Margarets Cl. CF14: Whit 1C **84**
CF83: Tret 3H **29**
St Margaret's Cres. CF23: Pen L 1D **96**
St Margaret's Pk. CF5: Ely 3A **94**
St Margaret's Pl. CF14: Whit 1C **84**
St Margaret's Rd. CF14: Whit 2C **84**
CF83: Caer 1B **46**
St Mark's Av. CF14: Card 4G **85**
St Mark's Cres. NP20: Newp 4A **36**
St Marks Gdns. CF14: Card 4G **85**
St Mark's Rd. CF64: P'rth 3D **108**
ST MARTINS 1C **46**
St Martin's Cl. CF64: P'rth 3C **108**
St Martins Ct. NP20: Newp 6H **35**
St Martin's Cres. CF14: L'shn 6H **71**
CF83: Caer 2C **46**
St Martin's Rd. CF83: Caer 2B **46**
St Mary's Av. CF63: Barry 2A **118**
St Marys Cl. CF5: Ely 6H **93**
CF37: R'fln 2F **25**
NP4: Grif 6D **6**
St Marys Ct. CF5: Ely 1G **99**
NP11: Ris 4D **16**
NP20: Newp 5B **36**
St Mary's Pl. NP26: Pskwt 5G **61**
(not continuous)
St Mary's Rd. CF14: Whit 1C **84**
NP44: C'iog 6G **9**
St Mary St. CF10: Card 4C **4** (4A **96**)
CF83: B'ws 3F **29**
NP4: Grif 6D **6**
NP11: Ris 4C **16**
NP16: Chep 2E **63**
NP20: Newp 5B **36**
St Mary's Well Bay Rd. CF64: Sul 4B **120**
St Matthew's Rd. NP4: P'pool 4D **6**
St Maur Gdns. NP16: Chep 1D **62**
ST MELLONS 1D **88**
St Mellons Bus. Pk. CF3: St M 5F **75**
St Mellons Cl. NP26: Undy 4E **59**
St Mellons Ct. CF83: Caer 1B **46**
St Mellons Interchange CF3: St M 4C **74**
St Mellons Rd. CF3: M'fld 6G **75**
CF14: L'vne 2C **72**
CF14: Pontp 3F **73**
CF23: Pontp 3F **73**
St Michael Gro. NP44: Oakf 6B **12**
St Michael's Av. CF37: T'rest 2D **24**
St Michaels Cl. CF15: Tong 4G **69**
CF38: Bed 5H **41**
CF62: St A 4D **112**
CF64: Mic P 4C **100**
St Michaels Ct. NP20: Newp 1D **54**
St Michaels Gdns. CF62: Barry 5G **105**
St Michaels M. NP20: Newp 1D **54**
St Michael's Rd. CF5: L'dff 2C **94**
St Michael St. NP20: Newp 1D **54**
St Nicholas Cl. CF62: Barry 4E **117**
CF64: Din P 2G **107**
St Nicholas Ct. CF5: Ely 5G **93**
CF23: L'dyrn 5E **73**
CF83: Caer 1B **46**
St Nicholas Rd. CF62: Barry 4E **117**
St Oswalds Cl. NP4: Grif 2E **9**
St Oswald's Rd. CF63: Barry 6C **106**
St Osyth Ct. CF62: Barry 5E **117**
St Paul's Av. CF62: Barry 3G **117**
CF64: P'rth 3D **108**
St Pauls Cl. CF64: Din P 3G **107**
St Peters Cl. NP44: F'wtr 3D **10**
St Peter's Rd. CF64: P'rth 3C **108**
St Peters St. CF24: Card 1F **5** (2B **96**)
St Philip Evans Cl. CF23: L'dyrn 1E **87**
St Phillip's Flats *NP19: Newp* *5F **37***
(off Cromwell Rd.)
St Pierre Cl. CF3: St M 5E **75**
St Quentins Cl. CF71: L'thian 4C **90**
St Quentins Hill CF71: L'thian 4B **90**
St Siors Meade CF62: Rho 5D **114**
St Stephen's Cl. NP26: C'went 1B **60**
St Stephens Ct. NP26: Undy 4F **59**
St Stephens Mans. CF10: Card 1B **102**

St Stephens Pl. NP26: Undy 4F **59**
St Stephens Rd. NP20: Newp 1D **54**
St Tanwg Rd. CF14: Heath 2G **85**
St Tathan's Pl. NP26: C'went 1B **60**
St Tecla Rd. NP16: Bul 4E **63**
St Teilo Av. CF62: Barry 1G **117**
St Teilo Cl. CF64: Din P 2H **107**
St Teilo Ct. NP26: Undy 4F **59**
St Teilos Ct. CF23: Pen L 1D **96**
St Teilo's Way CF83: Caer 2B **46**
St Tewdric Rd. NP16: Bul 3E **63**
St Tewdrics Pl. NP16: Math 6B **62**
St Thomas Cl. CF14: Heath 2E **85**
St Vincent Rd. NP19: Newp 4C **36**
St Vincents Ct. NP19: Newp 4C **36**
St Winifred's Cl. CF64: Din P 3G **107**
ST WOOLOS 6G **35**
St Woolos Cathedral 5B **36**
St Woolos Grn. NP44: C'brn 1G **11**
ST WOOLOS HOSPITAL 6B **36**
St Woolos Pl. NP20: Newp 5B **36**
St Woolos Rd. NP20: Newp 5B **36**
Salem La. CF38: Tont 2F **43**
Salem Row CF15: Gwae G 6D **44**
Salem Ter. CF15: Gwae G 6D **44**
Salisbury Av. CF64: P'rth 2D **108**
Salisbury Cl. CF64: P'rth 2D **108**
NP20: Newp 3C **36**
Salisbury Ct. CF64: P'rth 2D **108**
NP44: C'brn 2E **11**
Salisbury Rd. CF24: Card 1E **5** (2B **96**)
CF62: Barry 4E **117**
Salisbury St. NP11: C'keys 3A **16**
Sally, The NP4: P'pool 3A **6**
Salmon Cl. CF23: Pen L 6E **87**
Salop Pl. CF64: P'rth 6A **102**
Salop St. CF64: P'rth 6A **102**
CF83: Caer 1D **46**
Salvia Cl. CF3: St M 6E **75**
Samson St. CF71: Llan M 2B **110**
Samuels Cres. CF14: Whit 2A **84**
Sanatorium Rd. CF11: Card 4C **94**
Sanctuary, The CF5: Ely 6E **93**
Sanctuary Ct. CF5: Ely 1E **99**
Sandbrook Rd. CF3: St M 1E **89**
Sanderling Dr. CF3: St M 6C **74**
Sandon Rd. CF24: Card 4F **5** (3B **96**)
Sandon St. CF24: Card 4F **5** (4B **96**)
Sandown Ct. CF5: Ely 4A **94**
Sandpiper Cl. CF3: St M 5D **74**
Sandpiper Way NP10: Duf 5G **53**
Sandringham Cl. CF62: Barry 5E **105**
Sandringham Rd. CF23: Pen L 6C **86**
Sandwell Ct. CF64: L'dgh 5F **101**
Sandwick Ct. CF23: Cyn 6C **72**
Sandybrook Cl. NP44: C'brn 4E **11**
Sandy La. CF3: Cas 3G **75**
NP10: Duf 3H **53**
NP26: C'went 2C **60**
Sanquahar St. CF24: Card 5H **5** (4C **96**)
Sansom St. NP11: Ris 4D **16**
Sapele Dr. CF24: Card 5H **5** (4D **96**)
Sapphire St. CF24: Card 2D **96**
Sardis Rd. CF37: P'prdd 1B **24**
(not continuous)
Sardis Road Ground *1D **24***
(off Broadway)
Sarn Pl. NP11: Ris 4D **16**
Saron St. CF37: T'rest 2E **25**
Saundersfoot Cl. CF5: Ely 6H **93**
Saunders Rd. CF10: Card 6D **4** (5A **96**)
Sawtells Ter. NP4: P'nydd 1A **6**
Saxon Pl. NP16: Sed 3G **63**
Scala Cinema 2C **6**
Scarborough Rd. CF37: P'prdd 5E **15**
NP19: Newp 1D **36**
Scard St. NP20: Newp 5B **36**
School Cl. NP4: P'pool 3B **6**
School Ct. NP44: C'brn 3G **11**
School Cres. NP4: Grif 2E **9**
School Hill NP16: Chep 2E **63**
School Hill Trad. Est. NP16: Chep 2E **63**
School La. CF15: Taff W 1D **68**
CF37: R'fln 6H **25**
NP4: P'pool 2B **6**
NP20: Newp 4C **36**
School Rd. CF72: P'clun 1F **79**
NP4: P'nydd 1A **6**
School St. CF10: Card 6E **5** (5B **96**)
CF72: L'sant 2F **65**
CF72: P'clun 5D **64**
CF83: L'brad 1B **28**
School Ter. *NP4: P'nydd* *1A **6***
(off Old School Pl.)
NP10: Roger 4B **34**
School Vw. NP4: P'pool 4D **6**
Schooner Way CF10: Card 6G **5** (5C **96**)
Scotney Way CF23: Pontp 4G **73**
Scott Cl. CF62: St A 2D **112**
NP20: Newp 2G **53**
Scott Ct. CF23: Cyn 4B **86**
Scott Rd. CF10: Card 5C **4** (4A **96**)
Scott Wlk. NP10: Roger 2C **34**
Seabank CF64: P'rth 2F **109**
Seager Dr. CF11: Card 3H **101**
Sealawns CF62: Barry 6E **117**
Sea Point *CF62: Barry* *6E **117***
(off Sealawns)
Seasons Cl. NP26: Magor 4C **58**
Seaton's Pl. CF37: P'prdd 6B **14**
Seaton St. CF37: P'prdd 6A **14**
Sea Vw. NP26: Sud 6H **61**
Seaview Cotts. CF3: St M 6B **74**
Seaview Ct. CF64: P'rth 1F **109**
Seaview Ind. Est. CF24: Card 4E **97**
Seaview Pl. CF71: Llan M 3B **110**
Sea Vw. Ter. CF5: Wen 3C **98**
CF63: Barry 6C **106**
Seawall Rd. CF24: Card 4F **97**
Seawall Rd. Ind. Est. CF24: Card 3G **97**
SEBASTOPOL 2E **9**
Second Av. CF23: Pen L 6E **87**
CF83: Caer 6A **28**
Second St. NP19: Newp 3G **55**
SEDBURY 2H **63**
Sedbury Bus. Pk. NP16: Tut 1G **63**
Sedbury La. NP16: Sed 2H **63**
NP16: Tut, Sed 1G **63**
(not continuous)
Sedgemoor Ct. NP20: Newp 3A **36**
Sedgemoor Rd. CF3: L'rmy 6A **74**
Sefton Ct. *CF15: Rad* *1F **83***
(off Maes yr Awel)
Selby Cl. NP44: Llanf 3B **12**
Selwyn Morris Ct. CF24: Card 4E **97**
Senghennydd Ho. CF24: Card 2E **5** (3B **96**)
Senghennydd Pl. CF24: Card 1E **5** (2B **96**)
Senghennydd Rd. CF24: Card 1D **4** (2A **96**)
Senlan Ind. Est. CF23: Pen L 6G **87**
Senni Cl. CF62: Barry 1E **117**
Serpentine Rd. NP20: Newp 4B **36**
Sevenoaks Rd. CF5: Ely 4F **93**
Sevenoaks St. CF11: Card 1H **101**
Seven Stiles Av. NP19: Newp 1B **56**
Severn Av. CF62: Barry 2E **117**
NP16: Tut 1G **63**
Severn Bri. Ind. Est. NP26: Pskwt 6F **61**
Severn Cl. NP11: Ris 6F **17**
Severn Ct. CF11: Card 3F **95**
Severn Cres. NP16: Chep 3E **63**
Severn Gro. CF11: Card 2F **95**
Severn Rd. CF11: Card 3F **95**
CF37: Up Bo 1A **44**
Severn Ter. NP20: Newp 5B **36**
Severn Tunnel Junction Station (Rail) 6A **60**
Severn Vw. NP16: Chep 2D **62**
NP26: Cald 5B **60**
NP44: Up Cwm 5B **8**
Sevins *NP44: F'wtr* *4E **11***
(off Henllys Way)
Seymour St. CF24: Card 3E **97**
Seys Cl. CF71: C'bri 3B **90**
Seys Ct. CF71: Llan M 2D **110**
Sgubor Goch CF72: L'harry 4C **78**
Shackleton Cl. CF62: St A 2D **112**
Shadow Wood Dr. CF72: P'clun 5E **65**
Shaftesbury Cl. CF14: Thorn 2G **71**
Shaftesbury St. NP20: Newp 3C **36**
Shaftesbury Wlk. *NP20: Newp* *3C **36***
(off Shaftesbury St.)
Shakespeare Av. CF64: P'rth 1C **108**
Shakespeare Cl. NP26: Cald 5B **60**
Shakespeare Ct. CF24: Card 1G **5** (2C **96**)
Shakespeare Cres. NP20: Newp 1G **53**
Shakespeare Dr. CF71: Llan M 3D **110**
NP26: Cald 6B **60**
Shakespeare Ri. CF37: R'fln 3G **25**
Shakespeare Rd. CF62: Barry 5H **105**
NP44: C'brn, G'mdw 3E **11**
Shakespeare St. CF24: Card 1G **5** (2C **96**)
Shamrock Rd. CF5: F'wtr 1G **93**
Shannon Cl. NP20: Bet 5H **19**
Sharpe Cl. CF23: Pen L 6E **87**
Sharps Way NP16: Bul 5F **63**
Shaw Cl. CF3: L'rmy 6H **73**
Shaw Gro. NP20: Newp 1G **53**
Shawley Ct. NP44: G'mdw 3E **11**
Sheaf La. NP19: Newp 3D **36**
Shea Gdns. *NP20: Newp* *6C **36***
(off Francis Dr.)
Shearman Pl. CF11: Card 3A **102**
Shears Rd. CF5: F'wtr 2B **94**
Shearwater Cl. CF64: P'rth 6E **109**
Sheerwater Cl. CF3: St M 6C **74**
Shelburn Cl. CF11: Card 5G **95**
Shelley Cl. NP26: Cald 5B **60**
Shelley Ct. CF83: Mac 2C **30**
Shelley Cres. CF62: Barry 5G **105**
CF64: P'rth 1D **108**
Shelley Grn. NP44: G'mdw 3E **11**
Shelley Rd. NP19: Newp 4F **37**
Shelley Wlk. CF24: Card 1G **5** (2C **96**)
CF37: R'fln 3G **25**
Sheppard St. CF37: P'prdd 6B **14**
Sherborne Av. CF23: Cyn 6C **72**
Sherbourne Cl. CF62: Barry 5D **104**
Sherbourne Ct. NP4: Grif 2E **9**
Sherbourne Rd. NP4: Grif 2E **9**
Sheridan Cl. CF3: L'rmy 6H **73**
NP20: Newp 1G **53**
Sherman Theatre 1D **4** (2A **96**)
Sherwood Ct. CF5: F'wtr 6H **83**
Shetland Cl. NP19: Newp 2F **37**
Shetland Wlk. NP19: Newp 2F **37**
Shields Cl. CF23: Pontp 4H **73**
Ship La. *CF10: Card* *1C **102***
(off W. Bute St.)
Shirenewton Cvn. Pk. CF3: Rum 5E **89**
Shires, The CF3: M'fld 4H **75**
(not continuous)
Shirley Cl. CF63: Barry 5D **106**
Shirley Rd. CF23: Card 5A **86**
Short Path *NP44: F'wtr* *4D **10***
(off Jule Rd.)
Showcase Cinema 3D **44**
Showle Acre CF62: Rho 5D **114**
Shrewsbury Cl. NP20: Newp 3C **36**
Sickert Cl. NP19: Newp 3G **37**
Sidings, The *CF37: T'rest* *3E **25***
(off Park St.)
Sidney St. NP20: Newp 5B **36**
Sienna Ho. CF10: Card 5B **96**
Siloam Hill CF83: Mac 2F **31**
SILSTWN 6D **112**
Silure Way NP18: L'stne 1F **39**
Silurian Pl. CF10: Card 6B **96**
Silver Birch Cl. CF14: Llan N 4D **84**
NP18: C'ln 5E **21**
Silver Fir Sq. NP10: Roger 6D **34**
Silverhill Cl. CF37: C'fydd 3F **15**
Silver Jubilee Cotts. CF5: Ely 4H **93**
Silverstone Cl. CF3: St M 5B **74**
Silver St. CF24: Card 2H **5** (3D **96**)
NP11: P'waun 1A **16**
Silverton Rd. CF72: C Inn 3G **65**
Simpson Cl. NP20: Malp 4A **20**
Sims Sq. NP19: Newp 4B **38**
Sinclair Dr. CF23: Pen L 6E **87**
Sindercombe Cl. CF23: Pontp 4F **73**
Singleton Rd. CF24: Card 4E **97**
Sion St. CF37: P'prdd 6C **14**
Sir Alfred Owen Way CF83: Caer 3C **28**
Sir Charles Cres. NP10: Duf 5H **53**
Sir Charles Sq. *NP10: Duf* *5G **53***
(off Sir Charles Cres.)
Sirhowy Ct. NP44: G'mdw 1D **10**
Sirius Ho. CF10: Card 1D **102**
Sir Ivor Pl. CF64: Din P 3H **107**
Sir Stafford Cl. CF83: Caer 4E **29**
Sixth St. NP19: Newp 4H **55**
Skaithmuir Rd. CF24: Card 2F **97**
Skelmuir Rd. CF24: Card 2F **97**
Skibereen Cl. CF23: Pontp 4G **73**
Skillion Bus. Cen. NP19: Newp 2F **55**
(not continuous)
Skinner La. NP20: Newp 4C **36**
Skinner Row NP19: Newp 5A **38**
Skinner St. NP20: Newp 4C **36**
Skomer Rd. CF62: Barry 5H **105**
Slade Cl. CF64: Sul 1H **119**
CF71: C'bri 3D **90**
Slade Rd. CF62: Barry 6H **105**
Slade St. NP19: Newp 6F **37**
Slade Wood Ho. CF62: Barry 5A **106**
Slipway, The CF64: P'rth 6A **102**
Sloper Rd. CF11: Card 5F **95**
Sluvad Rd. NP4: New I 6H **7**
Smallbrook Cl. NP44: C'brn 2H **11**
Small Mdw. Ct. CF83: Caer 5D **28**
Smeaton Cl. CF62: Rho 6C **114**
Smeaton St. CF11: Card 4G **95**
Smithies Av. CF64: Sul 3H **119**
Smooth Stones NP16: Pwllm 3A **62**
Sneyd St. CF11: Card 2F **95**
Snipe St. CF24: Card 2C **96**
Snowden Ct. CF83: Caer 6E **29**
Snowden Rd. CF5: Ely 4F **93**
Snowdon Cl. NP11: Ris 5F **17**

Snowdon Ct. NP44: C'iog 6G **9**
Snowdrop La. NP10: Roger 2H **33**
Soane Cl. NP10: Roger 2C **34**
SOAR 2H **67**
Soar Cl. NP44: C'iog 5H **9**
Soarel Cl. CF3: St M 2D **88**
Soberton Av. CF14: Card 5H **85**
Soho St. NP19: Newp 4E **37**
(not continuous)
Solent Rd. CF63: Barry 5C **106**
Solva Av. CF14: L'shn 5A **72**
Solva Cl. CF62: Barry 6H **105**
Somerset Ct. CF3: L'rmy 6A **74**
Somerset Ind. Est. NP44: C'brn 1H **11**
Somerset Rd. CF62: Barry 1H **117**
NP19: Newp 2E **37**
NP44: C'brn, Pnwd 1H **11**
Somerset Rd. E. CF63: Barry 1H **117**
Somerset St. CF11: Card 5G **95**
Somerset Vw. CF64: Sul 3H **119**
Somerset Way NP16: Bul 6F **63**
SOMERTON 6H **37**
Somerton Ct. NP19: Newp 6G **37**
Somerton Cres. NP19: Newp 4H **37**
Somerton La. NP19: Newp 5G **37**
Somerton Pk. NP19: Newp 5G **37**
Somerton Pl. NP19: Newp 4H **37**
Somerton Rd. NP19: Newp 5G **37**
Sophia Cl. CF11: Card 2A **4** (3G **95**)
Sophia Gdns. 2A **4** (3G **95**)
Sophia Wlk. CF11: Card 3G **95**
Sorrel Dr. NP20: Newp 4A **36**
Sorrento Ho. CF10: Card 6F **5** (5B **96**)
Soudry Way CF10: Card 1B **102**
South Av. NP4: Grif 3D **8**
Southbourne Ct. CF62: Barry 5H **117**
Southbrook Vw. NP26: Pskwt 6F **61**
Sth. Clive St. CF11: Card 2H **101**
South Cl. NP44: Llanf 4B **12**
Southcourt Rd. CF23: Pen L 5D **86**
South Dr. CF72: L'sant 2G **65**
South East Wales Regional Swimming Pool 2G **55**
Southern St. CF83: Caer 1D **46**
Southern Way CF23: Pen L 4F **87**
Southesk Pl. CF62: Barry 5E **117**
Southey St. CF24: Card 1H **5** (2C **96**)
CF62: Barry 2H **117**
Southgate CF71: C'bri 3C **90**
Southgate Av. CF72: L'sant 2F **65**
South Glade CF15: Gwae G 2E **69**
Southglade CF64: Sul 1H **119**
(not continuous)
Sth. Lake Dr. NP10: Coedk 5F **53**
Sth. Loudoun Pl. CF10: Card 6B **96**
Sth. Luton Pl. CF24: Card 4H **5** (4C **96**)
Sth. Market St. NP20: Newp 6D **36**
Southminster Rd. CF23: Pen L 1D **96**
Sth. Morgan Pl. CF11: Card 4G **95**
Sth. Pandy Rd. CF83: Caer 4C **28**
South Pk. Rd. CF24: Card 4F **97**
South Point CF10: Card 6F **97**
Sth. Pontypool Ind. Pk. NP4: New I 5F **7**
SOUTHRA 3G **107**
Southra CF64: Din P 3G **107**
South Ri. CF14: L'shn 5A **72**
South Rd. CF64: Sul 2G **119**
NP44: Oakf 5H **11**
South St. CF37: P'prdd 6D **14**
NP4: Grif 2E **9**
South Vw. CF15: Taff W 1F **69**
CF62: Rho 6D **114**
NP4: P'pool 2B **6**
South Vw. Dr. CF3: Rum 2A **88**
SOUTHVILLE 3G **11**
Southville Rd. NP20: Newp 5H **35**
South Wlk. CF62: Barry 1G **117**
NP44: C'brn 2G **11**
Sovereign Gdns. CF72: P'clun 5F **65**
SOWHILL 3B **6**
Spartan Cl. NP18: L'stne 1G **39**
Speedwell Dr. CF62: Rho 6D **114**
Speke St. NP19: Newp 4E **37**
Spencer David Way CF3: St M 2D **88**
Spencer Dr. CF64: L'dgh 4F **101**
Spencer La. CF37: R'fln 5G **25**
Spencer Pl. CF37: R'fln 5G **25**
Spencer Rd. NP20: Newp 5A **36**
Spencer's Row CF5: L'dff 6C **84**
Spencer St. CF24: Card 6A **86**
CF62: Barry 2H **117**
Spillers & Bakers CF10: Card 6G **5** (5B **96**)
Spinney, The CF14: L'vne 3B **72**
NP20: Malp 5B **20**
Spinney Cvn. Pk., The CF64: Sul 3B **120**
Spinney Cl. CF5: Ely 3G **93**
Spires Wlk. CF63: Barry 5B **106**
Spitzkop CF71: Llan M 3B **110**
SPLOTT 3E **97**
Splott Ind. Est. *CF24: Card* 4E **97**
(off Portmanmoor Rd.)
Splott Rd. CF24: Card 3D **96**
Splott Swimming Pool 3F **97**
Spooner Cl. NP10: Coedk 5D **52**
Springfield Cl. CF5: Wen 5E **99**
NP10: R'drn 6H **33**
NP44: C'iog 5G **9**
Springfield Ct. CF38: Chu V 2E **43**
Springfield Dr. NP19: Newp 3B **38**
Springfield Gdns. CF15: Morg 5F **69**
Springfield La. NP10: R'drn 6H **33**
Springfield Pl. CF11: Card 3F **95**
Springfield Ri. CF63: Barry 6A **106**
Springfield Rd. NP4: Grif 2D **8**
NP10: R'drn 6H **33**
NP11: Ris 1F **33**
Springfields CF3: Cas 3H **75**
Springfield Ter. CF37: R'fln 3F **25**
NP4: New I 5G **7**
Spring Gdns. NP20: Newp 1C **54**
Spring Gdns. Pl. CF24: Card 2E **97**
Spring Gdns. Ter. CF24: Card 2E **97**
Spring Gro. CF14: Thorn 3H **71**
NP44: G'mdw 2C **10**
Springhurst Cl. CF14: Whit 6B **70**
Spring La. NP20: Newp 5A **36**
NP44: C'iog 6G **9**
Spring Mdw. Bus. Pk. CF3: Rum 5A **88**
Spring Mdw. Rd. CF3: Rum 5A **88**
Spring St. CF63: Barry 1C **118**
NP20: Newp 2B **36**
Spring Ter. NP4: Grif 1D **8**
Springvale NP44: C'brn 1E **11**
Springvale Ind. Est. NP44: C'brn 1E **11**
Springvale Way NP44: C'brn 1F **11**
Springwood CF23: L'dyrn 2D **86**
Spruce Cl. CF24: Card 5H **5** (4D **96**)
Spytty La. NP19: Newp 1G **55**
(not continuous)
Spytty Rd. NP19: Newp 1G **55**
Square, The CF38: Bed 4H **41**
CF62: St A 4D **112**
CF64: Din P 2G **107**
CF83: Abert 2D **26**
CF83: B'ws 3G **29**
NP26: Magor 4C **58**
Squires Cl. NP10: Roger 3D **34**
Squires Ct. CF38: Bed 6A **42**
Squires Ga. NP10: Roger 3C **34**
Stacey Rd. CF24: Card 2D **96**
CF64: Din P 2G **107**
Stadium Cl. CF11: Card 2G **101**
Stafford Rd. CF11: Card 6A **4** (5G **95**)
NP4: Grif, P'pool 5E **7**
NP19: Newp 2D **36**
NP26: Cald 6C **60**
Stag La. *CF71: Llan M* 3B **110**
(off Durrel St.)
Staines St. CF5: Card 2D **94**
Stallcourt Av. CF23: Pen L 1D **96**
CF71: Llan M 4B **110**
Stallcourt Cl. CF23: Pen L 6E **87**
CF71: L'thian 4B **90**
Stamford Ct. NP20: Newp 3A **36**
Standard St. CF83: Tret 3A **30**
Stanford Rd. NP19: Newp 4B **38**
Stanier Ct. CF24: Card 3D **96**
Stanley Dr. CF83: Caer 4B **28**
Stanley Pl. NP44: Pnwd 6E **9**
Stanley Rd. NP20: Newp 4B **36**
Stanton Way CF64: P'rth 5E **109**
Stanway Pl. CF5: Ely 4F **93**
Stanway Rd. CF5: Ely 4F **93**
Stanwell Cres. CF64: P'rth 6B **102**
Stanwell Rd. CF64: P'rth 1F **109**
Starbuck St. CF83: Rud 6B **30**
Star La. CF5: P'rch 1H **81**
CF15: P'rch 1H **81**
NP4: C'avn 1B **6**
Starling Rd. CF62: St A 3F **111**
Star St. CF24: Card 2H **5** (3D **96**)
NP44: C'brn 3G **11**
Star Trad. Est. NP18: C'ln 2G **21**
Star Vs. NP18: P'hir 2G **21**
Station App. CF64: P'rth 2E **109**
CF72: P'clun 5D **64**
NP10: Bass 6D **34**
NP18: C'ln 5H **21**
Station App. Rd. CF62: Barry 5G **117**
Station Farm NP44: C'iog 6F **9**
Station Ind. Est. NP16: Chep 2F **63**
Station Pl. NP11: Ris 5D **16**
Station Rd. CF14: Llan N 4B **84**
CF14: L'shn 5H **71**
CF15: Cre 6E **67**
CF15: Rad 2G **83**
CF38: Chu V, E Isaf 3F **43**
CF62: Rho 6E **115**
CF64: Din P 2G **107**
CF64: P'rth 2E **109**
CF71: Llan M 3B **110**
NP4: Grif 6E **7**
NP11: Ris 6D **16**
NP16: Chep 2E **63**
NP18: C'ln 4H **21**
NP18: L'wrn 6F **39**
NP18: P'hir 1E **21**
NP26: Cald 6B **60**
NP26: Pskwt 5H **61**
NP44: Pnwd 6E **9**
Station Rd. E. CF5: Wen 4E **99**
Station Rd. W. CF5: Wen 5E **99**
Station St. CF63: Barry 2A **118**
CF83: Mac 2G **31**
Station Ter. CF5: F'wtr 3B **94**
CF10: Card 3F **5** (3B **96**)
CF38: Llan F 4D **42**
CF64: P'rth 2E **109**
CF72: L'harry 4C **78**
CF72: P'clun 6D **64**
CF83: Caer 1D **46**
(Bartlett St.)
CF83: Caer 5A **28**
(Ty-Isaf)
NP44: Pnwd 6E **9**
Steepfield NP44: C'iog 5G **9**
Steep St. CF64: P'rth 6A **102**
NP16: Chep 2E **63**
Steer Cres. NP19: Newp 2G **37**
Steffani Ct. CF10: Card 6B **96**
Stella Cl. CF14: Thorn 2H **71**
Stella Maris Cl. CF15: Rad 2F **83**
Stelvio Gro. NP20: Newp 6H **35**
Stelvio Pk. Av. NP20: Newp 6H **35**
Stelvio Pk. Cl. NP20: Newp 6H **35**
Stelvio Pk. Ct. NP20: Newp 6H **35**
Stelvio Pk. Cres. NP20: Newp 6H **35**
Stelvio Pk. Dr. NP20: Newp 6H **35**
Stelvio Pk. Gdns. NP20: Newp 6H **35**
Stelvio Pk. Ri. NP20: Newp 6H **35**
Stelvio Pk. Vw. NP20: Newp 6H **35**
Stenhousemuir Pl. CF24: Card 2F **97**
Stephenson Ct. CF24: Card 2H **5** (3C **96**)
Stephenson Ind. Est. NP19: Newp 2F **55**
Stephenson St. CF11: Card 4G **95**
NP19: Newp 2D **54**
Ster Century Cinema 6B **4** (5H **95**)
Sterling Cl. CF24: Card 2G **97**
Sterndale Bennett Rd. NP19: Newp 4C **38**
Stevelee NP44: F'wtr 4E **11**
Stevenson Cl. NP10: Roger 3C **34**
Stevenson Ct. NP10: Roger 3C **34**
Stevenson St. Ind. Est. NP19: Newp 3E **55**
Steven Wlk. *NP10: Roger* 5D **34**
(off Ebenezer Dr.)
Stewart Rd. CF62: Rho 6E **115**
Steynton Path NP44: F'wtr, G'mdw 3E **11**
Stiels NP44: F'wtr 5D **10**
Stirling Rd. CF5: Ely 5E **93**
CF62: Barry 6E **105**
Stirling Rd. Shop. Cen. CF62: Barry 6E **105**
Stockland St. CF11: Card 1H **101**
CF83: Caer 1C **46**
Stockton Cl. NP19: Newp 6E **21**
Stockton Rd. NP19: Newp 2D **36**
Stockwood Cl. NP18: L'stne 6F **23**
Stockwood Way NP18: L'stne 1F **39**
Stokes Ct. NP18: P'hir 1F **21**
Stokes Dr. NP18: P'hir 1F **21**
Stonebridge Pk. NP44: C'iog 6F **9**
Stonechat Cl. CF3: St M 1E **89**
Stone Cotts. NP26: Sud 6H **61**
Stoneleigh Ct. CF11: Card 2F **95**
Stone Yd., The CF11: Card 4F **95**
Storehouse Row *CF15: N'grw* 4D **44**
(off Tyla Gwyn)
Storrar Pl. CF24: Card 1G **97**
Storrar Rd. CF24: Card 1G **97**
Stour Ct. NP44: G'mdw 1C **10**
Stowepath NP44: Llan 3B **12**
Stow Hill CF37: T'rest 2D **24**
NP20: Newp 5A **36**
STOW PARK 6A **36**
Stow Pk. Av. NP20: Newp 5A **36**
Stow Pk. Circ. NP20: Newp 6A **36**
Stow Pk. Cres. NP20: Newp 5A **36**
Stow Pk. Dr. NP20: Newp 6A **36**
Stow Pk. Gdns. NP20: Newp 6A **36**

Stow Pas. NP20: Newp 5B 36
Stradling Cl. CF62: Barry 1D 116
CF64: Sul 2G 119
CF71: C'bri 3B 90
Stradling Pl. CF71: Llan M 4C 110
Stradmore Cl. CF15: Taff W 6E 45
Straits La. NP18: Newp 6B 56
Strand, The *CF71: Llan M* *3B 110*
(off East St.)
NP44: C'brn 1G 11
Stratford Grn. CF63: Barry 5C 106
Stratford Ho. NP20: Newp 6G 35
Strathnairn St. CF24: Card 1B 96
Strathy Rd. CF3: St M 6E 75
Striguil Rd. NP16: Bul 4E 63
Strongbow Rd. NP16: Bul 4E 63
Stryd Silurian CF72: L'harry 5C 78
Stryd y Berllan CF72: L'harry 5A 78
Stryd-y-Gollen CF72: L'harry 5A 78
Stuart Av. NP16: Chep 1D 62
Stuart Cl. CF11: Card 3F 101
Stuart Crystal *1F 63*
(off Bridge St.)
Stuart Pl. CF10: Card 2C 102
Stuart St. CF10: Card 2B 102
(not continuous)
CF72: P'clun 6C 64
Stuart Ter. *CF72: T Grn* *3D 64*
(off Cowbridge Rd.)
Sturminster Rd. CF23: Pen L 1E 97
Stuttgarter Strasse CF10: Card 2E 5 (3B 96)
Subway Rd. CF63: Barry 3A 118
SUDBROOK 6H 61
Sudbrook Rd. NP26: Pskwt, Sud 5G 61
Sudbury Wlk. NP20: Newp 2C 36
Sudcroft St. CF11: Card 5E 95
Sufflex Est. NP11: Ris 1F 33
Suffolk Ho. CF5: Card 2E 95
Sullivan Circ. NP19: Newp 5B 38
Sullivan Cl. CF3: L'rmy 6B 74
CF64: P'rth 4D 108
SULLY 3H 119
Sully Moors Rd. CF64: Sul 6F 107
Sully Pl. CF64: P'rth 2E 109
Sully Rd. CF64: P'rth, Sul 1A 120
Sully Ter. CF64: P'rth 3E 109
Sully Ter. La. CF64: P'rth 3E 109
Sully Vw. CF63: Barry 6E 107
Summerau Ct. CF5: Card 2E 95
Summer Dale Cl. CF38: Tont 2F 43
Summerfield Av. CF14: Card 5H 85
Summerfield Dr. CF72: L'sant 3G 65
Summerfield La. CF83: Mac 3C 30
Summerfield Pl. CF14: Heath 2F 85
SUMMER HILL 3E 37
Summerhill Av. NP19: Newp 3E 37
Summerhill Cl. CF3: St M 6E 75
Summerhill Ho. NP19: Newp 3E 37
Summerhouse La. NP16: Bul 6F 63
Summerland Cl. CF64: L'dgh 5F 101
Summerland Cres. CF64: L'dgh 5F 101
Summerwood Cl. CF5: F'wtr 1F 93
Sumner Cl. CF5: L'dff 5A 84
Sunbeam Cl. NP19: Newp 5E 37
Sundew Cl. CF5: F'wtr 5H 83
CF64: P'rth 6G 101
Sunlea Cres. NP4: New I, P'pool 3F 7
Sunningdale CF83: Caer 1A 46
Sunningdale Cl. CF23: Cyn 3B 86
Sunningdale Ct. NP19: Newp 3A 38
Sunnybank CF64: Din P 1A 108
CF83: Abert 2F 27
NP10: Bass 1B 52
Sunnybank Cl. CF14: Whit 4F 85
Sunnybank Ct. NP4: Grif 6E 7
Sunnybank Rd. NP4: Grif 6D 6
Sunny Bank Ter. CF83: Mac 2F 31
Sunnybank Way NP4: Grif 1D 8
Sunnybrook Ct. CF5: F'wtr 6H 83
Sunnycroft NP26: Pskwt 5H 61
Sunnycroft Cl. CF64: Din P 2H 107
Sunnycroft La. CF64: Din P 2H 107
Sunnycroft Ri. CF64: Din P 2H 107
Sunny Pl. NP18: P'hir 6E 13
Sunny Side *CF37: P'prdd* *5B 14*
(off Mayfield Rd.)
Sun St. CF24: Card 2H 5 (3D 96)
Suran-y-Gog CF63: Barry 4B 106
Surrey Pl. NP19: Newp 2E 37
Surrey St. CF5: Card 3D 94
Sussex Cl. NP19: Newp 1G 55
Sussex St. CF11: Card 6A 4 (5H 95)
Sutherland Cres. NP19: Newp 2G 37
Sutton Gro. CF23: Pontp 4D 72
Sutton Rd. NP19: Newp 2D 36
Swallow Dr. NP26: Cald 6D 60
Swallowhurst Cl. CF5: Ely 5D 92
Swallow Way NP10: Duf 3G 53
Swanage Cl. CF3: St M 6E 75
SWANBRIDGE 3B 120
Swanbridge Gro. CF64: Sul 2A 120
Swanbridge Rd. CF64: Sul 1A 120
Swan Cl. NP26: Cald 6D 60
Swansea St. CF24: Card 4E 97
Swan St. CF72: L'sant 2F 65
Sward Cl. NP10: Roger 2C 34
Sweldon Cl. CF5: Ely 6F 93
Swift Bus. Cen., The CF24: Card 4D 96
Swift Cl. CF3: L'rmy 6H 73
Swinburne Cl. NP19: Newp 4G 37
Swinton St. CF24: Card 2E 97
Swn-y-Mor CF62: Barry 5C 116
Swn-y-Nant CF38: Chu V 2E 43
Sword Hill CF83: Caer 1H 45
Sycamore Av. CF62: St A 2B 112
NP16: Bul 5E 63
NP19: Newp 5G 37
NP26: Cald 4B 60
Sycamore Cl. CF64: Din P 3H 107
CF64: L'dgh 5G 101
CF72: P'clun 6F 65
Sycamore Ct. NP44: H'lys 5B 10
Sycamore Cres. CF62: Barry 6A 106
NP11: Ris 6F 17
Sycamore Ho. CF14: Whit 1A 84
Sycamore Pl. CF5: F'wtr 1H 93
NP44: Up Cwm 6B 8
(not continuous)
Sycamore Rd. CF72: L'harry 5A 78
NP4: Grif 2D 8
Sycamore Rd. Sth NP4: Grif 2D 8
Sycamore St. CF15: Taff W 1E 69
CF37: R'fln 4G 25
Sycamore Ter. NP26: Undy 4D 58
Sycamore Tree Cl. CF15: Rad 1E 83
Sylvan Cl. CF5: F'wtr 6A 84
NP20: Malp 4B 20
Symondscliff Way NP26: Pskwt 6F 61
Syon Pk. Cl. CF3: St M 6E 75
Syr Dafydd CF71: Llan M 2B 110
Syr David's Av. CF5: Card 2D 94
Syr David's Ct. CF5: Card 2D 94
System St. CF24: Card 2H 5 (3C 96)

T

Tabor St. CF15: Taff W 1E 69
Tacoma Sq. CF10: Card 2C 102
Taf Cl. CF62: Barry 1E 117
Taff Bus. Cen. CF37: Up Bo 6A 26
Taff Cotts. CF72: C Inn 3G 65
Taff Ct. NP44: G'mdw 6A 8
Taff Emb. CF11: Card 6H 95
Taff Gorge Countryside Cen. 2H 69
Taff Rd. NP26: Cald 4D 60
Taffs Fall Rd. CF37: Up Bo 1B 44
Taffs Mead Emb. CF11: Card 6B 4 (5H 95)
Taffs Mead Rd. CF37: Up Bo 1A 44
Taff St. CF10: Card 5F 5 (4B 96)
CF15: Tong 4G 69
CF37: P'prdd 1C 24
TAFF'S WELL 2E 69
Taff's Well Station (Rail) 2E 69
Taff Ter. CF11: Card 1A 102
CF15: Rad 2G 83
Taff Va. Flats CF37: P'prdd 1C 24
Taff Va. Shop. Cen. CF37: P'prdd 6C 14
Taff Valley Quad Bike & Activity Cen. 4B 26
Tafwy's Wlk. CF83: Caer 6C 28
Tai Duffryn CF15: N'grw 4E 45
Tair Erw Rd. CF14: Heath 3F 85
Tair Gwaun CF64: P'rth 4C 108
Talbot Cl. CF72: L'sant 2E 65
TALBOT GREEN 3D 64
Talbot Grn. Retail Pk.
CF72: T Grn 3E 65
Talbot La. NP20: Newp 5C 36
Talbot Pl. CF11: Card 3G 95
Talbot Rd. CF72: T Grn, L'sant 3E 65
Talbot Sq. CF72: T Grn 3D 64
Talbot St. CF11: Card 3G 95
Talgarth Cl. NP44: C'brn 3G 11
Taliesin NP44: C'brn 1G 11
Taliesin Cl. NP10: Roger 3D 34
Taliesin Ct. CF10: Card 1B 102
Taliesin Dr. NP10: Roger 3D 34
Tallard's Pl. NP16: Sed 2G 63
Tallis Cl. NP19: Newp 4C 38
Talworth St. CF24: Card 1G 5 (2C 96)
Talybont Cl. CF62: St A 2D 112
Talybont Ct. CF10: Card 1G 95
Talybont Rd. CF5: Ely 4H 93
Tal-y-Bryn CF64: P'rth 3C 108
Talyfan Cl. CF71: C'bri 4D 90
Talygarn Cl. CF72: P'clun 2B 78
Talygarn Ct. CF72: P'clun 2C 78
Talygarn Dr. CF72: P'clun 1B 78
Talygarn M. CF72: P'clun 2C 78
Tal-y-Garn St. CF14: Card 5H 85
Tamar Cl. NP20: Bet 5G 19
Tanglewood Cl. CF14: L'vne 3A 72
Tangmere Dr. CF5: F'wtr 5H 83
Tanhouse Dr. NP18: C'ln 5A 22
Tansy Cl. CF14: Thorn 2F 71
Tanybryn NP11: Ris 1G 33
Tan-y-Bryn CF38: Bed 4A 42
CF83: Sen 1E 27
Tan-y-Fron CF62: Barry 4D 116
Tan-yr-Allt CF72: C Inn 3G 65
Tapley Cl. CF5: Ely 6H 93
Tarragon Way CF23: Pontp 4E 73
Tarrws Cl. CF5: Wen 4E 99
Tarwick Dr. CF3: St M 6C 74
Tasker Sq. CF14: L'shn 6F 71
Tatem Dr. CF5: F'wtr 2F 93
Tathan Cres. CF62: St A 4D 112
Tatton Rd. NP19: Newp 3B 56
Taunton Av. CF3: L'rmy 2H 87
Taunton Cres. CF3: L'rmy 2A 88
Taverner Trad. Est. NP18: C'ln 4H 21
Tavistock St. CF24: Card 1F 5 (2B 96)
Taylor St. NP11: Ris 4D 16
Taymuir Grn. Ind. Est.
CF24: Card 1F 97
Taymuir Rd. CF24: Card 1F 97
Teal Cl. NP26: Undy 4E 59
Tealham Dr. CF3: St M 6F 75
Teal St. CF24: Card 1H 5 (2C 96)
Teamans Row CF15: Morg 5F 69
Teasel Av. CF64: P'rth 6G 101
Techniquest 2B 102
Tedder Cl. CF14: L'shn 6H 71
Tees Cl. NP20: Bet 5H 19
Tegfan CF11: Card 3F 95
CF72: P'clun 1C 78
CF83: Caer 6A 28
Tegfan Cl. CF14: L'shn 5G 71
Tegfan Ct. NP44: H'lys 5B 10
TEGFAN DAY HOSPITAL 2A 84
Teifi Dr. CF62: Barry 2E 117
Teifi Pl. CF5: Ely 4H 93
Teilo St. CF11: Card 2F 95
Telelkebir Rd. CF37: P'prdd 5A 14
Telford Cl. NP10: Roger 3D 34
Telford St. CF11: Card 4G 95
NP19: Newp 5E 37
Temperance Ct. CF15: P'rch 4H 67
Temperance Hill NP11: Ris 4D 16
Temperance Pl. CF37: P'prdd 6C 14
Temperance Rd. CF15: P'rch 4H 67
Tempest Dr. NP16: Chep 2D 62
Templar Pk. Ind. Est.
CF24: Card 6H 5 (5C 96)
Temple St. NP20: Newp 1C 54
Templeton Av. CF14: L'shn 4F 71
Templeton Cl. CF14: L'shn 4G 71
Tenby Cl. CF64: Din P 2A 108
NP44: Llan 2A 12
Tenby Ct. CF83: Caer 5H 27
Tenison Rd. NP4: C'avn 1D 6
Tennyson Av. NP18: L'wrn 5E 39
Tennyson Cl. CF37: R'fln 3G 25
NP26: Cald 5B 60
Tennyson Rd. CF62: Barry 5G 105
CF64: P'rth 1C 108
NP19: Newp 4G 37
NP26: Cald 5B 60
Tennyson Way CF71: Llan M 4D 110
Tensing Cl. CF14: L'shn 4H 71
Tensing Ter. CF63: Barry 1B 118
Tern Cl. CF3: St M 5D 74
Tern Ct. NP44: G'mdw 6A 8
Terrace, The CF15: Cre 5E 67
NP26: Sud 6H 61
Terra Nova Way CF64: P'rth 5H 101
Tetbury Cl. NP20: Newp 2C 36
Tewdric Ct. NP44: C'iog 6H 9
Tewdrig Cl. CF71: Llan M 4B 110
Tewends NP44: F'wtr 4D 10
Tewkesbury Pl. CF24: Card 5A 86
Tewkesbury St. CF24: Card 6A 86
Tewkesbury Wlk. *NP20: Newp* *3C 36*
(off Shaftesbury St.)
Teynes NP44: F'wtr 4D 10
Thackeray Cres. CF3: L'rmy 6H 73
Thames Cl. NP20: Bet 6G 19
Tharsis Cl. CF24: Card 4G 5 (4C 96)

Thaw Cl. CF62: Rho . . . 6C **114**
The.......
Names prefixed with 'The' for example 'The Acorns' are indexed under the main name such as 'Acorns, The'
Theatre Royal Cinema . . . **3G 117**
Theobald Rd. CF5: Card . . . 4E **95**
Theodora St. CF24: Card . . . 2E **97**
Thesiger St. CF24: Card . . . 1A **96**
Third Av. CF83: Caer . . . 6A **28**
Third St. NP19: Newp . . . 3G **55**
Thirlmere Pl. NP19: Newp . . . 1F **37**
Thistle Cl. CF62: Barry . . . 1F **117**
Thistle Ct. NP44: F'wtr . . . 3B **10**
Thistle Way CF5: L'dff . . . 1C **94**
NP11: Ris . . . 6F **17**
Thomas Davies Ct. CF3: Rum . . . 4H **87**
Thomas Gro. NP10: Roger . . . 5D **34**
Thomas St. CF11: Card . . . 6H **95**
CF37: P'prdd . . . 6C **14**
CF83: Abert, Caer . . . 2E **27**
CF83: L'brad . . . 1B **28**
CF83: Tret . . . 3A **30**
NP16: Chep . . . 2E **63**
Thomasville CF83: Caer . . . 5A **28**
Thompson Av. CF5: Card . . . 2C **94**
NP19: Newp . . . 6H **37**
Thompson Cl. NP19: Newp . . . 6A **38**
Thompson Pl. CF5: Card . . . 2C **94**
Thompson St. CF37: P'prdd . . . 6A **14**
CF63: Barry . . . 2H **117**
Thorley Cl. CF23: Cyn . . . 3B **86**
Thornaby Ct. CF10: Card . . . 6F **5** (5B **96**)
Thornbury Cl. CF14: Heath . . . 1E **85**
Thornbury Pk. NP10: Roger . . . 5C **34**
(not continuous)
Thorncliff Ct. NP44: G'mdw . . . 3E **11**
Thorne Way CF5: Ely . . . 6F **93**
Thorn Gro. CF64: P'rth . . . 5F **109**
THORNHILL
Caerphilly . . . **5D 46**
Cardiff . . . **3G 71**
Cwmbran . . . **1D 10**
Thornhill Cl. NP44: Up Cwm . . . 5B **8**
Thornhill Ct. CF14: Rhiw . . . 5F **71**
Thornhill Crematorium & Cemetery
CF14: Rhiw . . . 3E **71**
Thornhill Gdns. NP10: Roger . . . 2A **34**
Thornhill Rd.
CF14: L'shn, Rhiw, Thorn . . . 4D **46**
CF83: Caer, Rhiw . . . 4D **46**
NP44: G'mdw, Up Cwm . . . 1D **10**
Thornhill St. CF5: Card . . . 3E **95**
Thornhill Way NP10: Roger . . . 2A **34**
Thorntree Dr. NP16: Bul . . . 6F **63**
Thornwell Rd. NP16: Bul . . . 4E **63**
Thornwood Cl. CF14: Thorn . . . 2G **71**
Three Arches Av. CF14: Cyn . . . 6A **72**
Three Oaks Cl. CF83: B'ws . . . 2E **29**
Threipland Dr. CF14: Heath . . . 2F **85**
Thrush Cl. CF3: St M . . . 6E **75**
Thurston Rd. CF37: P'prdd . . . 5D **14**
Thurston St. CF5: Card . . . 4E **95**
Tidal Sidings CF24: Card . . . 5E **97**
Tide Flds. Rd. CF24: Card . . . 4G **97**
Tidenham Ct. CF5: Ely . . . 5H **93**
Tidenham Rd. CF5: Ely . . . 5H **93**
Till Gro. NP18: C'ln . . . 4F **21**
Tillsland NP44: F'wtr . . . 5E **11**
Timbers Sq. CF24: Card . . . 1D **96**
Timothy Rees Cl. CF5: L'dff . . . 4H **83**
Tin St. CF24: Card . . . 3D **96**
Tintagel Cl. CF14: Thorn . . . 4F **71**
Tintern Cl. CF62: St A . . . 2C **112**
NP44: C'brn . . . 3G **11**
Tintern St. CF5: Card . . . 3E **95**
Tippet Cl. NP19: Newp . . . 4C **38**
Tir-Afon Ct. CF72: P'clun . . . 6D **64**
Tir Coed CF83: Caer . . . 4A **28**
Tir Meibion La. CF72: L'sant . . . 2F **65**
Tir-y-Cwm La. NP11: Ris . . . 6D **16**
Tir-y-Cwm Rd. NP11: Ris . . . 5D **16**
Tir-y-Graig CF38: Tont . . . 1G **43**
Titan Rd. CF24: Card . . . 5D **96**
Tiverton Dr. CF3: Rum . . . 3G **87**
Toftingall Av. CF14: Heath . . . 2F **85**
Toghill Dr. CF15: Taff W . . . 2F **69**
Tollgate Cl. CF11: Card . . . 2F **101**
CF83: Caer . . . 4F **29**
Tolpath NP44: F'wtr . . . 4C **10**
Tom Mann Cl. NP19: Newp . . . 2B **38**
Ton, The CF3: St M . . . 6B **74**
Tone Cl. NP20: Bet . . . 5F **19**
Tone Rd. NP20: Bet . . . 5F **19**
Tone Sq. NP20: Bet . . . 5F **19**
TONGWYNLAIS . . . **4G 69**
Ton Rd. NP44: C'brn . . . 4E **11**
NP44: F'wtr . . . 3C **10**
TON-TEG . . . **2G 43**
Tonteg Cl. CF38: Tont . . . 1G **43**
Tonteg Ind. Est. CF37: Up Bo . . . 6H **25**
Tonteg Rd. CF37: Tont, Up Bo . . . 1H **43**
Ton y Felin CF37: R'fln . . . 3G **25**
Ton-y-Felin Rd. CF83: Caer . . . 6D **28**
TONYREFAIL . . . **2A 40**
Tonyrefail Rd. CF37: P'cae . . . 5A **24**
Ton-yr-Ywen Av. CF14: Heath . . . 2G **85**
Topaz St. CF24: Card . . . 3D **96**
Torbay Ter. CF62: Rho . . . 6E **115**
Tordoff Way CF62: Barry . . . 1G **117**
Torfaen Bus. Cen. NP4: New I . . . 5F **7**
TORFAEN COMMUNITY HOSPITAL (TALYGARN) . . . **5E 7**
Toronto Cl. NP20: Newp . . . 6F **35**
Torrens Dr. CF23: Cyn . . . 3B **86**
Torridge Rd. NP20: Bet . . . 4E **19**
Torrington Rd. CF3: L'rmy . . . 6A **74**
Tor Vw. CF83: B'ws . . . 2E **29**
Tourist Info. Cen.
Barry Island . . . **5G 117**
Caerleon . . . **5H 21**
Caerphilly . . . **1C 46**
Chepstow . . . **1E 63**
Magor Service Area . . . **3C 58**
Newport . . . **5C 36**
Penarth . . . **2F 109**
Pontypridd . . . **5C 14**
Tower Hill CF64: P'rth . . . 2F **109**
Towers, The NP44: C'brn . . . 2H **11**
Tower St. CF37: T'rest . . . 2D **24**
Tower Way CF64: Sul . . . 1E **119**
Town Hall Sq. CF71: C'bri . . . 3D **90**
Town Mill Rd. CF71: C'bri . . . 4C **90**
Town Wall CF10: Card . . . 4D **4** (4A **96**)
Towyn Rd. CF3: Rum . . . 3A **88**
Towyn Way CF38: Tont . . . 1G **43**
Towy Rd. CF14: L'shn . . . 6A **72**
Trade La. CF10: Card . . . 6A **96**
Trade St. CF10: Card . . . 5A **96**
Trafalgar Rd. CF23: Pen L . . . 1D **96**
Trafalgar St. NP11: Ris . . . 1E **33**
Traherne Dr. CF5: Ely . . . 5D **92**
TRALLWNG . . . **5D 14**
Tram La. NP18: C'ln . . . 5A **22**
NP44: Llanf . . . 6C **12**
Tramore Way CF23: Pontp . . . 4G **73**
Tram Rd. NP18: C'ln . . . 5A **22**
NP44: Up Cwm . . . 5B **8**
Tramway Cl. NP44: F'wtr . . . 4C **10**
TRANCH . . . **3A 6**
Tranch Rd. NP4: P'pool . . . 3A **6**
Trannon Ct. NP44: G'mdw . . . 1D **10**
Tranquil Pl. NP44: Oakf . . . 4G **11**
Transporter Bridge . . . **2D 54**
Tranters Ter. *NP44: Up Cwm . . . 5C 8*
(off Ty Pwca Rd.)
Trap Well CF83: Caer . . . 4F **29**
Traston Av. NP19: Newp . . . 2H **55**
Traston Cl. NP19: Newp . . . 2H **55**
Traston La. NP19: Newp . . . 2H **55**
Traston Rd. NP19: Newp . . . 3F **55**
(not continuous)
Traws Mawr La. NP20: Bet, Oakf . . . 4F **19**
NP44: Oakf . . . 4F **19**
Trebanog Cl. CF3: Rum . . . 1C **88**
Trebanog Cres. CF3: Rum . . . 2C **88**
Tre-Beferad CF71: Bov . . . 4E **111**
TREBEFERED . . . **4E 111**
Treberth Av. NP19: Newp . . . 3C **38**
Treberth Cl. NP19: Newp . . . 3C **38**
Treberth Ct. NP19: Newp . . . 3C **38**
Treberth Cres. NP19: Newp . . . 3B **38**
Treberth Dr. NP19: Newp . . . 3C **38**
Treberth Est. NP19: Newp . . . 3C **38**
Treberth Gdns. NP19: Newp . . . 3C **38**
Treberth Gro. NP19: Newp . . . 3C **38**
Treberth Ri. NP19: Newp . . . 3C **38**
Treberth Vw. NP19: Newp . . . 3B **38**
Treborth Rd. CF3: Rum . . . 2C **88**
Trecastle Av. CF14: L'shn . . . 4G **71**
TRECENYDD . . . **6A 28**
Trecenydd Ind. Est. CF83: Caer . . . 6A **28**
Trecinon Rd. CF3: Rum . . . 2D **88**
Tredegar Ct. CF14: Whit . . . 2B **84**
NP11: C'keys . . . 4A **16**
NP20: Newp . . . 1C **54**
Tredegar Dr. NP26: Undy . . . 4F **59**
Tredegar Fort . . . **1F 53**
Tredegar House . . . **4F 53**
Tredegar House Country Pk. . . . **4F 53**
Tredegar Ho. Dr. NP10: Duf . . . 4F **53**
TREDEGAR PARK . . . **2F 53**
Tredegar Pk. Vw. NP10: Roger . . . 5E **35**
Tredegar St. CF10: Card . . . 5E **5** (4B **96**)
NP10: R'drn . . . 6A **34**
NP11: C'keys . . . 3A **16**
NP11: Ris . . . 5D **16**
NP20: Newp . . . 6C **36**
Tredegar Ter. NP11: C'keys . . . 3A **16**
NP11: Ris . . . 6D **16**
Tredelerch Rd. CF3: Rum . . . 5G **87**
TREDOGAN . . . **3G 115**
Tredogan Rd. CF62: Rho . . . 1E **115**
Tree Tops NP26: Pskwt . . . 5G **61**
Treetops Cl. CF5: F'wtr . . . 6F **83**
Trefaser Cres. CF3: Rum . . . 1C **88**
TREFOREST . . . **2E 25**
Treforest Estate Station (Rail) . . . **2B 44**
Treforest Ind. Est. CF37: Up Bo . . . 1C **44**
(Main Av.)
CF37: Up Bo . . . 6A **26**
(Severn Rd., not continuous)
Treforest Station (Rail) . . . **3E 25**
Tregare St. NP19: Newp . . . 3D **36**
Tregarn Rd. NP18: L'stne . . . 6H **23**
Tregaron Rd. CF5: Ely . . . 4F **93**
Tre Garth Cl. CF15: Cre . . . 5D **66**
Tre Garth Ct. CF15: Cre . . . 5D **66**
Tregwilym Cl. NP10: Roger . . . 5D **34**
Tregwilym Ind. Est. NP10: Roger . . . 6C **34**
Tregwilym Rd. NP10: Roger . . . 4B **34**
(not continuous)
Tregwilym Wlk. NP10: Roger . . . 5C **34**
Treharne Flats CF37: R'fln . . . 4H **25**
Treharne Rd. CF63: Barry . . . 6A **106**
Treharris St. CF24: Card . . . 2B **96**
Tre-Herbert Rd. NP18: C'iog, P'hir . . . 2G **13**
NP44: C'iog . . . 4H **9**
NP44: C'iog, P'hir . . . 1F **13**
Treherbert St. CF24: Card . . . 1H **95**
Trelai Ct. CF5: Ely . . . 6G **93**
Trelawney Av. CF3: Rum . . . 4H **87**
Trelawney Cres. CF3: Rum . . . 4H **87**
Trelech Cl. NP44: C'brn . . . 3H **11**
Tremadoc Wlk. CF3: Rum . . . 2C **88**
Trem Echni CF62: Rho . . . 6F **115**
Trem Mapgoll CF63: Barry . . . 4A **106**
TREMORFA . . . **2F 97**
Tremorfa Ind. Est. CF24: Card . . . 5F **97**
Trem Powys CF63: Barry . . . 5C **106**
Trem Twynbarlwm NP44: C'brn . . . 4G **11**
Trem y Castell CF83: Caer . . . 2H **45**
Trem-y-Coed CF63: Barry . . . 4B **106**
Trem-y-Cwm CF38: Bed . . . 5A **42**
Trem-y-Don CF62: Barry . . . 5C **116**
Trem-y-Garth CF72: L'harry . . . 5C **78**
Trenchard Dr. CF14: L'shn . . . 6H **71**
Trenewydd Rd. CF3: Rum . . . 2C **88**
Trent Rd. NP20: Bet . . . 5F **19**
Treorchy St. CF24: Card . . . 1H **95**
Treseder Way CF5: Ely . . . 4A **94**
Tresigin Rd. CF3: Rum . . . 1C **88**
Tresilian Cl. CF71: Llan M . . . 4B **110**
Tresillian Ter. CF10: Card . . . 6D **4** (5A **96**)
Tresillian Way CF10: Card . . . 6D **4** (5A **96**)
Tresillian Way Ind. Est. CF10: Card . . . 5A **96**
TRETHOMAS . . . **3A 30**
Tretower Ct. NP44: Llan . . . 2B **12**
Trevelyan Ct. CF71: Bov . . . 2D **110**
CF83: Caer . . . 6E **29**
Trevethick St. CF11: Card . . . 4G **95**
Trevine Path NP44: F'wtr . . . 3E **11**
Trevithick Cl. NP20: Malp . . . 4H **19**
(not continuous)
Trewartha Ct. CF14: Whit . . . 2D **84**
Triangle, The *CF62: Barry . . . 5H 117*
(off Redbrink Cres.)
Triassic Towers . . . ***5G 117***
(in Esplanade Bldgs.)
Trident Ct. CF24: Card . . . 6H **5** (4C **96**)
Tridwr Rd. CF83: Abert . . . 2D **26**
Trinity Ct. CF62: Barry . . . 3G **117**
NP11: Ris . . . 5D **16**
NP20: Newp . . . 1D **54**
Trinity La. NP18: C'ln . . . 4F **21**
Trinity Pl. NP20: Newp . . . 1D **54**
Trinity Rd. NP44: Pnwd . . . 6D **8**
Trinity St. CF10: Card . . . 4D **4** (4A **96**)
CF62: Barry . . . 3F **117**
Trinity Vw. NP18: C'ln . . . 4E **21**
Triscombe Dr. CF5: L'dff . . . 6A **84**
Tristram Cl. CF14: Thorn . . . 3F **71**
Troddi Cl. NP26: Cald . . . 4C **60**
TROEDRHIW-TRWYN . . . **5A 14**
Troed-y-Bryn CF83: Caer . . . 4A **28**
Troed-y-Garth CF15: P'rch . . . 4H **67**
Troed y Rhiw CF14: Rhiw . . . 4C **70**
TROSNANT . . . **4C 6**

Trosnant St. NP4: P'pool 3C **6**
(not continuous)
Trostrey NP44: F'wtr 5E **11**
Trostrey Cl. NP4: New I 5H **7**
Trostrey St. NP19: Newp 3D **36**
Trotman Dickenson Pl. CF14: Card 6G **85**
TROWBRIDGE 2C **88**
Trowbridge Grn. CF3: Rum 1C **88**
TROWBRIDGE MAWR 3C **88**
Trowbridge Rd. CF3: Rum 2B **88**
Trussel Rd. NP44: C'brn 1G **11**
Tubular Cotts. NP16: Tut 1G **63**
Tudor Cl. CF5: F'wtr 2H **93**
CF64: P'rth 4E **109**
Tudor Ct. NP26: Undy 5F **59**
Tudor Cres. NP10: Roger 5D **34**
Tudor Dr. NP16: Chep 1C **62**
Tudor Gdns. CF83: Mac 3F **31**
Tudor La. CF11: Card 6A **4** (5H **95**)
Tudor M. CF72: P'clun 6F **65**
Tudor Pl. CF71: Llan M 4C **110**
Tudor Rd. NP19: Newp 1E **37**
NP44: C'brn 2G **11**
Tudors, The CF23: Pen L 6C **86**
Tudor St. CF11: Card 6A **4** (4G **95**)
CF37: R'fln 5G **25**
Tudor Way CF38: Llan F 5C **42**
Tudor Woods NP44: Llan 3B **12**
Tulip Wlk. NP10: Roger 3H **33**
Tullock St. CF24: Card 6C **86**
Tummel Cl. CF23: Cyn 2C **86**
Tump La. NP26: Undy 4E **59**
Tunnel Ter. NP20: Newp 5B **36**
Turberville Pl. CF11: Card 3F **95**
Turberville Rd. NP44: C'brn 1H **11**
Turkey St. CF71: Llan M 2B **110**
Turner Ho. CF64: P'rth 2F **109**
Turner Rd. CF5: Card 3D **94**
Turners End NP44: F'wtr 4D **10**
Turner St. NP19: Newp 3D **36**
Turnham Grn. CF23: Pen L 5E **87**
Turnpike Cl. CF64: Din P 1G **107**
NP4: P'pool 3F **7**
NP16: Chep 1C **62**
Turnpike End NP16: B'ly 6H **63**
Turnpike Rd. NP44: C'iog, Llanf 1B **12**
Turnstiles, The NP20: Newp 2C **36**
Tuscan Cl. CF64: L'dgh 4F **101**
TUTSHILL 1G **63**
Tutshill Gdns. NP16: Tut 1G **63**
Tweedsmuir Rd. CF24: Card 2F **97**
Tweedy La. NP19: Newp 4F **37**
Twinings, The NP44: G'mdw 2D **10**
Twissell's Rd. NP4: P'pool 3A **6**
Twm Barlwm Cl. NP11: Ris 5G **17**
Twmbarlwm Ri. NP44: H'lys 4A **10**
Twm Barlwm Vw. NP44: Llanf 3B **12**
Twmpath Gdns. NP4: P'pool 3B **6**
Twmpath Rd. NP4: P'pool 3B **6**
TWO LOCKS 4G **11**
Two-Locks Rd. NP44: C'brn 4F **11**
Twyn, The CF83: Caer 1D **46**
Twyncarn Rd. NP11: C'crn, P'waun 1A **16**
TWYNCYN 2F **107**
Twyncyn CF64: Din P 2F **107**
Twyn Oaks NP18: C'ln 4B **22**
TWYN Y CADNO 4G **33**
Twyn-y-Fedwen Rd. CF14: Whit 4F **85**
Ty Box Cl. NP44: Pnwd 6D **8**
Ty Box Rd. NP44: Pnwd 6D **8**
(not continuous)
Ty Camlas CF63: Barry 3H **117**
Ty-Canol Ct. NP44: F'wtr 4C **10**
Ty Canol La. CF83: Mac 2F **31**
Ty-Canol La. CF83: Tret 1A **30**
Ty-Canol Row NP44: F'wtr 4C **10**
Ty-Canol Way NP44: F'wtr, G'mdw 3B **10**
Ty-Cefn Rd. CF5: Ely 3H **93**
Ty Cerrig CF23: L'dyrn 5E **73**
Ty-Cerrig CF63: Barry 6B **106**
Ty Ceyln M. CF14: Whit 6B **70**
Ty Charlotte CF64: P'rth 5A **102**
TY-COCH 5G **11**
Ty-Coch Cl. NP10: Bass 1B **52**
NP44: Oakf 1A **20**
Ty Coch Ct. CF3: St M 1B **88**
Ty-Coch Distribution Cen. NP44: C'brn 5G **11**
Ty-Coch La. NP44: C'brn 5F **11**
NP44: Oakf 6H **11**
Ty-Coch Rd. CF5: Ely 3G **93**
Ty-Coch Way NP44: C'brn, Oakf 4G **11**
Ty Coed NP44: G'mdw 6B **8**
Ty Crwyn CF38: Chu V 3E **43**
Ty Dewi Sont CF64: P'rth 3C **108**
Tydfil Pl. CF23: Card 5B **86**
Tydfil Rd. CF83: B'ws 2F **29**
Tydfil St. CF63: Barry 1B **118**
Tydies NP44: F'wtr 5D **10**
Ty Draw CF38: Chu V 2E **43**
Ty-Draw Pl. CF23: Pen L 6C **86**
Ty-Draw Rd. CF23: L'vne, Pontp 4D **72**
CF23: Pen L 5B **86**
Tydu Vw. NP10: Roger 4D **34**
Ty-Dyfan CF63: Barry 5A **106**
Ty Enfys CF23: L'dyrn 5F **73**
Tyfica Cres. CF37: P'prdd 6C **14**
Tyfica Rd. CF37: P'prdd 6B **14**
Ty-Fry Av. CF3: Rum 4H **87**
Ty Fry Cl. CF3: Rum 3H **87**
Ty-Fry Gdns. CF3: Rum 3H **87**
Ty-Fry Rd. CF3: Rum 4H **87**
Ty Gambig CF62: Barry 6H **117**
Ty-Glas Av. CF14: L'shn 5G **71**
Ty-Glas Rd. CF14: L'shn 6F **71**
Ty-Glas Station (Rail) 1G **85**
Ty Gwenfo CF63: Barry 1C **118**
Ty-Gwyn Av. CF23: Pen L 5C **86**
Ty-Gwyn Cres. CF23: Pen L 4C **86**
Ty Gwyn Rd. NP44: F'wtr 3C **10**
NP44: G'mdw 2D **10**
Tygwyn Rd. CF37: P'prdd 6E **15**
Ty-Gwyn Rd. CF14: Rhiw 6E **71**
CF23: Pen L 4C **86**
CF38: Chu V 2E **43**
Ty Gwyn Way NP44: G'mdw 2C **10**
TY HAFAN CHILDREN'S HOSPICE 3E **119**
Ty Isaf CF72: L'harry 5A **78**
Ty-Isaf CF83: Caer 4H **27**
NP11: Ris 1F **33**
Ty-Isaf Bungs. CF83: Caer 4H **27**
Ty-Isaf Circ. NP11: Ris 1F **33**
Ty-Isaf Cres. NP11: Ris 1F **33**
Ty-Isaf Pk. Av. NP11: Ris 1F **33**
Ty-Isaf Pk. Cres. NP11: Ris 1F **33**
Ty-Isaf Pk. Rd. NP11: Ris 1F **33**
Ty-Isaf Pk. Vs. NP11: Ris 1F **33**
Tylacoch CF72: L'harry 5B **78**
Tylagarw Ct. CF72: P'clun 5C **64**
Tylagarw Ter. CF72: P'clun 5B **64**
Tyla Glas CF83: Caer 3B **46**
Tyla Gwyn CF15: N'grw 3D **44**
Tyla La. CF3: Cas, St M 1E **75**
Tyla Rhosyr CF71: C'bri 3B **90**
Tyla Teg CF14: Rhiw 5B **70**
Tylcha Fach Cl. CF39: T'fail 1A **40**
Tyle Garw CF72: P'clun 5B **64**
Tyle Ho. Cl. CF71: L'maes 1D **110**
Tyle'r Hendy CF72: P'clun 6E **65**
Tyler St. CF24: Card 2E **97**
Tylers Way NP16: Sed 2H **63**
Tyllwyd Rd. NP20: Newp 5H **35**
Ty-Mawr Av. CF3: Rum 5G **87**
Ty-Mawr Cl. CF3: Rum 5G **87**
Tymawr La. CF3: M'fld 5A **76**
NP10: M'fld 3B **76**
Ty Mawr Parc CF37: P'prdd 5A **14**
Ty-Mawr Rd. CF3: Rum 4G **87**
CF14: Llan N, Whit 2A **84**
CF37: P'prdd 5A **14**
Tymawr Ter. CF37: P'prdd 5A **14**
Ty Mawr Uchaf CF37: P'prdd 5A **14**
Ty Mynydd NP44: Pnwd 6E **9**
Tymynydd Cl. CF15: Rad 6F **69**
TYNANT 4A **42**
Ty Nant CF83: Caer 5A **28**
Tynant CF14: Whit 3D **84**
Ty Nant Ct. CF15: Gwae G 4F **69**
Ty Nant Ddu NP4: P'nydd 1B **6**
Tynant Rd. CF15: Cre 1D **80**
CF38: Bed 5A **42**
Ty-Nant Rd. CF15: Gwae G, Morg 4F **69**
Ty-Nant St. CF11: Card 6G **95**
Tyndall St. CF10: Card 6F **5** (5B **96**)
CF24: Card 5H **5** (5B **96**)
(not continuous)
Tyndall St. Ind. Est. CF10: Card 5F **5** (4B **96**)
Tyne Cl. NP20: Bet 6F **19**
Tyneside Rd. CF10: Card 1D **102**
Tynewydd CF14: Whit 3C **84**
Tynewydd Av. NP44: Pnwd 5E **9**
Ty-Newydd Ct. NP44: Pnwd 6E **9**
Tynewydd Dr. CF3: Cas 2G **75**
Tynewydd Farm Cl. NP44: Pnwd 5E **9**
Tynewydd Grn. NP44: Pnwd 5E **9**
Ty-Newydd Ho. NP44: Pnwd 6E **9**
Tynewydd Nth. Cl. NP44: Pnwd 5E **9**
Ty-Newydd Rd. CF62: Barry 1H **117**
NP44: Pnwd 6E **9**
Tynewydd Sth. Cl. NP44: Pnwd 5E **9**
Ty'n-y-Cae Gro. CF14: Rhiw 1E **85**
Ty'n-y-Coedcae CF83: Mac 4D **30**
Ty'n-y-Coed La. CF24: Card 6B **86**
Ty'n-y-Coed Pl. CF24: Card 6B **86**
Tyn-y-Coed Rd. CF15: Cre, P'rch 3D **66**
Tyn-y-Cwm Rd. NP11: Ris 1G **33**
Tyn y Parc CF83: Abert 1D **26**
Tyn-y-Parc Rd. CF14: Rhiw, Whit 2D **84**
Ty'n-y-Pwll Rd. CF14: Whit 2C **84**
Tyn y Waun Rd. CF83: Mac 2G **31**
Tynywern Ter. CF83: Tret 2A **30**
Ty Parc Cl. CF5: L'dff 4H **83**
Ty-Pica Dr. CF5: Wen 4E **99**
Ty Pont Haearn CF10: Card 5F **5**
Ty Pucca Cl. CF83: Mac 3G **31**
Ty Pwca Pl. NP44: Pnwd, Up Cwm 5C **8**
Ty Pwca Rd. NP44: Pnwd, Up Cwm 5C **8**
TY RHIW 1F **69**
Ty-Rhiw CF15: Taff W 1F **69**
Tyrhiw Est. CF15: Taff W 1F **69**
Ty'r Person CF38: Chu V 2E **43**
Tyr Sianel CF63: Barry 3H **117**
Ty'r Waun CF15: N'grw 3F **45**
Tyrwhitt Cres. CF23: Cyn 2A **86**
Tyr Winch Rd. CF3: St M 6B **74**
Tyr-y-Sarn Rd. CF3: Rum 4H **87**
Ty'r Ysgol CF24: Card 4H **5**
TY-SIGN 5F **17**
Ty-to-Maen Cl. CF3: St M 5C **74**
Ty Trappa NP44: Pnwd 5C **8**
Ty Trappa Pl. NP44: Pnwd 5C **8**
Ty Tudor NP44: C'brn 2H **11**
Ty Twyn CF38: Chu V 2D **42**
Ty Uchaf CF64: P'rth 3C **108**
Ty Verlon Ind. Est. CF63: Barry 6E **107**
Ty-Wern Av. CF14: Rhiw 1E **85**
Ty-Wern Rd. CF14: Rhiw 1E **85**

U

Ullswater Av. CF23: Cyn 4A **86**
Ullswater Ct. NP44: G'mdw 2E **11**
Underhill Dr. CF38: Tont 2G **43**
UNDERWOOD 3H **39**
Underwood CF83: Caer 2D **46**
Underwood Leisure Cen. 2H **39**
Underwood Ter. CF37: P'prdd 5A **14**
CF83: Abert 2F **27**
UNDY 4F **59**
Union St. CF37: P'prdd 1C **24**
Universal St. CF11: Card 5H **95**
UNIVERSITY DENTAL HOSPITAL 4G **85**
UNIVERSITY HOSPITAL OF WALES (YSBYTY ATHROFAOL CYMRU) 4H **85**
University of Glamorgan 3D **24**
University of Wales College (Newport) 4G **21**
University of Wales College (Newport) Sports Cen. 4G **21**
University of Wales Institute 3G **5** (3C **96**)
University of Wales Institute, Cardiff
Colchester Avenue Campus 6E **87**
Cyncoed Campus 3C **86**
Llandaff Campus 6D **84**
University Pl. CF24: Card 3E **97**
Uphill Cl. CF64: Sul 1H **119**
Uphill Rd. CF3: L'rmy 2H **87**
Upland Dr. NP4: C'avn 1B **6**
UPLANDS, THE 3B **34**
Uplands, The CF15: Rad 1F **83**
NP10: Roger 3B **34**
Uplands Ct. NP10: Roger 3B **34**
NP19: Newp 3F **37**
Uplands Cres. CF64: L'dgh 5G **101**
Uplands Rd. CF3: Rum 5G **87**
Uplands Ter. NP44: C'brn 2E **11**
Up. Alma Ter. CF37: T'rest 1D **24**
UPPER BOAT 6B **26**
Up. Boat Ind. Pk. CF37: Up Bo 6A **26**
Up. Bridge St. NP4: P'pool 3C **6**
Up. Church St. CF37: P'prdd 6C **14**
NP16: Chep 1E **63**
UPPER CHURCH VILLAGE 2E **43**
Uppercliff Cl. CF64: P'rth 6B **102**
Uppercliff Dr. CF64: P'rth 1G **109**
Up. Clifton St. CF24: Card 1H **5** (2D **96**)
Up. Cosmeston Farm CF64: P'rth 6E **109**
UPPER CWMBRAN 5B **8**
Up. Cwmbran Rd. NP44: Up Cwm 5A **8**
Up. Dock St. NP20: Newp 4C **36**
Up. Francis St. CF83: Abert 2D **26**
Up. Glyn Gwyn St. CF83: Tret 2A **30**
Up. Kincraig St. CF24: Card 1C **96**
Upper Mdw. CF5: Ely 6F **93**
Up. Nelson St. NP16: Chep 2E **63**
UPPER OCHRWYTH 2D **32**
Up. Park Ter. NP4: P'pool 3C **6**
Up. Power St. NP20: Newp 3B **36**
UPPER RACE 5A **6**

Up. Tennyson Rd. NP19: Newp 4F **37**
Up. Trosnant St. NP4: P'pool 3C **6**
Up. Tyn-y-Parc Ter. CF14: Rhiw 1D **84**
Up. Vaughan St. CF37: P'prdd 6B **14**
Upton La. NP20: Newp 5H **35**
Upton Pl. CF38: Bed 5A **42**
Upton Rd. NP20: Newp 5H **35**
Usk Cl. NP26: Cald 3D **60**
Usk Ct. NP44: G'mdw 1D **10**
Uskley Ct. CF3: St M 1C **88**
Usk Rd. CF14: L'shn 5A **72**
NP4: Lit M, New I, P'pool 4E **7**
NP16: Chep, Pwllm 1A **62**
NP18: C'ln 5H **21**
Uskside NP18: C'ln 6A **22**
Usk St. NP19: Newp 3D **36**
Usk Va. Cl. NP18: C'ln 4H **21**
Uskvale Ct. NP4: P'pool 3F **7**
Usk Va. Dr. NP18: C'ln 4H **21**
Usk Va. M. NP18: C'ln 4H **21**
Uskvale Vw. NP18: C'ln 6A **22**
Usk Vw. NP19: Newp 1G **37**
Usk Way CF62: Barry 1E **117**
NP20: Newp 5C **36**
Usk Way Ind. Est. NP20: Newp 6D **36**
UWIC Inter Cardiff FC 3D **86**

V

Vachell Ct. CF71: Bov 3D **110**
Vachell Rd. CF5: Ely 4G **93**
Vaindre Cl. CF3: St M 5E **75**
Vaindre Dr. CF3: St M 5E **75**
Vaindre La. CF3: St M 5E **75**
(Cypress Dr.)
CF3: St M 5D **74**
(Newport Rd.)
Valarian Cl. CF3: St M 1F **89**
Vale Ct. CF64: Din P 2H **107**
CF71: C'bri 4E **91**
Vale Enterprise Cen. CF64: Sul 2F **119**
Vale Gdns. CF37: P'prdd 5B **14**
Valegate Bus. Pk. CF5: Ely 1D **98**
Valegate Retail Pk. CF5: Ely 1C **98**
Valentine La. NP16: Bul 6F **63**
Vale of Glamorgan Golf & Country Club 6E **79**
Vale of Glamorgan Health and Racquets Club 6F **79**
Vale of Glamorgan Steam Railway and Heritage Cen. 5H **117**
Vale Rd. CF24: Card 2E **97**
Vale St. CF62: Barry 3E **117**
Vale Vw. CF62: Barry 5F **105**
NP11: Ris 5E **17**
NP19: Newp 2G **37**
NP44: H'lys 5B **10**
Vale Vw. Cl. CF64: L'dgh 5F **101**
Vale Vw. Cres. CF64: L'dgh 5F **101**
Valley Ent. CF83: B'ws 3F **29**
Valley Vw. CF3: Rum 3B **88**
VAN 1E **47**
Vanbrugh Cl. NP10: Roger 3D **34**
Vanbrugh Gdns. NP20: Newp 2G **53**
Vancouver Dr. NP20: Newp 6F **35**
Van Dyke Cl. NP19: Newp 2F **37**
Vanfield Cl. CF83: Caer 1E **47**
Vanguard Way CF24: Card 5D **96**
Van Ind. Est. CF83: Caer 1E **47**
Van Rd. CF83: Caer 1D **46**
Van St. CF11: Card 6G **95**
Van Ter. CF83: Caer 1F **47**
Vaughan Av. CF5: L'dff 1B **94**
Vaughan St. CF37: P'prdd 6B **14**
Vaughan Williams Dr. NP19: Newp 4A **38**
Vauxhall La. NP16: Chep 2D **62**
Vauxhall Rd. NP16: Chep 3D **62**
Vega Ho. CF10: Card 1D **102**
Velindre Ct. CF14: Whit 2B **84**
VELINDRE HOSPITAL 2B **84**
Velindre Pl. CF14: Whit 2B **84**
Velindre Rd. CF14: Whit 2A **84**
Vellacott Cl. CF10: Card 5B **96**
Vendre Cl. CF3: St M 4E **75**
Venosa Trad. Est. CF83: Caer 5D **28**
Ventnor Pl. CF14: Card 5F **85**
Ventnor Rd. NP44: C'brn 3G **11**
Venture Pk. NP19: Newp 5E **37**
Venwood Cl. CF5: Wen 5E **99**
Verallo Dr. CF11: Card 4D **94**
Verbena Cl. CF3: St M 5E **75**
Vere St. CF24: Card 1G **5** (2C **96**)
CF63: Barry 1C **118**
Veritys Ct. CF71: C'bri 3C **90**
Verlands, The CF71: C'bri 3B **90**
Verlands Cl. CF5: L'dff 1C **94**
Verlon Cl. CF63: Barry 6E **107**
Vermeer Cres. NP19: Newp 2G **37**
Vernon Gro. NP26: C'went 1B **60**
Verona Ct. CF10: Card 5B **96**
Verona Pl. CF63: Barry 6C **106**
Veronica Cl. NP10: Roger 6D **34**
Vervain Cl. CF5: Ely 4E **93**
Viaduct Cl. NP10: Bass 6D **34**
Viaduct Ct. NP4: P'pool 4D **6**
Viaduct Rd. CF15: Gwae G 3E **69**
CF63: Barry 3B **118**
Viaduct Vw. NP10: Bass 6D **34**
Viaduct Way NP10: Bass 6D **34**
Vibernum Ri. CF38: Llan F 6C **42**
Vicarage Cl. NP10: Bass 1D **52**
Vicarage Ct. CF3: M'fld 3H **75**
CF38: Tont 1F **43**
Vicarage Gdns. CF3: M'fld 4H **75**
NP10: Roger 3A **34**
NP26: C'went 1B **60**
Vicarage Hill NP20: Newp 5B **36**
(not continuous)
Victoria Av. CF5: Card 3D **94**
CF64: P'rth 2E **109**
NP19: Newp 4E **37**
Victoria Bri. CF64: P'rth 1E **109**
Victoria Cl. NP20: Newp 5C **36**
Victoria Ct. NP19: Newp 4E **37**
Victoria Cres. NP20: Newp 5B **36**
Victoria Hall CF10: Card 1H **95**
Victoria Ho. CF11: Card 6A **4** (5H **95**)
Victoria La. NP19: Newp 3F **37**
(not continuous)
Victoria M. CF14: Card 5G **85**
Victoria Pk. Rd. CF63: Barry 6B **106**
Victoria Pk. Rd. E. CF5: Card 3D **94**
Victoria Pk. Rd. W. CF5: Card 2C **94**
Victoria Pl. CF10: Card 4D **4** (4A **96**)
NP20: Newp 5C **36**
Victoria Rd. CF14: Whit 2C **84**
CF62: Barry 4E **117**
CF64: P'rth 3D **108**
NP4: P'pool 4D **6**
NP16: Bul 5F **63**
NP20: Newp 5C **36**
Victoria Sq. CF64: P'rth 2E **109**
Victoria St. NP4: Grif 6E **7**
NP44: C'brn 3G **11**
Victoria Wlk. NP20: Newp 5C **36**
Victoria Way NP26: Undy 4E **59**
Vigar Ter. NP11: Ris 6E **17**
Viking Pl. CF10: Card 1F **103**
Village Way CF14: Tong 5A **70**
Villas, The NP26: Sud 6H **61**
Vincent Cl. CF63: Barry 5C **106**
Vincent Ct. CF5: Ely 3A **94**
Vincent Rd. CF5: Ely 3A **94**
Vine Cotts. *NP16: Chep* *2E **63***
(off Portwall Rd.)
VINEGAR HILL 4E **59**
Vinegar Hill NP26: Undy 3E **59**
Vine Pl. NP19: Newp 3E **37**
Violet Pl. CF14: Whit 3F **85**
Violet Row CF24: Card 1B **96**
Violet Wlk. NP10: Roger 2G **33**
Virgil Ct. CF11: Card 6G **95**
Virgil St. CF11: Card 6G **95**
Virginia Cl. CF83: Caer 5D **28**
Virginia Ter. CF83: Caer 5C **28**
Virginia Vw. CF83: Caer 5D **28**
Viscount Evan Dr. NP10: Duf 4H **53**
Vishwell Rd. CF5: Card 2D **94**
CF5: Wen 6E **99**
Vista Ri. CF5: F'wtr 5H **83**
Vivian Rd. NP19: Newp 5E **37**
Voss Pk. Cl. CF71: Bov 3D **110**
Voss Pk. Dr. CF71: Llan M 3D **110**
Voysey Pl. CF5: F'wtr 2G **93**

W

Wades, The *NP44: F'wtr* *4D **10***
(off Rede Rd.)
Waghausel Cl. NP26: Cald 5C **60**
Wagtail Rd. CF62: St A 3G **111**
Wain Cl. CF23: Pontp 4H **73**
WAINFELIN 2A **6**
Wainfelin Av. NP4: P'pool 2A **6**
Wainfelin Rd. NP4: P'pool 1B **6**
Wakehurst Pl. CF3: St M 6D **74**
Wakelin Cl. CF38: Chu V 3E **43**
Walden Grange Cl. NP19: Newp 4H **37**
Wales Millennium Cen. 1C **102**
Wales National Ice Rink 5E **5** (4B **96**)
Wales National Velodrome 1H **55**
Wales Sports Cen. for the Disabled 3C **86**
Walford Davies Dr. NP19: Newp 4A **38**
Walford Pl. CF11: Card 4F **95**
Walford St. NP20: Newp 2B **36**
Walk, The CF3: Rum 4G **87**
CF24: Card 2F **5** (3B **96**)
NP4: New I 5G **7**
Walkdens NP44: F'wtr 4D **10**
Walker Flats NP26: Sud 6H **61**
Walker Rd. CF24: Card 4E **97**
CF62: Barry 1G **117**
Walk Farm Dr. CF3: Cas 1G **75**
Wallis St. NP20: Newp 1D **54**
WALLSTON 4D **98**
Wallwern Wood NP16: Chep 1C **62**
Walmer Rd. NP19: Newp 4F **37**
Walnut Cl. CF72: P'clun 5F **65**
Walnut Dr. NP18: C'ln 5E **21**
Walnut Gro. CF62: St A 2B **112**
NP26: C'went 1E **61**
Walnut Tree Cl. CF15: Rad 6E **69**
Walpole Cl. CF3: L'rmy 5A **74**
Walsall St. NP19: Newp 5E **37**
Walston Cl. CF5: Wen 4E **99**
Walston Rd. CF5: Wen 4D **98**
Walters Rd. CF37: P'prdd 2B **24**
Walton Cl. NP19: Newp 5A **38**
Walton Pl. CF11: Card 6F **95**
Waltwood Rd. NP18: Under 3H **39**
Walwyn Pl. CF3: St M 2D **88**
Wanderers Cres. CF5: Ely 5E **93**
Ward Cl. NP19: Newp 2G **37**
Ware Rd. CF83: Caer 2A **46**
Warlock Cl. NP19: Newp 3D **38**
Warlow Cl. CF62: St A 5D **112**
Warren Cl. CF37: R'fln 4G **25**
Warrendale *NP44: F'wtr* *4D **10***
(off Rede Rd.)
Warren Dr. CF83: Caer 2D **46**
Warren Evans Ct. CF14: Whit 3D **84**
Warren Slade NP16: Bul 5F **63**
Warwick Cl. NP4: New I 1G **9**
NP16: Bul 4D **62**
NP44: G'mdw 2C **10**
Warwick Ho. CF10: Card 4B **4**
Warwick La. NP19: Newp 4G **37**
Warwick Pl. CF11: Card 6H **95**
Warwick Rd. NP19: Newp 4G **37**
Warwick St. CF11: Card 6H **95**
Warwick Way CF62: Barry 1H **117**
Wasdale Cl. CF23: Pen L 5B **86**
Washford Av. CF3: L'rmy 6A **74**
Watchet Cl. CF3: L'rmy 2H **87**
Watch Ho. Pde. NP20: Newp 2C **54**
(not continuous)
Water Avens Cl. CF3: St M 1F **89**
Waterfall M. CF71: Llan M 4C **110**
Waterford Cl. CF11: Card 5G **95**
Waterhall Rd. CF5: F'wtr 6H **83**
Waterhouse Dr. CF11: Card 6F **95**
WATERLOO 4D **30**
Waterloo Cl. CF23: Pen L 6E **87**
Waterloo Ct. NP4: Grif 3E **9**
Waterloo Gdns. CF23: Pen L 1D **96**
Waterloo Pl. CF83: Mac 4D **30**
Waterloo Rd. CF23: Pen L 5D **86**
NP20: Newp 1A **54**
Waterloo Ter. Rd. CF83: Mac 4D **30**
Waterside Cl. NP10: Roger 2C **34**
Waterside Ct. NP20: Newp 1C **36**
Waterside Wlk. W. NP10: Roger 3C **34**
Waters La. NP20: Newp 4B **36**
Waters Rd. NP16: Chep 3E **63**
Waterston Ct. CF14: Llan N 5D **84**
Waterston Rd. CF14: Llan N 5D **84**
Watery La. CF71: A'thin 1G **91**
Watford Cl. CF83: Caer 2B **46**
WATFORD PARK 2B **46**
Watford Ri. CF83: Caer 2C **46**
Watford Rd. CF24: Pen L 1F **97**
CF83: Caer 3B **46**
Watkins La. NP20: Newp 5H **35**
Watkins Sq. CF14: L'shn 6F **71**
Watkins Wlk. *NP10: Roger* *5D **34***
(off Ebenezer Dr.)
Watkiss Way CF11: Card 4H **101**
Watson Rd. CF14: Llan N 5C **84**
Watson St. CF63: Barry 2A **118**
Watt Cl. NP20: Malp 4A **20**
Watton Cl. CF14: L'shn 5G **71**
Watts Cl. NP10: Roger 3D **34**
Waun Ddyfal CF14: Heath 1F **85**
Waun Erw CF83: Caer 4D **28**
Waun Fach CF23: L'dyrn 6E **73**
Waunfach Flats CF83: Caer 5C **28**
Waunfach St. CF83: Caer 5C **28**

Waun Fain CF83: Caer 3B **28**
Waunfawr Gdns. NP11: C'keys 4B **16**
Waunfawr Ho. NP11: C'keys 4A **16**
Waunfawr Park Rd. NP11: C'keys 3A **16**
Waunfawr Rd. NP11: C'keys 3A **16**
Waun-Fawr Rd. CF14: Rhiw 1F **85**
Waunfawr Ter. NP11: C'keys 3A **16**
Waun Ganol CF64: P'rth 4C **108**
Waunganol St. CF83: Caer 5D **28**
Waun Gron CF71: Llan M 2C **110**
Waun-Gron Park Station (Rail) 2B **94**
Waun Gron Rd. CF5: L'dff 2B **94**
Waun Hir CF38: E Isaf 6F **43**
Waun Hywel Rd. NP44: Pnwd 5C **8**
Waun Lee Ct. CF23: L'dyrn 5E **73**
Waun Rd. NP44: C'brn 4E **11**
Wauntreoda Rd. CF14: Whit 3E **85**
Waunwaelod Way CF83: Caer 5A **46**
Waunwern Pk. Cvn. Site NP4: P'pool 4A **6**
Waun-y-Groes Av. CF14: Rhiw 6E **71**
Waun-y-Groes Rd. CF14: Rhiw 6E **71**
Wavell Cl. CF14: L'shn 1H **85**
Wavell Dr. NP20: Malp 3A **20**
Waveney Cl. NP20: Bet 5E **19**
Waverley Cl. CF64: L'dgh 5G **101**
Waverley Sq. CF10: Card 2B **102**
Waycock Cross CF62: Rho 1C **116**
Waycock Rd. CF62: Barry 6C **104**
Wayfield Cres. NP44: Pnwd 6E **9**
Weare Cl. NP20: Bet 5E **19**
Webley Cl. NP18: C'ln 3G **21**
Webley Gdns. NP18: C'ln 3G **21**
Wedal Rd. CF14: Card 5A **86**
Wedgewood Ct. CF83: Caer 6F **29**
Wedgewood Dr. NP26: Pskwt 5H **61**
Wedmore Rd. CF11: Card 6A **4** (5G **95**)
Weekes Cl. CF3: L'rmy 6B **74**
Welby Rd. CF5: Card 4F **95**
Welch Regiment Mus., The 3C **4** (3A **96**)
Weldon Cl. NP44: C'iog 6H **9**
Welford St. CF62: Barry 4F **117**
Welland Circ. NP20: Bet 5E **19**
Welland Cres. NP20: Bet 5E **19**
Well Cl. NP16: Bul 6F **63**
Wellfield CF38: Bed 3A **42**
Wellfield Ct. CF3: M'fld 5H **75**
CF38: Chu V 1E **43**
CF62: Barry 4A **106**
Wellfield La. NP4: Grif 2D **8**
Wellfield M. CF38: Bed 3A **42**
Wellfield Pl. CF24: Card 1C **96**
Wellfield Rd. CF3: M'fld 5H **75**
CF24: Card 1C **96**
Wellington Dr. NP44: G'mdw 2C **10**
Wellington La. NP4: P'pool 3A **6**
Wellington Rd. NP20: Newp 6F **35**
Wellington St. CF11: Card 4F **95**
CF15: Tong 4G **69**
Wells Cl. NP20: Newp 2G **53**
Wellspring Ter. NP11: Ris 6E **17**
Wells St. CF11: Card 4G **95**
Wells St. La. *CF11: Card 4G 95*
(off Wyndham Pl.)
Well Wlk. CF62: Barry 5E **117**
Wellwood CF23: L'dyrn 4E **87**
Well Wood Cl. CF23: Pen L 5E **87**
Well Wood Dr. CF64: Din P 3G **107**
Wellwright Rd. CF5: F'wtr 2H **93**
Welsh Folk Mus. 2D **92**
Welsh Hawking Cen. 6C **104**
Welsh Institute of Sport 1A **4** (3G **95**)
Welsh National Tennis Cen. 6H **5** (5D **96**)
Welsh St. NP16: Chep 1C **62**
Welwyn Rd. CF14: Heath 2E **85**
Wembley Rd. CF5: Card 4E **95**
Wenallt Ct. CF14: Rhiw 5D **70**
Wenallt Mans. *CF14: Thorn 1G 71*
(off Heol Llinos)
Wenallt Rd. CF14: Rhiw 3C **70**
Wendesbury St. NP19: Newp 5E **37**
WENTLOOG 5A **88**
Wentloog Av. CF3: Pet W, Rum 6A **88**
Wentloog Cl. CF3: Rum 4H **87**
NP44: C'brn 2G **11**
Wentloog Corporate Ind. Pk. CF3: Rum 4D **88**
Wentloog Ct. CF3: Rum 4H **87**
Wentloog Ri. CF3: Cas 2G **75**
Wentloog Rd. CF3: Rum 4H **87**
Wentsland Cres. NP4: P'pool 3A **6**
Wentsland Rd. NP4: P'pool 3A **6**
Wentwood Cl. NP44: Pnwd 5C **8**
Wentwood Pl. NP11: Ris 6G **17**
Wentwood Rd. NP18: C'ln 5E **21**
Wentwood Vw. NP26: Cald 3C **60**
Wentworth Cl. CF3: St M 5E **75**
NP10: Bass 6B **34**
Wentworth La. CF3: St M 5E **75**
WENVOE 5E **99**
Wenvoe Cl. CF5: Wen 5E **99**
Wenvoe Ct. CF5: Ely 5G **93**
Wenvoe Ter. CF62: Barry 3F **117**
Werfa St. CF23: Card 6B **86**
WERN DDU 3H **47**
Wernddu Ct. CF83: Caer 1F **47**
Wern-ddu Row CF83: Caer 2G **47**
Wern Fach Ct. NP44: H'lys 5B **10**
Wern Fawr Cl. CF3: St M 5C **74**
Wern Fawr La. CF3: St M 5C **74**
Wern Gethin La. CF3: St M 1E **89**
Wern-Gethin La. CF3: Rum 2C **88**
CF3: St M 1D **88**
Wern Goch E. CF23: L'dyrn 1E **87**
Wern-Goch Rd. CF23: Cyn 1C **86**
Wern Goch W. CF23: L'dyrn 1D **86**
Wern Hill NP4: P'pool 3B **6**
Wern Ind. Est. NP10: Roger 3C **34**
Wern Migna CF5: St F 2C **82**
Wern Rd. NP4: Grif 2E **9**
Wern School Cl. NP4: Grif 2E **9**
Wern Ter. NP4: P'pool 3B **6**
NP10: Roger 3B **34**
Wern Trad. Est. NP10: Roger 4C **34**
Wesley Av. CF62: Rho 5D **114**
Wesley Bldg. NP26: Cald 5C **60**
Wesley Cl. NP44: C'brn 3F **11**
Wesley Ct. CF3: L'rmy 2A **88**
CF64: Din P 2G **107**
Wesley Hill CF83: Mac 2E **31**
Wesley La. CF10: Card 4E **5** (4B **96**)
(not continuous)
Wesley Pl. NP11: Ris 6D **16**
NP20: Newp 5B **36**
Wesley Rd. CF83: Caer 2H **45**
Wesley St. CF71: Llan M 3B **110**
NP44: C'brn 3G **11**
Wessex Pl. CF62: Barry 5E **117**
Wessex St. CF5: Card 3D **94**
WEST ABERTHAW 6E **113**
West Acre CF71: L'maes 1D **110**
West Av. CF83: Caer 6A **28**
NP4: Grif 2D **8**
West Bank NP44: Llanf 3B **12**
Westbourne Ct. CF3: Rum 5A **88**
CF63: Barry 5C **106**
Westbourne Cres. CF14: Whit 3A **84**
Westbourne Rd. CF14: Whit 3B **84**
CF64: P'rth 4E **109**
Westbury Cl. CF63: Barry 6B **106**
Westbury Ter. CF5: Card 2D **94**
W. Bute St. CF10: Card 1C **102**
W. Canal Wharf CF10: Card 6D **4** (5A **96**)
West Cl. CF10: Card 1B **102**
West End NP26: Magor 5C **58**
NP26: Undy 5E **59**
West End Gdns. NP26: Undy 4E **59**
West End Ter. CF71: Llan M 3A **110**
WEST-END TOWN 3A **110**
Western Av. CF5: F'wtr, L'dff 2B **94**
CF14: Llan N 1D **94**
NP16: Bul 5E **63**
NP20: Newp 5E **35**
Western Av. Ct. CF5: L'dff 2B **94**
Western Av. Nth. CF14: Llan N 6E **85**
Western Dr. CF14: Llan N 6E **85**
CF83: Caer 2A **46**
Western Ind. Est. CF83: Caer 2A **46**
NP18: C'ln 3H **21**
Western Leisure Cen. 5H **93**
Western Ter. NP11: C'keys 2A **16**
Western Valley Rd. NP10: Roger 5D **34**
Westfield NP26: Cald 5B **60**
Westfield Av. CF14: Heath 2E **85**
NP20: Malp 5A **20**
NP26: Cald 5B **60**
Westfield Cl. NP18: C'ln 3F **21**
Westfield Ct. CF72: L'sant 3G **65**
Westfield Dr. CF64: P'rth 3C **108**
NP20: Malp 5A **20**
Westfield Rd. CF14: Whit 3E **85**
CF37: Glyn 2C **14**
NP18: C'ln 4F **21**
NP20: Newp 5A **36**
Westfield Way NP20: Malp 5A **20**
Westgate CF71: C'bri 3B **90**
Westgate Ct. NP18: C'ln 5H **21**
Westgate St. CF10: Card 4B **4** (4H **95**)
West Gro. CF5: Ely 1D **98**
CF24: Card 2F **5** (3B **96**)
West Gro. Ct. CF24: Card 2F **5** (3B **96**)
Westhill Dr. CF72: L'sant 3G **65**
Westhill St. CF71: Llan M 3B **110**
Westland Cl. CF24: Card 2G **97**
West Lee CF11: Card 3A **4** (3G **95**)
W. Luton Pl. CF24: Card 4H **5** (4C **96**)
W. Market St. NP20: Newp 6C **36**
(not continuous)
Westminster Cres. CF23: Cyn 6C **72**
Westminster Dr. CF23: Cyn 5C **72**
CF64: Sul 2H **119**
Westmoor Cl. NP19: Newp 6A **38**
Westmoreland St. CF5: Card 4E **95**
W. Mound Cres. CF38: Tont 2G **43**
West Nash Rd. NP18: Newp 6B **56**
Weston Av. CF64: Sul 3H **119**
Westonbirt Cl. CF3: St M 1D **88**
Weston Rd. CF3: L'rmy 2H **87**
Weston Sq. CF63: Barry 1B **118**
Weston St. CF63: Barry 1B **118**
W. Orchard Cres. CF5: Card 2C **94**
West Pk. La. NP20: Newp 5H **35**
West Pk. Rd. NP20: Newp 5H **35**
West Pl. NP4: P'pool 3C **6**
W. Point Ind. Est. CF11: Card 4G **101**
WEST PONTNEWYDD 6C **8**
WESTRA 2E **107**
Westra CF64: Din P 3D **106**
Westray Cl. NP19: Newp 2F **37**
West Ri. CF14: L'shn 5A **72**
West Rd. CF14: Llan N 4B **84**
CF64: Sul 1E **119**
West Roedin NP44: F'wtr 5E **11**
West St. CF37: P'prdd 6D **14**
CF71: Llan M 3B **110**
NP20: Newp 4B **36**
West Ter. CF64: P'rth 1E **109**
West Vw. CF15: Taff W 1F **69**
NP44: C'brn 2E **11**
Westview Ter. CF83: Caer 4F **29**
WEST VILLAGE 3B **90**
Westville Rd. CF23: Pen L 6C **86**
NP20: Newp 5H **35**
Westville Wlk. CF23: Pen L 6C **86**
West Wlk. CF62: Barry 1F **117**
Westward Ri. CF62: Barry 5C **116**
Westway NP26: Rog 6A **60**
Westway Rd. NP20: Newp 2B **54**
W. Wharf Ter. CF10: Card 5A **96**
Westwood Ct. CF64: P'rth 1E **109**
Wexford Ct. CF23: Pontp 3G **73**
Wharfedale Rd. CF23: L'dyrn 5F **73**
Wharf La. NP19: Newp 4E **37**
Wharf Rd. NP19: Newp 4E **37**
Wharf Rd. E. CF10: Card 6H **5** (5C **96**)
Wharton Cl. CF62: Rho 6C **114**
Wharton St. CF10: Card 4D **4** (4A **96**)
Wheate Cl., The CF62: Rho 5E **115**
Wheatley Rd. CF5: Ely 5G **93**
Wheatsheaf Ct. NP26: Magor 4D **58**
Wheeler St. NP20: Newp 2C **36**
Wheel La. NP10: St Bri 3E **77**
Whinberry Way CF5: Ely 4E **93**
Whinchat Cl. CF3: St M 6E **75**
Whistler Cl. NP19: Newp 2F **37**
Whitaker Rd. CF24: Card 1G **97**
Whitby Pl. NP19: Newp 3D **36**
WHITCHURCH 3D **84**
WHITCHURCH HOSPITAL
(YSBYTY EGLWYS NEWYDD) 2B **84**
Whitchurch Pl. CF24: Card 6A **86**
Whitchurch Rd. CF14: Card 4G **85**
Whitchurch Station (Rail) 1C **84**
Whiteacre Cl. CF14: Thorn 3H **71**
White Ash Glade NP18: C'ln 5F **21**
White Av. NP10: Coedk 6G **53**
White Barn Rd. CF14: L'shn 5F **71**
Whitebrook Way NP44: C'brn 3G **11**
Whitechapel Wlk. NP26: Undy 3E **59**
Whitecliffe Dr. CF64: P'rth 5F **109**
White Cross La. CF83: Caer 5H **27**
Whitefield Rd. CF14: Llan N 5C **84**
Whitehall Av. CF3: Rum 4G **87**
Whitehall Cl. CF5: Wen 4D **98**
White Hall Gdns. NP26: Undy 5F **59**
White Hall La. NP44: Llanf 3B **12**
Whitehall Pde. CF3: Rum 4H **87**
Whitehall Pl. CF3: Rum 4G **87**
Whitehall Rd. CF5: L'dff 6B **84**
White Hart Dr. CF83: Mac 2E **31**
White Hart La. NP18: C'ln 6A **22**
White Ho. CF62: Barry 6E **117**
Whitehouse Cl. NP44: C'iog 6G **9**
Whitehouse Rd. NP44: C'iog 6G **9**
White Oaks Dr. CF3: St M 5C **74**
Whiterock Av. CF37: P'prdd 5B **14**
Whiterock Cl. CF37: P'prdd 5B **14**
Whiterock Dr. CF37: P'prdd 5B **14**
Whitesands Rd. CF14: L'shn 4F **71**
White St. CF83: Caer 1D **46**

Whitethorn Way CF3: M'fld 5A **76**
Whitewall NP26: Magor 5D **58**
Whiteways CF71: Llan M 2D **110**
Whitewell Dr. CF71: Llan M 4B **110**
Whitewell Rd. CF62: Barry 6F **105**
Whitland Cl. CF5: F'wtr 6H **83**
Whitland Cres. CF5: F'wtr 6A **84**
Whitmore Pk. Dr. CF62: Barry 6E **105**
Whitmuir Rd. CF24: Card 2F **97**
Whitstone Rd. NP19: Newp 3H **37**
Whittan Cl. CF62: Rho 6C **114**
Whittle Ct. NP20: Malp 4A **20**
Whittle Dr. NP20: Malp 4H **19**
Whittle Rd. CF11: Card 6E **95**
Whitworth Ct. CF11: Card 6A **4** (5H **95**)
Whitworth Sq. CF14: Whit 6A **70**
Wicken Cl. CF3: St M 6E **75**
Wicklow Cl. CF23: Pontp 4G **73**
Wick Rd. CF71: Llan M 2A **110**
Wick St. CF71: Llan M 2A **110**
Widecombe Dr. CF3: Rum 4G **87**
Wiesental Cl. NP26: Cald 4D **60**
Wigmore Cl. CF14: Thorn 3G **71**
WILCRICK 2A **58**
Wilcrick Way NP44: Pnwd 6F **9**
Wilde Ct. CF15: Rad 3H **83**
Wild Gdns. Rd. CF23: Cyn 2A **86**
Wilfred Brook Ho. CF11: Card 1H **101**
Wilfred St. CF63: Barry 2B **118**
Wilkinson Cl. CF24: Card 4D **96**
Wilkins Ter. CF83: Caer 3B **28**
Willenhall St. NP19: Newp 5E **37**
William Belcher Dr. CF3: St M 2E **89**
William Brown Cl. NP44: Oakf 6A **12**
William Harris Bungs. CF83: Abert 2E **27**
William Lovett Gdns. NP20: Newp 5B **36**
William Morris Dr. NP19: Newp 3B **38**
William Nicholls Dr. CF3: St M 5C **74**
Williams Cl. *NP20: Newp 6C 36*
(off Francis Dr.)
Williams Cres. CF62: Barry 2G **117**
Williams Pl. CF37: Up Bo 6A **26**
(not continuous)
William St. CF11: Card 2F **95**
CF37: C'fydd 2F **15**
CF83: Abert 2E **27**
CF83: Tret 2A **30**
NP44: Pnwd 6E **9**
Williams Way CF10: Card 6A **96**
Willie Seager Cotts. CF23: Pen L 6D **86**
Willie Seager Memorial Homes
CF23: Pen L 6F **87**
Willins NP44: F'wtr 5D **10**
Williton Rd. CF3: L'rmy 6A **74**
Willowbrook NP20: Bet 5F **19**
Willowbrook Dr. CF3: St M 6C **74**
Willowbrook Gdns. CF3: St M 6D **74**
Willowbrook Laboratory Units
CF3: St M 6D **74**
Willow Cl. CF38: Bed 6H **41**
CF64: P'rth 2C **108**
NP16: Bul 4E **63**
NP19: Newp 1H **55**
NP26: Cald 4C **60**
Willow Ct. CF24: Card 1H **5** (2C **96**)
Willow Cres. CF63: Barry 6A **106**
Willowdale Cl. CF5: F'wtr 1G **93**
Willowdale Rd. CF5: F'wtr 1F **93**
Willowdene Way CF3: St M 5E **75**
Willowfield Ct. CF23: Cyn 1C **86**
WILLOWFORD, THE 2C **44**
Willowford CF37: Up Bo 3C **44**
Willowford, The CF37: Up Bo 3C **44**
Willowford Rd. CF38: Up Bo 1A **44**
Willow Grn. NP18: C'ln 4F **21**
Willow Gro. CF3: St M 5E **75**
Willowherb Cl. CF3: St M 1F **89**
Willowmere CF64: L'dgh 4F **101**
Willow Rd. CF72: L'harry 5B **78**
Willows, The *CF62: St A 5D 112*
(off Gileston Rd.)
CF83: B'ws 2G **29**
NP26: Undy 4D **58**
Willows Av. CF24: Card 3F **97**
Willow St. CF37: R'fln 4G **25**
Willow Tree Cl. CF15: Rad 1D **82**
Willow Wlk. CF71: C'bri 3D **90**
NP10: Roger 2H **33**
Will Paynter Wlk. *NP19: Newp 2B 38*
(off Kier Hardie Dr.)
Wills Row NP10: Roger 4D **34**
Wilson Pl. CF5: Ely 5G **93**
Wilson Rd. CF5: Ely 4F **93**
NP19: Newp 2G **37**
Wilson St. CF24: Card 2E **97**
NP20: Newp 1D **54**
Wimborne Cres. CF64: Sul 2H **119**
Wimborne Ri. NP44: Pnwd 6C **8**
Wimbourne Cl. CF71: Llan M 4B **110**
Wimbourne Rd. CF63: Barry 2C **118**
Winchester Av. CF23: Pen L 5D **86**
Winchester Cl. CF62: Barry 2F **117**
NP20: Newp 2A **54**
Windermere Av. CF23: Cyn 3A **86**
Windermere Ct. NP44: G'mdw 2E **11**
Windermere Sq. NP19: Newp 1E **37**
Windflower Cl. CF3: St M 6E **75**
Windhover Cl. CF3: St M 1E **89**
Windlass Ct. CF10: Card 6C **96**
Windmill Cl. CF14: Thorn 3G **71**
CF71: Llan M 2C **110**
Windmill Ind. Area CF64: Sul 3D **118**
Windmill La. CF71: Llan M 2C **110**
(not continuous)
CF71: L'thian 4C **90**
Windmill Sq. *NP20: Newp 6C 36*
(off Commercial Rd.)
Windrush Cl. NP20: Bet 5G **19**
Windrush Pl. CF5: F'wtr 1H **93**
Windsor Arc. CF64: P'rth 1E **109**
Windsor Av. CF15: Rad 1F **83**
Windsor Clive Dr. CF5: St F 2C **82**
Windsor Cl. CF15: Rad 1F **83**
CF71: Bov 3D **110**
NP26: Magor 4C **58**
Windsor Ct. CF15: Rad 1F **83**
CF24: Card 3G **5** (3C **96**)
CF64: P'rth 2F **109**
CF72: P'clun 6D **64**
Windsor Cres. CF15: Rad 2G **83**
Windsor Dr. CF72: P'clun 6F **65**
NP26: Magor 4C **58**
Windsor Esplanade
CF10: Card 2B **102**
Windsor Gdns. CF5: Ely 3A **94**
CF38: Bed 3A **42**
NP26: Magor 4C **58**
Windsor Grn. CF5: Ely 3A **94**
Windsor Gro. CF15: Rad 1F **83**
Windsor Ho. CF10: Card 4B **4** (4H **95**)
Windsor La. CF10: Card 3E **5** (3B **96**)
CF64: P'rth 6A **102**
Windsor M. CF24: Card 4H **5** (4C **96**)
Windsor Pk. NP26: Magor 4C **58**
Windsor Pl. CF10: Card 2E **5** (3B **96**)
CF64: P'rth 1E **109**
CF83: Abert 2D **26**
NP10: Roger 5D **34**
WINDSOR QUAY 2A **102**
Windsor Rd. CF15: Rad 2F **83**
CF24: Card 4G **5** (4C **96**)
CF37: T'rest 2E **25**
CF62: Barry 4F **117**
CF64: P'rth 5G **101**
NP4: Grif 6E **7**
NP19: Newp 5F **37**
NP44: F'wtr, G'mdw 3D **10**
Windsor St. CF83: Caer 1D **46**
Windsor Ter. CF10: Card 2B **102**
CF64: P'rth 1F **109**
NP20: Newp 5B **36**
Windsor Ter. La. CF64: P'rth 1F **109**
Windway Av. CF5: Card 3C **94**
Windway Rd. CF5: Card 2B **94**
Windyridge CF64: Din P 3A **108**
Wine St. CF71: Llan M 3B **110**
Wingate Dr. CF14: L'shn 1H **85**
Wingate St. NP20: Newp 2C **54**
Wingfield Av. CF38: Bed 4H **41**
Wingfield Cl. CF37: P'prdd 6E **15**
Wingfield Rd. CF14: Whit 3B **84**
Winifred Av. CF62: Barry 5G **105**
Winnipeg Dr. CF23: Cyn 2C **86**
Winsford Rd. CF64: Sul 3A **120**
Winston Av. CF5: Ely 1E **99**
Winston Rd. CF62: Barry 5G **105**
Wintour Cl. NP16: Chep 1D **62**
Wisley Pl. CF23: Pontp 4E **73**
Wistaria Cl. NP20: Malp 4B **20**
Wiston Path NP44: F'wtr 3D **10**
Witham St. NP19: Newp 5E **37**
Withy Cl. NP26: Magor 4C **58**
Withycombe Rd. CF3: L'rmy 5A **74**
Withy Wlk. NP26: Magor 4C **58**
Witla Ct. Rd. CF3: Rum 2A **88**
Wolfe Cl. CF63: Barry 6C **106**
Wolffe Cl. CF71: C'bri 3B **90**
Wolfs Castle Av. CF14: L'shn 4G **71**
Wolseley Cl. NP20: Newp 2C **54**
Wolseley St. NP20: Newp 2C **54**
Womanby St. CF10: Card 4C **4** (4A **96**)
Woodbine Gdns. NP26: Undy 4D **58**
Wood Cl. CF14: L'vne 4B **72**
NP10: Roger 2C **34**
NP44: Llanf 4B **12**
Woodcock St. CF24: Card 2C **96**
Wood Cotts. CF15: Taff W 1F **69**
Wood Cres. NP10: Roger 2C **34**
Woodfield Av. CF15: Rad 3G **83**
Woodfield Cl. CF3: M'fld 4A **76**
Woodfield Rd. CF72: T Grn 3C **64**
NP4: New I 5G **7**
Woodford Cl. CF5: L'dff 6A **84**
Woodham Cl. CF62: Barry 1F **117**
Woodham Pk. CF62: Barry 1F **117**
Woodham Rd. CF63: Barry 3A **118**
(not continuous)
Woodhouse CF62: Rho 2B **114**
Woodland Ct. NP44: C'iog 1A **12**
(not continuous)
Woodland Cres. CF15: Cre 5E **67**
CF23: Cyn 3C **86**
Woodland Dr. CF64: P'rth 1E **109**
NP10: Bass 6B **34**
NP10: Roger 2A **34**
Woodland Pk. Rd. NP19: Newp 3F **37**
Woodland Pk. Vw. NP19: Newp 3F **37**
Woodland Pl. CF24: Card 1H **5** (2C **96**)
CF64: P'rth 1E **109**
Woodland Rd. CF14: Whit 3B **84**
CF38: Bed 5A **42**
NP19: Newp 3F **37**
NP44: C'iog 6G **9**
Woodlands CF15: Gwae G 4F **69**
Woodlands, The CF14: L'vne 3B **72**
CF38: Llan F 4B **42**
NP4: P'pool 2D **6**
Woodlands Cl. CF71: C'bri 3B **90**
Woodlands Ct. CF62: Barry 2H **117**
Woodlands Dr. NP20: Malp 3A **20**
Woodlands Pk. Dr. CF5: Ely 6G **93**
Woodlands Rd. CF62: Barry 2H **117**
CF63: Barry 2H **117**
Woodland St. NP44: C'brn 1E **11**
Woodland Ter. CF37: P'prdd 1B **24**
(not continuous)
CF83: Abert 2D **26**
Woodland Valley NP26: C'went 2C **60**
Woodland Vw. CF38: Chu V 3D **42**
NP4: P'pool 1B **6**
NP26: Cald 4B **60**
NP26: Rog 6A **60**
Woodlawn Way CF14: Thorn 2G **71**
Wood Path NP44: C'iog 5G **9**
Woodpecker Sq. CF62: St A 3G **111**
Wood Rd. CF37: T'rest 1D **24**
Woodruff Way CF14: Thorn 2F **71**
Woodside CF5: Wen 5E **99**
NP10: Duf 4G **53**
(not continuous)
Woodside Ct. CF14: L'vne 4A **72**
Woodside Rd. NP44: C'brn 1G **11**
Woodside Ter. NP44: C'brn 1F **11**
Woodside Way NP44: C'brn 1E **11**
Woodstock Cl. CF62: Barry 2F **117**
NP26: Cald 6C **60**
Woodstock Ct. NP26: Cald 6C **60**
Woodstock Way NP26: Cald 6C **60**
Wood St. CF10: Card 6B **4** (5H **95**)
CF37: C'fydd 2F **15**
CF64: P'rth 1E **109**
Woodsy Cl. CF14: Pontp 3G **73**
CF23: Pontp 3G **73**
Woodvale Av. CF23: Cyn 6C **72**
Woodview Ct. NP4: P'pool 3B **6**
Wood Vw. Cres. NP11: Ris 6E **17**
Wood Vw. Rd. NP11: Ris 5E **17**
Woodview Ter. NP4: P'pool 3B **6**
Woodville Ct. CF24: Card 1A **96**
Woodville Rd. CF24: Card 1A **96**
NP20: Newp 5H **35**
Woodward Av. NP11: C'keys 3A **16**
Woodward Rd. NP11: C'keys 3A **16**
Woolacombe Av. CF3: L'rmy 2A **88**
Woolaston Av. CF23: Cyn 2B **86**
Woolmer Cl. CF5: L'dff 5H **83**
Woolos Ct. NP20: Newp 5B **36**
Woolpitch NP44: G'mdw 2D **10**
Woolpitch Wood NP16: Chep 2C **62**
Woosnham Cl. CF23: Pen L 5E **87**
Worcester Cl. CF11: Card 1H **101**
NP44: Llan 2A **12**
Worcester Ct. CF11: Card 2H **101**
Worcester Cres. NP19: Newp 1F **37**
Worcester Path NP44: Llan 2A **12**
Worcester St. CF11: Card 1H **101**
Wordsworth Av. CF24: Card 1H **5** (2C **96**)
CF64: P'rth 1C **108**

Wordsworth Cl. CF71: Llan M 3D **110**
NP26: Cald 6B **60**
NP44: C'brn 3F **11**
Wordsworth Gdns. CF37: R'fln 3H **25**
Wordsworth Rd. NP19: Newp 4F **37**
Working St. CF10: Card 4D **4** (4A **96**)
Worle Av. CF3: L'rmy 2H **87**
Worle Pl. CF3: L'rmy 2H **87**
Worrells Pl. CF5: Ely 1F **99**
Wren Cl. CF3: St M 1E **89**
Wrenford Ct. *NP20: Newp 5C* ***36***
(off Commercial St.)
Wren Rd. CF62: St A 3G **111**
Wrexham Ct. CF3: Rum 2C **88**
Wright Cl. NP19: Newp 6H **37**
Wroughton Pl. CF5: F'wtr 2A **94**
Wyebank Av. NP16: Tut 1G **63**
Wyebank Cl. NP16: Tut 2G **63**
Wyebank Cres. NP16: Tut 2G **63**
Wyebank Dr. NP16: Tut 1G **63**
Wyebank Pl. NP16: Tut 2G **63**
Wyebank Ri. NP16: Tut 2G **63**
Wyebank Rd. NP16: Tut 2G **63**
Wyebank Vw. NP16: Tut 2G **63**
Wyebank Way NP16: Tut 2G **63**
Wye Cl. CF62: Barry 1E **117**
Wye Ct. NP44: G'mdw 1D **10**
Wye Cres. NP16: Chep 3E **63**
NP20: Bet 5G **19**
Wyelands Vw. NP16: Math 6B **62**
Wye Valley Link Rd.
NP16: Chep, Math, Pwllm 3D **62**
Wye Valley Wlk. NP16: Chep 1D **62**
Wyeverne Ct. CF24: Card 2A **96**
Wyeverne Rd. CF24: Card 1A **96**
NP19: Newp 4G **37**
Wyfan Pl. CF14: Card 5F **85**
Wyncliffe Gdns. CF23: L'dyrn 5F **73**
Wyncliffe Rd. CF23: L'dyrn 5G **73**
Wyndham Arc. CF10: Card 5D **4** (4A **96**)
Wyndham Cres. CF11: Card 3F **95**
Wyndham Pl. CF11: Card 4G **95**
Wyndham Rd. CF11: Card 3F **95**
Wyndham St. CF11: Card 4G **95**
(not continuous)
CF15: Tong 4G **69**
CF63: Barry 2H **117**
CF83: Mac 2F **31**
NP20: Newp 3C **36**
Wyndham Ter. CF14: L'shn 5A **72**
NP11: Ris 6F **17**
Wynd St. CF63: Barry 1B **118**
Wynnstay Cl. CF11: Card 6G **95**
Wyon Cl. CF5: L'dff 4H **83**

Y

Yarrow Cl. CF5: Ely 4E **93**
Y BONT-FAEN 3D **90**
Y Cerigos CF62: Barry 5D **116**
Y Cilgant CF83: Caer 3A **28**
Y Clifordd CF83: Caer 5B **28**
Y Deri CF38: Llan F 5C **42**
Y Dolydd CF83: Caer 2B **46**
Yellow Row *NP4: P'pool 4A* ***6***
(off Crumlin Rd.)
Yeo Cl. NP20: Bet 6F **19**
Yeo Rd. NP20: Bet 6G **19**
Yetts, The NP16: Sed 3H **63**
Yewberry Cl. NP20: Malp 5B **20**
Yewberry La. NP20: Malp, Newp 5B **20**
(not continuous)
Yew St. CF15: Taff W 1E **69**
Yew Tree Cl. NP26: Cald 6C **60**
Yewtree Cl. CF5: F'wtr 1G **93**
NP26: Undy 5E **59**
Yew Tree Ct. CF23: Pen L 5C **86**
CF62: Barry 4E **117**
Yewtree Gro. CF62: St A 2B **112**
Yew Tree La. NP18: C'ln 4H **21**
Yew Tree Ri. NP26: Rog 6A **60**
Yew Tree Ter. NP44: C'brn 3F **11**
NP44: C'iog 6G **9**
Yew Tree Wood NP16: Chep 2B **62**
Y Felin Ffrwd CF83: Caer 5A **28**
Y Goedwig CF14: Rhiw 5C **70**
Y Groes CF14: Rhiw 6D **70**
Y GROES-WEN 1E **45**
Ynysangharad Rd. CF37: P'prdd 6D **14**
Ynysangharad Swimming Pool 6C **14**
Ynys Bri. Ct. CF15: Gwae G 3F **69**
Ynysbryn Cl. CF72: L'sant 2E **65**
Ynys Cl. CF37: R'fln 3F **25**
Ynys Coed CF5: L'dff 1C **94**
Ynyscorrwg Rd. CF37: R'fln 5H **25**
Ynysddu CF72: P'clun 5C **64**
Ynysfach Yd. CF15: Tong 4F **69**
Ynys-Gyfelin Rd. CF37: P'prdd 5C **14**
Ynys Hir CF37: Glyn 1D **14**
Ynys La. NP44: C'iog 6G **9**
Ynyslyn Rd. CF37: R'fln 5H **25**
YNYSMAERDY 6C **40**
Ynysmaerdy Ter. CF72: L'sant 6C **40**
Ynys Ter. CF37: R'fln 4F **25**
Ynys Wlk. NP26: Magor 6B **58**
Ynysybwl Rd. CF37: Y'bwl, P'prdd, Glyn 1B **14**
Yorath Rd. CF14: Whit 2D **84**
York Cl. NP44: G'mdw 2C **10**
York Ct. CF10: Card 6G **5** (5C **96**)
CF15: Rad 1F ***83***
(off Maes yr Awel)
York Dr. CF38: Llan F 5D **42**
York Pl. CF11: Card 2H **101**
CF62: Barry 4F **117**
NP11: Ris 4D **16**
NP20: Newp 5B **36**
York Rd. NP19: Newp 2E **37**
York St. CF5: Card 4E **95**
(not continuous)
Youghal Cl. CF23: Pontp 3G **73**
Youldon Ho. CF64: Din P 2H **107**
Y Parc CF72: Groes F 6B **66**
Yr Allt CF72: L'sant 2F **65**
Yr Graig CF72: L'sant 2E **65**
Y RHATH 1C **96**
Yr Hendre CF15: N'grw 3E **45**
Y Rhodfa CF63: Barry 3H **117**
Y RHWS 5F **115**
Ysgol Pl. NP44: Up Cwm 5C **8**
Ysgubor Fach CF83: Mac 2F **31**
Ystradbarwig Dr. CF38: Llan F 5C **42**
Ystradbarwig Ter. CF38: Llan F 5C **42**
Ystrad Bldgs. *CF83: Tret 3A* ***30***
(off Newport Rd.)
Ystrad Cl. CF3: St M 6E **75**
Ystrad St. CF11: Card 1A **102**

Z

Zinc St. CF24: Card 3D **96**
Zion Hill *NP4: P'nydd 1A* ***6***
(off Pentrepiod Rd.)

Printed and bound in the United Kingdom by Polestar Wheatons Ltd., Exeter.